THE REINVENTION OF THEATRE IN SIXTEENTH-CENTURY EUROPE
TRADITIONS, TEXTS AND PERFORMANCE

LEGENDA

LEGENDA, founded in 1995 by the European Humanities Research Centre of the University of Oxford, is now a joint imprint of the Modern Humanities Research Association and **Routledge**. Titles range from medieval texts to contemporary cinema and form a widely comparative view of the modern humanities, including works on Arabic, Catalan, English, French, German, Greek, Italian, Portuguese, Russian, Spanish, and Yiddish literature. An Editorial Board of distinguished academic specialists works in collaboration with leading scholarly bodies such as the Society for French Studies, the British Comparative Literature Association and the Association of Hispanists of Great Britain & Ireland.

MHRA

The Modern Humanities Research Association (MHRA) encourages and promotes advanced study and research in the field of the modern humanities, especially modern European languages and literature, including English, and also cinema. It also aims to break down the barriers between scholars working in different disciplines and to maintain the unity of humanistic scholarship in the face of increasing specialization. The Association fulfils this purpose primarily through the publication of journals, bibliographies, monographs and other aids to research.

LONDON AND NEW YORK

Routledge is a global publisher of academic books, journals and online resources in the humanities and social sciences. Founded in 1836, it has published many of the greatest thinkers and scholars of the last hundred years, including adorno, einstein, Russell, Popper, Wittgenstein, Jung, Bohm, Hayek, Mcluhan, Marcuse and Sartre. Today Routledge is one of the world's leading academic publishers in the Humanities and Social Sciences. It publishes thousands of books and journals each year, serving scholars, instructors, and professional communities worldwide.

www.routledge.com

EDITORIAL BOARD

Chairman
Professor Colin Davis, Royal Holloway, University of London

Professor Malcolm Cook, University of Exeter (French)
Professor Robin Fiddian, Wadham College, Oxford (Spanish)
Professor Anne Fuchs, University of Warwick (German)
Professor Paul Garner, University of Leeds (Spanish)
Professor Andrew Hadfield, University of Sussex (English)
Professor Marian Hobson Jeanneret,
Queen Mary University of London (French)
Professor Catriona Kelly, New College, Oxford (Russian)
Professor Martin McLaughlin, Magdalen College, Oxford (Italian)
Professor Martin Maiden, Trinity College, Oxford (Linguistics)
Professor Peter Matthews, St John's College, Cambridge (Linguistics)
Dr Stephen Parkinson, Linacre College, Oxford (Portuguese)
Professor Suzanne Raitt, William and Mary College, Virginia (English)
Professor Ritchie Robertson, The Queen's College, Oxford (German)
Professor David Shepherd, Keele University (Russian)
Professor Michael Sheringham, All Souls College, Oxford (French)
Professor Alison Sinclair, Clare College, Cambridge (Spanish)
Professor David Treece, King's College London (Portuguese)

Managing Editor
Dr Graham Nelson
41 Wellington Square, Oxford OX1 2JF, UK

www.legendabooks.com

The Reinvention of Theatre in Sixteenth-Century Europe

Traditions, Texts and Performance

❖

EDITED BY T. F. EARLE AND CATARINA FOUTO

LEGENDA

Modern Humanities Research Association and Routledge
2015

First published 2015

Published by the
Modern Humanities Research Association and Routledge
2 Park Square, Milton Park, Abingdon, Oxon OX14 4RN
711 Third Avenue, New York, NY 10017, USA

LEGENDA is an imprint of the
Modern Humanities Research Association and Routledge

Routledge is an imprint of the Taylor & Francis Group, an informa business

© *Modern Humanities Research Association and Taylor & Francis 2015*

ISBN 978-1-907975-76-9 (hbk)

All rights reserved. No part of this publication may be reproduced, stored in a retrieval system,
or transmitted in any form or by any means, electronic, mechanical, including photocopying,
recordings, fax or otherwise, without the prior written permission of the copyright owner and the
publisher.

Product or corporate names may be trademarks or registered trademarks, and are used only for
identification and explanation without intent to infringe.

Disclaimer: Statements of fact and opinion contained in this book are those of the author and
not of the editors, Routledge, or the Modern Humanities Research Association. The
publisher makes no representation, express or implied, in respect of the accuracy of the
material in this book and cannot accept any legal responsibility or liability for any errors or
omissions that may be made.

CONTENTS

Acknowledgements — ix

Introduction
T. F. EARLE and CATARINA FOUTO — 1

PART I: LITERARY TRADITION AND THE THEATRE

1 Sooner than Shakespeare: Inwardness and Lexicon in the Drama of Gil Vicente and António Prestes
HÉLIO J. S. ALVES — 11

2 The *Auto da Festa* and the (Well-stocked) Workshop of Gil Vicente
JOSÉ AUGUSTO CARDOSO BERNARDES — 27

3 The *Auto de la huida a Egipto*: Italian and Other Connections
JANE WHETNALL — 41

4 Who is Júlio? Plot and Identity in António Ferreira's Comedies
T. F. EARLE — 73

5 The Reinvention of Classical Comedy and Tragedy in Portugal: Defining Drama in the Work of Sá de Miranda, António Ferreira and Diogo de Teive
CATARINA FOUTO — 89

6 The Recovery of Terence in Renaissance Italy: From Alberti to Machiavelli
MARTIN MCLAUGHLIN — 115

7 Palimpsestuous Phaedra: William Gager's Additions to Seneca's Tragedy for his 1592 Production at Christ Church, Oxford
ELIZABETH SANDIS — 141

8 The Power of Transformation in Guillén de Castro's *El caballero bobo* (1595–1605) and *La fuerza de la costumbre* (1610–15): Translation and Performance
KATHLEEN JEFFS — 161

PART II: THEATRE AND PERFORMANCE

9 Amateurs Meet Professionals: Theatrical Activities in Late Sixteenth-Century Italian Academies
LISA SAMPSON — 187

viii   CONTENTS

10   Competing with Continentals: The Case of William Kemp
     KATHERINE DUNCAN-JONES   219

11   Gil Vicente, a Source for a Heritage Made of Scraps
     JOSÉ CAMÕES   239

     PART III: THEATRE AND SOCIETY

12   Plautus and Terence in Tudor England
     PETER BROWN   255

13   Diffusing Drama: Manuscript and Print in the Transmission of
     Camões's Plays
     VANDA ANASTÁCIO   281

14   From the Catholic Mystery Play to Calvinist Tragedy, or the
     Reinvention of French Religious Drama
     MICHAEL MEERE   297

15   The Renaissance Meets the Reformation: The Dramatist Thomas
     Naogeorg (1508–1563)
     HELEN WATANABE-O'KELLY   317

     Index   333

ACKNOWLEDGEMENTS

The history of this book began in October 2011, when a successful two-day conference entitled 'Sixteenth-Century Theatre in Europe: the Latin and the Vernacular Traditions' was held at St John's College, Oxford. Eleven of the contributors to this volume presented their research at the conference and plans to publish a volume entirely devoted to sixteenth-century theatre stemmed from the lively discussion which followed between the speakers and the audience. The editors are grateful to everyone who shared their expertise and interest with us on that occasion and afterwards, especially the editorial team at Legenda led by Graham Nelson. We wish to thank also the contributors to this volume, both those who read papers at the conference and those who joined the project later. Oxford bodies — St John's College and the Faculty of Medieval and Modern Languages — and agencies of the Portuguese government — the Instituto Camões and the Imprensa Nacional — all contributed handsomely to the costs of the 2011 conference. Finally, the publication of this volume was made possible thanks to the generous support of the Oxford Faculty of Medieval and Modern Languages and the School of Arts & Humanities, King's College London.

T.E. & C.F., Oxford, November 2014

INTRODUCTION

T. F. Earle and Catarina Fouto

There is very little in the history of the theatre in Western Europe that has escaped academic attention, and the sixteenth century is no exception. Even so, traditionally it is a rather neglected period, especially by comparison with the century which followed — the age of Shakespeare and Jonson, Corneille and Racine, Lope and Calderón. Recently, however, a number of surveys have been published with much information about the rich theatrical life of the years before 1600. The present book builds on the work of its predecessors, but is not like them, because what we have tried to do is not to present a comprehensive account of this or that aspect of sixteenth-century drama, but to try to see it in the round.

We believe that this approach provides innovative perspectives on European theatre of the sixteenth century, and is distinct from other publications, valuable though these are. Therefore, we do not seek to be encyclopaedic, like Philip Freund's *Dramatis Personae: The Rise of Medieval and Renaissance Theatre*.[1] On the other hand, we have tried to go beyond those collections of essays which focus on specific European dramatic traditions,[2] or on a single language, like the recent *Neo-Latin Drama and Theatre in Early Modern Europe* and *The Early-Modern Cultures of Neo-Latin Drama*.[3] Equally, our book has a wider focus than the monographs which discuss particular aspects of the writing and publishing of theatre in this period,[4] or which have a thematic approach to European theatre.[5] The aim of this volume is, rather, to explore the development of sixteenth-century theatre and to contribute to the understanding of its specificity, rather than to present it as the predecessor of the better-known and more studied dramatic tradition of the seventeenth century.[6]

The book is divided into three main sections. The first, and longest, 'Literary Tradition and the Theatre', is made up of studies which focus on one or more play texts in a way which emphasizes their aesthetic significance. It is true that Shakespeare was active in the 1590s, and no one doubts that *Romeo and Juliet* or *A Midsummer Night's Dream* or even *Love's Labour's Lost*, which is discussed in the present volume, have received ample critical attention. But there are so many other plays, in so many different languages (including Latin), which merit close reading, even if the conventions of performance make them difficult to realize on the modern stage. In this part of the volume the reader will find readings of individual plays in a broad geographical frame, which includes works written in the familiar territories of England and Italy, France, Germany and Spain, but also in Portugal, the country that produced one of the greatest dramatists of the century — Gil Vicente — but which surveys touch only fleetingly, or not at all.

In the second section, 'Theatre and Performance', our contributors discuss the styles of performance that developed in different European countries in response to prevailing conditions, drawing attention to the complex relationship between scripted text and improvisation. The third and final section is concerned with drama as a means of reflecting, promoting and questioning social and political change. Plays sometimes had an immediate polemical and subversive function in the struggle between competing confessional loyalties, but they also had a role in the formation of taste, and could themselves be modified as tastes changed.

The three sections are loose ones, and contributors have not been subject to rigorous editorial control. They have, on the contrary, been encouraged to write freely, and at length, about the aspects of sixteenth-century theatre that interest them. Throughout the book, generous space has been allowed for quotation and, where necessary, translation into English. As a consequence, certain lines of force have emerged which cut across the book's formal divisions and also the national frontiers which have impeded the study of European drama as a whole. Cross-references, supplied by the editors, draw attention to these common themes.

The most obvious of these is the classical, Greco-Roman tradition. More than anything else, it was that tradition that dramatists reinvented in the sixteenth century. Latin was, after all, the language of many plays written in every western European country between 1500 and 1600. That did not stop the classical language being used for purposes unimaginable to a Roman, for example, by the Lutheran dramatist Thomas Naogeorg to attack the papacy. It was in the sixteenth century, too, that the five-act form recommended by Horace became widespread, for tragedy, with or without a chorus, and for comedy. Seneca, afforced sometimes by Euripides in Latin translation, also provided plot, characters and turns of phrase, visible even in the vernacular, for tragedy, and Plautus and Terence did the same for comedy. However, sixteenth-century dramatists were not overawed by the weight of tradition, and their inventive response to the classics is discussed in a number of the studies in this book.

The learned tradition of theatre did not exist alone. Popular traditions across Europe remained vibrant: the medieval farces and allegorical religious dramas continued to be written and performed throughout the period, and medieval forms were still employed. In Portugal, that medieval form was the one-act *auto*, mainly in verse though sometimes with interpolated dialogue in prose. One of the greatest playwrights of the sixteenth century, the Portuguese Gil Vicente, was essentially a medieval writer and a master of the *auto* which could be used for any kind of content, serious or comic.

The farce was, and remains, popular, and it appeals to a wide audience. Gil Vicente wrote a number of brilliant pieces in that genre — one, the *Auto da Índia*, is discussed in Chapter 1 — but he was employed throughout his career by the Portuguese Court and cannot be considered an exclusively popular writer. Everywhere in the sixteenth century it was very easy for popular and courtly or learned genres to merge. The polemic religious theatre of France and Germany combines Senecan structures with allegory, and farcical elements could be included in otherwise serious plays, as for example in the Spanish *comedia*. In Italy the literary academies, highly conscious of their social prestige and theoretical orthodoxy, tried to exclude popular performers (men and women), but the distinction between professional and amateur soon became blurred, and the paid actors of the *commedia dell'arte* took part in erudite productions if they were sufficiently talented.

The study of the theatre across different European countries varies greatly in proportion to the amount of accessible archival material available. In Portugal, almost nothing is known apart from the play texts themselves and the paratexts — prologues, dedications and the like — that are associated with them. In Italy and England, on the other hand, there is a wealth of information which reveals, in the Italian case at least, how in the sixteenth century women, both as actors and writers, became increasingly visible. All the same, even if the conditions of performance often remain obscure, this was a time when playwrights greatly extended the importance and the emotional weight of female roles.

The culture associated with the Latin language was necessarily international, and an international outlook prevailed also in forms of drama that were not erudite. English strolling players were popular in the Low Countries and the German-speaking lands, at least partly because of their athletic skills, and the *commedia dell'arte*, with its easily recognizable stock characters, was known outside Italy. On a different level, the classicism which is so marked a characteristic of Tudor drama was sometimes mediated through Italian or Spanish, so that an English adaptation of a scene from the *Celestina*, for example, can sometimes reveal a Roman substratum. Multilingualism of a different kind can be found in plays by Gil Vicente, who mixes Spanish and Portuguese speakers (and sometimes speakers of other languages), partly to emphasize the strangeness of the foreigner, but also to draw social distinctions in a country where more than one language was in common use. Plays otherwise dissimilar, like *Love's Labour's Lost* and António Ferreira's *Comédia do Cioso*, are alike in exploiting a foreign, French or Italian setting.

Although Aristotle's *Poetics* became quite widely studied (but not fully understood) in the later decades of the sixteenth century, the dead hand of theory did not weigh as heavily on dramatists as it came to do later. This partly explains why the earlier forms of sixteenth-century drama tend to be hybrid and original in their handling of tradition and the demands of the public. That public was very varied, for theatre at this period was not the concern of professionals only. Indeed, in some countries, like Portugal, the professional theatre hardly existed. Instead, plays were promoted by the Court, the Church, the universities and by wealthy private individuals, or groups of individuals, like the Italian academies, all of whom had different expectations, and welcomed audiences of different kinds. The playwrights discussed in this book had to be flexible, and the strict separation of genres was not one of their major aesthetic concerns. Instead, they were mostly uninhibited creators, eclectic and resourceful in their attitude to tradition and to stage-craft, capable of pathos — and often very funny. Ample space has been given to contributors for quotation, either in the body of articles or in appendices, and English translations are provided throughout.

There now follow brief summaries of the fifteen chapters which make up the book.

Part I: Literary Tradition and the Theatre

Gil Vicente is discussed by two writers, whose completely different approaches give some idea of the vast range of his writing. In his study of two plays Hélio Alves shows how the characters' statements about the passing of time are rather indications of their perceptions of time and can be related to similar passages in *Hamlet*, written nearly a hundred years later. Gil Vicente was fully conscious of the possibilities of the dramatic monologue and was able to explore them in a way that anticipated several aspects of the soliloquy as it went on to be performed on the English stage. However, the intention of articles such as this is not to show how Vicente in some way foreshadowed Shakespeare, which in any case is a rather absurd notion; it is rather that some of what we admire in Shakespeare already existed in other parts of Europe long before his time. This includes his use of language, a point made by Alves in the section of his chapter that is devoted to António Prestes.

José Cardoso Bernardes discusses a single play, the *Auto da Festa*, and its relation to the *Copilaçam*, the compilation of Vicente's writings which was published in 1562, about twenty-five years after his death. Even though this particular play was excluded from the *Copilaçam*, its central theme, the flight of Truth from the Portuguese Court, illustrates the perfect integrity of Vicente's medieval world in its mixture of the allegorical and the representational, and the comic and the serious. Yet even as Vicente expresses the religious certainty of a world that was passing, he seems to look forward to the psychologically complex drama of the century that was to come.

The sophistication of Spanish medieval theatre is the theme of Jane Whetnall's article. The *Auto de la huída en Egipto* is the product of wide reading in the devotional literature of the Middle Ages, and the anonymous author shows knowledge of both Latin and Italian. Sixteenth-century theatre was not an exclusively masculine affair, and there are hints that the play was written by a woman for performance in a convent.

Neoclassical comedy and tragedy developed early in Portugal — in the vernacular, perhaps earlier than in any other European country outside Italy. António Ferreira wrote his *Comédia do Cioso* [Comedy of the Jealous Man], here discussed by Tom Earle, in Portuguese in the 1550s. It is clearly influenced by Plautus and Terence, but in its portrayal of the actions of an obsessive — the jealous man of the title — it rewrites the conventions of the classic comic plot. Considered on its own, it is a satisfying play, and can be compared to other, later plays which depend on the psychological disorder of the hero, like *Othello*, *Volpone* and *L'Avare*. The Neo-Latin writer Diogo de Teive, a friend of Ferreira's, composed the only Latin tragedy to have survived in Portugal before the onset of Jesuit drama. Catarina Fouto shows that prologues and liminary texts penned by the Portuguese playwrights Sá de Miranda and Diogo de Teive are valuable contributions to the otherwise insignificant production of literary theory in that country in the early modern period. Teive's tragedy *Iohannes Princeps*, in particular, is unusual in being written in immediate reaction to a contemporary event, the death of the prince D. João, in January 1554. Far from being a piece of conventional moralizing, the tragedy is unsettling in laying the blame for the death of the heir to the throne on the Portuguese people as a whole, and especially on their obsession with the wealth of their Indian empire.

It was in Italy, however, that the first vernacular imitations of ancient comedy were written, and as early as 1424 Alberti had composed his *Philodoxeos*. Alberti uses many aspects of the ancient model to produce an allegorical comedy that revolves around his pessimistic obsessions, with virtue pitted against power, wealth and chance, as Martin McLaughlin explains. Nearly a century later, in *La Mandragola*, Machiavelli also extracts his own favourite themes from the classical original (including, of course, virtue and fortune), but he blends this with a striking modernity of character and message.

Wherever you look in sixteenth-century Europe you find playwrights recreating the legacy of Greece and Rome in the light of the preoccupations of their age. The English universities were great centres for the production, in the sense of writing and of performance, of drama in Latin, and this is the theme of Elizabeth Sandis's chapter. At Oxford, William Gager's additions to Seneca's *Phaedra*, composed for a festival in 1592, problematize the moral structure of the play in the interests of meta-literary conversations which take place between his own plays, the Senecan corpus, and the canonical texts which feed the work of both playwrights. Here again is a piece which might seem just one of many academic dramas but which when read for itself proves to have an individuality and force of its own.

In her study of two plays by Guillén de Castro, *El caballero bobo* [The Foolish Gentleman] and *La fuerza de la costumbre* [The Force of Habit], Kathleen Jeffs reminds us how the Spanish *comedia* was already well developed by the end of the sixteenth century. Very different both from the medievalism of Vicente and from the neoclassicism to be found in Portugal, Italy and England, Castro's melodramatic plays are full of violent action, cross-dressing and a concern for honour.

Part II: Theatre and Performance

The extraordinary riches of Italian archives allow Lisa Sampson to explore the great variety of performance styles which coexisted in Italy. The learned amateurs of the academies, the professional actors, especially the comic players in the popular *commedia dell'arte* tradition, and the performers in Court spectacles provided three different spheres for theatre. Although at first professionals and amateurs kept their distance from each other, the two categories began to merge towards the end of the sixteenth century, helping to create the climate of cultural experimentation which resulted, amongst other things, in the growth of Italian opera.

Katherine Duncan-Jones describes the world of three English clowns, Richard Tarlton, Robert Armin and, especially, William Kemp. English actors were in demand abroad, and Kemp was well travelled. A good improviser, Kemp was an athlete with a strongly physical style of performance, which linked him to the *commedia dell'arte*, in which he may even have taken part. In his sophisticated and cosmopolitan comedy *Love's Labour's Lost*, written nearly at the end of the sixteenth century, Shakespeare seems to use the clown Costard to promote a kind of bluff

6 T. F EARLE AND CATARINA FOUTO

Englishness. However, by the end of the play Shakespeare gives the idealistic Spaniard Armado the advantage.

In Portugal, contextual information about the theatre in the sixteenth century is in short supply. However, José Camões makes use of the 'play within a play' device, found in a number of *autos*, to discover something about the conditions of performance in a country without a professional theatre. Though there are risks in mining artistic works in this way, it would be too much of a coincidence if these examples were merely a literary convention and were not the reflection of everyday life when private houses were used as settings, for which plays were certainly commissioned.

Part III: Theatre and Society

Sixteenth-century dramatists were not just entertainers, academic or popular. Theatre was a way of transmitting urgent religious and political messages, and both sides in the conflict between Catholics and Protestants used it for that purpose. Michael Meere has investigated the French Calvinist writers Joachim de Coignac and Louis des Masures, who wrote plays based on the Biblical story of David and Goliath with a clear political as well as religious intent. Catholic playwrights used the same story, but without exploiting to the same extent its violence or its political implications.

Vernacular drama in German was largely confessional in the sixteenth century, and so was much that was written in Latin. Thomas Naogeorg (1508–1563), studied by Helen Watanabe-O'Kelly, was a humanist who translated Sophocles into Latin, but his own plays, for all that they were composed in the classical language, were allegorical assaults on the papacy, written from the Lutheran perspective. *Pammachius* is a true call to arms where, instead of the expected fifth act, an epilogue tells the audience to go out into the real world to see how the action continues.

In England and in Portugal in the sixteenth century there were religious tensions of various kinds, but no open warfare like in France and Germany, and the relationship between theatre and society took on different forms. Peter Brown's investigations of the influence of Latin comedy in the period show that it was thoroughly embedded in the developing dramatic culture of Tudor England. The taste of whole generations of theatre-goers was formed to some extent by Plautus and Terence, from schoolboys — for whom the comedies were part of the curriculum — to the audiences of both academic and popular plays, in Latin or in the vernacular.

Finally, Vanda Anastácio shows not so much how theatre influenced society but how a play could be modified by a variety of social pressures. Camões's *Auto de Filodemo* was not published until after the author's death and was subject to interventions by copyists, the inquisitorial censor and by producers, who added material or altered the text to suit the changing tastes of audiences.

★   ★   ★   ★   ★

It was not the intention of the editors and contributors to this volume to exhaust all the possible — and exciting — avenues of research into the theatre of sixteenth-century Europe. Rather, our book is intended to stimulate a critical dialogue into the rich and varied dramatic production of this period across many boundaries, not forgetting the traditional political and geographical frontiers, but involving other dividing lines: between elite and popular practices and dramatic forms, between sacred and secular traditions, including the confessional divisions between different parts of Europe, and between disciplinary approaches. We hope that the fruits of this work, which started in October 2011 at a conference held in St John's College, Oxford and developed into a more ambitious project, may contribute to a new critical appreciation of sixteenth-century theatre in its own right.

Notes to the Introduction

1. (London: Owen, 2006).
2. For example, *Tragedie Popolari del Cinquecento Europeo*, edited by Maria Chiabò and Federico Doglio (Rome: Torre d'Orfeo, 1997) or *Aspects du Théâtre Populaire en Europe au XVIème siècle*, edited by Madeleine Lazard (Paris: SEDES, 1989).
3. Edited by Jan Bloemendal and Howard B. Norland (Leiden: Brill, 2013), and by Philip Ford and Andrew Taylor (Leuven: Leuven University Press, 2013), respectively.
4. Examples are Roger Chartier, *Publishing Drama in Early-Modern Europe* (London: British Library, 1998) or Véronique Lochert, *L'écriture du spectacle : les didascalies dans le théâtre européen aux XVIe et XVIIe siècles*, originally presented as the author's thesis in 2009.
5. See A. Robert Lauer's *Tyrannicide and Drama* (Stuttgart: Steiner, 1987), or the collection of essays, edited by Jean-Pierre Bordier and André Lascombes, *Dieu et les dieux dans le théâtre de la renaissance* (Turnhout: Brepols, 2006).
6. See, for example, the collection edited by Silvia Carandini, *Teatri barocchi : tragedie, commedie, pastorali nella drammaturgia europea fra '500 e '600* (Rome: Bulzoni, 2000).

PART I

❖

Literary Tradition and the Theatre

CHAPTER 1

Sooner than Shakespeare:
Inwardness and Lexicon in the Drama of
Gil Vicente and António Prestes

Hélio J. S. Alves
Universidade de Évora

Gil Vicente and the Representation of Self

> The lights burn blue, it is now dead midnight.
> Cold fearful drops stand on my trembling flesh.
> What do I fear? Myself? There's none else by;
> Richard loves Richard, that is, I am I.
> Is there a murderer here? No. Yes, I am!
> Then fly. What, from myself? Great reason why,
> Lest I revenge? What, myself upon myself?
> Alack, I love myself. Wherefore? For any good
> That I myself have done unto myself?
> O, no, alas, I rather hate myself
> For hateful deeds committed by myself.
> [...]
> I shall despair. There is no creature loves me,
> And if I die, no soul will pity me —
> And wherefore should they, since that I myself
> Find in myself no pity to myself?[1]

It has been said that this speech's 'peculiar badness is difficult to describe'. The sentence comes from a peculiarly extreme critic of Shakespeare, Harold Bloom. The words 'dreadful' and worse also occur to him when faced with this play. Bloom's critical assault on Shakespeare's 'exorbitantly lengthy, cumbersome and overwritten *Richard III*' does not end here, however. On the particular speech quoted above, he says that 'no actor can salvage Richard from sounding silly', a risk that obviously I believe to be worth taking, though only for a less than Bardolatric purpose. As for women, it seems we should reach no further: the play is 'any actress's nightmare, for none of the women's parts are playable', he says. He even goes as far as stating that, for the 'ghastly' widow of Henry VI, 'Shakespeare never could compose a decent line'.[2] These are, of course, rather carefully chosen items from Harold Bloom's Shakespearean worship, but they are nonetheless comforting for those of us who think that the study and performance of plays other than Shakespeare's can be as rewarding. Bloom's derogatory opinions about *Richard III* help us believe that there may be more to early modern theatre than the categories 'before', 'during' and 'after' Shakespeare.

As early plays go, it seems from Bloom's analysis that Shakespeare is beginning something in English, even in world, literature, that being the explanation of why he is so inept in *Richard III*. The word goes that the playwright was experimenting with something utterly new. As with all experiments, the first attempts should be expected to be mediocre. Nevertheless, Shakespeare's originality, in this and other matters, has been generally challenged, even within the field of English studies.[3] If there is an introductory nature to *Richard III* in its attempts at conceiving dramatic inwardness, then it should apply only to the author's own development. If one goes to the trouble of looking at writing in languages other than English, the notion of Shakespeare's uniqueness is bound to be reduced even further, since a much clearer perception of historical development, dramatic techniques and expressions of inwardness in other literatures puts into a much more knowledgeable perspective his unquestionable artistic successes.

Academic convention tends to be so powerful, however, that even some comparative studies fail to achieve a wide enough range. In an otherwise perceptive book released in the current decade (effectively, only the other day), Robert Ellrodt attributes to the playwright from Stratford a language of the self which is initiated in the *Sonnets* and developed into higher degrees of introspection and dissolution of self in *Hamlet*, under the new influence of Montaigne.[4] A critique of such notions had been formulated earlier by comparatists who showed how far the arguments in favour of the exceptional features of the *Sonnets* represent a misunderstanding of how the early modern lyric was formed and developed, both historically and poetically, in a much wider geo-cultural scenario.[5] The argument against the uniqueness of *Hamlet* and other Shakespearean plays in this respect has been less visible, perhaps because it counters the widely held belief about the innovative genius of Shakespeare in this particular field as well as in others. And yet, the study of sixteenth-century drama and 'character poetics' in various literatures may just require inspection. It is one thing to recognize intertextuality, although slight in the case of Montaigne and Shakespeare; it is quite another to find out how a discourse about a living existence interested in talking about himself (Montaigne) becomes a fictional character inserted into a dramatic plot for the stage. The *Essais* are undoubtedly crucial to the early modern language of self, but the transfer between genres, from the essay to the drama, implied in their influence over Shakespeare, has not been explained. Again, the lack of a wider perspective transforms into a peculiar phenomenon of single minds what is, rather differently, a movement or tendency in poetics and general literary composition, occurring at certain points in time. What is lacking, in a word, is a good look at the neighbourhood.

In a book published some years ago, I argued that the so-called 'new' language of the performed self is a phenomenon clearly discernible in poetical compositions published during or just before the time of Shakespeare's literary activity.[6] I suggested that one could write a history of fictional third-person self-consciousness in European literature, with examples of characters who seem to be questioning their own thoughts, in played monologues and soliloquies. I called specific attention to the fact that one poet, Vasco Mouzinho, could be held responsible for introducing into Portuguese literature fictional characters with a modern inwardness of the kind Bloom finds in Shakespearean theatre. Mouzinho was an exact contemporary of Shakespeare's. The coincidence would be remarkable — we can be reasonably sure that neither of them ever heard about the other — if it were not for the fact that, as I attempted to show, both writers were part of the same historical current, the more or less conscious attempt to overwrite a rhetoric of speech by poetic elaborations of a self-overhearing presence. I then proposed that this new kind of complexity in fictional personality, this 'Hamletian' trait, was very much alive and 'in the air', so to speak, at the close of the sixteenth century across widely different parts of Europe, in a way that would imply a general tendency stimulated by a range of favourable circumstances, artistic and otherwise.

But did this modern individual character emerge suddenly, brought in by great authors such as Montaigne and (as I argued then) Torquato Tasso, or was it the result of a gradual acquisition, depending on public expectations? An enquiry into earlier stages of literary history presents us with a far from simple general picture of the construction of dramatic character. Before the late sixteenth century, there seems to have been no fully formed representations of self-consciousness, of inwardness or of 'the birth of the modern conscience' as some would call it, but it is certainly untrue that a shift from a plot-based structure to a logic of psychic development in drama occurs only with and from Shakespeare. A change from typical or even stereotypical character to a mimesis of modern psychology was happening long before *Richard III* was written and performed.

In my argument, the poet and dramatist Gil Vicente is a case in point. Some eighty years before Shakespeare began his writing career, this Portuguese author, celebrated within a restricted circle of performers and connoisseurs, but reduced to hardly more than a name in most of today's widely circulated histories of Western theatre,[7] introduced characters in his plays who reveal closeness to self-consciousness in the modern sense, characters capable of building shifting perspectives and reflections with an individual psychological depth way beyond that which is generally expected from medieval drama. Some characters in these Portuguese plays transcend the limits of rhetorical exemplarity, and typological personification or allegory, to become gifted with what looks like a 'personality'. Yet, school curricula and standard criticism taught most people to appreciate Vicentine characters as social types. These types do exist, and sometimes they dominate entire plays, as is to be expected from a late-medieval dramatist. But the generalization of this standard point of view has blinded both reading and performance to the inner life represented in many characters and to its importance in the historical development of Western theatre.

In what follows, I shall comment on two of Gil Vicente's plays: the first is one of his most discussed, the farce known as *Índia*, while the other is one of the most obviously allegorical of all his texts, the play on a city's shield of arms, *Divisa de Coimbra*. In both cases, genre and tradition would seem to discourage individuality

14 HÉLIO J. S. ALVES

in characters, not to speak of any kind of inwardness. Those plays are, however, proof that the stock characters of medieval farce and that long-deprecated mode of allegorical personification, with its direct and barren translation of abstractions into sensible images, are able to conflate with other, more modern expressions of human consciousness and inner perplexities.

What Shakespearean critic Joel Fineman[8] calls a theatre organized by a logic of personality as opposed to a theatre of logical action is precisely what can be found in the short play *Índia*, first performed in 1509.[9] Despite all efforts, no critic of this remarkable text has been able to explain its glaring distortions, implausibilities, not to say impossibilities, of chronology. Regarding linear and cyclical time, *Índia* seems to be a complete mess. True enough, some commentators have tried to make sense of the play in that respect, and they have achieved partial successes. But perhaps because Vicente has been constantly placed within the context of the Middle Ages or of the early Renaissance, nobody apart from the present writer has found it possible to show how the sense of time in *Índia* has got some points in common with *Hamlet*. As I hope to have explained at length elsewhere, the disruptions of time in Vicente's play are really disruptions *in the perception* of time by the characters. As such, they should be explained in the same ways as Hamlet's contrasting, even paradoxical, references to chronology: the absurdities and incompatibilities are manifestations of a psycho-logic of time dramatically exercised.

In *Índia*, a character like the Young Maid (the *Moça*) becomes far more complex and poetically successful when we understand how she plays, somewhere between the voluntary and the instinctive, on words about the passing of time. In fact, those words make sense only when they reflect psychological truths about herself and about her interlocutors, namely Constança, the Mistress (*Ama*). The entire initial scene of the play and the last, dense, dialogue between the two women, move around differing perceptions of time. But the point is not just that the Maid and her Mistress perceive time differently; in reality, even within each of these two characters there is no ultimate ground to settle quantifiable, 'real', time. The Maid tries to deal with the difference between her own perception of time, the understanding of chronology that will best guarantee her enjoyment of her Mistress's good graces and the preservation of a mental reserve of irony and critique which hardly coincides with the previous two apprehensions of time.

The Mistress called Constança (in English, *Constance* or *Constancy*), on the other hand, is anything but constant in the ticking of her clock. She suspects that time does not pass as she perceives it bodily, but she goes to a lot of trouble to face objectively, in her mind, the measurable passing of time. The initial scene of the play, her husband's departure to India in May 1506, is interpreted by Constança as essentially a discrepancy: spring, the month of May, is being overrun by political, economic or strategic convenience; natural time is being violated by human artifice. She recalls spring as the season when 'new blood is kindled' [*atiçar do sangue novo*], the season when men and women should get together and make love; she complains, not without reason, that the opposite happens when her husband sails off. From the beginning, therefore, Constança's biological clock, the clock of her desire, is radically altered by the outer circumstances forced upon it. Since she is at the centre of the play both physically and dramatically, her distorted psychological perception of reality is reflected by doubts and disagreements over when things happen and how long they take.

One of her lovers, the Castilian braggart, provides one more opportunity to enhance this psycho-logic at the level of discourse. He too thinks that 'the time is out of joint', as he becomes so anxious waiting for Constança's sexual favours that a short night of spring becomes to him a lengthy night at Christmas time [*noches de Navidá*]. The idea is reinforced by the contrast between the impression of a long winter night and the knowledge we get as spectators that the morning arrives fast (*quiere amanecer ya | que no tardará media hora*). The contrast, therefore, occurs in the Spaniard's discourse and *within* his mind. He feels that the night is very long but he also senses that Nature is bringing him the morning too early. Why too early? Because an entire night of waiting outside Constança's house was not enough to secure her permission for him to climb into her bedroom.

The reader or the spectator of this play gets involved in a dramatic structure highly dependent on differing perceptions of time subject to various interchanges between characters like the Mistress, the Maid and the Castilian, and even differing perceptions struggling inside each of these characters. The play dramatizes those different and interchanging psyches, enriching them with lines packed full of psychological uncertainties. A particularly extreme example is that afforded by lines 356 to 387: we know that the almost paranoid counting and recounting of time in the dialogue is a sign of the prime materials with which Vicente built characters already as repositories of psychology. 'The time is out of joint' already in Vicente's theatre, and it is disjointed in *Índia* for the purpose of rounding off characters whose behaviour reflects a complexity which goes some way towards reaching modern self-consciousness.

But it is not just in the mode of interchange between characters and action that Gil Vicente expresses something approaching modern inwardness. Despite their allegorical and even anagogical frameworks, soliloquies and other forms of monologue make their way into these Portuguese plays with unmistakable overtones of individual thought. My next example is Liberata from *Divisa de Coimbra*. The play reworks narratively and dramatically the symbols included in the shield of the city. However, no stock character from blazonry would ever be expected to say the words Liberata utters in the play. Placed in the isolated environment of the 'serra de Coimbra' (in this mythical past, the area where Coimbra now lies is a range of mountains in the play), left alone, Liberata, afraid of the surroundings, cannot afford to fall asleep. So, she decides instead to think:

> *Fica só Liberata e diz*:
>
> > En montaña tan terrible
> > no me conviene dormir
> > quiero pensar
> > por no dormir... (ll. 415–18)

If sleep brings death, or the fear that it may, we are one stage behind Hamlet's fear of what may come *after* death. But it is a similar need for exercising thought, occasioned by the fear of some sort of deathlike sleep that one finds in the introduction of

16 HÉLIO J. S. ALVES

Liberata as an individual character. We shall see that the parallel between the prince of Denmark and the princess from would-be Portugal is not as far-fetched as it may seem at first glance. Initially, we hear from Liberata about feelings quite common at this stage of the plot, without any philosophical abstractions. She simply misses her sister Heridea and she wonders whether circumstances again will allow for them to be together as they used to (lines 421–32). What happens next, however, is quite extraordinary. Although she is still thinking about her family, it is abstract thought that now comes to the fore. In a few extremely packed lines, Liberata produces not only a meditation on time and its powers, but also, more significantly, a commentary on that meditation:

> Lo que fue, si vuelve a ser
> lo mismo, creo que no,
> si será,
> qu'el tiempo tiene poder,
> no puede, mira en esto
> quizás podrá. (ll. 433–38)[10]

[If the past returns (literally: if what it was again becomes), I don't believe it will be the same, for time has power if it is that time has power. No it doesn't! Look at this — perhaps it does.]

The concrete action is clear enough: she merely wishes for a happy life again with her family. But although *esto* (l. 437) reminds us of the plain facts, they are suddenly absent and almost forgotten in the middle of these dense considerations. As in *Hamlet*, a situation derived from the plot provokes abstract thought, but this thought overwhelms action to the point of making us forget it. Liberata is discussing the powers of time in self-contradictory statements, already showing at least three properties of the modern monologue: hesitation, self-questioning and abstraction. She addresses herself more than she addresses time, and she does so in both the first person present (*creo*) and in the second person imperative (*mira*). She attempts an if-clause twice, twice she interrupts and refuses an if-clause. Time is the object, but in spite of the fact that it is a real situation that sparks off reflection, the philosophical issues are at the forefront. In the end, possibility is confronted with impossibility and the result is undecided (*quizás*), undecided within herself.

Liberata is not the only instance where complexity of character is shown in *Divisa de Coimbra*. The 'savage' Monderigón she meets in the mountains is a cruel tyrant [*cruel tirano*, l. 352] and a prisoner of love simultaneously. He behaves as a master *and* as a slave. But if this combination of contradictory stances and feelings may be explained in terms of a fusion of genres or stock characters (the monster of chivalric romance combined with the lover from courtly poetry and narrative), Liberata's monologue after meeting him is harder to pin down:

Partido Monderigón, fica Liberata a solas falando consigo e diz [Monderigón exits, and Liberata, alone on stage, soliloquizes]:

Es ido pues por mi fe	*By my faith, he has gone,*
que no sé por qué interese	*and I do not know why*
deseaba que se fuse	*I wanted him to go.*
y pésame porque se fue	*I am sorry he went*

como si bien le quisiese	*as if I meant him well,*
y pluguiese all alma mía	*and I wish with all my soul*
que ya pudiese librarme	*that I could be free,*
que esto que hace pesarme	*because what grieves me*
porque se fue algún día	*is that one day he left,*
quizá podrá amargarme.	*and that may make me bitter.*
Mas qué digo?	*But what am I saying?*
Por ventura es enemigo	*Perhaps he is an enemy*
que quiere hacerme hereje	*who wants to make me a sinner*
mas no rege	*but it doesn't follow*
qu'el amor siento comigo.	*if I feel love within me.*
Qué haré?	*What shall I do?*
Si volviere mostrarle he	*If he returns, shall I show him*
manso corazón o blavo?	*a tender heart or a fierce one?*
Mas él hácese mi escravo	*But he makes himself my slave,*
para qué m'ablandaré?	*so why should I show tenderness?*
Todavía	*All the same*
seguiré la tema mía	*I will follow my inclinations,*
no me quiero condenar	*I don't want to condemn myself*
ni pensar	*or to think*
neste hombre hora ni día.	*about this man for a minute.*
Bien mirado	*All things considered*
es tan dulce y bien hablado	*he is so sweet and well spoken.*
que lo sea norabuena	*Let him be like that,*
que esta lena	*For this talk*
después da luengo cuidado.	*is the cause of much thought.* (ll. 531–60)

Monderigón's complexities have disturbed Liberata's notions of behaviour and feeling. Fear and love seem well defined as poles in her thought, but it is clear that her own soul [*alma mía*] is being shaken by the contradictions of which this soliloquy is the expression. Most features of the modern dramatic monologue are present here again. Hesitation begins in the first line, with *pues*, to reappear further on in interruptions, repetitions of *mas*, and contrasting thoughts. Self-questioning is patently evident, as Liberata hears herself say and think things that she dares not agree with, leaving doubts and unanswered puzzles throughout. Only abstraction is less clear or absent, since she does not here address any philosophical issues directly. In any case, the soliloquy reaches beyond codified standards of the love lyric as understood, and practised, at the time, and even much later. Such concentrated expressions of inner feeling as inherently contradictory to the point of obscurity seem to arise from a need to expose complex individuality and sophisticated self-analysis on the stage, as opposed to a philosophical novel or a book of first-person poems. The medium of drama itself, with its peculiarities of exposition, should be regarded as the main source for these intense moments of self-representation.

These are not the only monologues uttered by Liberata. In all, she has got four longer or shorter speeches of this kind in the play. This means that Gil Vicente was fully conscious of the possibilities of the dramatic monologue and was able to explore them in a way that anticipated, by almost a century, several aspects of the soliloquy as it went on to be performed on the English stage. Even the sense of inscrutability which is such an emphatic feature of modern character-building is

18 HÉLIO J. S. ALVES

touched upon in Liberata's words, as they lack most punctuation, permit differing syntactic breaks and caesurae, and, in the end, leave an obscure recess inside her 'mind' that the character herself is unable to clarify. This is not to say, of course, that the same degree of inwardness exists in Gil Vicente as it does in Shakespeare, Montaigne, Tasso or Vasco Mouzinho. What can and should be said, however, is that Shakespeare's great monologues are better understood when placed in their adequate historical position within a theatrical practice beginning much earlier.

António Prestes and the Pre-eminence of Language[11]

'Words, words, words', says Hamlet (II. 2. 192). The astounding vocabulary and almost superhuman variety of imagery in Shakespeare's output are one of the commonplaces of literary criticism and one of the foundations on which the supremacy of the Stratford bard is laid. Suspicious as I am of all statements which individualize so much that they seem to detach the artist from his time, I'd like to see more work done on the artistic background to Shakespeare's own preferred territory of drama, contemporary and earlier. Part of this work, the part which specifically addresses language, has been done by David Crystal and his conclusion is interesting: since the poet was writing in one of the most creative times in the development of the English language, his achievement makes him more typical than exceptional.[12] This same conclusion is supported by electronic analysis of vocabulary. Hugh Craig wrote:

> One of the staples of Shakespeare commentary for the past century and more has been the idea that Shakespeare had an exceptionally large vocabulary. Now that electronic texts of early modern English drama are available in quantity, it is possible to check this claim. Comparing Shakespeare's plays to a large group of plays by other writers from the period shows that his vocabulary is indeed large, but this would seem to be only because his canon of surviving single-author plays is larger than his contemporaries. Play for play, Shakespeare's dramatic works fit well with the pattern of others in the number of different words used. The same can be said of the number of new words he introduces into successive plays. Looking at a different measure — the extent to which a playwright's rate of use of individual words deviates from the average — Shakespeare is remarkable for the closeness of his practice to that of his peers. Whatever quantitative measures reflecting Shakespeare's acknowledged exceptional status are explored in the future, the evidence of vocabulary size and word-use frequency places Shakespeare with his contemporaries, rather than apart from them.[13]

So the myth of a superhuman vocabulary, way beyond anything that could be found in the English language as used by a single individual, becomes rather a recognition of an entire era's linguistic vitality, quite superior, for example, to today's. This conclusion does not diminish the playwright's linguistic performance in the eyes of Bardolaters, it just redirects our attention, from merely quantitative statistics to the rich and inventive ways in which Shakespeare used words. For his ability to make nouns from verbs, verbs from nouns, change a term's morphology and reposition it syntactically is, according to Crystal, the hallmark of the playwright's creativity in language.

There are no remotely similar studies of António Prestes's seven surviving plays, an *oeuvre* which precedes Shakespeare's by anything between fifteen years and half a century.[14] Yet it can be safely assumed that one of the most remarkable features of Prestes as a dramatist is the strength of his grammatical inventiveness and the variety and semantic flexibility of his lexicon. It may yet be discovered that much of this vocabulary is shared with other more or less contemporary authors. However, it is clear thus far that Prestes's lexicographical creativity is quite his own, with a few words unknown elsewhere and an exuberance, especially in the quickness and intensity of figures of speech, that goes beyond even his closest rivals.[15] In addition, combinations of fresh words with puns, tropes, sound effects and the rhythm provided by the verse make the work of this Portuguese playwright a special case of achievement in language and prosody.

Here is an example from *Dois Irmãos* [Two Brothers], part of a portrait of married life created by the character called Confiado [Trusting]:

> J'agora o frio entra em custo
> à vida das vidas fartas
> vez de sol, roupão de martas
> campo mendes com magusto
> sobre triunfinho de cartas
> depois gato repelado
> sol posto na pousadinha
> ceazinha
> de lombo de porco assado
> e quando pior galinha
> ou coelho ou bom-bocado. (ll. 188–98)

Closely related in subject is this other example, from another play, *Procurador* [The Lawyer] on the art of being a husband:

> BRÁS: Tem arte de penteá-la
> em eirado ao soalheiro
> e depois disso enfeitá-la
> e andar rededor olhá-la
> se está bem, qu'é d'escudeiro
> aparar-lhe pêro à mesa
> chamar-lhe minha marquesa
> estáveis hoje na igreja
> ua dama. E a boneja
> guarda isto de salpresa. (ll. 401–10)

In these excerpts, lines such as 'à vida das vidas fartas', 'campo mendes com magusto' and 'aparar-lhe pêro à mesa' not only raise issues of lexicography and idiom, but are also evidently charged with a sense of musical euphony which has not even begun to be appreciated in modern critical writing. Prestes evidently enjoys language as an end in itself, in much the same way as a painter would work on a portrait or a view, not because the particular person or sight are interesting in themselves, but because they provide the adequate opportunity to display whatever resources may exist in the painter's art. This is not to say that such displays are empty of content, of course. But they certainly do not forfeit their character as display. I would qualify the use of language in Prestes as a sort of ballet. Meaning moves about, whirls and whooshes, as in a dance. It is as if the playwright wished to try the various shadings of a subject by exploring their potential to say more. In turn, this leads to almost inevitably strong demands in terms of an actor's bodily expression. The last excerpt is typical: Brás is simply saying that a good husband pays proper attention to his wife. But he expresses this in several gestures of a realistic sort: combing, making up, glancing at her from several angles, pronouncing courteous words, all of these actions and some more in quick succession and few lines. In such cases, variety in lexicon and semantics corresponds to considerable physical effort on the part of the actor. Display of language is bound to result in gestural display.

The high intensity of vocabulary and meaning in Prestes's plays, however, is not restricted to monologue. Quick and dense exchanges between two or more characters occur often. The following example comes from *Ave Maria* [Hail Mary]:

> Bom Trabalho: Bofá senhor, que quando ele
> gasta o pão com tal borrego
> que o gaste com um morcego.
> Ah i de puxa, que pele
> que pendão pera penego.
> Bom Serviço: Este com cepo e cadea será mona.
> Bom Cuidado: Almanjarra d'atafona.
> Bom Serviço: Parece pai de çantopea.
> Bom Trabalho: E casou co' azeitona. (ll. 1644–53)

In a single rhyming stanza, Prestes includes three characters speaking figuratively about personality and behaviour. The glossary in the 2008 edition *Autos de António Prestes* — from now on called *GAAP* for convenience — helps the reader somewhat. Bom Cuidado's sentence, for instance, can be explained in full: 'almanjarra' is described as 'peça de pau a que se prendem os animais que fazem andar a nora; pessoa grande e feia; coisa mal feita, disforme' [piece of wood to which animals are tied when they are drawing water from a well [...]]. 'Atafona', on the other hand, means 'moinho' [mill]. In the context, then, 'almanjarra d'atafona' is a rustic way of saying that the person discussed is large and ugly. Most of the expressions in the passage, however, are not so easily accessible. 'Gastar o pão' [to spend the bread] and 'azeitona' [olive], for example, suppose, in all probability, respectively a synecdoche for 'spending all the money' and a metaphor for 'coloured woman'. 'Puxa' is a euphemism for a slightly different four-letter word (explained in *GAAP* as 'filho' [son]). But the rest is mostly a question of guesswork. The contrast between 'borrego' and 'morcego' may mean that between a lame person and a predator, or a man of principle and an opportunist, or even between a subservient follower and a capricious entrepreneur; the expression 'pendão pera penego' perhaps implies giving high value to something worthless; 'pai de çantopea' could possibly translate as progenitor of a horrible woman, and so on. Despite the difficulties of interpretation, and the general intractability, in an interchange such as this the playwright's interest in intensifying meaning through quick-witted dialogue remains. The passage is typical in its purpose of enrichment and transformation of sense, but also in the wild competitiveness of the words. The characters seem to be in a race to find the best description, not in the sense of the most adequate to the object, nor even of a

SOONER THAN SHAKESPEARE   21

show of virtuosity and repertoire, but in the sense of finding the liveliest, freshest and most revealing.

Most of what I have qualified as a 'ballet' (in monologue) or a 'race' (in dialogue) of words and figures still awaits decoding. As we have seen, the *GAAP* can be helpful for this task, and so can the notes appended to the Camões-Reis Silva edition. Nevertheless, a running commentary is required to make us understand many of the lines in Prestes's plays. My own example will come from the beginning of one of the most interesting of his texts, a play with a ghost quite unlike Hamlet's, called *Mouro Encantado* [Enchanted Moor]. It begins with a monologue of about seventy lines. I shall quote and comment on its first twenty-two lines, as a sample of the kind of work Prestes's language requires.

> Como lá diz o rifão
> nam fez Deos quem desempare.
> Crê-lo assi tenho rezão
> que em mi o mostrou tam chão
> que escusa que o mais decrare.   5
> Um pintor tal não entrapa:
> sendo de tudo orfãzinho
> muito inho
> sem ter lapa nem solapa
> eira nem Beira nem Minho   10
> foi comigo sam Martinho
> em partir c'o pobre a capa.
> Deu-me aqui de sesmaria
> em mato maninho, pobre
> lazarilho, ũa estria   15
> a um senhor, enfim o bom dia
> é senhor, senhora, nobre.
> Entrei ali tam gentil peça
> tam paralítico, tão mosto
> tam desgosto   20
> que chamava aos pés cabeça
> e ao meu toutiço rosto.

These are the words of Fernão Varela as the play begins. He is telling his own story of social advancement, how he grew from humble origins to a comfortable bourgeois position in life. Apart from what Varela's story can tell us about sixteenth-century Portuguese society and class relations, its interest resides entirely in the play on language. Commentary must clarify, as far as possible, the lexicographical peculiarities of these lines, before attempting even the mildest approach to them from the point of view of social history or cultural studies. The basic work of philological understanding is required here as much as anywhere else, and possibly more.

Some lines are quite devoid of interpretive difficulties. Others, however, require special comment:

l. 2   both the paper and the online edition inform us, in a note, about the occurrence of a similar proverb (*rifão*) in other contemporary plays. It means that God did not create people to leave them helpless.

l. 5   *decrare* is for *declare* (a known phonological case of rhotacism).

22   HÉLIO J. S. ALVES

l. 6   *entrapa*: *GAAP* gives *inventa, concebe*. The overall meaning of the line is that no painter, however great a master, could ever conceive something like what follows (Varela's tale).

l. 8   *inho*: *GAAP* says nothing. It is an adjective for *orfãzinho* [little orphan] and it qualifies, through emphasis, how young, small and lonely he was when left without home and family.

l. 9   *solapa*: *GAAP* gives *disfarce* [mask]. *Sem lapa nem solapa* has certainly got a similar meaning to the next line, as reinforcement. *Lapa* is a kind of shell and *solapa* is a kind of hole. According to the Moraes dictionary, *solapa* is 'cova por baixo, e tapada, que se não vê'. But *solapa* could mean also something used to cover or hide a hole, as today. In which case, *lapa* would mean cave, cavity or, in a sense, 'hole'; again, in modern usage. So, *sem lapa nem solapa* could just mean literally 'neither with a hole to live in nor with something to cover it', i.e., lacking in all welfare. It could have been a popular expression, although no evidence of its presence in other texts is known.

l. 10 this is a mixture of a popular saying and an invention of Prestes's. *Sem eira nem beira* is a popular expression to describe someone who is homeless. Prestes transforms *beira* ('a place next door') into Beira (a region of Portugal) and adds another Portuguese name to this, creating a new meaning to the word *Minho*, which now becomes not only the river and the region of Portugal and Galicia of that name, but also a synonym of 'place' or even 'home'.

l. 13 *deu-me*: the subject is Sam Martinho [Saint Martin]; *sesmaria*: *GAAP* gives *concessão, obrigação*. However, its meaning here must be the traditional one, land without culture or use. In one of the plays by Gil Vicente, *Romagem dos Agravados*, *sesmaria* is used as the opposite of *empreitada* (ll. 39–40), that is free land as opposed to land for contracted work. In Prestes, *sesmaria* appears as a synonym for *mato maninho* [barren scrubland] in the next line. Both follow metaphorically from the references to geography earlier on.

l. 15 *lazarilho*: from the hero of the anonymous mid-sixteenth century Castilian novel *Lazarillo de Tormes*, meaning wretch, beggar (*GAAP*), depending on others to survive. *estria*: possibly a groove. Absent in *GAAP*. However, it is part of the play on words coming from *sesmaria* and *mato* and so, by hyperbaton, a narrow stretch (of land).

ll. 16–17 These lines are so concise that they become quite obscure, if not inscrutable. It is clear enough that Varela is saying that fortune gave him a master, in this case, two masters, a couple (*senhor, senhora*). *Bom dia* is, I think, being used as a synonym for 'morning' (this is the time of day when one says *bom dia*) and a metaphor for the beginning of the subject's life. Prestes frequently transforms expressions (such as a greeting) into a noun.

l. 18 *gentil*: probably in the sense of 'fragile' or 'delicate'; the adjective applies usually to boys and educated young ladies.

l. 19 *mosto*: a case of what Eugenio Asensio called 'adjectivization of the noun' (as also in the next line: *tam desgosto*). From the noun *mosto* [must, grape juice], implying that Varela was then more like must than like good wine. *GAAP* gives *rude* [crude, rustic] as synonym.

The type of figurativeness featuring most in the theatre of António Prestes is linguistic. For him, words are meant to be moulded: Eugenio Asensio called attention to the way he tortures and disjoints them in a thousand ways.[16] The quotations given above have already shown how Prestes pays at least as much attention to the rhythm and the sound of discourse as he does to literal and metaphorical meaning. Alliteration, assonance and puns, combined in ever fresher forms, are at least as central to this Portuguese playwright as they will later be to William Shakespeare.

In the famous graveyard scene, Hamlet speculates that one of the skulls might have been that of a lawyer, and we hear this volley of alliterations and puns:

> Where be his quiddities now — his quillets, his cases, his tenures and his tricks [...] Hum! This fellow might be in's time a great buyer of land, with his statutes, his recognizances, his fines, his double vouchers, his recoveries: is this the fine of his fines, and the recovery of his recoveries, to have his fine pate full of fine dirt! (*Hamlet*, v. 1. 93–101)

In this explosion of semantic variety, Hamlet uses 'recovery' in two senses and 'fine' in no less than four. 'Fine of fines' requires a stretch of interpretation, as 'fine' acquires the sense of 'end' or 'outcome' (as in 'final') which may just be guessed from the context of the graveyard, albeit with difficulty. Shakespeare is re-creating vocabulary out of etymology and figure, and making Hamlet produce dark humour with them.

The same thing happens in Prestes's drama a few decades earlier. Precisely in the play where the protagonist is a lawyer (*Procurador*), João Gaspar, a peasant rather than a prince, but almost a representation of Everyman (he says he belongs to the 'concelho d'Elva e Aldrão', something like 'the constituency of Elve and Aldam'), wonders aloud about the nature of the legal system that is supposed to serve him:

> E como demanda é já
> ougir dor, estreguir dor
> que mais desembargador?
> Tudo é dor e dor não há
> De quem s'há de ter à dor.
> [...]
> Eu lhe direi o que vai:
> Que pois é proculador
> Que me não procule dor
> Sem me aproveitar no ai.
> (ll. 1037–41 & 1063–66)

While Hamlet contaminates the vocabulary of courts of law with that of graveyards, João Gaspar mixes the legal with the rural. But it is the puns and the thorough delight in them that brings both dramatists together. Even absent words from legal terminology, like *ouvidor* (punned by *ougir dor*) are present in the Portuguese text, allowing João Gaspar to make puns on the identical endings of the words describing legal professions: *ouvidor, procurador, desembargador*. 'Dor', which by itself means 'pain', becomes an interjection reacting to pain ('ai'). Just like Hamlet's 'fine' means 'final' at one point, João Gaspar's 'dor' [pain] can become a pun on 'dó' [pity]: *e do(r) não há de quem...*

Examples of puns in the drama of Prestes abound to such an extent that one can perhaps say that a large part of his style is, so to speak, 'punny'. The author is fully conscious of this. He calls these puns *derivados* (probably from the Latin *derivatio*,

24 HÉLIO J. S. ALVES

which is the rhetorical term for figurative playing with etymology) and is fond of making his characters comment on them. Look at the following example from *Auto do Procurador*, where the daughter of the protagonist puns her father's Latin:

> PROCURADOR: Não sei se os fados lhe deram
> suma fastigia rerum.
> FILHA: Rerum não sei, mas eu fio
> darem-lhe suma fastio
> e nõ già ser burrerum. (ll. 1267–71)

This said, the father cannot avoid making a comment on his daughter's punning talent:

> PROCURADOR: Já eu vi pior derivado
> do que é esse. (ll. 1272–73)

And he goes on, praising his daughter's powers of expression and commenting on true and false eloquence, as if the *derivados*, or puns, were the privileged means to ascertain that difference.

Indeed, if one were neoclassically minded and not at all fond of wordplay, one could say of António Prestes what Samuel Johnson said of the Stratford playwright:

> A quibble is to Shakespeare, what luminous vapours are to the traveller; he follows it at all adventures, it is sure to lead him out of his way, and sure to engulf him in the mire. It has some malignant power over his mind, and its fascinations are irresistible. [...] A quibble poor and barren as it is, gave him such delight, that he was content to purchase it, by the sacrifice of reason, propriety and truth. A quibble was to him the fatal Cleopatra for which he lost the world, and was content to lose it.[17]

In this too, Prestes is a predecessor of Shakespeare's, a predecessor who shows that a heavy interest in punning was quite clearly present in non negligible areas of European drama just before the Stratford playwright began his theatrical career. It is only fair to say, then, that the theatre of António Prestes, like that of Gil Vicente, arrived *sooner than Shakespeare* and thus made justice to another pun, that of the playwright's own name: *prestes* can be translated as 'early'.

Bibliography

ALVES, HÉLIO J. S., *Tempo para entender: história comparada da literatura portuguesa* (Casal de Cambra: Caleidoscópio, 2006)

ASENSIO, EUGENIO, 'El teatro de António Prestes: notas de lectura', *Estudios Portugueses* (Paris: Calouste Gulbenkian Foundation, 1974), pp. 349–80

BLOOM, HAROLD, *Shakespeare: The Invention of the Human* (New York: Riverhead Books, 1998)

CAMÕES, JOSÉ, and JOSÉ AUGUSTO CARDOSO BERNARDES (eds), *Compêndio de Gil Vicente* (Coimbra: Imprensa da Universidade, forthcoming)

CRAIG, HUGH, 'Shakespeare's Vocabulary: Myth and Reality', *Shakespeare's Quarterly*, 62.1 (2011), 53–74

CRYSTAL, DAVID, *Think on my Words: Exploring Shakespeare's Language* (Cambridge: Cambridge University Press, 2008)

SOONER THAN SHAKESPEARE   25

EARLE, THOMAS F., 'The Ending of Three Plays by Gil Vicente: *Auto da Índia*, *Quem Tem Farelos?* and *Auto da Sibila Cassandra*', in *Por S'Entender Bem a Letra: homenagem a Stephen Reckert*, ed. by Manuel Calderón et al. (Lisbon: Imprensa Nacional — Casa da Moeda, 2011), pp. 701–14

ELLRODT, ROBERT, *Montaigne et Shakespeare. L'Émergence de la conscience moderne* (Paris: José Corti, 2011)

FINEMAN, JOEL, *Shakespeare's Perjured Eye: The Invention of Poetic Subjectivity in the Sonnets* (Berkeley: University of California Press, 1986)

GREENE, ROLAND, 'The Lyric', in *The Cambridge History of Literary Criticism: The Renaissance*, ed. by Glyn Norton (Cambridge: Cambridge University Press, 1999)

JOHNSON, SAMUEL, *Prose and Poetry*, ed. by Mona Wilson (London: Hart-Davis, 1968)

PRESTES, ANTÓNIO, *Auto dos Dous Irmãos*, in *Autos de António Prestes*, ed. by José Camões and Helena Reis Silva (Lisbon: Imprensa Nacional — Casa da Moeda, 2008), pp. 261–325

——*Auto do Procurador*, in *Autos de António Prestes*, ed. by José Camões and Helena Reis Silva (Lisbon: Imprensa Nacional — Casa da Moeda, 2008), pp. 127–96

——*Auto da Ave Maria*, in *Autos de António Prestes*, ed. by José Camões and Helena Reis Silva (Lisbon: Imprensa Nacional — Casa da Moeda, 2008), pp. 23–125

——*Auto do Mouro Encantado*, in *Autos de António Prestes*, ed. by José Camões and Helena Reis Silva (Lisbon: Imprensa Nacional — Casa da Moeda, 2008), pp. 391–474

SHAKESPEARE, WILLIAM, *Hamlet*, ed. by Ann Thompson and Neil Taylor (London: The Arden Shakespeare, 2006)

——*The Norton Shakespeare*, ed. by Stephen Greenblatt et al. (New York and London: Norton, 1997)

SINFIELD, ALAN, *Faultlines* (Oxford: Clarendon Press, 1992)

WIGGINS, MARTIN, *Shakespeare and the Drama of his Time* (Oxford: Oxford University Press, 2000)

VICENTE, GIL, *Devisa de Coimbra*, in *As Obras de Gil Vicente*, ed. by José Camões (Lisbon: Centro de Estudos de Teatro/Imprensa Nacional — Casa da Moeda, 2002), vol. I, pp. 451–77 and vol. III (facsimile of the 1562 edition), pp. 224–38

——*Índia, ibidem*, in *As Obras de Gil Vicente*, ed. by. José Camões (Lisbon: Centro de Estudos de Teatro/Imprensa Nacional — Casa da Moeda, 2002), vol. II, pp. 171–86

Online Sources

Teatro de Autores Portugueses do Séc. XVI — Online Database <http://www.cet-e-quinhentos. com/> [accessed December 2013]

Notes to Chapter 1

1. William Shakespeare, *Richard III*, v. 3. 181–91 and 201–04.
2. Harold Bloom, *Shakespeare: The Invention of the Human* (New York: Riverhead Books, 1998), pp. 67–68.
3. An excellent example is Martin Wiggins, *Shakespeare and the Drama of his Time* (Oxford: Oxford University Press, 2000).
4. Robert Ellrodt, *Montaigne et Shakespeare. L'Émergence de la conscience moderne* (Paris: José Corti, 2011).
5. 'The subject of Shakespeare's sonnets experiences himself *as* his difference from himself', says Joel Fineman in *Shakespeare's Perjured Eye: The Invention of Poetic Subjectivity in the Sonnets* (Berkeley: University of California Press, 1986), p. 25; *apud* Roland Greene, 'The Lyric', in *The Cambridge History of Literary Criticism: The Renaissance*, ed. by Glyn Norton (Cambridge: Cambridge University Press, 1999), p. 226. 'One needs to detach Fineman's argument from the text to which it emphatically joins itself, and retell the unsettling of lyric subjectivity through many more examples over a larger time-line. The revision he describes begins much earlier, with Petrarch himself' (R. Greene, ibid.).

6. Hélio J. S. Alves, *Tempo para entender: história comparada da literatura portuguesa* (Casal de Cambra: Caleidoscópio, 2006).
7. I have written on the presence of Gil Vicente in European theatre histories of the last thirty to forty years in a chapter of the *Compêndio de Gil Vicente*, ed. by José Camões and José Augusto Cardoso Bernardes (Coimbra: Imprensa da Universidade, forthcoming).
8. Fineman, *Shakespeare's Perjured Eye, apud* Alan Sinfield, *Faultlines* (Oxford: Clarendon Press, 1992), p. 59.
9. This is not to say that 'psychology' is the only organizing element in the play. As I hope to have demonstrated elsewhere, together with its farcical surface meanings, *Índia* is structured, at a deep level, like a re-enactment of biblical and theological subjects, as a kind of mystery play (see 'A arte do tempo no *Auto da Índia*', in my *Tempo para entender*, pp. 47–59). On this subject and, in general, on anagogical readings of Vicente's theatre, one can now read T. F. Earle, 'The Ending of Three Plays by Gil Vicente: *Auto da Índia, Quem Tem Farelos?* and *Auto da Sibila Cassandra*', in *Por S'Entender Bem a Letra: homenagem a Stephen Reckert*, ed. by Manuel Calderón et al. (Lisbon: Imprensa Nacional — Casa da Moeda, 2011), pp. 701–14.
10. I transcribe from the facsimile of the first edition of the *Compilaçam* (1562) in vol. III of *As Obras*, p. 231. The modern transcription in the same edition (vol. I, p. 464) includes no punctuation marks, except for a comma after *puede* and the full stop at the end. This option allows for the syntactic flexibility and semantic oscillations in the text, but it makes translation into another language such as English more difficult than perhaps it could be.
11. For reasons which will become obvious to the reader, not all the excerpts from Prestes have been translated.
12. David Crystal, *Think on my Words: Exploring Shakespeare's Language* (Cambridge: Cambridge University Press, 2008).
13. Hugh Craig, 'Shakespeare's Vocabulary: Myth and Reality', *Shakespeare's Quarterly*, 62.1 (2011), 53–74.
14. The texts can be read both in the modern edition by José Camões and Helena Reis Silva of the *Autos de António Prestes* (Lisbon: Imprensa Nacional — Casa da Moeda, 2008) and in the remarkable website *Teatro de Autores Portugueses do Séc. XVI* <http://www.cet-e-quinhentos. com>, where all Portuguese sixteenth-century plays are collected.
15. 'Abunda en términos únicos, tortura de diccionarios' says Eugenio Asensio, 'El teatro de António Prestes: notas de lectura', *Estudios Portugueses* (Paris: Calouste Gulbenkian Foundation, 1974), p. 377. Asensio's statement may yet be proven to be incorrect, although not in the context of what scholarship has determined so far. As for his possible rivals in Portuguese, I am thinking particularly of Jorge Ferreira de Vasconcelos, whose three plays in prose are well known for their exuberance of speech. But in the mass of reminiscences, commonplaces, *adagia*, and wealth of characterization which abound in *Eufrosina, Ulissipo* and *Aulegrafia*, vocabulary and wordplay are not features as distinguishing as they are in Prestes.
16. 'La palabra es para él plástica: puede ser torturada y descoyuntada de mil maneras' (Asensio, 'El teatro de António Prestes', p. 377).
17. 'A Preface to Shakespeare', in Samuel Johnson, *Prose and Poetry*, ed. by Mona Wilson (London: Hart-Davis, 1968), p. 500.

CHAPTER 2

The *Auto da Festa* and the (Well-stocked) Workshop of Gil Vicente

José Augusto Cardoso Bernardes
Centro de Literatura Portuguesa, Universidade de Coimbra

The *Auto da Festa* in the Context of Gil Vicente's Dramatic Work

Gil Vicente (1465?–1536?) is still today the best-known name in the history of Portuguese theatre. This prominence is explained, first and foremost, by the fact that Portuguese dramaturgy as a whole is rather irregular and impoverished, at least in comparison with what was produced in Spain or England. But there is also another reason that justifies this playwright's importance almost half a millennium after his death. Gil Vicente was writing in the first third of the sixteenth century, which, as we know, was the most glorious period of Portugal's history, due to its control of the maritime spice route. In fact, Vicente's *oeuvre* is often read as a kind of sociological tract, reflecting the great transformations that occurred in the kingdom in the wake of the so-called Discoveries. It has been understood in this way by many historians, who invoke one or another play (or sometimes only a particular character) to illustrate the socio-economic situation of the period, and by literary and theatre scholars, who like to draw attention to the *testimonial* side of Gil Vicente's theatre. However, neither readings are completely convincing; for, rather than being an accurate portrait of Portugal at the time, Gil Vicente's theatre is a kind of *caricature*. This means that, though it is strongly related to reality (for that is a property of all good caricatures), it does not reflect it faithfully.

But Vicente's worth should not be gauged only by his supposed realism. Before him, there was, to our knowledge, no one in Europe that produced an *oeuvre* that is simultaneously so *extensive* (around fifty plays), so *coherent* (to the extent that his plays are like continuous chapters of the same work), and yet so *varied* (in that they make use of a whole range of medieval theatre genres from farce, mystery and *sottie* to the morality play and chivalric fantasy).[1]

These characteristics (extension, coherence and diversity) constitute the true basis for valuing Vicente's *oeuvre*. But, as if this were not enough, others also indicate *originality* as an important factor, considering him to be an *original* creator in the Romantic sense of the word, that is, someone who does not follow models, but whose art constantly and freely comes up against reality or the imagination. But

28   JOSÉ AUGUSTO CARDOSO BERNARDES

this needs to be qualified. While his work is undoubtedly very inventive (an aspect that has been insufficiently studied to date), this does not mean that there are no underlying models. On the contrary, in recent times both formal and thematic/ morphological sources have been identified: the Iberian song books, in the first case (at least as regards versification), and a wide range of references in the second that extends from fifteenth-century Iberian theatre to medieval drama from the north of France.

As Gil Vicente's *oeuvre* as a whole came to light for the first time only in 1562 (twenty-five years after his death), there have always been doubts as to the extent to which the published material was exclusively by him. It seems that one of his sons (Luís Vicente) may have intervened, at least in the arrangement of the text. The only thing we know for sure is that Gil Vicente had begun the task of organizing and editing his plays with a view to publishing them in a complete edition. But he most probably did not finish the job himself, and it seems to have been taken over and completed by his son. Though we cannot determine exactly the extent of Luís's intervention in the texts, it is generally considered to be minimal.

However, rather than speculating about the role played by father and son in the editing of the former's plays, it is more important to try to identify the *stability* of the texts that figure in the *Copilaçam*. Are these exactly the same texts that were used for the theatrical performances, or have they been adapted from a literary or rhetorical perspective? Unfortunately, we do not have enough data to be able to answer this question definitively. All that we know is derived from a comparative study of a very small set of plays that have survived in more than one version, such as the *Auto da Barca do Inferno* and *Farsa de Inês Pereira*. In both of these cases, there are reasons to believe that the versions collected in the 1562 edition underwent some alterations, which included literary or rhetorical improvements to highlight their relationship with the works of the *Cancioneiro*,[2] and the suppression of the stage directions.

However, there is one case that could be understood quite differently. While the vast majority of the plays are only available in the *Copilaçam*, which means we cannot compare them with other versions (if these existed, they have not survived or have not been found), there is one text (only) that was not included in the 1562 collection, or at least not in its entirety. I am referring to the *Auto da Festa*, which is one of this author's least-read plays, despite the fact that it has particular points of interest, at least as refers to the *workshop aspect* of the playwright's creation. The *Auto da Festa* came to light in 1906, having been kept for years in a private library. It was part of a miscellany of twenty-one texts that had been printed in the late sixteenth or early seventeenth centuries, most of them being sixteenth-century dramatic works.[3]

Unsurprisingly, this find was greeted with great enthusiasm, as the early twentieth century was a very propitious period for events of this kind. We should remember that less than a century had elapsed since the Hamburg edition (of 1834) had generated a spectacular revival of interest in Gil Vicente;[4] while the 400th anniversary of the *Monólogo do Vaqueiro*, in 1902, had also generated considerable public interest.[5] Indeed, those latter commemorations proved to be an inaugural moment for an intense activity that continued unabated for thirty-five years, and which was unusual in its continuity and coverage. In order to better understand the sense of opportunity generated by this event, we should remember that this was a time of great philological excitement, when there was great receptivity to anything that could be added to the very special heritage that was sixteenth-century literature in Portugal.

The owner of the miscellany in question was the Count of Sabugosa, a prestigious aristocrat and polymath (himself a poet, though perhaps more persistent than inspired), who threw himself energetically into the publication of the work. In fact, he not only transcribed the text with remarkable zeal, but also wrote a long introductory essay, characterized by the clarity, the sound research and the caution typical of the philology of the day.

The essay does not avoid some of the more intriguing questions. It was not known, for example (nor is it yet), why the play was not included in either of the two editions of Vicente's complete works. Various hypotheses have been put forward, some of which may still be considered valid. Perhaps Gil Vicente had himself rejected it? Or perhaps it was rejected by his children who, as we have seen, edited his *oeuvre* after his death (though in that case, we might ask why this play in particular attracted such censorship)? Could it be that the play, in its present form, resulted from the cobbling together of disconnected scenes, perhaps undertaken in the author's absence (for example, after his death)?[6]

All of these hypotheses are plausible. However, no evidence has emerged to date that definitively proves any one of them. In fact, the text contains materials (characters, situations, phrases) that can be found in Vicente's other plays (in various degrees of transposition), which might have been sufficient in itself for the dramatist to have left them out of the edition of his collected works (which, everything suggests, was in an advanced stage of preparation). We also know the letter addressed to the king that he composed as a preface to the work. But there may be other reasons for its non-inclusion. In fact, despite the high degree of impunity that Gil Vicente seems to have enjoyed, the play undoubtedly contains scandalous material. The play opens with the figure of Truth, who has been driven out of the Portuguese Court, no less![7] But the denunciation goes even further. Behind the criticism of 'bad times', there is a strong hint that the King himself had been complicit in the rejection of Truth (or at least had accepted it passively):

> Oh grã crueldade
> Que o tempo de agora tem tal calidade
> Que cedo no paço já trazem por Lei
> Que todo aquele que falar verdade
> É logo botado da graça d'el rei. (p. 656)[8]

[Oh, great cruelty! The times now are of such a sort that soon in the royal palace they will make a law that anyone who speaks the truth will immediately lose the king's favour.]

Even though the monarch is absent, he is nevertheless invoked in various ways.[9] For example, Truth addresses a certain lord in terms that would seem to rank him above the king, D. João III. After the comment about her poor relationship with the king, she immediately refers to that lord in terms that exceed what one might expect in the circumstances. As well as praising him for his intrinsic virtues, the character also recognizes him as an *alternative protector*, declaring herself prepared to move her seat ('assento') from the royal palace to other lodgings ('pousada'):

> E tendo sabido que vós, meu senhor,
> Me tendes amizade e fé verdadeira,
> E por isso venho de aquesta maneira
> Dar-vos as graças por tão grande amor.
> E com pensamento
> De em vossa pousada fazer aposento,
> Pois me amais com tanta firmeza,
> De vossa boca farei fortaleza
> Para estar nela sempre de assento. (pp. 656–57)

[Since I know that you, my lord, feel genuine friendship and loyalty towards me, I have come to thank you for your great affection. My idea is to take up my lodging in your house, since you love me so constantly. Your word will be my protection so that I can always remain there.]

In addition to these implications (which were potentially scandalous politically), there are others of a moral nature. We only have to recall the first peasant (João Antão, from Beira), who brags shamelessly about a sexual encounter he had with the judge's wife, no less, one Sunday. Of course the theme of the peasant who sleeps with a married woman of a higher social standing is a common one in medieval farce;[10] but even so, there are a number of contextual differences here that should be pointed out. The burlesque and inversion of values that characterize farce (which of course was a popular urban tradition) may not have gone down well at Court, particularly in a book composed at the king's request and dedicated to him. Furthermore, in its crudeness, an allusion of this type would have been inconvenient, not only on the abstract plane but also as regards the personal references that are brought into play.[11] In the light of this, if the *Auto da Festa* had been included in the *Livro das Obras*, it would have seemed out of place, alien to the logic of the whole.

In order to shed light on these questions, it would be useful to know more about the circumstances surrounding the play's performance. But this does not seem to be possible. We do not know with any accuracy when and for whom the text was performed for the first time. Following Óscar de Pratt, José Camões (who has undoubtedly produced the most important study of this text of all those published since 1906) thought that it was performed one Christmas, some time after 1526. However, with his habitual caution, he hesitates to specify the place and audience. For my part, I would go a little further. On the basis of all the various textual and extratextual elements that are available to us, I might risk suggesting that the play was performed outside the royal space, quite probably in a lord's court. That in itself would be enough to endow the text with a relatively exceptional status.[12]

After some hesitation (hesitation seems to plague philology in all periods!), the Count of Sabugosa suggested that the play might have been performed in Évora at Christmas 1535 for the 1st count of Vimioso, D. Francisco de Portugal. In support of this thesis, there exists a curious similarity between Truth's encomium to the dedicatee of the play and the words that Gil Vicente places in the mouth of the

THE *AUTO DA FESTA* AND THE WORKSHOP OF GIL VICENTE   31

same character in the lines he composed to celebrate the acclamation of the king, D. João III (cf. p. 87).

However, more important than knowing if this play was rejected, banned or merely forgotten (and the three possibilities may be complementary), it is worth exploring the text itself with a view to establishing its usefulness for capturing something of Gil Vicente's creativity 'in process'. In fact, as there are few doubts about the authorship of the play, someone must have decided that this particular work by Gil Vicente should not figure in the *Copilaçam*. We do not know who took that decision, nor even if it was taken freely or conditioned in some way. Given the lack of evidence to help us answer these questions, the best thing is to focus, for now, on another type of problem. Despite the various unknowns that I have been highlighting, and which have almost entirely occupied the attention of Vicente scholars, it is very likely that the text that we have today may tell us something new about another aspect: I am referring specifically to the way in which it functioned as a kind of workshop for the dramatist. This is not a minor point. On the contrary, the possibilities it offers for understanding the dramatist's creative processes may be a particularly promising line of research. It could help solve some of the dramaturgical and theatrical mysteries of this play and of the *autos* as a whole. Moreover, provided that certain precautions are taken, an inquiry into this material could also yield a better understanding of Gil Vicente's place in the artistic panorama of the sixteenth century, possibly thereby helping him achieve the recognition that is due to him in the history of European theatre.

In the light of this encouraging prospect, I shall, therefore, formulate some questions, which to date have scarcely been raised. In other words, I propose to use the *Auto da Festa* to take a peep into Gil Vicente's workshop, as this play that seems to have emerged from it in a very different state to the others that we know.

As has been repeatedly noted since 1906, this play may indeed be perceived as a kind of mosaic of a significant part of Vicente's dramatic works. I propose to look at how the pieces of that mosaic fit together, resorting not only to the most obvious analogies but also to others that are less visible. Let us begin with the gypsy women. As in the short farce entitled precisely the *Farsa das Ciganas* [Farce of the Gypsy Women], the *Festa* also has gypsies who have gifts of divination.[13] Differences have been pointed out, which I shall return to later. But we cannot ignore the fact that clever gypsy women who are well-spoken and claim to understand the arts of divination only appear in two of Vicente's plays.[14] Still with regard to the characters, there is a peasant (the second, called Janafonso), who is undoubtedly a typical example of the displaced rustic — displaced not only in space (though unfortunately we don't know exactly where he is from) but also in terms of his speech and values. In this case, the peasant makes the effort to travel from Braganza to ask the newborn God to marry him, refusing not to be received:

> Ca se Deus fosse ocupado
> Como homem diz a respeito,
> Mas ele tem tudo feito
> Dantes que ele fosse nado
> E meu visavô desfeito. (p. 668)

32 JOSÉ AUGUSTO CARDOSO BERNARDES

[For if God was busy, as people say... But he has done everything since before
he was born and my great-granddad died.]

In terms of its discourse and theatricality (which is clearly parodic), this is in fact the
clearest example of duplication. The *Templo de Apolo*, which had been performed
in 1525, included a peasant of this type, a parody that would naturally have amused
the audience.[15]

This calquing of roles, which has been repeatedly pointed out by critics, raises
a larger problem — the question of Gil Vicente's originality. There are so many
aspects to this that I cannot analyse them all here. However, it does appear that
we might have given too much credence to the simplified notion that such issues
were not important at the time Vicente was writing; that literary composition was
still formulaic in nature and the concept of the *author* (at least as conceived from
the eighteenth century onwards) was largely dispensable; and also that Vicente's
creation was defined more by political commitment than by aesthetic criteria (in
the Romantic sense). However, the sensation I have is that it was not entirely like
that. As Daniel Arasse, Andrew Bennett and others have shown, the modern idea
of the author developed gradually, and in literary creation and the arts generally,
important changes took place precisely in the course of the fifteenth and sixteenth
centuries.[16] (This very question has been recently reassessed in the context of late
medieval theatre.) Without going into aspects that I have developed in more detail
elsewhere,[17] it seems to me perfectly reasonable that the *Livro das Obras* should have
obeyed a civic, ideological and aesthetic plan that includes the very idea of *originality*,
expressly invoked in some of the paratexts of that book.

But let us return to our inventory of similarities between the *Festa* and the other
autos, because that will form the basis for the conclusions that I hope to propose
shortly. Like the *Barca do Inferno* [Boat of Hell], *Juiz da Beira* [Judge from Beira] and
Floresta de Enganos [Forest of Deceits], this play criticizes the functioning of justice
(this time it is Truth that points out that João Antão has to 'buy' the Judge's favour
with partridges); the peasant for his part, following in the footsteps of Pêro Marques
(the famous husband of Inês Pereira, later the magistrate of Beira), compares the
justice of the codes with the justice of nature — if the judge's wife had agreed and
enjoyed the relationship, then why should he be condemned?[18]

Still within this sphere of analysis, we should not forget to mention the figure of
the Fool. Various models of the Fool exist in Gil Vicente, of course, almost all taken
from the medieval *sotties*. However, the character that appears in the *Festa*, though
occasionally showing a more sensitive side, is above all both *evangelical* and *obscene*,
evoking in this duality the famous Joane in the *Barca do Inferno*. In this case, the
Fool even proposes marriage to Truth, who is not aghast at the idea (a complicity
that reminds us of the heavenly guarantee that the Angel grants Joane in the first
Barca). Another affinity between the two fools results from the fact that, in both
cases, the character remains on stage even after having obtained his orders to leave:
in the *Barca do Inferno*, Joane stays at the Angel's side, while in this play the Fool
remains with Truth, conversing with Janafonso and old Filipa Pimenta (his mother).

The parallels (and I am not speaking of pure transpositions) are coming to an
end. Even so, we should not overlook old Filipa Pimenta who, in her amorous

THE *AUTO DA FESTA* AND THE WORKSHOP OF GIL VICENTE   33

folly, is akin to Brásia Caiada of *Triunfo do Inverno*. Both represent the same grotesque subversion of nature and are prepared to make all sacrifices to fulfil their belated desires. Another common topic (though one that is even more diffuse) is the connection between punishments from God ('que é verdade acabada' [who is perfect truth]) and the flight from Truth. This same punitive logic is applied throughout the whole of the *Auto da Feira* [*Auto* of the Fair] and, in particular, to the character of Rome, chastised by Providence for having made a pact with the Devil. If we want to take this parallelism to the extreme, we could call attention to the scene immediately preceding the nativity scene. I am referring to the group of nine shepherds that come to the Fair (in the *Auto da Feira*) not to buy and sell but only to show their unconditional devotion to the Virgin, thereby revealing themselves to be the antithesis of all the other unsatisfied characters who cultivate deceptive appearances to the detriment of their true essences (Rome, the *compadres* and *comadres*). As in the *Feira*, the *Festa* also finishes with a group of shepherds (in this case a boy and three girls) who in fact celebrate Christmas and Truth on the pretext of a marriage between the shepherd Gil Tibabo and Filipa Pimenta.

The Allegorical Figure of Truth

In the light of this, it is tempting to suggest that this *auto* is, in a sense, a 'repetition' or 'duplication', and that it was for this reason that it was considered to have no place, either in the *Copilaçam* or in Vicente studies in general. Indeed, this has been the general tone of the assessments made hitherto, with some basis. But we should not confuse the various dimensions on which these plays operate. While this might be the effect of the play on the common reader (the kind of public that Gil Vicente or his sons would have had in mind when they put together the *Copilaçam*), it is not the case for the more demanding reader. The echoes and foreshadowings of other texts, which appear to subvert the basic precepts of authorial originality, might have been a reason for excluding it from the book that was edited in 1562. But as this play is effectively an extensive repository of theatrical formulae, it occupies a unique position in relation to the other Vicente plays that we know. If we discount the very particular case of the *Barcas* and the holy, angelic and diabolic characters that appear in the morality plays, the presence of the same character in more than one *auto* is really very rare (Pêro Marques and Inês Pereira are unique cases in the whole of the *Copilaçam*). This is surely significant, confirming what we said a short time ago about the idea of the author that underpins the whole of Gil Vicente's work.

In fact, although these similarities are important, they may mask an aspect that could prove decisive in our evaluation of this play. Firstly, it should be pointed out that the similarities indicated are not all of the same type. While the second peasant (Janafonso) recalls, in his speech and attitude, the peasant in the *Templo de Apolo* (performed in January 1526), and the two gypsy women, despite their differences in tone, are reminiscent of those others in the *Farsa das Ciganas*, all the other overlaps merely indicate the remarkable cohesiveness of the extraordinary edifice constructed by Gil Vicente. Indeed, we could go as far as to say that, across the *oeuvre* as a whole, such approximations can also be seen in other plays by this author

34   JOSÉ AUGUSTO CARDOSO BERNARDES

(discounting the cases already mentioned of Janafonso, the gypsy women and the old woman who wants to get married).

I would like to draw attention to the fact that the *Auto da Festa*, as well as displaying numerous marks of Vicente's vision, also bears important traces of individuality, which suggests that it would not have been impossible to eliminate the repetitions. The most impressive original feature is the character of Truth, a structuring allegory that does not feature in any of Vicente's other plays. As has already been noted, it is she that opens the play with a Prologue which is a kind of sermon about the state of the world and the Portuguese Court in particular; and she also presides over the procession of pilgrims, thereby linking together the different scenes. This prominence is also marked formally; for, as has been noted since 1906, Truth is the only character that expresses herself in lines of more than seven syllables (*versos de arte maior*), in keeping with the persuasive declamatory register of her speeches. This was a very common device in medieval theatre: a fixed character would have the function of connecting the movable parts of the play (as happens in *Agravados*, *Templo de Apolo*, *Cortes de Júpiter* and in the three *Barcas*). But in this case, there is more to it than that. In addition to the theatrical component, Truth also fulfils another function. On Christmas day, the character actually assumes the role of the Nativity, so that all meanings centre upon her. She speaks of herself, evidently, and of the lack of welcome she has received; but at the same time she also confronts the other characters with her presence. Thus, all the characters that arrive are necessarily identified by their relationship to the figure who has taken her seat on stage, dominating the scene even when she does not expressly intervene. In her axiological dimension, this allegorical character occupies the place that, in Vicente's other Christmas plays, is occupied by Christ or by the Virgin.

I have previously pointed out how Truth's lamentations are particularly incisive: the scorn she receives from all sides, including from the Court, makes her into a lyrical figure, an attribute straight from the field of Good. It is this that explains how she is affirmed as the direct daughter of the Holy Trinity, alongside faith. The fact that she addresses herself to a particular lord, after being expelled from other places, in the belief that she might find shelter with him, makes her indirectly the daughter of hope, another theological virtue. Thus, the allegory becomes so central that the two aesthetic pillars that sustain Vicente's whole *oeuvre* — satire and lyricism — are concentrated in her. In fact, she embodies not only the dimension of moral criticism directed at society (for having abandoned Truth), but also, in her moral appeals (and her marked affinity with the dispossessed Fool), the values of Humility and Justice, which in the sermon books of the era, so often function as conventional oppositions to the lie.

Thus defined, the allegory of Truth is not valid only for this play, but irradiates outwards to touch Gil Vicente's whole *oeuvre*. In the end, this is the same Truth that was put to the test in the *Auto da Alma* [*Auto* of the Soul] (where she is antagonized by the Devil's lie); and in the *Barcas*, it is the lack of Truth that causes those condemned to Hell and Purgatory (many of whom are liars, flatterers or alienated souls) to enter the boat of the damned. On the other hand, it was for having recognized Truth *in extremis* that the great of the world are touched by the gesture

THE *AUTO DA FESTA* AND THE WORKSHOP OF GIL VICENTE   35

of mercy in the *Barca da Glória*. Proclaiming himself the lover of truth, the shepherd Gil (who in Christmas 1502 was played by Gil Vicente himself) crafts his image before the royal Court, declaring that he is ready to distance himself from the lying hubbub of the world and detach himself from his companions in order to decipher the mysteries of the Nativity.[19] It was also for having proclaimed the truth that the Philosopher in *Floresta de Enganos* (the author's last play, performed in Évora in 1536) complains of having been put 'en cárcel muy tenebloso' [in a very dark gaol], bound to a simple-minded fool who humiliates and represses him, thereby preventing him from continuing to express himself in the Court (and only in the Court).

The *Livro das Obras* obviously contains other characters of this type. But there is no doubt that the presence of one more reinforces the gallery of moralizing characters, which are clearly unifying factors in such a heterogeneous *oeuvre*, as well as being extensions of the author's own thought.

The Theatricality of the *auto*

The effect of this unique character is not only semantic in nature; there are also theatrical consequences. By concentrating the message of the whole play onto a single figure, the dramatist achieves another unexpected result: he reinforces the theatricality of all the other characters. We should note that the scenes were also punctuated by music, which also served as an emblem for some of the pilgrims. There are also elements of pure theatre, which go beyond the words pronounced. For example, the gypsy women have little value dramaturgically, but are important devices from the theatrical perspective; the fool, an accident-prone swineherd, who is distracted and often fails to perceive the meaning of what is said to him, is a source of amusement amongst the audience, generating ambiguity; while the peasant Janafonso is not only there for his social representativity, but also because he is the most festive and parodic peasant in Gil Vicente, not only for what he says but also for what he suggests (going, in this respect, further than his predecessor in the *Templo de Apolo*). The same happens with the grotesque Filipa Pimenta who, giving up as lost the time when she raised the Fool (her son), now tries obsessively to recover the fires of passion; transcending the conventional representation of the old woman crazed by love, she becomes yet another of the many foolish figures that abound in the theatre of Gil Vicente.[20] But irrespective of the relationship that any of these characters might maintain with others in this vast frieze of Vicentine action, they are clearly less bound in this play to the rhetoric of the message, appearing more detached and genuine. That is to say, they seem to be endowed with a greater degree of theatricality than what we have been used to in the *Copilaçam*.

Conclusion

Strictly speaking, nothing that I have said up to now has undermined the two hypotheses already put forward to justify the non-inclusion of the *Auto da Festa* in the *Copilaçam* of 1562 and 1586, and its disappearance for over three centuries. Nevertheless, I think it is legitimate to propose a third possible explanation, not to exclude any of those that are under appreciation, but to complement them. As we have known since 1906, the *Auto da Festa* consists of unworked theatrical material that the author had not intended to appear in the printed book and song book that would later collect together most of his *oeuvre*. Vicente's creative process would probably have involved several different phases. Firstly, there would have been the theatrical invention, often done quickly. Only later would that be subjected to literary treatment, which would operate on two levels: technical and formal improvement, which would bring gains in the rhetorical and expressive dimensions though with some possible loss of theatricality,[21] and preparation for inclusion in the macrotext (the *Copliaçam*), which would involve reinforcing internal connections and accentuating parallelisms with other works.[22]

Before or after the death of Gil Vicente, the *Auto da Festa* was a theatrical performance. For one reason or another, it remained in that state, and was never reworked dramaturgically. In the form that we know it today, this play is an important vestige of the abundant material that Gil Vicente kept in his prodigious workshop. Everything suggests that this workshop was not so different from other workshops, in that it contained raw material for later use mixed up with vestiges of other things that may occasionally have been taken advantage of and then dismantled for convenience. This was a mental and material workshop, and I imagine it as having many ordered shelves, labelled to distinguish the various genres (Gil Vicente had a keen awareness of genre), formulas, characters and topics. In this type of workshop, there is always a place for recyclable materials. And, as all of us that work with literature and the products of the mind know well, that type of material may constitute not only an opportunity and comfortable reserve, but also a form of moral martyrdom. They are materials which, today, we would save on a back-up disk, awaiting the long summer holidays. I am speaking of those things that people our memory, but which, with the passing of time, gradually become pure nostalgia. Yesterday, as today, the time for those tasks may never arrive, particularly when the task in question is not an easy one (as was definitely the case here), requiring not only time but also a creative spurt of the kind that only occurs once in a while. Parts of the play would have had to have been erased (Janafonso, undoubtedly), others adjusted (the gypsies and the old woman), and there would have had to have been a major reorganization of the whole in order to allow the rest to be preserved.

Although I have not seen any records to this effect, I believe that, at the time of Gil Vicente's death, the *Auto da Festa* was on that top shelf, the one containing the materials that had served a purpose for a particular occasion and were now awaiting an opportunity when they could be reworked. It was from that shelf that the work was taken, without Vicente's knowledge, for a one-off edition, later to end up in the so-called miscellany that the Count of Sabugosa inherited and published in the euphoric climate of the early twentieth century.

If this was indeed the case, two conclusions may be suggested. One, while neither consensual nor controversial, is already well known and has been put forward by a number of Vicente scholars; the other is more theoretical, and perhaps for this reason has attracted less attention. In fact, we might imagine that Vicente, like Camões,

Bocage and Almeida Garrett after him, worked in phases, with much trial-and-error (a vision that will not appeal to those that prefer the Romantic image of the inspired genius given to sudden spurts of inspiration). In this respect, common sense can come to our aid. As a man of the theatre, Gil Vicente would have been dependent on collective dynamics, and could only have worked in that way. But this little visit to his workshop has proved something else: that in his time, there was a clear awareness of the differences of register between the text that directly served the performance (whether published or not), and that other one that could be given to the public to read in the form of a book.[23] Very probably, the texts that figure in the *Copilaçam* derived from theatrical versions that have since disappeared. The *Auto da Festa* did not make it to that last phase; for that would have cost too much effort, and/or because the final result may not have pleased the king, D. João III, for whom Gil Vicente had worked hard for fifteen consecutive years and for whom, at the end of his days, he collected together his works 'out of pity for my old age'. Or even — and now it is merely my intuition speaking — because this work was produced during a period of bitter circumstances. As I interpret the material available, this play not only developed outside the royal Court but also against it — so outside it and against it, in fact, that it was not possible to give it, later, the rhetorical and moral varnishing that covers most of Gil Vicente's *Cancioneiro* — which, benefiting from protection at the highest level, came off the press of João Álvares ('printer to the king') in Lisbon in September 1562, exactly 452 years ago.

Bibliography

ARASSE, DANIEL, *Le Sujet dans le tableau* (Paris: Flammarion, 1997)

BENNETT, ANDREW, *The Author* (London: Routledge, 2005)

BERNARDES, JOSÉ AUGUSTO CARDOSO, 'O Juiz da Beira e os sentidos da sátira vicentina', in *Revisões de Gil Vicente* (Coimbra: Angelus Novus, 2003), pp. 89–111

——*Sátira e lirismo no teatro de Gil Vicente* (Lisbon: Imprensa Nacional — Casa da Moeda, 2004)

——'A *Copilaçam de todalas obras*: o livro e o projecto identitário de Gil Vicente', *Diacrítica. Ciências da Literatura*, 18–19 (2004–05), 179–98

BONFIM, ENEIDA DO REGO MONTEIRO, 'Uma leitura dos autos de Gil Vicente: o *Auto da Festa*', *Semear*, 8 (2003), 193–211

CAMÕES, JOSÉ, *Festa* (Lisbon: Quimera, 1992)

FAIBRE, BERNARD, *Répertoire des farces françaises. Des origines à Tabarin* (Paris: Imprimerie Nationale, 1993)

MATEUS, JORGE OSÓRIO, *Livro das Obras* (Lisbon: Quimera, 1993)

——'Teatro e Literatura', in *De teatro e outras escritas* (Lisbon: Quimera, 2004), pp. 212–18

MELLO MOSER, FERNANDO DE, 'Gil Vicente da Meia Idade ao Renascimento', in *Discurso Inacabado* (Lisbon: Fundação Calouste Gulbenkian, 2004), pp. 15–154

PRATT, ÓSCAR DE, 'Ainda o *Auto da Festa*', in *Gil Vicente: notas e comentários* (Lisbon: Livraria Clássica Editora, 1970), pp. 231–38

RECKERT, STEPHEN, '"Gil Terrón lletrudo está"', *Leituras. Revista da Biblioteca Nacional*, 11 (2002), 15–33

TISSIER, ANDRE (ed.), *Farces françaises de la fin du Moyen Age. Transcription en français moderne* (Geneva: Librairie Droz, 1999)

VICENTE, GIL, *Auto da Festa*, intro. and ed. by Count of Sabugosa (Lisbon: Imprensa Nacional, 1906)

38   José Augusto Cardoso Bernardes

———*As Obras de Gil Vicente*, ed. by José Camões, vols. II & IV (Lisbon: Imprensa Nacional — Casa da Moeda, 2002) [facsimile edition in vol. IV, pp. 675–90; transcription in vol. II, pp. 655–85)

Notes to Chapter 2

1. There is a full list of the plays in Chapter 11 (eds).
2. The name *Cancioneiro* may legitimately be applied to the *Copilaçam*, or *Libro das Obras*, not only because of the coherence of the texts included in it, but also because the word 'cancioneiro' is repeatedly used in the printing privilege of 3 September 1561.
3. The complete collection had been kept in the Palácio do Calvário. The text in question was in the form of a quarto volume, bound in calf, with gold lettering on the spine reading 'Varias crusid. Tom-III'. The miscellany also included texts of a lyrical nature, such as the famous 'Coplas por la muerte de su padre' by Jorge Manrique, plays by Ribeiro Chiado, Fernando Mendes, Afonso Álvares and Baltasar Dias, and other works by Gil Vicente (*Fé, Breve Sumário, Cananeia* and *Barca do Inferno*). There also two *autos* of uncertain authorship (*Deus Padre* and *Geração Humana*).
4. The person who discovered the *auto* described the circumstances of the find in the following terms: 'The atmosphere generated in cultured circles in both Europe and Brazil by that group of Lusophiles [he is referring to figures such as Alexandre Herculano, Gama Barros, Teophilo Braga and Carolina M. de Vasconcelos] meant that the neo-Vicentine movement was followed sympathetically, as can be seen in the celebration of his fourth centenary [...] This will certainly favour the reception of this play, the publication of which will bring a lost jewel of no mean value to the treasure hoard of Literature' (Count of Sabugosa, in *Auto da Festa*, p. 519).
5. The Hamburg edition, produced by Gomes Monteiro and Mascarenhas Barreto, had, nevertheless, limited circulation. As if this were not enough, a fire in the depository also meant that the book soon became a relative rarity. Under those circumstances, the appearance of the 1852 edition, which formed part of the prestigious collection known as the 'Bibliotheca Portuguesa' [Portuguese Library], was also important in affirming the canonical status of Vicente's *oeuvre* in Portugal and Brazil.
6. Óscar de Pratt, 'Ainda o *Auto da Festa*', in *Gil Vicente: notas e comentários* (Lisbon: Livraria Clássica Editora, 1970) has expressed a somewhat depreciative opinion of this play: '[...] curiously, despite its portrayal of the times and customs (which in fact do not add anything new to what we already know from Vicente's other canvases), this is perhaps the least carefully wrought of all that poet's works' (p. 235). The list of Vicente's works does not even mention the piece, which might mean that he did not recognize it as one of his — see *Livro das Obras* (Lisbon: Quimera, 1993). For another example of a text altered after the author's death, see Chapter 13 (eds).
7. For the allegorical figure of Truth in Protestant drama, see Chapter 15 (eds).
8. The quotations from the play are taken from the transcription by José Camões in vol. II of *Obras*.
9. Referring to expressions such as 'vim-me à Corte' [I came to the Court] or 'vós outros que andais no paço' [you others that are at the palace], José Camões does not seem to exclude that possibility, though he recognizes that the allusions could have been transposed from other plays (p. 3).
10. For the reader who does not have time to consult a complete edition of the farces (I am thinking particularly of the magnificent edition that André Tissier began to publish with Editorial Droz in 1999), there exists a useful directory of topics, involving 176 texts, which makes it possible to explore systematically the affinities with the Vicente *corpus*, in the certainty that there is no material missing. See Bernard Faibre, *Répertoire des farces françaises. Des origines à Tabarin* (Paris: Imprimerie Nationale, 1993).
11. A similar situation is of course evoked in the *Juiz da Beira*. I am referring to the complaint lodged by the procuress Ana Dias, involving a son of Pero Amado who has taken advantage of the fact that the wheat he had been tending was now 'grown' to embark on a sexual relationship with her daughter, Beatriz. Faced with the mother's protestations (now that her ambitions of marrying

The *Auto da Festa* and the Workshop of Gil Vicente 39

her daughter into a different social level have been thwarted), the Judge ignores the Ordinances, which lay down harsh penalties in such cases, and merely orders that it be determined whether the girl put up any resistance or if, on the contrary, the act occurred with mutual consent. Despite the similarity of the situation, the terms in which the episode is narrated (by the mother) and commented on (by Pero Marques) seem to reveal that some effort had been made to achieve that moral nuancing (the act occurred between peasants) and literary adaptation which, despite everything, can be detected in the texts of the *Copilaçam*.

12. In the study mentioned above, the first modern editor suggested that this might explain why the text was lost: 'it was perhaps because it had not been engendered in the noisy atmosphere of the Court, because the original was not stowed away in the council chests, that it was condemned to oblivion' (Pratt, 'Ainda o *Auto da Festa*', p. 67). In fact, we have information of only one such play that appeared in the *Livro das Obras*, but was not performed at Court. That was the *Cananeia*, a mystery play staged at the Monastery of Odivelas in 1534 or 1535.

13. As we know, divination, like astrology and presumption, was a common target of Vicente's satire.

14. As Eneida Bonfim has pointed out, the gypsy women in the *Festa* (Lucinda and Graciana) are less polite (or coarser) than their counterparts in the *Farsa das Ciganas* ('Uma leitura dos autos de Gil Vicente: o *Auto da Festa*', *Semear*, 8 (2003), 193–211 (p. 200 ff.)). However, given the uncertainty surrounding the date when the *Festa* was first performed, José Camões speaks both in terms of 'memory' (in the event that the *Farsa das Ciganas* had been performed earlier) and of 'anticipation' (to account for the scenario — less plausible to my mind — of it having been performed afterwards).

15. See Bonfim, 'Uma leitura' for a detailed comparison of Janafonso of the *Festa* and the peasant in the *Templo de Apolo*.

16. See in particular the detailed introduction to Daniel Arasse's *Le Sujet dans le tableau* (Paris: Flammarion, 1997), and Chapters 2 and 3 of Andrew Bennett's *The Author* (London: Routledge, 2005).

17. 'A *Copilaçam de todalas obras*: o livro e o projecto identitário de Gil Vicente', *Diacrítica. Ciências da Literatura*, 18–19 (2004–05), 179–98.

18. I have written elsewhere (2003) about the satirical logic that inspires the sentences issued by the Judge of Beira.

19. See Stephen Reckert, ' "Gil Terrón lletrudo está" ', *Leituras. Revista da Biblioteca Nacional*, 11 (2002), 15–33, and Cardoso Bernardes, 'A *Copilaçam de todalas obras*: o livro e o projecto' on the significance of this character in the *Auto Pastoril Castellano* and in Vicente's *oeuvre* as a whole.

20. Unreasonableness is of course a powerful generator of theatricality in itself, and is much satirized in Vicente's theatre. For an overview of the different satirical foci in Vicente's *corpus*, see my *Sátira e lirismo no teatro de Gil Vicente* (Lisbon: Imprensa Nacional — Casa da Moeda, 2004), pp. 303 ff.

21. These are also the conclusions that may be drawn by comparing most of the texts that figure simultaneously in the *Copilaçam* and outside it: *Maria Parda*, *Histórias de Deus*, *Ressurreição*, *Barca do Inferno* and above all, *Inês Pereira*.

22. This is what happened, very visibly, with the *Barcas*. We can see from the stage directions and through various internal corrections and omissions that the versions that appeared in the *Livro* offered the reader a much more interconnected piece of theatre.

23. In Portugal, it was Osório Mateus who most frequently emphasized that difference. Indeed, he did so repeatedly throughout his Vicente studies and even wrote a complete article on the subject: 'Teatro e Literatura', in *De teatro e outras escritas* (Lisbon: Quimera, 2004), pp. 212–18.

CHAPTER 3

The *Auto de la huida a Egipto*: Italian and Other Connections

Jane Whetnall

Queen Mary University of London

Despite the ample documentation of theatrical and paratheatrical activity in Court, convent, and cathedral in late medieval Castile, the corpus of surviving play texts is extremely thin.[1] Outside the so-called Salamancan school of Juan del Encina (1468–1529/30) and Lucas Fernández (1474–1542) there are only five short plays that are regarded as representing a Spanish tradition of early religious drama in the vernacular. Alongside the anonymous twelfth-century *Auto de los Reyes Magos*, the *Representación del Nacimiento de Nuestro Señor* and the *Lamentaciones fechas para Semana Santa* by Gómez Manrique (*c.* 1412–*c.* 1491), and Alonso de Campo's *Auto de la Pasión* of 1485–86, we have the anonymous *Auto de la huida a Egipto*, the latest of the five, but of uncertain date.

The *Auto de la huida a Egipto* (*Auto*) exists in a single manuscript witness of ten leaves which was bound together with two printed books of 1510. According to an inscription on the title page of one of these books it was donated to the Poor Clare convent of La Bretonera, in the province of Burgos, in 1512. On this basis, the margin of dating for the composition of the *Auto* was fixed by its first editor, Justo García Morales, at between 1446 (date of the supposed foundation of La Bretonera) and 1512.[2] Although José Amícola, who edited it for a second time, satisfactorily discounted García Morales's provisional attribution of the *Auto* to Manrique, he still considered the play roughly contemporary with Manrique, that is, as belonging to the second half of the fifteenth century, partly because it shows none of the features associated with the religious drama of Encina.[3] Since the early 1980s the *Auto* has formed an integral part of the canon of medieval Spanish drama and has been re-edited several times. I shall quote from Ronald Surtz's revised and expanded edition of 1992.[4]

However, this wide dating window of 1446–1512 for the play has come under scrutiny. New studies based on an examination of the volume have shifted the date of the manuscript towards the beginning of the sixteenth century: the *a quo* date has been rejected as unrealistic (the convent was founded much earlier); the second date means little, as the volume could have been bound at any time after 1512.[5] Critical assessments of the work itself have also tended to bring the date of composition

42   JANE WHETNALL

forward. Whereas in 1948 García Morales referred to its 'obvious medieval character', and Amícola in 1971 referred to the complexity of its staging as medieval, a consensus view has begun to emerge of its maturity and sophistication.[6] For Josep Lluís Sirera, writing twenty years after Amícola, the play is constructed 'with sufficient skill and technical knowhow for us to be able to regard it as theatrically mature'.[7] And, ten years on, Pedro Cátedra has said that, of the five plays, its *mise en texte* is closest in style to that of the post-medieval, professional theatre, 'perhaps because it is a much later work than all the others'.[8] For Cátedra it is unequivocally a work of the early sixteenth century. I hope to bring further evidence to bear in support of a sixteenth-century date of composition.

The *Auto* is made up of 384 lines of octosyllabic verse, which include 88 lines intended for singing. García Morales divided the action into twelve scenes; subsequent editors have followed this scheme.[9] Ten characters have speaking parts: in order of size, the Peregrino [Pilgrim] (138 lines), San Juan (82), Josepe (74), the Angel (32), the Virgin Mary (24), Zacarías (8), Isabel [St Elizabeth] (8), and the Ladrón Mozo [Robber Boy] (8); two other Robbers speak in unison with the Ladrón Mozo (8). The Child Jesus, who is on stage throughout the Flight scenes and the Peregrino's visit to Egypt, does not speak.

The backbone of the plot is the Gospel story of the Holy Family's Flight into Egypt to escape Herod's murderous decree. It begins with an Angel appearing to Josepe in a dream and ends after the same Angel announces that it is safe for the Family to return home. Between these two framing points the play inserts a less familiar, parallel, story, that of the young St John the Baptist's withdrawal to the desert, a stay which overlaps with the Holy Family's sojourn in Egypt. These two plots are linked by the intervention of a nameless Peregrino. On his way from Egypt to Judea he crosses the desert and comes across Juan, the future Baptist, with whom he conducts a question-and-answer session which proves the turning point of the action. When Juan mentions that the Holy Family is living in Egypt the Peregrino recognizes them as his neighbours. He goes back to greet them, taking news of Juan. The Virgin responds with messages for Juan and the Peregrino goes back to Juan in the desert. Juan invites him to share his hermit life and together they look forward to the return of the Messiah. The Angel then appears to Josepe for the second time, and the Family sets off for home, with Josepe singing the closing song, 'Alegrarte has, tierra mía, | porque a visitarte va | el que te redimirá' [Rejoice, my country, for your Redeemer is on his way].

This is an upbeat and uplifting play, with never a dull moment, no longueurs, no long speeches.[10] It is full of movement, journeys, visitations: the Angel to Josepe, the Holy Family to Egypt, Juan to the desert, the Peregrino to the desert, back to Egypt, back to the desert again, the Angel to Josepe again, the Holy Family back to Judaea. Apart from these comings and goings, other events are described or alluded to, such as the Nativity (167–72), the Visitation (295–97), the Holy Family's life in Egypt (181–86), Juan's life in the desert (244–45; 250–55), and two apocryphal incidents that occur during the Flight (71–86). The action is punctuated with five *villancicos* [rustic songs], which mark points of transition between scenes, four of them being sung by characters on the move from one place to another. And there

THE *AUTO DE LA HUIDA A EGIPTO*   43

are several comic touches, such as when the repentant robbers offer to share their swag with the Holy Family: 'Si queréis de lo hurtado, | con vós queremos partir' [If you'd like some of what we've stolen, we'll gladly share it with you] (101–02).

Scholars have been unanimous in proclaiming the originality of the *Auto* and the inventiveness of its unknown author. A number of important studies have opened out our appreciation of the play. Amícola is impressed by its metrical variety and the shifts in pace and tempo as it moves from strophic speeches to the rapid-fire exchange between San Juan and the Peregrino: 'an example of sparkling dialogue that is unique in early Spanish verse drama'.[11] Surtz has explored its Franciscan affiliations and highlighted the importance of the figure of the Peregrino as key to an interpretation of the play's dynamic.[12] In a sensitive analysis of the text for clues to its original staging, Sirera has brought the *Auto* to life with a convincing reconstruction of an early performance.[13]

While other aspects of the work have been the subject of critical attention, the quest for sources has not kept pace. Nonetheless, since García Morales's first tentative observations, the archive of biblical citations has been gradually growing. Editors have noticed that apart from the basic skeleton debt to Matt. 2 and 3 (for the Flight into Egypt and John the Baptist's desert calling), the text is threaded through with biblical allusions: from the unborn John leaping in his mother's womb at the Visitation (*Auto* 295–97; cf. Luke 1. 41) to the temptation of Christ (*Auto* 333–34; cf. Matt. 4. 1–11, Mark 1. 12–13, Luke 4. 1–13).[14] To these I would add that 'Dios me puso nombre: Juan' (*Auto* 207) must refer to the miraculous naming of John (Luke 1. 13; 59–63). From the apocryphal tradition, the *Gospel of Pseudo-Matthew* and the *Arabic Gospel of the Infancy* have been suggested as sources for incidents on the Flight into Egypt (*Auto* 71–72; 73–110).[15]

But I am not sure how many of these canonical or apocryphal texts can be regarded as sources in any practical sense. I prefer to think of them as authorities. Most of the relevant biblical references belong to the liturgy of the Christmas cycle, and are therefore too commonplace to count as sources. Conversely, even if the *Gospel of Pseudo-Matthew*, for example, is the earliest written authority for lines 71–72 of the play, 'Los tigres y los leones | se umilian al poderoso' [Lions and tigers bow down before the Almighty], it is unlikely to have been consulted directly by the author of the *Auto*.[16] Apocryphal material was disseminated during the Middle Ages via compilations such as the *Golden Legend* of Jacobus de Voragine and through oral and iconographic tradition, and this particular motif will have reached the dramatist by some such intermediate route.

No doubt inhibited by the play's uncertain date, editors have seemingly been reluctant to look for sources among the mass of devotional writings at large in the late fifteenth century, many of which were given a new lease of life with the advent of printing. García Morales refers to a series of medieval works in fairly general terms, but without following through his observations.[17] Surtz mentions some of them as Franciscan analogues for the *Auto*, but without considering them as sources.[18]

From what I have been able to discover, however, the principal sources of the *Auto* are all medieval texts and therefore more nearly contemporary with the com-

44 JANE WHETNALL

position of the *Auto* than the Gospels or the apocryphal gospels, or the fourth-century New Testament commentaries adduced as secondary influences in a recent study.[19] I have found textual parallels in four devotional works which, directly or indirectly, fed into the composition of the *Auto*: two *Vitae Christi*, one hagiographical narrative and one play. None of them is Spanish in origin and only one of them (*pace* Surtz) bears a Franciscan stamp. The *Auto* also shows a degree of affinity with the liturgical drama of previous centuries. The *Ordo Rachelis* and the *Peregrinus* both harbour precedents for certain features of the *Auto*: its bipartite structure and the idiosyncratic figure of the Peregrino.

Identifying some of the elements that pre-existed the *Auto* casts fresh light on its originality and helps to build up a picture of the cultural environment in which it was written and performed. Perhaps more importantly, it gives us some indication of the choices and constraints that the author was faced with in constructing the play.

1. The Episode of the Robbers

The apocryphal legend which is most developed in the play, half narrated and half acted, is the Episode of the Robbers. In Scene 4 of the *Auto* Josepe starts to tell the audience how the Family were set upon by bandits (lines 73–78). Then, turning to the Child, he reminds him of the happy outcome, how the older villain and his two sons, 'viéndote, ellos confesaron | los altos secretos tuyos' [seeing you, declared your deepest secrets] (81–82). This narrative flashback is the prologue to a re-enactment of the robbers' change of heart. Josepe next introduces one of the boys as the future Good Thief of the Crucifixion:

> Y un hijo d'este ladrón,   [And a son of this robber,
> de tu graçia inspirado,   inspired by your grace,
> quesiste fuese salvado   you chose to be saved
> en el día de la Pasión.   on the day of the Passion.]
> (lines 83–86)

At this the Ladrón Mozo materializes and speaks to the Child:

> De ti, niño, veo salir   [Shining from you, child, I see
> atán grande resplendor,   a radiance so bright
> que me pone tal temor,   that it makes me more in awe
> cuanto no puedo dezir.   than I can say.]
> (lines 87–90)

As we have seen, the legend of the robbers derives ultimately from the *Arabic Gospel of the Infancy*. But the account which has as its climax the conversion of the robber boy, struck by the radiant beauty of the Holy Child, can be traced to the writings of an English Cistercian, Aelred of Rievaulx, in his *De vita eremitica ad sororem* [*A Letter to His Sister*], also known as *De institutione inclusarum* [*A Rule of Life for a Recluse*], of 1160–62. It is addressed to his sister, who was a hermit.

Part 3 of this devotional treatise comprises a threefold meditation on the life of Christ from the Annunciation to his appearance to Mary Magdalen after the Resurrection. Like the author of the *Meditationes vitae Christi* a century later Aelred uses the technique of bringing the female reader as it were bodily into the scenes

THE *AUTO DE LA HUIDA A EGIPTO*   45

she is invited to contemplate: 'Next with all your devotion accompany the Mother as she makes her way to Bethlehem. Take shelter in the inn with her, be present and help her as she gives birth.'[20] So too, she is to witness and wonder at the incident on the road to Egypt:

> Do not in thy meditation pass over the gifts of the Magi: nor leave him without company when he flees into Egypt. Think that to be true which is told, that he was captured by robbers in the way and saved by the kindness of a youth. This was, they say, the son of the chief of the robbers, and when he got possession of his prey, and found the child on his mother's breast, *such splendour of majesty appeared in his lovely face* that [the youth], not doubting that he was more than man, inflamed with love embraced him and said: O most blessed of children, if ever there come a time for having mercy on me, then remember me and forget not this hour. This they say was the robber who was crucified on Christ's right hand.[21]

There can be no doubt that the phrase 'atán grande resplendor' [such great splendour] echoes the words of Aelred, but it seems unlikely that the author of the *Auto* would have known *De institutione inclusarum* at first hand.[22] However, Aelred's version of the robber episode circulated widely in the later Middle Ages through a readily accessible intermediary, the *Vita Christi* of Ludolph of Saxony (*c.* 1295–1378). The Castilian translation by Fray Ambrosio Montesino was printed in Spain in 1502. Ludolph lifts the whole of the Aelred story into his chapter on the Flight into Egypt, although he attributes it to St Anselm:[23]

> Item es de notar (según dize san Anselmo), que la gloriosa Virgen con su hijo e con su esposo fue en aquel camino presa de unos ladrones. Pues piensa cómo fue verdad esto que se dize que aquel infante fue preso con su madre de unos ladrones en la vía de Egipto e cómo fueron libres por ruego de un mancebillo que allí estava entre los ladrones. Este moço (según que se afirma) era hijo del capitán de aquellos salteadores, e como ya toviesse recebida la parte que le cupo del robo e mirasse bien al niño en los braços de su madre, *tan grande majestad aparesció de resplandor en su cara muy hermosa* que, no dubdando ser él alguna cosa más que hombre, se allegó a él con acelerado fervor de amor e lo abraçó, diziéndole: O más bienaventurado que todos los niños, si en algun tiempo después d'este se ofresciere caso en que puedas obrar misericordia comigo, pídote por merced que te acuerdes de mí e no te olvides d'esta hora presente *en que a ti e a tus padres os hago soltar e tornar lo vuestro.* O cosa maravillosa que cuentan que este ladrón fue él que, a la diestra de Dios crucificado...[24]

> [Note also that (according to St Anselm) the glorious Virgin, with her son and her husband, was captured by robbers on that journey. Think that to be true which is told, that the child with his mother was captured on the way to Egypt, and how they were freed thanks to a young lad who was there among the robbers. This lad (they say) was the son of the chief of those bandits, and when he had received his share of the spoils and had gazed at the child in the arms of his mother, *such great majesty of brightness shone in his lovely face* that, not doubting that he was something more than man, he was overcome with a sudden fervour of love, embraced him and said: O most blessed of children, if there ever come a time after this for having mercy on me, I entreat you to remember me and forget not this hour *in which I set you and your parents free and restore your property.* O wondrous thing they tell that this thief was the one who, crucified on God's right hand ...]

46   JANE WHETNALL

That Montesino's translation was the immediate source for the *Auto* seems to be confirmed by the rider, 'en que a ti e a tus padres os hago soltar e tornar lo vuestro' [in which I set you and your parents free and restore your property]. This clause is an addition by Montesino which does not appear in Aelred or Ludolph, and it corresponds to the pledge by the three Robbers in the play: 'Queremos restituir | lo que a vós hemos tomado' [We wish to give you back what we've taken from you] (100–01). This has a bearing on the date of the *Auto*: according to Keith Whinnom, 'There was indubitably a sixteenth-century vogue of "el Cartuxano" ['the Carthusian' = Ludolph's *Vita Christi*]; but one does not begin to find references to the work in Spain before the end of the fifteenth century'.[25]

According to Émile Mâle, the episode of the robbers is found in very few written sources. It is one of only two apocryphal legends relating to the Flight into Egypt — the other being the miracle of the wheatfield — which were transmitted in iconographical tradition but escaped the great compilations of the thirteenth century, Vincent de Beauvais and the *Golden Legend*.[26] At least three other literary treatments of the robbers episode surfaced in Spain in the late Middle Ages, all of which help throw into relief the *Auto*'s debt to Aelred, via Ludolph and Montesino.[27]

2. Egypt and After

A more important and extensive source of the *Auto* is the *Meditationes vitae Christi* (*MVC*), once attributed to St Bonaventure and now said to be the work of Johannes de Caulibus of San Gimignano, a Franciscan friar living in Tuscany during the second half of the thirteenth century. One of the international best-sellers of the Middle Ages, its impact was immediate, 'the text spread widely and rapidly and its early popularity [...] has left a rich depository of manuscripts throughout Europe'.[28] I have used the modern English translation of the text made from an Italian manuscript with the fullest series of illustrations.[29]

The *MVC* has not been formally proposed as a source by any of the editors of the *Auto*.[30] Ronald Surtz has drawn attention to several parallels between the two works, but he suggests no more than that the author of the play shares a common Franciscan tradition — the legend of the encounter between Jesus and John in the desert — and a common purpose — the edification of a Poor Clare community — with the author of the *MVC*.[31] I believe that it is possible to show that the *MVC* was a direct inspiration for the *Auto*, that its influence is apparent in a number of small ways where there is an overlap in content, and even that it may have provided a model for one aspect of the characterization of the Peregrino.

Chapters 12 and 13 of the *MVC* cover the Flight into Egypt and the Holy Family's return to Judaea. The author dwells upon the practical hardships of the outward journey (there is no mention of robbers or lions) and then gives a lively and imaginative account of the Holy Family's life in Egypt. The *Auto*'s treatment of the *Egyptian* sojourn is consistent with the tone and the emphasis of the *MVC*: Joseph finds carpentry work there and the Holy Child runs errands for his Mother. But particular stress is laid on the Virgin's role as breadwinner:

> How did they live all this time, or did they beg? We read that she provided
> the necessities for herself and the Son with spindle and needle; the Lady of the

The *Auto de la huida a Egipto*   47

world sewed and spun for money, for love of poverty [...] Did she not go from house to house asking for cloth or spinning work?[32]

This passage seems to have been the direct source for the following exchange between San Juan and the Peregrino. At their first meeting, when Juan enquires after the well-being of the Holy Family in Egypt, the Peregrino seeks to reassure him:[33]

San Juan: Así Dios te dé alegría, que me cuentes cómo están.	For heaven's sake, please tell me, how are things with them?
Peregrino: No les falta vino y pan; la dueña les mantenía.	They do not want for bread or wine; the Lady provides for them.
San Juan: Dime, ermano, ¿qué hazía o a qué gana de comer?	Tell me, brother, what does she do? How does she earn their keep?
Peregrino: A hilar y a coser, travajando noche y día.	By spinning and sewing: she works day and night.

(179–86)[34]

The question-and-answer format, which was designed to draw the reader into the *MVC*, serves as an ideal model for the staged dialogue of the *Auto*.[35] This would be a good example, then, of the way that the 'narrative and dramatic function embraced in the *Meditations* accord with the unique presentation of the Gospel story which occurs in medieval religious drama'.[36]

The *MVC* is also the first medieval text to give sanction, albeit cautiously, to the apocryphal tradition that the Holy Family met John the Baptist on their way back to Judaea:[37]

> When they came close to the edge of the desert they found John the Baptist, who had already begun to do penance there, although he had not committed any sin. [...] Thus it is likely that the boy Jesus, passing it on His return, found him there. Meditate on how he received them joyfully and how, resting a little, they ate with John those raw foods that he usually ate. Finally, after enjoying great refreshment of the spirit together, they bade farewell to him.[38]

Now, as far as the plot of the *Auto* is concerned, its debt to the *MVC* narrative stops short of the actual encounter between Juan and the Holy Family, which is to take place beyond the action of the play. As Surtz has pointed out, the meeting is heralded in several lines of dialogue between the Virgin and the Peregrino, and the Peregrino and Juan.[39] But if we disregard for a moment the fact that the meeting of the two cousins remains unstaged in the *Auto*, there are further textual parallels at this point that reveal an interesting structural correspondence between the devotional narrative and the drama. A conspicuous feature of the *MVC* is the active role assigned to the reader, who is constantly exhorted to participate imaginatively in the scenes described.[40] Thus after the description of the meeting in the desert the reader is presumed to be present too: 'You, therefore, on greeting him and on departing, kneel before John to kiss his feet, ask for his blessing, and commend yourself to him.'[41]

In an earlier passage the link with the *Auto* is unmistakeable:

> Go back to Egypt to visit the child Jesus. [...] Kneel before Him and kiss His feet, then take Him in your arms and repose with Him. Then He will say to

you, 'We have been given permission to return to our land, and tomorrow we must leave here. You have come at the right time to return with us.' To this you will answer cheerfully that you are very happy about it and wish to follow Him wherever he goes. [...] Then He will take you to His mother, who will honor you with courtesy. You will kneel to do reverence to her and the saintly old Joseph and you will rest with them.[42]

In the context of the *MVC*, 'Go back' requires the reader to resume the narrative after a digression, but it relates uncannily to what happens in Scene 8 of the play (lines 230–69), in which the Peregrino does indeed go back to Egypt, kisses the feet of the Child on behalf of Juan (246), and offers to remain there with the Holy Family (258–59). The Virgin sends him back to Juan, but with the promise that they are to return home soon.[43]

If there were no intervening texts between the *MVC* and the *Auto* we would have to say that in creating the character of the Peregrino the author was translating into dramatic terms the role of the reader of the *MVC*. However, the author of the *Auto* did have other sources to draw on, one of which was itself dependent on the *MVC*.

3. John the Baptist, the Boy Hermit

3.1. Vita di Sangiovambatista

The second most important source which must have been known, directly or indirectly, to the author of the *Auto* is an anonymous prose life of St John the Baptist written in Italian in the early fourteenth century, the *Vita di Sangiovambatista*.[44] I shall refer to it as the *Vita*. It survives only in the vernacular, but it is presumed to derive from a lost Latin original. This work was enormously influential in Renaissance Italy. Marilyn Aronberg Lavin documents its impact in the field of the pictorial arts in two articles about the infant St John the Baptist;[45] and it was also the inspiration for at least one poem and one play.[46] For a long time it was attributed to the prolific Dominican writer Fra Domenico Cavalca, author of other saints' lives, the *Vite de' santi padri*, but is now known not to be by him.[47] Lavin describes it as a 'vernacular translation of what was presumably an anonymous Latin life of St. John dependent on the rich legacy of eastern legends. The Italian translation, while amalgamating nearly all the elements of the medieval tradition, also adds many embellishments of its own'.[48]

The *Vita* provides a lavish and endearing account of the childhood of Giovanni and his early ventures into the desert, full of picturesque detail, dialogue, and interior monologue. From the age of three or four he seems naturally drawn to the wild and the solitude it offers. We are told of his sallies into a nearby wood to try out his vocation, the alarm this provokes in family and friends when he takes to spending nights at a time there, and, after much heart-searching, his eventual decision at the age of seven to adopt the life of a hermit: 'Adunque nel diserto me ne voglio andare sanza tornare mai più a casa, infinoattantochè'l Signore mio Giesù verrà e dirammi quello che vorrà ch'io faccia' [Right, I want to go off to the desert and not come home any more, until my Lord Jesus comes and tells me what he

THE *AUTO DE LA HUIDA A EGIPTO*   49

wants me to do]. The leave-taking from his parents is (relatively) short and decisive: 'Ecco, io me ne vado al diserto; datemi la vostra benedizione' [Look, I'm off to the desert; give me your blessing]. Zaccheria is prompt to give his, 'E la madre fece il simigliante' [And his mother did likewise], whereupon Giovanni goes off happily and his parents watch from a window until he is out of sight.[49]

This work may be the earliest extant authority for Scene 5 of the *Auto*, in which Juan seeks permission from his parents to go and live in the desert.[50] It is more difficult to pinpoint smaller textual affinities, but there is one passage which seems to anticipate Juan's frame of mind in the *Auto*:

> E andava il fanciullo a questo bosco [...] e recavasi a memoria le cose ch'egli aveva lette di Dio e del Figliuolo suo, e sapeva che la nostra Donna era già fuggita in Egitto col Figliuolo suo, ed egli disiderava di vederlo, e diceva a Dio: *O Signore, quando potrò vedere il Figliuolo e la Madre, e quando mi ritroverrò con lui?*[51]

> [And the little boy would go to this wood [...] and mull over in his mind the things he had read about God and his Son, and he knew that Our Lady had already fled into Egypt with her Son, and he longed to see him, and he would say to God: *O Lord, when shall I be able to see the Son and his Mother, and when shall I meet him again?*]

The last sentence corresponds to San Juan's words in Scene 6 after he learns of the proximity of the Holy Family as neighbours of the Peregrino: '¡O quién te viese Jesú! | ¡O quién te viese María!' [Oh if only I could see you, Jesus! Oh if only I could see you, Mary!] (187–88). These fervent wishes are not addressed to the Peregrino, but his puzzled rejoinder is the response of someone who has noticed an oversight in the *Vita*: '¿Y al viejo querrías ver tú, | que Josepe se dezía?' [What about the old guy? Don't you want to see Joseph too?] (189–90).[52]

In telling of the encounter between Jesus and John in the desert the author of the *Vita* explicitly defers to the authority of the *MVC*, but the narrative is much fuller and more detailed.[53] Whereas in the *MVC* the meeting is part of the Holy Family's story, in the *Vita* it is told from Giovanni's point of view:

> Passando [Giuseppo colla Madre e col Figliuolo] per questo diserto, come Iddio volle, venne là dov'era Giovanni Batista, e incontanente che vide venire da lungi la Madre e il Figliuolo, ispirato da Dio, conobbegli, e incontanente cominciò a correre inverso di loro [...], e giunse Giovanni e gittossi tutto quanto in terra a baciare i piedi di Messer Giesù; e Giesù il prese per le braccia e levollo suso e baciollo nella fronte e poi gli diede la pace: Pace teco, *apparecchiatore della via mia.*[54]

> [When the Holy Family were passing through this desert, in accordance with God's will, they came to where John the Baptist was; and as soon as he saw the Mother and Son in the distance, inspired by God he recognized them, and straight away began to run towards them [...] and John reached them and threw himself on the ground and kissed the feet of Lord Jesus; and Jesus took him by the arms and raised him up and kissed him on the forehead and then he blessed him, saying: Peace be with you, *Preparer of my Way.*]

The parallel with the *Auto* in this case has far-reaching implications. In the Spanish

50 JANE WHETNALL

play these words are given to the Peregrino, who brings Juan messages from his cousin in Egypt:

> Dize que eres su vandera,
> que levantes su pendón.
> Invíate su vendiçión,
> *que aparejes su carrera.*
>   (305–08)

> [He says you are his banner,
> you are to raise his pennant.
> He sends you his blessing:
> *you are to prepare his way.*]

If the dramatist had the *Vita* in mind when planning the play it is Jesus's role he or she is assigning to the Peregrino.

3.2. *Rappresentazione di San Giovanni nel deserto* [Play of St John in the Desert]

These few parallels are close enough to persuade me that the *Vita* was the inspiration for part of the *Auto*, although a plausible intermediary, another Italian text, may have provided the model. This is a fifteenth-century drama about the desert meeting of Jesus and John, the *Rappresentazione di San Giovanni nel deserto* by Feo Belcari (1410–84) and Tommaso Benci (†1470).[55] It is very faithful to the text of the *Vita*, apparently its sole source, but it dramatizes only John's leave-taking of his parents and the subsequent encounter with Jesus.[56]

Because both the *Rappresentazione* and the *Auto* are plays and in verse it is easier to find similarities between them, the most striking coincidence being their length. The *Rappresentazione* is made up of 48 eight-line stanzas, exactly the same number of lines (384) as the *Auto*. Like the *Auto*, its main action is framed by two angelic interventions: a prologue announcing the Return from Egypt, and an epilogue containing the moral of the play. Within this frame, the shape of the *Rappresentazione* is comparable to the corresponding portions of the *Auto*, Scenes 5 and 6: a leave-taking closely followed by an encounter between two interlocutors.[57] But in relation to the Italian play the equivalent sections of the *Auto* are much more compact. The three-way scene of leave-taking between Juan, Zacarías, and Isabel condenses the sixteen Italian stanzas into three *octavas*. The twenty-two-stanza exchange between Gesù and Giovanni, dominated by Gesù, with thirteen stanzas to Giovanni's nine, has been reduced to forty couplets in the *Auto* (lines 135–214), which are divided equally between Juan and the Peregrino.

Despite considerable differences in scale between the two treatments of these scenes, three verbal coincidences are, to my mind, incontrovertible. In Scene 5 of the *Auto*, the leave-taking, the opening lines of Juan's and Zacarías's speeches, 'Padre mío, Zacarías, | señor, dé vuestra liçençia, | y vós, madre [...] Pido liçençia a los dos' [Zachariah, my father, sir, give me leave, and you, mother [...] I ask you both] (111–13; 115), and 'Hijo, la buestra niñez | no os engaña, según creo' [Son, your infant years do not mislead you, I believe] (119–20), even allowing for the formulaic nature of the occasion, plainly recall the words used by their characters in the *Rappresentazione*:

> *Santo Giovanni dice*
> *al padre e alla madre:*
> O venerabil padre Zacheria,

> [*St John says to his*
> *father and mother:*
> O venerable father, Zachariah,

o santa Lisabetta dolce madre,	O Saint Elizabeth, dear mother,
io son mandato a preparar la via [...]	I have been sent to prepare the way [...]
datemi dunque la bendizione.	so give me your blessing. (4.1–4; 5.8)

Zaccaria gli risponde e dice: *Zachariah replies, saying:*
Dolce figliuol, la tu tenera etade   Dear little son, your tender age
non è ancor forte a così aspra vita.   isn't strong enough for so harsh a life.]

(6.1–2)

But it is the desert encounter between the cousins that reinforces our impression that the Italian Gesù of the *Rappresentazione*, as of the *Vita*, is the forerunner of the Spanish Peregrino. This occurs in an exchange between Gesù and Giovanni that reads like the template for one of the jokes in the *Auto*. In Scene 6, when the Peregrino enquires how Juan manages to live in the desert, 'Pues, dezime, ¿qué coméis | en esta fiera montaña?' [So tell me, what do you eat on this wild mountain side?] (145–46), Juan draws himself up to his full height and claims he lives on God's fresh air: 'La graçia de Dios tamaña | me sostiene, como veis' [God's amazing grace sustains me, as you see] (147–48). This leads the Peregrino to reply incredulously: 'Dezime, ¿con esa graçia | sin comer os sostenéis?' [What, on grace alone you survive without food?] (149–50). The equivalent passage in the *Rappresentazione* shows Giovanni similarly failing to give a straight answer to a straight question, in this case posed by Gesù:

> *Gesù*: dimmi, ti prego, tua vita e costume,
>   con che modo ti reggi e con qual lume. (21.7–8)
> *Giovanni*: Tal grazia porge tua dolce presenza
>   che tutto il cor mi sento in allegreza. (22.1–2)
>
> [*Jesus*: tell me, please, about your life and how you live,
>   how you support yourself, and with what guidance.
> *John*: The grace that flows from your dear presence
>   fills my whole heart with joy.]

Although the answers are different, the idea of grace figures in both.

Among Giovanni's first words to his cousin in the *Rappresentazione* we have an unexpected echo of Aelred: 'tanto splendor mi getta tua belleza' [your beauty casts such radiance upon me] (22.4).[58] This avowal has no reflex in the *Auto*, but a second echo does, when he goes on to tell Gesù about his moment of recognition in the womb:

Dalla tua somma luce uno splendore	[From your bright eyes a radiance
mi venne, essendo in corpo di mia madre,	reached me in my mother's womb,
in modo ch'io mi vuolsi a te, Signore,	so that I turned to you, Lord,
che t'amo più che Zacheria mio padre.	for I revere you more than I do
(23.1–4)	my father, Zachariah.]

In the *Auto* this constitutes a message from Josepe, relayed to Juan by the Peregrino:

dize aquel su sancto padre	[his saintly father tells
que en el vientre de tu madre	how in your mother's womb
adoraste al infinito (lines 295–97)	you worshipped the Infinite One]

The pairing of *padre* in rhyme with *madre* is revealing. As well as helping to confirm the *Auto*'s debt to this model, it supplies the author of the *Auto* with a pretext for bringing Josepe in as a witness to the Visitation: a rather happier solution than the gratuitous disparagement of Zacheria by Giovanni. I have set the three parallel passages out in a chart for easy comparison (see Table 1).[59]

TABLE I. Parallel passages from *Rappresentazione* and *Auto de la huida*

	RAPPRESENTAZIONE		AUTO DE LA HUIDA
Gio	O venerabil padre Zacheria,	Ju	Padre mío, Zacarías,
	o santa Lisabetta dolce madre,		señor, dé vuestra liçençia,
	io son mandato a preparar la via		y vós, madre
	[...]		[...]
	datemi dunque la bendizione		Pido liçençia a los dos
	(4.1–3; 5.8)		(111–13; 115)
Zac	Dolce figliuol, la tua tenera etade	Zac	Hijo, la buestra niñez
	non è ancor forte a così aspra vita		no os engaña, según creo
	(6.1–2)		(119–20)
Ge	dimmi, ti prego, tua vita e costume,	Pe	Pues, dezime, ¿qué coméis
	con che modo ti reggi e con qual lume.		en esta fiera montaña?
	(21.7–8))		(145–46)
Gio	Tal grazia porge la tua dolce presenza	Ju	La graçia de Dios tamaña
	che tutto il cor mi sento in allegreza		me sostiene, como veis
	(22.1–2)		(147–48)
		Pe	Dezime, ¿con esa graçia
			sin comer os sostenéis?
			(149–50)
Gio	Dalla tua somma luce uno splendore	Pe	dize aquel su sancto padre
	mi venne, essendo in corpo di mia madre,		que en el vientre de tu madre
	in modo ch'io mi vuolsi a te, Signore,		adoraste al infinito (295–97)
	che t'amo più che Zacheria mio padre		
	(23.1–4)		

Both of these Italian works which deal with the legendary encounter between Jesus and John, one a prose narrative, the other a verse play, contain verbal coincidences with the *Auto*. The possibility of either text being available in Spain is something I have yet to explore, but both were in print by the early sixteenth century. The *Vita* has been dated to 1300–10 on linguistic grounds, a little earlier than Cavalca's *Vite de' santi padri* (c. 1330); Domenico Manni, who edited the text from two manuscripts in his edition of 1731–35, said he had also seen an undated printing of c. 1500.[60] According to Lavin, the *Rappresentazione*, which was probably completed before 1449, 'was frequently published from the late 15th century on'.[61]

Then again, the *Auto*'s association with La Bretonera suggests other channels of transmission. These devotional texts are precisely the sort of material that would have circulated in manuscript within the network of Poor Clare convents, some of which may have emanated from their mother house in Italy. Katherine Gill provides eloquent testimony to the heightened literary activities of women in general and Poor Clare nuns in particular in late medieval and early modern Italy.[62]

THE *AUTO DE LA HUIDA A EGIPTO* 53

That communities of women religious in Italy 'and beyond' copied, shared, and exchanged manuscripts of plays is clear from the research of Elissa B. Weaver.[63]

Whether or not we are able to establish a direct line of dependence on the part of the writer of the *Auto* — and I don't rule out an intermediate translation in either case — the *Vita* and the *Rappresentazione*, taken together, provide a template for one aspect of the role of the Peregrino in the Spanish play. In his interrogation of Juan at their first meeting (Scene 6), his visit to the Holy Family in Egypt (Scene 8), and the messages he brings back to Juan on his return (Scene 9), the Peregrino is a stand-in for Jesus in the legendary encounter with his cousin, as configured in the Italian texts.

4. The Figure of the Peregrino

The figure of the Peregrino and his role in the play are widely regarded as the most successful achievement of the unknown author: he is at the hub of the action, forming a bridge between the two halves of the plot, and his conversion to the ascetic life affords a model of conduct for the audience of the play. But he is also something of a puzzle: 'The character known only as the Peregrino seems to be the product of the playwright's imagination, for no such personage is to be found in the gospels, whether canonical or apocryphal.'[64] No one has noticed, however, that the Peregrino has a distinguished precursor in theatrical tradition dating back to the eleventh century.

As we have seen from a comparison between the *Auto* and the two Italian versions of the meeting between John and Jesus, the Peregrino has become the spokesman for the Christ Child in the *Vita* and the *Rappresentazione*: it is he who interrogates Juan about his life in the desert in Scene 6, and in Scene 9 he brings back the substance of the Holy Child's message about his own future mission and that of Juan. One passage I have already cited (lines 305–08; see above). Earlier in the same scene the Peregrino tells Juan:

En tu tan sancto vivir	In your saintly way of life
Dios manda que perseveres [...]	God says you must persevere [...]
Y más te quier[e] dezir	What's more, he wants you to know
qu'el mundo redimirá.	that he will redeem the world.
(280–81; 284–85)[65]	

To all intents and purposes a version of the legendary encounter between Jesus and John is portrayed in the *Auto*, but with the Peregrino taking Christ's role. Closer to home in one sense, but more remote in terms of its antiquity, there is a sort of inverted precedent for this, both on the stage and in the Gospels, whereby Christ assumes the role of a Peregrino.

The liturgical drama *Peregrinus* or *Officium Peregrini* was usually performed at Vespers on Easter Monday. It is a dramatization of Luke 24. 13–32. Two disciples on the road to Emmaus are joined by a stranger, who asks them what they are talking about. One of them replies with a question of his own: 'Tu solus peregrinus es in Jerusalem et non cognovisti quae facta sunt in illa his diebus?' [Are you a stranger in Jerusalem that you haven't heard about the things that have been happening there in the last few days?] (Luke 24. 18). To which the risen Christ replies, 'Quae?'

54   JANE WHETNALL

[What things?], and is accordingly given an account of his own death, burial, and resurrection before he reveals himself over supper at Emmaus.[66]

In the Latin of the Vulgate the noun *peregrinus* has an entirely secular meaning: visitor, stranger, foreigner, traveller. By the Middle Ages it had taken on a religious sense as well. Karl Young refers to a thirteenth-century *Peregrinus* from Padua which specifies that the priests playing Christ and the disciples should be dressed in pilgrim garb.[67] This convention must have been in place from the earliest times and will have had particular resonance in Spain. According to Julia Holloway, 'Depictions in art of the Emmaus Pilgrims are much influenced by the liturgical drama, the iconography being established by the eleventh and twelfth centuries'.[68] Among many such artworks the most relevant to our purpose and the most iconic is the eleventh-century bas-relief of the Journey to Emmaus in the cloister of Santo Domingo de Silos. In Italy the tradition is represented in a fourteenth-century panel of the Emmaus Pilgrims by Duccio di Buoninsegna.[69] In both of these images reflecting the *Peregrinus* drama, Christ is wearing a scallop shell on his scrip, the badge of a pilgrim to Santiago.[70]

The only textual witness of the *Peregrinus* on Spanish soil was found appended to the *Visitatio sepulchri* in a Ripoll troper of the second half of the twelfth century, complete with musical notation; but there is a reference to it as still belonging to the liturgical repertoire in a Vic *consueta* of 1413.[71] We can be fairly sure, then, that despite its poor survival rate *qua* text, *Peregrinus* was still part of a living tradition at the end of the Middle Ages, perhaps in the vernacular.[72] An idiosyncrasy of the Ripoll *Peregrinus* is that it follows seamlessly on from another scene in the cycle of Easter plays, *Hortulanus*: 'In no other play found to date does the episode of the journey to Emmaus follow a scene between Christ and Mary Magdalen'.[73] And one indication of its possible longevity is that Juan del Encina may have known an liturgical drama of this type. In his *Representación de la santíssima Resurrección de Cristo* [Re-Enactment of the Most Holy Resurrection of Christ] he juxtaposes the episodes of *Hortulanus* and *Peregrinus* in the same sequence as occurs in the text of the Ripoll troper. In this case, however, the encounter in the garden and the encounter at Emmaus are not acted out, but narrated. Joseph of Arimathaea and Mary Magdalen, Luke and Cleophas, first in pairs and then as a foursome, exchange accounts of their contact with the risen Christ. Christ is not a character in the play, but Luke says:

Quando ívamos camino	We were on our way
al castillo de Emaús,	to the village of Emmaus,
nos apareció Jesús	when Jesus appeared
en trage de peregrino.[74]	in pilgrim dress.

The equation of the Peregrino of the *Auto* with Christ the *Peregrinus* may seem far-fetched, but the notion of pilgrimage is inherent in medieval treatments of the Flight into Egypt story, not least in the some of the sources used by the author of the *Auto*.[75] In the *MVC*, 'Habitaverunt ibi per septem annos ut peregrini' [they stayed there for seven years as pilgrims];[76] and in Ludolph's *Vita Christi*, 'we are told that Mary, Joseph and the Child lived as "peregrini, pauperes et egini" [pilgrims, poor and destitute] after their arrival in Egypt'.[77] Similar references to Christ as a

THE *AUTO DE LA HUIDA A EGIPTO* 55

pilgrim and the Flight into Egypt as a pilgrimage can be found in the *Vita Christi* of Francesc Eiximenis.[78] Images of the Christ Child in pilgrim garb persist as objects of devotion in convents down to the present day.[79]

I can hardly argue that the Peregrino of the *Auto* is a direct descendant of the liturgical *Peregrinus*, but the dramatic function of the two is not dissimilar. Christ poses as a stranger in order to test the faith and loyalty of his followers; the Peregrino enters the *Auto* stage as a stranger from Egypt genuinely ignorant of recent events in Judaea. For the play's first audience the *Peregrinus* drama may have been no more than a shared cultural memory. For the unknown playwright, however, an awareness of this long tradition could well have informed the creation of an Everyman character who is also the occasional spokesman for Jesus.

5 The Massacre of the Innocents

The upbeat mood and tempo of the *Auto* encourage us to forget the grim premise for the framing plot: namely, that while the Holy Family is away Herod's soldiers will slaughter all the boy children of Jesus's generation. And this is what they duly did, on stage, in the *Ordo Rachelis*. For the Flight into Egypt also had its place in a liturgical drama, in this case one for which no text has been preserved in Spain.[80] From modest beginnings the *Ordo Rachelis* evolved to form part of a fully fledged Epiphany drama which was 'probably complete by the end of the eleventh century'.[81] Young's account of the Fleury version (thirteenth century) inevitably brings to mind the *Auto de la huida*:

> The action proper begins with a scene in which the angel appears above the *præsepe*, commanding Joseph to flee with Mary and Jesus into Egypt. As the Holy Family depart, Joseph sings the responsory *Ægypte, noli flere* [Egypt, do not weep] [...] The action ends with a scene representing the return of the Holy Family from Egypt and their departure into Galilee.[82]

As they set out again, Joseph sings the closing responsory, *Gaude, gaude, gaude, Maria virgo* [Rejoice, rejoice, rejoice, Virgin Mary].[83] Apart from Joseph's songs, the text of the *Ordo Rachelis* is a close dramatization of the Gospel narrative (Matt. 2. 13–21) that follows the visit of the Magi: Herod's wrath and its harrowing consequences — the Massacre of the Innocents and Rachel's Lament — are framed between the two angelic messages and the start of two journeys.[84]

The *Auto de la huida* is not only free from any direct representation of the atrocity, but the one allusion to it is extremely carefully phrased. The Angel's message to Josepe, 'que a Dios piensa de matar | el falso Erodes malvado' [for false, wicked Herod plans on killing God] (15–16) is oddly euphemistic if we compare it with the Biblical text it is based on.[85] The choice of words tends to gloss over the grim fact that it was a child that Herod was after: 'quaeret puerum ad perdendum eum' [he is seeking to do away with the child] (Matt. 2. 13); and that a great many other children were killed: 'omnes pueros qui erant in Bethlehem [...] a bimatu et infra' [all the boy children in Bethlehem [...] of two years and under] (Matt. 2. 16). On the Angel's return, 'volveos para Judea, | que Erodes ya es finado' [go back to Judaea, for Herod is dead] (359–60), there is no mention of the death threat.[86] Yet the slaughter was staged in the *Ordo Rachelis* and its vernacular offshoots.[87]

56 JANE WHETNALL

This circumspection is akin to that shown by John of Caulibus, and is another aspect of the *Auto* that could be ascribed to the influence of the *MVC*, both spirit and letter. In tailoring the *MVC* to its female reader, a nun, the author 'is careful not to offend her delicacy by details of too much brutality; and in the Herod scenes and the episode of the woman with the issue of blood, he chooses his words with great restraint'.[88] The one reference to the Crucifixion in the *Auto* is also carefully phrased ('quesiste fuese salvado | en el día de la Pasión' [you chose to save him on the day of the Passion], 85–86), in marked contrast to the stark candour of Gómez Manrique's *Representación*, in which the instruments of the Passion are paraded before the Baby.[89]

Of course, the author of the *Auto* need not have been reacting against any theatrical precedent in choosing to avoid the poignant backdrop to the story in Matthew's Gospel. However, some recollection of a liturgical drama on the lines of the *Ordo Rachelis* could help to account for the prominent role accorded to Joseph. He has the third-largest role of all the characters in the play, and sings three of the five *villancicos*, two as they set off for Egypt and one on their return. The musical success of the piece must stand or fall by his performance.[90]

6. The Real Role of the Peregrino

A more fundamental gap in the text of the *Auto de la huida* was first pointed out by Amícola and later articulated by Surtz.[91] Why does the author choose not to dramatize the actual encounter between St John and the Holy Family, which the whole plot seems to be building towards? One possible explanation is implicit in Surtz's theory that the Peregrino was devised as the *alter ego* of the audience: obviously, in a dramatic portrayal of a meeting between the two cousins there would be no place for the Peregrino — which would leave the audience, with the Peregrino, out in the cold. In other words, the apocryphal meeting has been suppressed in order to justify the intervention of the non-canonical Peregrino.

An alternative explanation arises from a comparison with the *Vita di Sangiovambatista* and the *Rappresentazione*. In both works St John's leave-taking from his parents is the prelude to an encounter which is shocking in its realization. The purpose of the meeting in the desert is to give Gesù the opportunity to instruct Giovanni as to the import of his hitherto instinctive mission, and it culminates in a blow-by-blow account of the Passion and Crucifixion.[92] If the *Auto* were to remain true to the Italian tradition of the life of St John, the consequences would be quite distressing and alien to the atmosphere the author has created. On the other hand, a version of the encounter that corresponded to its sketchy treatment in the *MVC* (quoted above) could produce only an anti-climax: the effect would be bathos.[93]

There is of course a more compelling reason why such a confrontation is not so much undesirable as impossible: the discrepancy between the ages of the children as they are presented in the *Auto*.[94] According to canonical tradition (Luke 1. 37), John is a mere six months older than Jesus. According to apocryphal tradition, both children will have been about seven years old at the time of their meeting in the desert.[95] But even if we allow for a time lapse of five or six years between Scene 4, when the Holy Child might be, at most, a toddler-in-arms, and Scene 5, when the

THE *AUTO DE LA HUIDA A EGIPTO*   57

Infant Juan takes leave of his parents (Zacarías refers to his 'niñez', line 119), there is no textual support for the idea that Jesus catches up with his precocious cousin.[96] Throughout the play he is referred to as 'niño' [child] (40, 77, 87, 97, 176, 195, 204, 246) or 'chiquito' [little one] (35, 44, 217, 294); and the age gap is made plain when in the same speech in Scene 8 the Peregrino refers to Juan a 'mançevo' [young lad] (238) and to Jesús as a 'niño' (246). Over the course of the play Jesús has remained a child while his cousin has aged prematurely into a 'mançevo'. No written tradition endorses this incongruity. So what was there to prevent the author from allowing the Holy Child to gain a few years during the play?

I can only think that the discrepancy was dictated by theatrical imperatives: Juan has a speaking part and could have been played by a young boy or girl; the part of Jesús, who does not speak, will have been represented by a small lay figure such as a doll or a statue. A confrontation between the two on the same stage would provoke unease: the Holy Child could only conduct a dialogue through a third party, as he has done in the rest of the play.

This difficulty suggests something new about the function of the Peregrino. Far from regarding him as a bridge or link between the two strands of the plot, I think we should consider that, on the contrary, his character has been devised to keep them apart, at a safe distance from each other. The Peregrino is a spokesman for Jesús in a way that both compensates for the lack of an actual meeting between Jesus and Juan and renders it unnecessary. The joyful reunion between Juan and the Holy Family has already been enacted in the content of the messages between Juan and the Holy Child as relayed by the Peregrino. Through this intermediary Jesús has already informed Juan of his vocation and of His own mission. In all its essentials the encounter has already taken place. But the potential awkwardnesses attendant on a staging of the encounter — whether emotional or mechanical — have been circumvented.

I believe that Sirera, who acknowledges the silence of the Child Jesus and the messenger role of the Peregrino, provides a constructive solution which will allow me (and the unknown author) to have it both ways.[97] After the last song had been sung:

> The performance would end with a *tableau vivant* of the adoration of the Child Jesus by the Peregrino and St John — a scene that could perfectly well be timed to synchronize with the last three lines of the play, and involve the whole of the audience in the act of adoration.[98]

Not an acted-out encounter, then, but an adoration scene in which the Holy Family, Juan and the Peregrino, and maybe the rest of the cast, all appear on stage together. It is more than possible that a final tableau of that kind was a foregone conclusion — like a curtain call — and was not written into the script because it had no words.[99]

7. The Child at the Heart of the Play

The figure of the Peregrino may be pivotal to the structure of the *Auto* and he may have the largest speaking part, but he is not the main character, much less the subject of the play. His most important function is to provide a voice for the Child

58   JANE WHETNALL

Jesus, who is the motor of both strands of the plot — the Family's Flight into Egypt and Juan's withdrawal to Judea — and at the heart of all the characters' thoughts, plans, and actions.

The nature of the role assigned to him presupposes that the part of the Holy Child in the *Auto* (as in so many Nativity plays up to the present day, or so-called 'live' cribs) would have been taken by a doll or a small statue.[100] This probably means that the play was designed expressly to showcase an effigy of the Christ Child belonging to the community for whom the *Auto* was written.[101] If we accept this condition as established from the outset, that is, before the dramatist put pen to paper, certain aspects of the Child's stage persona become clear. We can observe how his muteness is inscribed in the text and how it would be managed in performance. For although he does not speak he is still able to communicate.

In their scenes together, the Virgin is his mouthpiece. When the robbers kneel to beg forgiveness they ask the Virgin to ask the Child, 'al niño vos supliquéis | que seamos perdonados' [please entreat the Child to pardon us] (97–98), and she replies on his behalf: 'Mas si d'ello os apartáis, | Dios os querrá perdonar' [But if you mend your ways, God will pardon you] (105–06). When she sends the Peregrino back to Juan, 'Dile que presto hemos de ir' [Tell him we are coming soon] (266), she is again speaking for the Child, as we learn from the following scene. In passing on this news to John the Peregrino presents it as a message from the Child: 'Dize, Juan, que aquí le esperes, | que muy presto ha de venir' [He says, John, to wait for him here, he's coming very soon] (282–83).[102] We as readers have to work this out retrospectively, but in performance it would be solved by mime and puppetry, with the Child doll whispering to his mother the replies she is to give on his behalf.

When the Child is not on stage, the Peregrino is his mouthpiece. After his visit to the Holy Family, the Peregrino relays to Juan ten separate instructions or messages of encouragement from Jesus. Heading the list is: 'En tu tan sancto vivir | Dios manda que perseveres' [In your saintly way of life God says you must persevere] (280–81). This quirk of referring to the Child Jesus as God — as in the angel's warning, 'que a Dios piensa de matar' [plans on killing God] (15), the Virgin's pledge to the robbers, 'Dios os querrá perdonar' [God will pardon you] (106), and Juan's resolution to stay away from Judea, 'hasta que a ella vuelva Dios' [until God returns] (118), seems strange to us. But the Godhead of the Child Jesus is a leitmotiv of this play.

The noun 'Dios' occurs twenty-nine times in the script. It is not always easy to distinguish those instances which refer to the Holy Child from those which refer to God the Father, sender of angels, but on at least ten occasions the 'Dios' in the text is the Child whose movements on earth are tracked by Juan and the Peregrino.[103] Sometimes the connection is quite tortuous, as in: 'Dios me puso nombre: Juan' [God gave me the name John] (207). We know this 'Dios' must mean the Child Jesus because of the subsequent remark by the Peregrino to the Holy Child on his mother's lap, 'Un mançevo que hallé | [...] | al que distes nombre "Juan"' [A young lad I met [...] whom you named John] (238, 242).[104]

Although he is on stage for less than half of the running time of the *Auto*, over a quarter of the text is taken up with the Child: about a hundred lines in which he

THE *AUTO DE LA HUIDA A EGIPTO*   59

is addressed or described or alluded to.[105] In fact we are never far from a mention of the Holy Child, not just as 'niño' or 'chiquito', but as the Messiah (eight times), and most often as God, whether by name ('Dios'), or by some attribute or title connoting his divinity, such as 'A quien çielo y tierra adora' [Whom Heaven and Earth adore] (45), 'el rey de gloria' [King of Heaven] (271), 'aquel que el mundo regía' [Ruler of the World] (289).[106]

The whole play is a celebration of the mystery of the Incarnation, embodied in the central character, explicit in Juan's declaration, 'aquel niño, Dios e honbre' [that Infant, God and man] (204), and reinforced subliminally by the Eucharistic resonances of 'pan y vino' [bread and wine] in Scenes 6 and 8.[107] Towards the end of the play these references come together, as Juan announces to the Peregrino the theme of their meditation:

Començad a contemplar	[Begin to contemplate
en su sancta encarnaçión,	his holy Incarnation,
que por nuestra salvaçión	since for our salvation
quiso la carne tomar. (337–40)	he chose to become flesh.]

And they are crowned by the last words of the *Auto*, the burden of Josepe's third *villancico*:

Alegrate has, tierra mía,	[Rejoice, my country,
porque a visitarte va	for your Redeemer
el que te redimirá. (382–84)	is on his way.]

8. Conclusion

Although I am unable to bring any solid evidence to bear on the vexed questions of dating and authorship, my suggestions about some of its first-hand sources push the *Auto*'s date of composition more securely into the sixteenth century, when Castilian translations of the *MVC* and of Ludolph, the *Vita di Sangiovambatista* and the *Rappresentazione* were all in print. The unknown dramatist was conversant with a wide variety of material relevant to the different strands of the plot, much of which will have been in the vernacular, though not necessarily in Spanish. I used to think that the author must have been well-travelled but I am now persuaded that the Italian connections will have reached him or her in book form. Meanwhile, the nature of the sources and the way they have been handled create the firm impression that the writing was the work of a convent insider.

The glimpses we have of the playwright's background reading evince an eclectic use of sources: only the robbers episode from Montesino's Ludolph, only a few exchanges from the *Vita* and the *Rappresentazione*, just a chapter and a bit from the *MVC*. And in the process of registering the essential dynamic of the *MVC*, he or she was inspired to invent a neighbour for the Holy Family in Egypt who could take on the role of the suggestible, interactive reader. The sophisticated command of these texts shows an easy familiarity with them. Moreover, the humorous touches suggest that they were aimed at an audience who shared this knowledge, perhaps because the *MVC* and Ludolph (at least) would have been standard fare as communal reading in the convent refectory.

60 JANE WHETNALL

Identifying sources in no way detracts from the originality of the piece. On the contrary, the dramatist has displayed great ingenuity in harnessing these disparate elements and shaping them into something new and strange. The play is fast-moving, tightly constructed, with a lighthearted approach to sacred themes: doctrinally sound and rich in biblical allusion, but built upon a tissue of legend and make-believe. All this is achieved with extraordinary economy, the sign of an accomplished playwright, who also knew how to write speakable verse in colloquial and expressive language.

The upbeat treatment and a certain reticence about the dark side of the Gospel story, and of the legendary meeting of Jesus and John, may indicate a turning away from the Gothic in favour of a gentler, more humane approach to devotional themes; or it may simply mean that on the occasion for which it was written the recreational purpose of the piece was required to take precedence over the didactic. Descriptions of convent theatre in the early modern period invariably point out that entertainment went hand-in-hand with instruction. Of convents in Tuscany, Weaver says: 'theatrical productions were justified as a pedagogical tool for the education of young women and as an important moment of relaxation and enjoyment for all the convent sisters'.[108] Writing about Spanish nuns of the same era, Electa Arenal and Stacey Schlau are quite clear that 'Plays were a major form of monastic recreation [...] an effective means of accomplishing the goals of education and entertainment in the convent'.[109]

In looking to its convent provenance as a key to the *Auto de la huida a Egipto* it may be that critics have not gone far enough. Elissa B. Weaver's research on the theatre culture of Tuscan convents in the fifteenth and sixteenth centuries supplies us with a powerful incentive for an interpretation of the *Auto* that reflects the tastes and interests of its likely actors — novices, postulants, *educanda* — , its target audience — other nuns, both choir and lay sisters — , and its convent-commissioned, or even convent-educated author. Many of her observations on convent theatre resonate with what we might call the production values of this play, the unusual complement of musical numbers, for example, and the fact that it seems to be tailor made to accommodate a young cast. Weaver invokes earlier studies to demonstrate the widespread practice of drama performed in Tuscan convents, even in enclosed orders, involving nuns as actors, writers, and audience. Her findings are based on over fifty texts of plays from the late fifteenth to the mid seventeenth century, but many others await discovery:

> [It] is clear that the texts discussed in this study represent only a fraction of the theatrical repertoire of Tuscan women religious. Theirs is a tradition that still remains in large part to be discovered and which, to be properly understood, should be considered in the larger context of the religious theatre of convents throughout Italy, *if not the entire Catholic world of early modern times.*[110]

Convent archives in Spain may be slow to yield up their literary secrets to scholarly inquiry. But when more have done so the *Auto de la huida a Egipto* should find its true place in an adventurous, alternative theatre tradition with an international reach.

Bibliography

AELRED OF RIEVAULX, *A Rule of Life for a Recluse*, trans. by Mary Paul Macpherson OCSO, in Aelred of Rievaulx, *'Treatises' and 'The Pastoral Prayer'*, ed. by M. Basil Pennington, Cistercian Fathers Series, 2 (Kalamazoo, MI: Cistercian Publications, 1971), pp. 43–102

ÁLVAREZ PELLITERO, ANA MARÍA, ed., *Teatro medieval*, Colección Austral, 157 (Madrid: Espasa-Calpe, 1990)

AMÍCOLA, JOSÉ, 'El *Auto de la huida a Egipto*, drama anónimo del siglo XV', *Filología*, 15 (1971), 1–29

ARENAL, ELECTA, and STACEY SCHLAU, *Untold Sisters: Hispanic Nuns in their Own Works* (Albuquerque: University of New Mexico Press, 1989)

BANFI, LUIGI, ed., *Sacre rappresentazioni del Quattrocento* (Turin: Unione Tipografico-Editrice Torinense, 1963)

BARTLETT, ROBERT, *Why Can the Dead Do Such Great Things?* (Princeton, NJ: Princeton University Press, 2013), ch. 10, 'Pilgrimage', pp. 410–42

BELCARI, FEO, and TOMMASO BENCI, *La rappresentazione di San Giovanni nel deserto*, in *Sacre rappresentazioni del Quattrocento*, ed. by Luigi Banfi (Turin: Unione Tipografico-Editrice Torinense, 1963), pp. 85–105

CASTRO, EVA, ed. *Teatro medieval, 1: el drama litúrgico* (Barcelona: Crítica, 1997)

CÁTEDRA, PEDRO M., 'Liturgia, poesía y la renovación del teatro medieval', in *Actas del XIII Congreso de la Asociación Internacional de Hispanistas, Madrid (6–11 de julio de 1998)*, ed. by Florencio Sevilla and Carlos Alvar, 4 vols (Madrid: Castalia, 2000), I, 3–28

——*Liturgia, poesía y teatro en la Edad Media*, Biblioteca Románica Hispánica, Estudios y Ensayos, 444 (Madrid: Gredos, 2005)

——*Poesía de Pasión en la Edad Media: el 'Cancionero' de Pedro Gómez de Ferrol* (Salamanca: Seminario de Estudios Medievales y Renacentistas, 2001)

CHAMBERS, E. K., *The Medieval Stage*, 2 vols (London: Oxford University Press, 1967 [first published 1903])

CHAPLIN, MARGARET, 'The Episode of the Robbers in the *Libre dels tres reys d'orient*', *Bulletin of Hispanic Studies*, 44 (1967), 88–95

DONOVAN, RICHARD B., *The Liturgical Drama in Medieval Spain* (Toronto: Pontifical Institute of Mediaeval Studies, 1958)

EIXIMENIS, FRANCESC. *Vita Christi*, trans. by Fray Hernando de Talavera (Granada: Ungut & Pegnitzer, 1496).

ENCINA, JUAN DEL, *Teatro completo*, ed. by Miguel Ángel Pérez Priego, Letras Hispánicas, 339 (Madrid: Cátedra, 1991)

FALKENBURG, REINDERT L., *Joachim Patinir: Landscape as an Image of the Pilgrimage of Life*, trans. by Michael Hoyle (Amsterdam and Philadelphia, PA: John Benjamins, 1988)

FLEMING, JOHN V., *An Introduction to the Franciscan Literature of the Middle Ages* (Chicago, IL: Franciscan Herald Press, 1977)

FLORA, HOLLY, and ARIANNA PECORINI CIGNONI, 'Requirements of Devout Contemplation: Text and Image for the Poor Clares in Trecento Pisa', *Gesta*, 45.1 (2006), 61–76

GARCÍA MORALES, JUSTO, ed., *Auto de la huida a Egipto*, Colección Joyas Bibliográficas, 2 (Madrid: Marsiega, 1948)

GILL, KATHERINE, 'Women and the Production of Religious Literature in the Vernacular, 1300–1500', in *Creative Women in Medieval and Early Modern Italy: A Religious and Artistic Renaissance*, ed. by E. Ann Matter and John Coakley (Philadelphia: University of Pennsylvania Press, 1994), pp. 64–104

GÓMEZ MORENO, ÁNGEL, *El teatro medieval castellano en su marco románico* (Madrid: Taurus, 1991)

HOLLOWAY, JULIA BOLTON, 'The Pilgrim in the Poem: Dante, Langland, and Chaucer', in *Allegoresis: The Craft of Allegory in Medieval Literature*, ed. by J. Stephen Russell (New York & London: Garland, 1988), pp. 109–32

JAMES, M. R., ed. and trans., *The Apocryphal New Testament* (London: Oxford University Press, 1924)

—— *The Latin Infancy Gospels* (Cambridge: Cambridge University Press, 1927)

JANNELLA, CECILIA, *Duccio di Buoninsegna* (Sienna: Scala, 1991)

JEFFREY, DAVID L., 'Franciscan Spirituality and the Rise of Early English Drama', *Mosaic*, 8.4 (1975), 17–46

KLAPISCH-ZUBER, CHRISTIANE, 'Holy Dolls: Play and Piety in Florence in the Quattrocento', in her *Women, Family, and Ritual in Renaissance Italy*, trans. by Lydia G. Cochrane (Chicago, IL: University of Chicago Press, 1985), pp. 310–29

LAVIN, MARILYN ARONBERG, 'Giovannino Battista: A Study in Renaissance Religious Symbolism', *Art Bulletin*, 37 (1955), 85–101

—— 'Giovannino Battista: A Supplement', *Art Bulletin*, 43 (1961), 319–26

LÓPEZ ESTRADA, FRANCISCO, 'La *Representación del Nacimiento de Nuestro Señor*, de Gómez Manrique: estudio textual', *Segismundo*, 18 (1984), 9–30

LOWE, KATE, *Nuns' Chronicles and Convent Culture in Renaissance and Counter-Reformation Italy* (Cambridge: Cambridge University Press, 2003)

LUDOLPH OF SAXONY, *Vita Cristi cartuxano romançado por fray Ambrosio Montesino* (Alcalá de Henares: Stanislao Polono, 1502)

McNAMER, SARAH, 'The Origins of the *Meditationes vitae Christi*', *Speculum*, 84 (2009), 905–55

MÂLE, ÉMILE, *L'Art religieux du XIIIe siècle en France: étude sur l'iconographie du Moyen Âge et sur ses sources d'inspiration* (Paris: Armand Colin, 1948 [first published 1898])

MANNI, DOMENICO MARIA, ed., *Volgarizzamento delle vite de' santi padri di fra Domenico Cavalca*, 6 vols, IV, *Vite di alcuni santi*, Biblioteca Scelta di Opere Italiane Antiche e Moderne, 244, 6th edn (Milan: Giovanni Silvestri, 1830)

MATTER, E. ANN, and JOHN COAKLEY, eds, *Creative Women in Medieval and Early Modern Italy: A Religious and Artistic Renaissance* (Philadelphia: University of Pennsylvania Press, 1994)

Meditationes vitae Christi (Paris: Philippe Pigouchet, 1490)

MONTESINO: see LUDOLPH

MORENO, MANUEL, 'Descripción codicológica MN66. CsXV, II: 379–80. R-31133, Biblioteca Nacional, Madrid', in *An Electronic Corpus of 15th Century Castilian 'Cancionero' Manuscripts*, 20pp. <http://cancionerovirtual.liv.ac.uk>

PÉREZ PRIEGO, MIGUEL ÁNGEL, ed., *Teatro medieval*, Letras Hispánicas, 646 (Madrid: Cátedra, 2009)

—— *Teatro medieval, 2: Castilla* (Barcelona: Crítica, 1997)

PICKERING, F. P., ed., *The Anglo-Norman Text of the Holkham Bible Picture Book*, Anglo-Norman Texts, 23 (Oxford: Blackwell, 1971)

RAGUSA, ISA, and ROSALIE B. GREEN, eds, *Meditations on the Life of Christ: An Illustrated Manuscript of the Fourteenth Century (Paris, Bibliothèque Nationale, ms. ital. 115)*, trans. by Isa Ragusa (Princeton, NJ: Princeton University Press, 1961), pp. 65–75

SALVADOR MIGUEL, NICASIO, 'Gómez Manrique y la *Representación del Nacimiento de Nuestro Señor*', *Revista de Filología Española*, 92 (2012), 135–80

SIRERA, JOSEP LLUÍS, 'Sobre la estructura dramática del teatro medieval: el caso de *El auto de la huida a Egipto*', in *Actas del II Congreso Internacional de la Asociación Hispánica de Literatura Medieval (Segovia, del 5 al 19 de octubre de 1987)*, ed. by José Manuel Lucia Megías, Paloma García Alonso, and Carmen Martín Daza, 2 vols (Madrid: Universidad de Alcalá, 1992), II, 837–55

SURTZ, RONALD E., 'El *Auto de la huida a Egipto* como peregrinación virtual', *Boletín de la Real Academia Española*, 301 (2010), 121–30

THE *AUTO DE LA HUIDA A EGIPTO* 63

——'The "Franciscan Connection" in the Early Castilian Theatre', *Bulletin of the Comediantes*, 35.2 (Winter 1983), 141–52
——ed., *Teatro castellano de la Edad Media*, Clásicos Taurus, 13 (Madrid: Taurus, 1992)
——ed., *Teatro medieval castellano*, Temas de España, 125 (Madrid: Taurus, 1983)
——*Writing Women in Late Medieval and Early Modern Spain: The Mothers of Saint Teresa of Avila* (Philadelphia: University of Pennsylvania Press, 1995)
TALAVERA: see EIXIMENIS
TALBOT, C. H., ed. and study, 'The *De institutis inclusarum* of Ailred of Rievaulx', *Analecta Sacri Ordinis Cisterciensis*, 7.3–4 (1951), 167–217
TORROJA MENÉNDEZ, CARMEN, and MARÍA RIVAS PALÁ, *Teatro en Toledo en el siglo XV: 'Auto de la Pasión' de Alonso del Campo*, Anejos del *BRAE*, 35 (Madrid: *Boletín de la Real Academia Española*, 1977)
URÍA MAQUA, ISABEL, 'Fuentes básicas y fuentes secundarias en la composición del *Auto de la huida a Egipto*', in *Actas del IX Congreso Internacional de la Asociación Hispánica de Literatura Medieval (A Coruña, 18–22 de septiembre de 2001)*, ed. by Carmen Parrilla and Mercedes Pampín, 3 vols, Biblioteca Filológica, 13–15 (A Coruña: Universidade da Coruña and Toxosoutos, 2005), I, 199–224
——'Una nota sobre la fecha del *Auto de la huida a Egipto*', in *Lengua, variación y contexto: estudios dedicados a Humberto López Morales*, ed. by Francisco Moreno Fernández et al., 2 vols (Madrid: Arco Libros, 2003), II, 1087–90
VILLENA, ISABEL DE, *Vita Christi*, selected chapters, ed. by Albert-Guillem Hauf i Valls (Barcelona: edicions 62, 1995)
Vita di Sangiovambatista: see MANNI
WARNER, MARINA, *Alone of All Her Sex: The Myth and Cult of the Virgin Mary* (London: Picador, 1985 [first edn 1976])
WEAVER, ELISSA B., *Convent Theatre in Early Modern Italy: Spiritual Fun and Learning for Women* (Cambridge: Cambridge University Press, 2002)
WHINNOM, KEITH, 'The Supposed Sources of Inspiration of Spanish Fifteenth-Century Narrative Religious Verse', in his *Medieval and Renaissance Spanish Literature: Selected Essays*, ed. by Alan Deyermond, W. F. Hunter, and Joseph T. Snow (Exeter: University of Exeter Press & *Journal of Hispanic Philology*, 1994), pp. 46–71; first published in *Symposium*, 17 (1963), 268–91
YOUNG, KARL, *The Drama of the Medieval Church*, 2 vols (Oxford: Clarendon Press, 1933)

Notes to Chapter 3

1. For an overview of the evidence for late-medieval religious drama in Castile see especially Carmen Torroja Menéndez and María Rivas Palá, *Teatro en Toledo en el siglo XV: 'Auto de la Pasión' de Alonso del Campo*, Anejos del *BRAE*, 35 (Madrid: *BRAE*, 1977); Ángel Gómez Moreno, *El teatro medieval castellano en su marco románico* (Madrid: Taurus, 1991); and *Teatro medieval*, ed. by Miguel Ángel Pérez Priego, Letras Hispánicas, 646 (Madrid: Cátedra, 2009).
2. See Justo García Morales's introduction to his edition, *Auto de la huida a Egipto*, Colección Joyas Bibliográficas, 2 (Madrid: Marsiega, 1948), pp. xi–xxxiv.
3. Amícola judged the *Auto* to be the work of an unknown author, contemporary with Gómez Manrique or a little later ('El *Auto de la huida a Egipto*, drama anónimo del siglo XV', *Filología*, 15 (1971), 1–29 (pp. 3–4)). The first edition of Encina's *Cancionero* [Collected Poems], containing eight of his early *églogas* (shepherd plays), appeared in 1496.
4. *Auto de la huida a Egipto*, in his *Teatro castellano de la Edad Media*, ed. by Ronald E. Surtz, Clásicos Taurus, 13 (Madrid: Taurus, 1992), pp. 37–42 (study); pp. 127–49 (text).
5. The volume has been rebound since it was described by García Morales, and the original binding lost. On the problems of dating, see Isabel Uría Maqua, 'Una nota sobre la fecha del *Auto de la huida a Egipto*', in *Lengua, variación y contexto: estudios dedicados a Humberto López Morales*, ed. by

Francisco Moreno Fernández et al., 2 vols (Madrid: Arco Libros, 2003), II, 1087–90; and Manuel Moreno, 'Descripción codicológica MN66. CsXV, II: 379–80. R-31133, Biblioteca Nacional, Madrid', in *An Electronic Corpus of 15th Century Castilian 'Cancionero' Manuscripts*, 20pp., <http://cancionerovirtual.liv.ac.uk>.

6. See García Morales, *Auto de la huida*, p. xii; (Amícola, 'El *Auto de la huida*', p. 5). Except where indicated, all translations are mine.

7. Josep Lluís Sirera, 'Sobre la estructura dramática del teatro medieval: el caso de *El auto de la huida a Egipto*', in *Actas del II Congreso Internacional de la Asociación Hispánica de Literatura Medieval (Segovia, del 5 al 19 de octubre de 1987)*, ed. by José Manuel Lucia Megías, Paloma García Alonso, and Carmen Martín Daza, 2 vols (Madrid: Universidad de Alcalá, 1992), II, 837–55 (p. 851). According to Ana María Álvarez Pellitero, its dramatic structure is much richer and more complex than that of the shepherd plays (*Teatro medieval*, ed. by Ana María Álvarez Pellitero, Colección Austral, 157 (Madrid: Espasa-Calpe, 1990), p. 146); and for Miguel Ángel Pérez Priego, the *Auto* is remarkable for the complexity of its plot and its artistry (*Teatro medieval, 2: Castilla*, ed. by Miguel Ángel Pérez Priego (Barcelona: Crítica, 1997), p. 29).

8. Pedro M. Cátedra, 'Liturgia, poesía y la renovación del teatro medieval', in *Actas del XIII Congreso de la Asociación Internacional de Hispanistas (Madrid, 6–11 de julio de 1998)*, ed. by Florencio Sevilla and Carlos Alvar, 4 vols (Madrid: Castalia, 2000), I, 3–28 (p. 4; see also p. 3).

9. The play is untitled in the manuscript, rubrication is erratic, and stage directions are minimal. Sirera ('Sobre la estructura dramática') regroups these twelve scenes into six larger units which he calls *cuadros*.

10. In terms of length alone it is a substantial piece, more than twice as long as the *Auto de los reyes magos* (147 lines), more than three times as long as Manrique's *Representación del Nacimiento de Nuestro Señor* (115 lines), and longer than all but one of the early plays of Juan del Encina. The *Égloga de Mingo, Gil y Pascuala* has 557 lines; see his *Teatro completo*, ed. by Miguel Ángel Pérez Priego, Letras Hispánicas, 339 (Madrid: Cátedra, 1991), pp. 171–89.

11. Amícola, 'El *Auto de la huida*', p. 7. The dialogue between San Juan and the Peregrino lasts for 40 lines (135–214). I have looked for equivalent passages of stichomythia in Encina but it is never sustained for more than four or five exchanges.

12. Surtz, 'The "Franciscan Connection" in the Early Castilian Theatre', *Bulletin of the Comediantes*, 35.2 (Winter 1983), 141–52 (pp. 144–47). See also his *Teatro medieval castellano*, Temas de España, 125 (Madrid: Taurus, 1983), p. 33.

13. Sirera, 'Sobre la estructura dramática', pp. 844–51.

14. Surtz's edition gives the most complete account of these biblical echoes in his *Teatro castellano* (1992), pp. 129–44; see also his footnotes to lines 49, 304, and 308.

15. Amícola, 'El *Auto de la huida*', p. 16. For the full text of these in Spanish see *Auto de la huida a Egipto*, ed. by Pérez Priego, in his *Teatro medieval, 2: Castilla*, pp. 104–06.

16. 'In like manner lions and leopards adored him and accompanied them, showed them the way, and bowed their heads to Jesus', *Gospel of Pseudo-Matthew*, in *The Apocryphal New Testament*, ed. and trans. by M. R. James (London: Oxford University Press, 1924), p. 75.

17. García Morales mentions as possible influences the *Meditationes vitae Christi* of pseudo-Bonaventure, a vernacular *Infancia del Salvador* attributed to St Bernard, the *Vitae Christi* of Ludolph of Saxony and Fray Íñigo de Mendoza; he discounts the two Catalan *Vitae Christi* by Francesc Eiximenis and Isabel de Villena (*Auto de la huida*, pp. xxiii–xxiv).

18. Surtz points out that the juxtaposition of the Flight into Egypt and John's withdrawal to the desert first appears in the *Meditationes* of Pseudo-Bonaventure, then in the *Vita Christi* of Francesc Eiximenis, but not in the *Vita Christi* of Ludolph of Saxony. He refers in a note to Feo Belcari's play, but does not relate this to the *Auto* ('The "Franciscan Connection"', p. 145 and notes 13–15).

19. Uría Maqua invokes motifs from the Gospel commentaries of St John Chrysostom and St Ambrose as aids to finer points of interpretation, but not all of them convince. See 'Fuentes básicas y fuentes secundarias en la composición del *Auto de la huida a Egipto*', in *Actas del IX Congreso Internacional de la Asociación Hispánica de Literatura Medieval (A Coruña, 18–22 de septiembre de 2001)*, ed. by Carmen Parrilla and Mercedes Pampín, 3 vols, Biblioteca Filológica, 13–15 (A Coruña: Universidade da Coruña and Toxosoutos, 2005), I, 199–224.

THE *AUTO DE LA HUIDA A EGIPTO*   65

20. *A Rule of Life for a Recluse*, trans. by Mary Paul Macpherson, OCSO, in Aelred of Rievaulx, *'Treatises' and 'The Pastoral Prayer'*, ed. by M. Basil Pennington, Cistercian Fathers Series, 2 (Kalamazoo, MI: Cistercian Publications, 1971), pp. 43–102 (p. 81).

21. Aelred, *De vita eremitica ad sororem*, version in James, *The Apocryphal New Testament*, p. 81. The Latin reads: 'Noli in tua meditacione magorum munera preterire, nec fugientem in Egyptum incomitatum relinquere. Opinare uerum esse quod dicitur, eum a latronibus deprehensum in uia, et ab adolescentuli cuiusdam beneficio ereptum. Erat is ut dicunt principis latronum filius, qui preda potitus, cum puerulum in matris gremio conspexisset *tanta ei in eius speciosissimo uultu splendoris maiestas apparuit*, ut eum supra hominem esse non ambigens, incalescens amore amplexatus est eum, et: "O, inquit, beatissime paruulorum, si aliquando se tempus obtulerit michi miserendi, tunc memento mei, et huius temporis noli obliuisci". Ferunt hunc fuisse latronum qui ad Christi dexteram crucifixus', in 'The *De institutis inclusarum* of Ailred of Rievaulx', ed. by C. H. Talbot, *Analecta Sacri Ordinis Cisterciensis*, 7 (1951), 167–217 (p. 201). The canonical reference to the Good Thief crucified with Jesus is Luke 23. 39–43.

22. James cites Aelred as the source for an image of the episode in the Holkham Bible: 'where the robber's young son is captivated by the beauty of the Child' (*The Latin Infancy Gospels* (Cambridge: Cambridge University Press, 1927), pp. 120–21). The robber boy has clambered on to the back of the ass carrying the Virgin and Child and is peering down into the Child's face. For the accompanying verse, see *The Anglo-Norman Text of the Holkham Bible Picture Book*, ed. by F. P. Pickering, Anglo-Norman Texts, 23 (Oxford: Blackwell, 1971), pp. 23–24.

23. The misattribution to Anselm was common: 'Early mss ascribed this work to St Augustine and to St Anselm. It is therefore in Migne twice, PL 32:1451–74 and PL 158:785–94' (Aelred, *'Treatises' and 'The Pastoral Prayer'*, p. 120).

24. *Vita Cristi cartuxano romançado por fray Ambrosio Montesino* (Alcalá de Henares: Stanislao Polono, 1502), ch. 13. I have checked Ludolph's Latin (Lyon, 1522, ch. 13, fols 35^v–36^r) against Aelred's to find that Ludolph has reproduced the text of *De institutione inclusarum* almost verbatim and embedded it in further commentary of his own. Montesino's translation cuts some of this commentary.

25. Keith Whinnom, 'The Supposed Sources of Inspiration of Spanish Fifteenth-Century Narrative Religious Verse', in his *Medieval and Renaissance Spanish Literature: Selected Essays*, ed. by Alan Deyermond, W. F. Hunter, and Joseph T. Snow (Exeter: University of Exeter Press & *Journal of Hispanic Philology*, 1994), pp. 46–71 (p. 47); first published in *Symposium*, 17 (1963), 268–91.

26. Émile Mâle, *L'Art religieux du XIIIe siècle en France: étude sur l'iconographie du Moyen Âge et sur ses sources d'inspiration* (Paris: Armand Colin, 1948 [first published 1898]), pp. 412–14.

27. Compare Eiximenis's account of the Holy Family's release: 'E la Virgen gloriosa, fincados los ynojos a sus pies, rogava que los dexassen yr, diziendole que eran personas pobres e que no les podían dar ninguna cosa' (*Vita Christi*, trans. by Fray Hernando de Talavera, Granada, 1496, fol. 129^v). On this hint Isabel de Villena puts an entirely different slant on the adventure in her *Vita Christi* (Valencia, 1497), with the Virgin taking a dominant role in persuading the robbers to spare her family (Villena, *Vita Christi*, selected chapters, ed. by Albert-Guillem Hauf i Valls (Barcelona: edicions 62, 1995), pp. 156–82). See also Margaret Chaplin, 'The Episode of the Robbers in the *Libre dels tres reys d'orient*', *Bulletin of Hispanic Studies*, 44 (1967), 88–95.

28. John V. Fleming, *An Introduction to the Franciscan Literature of the Middle Ages* (Chicago, IL: Franciscan Herald Press, 1977), p. 246.

29. Isa Ragusa and Rosalie B. Green, *Meditations on the Life of Christ: An Illustrated Manuscript of the Fourteenth Century (Paris, Bibliothèque Nationale, ms. ital. 115)* (Princeton, NJ: Princeton University Press, 1961). For bibliography on the dating of this manuscript (c. 1350) and on the attribution of the *MVC* to John of Caulibus see Holly Flora and Arianna Pecorini Cignoni, 'Requirements of Devout Contemplation: Text and Image for the Poor Clares in Trecento Pisa', *Gesta*, 45.1 (2006), 61–76.

30. Two fifteenth-century Spanish translations are commonly cited, the *Contemplación de la vida de nuestro Señor Jesucristo*, Madrid, BNE, MS 9560 (see Surtz, 'The "Franciscan Connection"', p. 151, n. 13); and an abridged version, attributed to St Bernard and known as the *Infançia Salvatoris*, which was printed in Burgos, c. 1493. I have been unable to consult either of these. On the diffusion of the *MVC* in Spanish translation see Pedro M. Cátedra, *Liturgia, poesía y teatro*,

66   JANE WHETNALL

pp. 80–85, and *Poesía de Pasión en la Edad Media: el 'Cancionero' de Pedro Gómez de Ferrol* (Salamanca: Seminario de Estudios Medievales y Renacentistas, 2001), pp. 206–09.

31. Surtz, 'The "Franciscan Connection"', p. 145 and note 13.

32. Ragusa and Green, *Meditations,* pp. 68–69. The Latin text reads: 'Unde enim et quomodo vivebant isti tanto tempore et numquid mendicabant? Legitur enim de domina quod colo, acu, et opere textrino sibi et filio querebat necessaria. Suebat ergo et filabat domina preciosa mundi amore paupertatis. [...] Sed numquid ipsa ibat per domos petendo pannos et alia in quibus operaretur?', *Meditationes vitae Christi* (Paris: Philippe Pigouchet, 1490), fol. b6^v.

33. The Peregrino repeats this observation of the Virgin at work on his return from Egypt: 'la madre estava cosiendo' (287); as does the author of the *MVC*: 'Look at her as she works at sewing and spinning with constancy, humility, and promptness' (Ragusa and Green, *Meditations*, p. 75); 'conspice dominam in laboribus suis suendo, filando, texendo: quomodo facit omnia, humiliter, fideliter, et sollicite' (*Meditationes*, fol. b7^v.). Surtz notes the parallel with the *MVC* but he highlights one difference, in that Josepe's work as a carpenter is not mentioned in the *Auto*: 'The *Auto*, aimed at an audience of nuns, stresses the role of a woman, the Virgin Mary, as the sole breadwinner of the family' (*Teatro castellano*, p. 136, note to line 185). In fact the emphasis is the same in both texts. Mary's industry is the theme of the Egypt chapter of the *MVC* and Joseph's carpentry is mentioned almost as an afterthought, in one short sentence towards the end (Ragusa and Green, *Meditations*, p. 76).

34. Fluctuating verb tenses in rhyme position are a feature of the ballad genre. I have ignored them in my translation.

35. In the words of Keith Whinnom, 'the Franciscan author of the *Meditationes* has the instinct of a dramatist: dialogue abounds' ('The Supposed Sources of Inspiration', p. 56).

36. David L. Jeffrey, 'Franciscan Spirituality and the Rise of Early English Drama', *Mosaic*, 8.4 (1975), 17–46 (p. 22).

37. The legend goes back to an Eastern tradition that sought to explain how the infant John survived Herod's murderous decree: Elizabeth and the baby sought refuge in the desert. Marilyn Aronberg Lavin gives a lucid account of the development of this legend from its first appearance in the second-century *Book of James* or *Protoevangelium* to a fourth-century *Life of St John the Baptist* by an Egyptian bishop, Serapion ('Giovannino Battista: A Study in Renaissance Religious Symbolism', *Art Bulletin*, 37 (1955), 85–101 (pp. 85–86, note 5)).

38. Ragusa and Green, *Meditations*, pp. 81–83. 'Cum autem fuerunt prope finem deserti invenerunt Sanctum Iohannem Baptistam qui iam inceperat agere ibidem penitentiam cum tamen nullum haberet pecatum. [...] Unde possibile est quod puer Iesus inde transiens in reditu suo invenit eum ibidem. Mediteris ergo quomodo suscepit eum alacriter et ibi aliquantulum subsistens comedunt cum illo illa cruda cibaria que Iohannes alias ibi comedebat. Tandem inmensa recreatione spiritus habita valefaciunt ei. Tu autem in adventu et in recessu genuflectens Iohanni: deosculeris pedes eius benedictionem petens et ei te recommendans' (*Meditationes*, fol. b8^v).

39. Surtz, 'The "Franciscan Connection"', pp. 145–46 and note 17. The relevant lines of the *Auto* are 266–69 (spoken by the Virgin), 282–83; 299–300; 323–24 (spoken by the Peregrino); 316 (spoken by Juan).

40. The phrase 'participate imaginatively' comes from Surtz: 'Just as the eminently Franciscan *Meditationes* constantly invites the reader or listener to participate imaginatively in the events of Christ's life [...], so Franciscan plays often invite the audience to participate in the unfolding of the dramatic action' ('The "Franciscan Connection"', p. 152, note 20).

41. Ragusa and Green, *Meditations*, p. 84.

42. Ragusa and Green, *Meditations*, p. 78. 'Redeas igitur in Egyptum ad visitandum puerum Iesum [...] Tu vero genuflectens osculeris pedes eius et post inter brachia tua ipsum suspicias, et aliquantulum cum eo quiescas. Tunc dicet tibi. Data est nobis licentia redeundi ad patriam nostram et cras hinc recedere debemus. Bona hora venisti quare nobiscum iturus es. Cui alacriter respondeas te ex hoc multum gaudere, et quod eum optas sequi quocunque ierit. [...] Postea ducet te ad matrem et curialiter honorabit te. Tu vero genuflectens fac reverentiam eis et sancto seni Ioseph et requiesce cum eis', *Meditationes*, b8^r.

43. One significant departure from the *MVC*'s presentation of this virtual meeting is that the Holy Child's assurance to the reader about the return from Egypt is voiced by the Virgin in the *Auto* (266–67).

THE *AUTO DE LA HUIDA A EGIPTO* 67

44. *Vita di san Giovambatista*, in *Volgarizzamento delle vite de' santi padri di Fra Domenico Cavalca*, ed. by Domenico Maria Manni, 6 vols, Biblioteca Scelta di Opere Italiane Antiche e Moderne, 244, 6th edn (Milan: Giovanni Silvestri, 1830), IV: *Vite di alcuni santi*, pp. 259–369.

45. Lavin, 'Giovannino Battista: A Study', and 'Giovannino Battista: A Supplement', *Art Bulletin*, 43 (1961): 319–26.

46. According to Lavin the *Vita* was 'the fountainhead of the entire subsequent development of the iconography of the Infant St. John in the West' ('Giovannino Battista: A Study', p. 87).

47. On the mistaken attribution and its cause Lavin says: 'In mentioning the *Vita* earlier I assumed the translation to be the work of Fra Domenico Cavalca (ca. 1260–1342), the Pisan monk whose literary efforts include many such translations. It has since become evident that this attribution, which many other scholars have followed, is unfounded' ('Giovannino Battista: A Supplement'. p. 320b).

48. Lavin, 'Giovannino Battista: A Supplement', p. 320b.

49. *Vita*, in Manni, *Volgarizzamento*, IV, 288–89.

50. This is an episode for which scholars have been unable to locate a precedent (Álvarez Pellitero, *Teatro medieval*, p. 145, note 9) or a source (Uría Maqua, 'Fuentes básicas', p. 214).

51. *Vita*, in Manni, *Volgarizzamento*, IV, 281. The phrase 'mi ritroverrò con lui' [shall I meet him again] needs some explanation. Earlier in the *Vita*, the infant John is taken to see the newborn Jesus, so the two cousins have met before.

52. Twice Josepe is the butt of gentle irony voiced by the Peregrino. A few lines later he says to Juan, '¿Y al viejo no dizes nada? | Tanvién creo que sancto es' [Haven't you a message for the old guy? I'm sure he's saintly too] (197–98). This mischief on the part of the dramatist could well have been suggested by the neglect of Joseph in the *Vita*.

53. 'Dice nel libro della Vita di Cristo che questo diserto è di là dal fiume Giordano e per questo diserto passò la nostra Donna e Giuseppo col Fanciullo Giesù quando fuggirono in Egitto' [It says in the book of the Life of Christ that this desert is on the other side of the river Jordan and it was through this desert that Our Lady and Joseph and the Child Jesus passed when they fled into Egypt] (*Vita*, in Manni, *Volgarizzamento*, IV, 290). Lavin identifies the 'libro della Vita di Cristo' as the *MVC* ('Giovannino Battista: A Study', p. 90, n. 31). In the *MVC* no background is provided for John's sojourn in the desert; he is simply there, doing penance, when the Holy Family come across him.

54. *Vita*, in Manni, *Volgarizzamento*, IV, 292.

55. Feo Belcari and Tommaso Benci, *La rappresentazione di San Giovanni nel deserto*, in *Sacre rappresentazioni del Quattrocento*, ed. by Luigi Banfi (Turin: Unione Tipografico-Editrice Torinense, 1963), pp. 85–105. Benci added sixteen stanzas of leave-taking to the text of Belcari, which consisted of a prologue, the meeting of Gesù and Giovanni, an exchange between Giovanni and the Virgin, and an epilogue.

56. 'It is obvious that Belcari found his inspiration in the fourteenth century *Vita*, since every detail of the action and whole sections of dialogue are taken directly from it' (Lavin, 'Giovannini Battista: A Supplement', p. 323b).

57. The Virgin Mary and Joseph are silent witnesses to the encounter, but afterwards Giovanni greets them both and the Virgin has a one-stanza speech commending his chosen path.

58. This vignette occurs later in the meeting in the *Vita*: 'Ed istava Giovanni dinanzi alla faccia di Giesù e guardandolo gli parea essere in paradiso e quasi temeva di reverenzia, perocchè Messere Giesù gli mostrava un pochetto della *signoria sua e dello splendore della faccia sua*' [And John was face to face with Jesus, and as he looked at him he felt as though he were in paradise and almost trembled with awe, for Lord Jesus was showing him a little of *his majesty, and the radiance of his face*] (*Vita*, in Manni, *Volgarizzamento*, IV, 296). The *signoria* and the *splendore della faccia* are undeniably Aelred's 'speciosissimo uultu splendoris maiestas' (see note 21, above), and it cannot have been mediated through Ludolph, whose *Vita Christi* was written later than the *Vita*. Incidentally, John here seems to have taken on the fate as well as the attitude of the robber boy, since 'parea esser in paradiso' recalls Jesus's assurance to the Good Thief at the Crucifixion, 'Hodie mecum eris in paradiso' [Today you will be with me in Paradise] (Luke 23. 43).

59. A fourth textual correspondence between the two plays occurs in a concern shared by both of St John's interlocutors. When he first approaches Giovanni in the desert, Gesù worries lest his cousin has fallen prey to the devil: 'La carne inferma e i diabolici inganni | fanno spesso cader

68   JANE WHETNALL

per tal camino' [The flesh being weak and the devil's wiles often cause stumbles on that path] (*Rappresentazione*, 21.5–6). This could be why the Peregrino suggests to Juan they hide out in a cave, 'que el diablo con su maña | tengo temor que me mueva' [for the devil with his wiles I fear will tempt me] (*Auto*, 327–28).

60. Manni, *Volgarizzamento*, IV, p. X. From its impact on the visual arts we have to infer its widespread circulation in Italy. Lavin (who refers to the text as 'Cavalca') deems its influence responsible for the composition of Florentine artworks from as early as *c.* 1334 ('Giovannino Battista: A Study', p. 87, note 20).

61. 'Giovannino Battista: A Supplement', p. 323, note 22, and cf. note 24.

62. 'A proliferation of vernacular works written or translated for women, commissioned or purchased by women, copied or illustrated by women can be documented to varying degrees *in every region of late medieval Europe*' [...] 'At Monteluce in Perugia, as with a conspicuous number of fifteenth-century Clarissan monasteries [...], writing and commissioning literary works accompanied this busy production and consumption of manuscripts and books' (my emphasis) (Katherine Gill, 'Women and the Production of Religious Literature in the Vernacular, 1300–1500', in *Creative Women in Medieval and Early Modern Italy: A Religious and Artistic Renaissance*, ed. by E. Ann Matter and John Coakley (Philadelphia: University of Pennsylvania Press, 1994), pp. 64–104 (pp. 65–66; 67)).

63. '[W]omen in convents throughout Italy *and beyond* shared a theatrical tradition and propagated it' (my emphasis); 'There is abundant evidence that plays circulated among the convents' (Elissa B. Weaver, *Convent Theatre in Early Modern Italy: Spiritual Fun and Learning for Women* (Cambridge: Cambridge University Press, 2002), pp. 6; 71).

64. Surtz, 'The Franciscan Connection', p. 146; see also his *Teatro medieval* (1983), p. 33; and his *Teatro castellano* (1992), p. 40.

65. I have made a small adjustment to line 284 (MS: 'Y mas te quiero dezir' [What's more, I want to tell you]), as this prophecy, relayed by the Peregrino, can only come from the Holy Family: 'Tal nueva save de allá' [That's the news from there] (286).

66. See Richard B. Donovan, *The Liturgical Drama in Medieval Spain* (Toronto: Pontifical Institute of Mediaeval Studies, 1958), p. 13; and pp. 172–73 for the text of a thirteenth-century *Peregrinus* from Rouen.

67. 'Et tunc associat se eis ipse Christus cum sclavina, burdone, et barisello vini ad modum Peregrini' [And then Christ himself joins them with a cape, a staff, and a little barrel of wine, in the manner of a Pilgrim] (Karl Young, *The Drama of the Medieval Church*, 2 vols (Oxford: Clarendon Press, 1933), I, 482).

68. Julia Bolton Holloway, 'The Pilgrim in the Poem: Dante, Langland, and Chaucer', in *Allegoresis: The Craft of Allegory in Medieval Literature*, ed. by J. Stephen Russell (New York & London: Garland, 1988), pp. 109–32 (p. 117).

69. Now in the Museo dell' Opera del Duomo, Sienna, it once formed part of the back of his *Maestà* (Cecilia Jannella, *Duccio di Buoninsegna* (Sienna: Scala, 1991), pp. 21–25).

70. On the motif of Christ the Pilgrim in medieval art and literature, see Holloway, 'The Pilgrim in the Poem', pp. 114–18.

71. The *Versus de Pelegrino* of the Ripoll (or Vic) tropery is reproduced in Donovan, *The Liturgical Drama*, pp. 84–86, and in *Teatro medieval, 1: el drama litúrgico*, ed. by Eva Castro (Barcelona: Crítica, 1997), pp. 252–57.

72. Donovan surmises that the absence of liturgical drama in Western Iberia could be partly because it was overtaken by the early rise of vernacular drama, texts of which would have been unlikely to survive (*The Liturgical Drama*, p. 73).

73. Donovan, *The Liturgical Drama*, p. 86. The more usual sequence in *Peregrinus* texts is the Emmaus episode 'followed by a second scene between Christ and Mary Magdalen, and a third between Christ and St. Thomas' (p. 103). There is no canonical sequence. Christ's appearance to Mary Magdalen is reported only in St John's Gospel (20. 11–18), the Emmaus episode only in Luke. The Ripoll sequence, however, is authorized by Mark, who gives a summary of these two appearances, with no dialogue, and in the case of Emmaus, without naming the place or either disciple (Mark 16. 9–11; 12–13).

74. Encina, *Teatro completo*, pp. 131–37, lines 82–85. See also Pérez Priego's comments in his

THE *AUTO DE LA HUIDA A EGIPTO*   69

introduction, pp. 47–48, and p. 134, note to line 83. This play was included in Encina's *Cancionero* of 1496.

75. See Reindert L. Falkenburg, *Joachim Patinir: Landscape as an Image of the Pilgrimage of Life*, trans. by Michael Hoyle (Amsterdam and Philadelphia, PA: John Benjamins, 1988), p. 98. This study devotes five chapters to the theme of the Flight into Egypt in Netherlandish painting and devotional literature, paying special attention to Patinir's *Rest on the Flight into Egypt* in the Prado, details of which 'place this particular Flight into Egypt in the context of a pilgrimage [...] Joseph [...] is clad entirely in pilgrim's garb. He is wearing a cloak with "pelerine" of the type worn by pilgrims around 1500, and on his back is the distinctive broad-brimmed hat' (p. 18). Motifs in paintings by other Flemish artists 'identify the fugitives as pilgrims, and the Flight into Egypt as a pilgrimage' (p. 97).

76. *Meditationes*, fol. b6^v; Ragusa and Green, *Meditations*, p. 68.

77. Falkenburg, *Joachim Patinir*, p. 98.

78. For example, he refers to Jesus having spent seven years in Egypt, 'assi como peregrino e desterrado' [as a pilgrim and exile] (Eiximenis, *Vita Christi*, trans. by Talavera, ch. 215).

79. Electa Arenal and Stacey Schlau reproduce a photograph of a statue of the Child Jesus dressed as a pilgrim from a Carmelite Convent in Madrid, captioned 'Niño Peregrino' [Pilgrim Child], in *Untold Sisters: Hispanic Nuns in their Own Works* (Albuquerque: University of New Mexico Press, 1989), p. 190.

80. The *Ordo Rachelis* survives in four different stages of development in four different places: Laon, Limoges, Fleury and Freising. Only the second two of these incorporate the Flight into Egypt. See Young, *The Drama of the Medieval Church*, II, ch. 20, 'The Slaughter of the Innocents' (pp. 102–24).

81. E. K. Chambers, *The Medieval Stage*, 2 vols (London: Oxford University Press, 1967 [first published 1903]), II, 45.

82. Young, *The Drama of the Medieval Church*, II, 113, 114.

83. Young, *The Drama of the Medieval Church*, II, 113. In the earlier (eleventh- to twelfth-century) version of the drama from Freising, 'The flight of the Holy Family is somewhat more fully developed than the parallel part of the Fleury play, in that it contains a dialogue between Joseph and Mary; but the absence of provision for the return from Egypt conveys an impression of incompleteness' (p. 122).

84. 'As the slayers approach, the lamb is removed, and the destruction of the boys promptly begins, the mother uttering a vain prayer for mercy. [...] Over the bodies of the dead boys Rachel sings a succession of four laments, interrupted by comforting assurances from her companions, and supported by them in her moments of fainting' (from Young's synopsis of the Fleury version, *The Drama of the Medieval Church*, II, 114).

85. The phrasing does of course serve to emphasize that this is the aspiration of a blasphemer and lunatic. There is a precedent for this in Ludolph. In modifying Aelred, he has the Good Thief crucified on 'God's right hand' instead of 'Christ's right hand'.

86. Compare: 'defuncti sunt enim, qui quaerebant animam pueri' [for they are dead who were seeking the life of the child] (Matt. 2. 20).

87. For example, an anonymous fifteenth-century Italian play, the *Rappresentazione della Natività di Cristo*, has a brief Flight into Egypt section that climaxes in the Massacre of the Innocents, during which babies are snatched out of their mothers' arms and put to the sword (Banfi, *Sacre rappresentazioni*, pp. 153–82).

88. Ragusa and Green, *Meditations*, p. xxxi. Recent research on the textual history of the *MVC* recasts John of Caulibus as editor of the work rather than author. Sarah McNamer makes a strong case for the original having been composed in the Tuscan vernacular by a nun, probably a Poor Clare. This primitive version, which survives in a single manuscript witness, was subjected, McNamer argues, to two phases of correction and interpolation before being translated into Latin and launched on a wider public some time after 1336. See Sarah McNamer, 'The Origins of the *Meditationes vitae Christi*', *Speculum*, 84 (2009), 905–55.

89. Manrique, *Representación*, lines 129–60 (Pérez Priego, *Teatro medieval*, pp. 141–43). See Surtz, 'The "Franciscan Connection"', pp. 142–44.

90. One of the distinguishing features of the *Auto* is the sympathetic portrayal of St Joseph, especially

70 JANE WHETNALL

when compared with the Joseph of Manrique's *Representación* (see Amícola, 'El *Auto de la huida*', p 16; Surtz, *Teatro castellano* (1992), p. 129, note). Uría Maqua ascribes it to the influence of a commentary by John Chrysostom ('Fuentes básicas', pp. 210–12), but I think it is more likely to reflect a new respect for the Saint that gathered impetus towards the end of the fifteenth century and led to the rejuvenation of his image in art. On the contrast between the medieval Joseph and the early modern Joseph see Marina Warner, *Alone of All Her Sex: The Myth and Cult of the Virgin Mary* (London: Picador, 1985 [1st edn 1976]), pp. 188–89.

91. Amícola, 'El *Auto de la huida*', p. 6; Surtz, *Teatro medieval* (1983), p. 33.

92. In the *Vita* Giovanni collapses in shock (Manni, *Volgarizzamento*, IV, 298); a stage direction in the drama says he is 'tutto stupefatto ad udire le [...] parole di Gesù Cristo' [stunned on hearing the words of Jesus Christ]; weeping and sighing he goes on to describe his condition as close to death (Belcari and Benci, *Rappresentazione*, pp. 101–02).

93. In the *MVC* the Holy Family and St John share a frugal picnic before parting (Ragusa and Green, *Meditations*, p. 83). Eiximenis's account of the meeting, while clearly indebted to the *MVC*, adds details that seem to derive from the Italian *Vita* of St John the Baptist (*Vita Christi*, ch. 219).

94. Sirera notes the discrepancy in age between the two cousins: 'John, barely a few months older than Jesus, behaves like an adult' ('Sobre la estructura dramática', p. 855, note 34). Uría Maqua denies the existence of any incongruity or anachronism in making John's sojourn in the desert coetaneous with Jesus's sojourn in Egypt (both are children, between four and five years old), though it is not clear whether she is reckoning by the bible commentaries or the terms of the *Auto* ('Fuentes básicas', p. 217).

95. According to the *Gospel of Thomas*, Jesus was seven years old when the Holy Family returned home (James, *The Apocryphal New Testament*, p. 59); according to the *MVC*, the Child was 'not yet two months old', when they set off for Egypt (Ragusa and Green, *Meditations*, p. 67), and the stay in Egypt lasted seven years (pp. 68, 76, 77). The image of the encounter in the manuscript edited by Ragusa and Green (Paris: Bibliothèque nationale de France, ital. 115) depicts both children as roughly seven or eight (*Meditations*, p. 80, figure 68). In Belcari and Benci's *Rappresentazione* the initial rubric introduces Giovanni as 'essendo piccolino' [when he was very small]. In the leave-taking (stanzas 1–16), Giovanni is consistently 'figliuolo' [little son] to his parents. Both Gesù and Giovanni refer to one another as children; and Giovanni, introducing himself to the Virgin Mary, says 'io son figliuol di Lisabetta' [I'm Elizabeth's little boy] (43.2).

96. Juan's status as a child is mentioned by Zacarías but in an emotive context that implies he has wisdom beyond his years: 'Hijo, la buestra niñez | no os engaña, según creo' [Son, your infant years do not mislead you, I believe] (lines 119–20).

97. 'The Child Jesus doesn't say a word in the whole work'; and 'with his comings and goings the Peregrino has an important role as messenger for the Virgin and for Juan' (Sirera, 'Sobre la estructura dramática', p. 855, note 34; p. 846).

98. 'Sobre la estructura dramática', p. 845, and cf. p. 849, where he points out that just such an adoration scene is implied by Juan's last words to the Peregrino, 'y después contemplaremos | el nuestro santo Mexía' [and afterwards we'll contemplate our holy Messiah] (347–48).

99. This kind of ending has also been conjectured as providing the missing final scene for the *Auto de los Reyes Magos* (see Pérez Priego, *Teatro medieval* (2009), p. 63).

100. Francisco López Estrada refers to the use of a special figurine of the Child Jesus in Manrique's Nativity play, 'La *Representación del Nacimiento de Nuestro Señor*, de Gómez Manrique: estudio textual', *Segismundo*, 18 (1984), 9–30 (p. 17).

101. On the use of life-like figurines of the Christ Child (*bambini*) in convent culture of the fifteenth century see Christiane Klapisch-Zuber, 'Holy Dolls: Play and Piety in Florence in the Quattrocento', in her *Women, Family, and Ritual in Renaissance Italy*, trans. by Lydia G. Cochrane (Chicago, IL: University of Chicago Press, 1985), pp. 310–29.

102. This information, to which only the Child can be privy, derives from the *MVC*, where Jesus tells the visiting reader: 'Tunc dicet tibi [...] cras hinc recedere debemus' (*Meditationes*, b8r); 'Then He will say to you "[...] tomorrow we must leave here"' (Ragusa and Green, *Meditations*, p. 78).

103. There are fifteen unambiguous references to God the Father (identified as Dios Padre in lines

The *Auto de la huida a Egipto* 71

39 and 368), mainly in speeches by the Angel, Joseph, and the Virgin in the opening and closing scenes. In four cases (lines 57, 321, 335, 356), the referent is not clear: it could be either the Child or the Father.

104. Other examples include: 'Estoy esperando a Dios' [I'm waiting for God] (163); 'Si quieres a Dios servir | esperemos a que venga' [If you want to serve God, let's wait until he arrives] (315–16), both spoken by Juan; cf. lines 65, 204, 330.

105. Sirera's interpretation of the staging has the Child on view throughout the *Auto* ('Sobre la estructura', p. 855, note 34). I am counting only the scenes in which he is addressed directly (Scenes 4 and 8), or in which his presence is implicit in the actions of others (Scenes 1–3 and 10–12).

106. There are ten of these; see also lines 49, 63, 66, 72, 297. He is referred to as 'Jesú' only four times, and only by his blood relatives, Isabel (134) and Juan (176, 187, 333).

107. Bread and wine are mentioned three times in the initial interchange between Juan and the Peregrino (143, 158, 181), and bread alone once (162). When the Peregrino describes Juan's life style to the Holy Family he says he has no meat or wine or bread (245). This motif may derive from the *Vita*, where Giovanni in the desert 'non aveva nè pane nè vino' [had neither bread nor wine] (*Vita*, in Manni, *Volgarizzamento*, iv, 305).

108. Weaver, *Convent Theatre*, pp. 6–7.

109. Arenal and Schlau, *Untold Sisters*, p. 148.

110. Weaver, *Convent Theatre*, p. 238, my emphasis. On convent theatre in Rome at the same period see Kate Lowe, *Nuns' Chronicles and Convent Culture in Renaissance and Counter-Reformation Italy* (Cambridge: Cambridge University Press, 2003), pp. 263–64.

CHAPTER 4

Who is Júlio? Plot and Identity in António Ferreira's Comedies

T. F. Earle

St Peter's College, Oxford

António Ferreira (1528–1569) was, of all the creative writers of the Portuguese Renaissance, the one most closely associated with the university. In his day, that meant Coimbra, because the second Portuguese university, the Jesuit college at Évora, was only founded in 1559. About three years before that Ferreira had completed his doctorate and had left, at the age of twenty-eight, to pursue a career as a lawyer in Lisbon. While at Coimbra, or very shortly afterwards, he wrote the bulk of his extensive poetic output — published in 1598, long after his death, as the *Poemas Lusitanos* — and three plays, a verse tragedy, *Castro*, and two comedies in prose. Though he claims in the prologue to the comedy *Bristo* that the play was his first literary work, the second comedy, *Cioso*, and the tragedy *Castro* were probably not the work of a very young man.[1]

In Ferreira's time there was no professional theatre in Portugal. Plays were written and performed at Court — though the Court's most celebrated playwright, Gil Vicente, had died around 1536 — in private houses and in the university.[2] Dramas in Portuguese and in Latin were performed in Coimbra, and Latin was the language used by the Jesuits when they came to dominate the serious theatrical scene in the final decades of the sixteenth century. Ferreira's plays, though, are all in Portuguese. They are academic dramas in the sense that they follow Latin models: Seneca, the neo-Latin playwright George Buchanan, and Euripides in translation for the tragedy, and Plautus and Terence for the comedies.[3] There are also some indications in the text of the tragedy *Castro*, for instance the chorus of Coimbra girls, that the play was set in the university city, but no record of performance of any of the plays there or elsewhere has survived. By the 1550s comedies in the Roman style were already established in Portugal, and Ferreira knew well the work of his predecessor, Francisco de Sá de Miranda (1485–1557), to whom he refers in the prologue to *Bristo* and whose work he to some extent rewrites.[4]

Though Ferreira's plays are associated with the university, they are not to be seen as just a licensed diversion for undergraduates or the product of an immature writer. Certainly he would not have seen it in that way. The plays form part of a carefully thought out and very ambitious literary project. That project had two aims, moral and aesthetic, though in practice it is not easy to distinguish between them. Ferreira hoped to raise the moral awareness, not of the Portuguese people as a whole, but of the *bons engenhos* [good spirits], who included important public figures, like the regent, Cardinal-Prince Henry, as well as the poet's friends and colleagues. At the same time Ferreira continued the process, begun by Sá de Miranda, of elevating the Portuguese language to the level of Latin by using it to compose in all the genres practised by the Romans, including drama.

Ferreira's conception of literature in rhetorical and moral terms makes it easy to classify him as a humanist, though it is uncertain whether he wrote anything in Latin. Christian Stoicism provided the basis of his moral thought, complicated — and made more interesting — by an awareness of the difficulty of living according to precept.

The *Poemas Lusitanos* have been republished many times and *Castro*, always included in the volume because it is in verse, has long been recognized as a masterpiece, in which Ferreira very skilfully integrates a famous incident from the history of Portugal into a Senecan structure. Through the conventions of Roman and neo-Latin tragedy — choruses, tirades and stichomythia — the play deals with the judicial murder of the heroine, Inês de Castro, and uncovers a complex web of motivation. Despite the absence of on-stage action the play is highly theatrical and is frequently performed.

The prose comedies, however, are known only to a handful of specialists. That is a pity, especially in the case of *Cioso*, in which Ferreira can be seen to move away from Plautus and Terence towards a new dramaturgy. Scholars have, not surprisingly, been reluctant to engage with it, because the earliest edition known to us is in the compilation, *Comédias famosas portuguesas*, printed in Lisbon in 1622, long after the playwright's death and, to judge by what happened to the other plays in the volume, subjected to censorship. Those other plays, by Sá de Miranda and by Ferreira himself, had all been printed previously, in the sixteenth century, and it is likely that *Cioso* was too, though no copy has yet come to light.

Critics have, therefore, to base their views on the probably bowdlerized edition of 1622, which itself was further censored following the publication of the Portuguese index of 1624.[5] All the same, it remains an extremely interesting play, in which Ferreira, probably for the first time in the history of Portuguese drama, was able to integrate plot and character successfully. The character in question is Júlio, the *cioso* [jealous man] of the title, and his violent mood-swings point to the underlying moral of the comedy — the need for a reasonable, balanced approach to life and its problems — and to the difficulty of achieving it.

The idea of the golden mean was very dear to Ferreira, because of his Stoic mistrust of passion and because of his admiration for Horace, probably the Roman writer who meant most to him. The need to avoid extremes turns up so frequently in the verse letters that he sent to friends, literary colleagues and patrons, and in such a variety of contexts, that the reader is bound to conclude that it was an issue that concerned him very deeply.

At some point between 1555 and 1557, he wrote to Dom João de Lencastre, the illegitimate son of the Duke of Aveiro, who was at once a potential patron but also a personal friend, a contemporary at Coimbra. The poet was now trying to make his way in the law in Lisbon, a career change which caused him much uncertainty, for the prospect of great material wealth was not one which he found attractive, as he explains to Dom João: 'Queria um estado meão, igual | em todo tempo, ũa fortuna honesta, | que bastasse livrar-me de obrar mal' [I would like a middling state, not subject to change, an honest fortune, to keep me free from crime].[6] He continues, in ll. 106–08, with a clear reference to Horace's 'Extremi primorum, extremis usque priores' [The last of the first, but always ahead of the last], *Ep.*, II, 2, l. 204, but the quotation does not indicate necessarily a lack of conviction on Ferreira's part. Around the same time he wrote to Manuel de Sampaio, one of his closest friends: 'Visse eu do que desejo santo efeito, | com saúde, com livros, com meã vida' [Let me see the holy results of my desire for health, books and a middling way of life], p. 297, ll. 175–76. Here the middling way is not just that between economic wealth and poverty, because in this highly personal poem Ferreira requests guidance from Sampaio as he begins married life, whose joys he both desires and fears, because they can lead to the loss of self-control. A few years later, in 1559, the context is political, the controversial appointment of the Jesuit Luís Gonçalves de Câmara as tutor to the still very youthful king, Dom Sebastião. Moderation in all things is the lesson proposed, not just in reducing the expenses of the Court to the levels practised in the more austere reigns of the medieval monarchs, but also in such matters as preparing for war in times of peace, and at the same time using reason to restrain the king's martial ardour.[7]

The moral message, the need for reason as the way to navigate between extremes, is a familiar one, and can be paralleled in much literature of the European Renaissance. However, there is a tension in Ferreira's poetry, and even more so in his dramatic work, which means that it does not read as the bland utterance of commonplaces. To find the middle way you must know, and fear the extremes, and the portrayal of extremes was one of Ferreira's principal preoccupations as a playwright.

That did not happen all at once, however, as an examination of the first comedy, *Bristo*, shows. Though that play contains a number of volatile characters, who fly from one emotional extreme to its opposite, thereby contributing to the humour of the piece, their abrupt changes of mood do not advance the plot, as in Ferreira's mature work. *Bristo*, though certainly comic, and with some original elements, is nevertheless highly predictable, so that the play's outcome would be the same whatever the emotional make-up of the characters.

Like many Roman comedies, *Bristo* presents the reader with contrasting pairs of characters, two young men, Lionardo and Alexandre, and their fathers, Roberto and Calidónio one — Roberto — severe, the other — Calidónio — more indulgent towards his offspring. The situation is reminiscent of Terence's *Adelphoe*. Lionardo is in love with the poor but respectable Camília and, despite the opposition of his father to the match and the competition of the soldier Aníbal, a ridiculous *miles gloriosus* like so many others, and, later, of his friend Alexandre, it is not hard to predict Lionardo and Camília's future happiness. The plot is complicated by the intervention of the servants of some of the principal characters and also, especially,

76   T. F. EARLE

by the intrigues of the go-between Bristo, who gives his name to the play, as in Terence's *Phormio*. As will appear in a moment, Bristo is a complex character, given to extremes of behaviour, but nothing that he does alters the dénouement, which is achieved, as frequently happens in Roman comedy, by the arrival of travellers from overseas. They turn out to be the long-lost father and brother of Camília, believed to have perished in India, whose return as wealthy nabobs legitimizes her marriage to Lionardo, and two other marriages between the young people of the play. The Indian experiences of Píndaro (Camília's father) and Arnolfo (her brother) give the final act a certain topicality, but at the same time the use of the convention of the returning traveller rather negates the interest of the rest of the play. It hardly matters what the characters say or do, since a university audience will always know that everything will turn out all right in the end.

However, even if the actions of the characters in the play cannot alter its outcome, Ferreira's men and women are interesting in themselves, and several of them reveal that tendency to extreme behaviour which so fascinated him. Take for example Alexandre, the foil to the love-sick Lionardo, who in Act I, Scene I, rebukes his friend for defying his father and insisting on his relationship with the beautiful and virtuous, but poor, Camília. In the rather smug monologue which follows the scene between the two young men Alexandre ponders the nature of love, to which he has never been subject, and then introduces the notion, so important in Ferreira's later work, that those who go to extremes lose the sense of who they really are: 'Quem se não espantará de ver andar homens perdidos após seus apetites, tão metidos neles, e tão esquecidos de si mesmos que é vergonha e piedade?' [Who will not be amazed to see men lost in their desires, so taken up with them, and so forgetful of themselves that it is a shame and a pity?] (p. 150). Yet even by the end of Act I Alexandre himself is beginning to change, after he too sees Camília, and by the time of his Act III monologue he is totally smitten by her, with the consequence that he too begins to lose his sense of identity: 'Não sou eu Alexandre? Não sou eu livre? Não me conheceis todos? Não me ouvíeis zombar sempre de homens perdidos? Ah, coitado de mim! Que já não sou esse, já sou outro, todo diferente do que dantes era!' [Aren't I Alexandre? Aren't I free? Doesn't everyone know me? Haven't you heard me invariably laughing at men who are lost [in love]? Oh, poor me! I'm no longer him, I'm someone else, quite different from what I used to be!] (p. 272).

In literature at least, falling in love usually means personality change, and the idea may have come to Ferreira from a passage like the following from Terence's *Eunuchus*, in which the slave Parmeno comments on his master Phaedria's love-affair: 'Adeon homines inmutarier | ex amore ut non cognoscas eundem esse! Hoc nemo | minus ineptu', mage severu' quisquam nec mage continens' [To think that men can be so changed by love that you can't recognize them to be the same person! No was ever less silly, more serious, or more self-controlled than he was].[8] However, Alexandre's self-awareness — or the awareness which Ferreira gives him — points towards the developments which are given a greater prominence in *Cioso*. Nor is Alexandre the only character to go from one extreme to another. In Act IV, Scenes 4 and 5, Roberto furiously disowns his son Lionardo, who has defied him through his clandestine marriage with Camília, but by Act V, Scene 2 he has

WHO IS JÚLIO? PLOT AND IDENTITY IN ANTÓNIO FERREIRA'S COMEDIES   77

changed completely, and taken to his bed out of grief that he might never see his son again. By this point the audience is clear that the play will end happily, because they have witnessed the recognition scene involving the girl's father and brother, but Roberto knows nothing about that. His shift of mood is internally produced, and is not provoked by any external cause.

The character most obviously without a centre is the go-between Bristo, after whom the play is named. There is an alternative title, *Comédia do fanchono,* used in the first edition of 1562, but subsequently censored, so that in 1622 the word *fanchono* is excised from the title and from the text of the play nearly every time it appears. The word, which is no longer in use, means either a go-between or else a homosexual. As Adrien Roig points out, Bristo is not actively homosexual, but he is something of a cross-dresser, who behaves like a woman in female company.[9] Rather more significant in the context of the play is his moral ambiguity, strictly honourable when dealing with the affair between Lionardo and Camília, but deceitful with regard to Alexandre, a course of conduct which results in a severe beating (Act IV, Scene 7).

Cioso, however, is less dependent on Roman comedy for characterization and plot, and events are driven only partly by the traditional pattern, and much more by the twists and turns of the hero's abnormal psychology. Where traditional elements are retained, their function is usually altered. Some of those elements are listed here.

There is, as there is in a great many other plays, a pair of young males, the Portuguese Bernardo and his Venetian friend Octávio. They are temperamentally different, in that Bernardo has a romantic view of the opposite sex, while Octávio has a much more physical approach. Contrasting personalities of this type were much explored by Portuguese dramatists, most famously by Camões in his *Filodemo,* also composed in the 1550s. What is more, Octávio is the lover of the courtesan Faustina, and this relationship, between an *adulescens* and a *meretrix,* is one inherited from ancient times, and revived in Portugal by Sá de Miranda in his *Vilhalpandos,* which was composed in the 1520s and, like *Cioso,* set in Italy. Although this is one of the more conventional relationships of the play, Faustina is a much stronger and better developed character than her Roman source, Philematium in Plautus's *Mostellaria.*[10]

In the secondary plot, involving Octávio and Faustina, Ferreira did not, therefore, move very far beyond accepted norms. However, the main plot, the relationship between Bernardo and Lívia, is a radical departure. Lívia, unhappily married to Júlio for the past five years, is quite unlike the inexperienced girls of Roman comedy and, though she seeks to renew the affair with Bernardo which had begun before her wedding, she and he both know that it cannot lead to marriage, the outcome of nearly all Plautus's and Terence's comedies.

An important figure of their plays is the *senex,* the father, usually of one of the male leads, who opposes, or is thought likely to oppose, his son's marriage plans. The corresponding character of *Cioso* is César, Lívia's father, who, long before the action of the play begins, had insisted that his daughter should marry the wealthy Júlio rather than the penniless foreigner Bernardo. In the comedy he is no longer

78   T. F. EARLE

the father of tradition, whose opposition has to be circumvented by the other characters, but rather a deeply troubled old man, all too conscious that his greed for a good dowry has brought his daughter lasting unhappiness. Instead, the ingenuity of the young lovers and their servants has to be employed in outwitting the jealous Júlio (of whom more presently), an extreme character with no close parallel in ancient comedy.

Brómia, the garrulous and strong-willed elderly servant, has a major role in *Cioso*, much greater than those given to female servants in ancient comedy. Though Ardélio, Bernardo's servant, is a typical *servus callidus*, some of the other types so common in Plautus and Terence are missing. There is no *servus edax*, the hungry slave, no go-between — in other words, no parallel to Bristo or Phormio — and no *miles gloriosus*.

Early in Act v, as in so many ancient comedies and in Renaissance imitations of them, comes the recognition scene, the arrival of the seaborne traveller with news that should resolve the conflicts of the plot. However, the news that Ignácio brings in *Cioso* is different and unexpected, even to an audience aware of the comic tradition. Ignácio, it turns out, has been sent by Bernardo's father to find his son, who has been away from home for five years, and bring him back to Lisbon. In the course of doing that he discovers that Octávio, Bernardo's friend, whom everyone believes to be a Venetian, is also Portuguese and actually Bernardo's brother.

The consequence of the recognition scene is that both young men are removed from the scene, without either having any immediate prospect of marriage. Nevertheless, they had become close friends before discovering their blood relationship, and in Lisbon they will have a future together. The contrasting ties of friendship between males and heterosexual love were explored by a number of writers in the Renaissance, and the final act of the comedy brings some consolation to Bernardo.[11] In *Cioso*, as also in *Castro*, Ferreira creates scenes which can be understood in more than one way, for if Bernardo has gained a brother, he has certainly lost any contact with Lívia. However, a comedy was expected to end happily, and the necessary happy end is achieved by an unexpected manoeuvre, a change of heart by Júlio, who promises to trust his wife in future and treat her with love and affection. The change of heart further complicates the situation, for it too can be understood in more than one way.

Abrupt shifts of personality are not unknown in ancient comedy, though they are not common. A famous example is provided by Demea, the stern father of Terence's *Adelphoe*, who, in the last scenes of the play, suddenly decides to change the habits of a lifetime and bring happiness to the younger members of his and his brother's family. However, Demea's final speech, ll. 985–95, suggests that the change is not as complete as it seems, and in any case his role in the comedy is very different from Júlio's, nor is unreasoning jealousy his dominant character trait.

In *Cioso* Ferreira achieved something quite novel in the comic tradition. The recognition scene is retained, but it does not render otiose the previous action of the play, as had happened in *Bristo* and in so many others. There is a resolution — probably only temporary, as will appear — but it is not due to the workings of chance, or fortune, outside the characters' control, the chance which brought

WHO IS JÚLIO? PLOT AND IDENTITY IN ANTÓNIO FERREIRA'S COMEDIES   79

Píndaro and Arnolfo back from India or which, in Roman comedies, reunites a child, previously thought lost or even dead, with its parents. In *Cioso* happiness is restored because Júlio resolves to behave better.

This is a good moment to pause and consider the moral implications of the action of the play. Underlying everything is that concern for reason and balance in life, mentioned earlier, which the three principal male characters might be said to learn. Júlio learns through the comments of the other characters because in the course of the play nearly of them, male and female, have the chance to tell him what they think of him. Eventually, after a number of humiliations, he understands that they are right and modifies his way of life accordingly. The other two young males, Bernardo and Octávio, learn to modify their behaviour as a consequence of the events they are caught up in. Bernardo's love for a married woman, though not in itself dishonourable, is shown to be impossible, while Octávio's affair with the courtesan Faustina, though it too has redeeming features, is nevertheless tainted by the mercenary element inherent in prostitution and cannot last. Since neither of them is altogether wicked they are rewarded by the discovery that they are brothers, which brings them closer to each other.

That is a possible reading of the play, but not the only reading. It is a bit glib to say that Bernardo, having lost Lívia, will be satisfied by a relationship with Octávio, even though the two get on well. His feelings for Lívia, and hers for him, are and remain very intense. In addition, the play is less concerned with putting Bernardo on the right course in life than it is with the social and moral evil of marriages arranged for the sake of a good dowry.[12]

Nor is Júlio's conversion from monster of jealousy to supportive husband straightforward. It is true that, for a moment at least, Júlio talks about himself in terms of sin and redemption: '[...] não me temia de mi mesmo, e do meu pecado, de que mais devera. Louvores a nosso Senhor que tanta mercê me faz, já sei que cousa é ser casado [...]' [I had no fear of myself, or of my sin, which was my chief obligation. Praise the Lord who has shown me such favour. Now I know what it is to be married] (fol. 150). However, the complexity of Júlio's character, his continuing problem of identity, his self-centredness and inability to sympathize with others, all suggest that the interest of the play is more psychological than moral. It is also possible to doubt whether the change of heart will be permanent, in other words, Lívia's new happiness may well not last long.

The next part of this article will examine how all the action of the comedy, not just its final scenes, is driven by Júlio's strange and disordered personality. He is not totally without precedent, because the jealous man was a character type of interest to writers and theorists in the Renaissance.[13] There is a parallel in ancient comedy also, though not a close one, because some of Júlio's traits are inherited from Euclio, the miser of Plautus's *Aulularia*. So in Act I, Scene 2 Júlio orders his servant Brómia to keep the house locked up, to prevent any possible contact between his wife Lívia and the outside world, using language which clearly derives from Plautus's play, ll. 89–102. However, in most respects Júlio and Euclio are quite different. And what is important is not so much whether or not Júlio is an original creation, but how he is the cause of events, even if chance cannot be entirely excluded from them.

Ferreira, like many in the sixteenth century, was keenly interested in the role of chance in human affairs, though he did not believe that it had a determining role. 'Sorte' [chance], or usually a more dignified term like 'fado' [fate] o or 'destino' [destiny] are words frequently used in *Castro*, nearly always by characters who wish for one reason or another to avoid taking responsibility for their actions.[14] It is chance that brings about the situation from which *Cioso* develops, though the way in which the situation develops is the result of decisions made by human beings, so references to fate or fortune are much more likely to reflect a character's weakness than a belief on the author's part in a transcendental destiny. It is, indeed, a pure accident that Bernardo, Lívia's boyfriend from five years ago, has returned to Venice on business. More precisely, he has been ordered by his employer, Benedito, who lives in Genoa, to deliver a letter to Júlio. That, however, is the extent of events outside the control of the characters who appear on stage.

When Bernardo arrives in Venice he has no intention of seeing Lívia. He treasures her memory, but thinks a meeting will only bring unhappiness (fol. 132). It is Lívia who is determined to see him, as she tells Bernardo's servant, Ardélio (fol. 138; the circumstances of their meeting will be explained in a moment), because she no longer loves her husband, whose unreasoning jealousy has turned him into a tyrant. But why is Júlio jealous? Certainly not because of any misdeed of Lívia's, who is never accused of anything, not even by her husband. And so we come back to Júlio's personality.

The audience first encounters him in Act I, furious because he has come home to find a window slightly open, to let in light. He upbraids his servant Brómia with this, because he insists that Lívia should be completely secluded. Brómia, who is not one to be bullied, asks him why. Didn't his own father allow his wife some liberty? She obeyed orders, replies Júlio (fol. 119). Left alone on stage, he explains himself, thereby revealing how he is torn between two extreme positions. On the one hand, in his view, he is the only sensible man alive, and everyone else is a fool because they expose their wives to the gaze of other men. However, excessive self-satisfaction is combined with neurotic fear that his street, more than any other, is beset with 'galantes, namorados, ociosos' [gallants, lovers, idlers] (fol. 120).

At the heart of Júlio's problems is his extraordinary self-centredness. For him, Lívia is not a person in her own right, with a life of her own, but his treasure which, like gold, has to be kept locked up (fol. 120). His feelings about his marriage preoccupy him, but not any thoughts his wife might have. His attitude towards her is one of disapproval, possibly extending to physical punishment, as Brómia hints in the opening scene (fol. 117). In general, Júlio avoids intimate relationships, whether with men or women, and he is seen alone on stage more often and for longer than any other character. In making statements of this kind one has to be aware of the convention of sixteenth-century Portuguese theatre, shared by a number of writers, that people who might have a sexual interest in one another can never be seen together on stage.[15] For this reason Júlio and Lívia are never seen together. Contact between the sexes is restricted to the elderly, and to people of different social status. Yet even bearing that in mind, Júlio is strangely solitary, and he lives largely in the street. The strict monogamy which he imposes on his wife does not apply to him, and he spends some time plotting a visit to the courtesan Faustina.

It is the paradox of the jealous man who spends as much time as possible away from home, shunning the intimacies of family life, including at night, that allows the plot to advance, and first Ardélio and then his master Bernardo visit Lívia. Before that happens, there is a scene between Júlio and Ardélio in which the complexities of the former's personality are further exposed (fols. 129–31).

Ardélio is looking for Júlio in relation to the letter requesting hospitality for Bernardo which had been handed over off-stage. Júlio has not met Ardélio before, and until he discovers the nature of the servant's errand is happy to talk to him and to admit to his identity. However, once he knows who his master is, and how that master might come to his house, he panics and denies that he is Júlio. It is a desperate measure, because it is a transparent lie, as Ardélio immediately recognizes, but it does at least serve to keep Bernardo away, for the moment. It also explains quite a lot about Júlio.

The dialogue confirms Júlio's extreme reluctance to reveal his thoughts to other people. By pretending not to be who is, he at least contrives to keep himself to himself, but he is extremely uncomfortable throughout, as his asides make clear. The clever servant, on the other hand, is enjoying himself hugely, especially when he gets Júlio to admit that, although he is not Júlio, he knows him, and he is a good and sensible man. This allows Ardélio to tell Júlio exactly what he, and everyone else in the play thinks of him: 'A um cioso malaventurado, desconfiado, que martiriza a mulher de dia e de noite, chamas bom e sesudo?' [An unlucky, mistrustful, jealous fellow, who makes a martyr of his wife day and night, you call him good and sensible?] (fol. 130). Júlio brazenly replies that he is the best and most sensible man around, but he now knows how he appears to others. Ardélio then adds a further dimension to the plot by telling Júlio that there is merchandize brought by Bernardo waiting in the harbour, and that it is a pity that, since Júlio is not Júlio, he won't be able to collect it. Júlio thinks of a way round this difficulty and goes to put it into effect, leaving Ardélio in command of the stage and, as it happens, right outside Júlio's house.

Clearly the scene is, first and foremost, an opportunity for comic fooling, but it also deepens our understanding of Júlio. By denying his own identity he rejects his positive self-image and consequently comes to learn what he perhaps expected to hear, that he is not the best man in Venice, but the worst. And by yielding to his greed and leaving the stage he is abandoning what he calls his treasure, Lívia, just at the moment when her virtue is most under threat. He is, therefore, shifting from one extreme to the other, and by denying his identity he is denying himself a stable centre, where contraries can be reconciled by reason.

The folly of Júlio's behaviour is such as to make one feel that, with one part of his mind at least, Júlio actively courts disaster, and disaster is what occurs. Both Ardélio and Bernardo enter his house, separately, and talk at length with his wife. The night-time meeting between Bernardo and Lívia is one of emotional, not sexual communion, and is chaperoned by Brómia, but it represents the overthrow of Júlio's authority all the same. While it is going on Júlio is with the courtesan

82   T. F. EARLE

Faustina, but he gets no joy from her, and instead is robbed of a valuable ring. In the middle of the night he returns home, but Brómia refuses to admit him, because she has orders not to admit anyone, even Júlio himself, because such a person will be an impostor. Júlio had indeed given orders to that effect (fols 142–43). In that scene Brómia raises all kinds of reasonable objections, but Júlio dismisses them. If he returns during the night, it will not be as himself. 'Crê que é o diabo, e não são eu' [Believe it to be the devil, and not me], he says (fol. 142). Here is another scene, not unlike the earlier one with Ardélio, in which Júlio's fear of self-revelation leads him to say the most extraordinary things about himself.[16]

The scene in which a master is refused entry to his own house by a servant derives ultimately from Plautus's *Amphitryo*, but in Ferreira's play it has a psychological depth quite absent from the original. Júlio's strange commands, and subsequent humiliation at the hands of his servant, indicate a man in the grip of unreasoning terrors, all too obvious to Brómia, and of profound uncertainty about his own identity. If that identity can be defined in social terms, Júlio as husband and master of his house, it is doubly shaken, because his wife receives a lover at home, while a servant compels him to spend the night in the street. Both these things happen, not because Júlio is outwitted by a go-between or someone else cleverer than he is, but because of his own decisions.

And so we come to Júlio's final appearance in Act V, and his decision to be a model husband henceforward. It is a decision which has given such few critics of the play as there have been great difficulty, because it does not derive from the action of the comedy.[17] However, if the play is driven, not by the mechanical working-out of a classical plot, but by the personality of its principal character, it seems in keeping. Júlio has not really learnt the lesson about balance and reason, even if he now knows things about himself of which he was previously ignorant. He has simply gone, once again, from one extreme to another, from devil to angel, as it were. He is still uncertain about who he really is: 'Se pudera tomar outro nome, deixara o que tenho, pera que em tudo parecera novo homem' [If I could take another name, I would drop the one I have, so as to seem a new man in everything] (fol. 150). Though he promises that he will be a better husband to Lívia in the future, he never thinks of her feelings, but only of his own. Particularly telling is the final speech of the play, a monologue delivered by César, Júlio's father-in-law. He rejoices in the change in his daughter's life, and in the newly discovered fraternal relationship between Bernardo and Octávio, and in the style of classical comedy summons everyone to a party. Yet he says of Júlio: '[...] segundo o que enxergo nele, vai já caindo em outro estremo demasiado' [from what I see in him, he is going too far towards the opposite extreme] (fol. 154).

The originality of Ferreira's play lies in the way the action is driven by the personality of its principal character, and in the nature of that personality, tormented, driven to extremes, and of uncertain identity. In some ways Júlio could be seen as the comic equivalent of Inês de Castro, Ferreira's tragic heroine. Inês is torn between the Stoic attitude of equanimity in the face of death, secure in the certainty of her innocence of any crime, and a much more human wish to prolong her life which leads her to beg the king Dom Afonso IV for mercy.[18] In his own

WHO IS JÚLIO? PLOT AND IDENTITY IN ANTÓNIO FERREIRA'S COMEDIES   83

way, Júlio too is unable to find a secure mid-point between emotional extremes.

The two plays are also alike in the prominence given to women and in their strength of character. In her famous scene in Act IV of *Castro* the heroine comes to dominate the weak king, who calls her a 'mulher forte' [strong woman] and gives her her liberty, only to change his mind when she is off stage. In *Cioso* all the main female roles — Lívia, the injured wife, Brómia, her servant, Faustina, her rival, and Pórcia, her mother-in-law — are much stronger and more stable characters than the men who are associated with them.[19] Though there is an underlying moral, both plays avoid easy solutions.

It is a pity that the accidents of printing history and the supposed immorality of classically inspired comic drama have prevented *Cioso* from being seen as what it is, one of the most interesting plays to have been written in Portugal during the Renaissance. With it, and with *Castro*, Ferreira escaped from the restraints of academic classicism and wrote a play comparable with the more problematic theatre of the seventeenth century.

84 T. F. EARLE

Appendix

The transcription and translation which follows, of Act IV, Scene 1, opens, as often in Roman comedy and in imitations of it, with a monologue. Then Júlio notices that his elderly servant, Brómia, is also on stage and a dialogue begins.

JÚLIO. Não cuidei que tão bem acabasse o dia. Forte cobiça de anel foi esta, que o não guardou Faustina para mais tarde. Logo eu enxerguei na moça bons desejos, e com tanto alvoroço me veio chamar agora, que parecia que lhe fugia. Mas com que mentira encobrirei eu minha ida a tais horas que me não entendam? Dou ao diabo esta velha que já estive por vezes pera a lançar fora de casa, e hei o de vir a fazer. Não sei quem a fez tão endiabrada, parece que tem algum esprito familiar que lhe diz quanto eu faço, que já agora no seu rosto e nos seus olhos entendo eu que me entende. Mas como a enganarei? Ora andar, boa dissimulação tenho. Brómia!

BRÓMIA. Já me chama, começará com seus esconjuros.

JÚLIO. Brómia!

BRÓMIA. Que mandas?

JÚLIO. Quanto me deves pela confiança que em ti tenho?

BRÓMIA. Deus o sabe.

JÚLIO. Eu são convidado pera ũa certa festa de um meu amigo, por isso vou assi de festa. Não me parece que tornarei esta noite.

BRÓMIA. Pera que me dás essas contas? Avezado és ires e vires quando e cada vez que queres. Achaste por ventura algũa hora as portas abertas a outrem, e fechadas a ti?

JÚLIO. Não papeies. Por isso to digo, porque durmas descansada de me vires abrir.

BRÓMIA. Quem tivesse o teu descanso!

JÚLIO. A porta, da maneira que a eu deixar, assi fique até que eu torne.

BRÓMIA. Que não seja mais que pelo costume. Ela o fará já de si.

JÚLIO. E, porque muitas vezes acontecem enganos, falo isso pelo que já vi. Ainda que outrem venha com recado meu, ou diga que são eu, não lho creias.

BRÓMIA. De que servem tantos medos? Por tua vida, quem vês, ou quem ouves, pera os teres de ninguém?

JÚLIO. Isto não são medos, mas sisos, às vezes acontece o que homem não cuida, e por não cuidar no que pode acontecer vem a cair no perigo sem remédio.

BRÓMIA. Bom é atalhar em tempo. Mas...

JÚLIO. E que melhor tempo que este? Sabes tu se está ali por ventura alguém espreitando quando eu saio, e me pode contrafazer também a fala, que te engane, e lhe vás abrir?

BRÓMIA. Ai, que mau homem! Ora, dou-lhe que aconteça isto, em entrando não haverá aí olhos que o conheçam?

JÚLIO. Em entrando! E querias que entrasse?

BRÓMIA. Que pecado era entrar, cuidando que eras tu?

JÚLIO. Mas que pecado é avisar-te eu, pera que não entre? Não poderá ele mais que ti, não te matará, ou não te tapará esta boca, para fazer tudo a seu salvo?

BRÓMIA. Como te pode isso cair no pensamento, que nunca se viu, nem se ouviu?

WHO IS JÚLIO? PLOT AND IDENTITY IN ANTÓNIO FERREIRA'S COMEDIES 85

[JÚLIO. I didn't think the day would end so well. Faustina really wanted the ring, because she didn't wait for later to have it. Right from the start I could the girl's mad with desire. She was very excited when she asked me to come to her, as if she thought I was going to run away from her. But what lie am I going to use to cover my absence at that sort of time that they won't see through? The devil take that old woman. More than once I've wanted to send her packing, and before long I will. I don't know who put the devil into her, she seems to have a familiar spirit who tells her everything I do, and I can see now in her face and her eyes that she understands me. How am I going to fool her? Well, I'm good at pretending. Brómia!

BRÓMIA. He's calling me, he's going to start cursing me.

JÚLIO. Brómia!

BRÓMIA. What is it?

JÚLIO. How much do you owe me for the confidence I have in you?

BRÓMIA. God knows.

JÚLIO. I've been invited to a party by a friend, that's why I'm all dressed up. I shan't be back tonight.

BRÓMIA. Why are you giving me all these explanations? You're in the habit of going and coming whenever you want. Have you ever found the door opened for someone else, and closed to you?

JÚLIO. Stop your wittering! I'm telling you this, so you can sleep in peace and not have to open up for me.

BRÓMIA. I wish I could have your peace!

JÚLIO. I want the door to stay exactly as it is, when I go and when I return.

BRÓMIA. That's no more than what always happens. The door can do that by itself.

JÚLIO. There are often scams, I'm telling you this from experience. Even if someone comes with a message from me, or says they're me, don't believe them.

BRÓMIA. What are you so afraid about? For goodness' sake, who do you see, or who do you hear, to be afraid of anyone?

JÚLIO. This is not being afraid, but common sense. Sometimes the unexpected happens, and because you haven't thought about what might happen you find yourself in danger and with no way out.

BRÓMIA. It's good to stop things in time. But...

JÚLIO. And what better time than the present? How do you know if maybe someone isn't watching when I go out, who can imitate my voice and trick you into opening the door to him?

BRÓMIA. What a dreadful fellow! All right, let's suppose that happens, if he comes in aren't there eyes here to recognize him?

JÚLIO. If he comes in! And you'd like him to come in?

BRÓMIA. Where's the sin in letting him in, thinking that it was you?

JÚLIO. Then where's the sin in warning you not to let him in? Won't he be stronger than you? He could kill you, or silence you, so's to be able to do everything in safety.

BRÓMIA. How did you get hold of this idea, of something which has never been seen or heard of?

JÚLIO. Porque o tu não viste, nem ouviste, crês logo que ninguém o veria nem faria. Por isso, eu digo que quem não vê não sabe o caso, e eu não quero que ainda que eu mesmo torne — olha o que te digo — ainda que eu mesmo torne, não quero que me abras.

BRÓMIA. Que dizes?

JÚLIO. Isto que ouves.

BRÓMIA. Ainda que tornes...

JÚLIO. Ainda que eu torne...

BRÓMIA. Que te não abra.

JÚLIO. Que me não abras.

BRÓMIA. Isso me mandas? Não cuidarás que te pode acontecer cousa por ventura que te obrigue a vir a casa, ou se te arrependerás da ida e do caminho?

JÚLIO. Eu que to digo, bem sei que não hei-de tornar.

BRÓMIA. Se tornares?

JÚLIO. Mata-me e não me abras, ainda que brade e que grite, e tu me vejas e conheças, crê que é o diabo e não são eu, porque eu vou pera não tornar, nem mandar recado algum, ouves-me tu?

BRÓMIA. Ouço, mas não sei como isso seja, não queria ter mais guerra contigo da que tenho. Hei-te de ver eu batendo a porta, e não te hei-de abrir?

JÚLIO. Se te digo. Esta é a mais perra velha do mundo, que nem hei-de tornar, nem me hás-de ver, e ainda que me vejas, me não abras.

BRÓMIA. Digo que assi o farei pois mo mandas. Quem crerá tal?

JÚLIO. Deitai-vos logo, apagai a candeia e dormi descansadamente.

BRÓMIA. Aosadas.

JÚLIO. E lembrei-vos o que vos sempre digo, que vivamos em paz.

BRÓMIA. De quantos desastres os bons acham pelo mundo, não haverá um só pera este mau que o mate? Homem é isto, alma tem este, razão tem este? Faz-me crer que cheirou já os recados de Bernardo, e que nos vai espreitar a todos. Coitada de mi, que nunca pude tirar Lívia de tamanho cometimento, oferecida está a seu perigo. O ódio que tem a este e o amor de Bernardo lhe dá este ânimo e afouteza. Hoje lhe mandou dizer que o desejava ver, hoje se foi ordenando como se vissem. Ó ciosos enganados, cegos! Quero ver, antes que o outro acerte de vir, se a posso tirar de sua teima.

Bibliography

EARLE, THOMAS F., 'António Ferreira's Castro: Tragedy at the Cross-Roads', in *Portuguese Humanism and the Republic of Letters*, ed. by Maria Berbara and Karl A. E. Enenkel (Leiden: Brill, 2012), pp. 289–318

——'As comédias em prosa de Francisco de Sá de Miranda e António Ferreira: um género clássico que se fez português', in *A literatura clássica ou os clássicos na literatura*, ed. by Cristina Pimentel and Paula Morão (Lisbon: Campo da Comunicação, 2012), pp. 29–44

——'"Oh morte, que vida é esta!": Relations between Women and Male Authority Figures in the Comedies of António Ferreira', *eHumanista*, 22 (2012), 155–64

FERREIRA, ANTÓNIO, *Castro*, ed. by Thomas F. Earle (Lisbon: Comunicação, 1990)

Who is Júlio? Plot and Identity in António Ferreira's Comedies 87

JÚLIO. Just because you haven't seen or heard of it, you immediately think that no one would. That's why I say that people who can't see don't know. Even if I come back myself — listen to what I'm saying — even if I come back myself, I don't want you to open the door to me.

BRÓMIA. What did you say?

JÚLIO. What you've just heard.

BRÓMIA. Even if you come back...

JÚLIO. Even if I come back...

BRÓMIA. I'm not to open the door to you.

JÚLIO. You're not to open the door to me.

BRÓMIA. You're asking me to do that? Don't you think that something might happen by chance which would make you return home, or you might change your mind about going and about the route?

JÚLIO. I'm telling you, I know very well that I'm not coming back.

BRÓMIA. And if you do?

JÚLIO. Kill me, and don't open the door, even if I shout and scream, and you see me and recognize me. Think it's the devil and not me, because I'm going and I'm not coming back, and I'm not sending any messages. Got that?

BRÓMIA. Yes, but I don't know how this is going to be, and I wouldn't want any more fights with you than those I have already. So I'm going to see you knocking at the door, and I'm not to open?

JÚLIO. If I say so. This is the most stiff-necked bitch in the world! I'm not coming back, and you're not going to see me, and even if you do, you're not to open the door.

BRÓMIA. Since those are your orders, I say that I'll do it. Who'd believe it?

JÚLIO. Go to bed now, blow out your candle and sleep tight.

BRÓMIA. Very good.

JÚLIO. And remember what I always say, let's live in peace.

BRÓMIA. Of all the disasters which happen to good people in this world, isn't there just one for this wicked fellow that will finish him off? Is he a man, does he have a soul, does he have any sense? It makes me think that he's sniffed out Bernardo's messages and he's going to spy on all of us. Poor me, since I could never talk Lívia out of this terrible business, she's exposed to danger. The hatred she feels for this fellow and her love for Bernardo give her this courage and boldness. Today she sent word to him that she wanted to see him, and today she made plans for the meeting. What blind fools jealous men are! I'm going to see is I can talk her out of what she's determined to do, before Bernardo arrives.

——— *Comédia de Bristo, ou do Fanchono*, ed. by Adrien Roig (Paris: Presses Universitaires de France, 1973)

——— *Comédia do Cioso*, Online database: 'Teatro de Autores Portugueses do Séc. XVI', Centro de Estudos de Teatro, <http://www.cet-e-quinhentos.com/>

——— *Poemas Lusitanos*, ed. by Thomas F. Earle (Lisbon: Fundação Calouste Gulbenkian, 2008)

HORACE, *Opera*, ed. by Edward Wickham and H. W. Garrod (Oxford: Clarendon Press, 1901)

REBELO, LUÍS DE SOUSA, *A tradição clássica na literatura portuguesa* (Lisbon: Horizonte, 1982)

ROIG, ADRIEN, *O teatro clássico em Portugal no século XVI* (Lisbon: Biblioteca Breve, 1983)

TERENCE, *The Comedies*, trans. by Peter Brown (Oxford: Oxford University Press, 2006)

——— *Comoediae*, ed. by Robert Kauer and Wallace M. Lindsay (Oxford: Clarendon Press, 1965)

88   T. F. EARLE

Notes to Chapter 4

1. See the dedication to Prince João printed in the good, though now somewhat out of date, edition by Adrien Roig (Paris: Presses Universitaires de France, 1973), p. 126. Further references to this edition are given after quotations in the text. To facilitate comprehension I have modernized the orthography. There are many editions of *Castro*. Here reference will be made to the one contained in António Ferreira, *Poemas Lusitanos*, ed. by Thomas F. Earle (Lisbon: Fundação Calouste Gulbenkian, 2008), pp. 379–460. For *Cioso*, see note 4.
2. There is more information about performing plays in Portugal in Chapter 11 (eds).
3. For a modern study of the sources of *Castro* see T. F. Earle, 'António Ferreira's *Castro*: Tragedy at the Cross-Roads', in *Portuguese Humanism and the Republic of Letters*, ed. by Maria Berbara and Karl A. E. Enenkel (Leiden: Brill, 2012), pp. 289–318.
4. For the reference to Sá de Miranda, see *Bristo*, ed. by Adrien Roig, pp. 130–32. For Ferreira's rewriting of the earlier dramatist, see Thomas F. Earle, 'As comédias em prosa de Francisco de Sá de Miranda e António Ferreira: um género clássico que se fez português', in *A literatura clássica ou os clássicos na literatura*, ed. by Cristina Pimentel and Paula Morão (Lisbon: Campo da Comunicação, 2012), pp. 29–44 (pp. 36–39).
5. The 1622 text is reprinted, with a few notes, in the excellent web-site Cet-e-Quinhentos, published by the Centro de Estudos de Teatro of the University of Lisbon. This is the edition followed here. References are to folio numbers, and are given after quotations in the text.
6. See António Ferreira, *Poemas Lusitanos*, p. 290, ll. 97–99. Further references to this edition are given after quotations in the text. For the biography of Dom João de Lencastre see idem, pp. 519–20. Except where indicated, all the translations in this chapter are mine.
7. *Poemas Lusitanos*, pp. 327–34. The word 'mediocridade' [mediocrity], in a positive sense, is found p. 330, l. 103.
8. The translation, of ll. 225–27, is by Peter Brown, *Terence: The Comedies* (Oxford: Oxford University Press, 2006).
9. *Bristo*, pp. 76–77.
10. See Thomas F. Earle, ' "Oh morte, que vida é esta!": Relations between Women and Male Authority Figures in the Comedies of António Ferreira', *eHumanista*, 22 (2012), 155–64 (p. 159).
11. For this theme in an English neo-Latin comedy of the 1540s, see Howard B. Norland, 'Terence "improved"? Form and Function in Foxe's *Titus et Gesippus*', in *Neo-Latin Drama: Forms, Functions, Receptions*, ed. by Jan Bloemandal and Philip Ford (Hildesheim: Olms, 2008), pp. 93–102 (pp. 98–99).
12. Other sixteenth-century writers condemned dowry hunting, notably Erasmus. See Earle, ' "Oh morte, que vida é esta!" ', p. 162.
13. See Earle, 'As comédias em prosa de Francisco de Sá de Miranda e de António Ferreira', p. 43.
14. A discussion of this question, with bibliography, can be found in António Ferreira, *Castro*, ed. by T. F. Earle (Lisbon: Comunicação, 1990), pp. 26–29.
15. An exception is Camões's *Auto de Filodemo*, in which pairs of lovers do appear together, but that play was written for performance in India, where standards may not have been so exacting.
16. The whole scene, with a translation, is transcribed at the end of this article.
17. See Luís de Sousa Rebelo, *A tradição clássica na literatura portuguesa* (Lisbon: Horizonte, 1982), p. 167, and Adrien Roig, *O teatro clássico em Portugal no século XVI* (Lisbon: Biblioteca Breve, 1983), pp. 50–51.
18. Further discussion in Earle, 'Tragedy at the Cross-Roads'.
19. Further discussion in Earle, ' "Oh morte, que vida é esta!" ', pp. 158–61.

CHAPTER 5

The Reinvention of Classical Comedy and Tragedy in Portugal
Defining Drama in the Work of Sá de Miranda, António Ferreira and Diogo de Teive

Catarina Fouto

King's College London

1.1. *Argumentum* and *Dramatis Personae*

Unlike in many parts of Europe, where the seventeenth-century is considered the 'golden age' of theatre, in Portugal it is the plays of the sixteenth-century that are unanimously regarded by critics as the best examples of the tradition of drama in that country. Contrastingly, the production of literary theory during the 1500s in Portugal was quite insignificant, with the few exceptions being published towards the turn of the century, and often published abroad.[1] Critics who have devoted their attention to the development of literary theory in the Portuguese Renaissance and Baroque have drawn attention to this absence of theoretical output by Portuguese humanists, and have highlighted the importance of non-theoretical writing to the understanding of the underlying principles of literary theory which guided Portuguese authors.[2]

If scholarly work has greatly enhanced our understanding of the Iberian *auto* tradition, the same degree of critical attention has not been given to the analysis of texts which might shed light on the concepts of dramatic theory shared by Portuguese humanist playwrights. This type of exploratory work is even more relevant if we bear in mind that the reception, commentary and understanding of the *Poetics* of Aristotle only truly had an impact in Portugal (as in many parts of Europe) at the turn of the seventeenth century.[3]

This analysis of the non-theoretical output of playwrights will be the starting point of this chapter, which will outline the development of classical drama in Portugal between the 1520s and 1555. After a summary examination of the history of the editions, translations and reading of classical drama in Portugal, I will explore the concepts of comedy and tragedy in the work of three Portuguese humanist playwrights who are representative of three different generations of Portuguese humanism: Francisco Sá de Miranda, Diogo de Teive and António Ferreira.

Sá de Miranda (1485–1558) played a pivotal role in the blossoming of classical letters in vernacular literature in Portugal. The Crown supported young men in their studies in Italy, where he was able move in the highest intellectual circles of that time in the service of the bishop Miguel da Silva (the celebrated dedicatee of Castiglione's *Il Cortegiano*). Upon returning to Portugal in 1526, Sá de Miranda's first literary experiments were in classical comedy (*Os Estrangeiros* and *Os Vilhalpandos*),[4] which were enthusiastically welcomed by a humanistic audience at the royal Court, then in Coimbra. It was around the same time that Diogo de Teive (*c.* 1514–1565?) left Portugal at the age of twelve on a royal scholarship to study in Paris, and then transferred to Bordeaux. There he made contact with the cream of European humanism, and became friends with André de Gouveia and George Buchanan, who accompanied him back to Portugal in 1547 to staff the newly founded Colégio das Artes in Coimbra, planned as a secular educational institution which would form young men to serve in the administration of the empire. Teive, a polymath, is credited with at least three neo-Latin tragedies: he experimented with biblical tragedy with great success at the Colégio (*Saul* and *Iudith*), but his historical play *Ioannes Princeps* (written in 1554, published in 1558, and the only one to survive to this day) was met with criticism and this chapter will explore the polemic surround the play in detail in Part II. Teive taught the young António Ferreira (1528–1569) in Coimbra where he also coincided with Buchanan, and Ferreira would certainly have been familiar with their plays, performed at the Colégio by the students, and even in manuscript form.[5] Before he left for Lisbon in 1556, Ferreira's interest was sparked by Sá de Miranda's comedies, and he experimented in this new dramatic form with success (*Bristo*, 1553; *Cioso*, early to mid-1550s),[6] but his best-known work is the tragedy *Castro* (a historical tragedy, drafted most likely between 1553 and 1555, and later revised).[7]

There was a gradual ideological shift in Portugal in the 1540s and more noticeably in the 1550s, resulting from a combination of factors. The political conflicts in Europe (which both Sá de Miranda and Teive witnessed closely) and the rise of the Reformation did not cause unrest or instability in Portugal. The king, Dom João III, made a point of avoiding European wars, but boosted his reputation as a devoutly Catholic king by declaring himself an enemy of heresy, both at home and in his growing imperial territories. The 1540s and 1550s were decades of increasing difficulties in the maintenance of the empire, and at home the Inquisition (created in 1536) targeted the Jewish and New Christian population but also the intellectual elite, showing that no deviation from strict orthodoxy would be tolerated. Cardinal Henrique, the king's brother, later appointed *Inquisidor-Mor*, had sponsored the publication of Sá de Miranda's *Os Estrangeiros* (1559), and was the dedicatee of Teive's *Ioannes Princeps* in 1558. There was a visible shift in the priorities of this important patron of the letters, as by the 1550s his interests were virtually restricted to moral or religious works. Thus, the study of how classical drama made a start on Portuguese stages and gradually developed aesthetically up to the 1550s takes us back to the years when both vernacular and neo-Latin literature were blossoming under the aegis of humanism, and when Portugal's cultural links with Italy, France and Spain gave a new impulse to different generations of writers.

THE REINVENTION OF CLASSICAL COMEDY AND TRAGEDY IN PORTUGAL 91

In this chapter I will focus on comedy as the first successful humanist adaptation of classical and Italian Renaissance theatre in Portugal, with particular attention to the earlier versions of the prologue of Sá de Miranda's *Estrangeiros*: it shows a clear attempt to bring something new to the Portuguese stage, drawing on the authoritative work of the Latin grammarians (Donatus and Evanthius) and especially the new Renaissance playwrights like Ariosto. Sá de Miranda's debt to their work in the prologue is greater than has been previously thought, as it shows his efforts to present the new dramatic genre to the Portuguese public, whilst still claiming his own originality on the basis of authorized imitation.

The concept of tragedy will be the subject of the final section of this chapter, where my discussion will focus exclusively on Teive's *Ioannes Princeps*, as this is the only classical tragic play by a Portuguese associated with a discussion about the nature of tragedy.[8] There I will explore the polemical choice of subject matter and the relation between rhetoric and drama which is illustrated by the play. As will be seen, Teive's play goes beyond the trite moralizing which some have attributed to it, but the close relationship which the play has with contemporary events is one of its shortcomings and the reason for its critical force having remained elusive to critics.

Delving into the works of Sá de Miranda, Ferreira and Teive will contribute to problematizing the reasons why the tradition of classical drama in Portugal was so short-lived, whilst engaging with its experimentalism, originality and sophistication, features which remain to be fully explored from a broader critical perspective.

I.2. Drama in Early Sixteenth-Century Portugal: Stage and Page

Long before the work of Plautus, Terence, Seneca and Euripides sparked the interest of the Portuguese elites, there was a thriving dramatic tradition, specific to the Iberian Peninsula, which was very popular across society and was supported at the highest level by the royal family: the Portuguese *auto* is, to this day, represented by the important and prolific playwright Gil Vicente (1465–c. 1536) and his acolytes, otherwise known as the 'Vicentine school'.[9] A great innovator of the 'auto' himself, and a playwright whose varied *Compilaçam de todalas obras* (posthumous edition, 1561–62) illustrates the reinvention that drama underwent in the sixteenth century, Vicente enjoyed the patronage of different generations of members of the Portuguese royal family, catering to their tastes with farces and tragicomedies, marking the religious calendar at Court with his plays, and celebrating important political events with made-to-order dramatic works. It was in competition with the tradition of the *auto* that the new humanist drama — comedy, in particular — came to develop:[10] despite the continued support from the Crown until his death, Vicente could not counter the enthusiasm surrounding the original plays by the young and well-travelled poet Francisco de Sá de Miranda, recently returned from Italy.

Conversely, scholars attempting to assess the reception of classical drama in sixteenth-century Portugal cannot rely on the study of the history of the printing press in that country. There were few classical manuscripts in Portugal, and it is

92   CATARINA FOUTO

well known that editing and printing were not developed there to a standard that would satisfy the more demanding humanists. Furthermore, patronage was limited to the royal family, to a very restricted number of important aristocratic houses (of Aveiro and Braganza), and to the higher members of the clergy, who used the printing press to accommodate their political, social and institutional interests.[11] Portuguese printing expanded in the second half of the sixteenth century at a time when the Portuguese Crown and its most distinguished members, who were able to monopolize it, were actively promoting the image of a nation firmly committed to fighting heterodoxy. Therefore, it is not surprising that Portuguese intellectuals rarely carried out this type of editorial work, and if they did so it was abroad.

There were virtually no editions of classical drama in Portugal. Their (late) appearance is linked to the teaching carried out in Coimbra, after the secular Colégio das Artes was handed over to the Jesuits. Seneca's tragedies *Thyestes* and *Troades* were printed in an edition intended for teaching in 1559 by Antonio de Mariz, followed in 1560 by *Hercules Furens* and *Medea*, also in Coimbra. Plautus was edited only in 1567 by João Barreira, under the sponsorship of the regent, Cardinal Henrique, at the request of the Jesuits: the four Plautine comedies (*Aulularia*, *Captivi*, *Stichus* and *Trinummus*) were 'acommodadas com o espaço necessareo pera os ouvintes poderem grosar' [printed with sufficient space for students to gloss the text], in the words of the Cardinal himself, but more significantly, we are told in the title page, 'delecta sunt, quae bonis moribus nocere possunt' [all things which can harm good customs have been deleted (from the edition)]. Censoring of classical works became the norm in the second half of the sixteenth century, and this, combined with the elaboration of anthologies with extracts of plays, impacted on the knowledge that pupils had of the vast corpus of classical authors and of the individual texts.[12]

As in England, few translations were published:[13] only one version, of Sophocles' *Electra*, appeared. The translation by the otherwise obscure Aires de Vitória was printed twice (1536 and 1555, Lisbon), and even though the title page states that the play was 'tirada de grego em linguagem, trovada' [translated from Greek and in verse], the very title of this work, *Tragédia da vingança que foi feita sobre a morte del rei Agamémnon* [*Tragedy of the vengeance taken after the death of King Agamemnon*] indicates that this is a Portuguese rendering of Fernán Pérez de Oliva's prose adaptation into Spanish (*Agaménon vengado*, 1528, Burgos). Both this and the *Tragedia de los amores de Eneas y de la Reyna Dido* [*Tragedy of the loves of Aeneas and Queen Dido*] (c. 1536–50?, Lisbon, Germain Gaillard) were composed in rhymed verse, and derived from previous Spanish texts: in the case of the *Tragedia de los amores de Eneas y de la Reyna Dido*, the author, who has been identified as the Portuguese João Cirne, worked with the Virgilian epic in mind, but was equally influenced by Torres Naharro's *Propalladia* (1526), and also the *Tragicomedia de Calixto y Melibea* (1499).[14]

Research in the special collections of Portuguese libraries reveals a very different reality, which contrasts with the image of a feeble printing industry: Portugal depended on the international book market, and there are many foreign editions of classical playwrights printed before 1555 in Portuguese libraries, in both Latin and Greek, and naturally intellectuals educated abroad also had access to the best

THE REINVENTION OF CLASSICAL COMEDY AND TRAGEDY IN PORTUGAL 93

scholarly editions available.[15] The number of extant sixteenth-century copies of editions of Terence, Plautus, Euripides and Seneca in Portuguese libraries indicates that, as throughout the rest of Europe, they were seen as model playwrights.

It was to these and to Horace's *Ars Poetica* that sixteenth-century intellectuals in Portugal turned when composing their plays, but also often appended to the editions of classical playwrights were texts which presented some form of exposition on the nature of ancient drama: Aelius Donatus's *Vita Terenti* and the fragment by him known as *De Comoedia et Tragoedia*, as well as Diomedes's *Ars Grammatica* book III. These appeared in virtually all the earlier editions of Terence, and were widely disseminated in Europe throughout the sixteenth century, particularly in Josse Bade's best-selling *Praenotamenta ascensiana* to the edition of Terence (1511), and also in the translations of the Euripides' *Hecuba* by Erasmus (Paris, 1544). Gustave Lanson has established that, for a substantial part of the sixteenth century, Donatus, Diomedes and Horace were the basis of any discussion on drama. In Portugal too, authors were indebted to this medieval line of transmission,[16] but not exclusively, and authors like Sá de Miranda, Ferreira and Teive highlight the novelty of these dramatic forms and the role of the author in adapting them to the new historical context.

I.3. Defining Comedy in Sixteenth-Century Portugal

The Portuguese elites would have been familiar with the work of Plautus and Terence, but the innovative Sá de Miranda aimed at more than an *imitation* of Roman comedy, showing the level of originality and literary ambition which is the trademark of his writing. Addressing his audience in the prologue of his *Estrangeiros*, Sá de Miranda introduces the comedy to the Portuguese public:[17]

> 'Prologo: A Comédia faz o prólogo.
> Estranhais-me, que bem o vejo, dais de cotovelo e d'olho uns aos outros. Quem será? Quem não será? Quis-me Deos bem que nam apodais já, porém nam há de falecer quem me remede. Agora vos digo que todos encrespais as sobrancelhas, porque vos falo português ou porque esperáveis de mim alguns trinquesfortes. Ora me escuitai se quiserdes, dir-vos-ei quem sam, donde venho e a que venho. Primeiramente sam, como vedes, ũa pobre molher antiga de dias e de nação estrangeira. Sei porém todas as línguas. Meu nome é Comédia. Nam abrais as bocas, nam cuideis por isso que me haveis logo de comer, porque eu naci em Grécia, e lá me foi posto o nome, por cousas que pertencem àquela língua e não a esta vossa. Naquela minha natureza vivi muitos anos, como dizem, à boca que queres. Depois, fui trazida a Roma pera onde entam corria tudo por mandado da fortuna. Cá também vos coube vossa parte de que esta linguagem a que inda chamais romance é mui grande testemunha. Ora eu assi trazida a Roma mal podereis agora crer quanto i fui estimada e em quanto tida. Que mais quereis? Não estive em um nada de ser deosa. Depois, a grandeza daquele império, que nunca parecia que houvesse d'acabar, todavia acabou e caiu sobre si mesmo. Entam me perdi eu ali juntamente com todas as boas artes. E i jouvemos um grande tempo, como enterradas entre as quedas daqueles edifícios altos e fermosos, que nam havia somente memória de nós nas outras partes, quando os vezinhos em que ficou sempre esta lembrança de uns nos outros, como o tempo deu lugar e inda às vezes contra o tempo, cavaram

CATARINA FOUTO

tanto que nos tornaram à vida, maltratadas e pouco pera ver. Agora que já íamos ganhando forças, sentimos outra vez aquela ĩmiga nossa poderosa que nos da outra vez destruía, bem deveis de crer que o digo pola guerra... Venho fogindo dela. Aqui que é cabo do mundo acho paz, nam sei se acharei assossego [...]. Nam sei se achastes em mim ũa grande mudança de vos falar em prosa, sabei que o faço à míngua de versos, que os nam tendes quais me a mim compriam, e assi fazia agora em Itália. Nos meus versos, assi latinos como gregos, sempre me cheguei à prosa quanto pude, eles davam-me tal lugar. Que nestas partes ainda há muito pouco que os conheceis por versos. Os vossos consoantes não me armam, são mui forçados e batem muito nas orelhas. Eu trato cousas correntes, sam amiga do povo, folgo de aprazer a todos...Finalmente, nunca me aprouveram escuridades, nenhuns trinquestroques de que se espantam e contentam os que menos sabem. Digo-vos que pera isso falo, pera que me entendais. Quem quiser que o nam entendam nam fale e tirará de trabalho a si e aos outros. Quando me passaram a Roma mudanças fiz e já dantes contra minha vontade tinha deixados os meus coros. Convém de obedecer aos tempos, queiramos ou nam queiramos'.

[Prologue. Comedy speaks:

You think that I am strange, I can see that clearly, nudging each other and looking at each other. 'Who is that? Who can that be?' I am very fortunate that you have not yet begun to mock me, but I won't be short of those who try to ape me... Now that I see you raising your eyebrows I will tell you why I speak in Portuguese, as maybe you were expecting wordplay. Now, if you please, listen to me, I will tell you who I am, where I have come from, and why I have come here. First, I am, as you can see, a poor old woman from a foreign land, but I can speak all languages. My name is Comedy. But keep your mouths closed, lest you think that I am a comestible, because I was born in Greece, and that is where I was given this name, for reasons that pertain to their language and not yours. I lived there very happily for many years. I was then taken to Rome, whereto at the time everything seemed destined to go. You too have your share of theirs, as the language you still call romance is a good witness to that. Now you would hardly believe how esteemed I was and how highly I was regarded there when I was taken to Rome. What else can I say? I became so great there that I was not far short of becoming a goddess. Then the greatness of that empire, which seemed eternal, in the end disappeared, and collapsed on itself. There I was lost with many of the fine arts, and there we remained buried for a long time, as if entombed amongst the ruins of those beautiful and magnificent buildings — and all recollection of our existence was almost gone until those to whom memory of our past had been handed on unearthed us in a race against time and brought us back to life, though downtrodden and defaced. Now that we were regaining our strengths, we heard the coming of that powerful enemy who in the past had us destroyed. You see that I am referring to war [the sack of Rome], the enemy of all good. I am running away from it. Here at the edge of the world I have found peace, but I don't know if I will enjoy some quiet [...]. I don't know whether you noticed a great change, which is that I am speaking to you in prose — be advised that I do so from the lack of metres, because you don't have those that suit me, and that is how I speak in Italy these days. In my metres, both Latin and Greek, I have always tried to be as close to prose as possible, which was how they saw me. Yes, because around here you have only recently discovered that they are verses! Your rhymes don't suit me; they are very forced and very unpleasant to the ear. My subject is the

> stuff of everyday life; I am a friend of the people, I am happy to please all [...].
> Finally, I have never been fond of obscurity nor wordplay, which amazes and
> pleases those less knowledgeable. Let me tell you — that is why I speak to you:
> so that you understand me. Those who don't wish to be understood should stop
> talking and they'd no longer burden themselves or those who listen to them.
> When I arrived in Rome I underwent changes and then against my will I had
> to let go of my choruses. One should adapt to the times, whether one likes it
> or not.]

Sá de Miranda's contacts with Giovanni Rucellai, Bembo, Sannazzaro and Ariosto during his trip in Italy were decisive to this literary experiment in comedy, and the role of the successive generations of Italian humanists in recovering classical literature is explicitly acknowledged in this prologue. The excerpt that I have selected here introduces a novel dramatic form to its audience, something which Sá de Miranda achieves with humour and a juxtaposing of his sources, Donatus, Horace and Ariosto. These would only be fully identifiable and understandable to a learned audience, a minority able to recognize the inventiveness of playwrights who were experimenting with a rediscovered and prestigious literary tradition.

Sá de Miranda drew inspiration from the prologue of Ariosto's *Cassaria* (1508), which circulated in a number of editions in prose before the author decided to rewrite it in *versi sdruccioli* in *c.* 1528–30 (i.e. after Sá de Miranda had returned to Portugal). In the prologue of the play, Comedy presents itself on stage, and defends the author's decision to compose the play in the vernacular in terms which surface in Sá de Miranda's own prologue: 'la volgar lingua di latino mista' [the vernacular, a language which is mixed with Latin] (fol. Ai^v). Comedy also defends the liberty which the author sees as his prerogative to innovate in accordance to the changes of time:

> Noua Comedia v'appresenta,
> [...] che ne mai Latine
> ne Greche lingue recitarno in scena
> parmi veder che la piu parte incline
> a riprenderla, subito ch'ho detto
> noua, senza ascoltarne mezzo o fine,
> che tal impresa non gli par soggetto
> delli moderni ingegni, e solo stima
> quel che gli antiqui han detto esser perfetto. (fol. Ai^v)[18]

[I here present you with a new comedy [...] which has never been recited in Latin or Greek on stage. I seem to see that the most part of you are inclined to criticize it as soon as I said 'new', without hearing me out to the end, since to you such an endeavour is not an appropriate subject in the eyes of the modern artists, and you only regard what the ancients have said to be perfect.]

In an epistle to Cardinal Henrique presenting his *Estrangeiros*, Sá de Miranda openly acknowledges Plautus, Terence and Ariosto as his models, and likewise defends his creative *imitatio* as authorized by literary tradition itself.[19] This too is a point recognized by Sá de Miranda's follower, António Ferreira, who, in the prologue of his *Comédia de Bristo ou do Fanchono*, praises the innovative character of his comedy, appropriate to contemporary life: 'em nossos dias vemos neste reino a honra e o louvor de quem novamente a trouve a ele, *com tanta diferença de tôdolos antigos quanta é a dos mesmos tempos'* [For today we see here in our kingdom the honour and glory of that man who recently introduced comedy, *which is as different from all the ancient comedies as the times themselves are different*] (my emphasis).[20] As will be seen, it is not just in this respect that Ariosto's work surfaces in the prologue of *Estrangeiros*.

In one of the versions of his epistle to Cardinal Henrique, Sá de Miranda defines comedy as follows: 'A comédia, tão estimada nos tempos antigos, que al disseram aqueles grandes engenhos que era senão ũa pintura da vida comum? À dos príncipes se repartiu a tragédia' [Comedy, so esteemed in ancient times, what did those great intellectuals say it was but a portrait of common life? The lives of princes pertain to tragedy].[21] This is a paraphrase of a remark of Cicero's, which is only preserved in the fragment 'De tragoedia et comoedia' by Evanthius, V.1, widely available to readers of Roman comedy in the Renaissance via Donatus's commentary on Terence.[22] The schematic distinction between the two dramatic forms, here only alluded to in regard to the characters' social status (and not the subject matter, plot or ending of the play), is typical of the Latin grammarians, and is repeated by many Renaissance dramatists in their writings. But Sá de Miranda shows that he had Donatus's text in mind (and not just a commonplace quotation) when he explains the history of the genre in Greece and Rome. His prologue follows the fragment closely, but adapted and rewritten for the stage: the complex discussion on the etymology of 'comedy' is avoided and replaced by wordplay to delight his audience ('My name is Comedy. But keep your mouths closed, lest you think that I am a comestible'). Sá de Miranda merely alludes to the existence of altars in the Roman comic stage ('I was not far short of becoming a goddess', Comedy says) — again something which is only found in the fragment by Evanthius. Finally, the disappearance of the chorus in the New Comedy is mentioned in the prologue (also explained in some detail in that fragment) as an example of the transformations which the genre has undergone through time.[23]

On the important subject of form, Sá de Miranda returns, understandably, to Ariosto: he also puts Latin and Greek verse and prose on a par, and points to the incipient development of metric forms in the vernacular as legitimizing his decision to compose the play in prose — according to Ariosto's practice during Sá de Miranda's visit to Italy. The Portuguese playwright goes further in his explicit rejection of rhyme ('versos consoantes') in the *auto* form, denounced as unpleasant to the ear ('batem muito nas orelhas') and 'forçados', i.e. artificial, and therefore unsuitable to represent the stuff of ordinary people's everyday lives.

Sá de Miranda's allusion in the prologue to the progress made in other countries with regard to the enrichment of the vernacular languages is an indication of how, for these intellectuals, *imitatio* of the classics was vital to that process. As in other parts of Europe, in Portugal too the discussion surrounding the status of the vernacular as a language of culture (and imperial power) was very much present. Portuguese intellectuals could choose to write in Portuguese, Spanish or Latin, and in the prologues of vernacular comedies linguistic choice is often discussed by playwrights in militant terms.[24] If the new humanist comedy showed a level of literary ambition which directly opposed and rejected the traditional *auto* form, that perhaps can be explained because it was the first field for literary and linguistic experimentation in the vernacular in Portugal.

The prologue of *Bristo* shows us that António Ferreira was not indifferent to the achievements of Sá de Miranda: 'Porque quem negará que na pureza de sua língua, na arte da composição naquele estilo tam cómico, no decoro das pessoas, na invenção, na gravidade, na graça, no artifício, nom possa triunfar de todos?' [For who could deny that, in the purity of his language, in the art of composition, in that truly comic style, in the decorum of his characters, in inventiveness, seriousness, grace and artifice, Sá de Miranda could triumph over all?]. Ferreira's Horatianism is clear in his praise of Sá de Miranda, but this passage also shows how (the teaching of) rhetoric was decisive in the early development of this renewed tradition of humanist drama. *Inventio, dispositio*, and *elocutio*, the first three canons of rhetoric, guide Ferreira's appreciation of the plays, and style is furthermore discussed by equally rhetorical parameters of correctness (*puritas*), propriety (*decorum*), and quality (*grauitas*, and rejecting *obscuritas*).

With regard to the function of comedy, both Ferreira and Sá de Miranda favour aesthetic pleasure as their primary concern, and there is no mention in the liminary texts and prologues that they saw it as a form of moralizing; in Sá de Miranda's words, comedy aims to 'please all'. This is an important fact to bear in mind, since this experience of individual creative freedom in the realm of classical comedy was soon replaced by a growing form of self-censorship which anticipated the institutionalized Jesuit drama and its moral and religious agenda from the mid-1550s.

Appropriately, both Sá de Miranda and Ferreira devoted great efforts to the careful revision of their writing, and this *limae labor* often took years to complete: in an illuminating, yet extreme, example, Sá de Miranda's *Os Estrangeiros* gave origin to three different versions of the play, with the same plot line and characters.[25] As T. F. Earle has shown, the much earlier first version of *Os Estrangeiros* is heavily tied to the technique of *amplificatio*, a rhetorical device much employed in Renaissance education, but as the author matured the text underwent significant revision and cutting, more in line with classical aesthetics. Amongst the material rejected by the playwright were 'the accumulation of *sententiae*, memorable and impressive quotations which illustrate and develop moral or psychological truths'.[26] This may explain the relatively static nature of the comedies of both authors, with an appreciable number of monologues and long speeches, which delay and occasionally suspend the dramatic action: adapting the classical models and their Italian continuators to an audience in sixteenth-century Portugal was far from a straightforward process. Sixteenth-century playwrights no longer thought of comedy and tragedy as narrative forms like Dante and Boccaccio, but they did not yet see them as fully *dramatic* forms, where action should take precedence over rhetorical declamation.

II.1. Defining Tragedy in Sixteenth-Century Portugal

This point has been explored in relation to the vernacular comedies of Sá de Miranda and Ferreira, as well as for the latter's tragic masterpiece, *Castro*.[27] But there has been no similar study of Teive's *Ioannes Princeps*, although his is the only known case of a sixteenth-century Portuguese writer who presents us with a discussion (albeit brief) of the concept of 'tragedy'. The *Ioannes Princeps* is a unique

98   CATARINA FOUTO

text in the panorama of humanist tragedy, the only play on a profane topic authored by a staff member of the Colégio das Artes to have survived from the times when it was a secular institution under royal privilege. Equally it is rare because it represents a contemporary historical event: the death of Prince João, the only heir to the Portuguese Crown, in 1554. This happened in the early days of January, at a time when his wife Joana, daughter of Philip II of Spain, was expecting their first child, the ill-fated Sebastião. There are many texts which commemorate the event, and which show the sadness which this sudden death brought upon the royal family and the country, and the blow it represented to different generations of humanists.

Teive's play has invariably been judged against a tradition to which it does not belong, and has been denounced as rhetorical and moralizing, as if a great deal of the literature of this period were much different. This brushing aside of the play has not taken into account a number of aspects which are of importance to ascertain its originality, as well as its shortcomings. The first is the choice of subject matter, which was the target of criticism. Secondly, Teive not only wrote a play commemorating the death of the prince — he also delivered an *oratio funebris* on this occasion, to a select audience in Coimbra. This circumstance offers a privileged opportunity to explore the relation between rhetoric and drama, and how Teive handles the same subject matter in different literary forms intended for the same audience. The two texts were subsequently printed together in the *Opuscula Aliquot* of 1558 (Salamanca), and I will attempt to show how the interaction between the *oratio* and the tragedy gives the play a critical force not yet explored by critics, as the eulogy pronounced to mark the death of the heir casts a shadow over the drama. Lastly, I shall ask if the play is as straightforwardly moralizing and trite as has been claimed, or whether Buchanan's friend was a more subtle writer than he has been given credit for.

In terms of choice of subject matter, the first tragedies printed in Portugal were mythological plays by Aires Vitoria's and Juan Cirne. These gave way to historical plays — Sá de Miranda's *Cleopatra* (now lost), Ferreira's *Castro* and Teive's *Ioannes Princeps* — and the biblical plays (exclusively in Latin) performed at the Colégio das Artes before it was handed over to the Jesuits in 1555 and their drama took centre stage in schools all over Portugal and her overseas territories. The reasons behind this shift from the 1530s to the 1550s are certainly manifold: the authors' personal taste, a growing confidence in not following in the footsteps of their literary models, a desire to experiment choosing well-known stories or entirely new ones, and an awareness of the development of a distinctively singular, national literature, inspired by the classics but not enslaved by them, whether in the vernacular or in Latin.

Unlike Erasmus or Buchanan who were drawn to translation in the first instance by their interest in developing their linguistic skills in Latin and Greek, Aires Vitória prefers to defend the role of the translator on the grounds of the moral value which could be found in classical tragedies — the argument used in the prologue of the second edition of his version of Sophocles' *Electra* is frequently used to justify the reading of non-Christian authors. There, Aires Vitoria revealingly conflates the meanings of *fabula*, 'story', and *fabella*, 'moral fable': 'acho nam haver aí nenhũa fábula escrita por qualquer daqueles antigos poetas, que eram grandes filósofos,

The Reinvention of Classical Comedy and Tragedy in Portugal   99

da qual nam possamos tirar grande dotrina moral' [I do not think that there is a story (*fabula*) written by one of those ancient poets, who were great philosophers, from which we cannot draw great moral teaching],[28] and thus he perpetuates the identification made by the grammarians Donatus and Diomedes who considered tragedy and comedy as varieties of the single genus *fabula*, a story with a clear moral truth. As Donald Stone Jr points out, this was one of the decisive elements in the perpetuation of 'that medieval tendency to moralize through art [...] that continued into the seventeenth century'.[29] It is worth pointing out in this respect that amongst the most popular characters of the first sixteenth-century tragedies are Sophonisba, Cleopatra, Medea, and Hecuba, all of whom are to be found among the morally improving biographies in Boccaccio's *De Claris Mulieribus* (1374). Both Petrarch and Boccaccio authored biographies of illustrious men and women, mythical, biblical, historical, past and present, in which a distinctive moral portrait of the protagonist was presented. As Stone argues, this moral lesson would also feature prominently in the sources used, making the continuity between classical, medieval and Renaissance literature an important, if often unacknowledged, dynamic of the development of humanist literature.[30] Whilst in comedy authors were free to create their own plot lines (even if often resorting to *contaminatio* of classical and Renaissance authors, especially Roman), this was not the case when it came to tragedy, as Renaissance authors would know from their reading of Donatus's commentary to Terence:

> Inter tragoediam autem et comoediam cum multa tum imprimis hoc distat, quod in comoedia mediocres fortunae hominum, parvi impetus periculorum, lactique sunt exitus actionum; at in tragoedia omnia contra: ingentes personae, magni timores, exitus funesti habentur. et illic prima turbulenta, tranquilla ultima, in tragoedia contrario ordine res aguntur. Tum quod in tragoedia fugienda vita, in comoedia capessenda exprimitur. Postremo quod omnis comoedia de fictis est argumentis; tragoedia saepe de historia fide petitur.[31]

> [Many things distinguish comedy from tragedy, especially the fact that comedy involves characters with middling fortunes, dangers of small moment, and actions with happy endings, whereas in tragedy it is just the opposite: imposing persons, great fears, and disastrous endings. Furthermore, in comedy what is turbulent at first becomes tranquil at the end; in tragedy, the action is just the reverse. Then too, tragedy presents the sort of life that one seeks to escape from, whereas the life of comedy is portrayed as desirable. Finally, all comedy is based on invented stories, whereas tragedy is often derived from historical truth.]

It should be pointed out that 'historical truth' meant that the plot of any tragedy should be faithful to its tradition and known to its audience, leaving the playwright to handle the writing of the characters' speeches and the dramatic denouement. The question of whether to favour old or new themes was not an obvious one for writers of this period and this ongoing debate is echoed in the prologue of Buchanan's *Baptistes*, a playwright whose work was well known to Teive:

> Nam si vetustam fabulam quis proferat,
> turbant molesti, tussiunt et nauseant.
> at si novam quis attulit, tum protinus
> vetera requirunt comprobant laudant amant.
> illiberali respuunt fastidio

> nova et, priusquam noscere queant, exigent,
> recteque dicta interpretationibus
> vitiant malignis, Omnia in peius trahunt;
> ipsique somno dediti ac ignaviae,
> vacui laboris invident laboribus
> aliorum, et omnem collocant operam suam
> ut deprehendant quod queant reprehendere.
> si quis sit error, antevortunt Lyncea
> visu, notaque perlinunt censoria;
> bene dicta surdis auribus praetervolant.
> horum severa supercilia nihil moror
> tristemque vultus taetrici arrogantiam.[32]

[If anyone produces an ancient plot, they [critics] make annoying interruptions, they cough and retch. But if anyone introduces a new one, they at once demand and approve and praise and love the old. They reject what is new with niggardly contempt, and drive it off-stage before they can make its acquaintance; they taint correct expressions by malicious interpretations. They criticize everything as inferior. They have abandoned themselves to sleep and sloth, and with no work to occupy them they are envious of the toils of others, and apply all their efforts to finding something to censure. Should there be an error, they excel Lynceus in sharpness of sight, and mark it with the censors' blot. Things happily expressed they flit by with deaf ears. The stern brows of these men and the pained arrogance of their crabbed countenances I disregard.]

The preference for the treatment of novel themes (i.e. not to be found in Greek or Roman tragedy) must have come as a valid option and a natural choice for those humanists who, like Ferreira and Teive, wished to write plays that were ultimately appealing to their audiences. Biblical and historical subject matter would be more credible, but even when attempting to discuss questions or events relevant to their times, authors avoided representing contemporary subjects and events — which is typical of self-censorship practices of this time in Portugal. Thus, in his *Castro* António Ferreira stages the conflict brought about by the Machiavellian exercise of political power, but the action takes place in a comfortably distant medieval Portugal. This is not, however, the case in the *Ioannes Princeps*.

The medieval grammarians and Horace offered no indication regarding this particular matter. Their words provided a comfortable (yet vague) definition of tragedy revisited by Renaissance playwrights and intellectuals, as can be seen in the summary exposé by the reputed humanist Josse Bade, in his printed edition of Terence (1502):

> Tragoedia est quidam ludus metrice compositus in quo principaliter ostenditur fragilitas humanarum rerum. Nam reges et principes qui se primum perbeatos et perquam felices arbitrantur, in fine tragoediarum in extremam miseriam redacti exclamationibus et dedignationibus caelum et terram confundunt, omniaque et caelestia et terrestria incusant.[33]

> [Tragedy is a metrical play in which the fragility of human affairs is mainly shown. For kings and princes, who initially considered themselves truly blessed and pre-eminently fortunate, at the end of tragedies are brought into extreme misery, moving heaven and earth with their wails and cries, and assailing all things celestial and terrestrial.]

The distinctive features of tragedy, then, are its form, the social status of its characters, a basic notion of how the reversal of fortune instructs men about the ephemeral nature of all things human, a sad ending and lamentations in an appropriately solemn style. In this light, Teive sees as valid his experiment in adapting a contemporary historical event, and defends his originality against *real* criticism. In the prologue of the *Opuscula Aliquot* he argues against his traditionalist detractors:

> Quibus etiam tragoediam addidi de acerbissimo illo principis nostri obitu, quam ante actis etiam illis temporibus exaraueram. [...] Tametsi satis intelligebam in grauium quorundam censorum reprehensiones me posse incidere, qui de hujusmodi argumento se nunquam tragoediam scriptam vidisse affirmare poterant, quibus nihil probatur, nec quicquam aequo animo ferendum putant, nisi quod ab antiquis scriptoribus usurpatum atque observatum vident. Et nonnunquam accidit, ut quod per ignauiam videre desierunt, perinde ac si nusquam reperiri posset, nescio qua freti authoritate temere reprehendunt. [...] In quo quidem scriptionis genere, quod ab antiquis imprimis celebratum et excultum, a nostris pene desertum ac neglectum est, in illo docendi munere, quod per multos annos obiui, me exercui, multaque argumenta ex sacris litteris, nonnulla ex profanis collegi, quae rerum magnitudine prope incredibili et inaudita nouitate admirationem excitant, multaque vitae documenta continent, quae tamen in publicum prodire non audent horum hominum reprehensionibus perterritae.[34]

> [To these [texts], I added the tragedy about that most grievous death of our prince, which I had written before as events were unfolding. [...] Notwithstanding that, I knew well that I would be subject to the reprimands of certain harsh critics, who had the opportunity to say that they had never seen a tragedy written about a subject such as this, they who approve of nothing, nor think that anything should be tolerated patiently, unless what they see has been employed and observed by ancient authors. And sometimes it happens that because they ceased to see it due to their laziness, as if it could be found nowhere, they condemn me thoughtlessly, relying on I know not what authority. [...] In my function as a teacher, in which I was engaged for many years, I practised precisely this literary genre [i.e. tragedy], which was especially celebrated and cultivated by the ancient writers, almost forgotten and abandoned by us, and I collected many stories from the Holy Scriptures, several from profane works, which rouse admiration for their almost incredible greatness and unheard of novelty, and which contain many examples for life. These, however, dare not come before the public, terrified by the reprimands of these men.]

Teive refers to the novelty of drama in Portugal, and uses his prestige as a staff member at the College de Guyenne and later at the Colégio das Artes to remind the readers of his extensive and successful curriculum as a playwright. At the time of the publication, Teive had already embraced the religious life after his dealings with the Inquisition (thus achieving a comfortable form of subsistence), and in this passage the emphasis on the choice of subject matter from the Holy Scriptures may be interpreted as a public display of orthodoxy. But there is more to it than meets the eye.

Teive's choice was acceptable in the light of a passage of *Ars Poetica* (285–88): 'Nil intemptatum nostri liquere poetae, | nec minimum meruere decus vestigia Graeca | ausi deserere et *celebrare domestica facta*, | *vel qui praetextas vel qui docuere togatas*' [Our own poets have left no style untried, nor has least honour been earned when they have dared to leave the footsteps of the Greek *and sing of deeds at home, whether they have put native tragedies or native comedies upon the stage*] (my emphasis). Seneca's *Octauia* could have provided a classical precedent in Teive's mind, but this is speculation as he makes no mention of it in the prologue. The fact that his detractors quote no *authoritas* to question his choice of a contemporary topic is an important point in Teive's defence in the prologue. His critics are denounced as subservient imitators of classical drama, supporters of worn-out subject matter, whereas Teive presents himself to his international readership as an innovative playwright. If it true that Teive composed no tragedies on a classical or pagan theme, we nevertheless learn from his own words that the reason for this is an underlying Horatian ideal: for the author, plays should combine novelty, seek to arouse admiration and pleasure from the audience, and at the same time, fulfil an important didactic function. Tragedy served a moral purpose, and the case of the *Ioannes Princeps* is no exception, as will be seen.

Teive was the only Portuguese writer to commemorate the death of the prince in a play. Considering that other writers opted for different forms of lyric poetry to do so, what might have prompted him to choose this genre? One of the reasons is the hope of different generations of humanists surrounding the young prince: despite his tender age, Prince João was already hailed as a new Maecenas and there is evidence to suggest that he greatly appreciated drama, as Ferreira's debut comedy was offered to the heir. But this alone does not explain it.

II.2. Drama, Rhetoric and Moralizing: Virtues and Vices of Teive's *Ioannes Princeps*

The heir's sudden death took the nation by surprise: a blow to one of the greatest in the kingdom, whose recent and happy marriage and impending fatherhood were cut short, leaving the desolated king and queen to bury their last of their nine children, and the country hopeless and anxious as to its own future. The heir's premature death was caused by illness, not by any act of passion or crime to be atoned. The prince had made no decisions in ignorance, no rash promises or impious remarks, nor was he a victim of adverse circumstances. However, in Teive's mind it was not significant that the prince himself had not played any role in this sudden calamity, as the general outline of the prince's biography fits neatly with the theme of the reversal of fortune, so dear to tragedy.

The plot of the Teive's play is easily summarized.[35] In Act I, the king and queen are the main characters on stage, and the atmosphere of foreboding is introduced with the opening speech by Queen Catherine (ll. 27–96), who speaks of Death's visit in her dreams, taking the lives of her 'lumina' [children] one by one, before launching a last fatal blow against her only surviving child, the prince. As pointed out by John R. C. Martyn, the dream is closely indebted to a similar dream in Buchanan's *Jephthes* (ll. 95–102), and this connection is furthermore reinforced by similar parallels between the Scotsman's play and António Ferreira's *Castro*.[36] While the main body of the play is composed in iambic trimeters throughout, the choral ode which contrasts the tyrant to the ideal king is in anapaestic dimeters, a favourite

THE REINVENTION OF CLASSICAL COMEDY AND TRAGEDY IN PORTUGAL 103

in Senecan choral odes.[37] Act II features Eubularchus and Philanax, the prince's faithful advisor and his closest friend, as well as the Medicus who announces that all hope of saving the heir is lost. The third act functions as an interlude. Princess Joana confesses her love for the prince, and her fear that some tragedy may have happened, because he has not paid her any visit for several days. The Nurse tries to comfort her, and reminds the princess that she should keep calm now that she is entering the final days of her pregnancy. A choral ode in Sapphic stanzas singing the power of Love (a parallel with Act III of *Thyestes*) closes this act. Eubularchus and Philanax return to the scene in Act IV, announcing that the prince has died, and how the news must be kept secret so that Princess Joana does not become aware of her husband's death. Closing the sequence of events, now that the death of the prince has been announced, the choral ode of Act IV is composed in anapaestic dimeters, mirroring the ode of Act I.[38] The final act of the play brings together on stage several characters, always in pairs, in a sequence of scenes presenting first Eubularchus and Philanax, then in a second scene (in iambic trimeters) the chorus and the queen, who stand before the coffin and take turns in lamenting the death of the prince. The final dialogue features the inconsolable queen and the king who acts as a model of temperance at such troubled times for the family and the nation. The closing stichomythic sequence of the play serves as an uplifting moment where king and queen invoke God and ask for His protection, while the birth of a male heir is anxiously expected.

The modern editor and the translators of the play have noted that there is no indication of a division between the choral ode of Act IV and the dialogue between two of the characters which immediately follows it. To the neo-Latinist playwright the five-act structure was not compulsory, and in *Jephtes* and *Baptistes* Buchanan follows the structure of Euripidean drama, separating the episodes of the play with interventions from the chorus. Yet, there are good reasons to think that Teive had in mind the advice of the *Ars Poetica*: 'Neve minor neu sit quinto productior actu | fabula quae posci volt et spectata reponi' [Let no play be either shorter or longer than five acts] (190–91). The most influential classical playwright of the period, Seneca, follows the five-act pattern, and the chiastic structure of the metrics of the choral odes in the *Ioannes Princeps* points to Seneca too: the anapaestic dimeters in the choral odes of Acts I and IV mark the sequence of premonition and death of the prince, contrasting with the absence of a closing choral ode in Act V. Teive is also careful not to have more than three characters interacting on stage at a time (*Ars Poetica*, 192), and he appears to follow Horace closely when using the chorus as an integral part of the plot, and not just as a spectator and commentator on the unfolding events. The best example of the complete transformation of the chorus takes place at the heart of Act V of the play, where the inconsolable queen and the chorus mourn the death of the prince in a continuous dialogue in iambic trimeters.

At the level of composition, Teive's play is largely Senecan, and his contemporaries were sensitive to this. In an epistle preserved in MS. F.G. 6368 BNL, entitled *Carmina de poetis Lusitanis ad Ignatium Moralem*, the neo-Latin poet Pedro Sanches lamented Teive's death in the following terms:

> Tevius attollit speciosae frontis honorem,
> qui Senecam verbis, et multo pondere rerum
> Pene pari sequitur gressu, paribusque cothurnis.
>
> [Teive lifts the honour of his beautiful forehead,
> he who follows Seneca almost with equal pace, and with equal buskin
> in the words, and in the weightiness of his topics.]

The exemplary Stoic reaction of the king and queen in the face of a political and private catastrophe reveals the appreciation of a man of the Renaissance for Seneca's work, and reflects the identification at that time of the playwright with the moral philosopher. But at the level of verbal expression and metrical practice, the *Ioannes Princeps* is equally indebted to the Roman playwright. Like Seneca, Teive favours the use of the same metre throughout each of the choral odes, particularly in his choice of anapaestic dimeters. Even the exceptional use of Sapphic stanzas in the choral ode of Act III replicates the first half of the metrical pattern adopted in a choral ode of Seneca's *Medea* (ll. 579 ff.). Comparing the recitatives and choral odes of both authors, it is possible to say that Teive's metrical technique in the play is, on the whole, Senecan, whereas his later *Epodon Iambicorum libri tres* (Lisbon, 1565) is more Horatian. In fact, Elaine Fantham's conclusions on Seneca's metrical technique in his *Troades* would suit Teive's *Ioannes Princeps* but for one or two aspects.[39] The use of stichomythia in the play is essentially Senecan, as are the changes of speaker — the antilabes, which always coincide with the caesura, never occur in a resolved foot.[40] From a selection of 200 lines from the five acts of the play, it is possible to draw more conclusions: like in Seneca, there is a clear distinction between the even and the odd feet of the line. The first foot is almost always a spondee, or more rarely an anapaest or a dactyl, whereas the second foot is almost always a pure iamb. In Seneca too, this is equally the most common position for a tribrach. The third foot is predominantly a spondee, but, unlike Seneca, there is a high number of iambs in this third foot. Again, an iamb will almost always occupy the fourth foot of the line, followed by a tribrach. Spondees are predominantly used in the fifth foot which has an unusually high number of iambs, replicating the metrical pattern of the third foot. However, Teive does use a sequence of two iambs in the fifth and sixth foot of the line, something which Seneca never does — he may have been influenced by Horace's iambic trimeters, which do not conform to this principle. These conclusions correspond essentially to the best practice of neo-Latin playwrights of the time, illustrated by Buchanan's plays as Stephen Berkowitz has shown.[41]

From form, let us move onto context and content, which brings us to the second issue to explore in this section of the chapter: the eulogy delivered by Teive before the entire humanist congregation in Coimbra, the *oratio funebris* which was published in the *Opuscula Aliquot*, immediately preceding the *Ioannes Princeps*. It had been the author's intention to have the play performed, as he informs us, which did not happen for reasons not entirely known. It could be that he missed the opportunity when the dead heir's son, Sebastião, was born, to the relief of the nation; or it could be that the criticism of the play prevented this from happening — Teive seems to suggest that this was the case in the prologue discussed earlier.

Teive's choice of a contemporary historical subject may have challenged the more

THE REINVENTION OF CLASSICAL COMEDY AND TRAGEDY IN PORTUGAL 105

conservative scholars. In his literary production, Teive rarely draws closely from classical, medieval and even Renaissance writers, and he is essentially an original author — his debt to specific literary models is more explicit at the level of metrical technique and structural allusion and emulation, as we have seen in relation to Seneca and Buchanan. It seems, however, unlikely that literary disputes alone could have prevented the performance of the play, or sparked such an unusual ferocity in an otherwise cordial soul as Teive. We do best to turn our attention to the *oratio funebris*, and its relation to the tragedy.

In his sober (and yet personal and heartfelt) eulogy to the prince, Teive advises his audience to grieve but to accept God's will — something his listeners would expect to hear from Teive, who at the time had already embraced the religious life. He argues, fittingly for a man of the cloth, that *fatum* is nothing other than God's spoken word (establishing a false etymology between *fatum*, 'fate', and *fari*, 'to speak', fol. 72^r). And yet, other aspects of this *oratio* go well beyond the conventions of the genre, and dwell on political, and even personal, issues close to Teive's heart. The rather unusual existence of an oration and a tragedy based on the same subject offers a unique opportunity to observe how the author handles his topic. The following comparative analysis illuminates to what extent the writing of the play is indebted to the set of rhetorical exercises known as *progymnasmata*, which were vital to the humanistic education. As one would expect both texts incorporate the *encomium* of the prince: in the *oratio* it is appropriately the first topic immediately after the exordium, and as Quintilian recommends in his *Institutio Oratoria* (2.4.20), the ancestry of the heir, his early years, upbringing and education are celebrated (fols 64^r–65^r). The praise of his physical beauty and moral virtues follows after that, and paves the way to the predicted future glory of the defunct prince (fols 65^r–66^r) — Teive had to improvise, since the prince had died a very young man, before being crowned, and recalling his *res gesta* would be inadequate. The *oratio* ends with a final prayer (fols 77^{r-v}), recommended by rhetoricians as an appropriate end to an encomium, and the tragedy also comes to a close with the king exhorting the audience to join him in prayer for God's help and mercy (ll. 1360–65). *Narratio* (Quint. 2.4.2, 2.4.15) and *prosopopoeia* (Quint. 9.2.29–38) feature prominently in early modern tragedy and in Filanax's speeches recording the final moments of the prince's life the exchange of the last words between father and son is reproduced in direct speech (ll. 989–1057). The vivid *descriptio* of the prince's ailment and his physical symptoms explained by the Doctor (ll. 383–450) are a good example of Quintilian's exposition on *ekphrasis* (*Inst.* 9.2.40–44), and would satisfy the curiosity of the people as to what had caused the death of the prince. The dialogue between the nurse and the princess (especially ll. 673–708) is constructed as a *refutatio* (Quint. 2.4.18–19), but the most illuminating example of this rhetorical exercise occurs at the end of the play, when Queen Catherine is exhorted to abandon her tears and grief, to accept the death as God's will, and to remain steadfast for the good of the people (ll.1307–59). The tense stichomythic exchange between king and queen mirrors the same argument presented in the *oratio* and the same logical and pathetic arguments are used, in both texts, near to the close. The practice of including 'commonplaces' in early modern tragedy has been very often condemned as empty rhetorical display, but, as Ann Moss reminds us, these were important means of communication and persuasion, a cultural code shared by writers and their public which fulfilled a specific ideological function.[42] If the contrasting choruses of Act I exploring the nature of kingly rule by means of opposition between the ideal king and the tyrant may come across as somewhat banal, the chorus of Act II (ll. 493–525, translated at the end of this chapter) shows how Teive could appropriate a commonplace such as the 'weakness of human nature' and develop it in meaningful terms for his audience. On this occasion, the maidens of the chorus affirm that all human life is ephemeral and feeble against the superior powers of nature, the evil caused by other men, and the diseases which affect young and old alike. Instead of discussing such reflections in broad general terms, the chorus identifies the extreme circumstances experienced by the crew of ships sailing in the vast Portuguese empire, the hunger and diseases suffered, and particular attention is paid to the loss of life in shipwrecks. The use of pastoral *topoi* gains further contemporary resonance when these disasters are explicitly exposed as a consequence of greed, licit *and illicit* enrichment, theft, pillage and war, and the catastrophe that affects the royal palace is linked to the events taking place throughout the empire. The publication of this play in Salamanca, distant from the Court circles, may have been imposed by the circumstances of the author's life, but it guaranteed that censorship could not silence the text definitively — as some of the audience in Coimbra seem to have wished.

As I have argued above, Teive's eulogy is, in many respects, conventional, but other aspects of this *oratio* go beyond the conventions of the genre. An important one was how to approach (and explain) the death of the royal couple's children, who had all died young, and were therefore free from sin. The devout king and queen were particularly shaken by the demise of the eldest prince, but the representation of this family tragedy had obvious political implications. If (as Teive assures us in his *Oratio*) the disaster could not be regarded as a punishment of any member of the royal family still living, and if the virtuous young prince himself could not have deserved such an untimely death, then how to explain and come to terms with the tragedy? The central section of the *oratio* delves into this particular subject, and makes up a total of almost a fifth of the text (fols 66^r–68^v). Those who heard the speech at first hand would not have expected the humanist to argue at such length and so outspokenly that the death of the heir was God's punishment for the sins of the Portuguese people. Teive's countrymen are reminded that the Portuguese had been blind to God's displeasure, and continued to act sinfully despite the warning signs manifested in the deaths that afflicted the royal household. Far from representing his countrymen as the forefront of the expansion of the Catholic faith or as paradigms of morally correct behaviour, as some contemporary writers do, Teive denounces jealousy, pride, greed, appetites, insolence, impudence and calumny. The preoccupation with slander is particularly noteworthy in the *oratio* (though Teive never names names, fol. 67^v), and may be explained by the recent experience of his trial at the hands of the Inquisition, falsely accused of Protestant leanings; in one of the hearings of his trial he complained that his countrymen are very prone to this type of defamation, often motivated by personal envy.[43] But Teive's concern was less with settling old scores than with the moral standing of the Portuguese,

THE REINVENTION OF CLASSICAL COMEDY AND TRAGEDY IN PORTUGAL   107

for him an increasingly important topic, and the criticism directed at his audience on this occasion was later expanded in works such as the *Institutio Sebastiani Primi* (a didactic work modelled on Erasmus's *Institutio Principis Christiani*), also published in the *Opuscula Aliquot* of 1558. In the *Institutio* Teive explicitly associates this moral and social degeneration to the overseas expansion and to the fast and easy profits to be made from the trade in exotic and luxurious goods — with great cost in human lives (fol. 52^r–52^v). This is an important aspect of his *oratio* which made its way into the play, significantly in the intervention of the chorus of Act II (previously discussed), but also fleetingly in the queen's emotional scene in front of the coffin of her son, when she admits the possibility that the prince's death was in fact the people's fault (ll. 1215–16). Yet again, the same idea resurfaces in the only soliloquy by the king, D. João, in the closing act of the play (ll. 1264–89, translated at the end of the chapter). The representation of the monarch as a *pater patriae* concerned with the destiny of his subjects, although a commonplace, has a powerful impact at this stage of the play: for the first time the circumscribed atmosphere of the Court is widened to include the nation, and the king, in a confessional passage, denies any responsibility for the deaths of so many Portuguese in shipwrecks and wars overseas, in pursuit of wealth. Significantly, this is the only long soliloquy in the play after the revelation of the death of the prince.

Critics have long pointed to the moralizing attitude of the play, namely 'the King's calm acceptance of calamity' and his 'Stoicism in the face of trouble',[44] and these observations are reasonable. However, there is more subtlety in the *Ioannes Princeps* than has been generally conceded: the *oratio funebris* which precedes the play in the *Opuscula Aliquot* affects the interpretation of the tragedy, and veiled criticisms in the interventions of the chorus and the king's speech gain intensity when read in its light. The king's Stoic attitude is commendable, and the queen's distress and grief are understandable, but the reader/spectator would no doubt feel uncomfortable at the king's monologue and be led to reflect on the public sins affecting Portuguese social life. The play's criticism of Portuguese contemporary life has not been identified or explored by critics, but this is one of the most unsettling aspects of the play, especially when considering it was written at a time of prevailing dogmatic orthodoxy in all spheres of Portuguese life. Undoubtedly, a sick prince on his deathbed could hardly have made for great dramatic action, but there is another important reason for the play's lack of success: because it uses a very specific historical episode and social context to fully achieve its subtle moralizing effect, it fails to attain the universalism which lies at the heart of classical tragedy.

Appendix

Actus Secundus

Chorus: Mortalis grauibus cincta periculis
uita est, siue oculis ignea sidera
lucentesque poli suspicias globos.
Hinc aestus rabidi, hinc aspera frigora
et nimbis tumidis, et gelida niue,
uentorum hinc furiis cuncta secantibus,
tempestas oritur. Vasta quid aequora
uerbis commemorem turbine fluctuum
concussa, aetheriam quae modo regiam
tangunt, ad Stygios nunc fugiunt lacus?
Vt qui ueliuolum per mare nauigant,
uiuos sit dubium, an dicere mortuos
possis, quod miseri funere ab impio
uno absint digito: si modo funeris
mors nomen capiat, qua nihil est ferum,
nil crudele magis. Ne memorem asperam
sub Cancro rabiem, quam miseri ferunt;
ne frigus memorem sub pluuialibus
Haedis neue grauem ac terribilem famem,
dum scindunt tabula pertenui freta,
ut cernant alium caelo alio polum,
per fas perque nefas ut cumulent opes,
quae sub Tartareas nos rapiunt aquas.
Aegri terram homines hanc humilem
                         incolunt,
ex qua mille homini pernicies fluunt,
ex qua mille lues milleque toxica,
fraudes, insidiae, furta, doli, neces
et spurcae innumeris criminibus manus
et Mars sanguineis agminibus furens,
aequans cuncta solo, moenibus efferus
nec parcens ualidis nec nitidis agris.
Hic uirtus uitium est, dedecus est decus;
hic laus uera sequi turpia crimina.

                               (ll. 493–525)

[Act II

Chorus: The life of mortals is surrounded by grave dangers, whether one looks up to the scintillating stars or to the sparkling spheres of the firmament. It is from there that the rabid summer heat proceeds, from there the harsh cold of winter, with swollen clouds and frosty snow, from there that storms arise, with the fury of the winds cutting through everything. With what words shall I evoke the vast ocean, agitated by the waves in a whirlwind, which at times reach the heavenly Court, and at others precipitate themselves towards the Stygian lakes? As such, one doubts whether to call those who navigate through the sail-covered oceans 'alive' or 'dead', for those wretches are one step away from an impious burial: if the word burial holds for a death that is more fierce and cruel than anything else. Neither will I recall the fierce heat that they endure at the tropic of Cancer; nor will I recall the cold under the rain-bringing Kids, nor the burdensome and terrible famine, while they plough through the sea in fragile wooden hulls, so they may see another region under another sky, so they may lawfully and unlawfully accumulate riches which precipitate us into the Tartarean waters. Miserable mortals inhabit this humble earth, whence a thousand calamities arise for man, whence a thousand plagues, and a thousand poisons, deceits, snares, thefts, deceptions, violent deaths and hands stained by countless crimes, and furious Mars with his blood-stained troops, razing everything to the ground, sparing neither the solid walls which he brings to ruin nor the fruitful fields. Here, virtue is vice, dishonour is honour, here true praise follows in the footsteps of despicable crimes.]

Actus Quintus

Rex: O sors acerba! Cur adeo saeuo impetu
adeoque ualidis deicere conatibus,
inimica, curas pectoris robur mei?
Sed firma mentis arx superbis machinis
usquam domari qui potest? O impia,
o saeua rerum domina! Quamquam
                    incusseris
tam saepe nobis multa et alta uulnera,
nullum fatebor grauius atque acerbius
mihi contigisse: mentis hoc ab intimos
abiit recessus. Tot mare obruit uiros,
tot opes uorauit totque puppes naufragas
submersit undis Indicis ac Persicis,
gazis refertas! Additae his clades malis
aliae fuere, quas modo Indus decolor,
modo fera uidit Lybia, quondam uiribus
superata nostris. Haec quidem acriter
                    animum
punxere, fateor, quae meo quia uitio
non contigerunt, pertuli multo aequius.
sunt rebus etiam liberorum funera
fratrumque multa, ceu cumulus, his addita,
nataeque maximae illius, quae Caroli
locata nato principi illustrissimo,
moriens nepotem praebuit parentibus
regnoque Hibero principem. Haec quidem
                    aspera
ac uix ferenda contigerunt iam mihi,
sed clade tanta hac nil fuit crudelius.
                (1264–89)

[Act v

King: Oh, cruel fortune! Why do you seek to bring down the vigour of my spirit with such ruthless impetus and with such strong blows? But how can the stronghold of the mind with its splendid devices ever be overcome? O impious, o ruthless mistress of things! Even though you have often inflicted upon me countless and deep wounds, I will confess that none more serious and crueller has hit me: it has penetrated into the deepest depths of my mind. So many men has the sea swallowed, so many riches has it devoured, and so many shipwrecked sterns has it submerged, filled with treasures, under the waves of the Indic and the Persian Gulf! To these misfortunes other calamities were added, witnessed at times by the swarthy Indus, at others by the savage Lybia, once defeated by our might. These events, I admit, troubled my mind greatly, but because it was not my fault they came to pass, I endured them much more patiently. To these, the many deaths of children and brothers were also added, and further to this, that of our eldest daughter, married to the most illustrious prince, son of Emperor Charles, who as she died left a son to her parents, and a prince to the Iberian kingdom. These events, bitter and difficult to endure, have already happened to me, but nothing was crueller than this great misfortune.]

110   CATARINA FOUTO

Bibliography

ALVES, HÉLIO, *Camões, Corte-Real e o sistema da epopeia quinhentista* (Coimbra: Imprensa da Universidade de Coimbra, 2001), pp. 105–23

ARIOSTO, LUDOVICO, *Comedia di messer Lodouico Ariosto intitolata Cassaria, con l'argumento aggiunto et non piu stampato* (Vinegia: Nicolo di Aristotile di Ferrara detto Zoppino, 1538)

BERKOWITZ, STEPHEN BENNET, 'A critical edition of George Buchanan's *Baptistes* and of the anonymous *Tyrannicall-government anatomized*' (unpublished doctoral thesis, Harvard University, 1986)

BISHOP, J. DAVID, 'The Meaning of the Choral Meters in Senecan Tragedy', *Rheinisches Museum für Philologie*, 111.3 (1968), 197–219

BORGES MACEDO, ANTÓNIO, 'Livros impressos em Portugal no século XVI: interesses e formas de mentalidade', *Arquivos do Centro Cultural Português*, 9 (1975), 183–221

BRANDÃO, MÁRIO, ed., 'O processo na Inquisição de Mestre Diogo de Teive', *Notícias Cronológicas da Universidade de Coimbra*, 4 (1943), 1–180

BUCHANAN, GEORGE, *Tragedies*, ed. by Peter Sharratt and Patrick Walsh (Edinburgh: Scottish Academic Press, 1983)

BUESCU, ANA, 'Aspectos do bilinguismo português-castelhano na Época Moderna', *Hispania* 64.1 (2004), 13–38

CARDINALI, GIACOMO, and GIANNI GUASTELLA, *Le rinascite della tragedia: origini classiche e tradizioni europee* (Rome: Carocci, 2006)

CRAWFORD, JAMES P., *Spanish Drama before Lope de Vega* (Philadelphia: University of Pennsylvania Press, 1968)

DE CASTRO, ANÍBAL, *Retórica e teorização literária em Portugal: do humanismo ao neoclassicismo* (Coimbra: Imprensa da Universidade, 1973)

—— 'Aquiles Estaço, o primeiro comentador da Arte Poética de Horácio', *Arquivos do Centro Cultural Português*, 10 (1976), 8–102

—— 'La Poétique et la Rhétorique dans la pédagogie et dans la littérature de l'Humanisme portugais', in *L'Humanisme portugais et l'Europe*, ed. by José Pina Martins (Paris: Centro Cultural Português), pp. 699–722

—— 'Os códigos poéticos em Portugal do Renascimento ao Barroco. Seus fundamentos. Seus conteúdos. Sua evolução', *Revista da Universidade de Coimbra*, 31 (1985), 505–31

DONATUS, *Aeli Donati quod fertur Commentum Terenti*, ed. by Paul Wesser (Leipzig: Teubner, 1902)

EARLE, THOMAS F., 'António Ferreira's *Castro*: Tragedy at the Cross-Roads', in *Portuguese Humanism and the Republic of Letters*, ed. by M. Berbara and K. Enenkel (Leiden and Boston, MA: Brill, 2012), pp. 289–318

—— 'The Two Versions of *Os Estrangeiros*', in *Culture and Society in Habsburg Spain*, ed. by N. Griffin et al. (London: Tamesis, 2001), pp. 35–44

—— 'Rhetoric and Scenic Form: The Castro, Act IV, Scene 1', in *Studies in Portuguese Literature and History in honour of Luís de Sousa Rebelo*, ed. by Helder Macedo (London: Tamesis Books, 1992), pp. 139–47

FANTHAM, ELAINE, 'Introductio' to *Seneca's Troades* (Princeton, NJ: Princeton University Press, 1982), pp. 3–124

FERREIRA, ANTÓNIO, *La Comédie de Bristo ou l'Entremetteur*, ed. by Adrien Roig (Paris: Presses Universitaires de France, 1973)

—— *Castro*, in *Poemas Lusitanos*, ed. by Thomas F. Earle (Lisbon: Fundação Calouste Gulbenkian, 2000), pp. 379 — 460

FERREIRA DE VASCONCELOS, JORGE, *Eufrosina* (Coimbra: João de Barreira, 1555)

KELLY, HENRY A., *Ideas and Forms of Tragedy from Aristotle to the Middle Ages* (Cambridge: Cambridge University Press, 1993)

LANSON, GUSTAVE, *Esquisse d'une histoire de la tragédie française* (New York: Columbia University Press, 1920)

LAWTON, HAROLD WALTER, *Handbook of French Renaissance Dramatic Theory* (Manchester: Manchester University Press, 1949)

MARTYN, JOHN R. C., 'The Influence of Buchanan and Teive', in António Ferreira, *The Tragedy of Ines de Castro*, trans. by John R. C. Martyn (Coimbra: Imprensa da Universidade de Coimbra, 1987), pp. 137–57

MENÉNDEZ PELAYO, MARCELINO, *Historia de las ideas estéticas en España* (Madrid: C.S.I.C., 1883–91)

MOREIRA DE SÁ, ARTUR, 'Livros de uso de Frei Diogo de Murça', *Boletim da Biblioteca de Coimbra*, 33 (1977), 69–109

MOSS, ANN, *Printed Common-Place Books and the Structuring of Renaissance Thought* (Oxford: Oxford University Press, 1996)

NASCIMENTO, AIRES AUGUSTO, 'A livraria de D. Teodósio I, Duque de Bragança', *Congresso de História no IV Centenário do Seminário de Évora. Actas, vols I–II* (Évora: Instituto Superior de Teologia — Seminário Maior de Évora, 1994), 209–20

PEREIRA, BELMIRO F., 'A livraria de Aquiles Estaco, *librorum uenator et helluo*', *Humanitas*, 45 (1993), 255–306

SÁ DE MIRANDA, FRANCISCO DE, *Comédias*, ed. by José Camões and Thomas F. Earle (Lisbon: Imprensa Nacional — Casa da Moeda, 2013)

STONE JR., DONALD, *French Humanist Tragedy: A Reassessment* (Manchester: Manchester University Press, 1974)

TEIVE, DIOGO DE, *Opuscula Aliquot* (Salamanca: Heirs of Juan de Junta, 1558)

—— *Tragédia do Príncipe João*, ed. by Nair de Castro Soares (Coimbra: Centro de Estudos Clássicos e Humanísticos — Universidade de Coimbra, 1977).

—— *Obra Completa*, trans. by António Guimarães Pinto (Lisbon: Esfera do Caos, 2011)

Tragedia de los amores de Eneas y de la reina Dido, ed. by J. E. Gillet and E. B. Williams, *PMLA*, 46 (1931), 353–431

WEINBERG, BERNARD, *Trattati di poetica e retorica del Cinquecento* (Bari: Laterza, 1974)

Websites

Teatro de Autores Portugueses do Século XVI — Centro de Estudos de Teatro, University of Lisbon: <www.cet-e-quinhentos.com> [accessed May 2014]

Hyperdonat: Collection d'éditions numériques de commentaires anciens avec traduction et annotation critique — Université Jean Moulin, Atelier des Humanités Numériques, ENS — Lyon, Université de Lyon: <http://hyperdonat.huma-num.fr/editions/index.html> [accessed April 2014]

112 CATARINA FOUTO

Notes to Chapter 5

1. Amongst these are commentaries to Horace's *Ars Poetica*, by Aquiles Estaço's *In Quintii Horatii Flacci Poeticam Commentarii* (Antwerp, 1553); Pedro da Veiga (*Horatius Flaccus Venusinus de Arte Poetica*, Antwerp, 1578); Tomé Correia (*In Librum de Arte Poetica Q. Horatii Flacci Explanationes*, Venice, 1587) — the latter has been analysed by Bernard Weinberg, *Trattati di poetica e retorica del Cinquecento* (Bari: Laterza, 1974), pp. 215–21. Another theoretical contribution to literary theory of the sixteenth century made by a Portuguese is that of Miguel Sanches de Lima's *El Arte Poetica en romance castellano* (1592).

2. Menéndez Pelayo's *Historia de las ideas estéticas en España* (Madrid: C.S.I.C., 1883–91) in five long volumes devotes very little attention to Portugal. For systematic and in-depth studies on literary theory in early modern Portugal, see the contributions by Aníbal de Castro: *Retórica e teorização literária em Portugal: do humanismo ao neoclassicismo* (Coimbra: Imprensa da Universidade, 1973); 'Aquiles Estaço, o primeiro comentador da Arte Poética de Horácio', *Arquivos do Centro Cultural Português*, 10 (1976), 83–102; and 'La Poétique et la Rhétorique dans la pédagogie et dans la littérature de l'Humanisme portugais', in *L'Humanisme portugais et l'Europe*, ed. by José Pina Martins (Paris: Centro Cultural Português), pp. 699–722 ; and 'Os códigos poéticos em Portugal do Renascimento ao Barroco. Seus fundamentos. Seus conteúdos. Sua evolução', *Revista da Universidade de Coimbra*, 31 (1985), 505–31. See also Hélio Alves, *Camões, Corte-Real e o sistema da epopeia quinhentista* (Coimbra: Imprensa da Universidade de Coimbra, 2001), pp. 105–23.

3. This is also the case in Italy, France and Spain, despite the access to the text, and later on to Robortello's commentary (1548) and Scaliger's *Poetices libri septem* (1561).

4. It is certain that Sá de Miranda wrote the plays whilst visiting Italy, from where he returned to Portugal in 1526. He revised his work insatiably throughout his life, very much like Ariosto, and editing the comedies is a particularly difficult task. The most recent and authoritative critical edition of the plays (including three manuscript versions of *Os Estrangeiros*) is that by José Camões and T. F. Earle published in 2013.

5. John R. C. Martyn, 'The Influence of Buchanan and Teive', in António Ferreira, *The Tragedy of Ines de Castro* (Coimbra: Imprensa da Universidade de Coimbra, 1987), pp. 137–57.

6. See the thorough critical edition by Adrien Roig: *La Comédie de Bristo ou l'Entremetteur* (Paris: Presses Universitaires de France, 1973). The *Comédia do Cioso* has not received the same degree of critical attention, but there is an excellent edition readily available at <www.cet-e-quinhentos.com>, the website of the Centro de Estudos de Teatro, University of Lisbon. There is a detailed discussion of António Ferreira's two comedies in Chapter 4 (eds).

7. The best critical edition of the play, with a commentary, is by T. F. Earle: *Poemas Lusitanos* (Lisbon: Fundação Calouste Gulbenkian, 2000), pp. 379–460.

8. The other sixteenth-century tragedy, *Castro*, by Ferreira, has attracted the attention of scholars and there are recent and excellent studies exploring the classicism of the play including T. F. Earle, 'António Ferreira's *Castro*: Tragedy at the Cross-Roads', in *Portuguese Humanism and the Republic of Letters*, ed. by M. Berbara and K. Enenkel (Leiden and Boston, MA: Brill, 2012), pp. 289–318.

9. See, in this volume, Chapters 1, 2 and 11 (eds).

10. The 'auto' was not by any means the only dramatic form to flourish in Portugal. Later in the sixteenth century, the *Tragicomedia de Calixto y Melibea* by Fernando de Rojas (1499) inspired the work of the Portuguese writer Jorge Ferreira de Vasconcelos (1515–?1565/85): though introduced by a prologue and divided into five acts, his 'comedias' *Eufrósina*, *Aulegrafia* and *Ulysippo* (1555, and posthumously, 1618 and 1620, respectively) are, in fact, dramatic novels (novels written in dialogue form), and display a wide range of erudition (namely of classical sources) which makes them impractical for performance on stage. The plays by Vasconcelos became popular and the dedication of the *Comédia Eufrósina* in 1555 to the heir to the throne, the prince D. João, is a clear sign of the author's success in Portugal.

11. A. Borges Macedo, 'Livros impressos em Portugal no século XVI: interesses e formas de mentalidade', *Arquivos do Centro Cultural Português*, 9 (1975), 183–221 (pp. 188–90).

12. Thanks to some of these anthologies, published in Portugal, students had access to the following

THE REINVENTION OF CLASSICAL COMEDY AND TRAGEDY IN PORTUGAL 113

classical playwrights: Seneca's *Troas*, Plautus's *Aulularia*, the prologues of all the plays by Terence (in *Sylva diversorum autorum, qui ad usum scholarum selecti sunt*, Lisbon, 1587), and later Plautus's *Captivi* and *Stichus*, Terence's *Andria*, *Eunuchus* and *Heautontimorumenos* (in *Sylvae variorum autorum, qui inferioribus classibus idonei sunt, tomus secundus*, Lisbon, 1593).

13. See Chapter 12 (eds).

14. It was James P. Crawford who attributed the authorship of the play to Juan Cirne, in *Spanish Drama before Lope de Vega* (Philadelphia: University of Pennsylvania Press, 1968), p. 160. A critical edition of the text and introductory study can be found in *Tragedia de los amores de Eneas y de la reina Dido*, ed. by J. E. Gillet and E. B. Williams, *PMLA*, 46 (1931), 353–431. The editors published the work as anonymous.

15. On the private libraries of some important intellectuals in the first half of the sixteenth-century, see Artur Moreira de Sá, 'Livros de uso de Frei Diogo de Murça', *Boletim da Biblioteca de Coimbra*, 33 (1977), 69–109; Belmiro F. Pereira, 'A livraria de Aquiles Estaço, *librorum uenator et helluo*', *Humanitas*, 45 (1993), 255–306; Aires Augusto do Nascimento, 'A livraria de D. Teodósio I, Duque de Bragança', *Congresso de História no IV Centenário do Seminário de Évora. Actas, vols I–II* (Évora: Instituto Superior de Teologia — Seminário Maior de Évora, 1994), 209–20.

16. A classic is Gustave Lanson, *Esquisse d'une histoire de la tragédie française* (New York: Columbia University Press, 1920). For a detailed analysis of this complex transmission, see Henry A. Kelly, *Ideas and Forms of Tragedy from Aristotle to the Middle Ages* (Cambridge: Cambridge University Press, 1993), pp. 5–15, especially pp. 10–13, and Giacomo Cardinali and Gianni Guastella, *Le rinascite della tragedia: origini classiche e tradizioni europee* (Rome: Carocci, 2006), pp. 125–66.

17. I have chosen to quote from the so-called ms. Asensio, considered to be the closest of the surviving copies to the first version of the text. For a discussion of the circulation and printing of Sá de Miranda's *Estrangeiros*, see José Camões, 'Com textos', in *Comédias*, pp. 24–31.

18. I quote from *Comedia di messer Lodouico Ariosto intitolata Cassaria, con l'argumento aggiunto et non piu stampato* (Vinegia: Nicolo di Aristotile di Ferrara detto Zoppino, 1538).

19. *Comédias*, pp. 114–15.

20. *Comédia de Bristo ou do Fanchono*, p. 4, apud Roig, *La Comédie de Bristo*, p. 130.

21. This is the text of the letter addressed to the Cardinal printed in the 1561 edition. The quotation is on p. 49 of the critical edition of the *Comédias* by Camões and Earle.

22. Donatus, 'Euanthi De comoedia excerpta', V.1: 'Comoediam esse Cicero ait imitationem uitae, speculum consuetudinis, imaginem ueritatis'. Accessed via the 'Hyperdonat' website: <http://hyperdonat.huma-num.fr/editions/html/DonEva.html#top>. The basis of the Latin text is the critical edition *Aeli Donati quod fertur Commentum Terenti*, ed. by Paul Wesser (Leipzig: Teubner, 1902), I, 13–31.

23. Donatus, 'Euanthi de fabula', III. 1, accessed via the 'Hyperdonat' website.

24. Jorge Ferreira de Vasconcelos, in his *Comédia Eufrosina* (Coimbra: João de Barreira, 1555) (I consulted the copy held at the Biblioteca Nacional de Portugal, shelfmark FG 6220) writes in his proemium to the Prince: 'Ca, por ser invenção nova nesta terra e em linguagem portuguesa, tam invejada e reprendida, por certo tenho ser salteada de muitos censores' [Given that it is a recent invention in our homeland, and because it is written in Portuguese, a language envied so much and criticized so heavily, I am sure that my play will be attacked by many censors]. In the prologue of the play, he addresses his audience, defending the importance of Portuguese as a language of culture and imperial power: 'Hei-vos de falar mera linguagem, nam cuideis que é isto tam pouco, que eu tenho em muito a portuguesa, cuja gravidade, graça lacónia e autorizada pronunciação nada deve à latina, que Vala exalça mais que seu império' [I will speak to you in the vernacular — think not that this is any mean feat, for I hold the Portuguese language in great esteem, as its gravity, laconic grace and authorized pronunciation owes nothing to Latin, which Valla exalts more highly than her empire] (p. 5). For a discussion on the use of Castilian by Portuguese intellectuals and the Court, see Ana Buescu, 'Aspectos do bilinguismo português-castelhano na Época Moderna', *Hispania*, 64.1 (2004), 13–38. For a discussion of bilingualism in Gil Vicente, see Chapter 11 (eds).

25. The recent critical edition by José Camões and T. F. Earle has identified a third, intermediary, version of the text of this play, complicating the history of the transmission and printing of the text, long thought to have existed in two different versions.

26. T. F Earle, 'The two versions of *Os Estrangeiros*', in *Culture and Society in Habsburg Spain*, ed. by N. Griffin et al. (London: Tamesis, 2001), pp. 35–44 (p. 37).

27. 'Rhetoric and Scenic Form: The Castro, Act IV, Scene 1', in *Studies in Portuguese Literature and History in honour of Luís de Sousa Rebelo*, ed. by Helder Macedo (London: Tamesis Books, 1992), pp. 139–47. However, (and this did not go unnoticed by the critics) Ferreira prefers to problematize rather than moralize, allowing conflicting points of view on stage, and exploring the drama of Castro's personal drama from different angles.

28. I am quoting from the critical edition available at <www.cet-e-quinhentos.com>, the website of the Centro de Estudos de Teatro, University of Lisbon.

29. On this crucial point, see Donald Stone Jr., *French Humanist Tragedy: A Reassessment* (Manchester: Manchester University Press, 1974), pp. 37–39.

30. See Stone Jr, *French Humanist Tragedy*, pp. 18–27.

31. Donatus, 'Euanthi de fabula', IV, 2. Accessed via the *'Hyperdonat'* website, see note 20.

32. I follow the edition and translation by Sharratt and Walsh in this chapter: George Buchanan, *Tragedies*, ed. by Peter Sharratt and Patrick Walsh (Edinburgh: Scottish Academic Press, 1983), p. 99; the translation of the passage can be found on p. 134.

33. *Apud* Harold W. Lawton, *Handbook of French Renaissance Dramatic Theory* (Manchester: Manchester University Press, 1949), p. 28.

34. Diogo de Teive, *Opuscula Aliquot* (Salamanca: Heirs of Juan de Junta, 1558), fols 2^v–3^v.

35. To this day, the play has only been critically edited by Nair de Castro Soares (Coimbra: Centro de estudos clássicos e humanísticos da Universidade de Coimbra, 1977). All references to the play follow her work. A more recent (and excellent) translation into Portuguese of the complete work of Teive, by António Guimarães Pinto, appeared in 2011 (Lisbon: Esfera do Caos), but the original Latin text does not appear to have been critically edited.

36. John R. C. Martyn, 'The Influence of Buchanan' appears to have followed the Portuguese translation by Nair de Castro Soares too closely when judging the overall effect of the prophetic dream on the play: 'The total effect of the dream is somewhat ludicrous, as the harpy-cum-archer picks off nine eyes, but leaves the tenth because she is tired!' (pp. 146–47, pp. 150–51). It seems that *lumina* has been rendered as 'eyes' and not 'loved ones'.

37. J. David Bishop, 'The Meaning of the Choral Meters in Senecan Tragedy', *Rheinisches Museum für Philologie*, 111.3 (1968), 197–219 (pp. 198–203).

38. The use of anapaestic dimeters may have been suggested to Teive by the choral ode of Act IV of *Phaedra* which also laments how Fortune affects the lives of the powerful. The use of anapaestic dimeters in choral odes expressing lamentation, loss, death and destruction are, however, common in Seneca's theatre. See note 37.

39. In fact, Elaine Fantham, 'Introductio' to *Seneca's Troades* (Princeton, NJ: Princeton University Press, 1982), pp. 3–124.

40. See the edition of the play by Castro Soares, pp. 135–37.

41. Stephen B. Berkowitz, 'A critical edition of George Buchanan's *Baptistes* and of the anonymous *Tyrannicall-government anatomized*' (unpublished doctoral thesis, Harvard University, 1986), pp. 515–17.

42. Ann Moss, *Printed Common-Place Books and the Structuring of Renaissance Thought* (Oxford: Oxford University Press, 1996).

43. Mário Brandão, ed., 'O processo na Inquisição de Mestre Diogo de Teive', *Notícias Cronológicas da Universidade de Coimbra*, 4 (1943), 1–180 (p. 11).

44. Both quotations from Martyn, 'The Influence of Buchanan', p. 149.

CHAPTER 6

The Recovery of Terence in Renaissance Italy: From Alberti to Machiavelli

Martin McLaughlin

Magdalen College, Oxford

The standard histories of Italian Renaissance theatre outline the growing understanding of ancient Latin comedy in the course of the fifteenth and sixteenth centuries.[1] Terence's six comedies had been well known in the Middle Ages, surviving in almost as many manuscripts as Virgil, over 650 of them in the period post-AD 800; they were a popular school text for teaching sound Latin and did not contain the risqué elements in Plautus's comedies.[2] However, the codex containing twelve new plays by Plautus brought to Italy by Nicolas Cusanus in 1429 aroused new interest in the older playwright, while the discovery of Donatus's commentary to Terence in 1433 further heightened interest in the genre.[3] Throughout the fifteenth century, Italian humanists wrote Latin plays in imitation of their ancient models, but interest in the originals of Plautus and Terence also continued: in 1476 there took place in Florence the first performance of Terence's *Andria* since the end of the ancient world, and Poliziano held a university course on the same play in 1484–85.[4] In Ferrara in the 1480s and '90s there were a number of performances of Plautus's plays in vernacular translation, as well as a performance of the *Andria* in 1491.[5] Finally, in the first decade of the sixteenth century, Ariosto wrote the earliest examples of 'commedia erudita', that is to say, a vernacular comedy imitating the topics and structure of ancient Latin comedy: *La cassaria* in 1508, and *I suppositi* in 1509, both written in prose, though he later recast them both in verse around 1530, as by then scholars had established that the plays of Plautus and Terence had been written in metre.[6]

Apart from Ariosto, two other major Renaissance writers who tried their hand at the new genre were Leon Battista Alberti (1404–1472), who wrote his only Latin comedy, *Philodoxeos fabula*, in 1424, and Niccolò Machiavelli (1469–1527), who almost 100 years later, around 1518, both translated Terence's *Andria* into the Florentine vernacular and wrote probably the most successful vernacular comedy of the Italian Renaissance, *La mandragola*. Needless to say, there have been many

116   MARTIN McLAUGHLIN

more studies of Machiavelli's play than of Alberti's comedy, but there are still some significant aspects to be explored even in the case of the former.

In what follows I examine in more depth these three play-texts, Alberti's *Philodoxeos*, Machiavelli's translation of the *Andria* and his own comedy *La mandragola*, primarily to consider how these two major Italian writers drew on their ancient model in very different ways, and learned crucial techniques from his plays. What I hope will emerge is a chapter on the precise recovery of Terence in Renaissance Italy; in particular an understanding of the sophistication of the young Alberti's attempt at a Terentian comedy and, in the case of Machiavelli, a recognition of the fact that some of the phrases that we think of as typical of the author of the *Prince* actually owe much to the ancient Latin comedian.

Alberti's *Philodoxeos fabula*

Most surveys of Alberti's life and works record the fact, mentioned in his autobiography, that he completed his first literary work, the Latin comedy *Philodoxeos fabula*, before the age of twenty, in other words before 1424.[7] In one of the play's paratexts, the prologue or *Commentarium* to the second version of the play, the author also tells us that ten years later he took the trouble to rewrite this first work, since the earlier redaction had been circulated without his consent, in a corrupt version, with obscene elements added to it by others.[8] However, the first redaction was considered to be such a good copy of an ancient comedy that it was originally attributed to a little known ancient writer, Lepidus.[9] The second and definitive version can be dated to between 1434 and 1437, the latter being the year in which he wrote a letter dedicating the comedy to Leonello d'Este, an appropriate patron since he was famous for his interest in Latin comedies, particularly those of Terence.[10] Clearly this was a work on which Alberti lavished considerable care in the first decade of his literary career, writing it in two different versions, the second one containing substantial changes. Nevertheless relatively few scholars have analysed the *Philodoxeos* in detail. The aim of the first half of this chapter is to consider the comedy in some depth, comparing the two versions and examining in more detail its intertextual allusions.

Partly because of this rewriting of the text, and partly because ancient Latin comedies, especially those of Terence, were always preceded in the manuscripts available to Alberti by both a prologue and a summary, the *Philodoxeos fabula* is accompanied by no fewer than five paratexts: a prologue and summary for each of the two versions, and a dedicatory letter accompanying the definitive redaction.[11] The first two paratexts are the prologue to the original redaction (*Prologus*, in *Philodoxeos*, pp. 148–49), and the plot summary (*Fabule Argumentum*, in *Philodoxeos*, p. 150). The first *Prologus* is a brief note of three paragraphs, written in a more vulgar tone than either the later prologue (which he calls *Commentarium*) or the dedicatory letter to Leonello d'Este. This early prologue opens with an allusion to the author being drunk, contains comic language ('ebibi', 'debibundo', the Plautine 'exanclarim', p. 148) and makes a striking contrast with the serious first sentence in the later *Commentarium*, which instead, as we shall see, echoes a work

THE RECOVERY OF TERENCE IN RENAISSANCE ITALY 117

by Cicero and emphasizes the moral allegory of the play. Here in the first prologue he claims that his comedy is 'pretty' ('bellula' is another word found only in Plautus), insists that it has the usual stock characters of comedies (lovers, deceivers and parasites) and he tells the audience its title: 'I'm telling you, it is quite a pretty play: it contains lovers, deceivers and those who make merry. I can inform you that this is a comedy, its title is *Philodoxeos*.'[12] In this list of stock types and the naming of the play he is following good Terentian precedent, since the Prologues to the *Eunuch* and *Heautontimoroumenos* also mention such traditional characters, while the first line of the prologue to *Hecyra* provides its title: 'Hecyra est huic nomen fabulae' [The title of this play is *The Mother-in-Law*] (*Hecyra*, Prologue, 1).[13] Alberti ends this first Prologue saying that if the audience wants to know his name, it is Lepidus [charming, witty], which he says is highly suitable for a play written for a charming audience. The name probably derives from the use of the adjective in several Terentian comedies, especially the *Adelphoe*.[14]

By contrast with the brief first prologue, the prologue to the second version is the lengthy *Commentarium*, probably written around 1434. This prologue/commentary explains the moral allegory behind the action and provides a summary of the plot, as well as recounting the work's genesis. Its opening sentence — 'Hec fabula pertinet ad mores' [This play deals with morals] (*Philodoxeos*, p. 144) — echoes, as has been noted, the first words in Cicero's lacunose *De fato* ('quia pertinet ad mores...'), and also now claims for this youthful comedy a serious moral purpose.[15] The rest of the *Commentarium* deals largely with the comedy's genesis. Alberti states that the first version of the *Philodoxeos* was received with enthusiasm, and when asked about its provenance, he had initially claimed that it had been found in an ancient manuscript where it was attributed to a little known Roman comedian called Lepidus. This proved credible, he claims, for a number of reasons: because the play conformed to the 'rules of comedy', because the language had an ancient aura ('et comicum dicendi genus et priscum quippiam redolebat', p. 147), and because it was unlikely that a student of canon law could have written such a work, indeed no one could believe that any contemporary writers were capable of this kind of achievement. Alberti tells us that he had, however, written a prologue to the first version (the first paratext discussed above) in which he recounted his studies and revealed his age so that he could prove the work was his when the time came. After finishing his legal studies, he polished and cleaned the play up ('elimatior et honestior', *Philodoxeos*, p. 147), but this second version, ironically, was now widely criticized, all of which makes the author bemoan the inconsistency of his critics. However, he ends the *Commentarium* on a positive note, saying that the criticisms of those who were jealous of his talents have spurred him on to creativity, and he appeals to good people to defend him from the sniping of the envious so that he can produce more comic works and more serious ones as well ('alia huiusmodi atque [...] maiora edere', *Philodoxeos*, p. 147).

As for the two plot summaries, they differ only in terms of language. In the first summary we find evidence of Terentian diction. The archaic form 'occipere' ('to begin') is a favourite verb in Terence and Plautus, often coupled with 'amare', so it is not surprising to find it here: 'hanc Doxiam cupere cum occeperit' [when he began to desire Doxia] (*Philodoxeos*, p. 150), echoing Terence's 'Amare occepit aliam' (*Adelphoe*, 327) and 'interea miles qui me amare occeperat' (*Eunuchus*, 125).[16] Like all humanists versed in the theory and practice of *imitatio*, the young Battista avoids too slavish an imitation of his model, and at the same time tones down the obscene elements of the first version, by changing two of Terence's other favourite verbs ('vitiare' and 'comprimere', meaning respectively 'to deflower' and 'to have sex with') which he had used in the first redaction, into their more classical but less explicit equivalent, 'rapere', meaning 'to abduct'.[17] Thus even these brief paratexts reflect the young Alberti's developing sense of appropriate language: the 1424 *Prologus* and *Fabule Argumentum* employ comic and explicit language, often echoing Plautus and providing only a literal summary of the play, while the later prologue, the *Commentarium*, opens on a moralizing note, echoing Cicero rather than Plautus, and stressing the allegorical meaning of the comedy, while the second summary tones down some strong language. The change of Latin style also mirrors the more serious intent of the second redaction and is appropriate to the elevated status of its dedicatee, Leonello. In addition, Alberti changes his 'signature': if in the first redaction he had used a Terentian pseudonym, Lepidus, in the later version dedicated to the Marquis of Ferrara he adopts his newly invented and more lofty tripartite name, Leo Baptista Albertus, with its echo of ancient tripartite names such as Marcus Tullius Cicero (a name repeated no fewer than four times in the paratexts that accompany the second version of the *Philodoxeos*).[18] The first redaction of the comedy, purportedly written by Lepidus, was thus in some sense an illegitimate work (Alberti himself had been born out of wedlock), whereas this new version is closely linked to his newly self-fashioned identity with his tripartite name, and his own 'logo': the presentation copy to Leonello contains Alberti's famous symbol of the winged eye just before and after the *Commentarium* which begins and ends with his new tripartite name being repeated several times. This first work by Alberti is thus not just a youthful imitation of a Terentian comedy but a work intimately connected with his emerging identity as an author, and deserves closer study than it has received hitherto.

The fifth and last paratext is the short dedicatory letter to Leonello d'Este, written in 1437 to accompany the second version of the comedy. Its main point is simply to note that since the play was much in demand amongst his friends, the author could think of no worthier patron to dedicate it to than to the virtuous Leonello. The latter, an enthusiast of Terence's comedies, was an appropriate dedicatee in many respects.[19]

There are many other areas that show Alberti's knowledge of the components of Latin theatre. The dramatis personae clearly include stock characters of ancient Latin comedy: a young man in love, his close friend and helper, a cunning servant, a rival for the girl's hand, a parasite, an angry old man, a forgiving mother. The plot also follows that of Roman comedy, and the setting is classical: ancient Rome (though classical Latin comedies were usually set in Greece), with piazzas, statues and alleyways ('angiportus'). By contrast, Alberti's predecessors in the genre — apart from Leonardo Bruni, whose *Poliscena* (*c.* 1408) also had a classical setting — had mostly dealt with 'goliardic' themes involving contemporary university settings or plots based on the novella tradition.[20] The text's editor suggests that the play

THE RECOVERY OF TERENCE IN RENAISSANCE ITALY   119

does not have an entirely happy ending as Philodoxus always remains pessimistic about how things will turn out,[21] and, it should be added, the violent Fortunius effectively gets away with rape and abduction, though this often happened in ancient comedy too. Other classical elements include Alberti's respect for the unities of place and plot, as well as his use of soliloquies: there are five monologues in the first ten scenes and another five in the last ten, with Philodoxus being accorded the highest number of them, with three soliloquies.

The Terentian influence continues throughout the play: this is immediately visible in the stock characters, and also in some of the names (Fortunius, the impetuous lover, has a patronymic 'Thrasis' which echoes the name of the boastful soldier Thraso in Terence's *Eunuchus*, and in the first redaction there was a brief anecdote about Gnatho, the name of the parasite in the same comedy). There are also many verbal echoes of the Roman playwright, including an allusion to Thais's famous flattering thanks from *Eunuchus*, 391–92, a passage cited by both Cicero (*De amicitia*, 98) and Dante (*Inferno*, 18.133–35).[22] Similarly at the end of the play, we can observe Alberti's closer imitation of the conclusions of Roman plays in the second redaction. At the end of the first version, Philodoxeos simply states: 'Plaudite hoc meo bono, plaudite!' [Applaud my good luck, applaud!] (1st version, *Philodoxeos*, p. 224), which is close enough to the endings of plays such as *Heautontimoroumenos*, *Eunuchus* and *Phormio*: 'Vos valete et plaudite.' However, the closing line in the final version is more elaborate and closer to the main intertextual source of the *Philodoxeos*: 'Plaudite, *spectatores*, hoc meo bono, plaudite. *Tuque, tibicen, precine hymeneum: nos sequemur. Valete*' [Applaud, spectators, my good luck, applaud! And you, flute-player, sound the marriage hymn: we will follow on. Farewell] (2nd version, *Philodoxeos*, p. 225). This clearly derives from the last scene of *Adelphoe*: 'That's what I want. But I am waiting for the flute-player and the chorus who will sing the wedding hymn' [Cupio; uerum hoc mihi moraest: | tibicina et hymenaeum qui cantent'] (*Adelphoe*, 904–05).

However, there are also areas that demonstrate that Alberti did not have complete mastery of all the elements of Latin comedy. For a start, the names of all the characters are allegorical names representing abstract qualities, such as glory, luck, wealth and so on: such names probably derive from medieval traditions of allegory, and seem to parallel the 'Cratylic' names used for other personified characters in medieval morality plays elsewhere in Europe.[23] These personifications were not a stock feature of Latin comedy: only in the Prologue to Plautus's *Trinummus* do we find two personified characters, such as Luxuria and Inopia, appearing on stage. Even although Alberti displayed his new humanist credentials by deriving the names of nine of the eleven characters from Greek, still the allegorical dimension clearly betokens a medieval rather than classical influence. In Alberti's comedy the protagonist's name Philodoxus means 'he who is in love with Doxia or Glory', and the meanings of the other characters' names provide a key to the fairly obvious allegory of the play. Philodoxus asks his friend Phroneus ('Intelligence') to persuade Doxia's neighbour Ditonus (a Latinate name meaning 'Wealthy') to let him use his house in order to observe his beloved. Ditonus initially agrees, but meantime Philodoxus's rival Fortunius (the other Latinate name, meaning 'Lucky'), son of

Tychia ('Chance'), is being helped by his slave Dynastes ('Power') also to gain access to Ditonus's house for the same reason. In the end Fortunius and Ditonus abduct Doxia's sister Phimia ('Fame'), while Doxia's chaperone Mnimia ('Memory') and her friend Alithia ('Truth') escape to tell the protagonist what has happened. They all report this to Alithia's father Chronos ('Time') who resolves matters by allowing Fortunius to keep Phimia and Philodoxus to marry Doxia. The allegorical meaning of this rather wooden plot can be worked out from the names alone: a young man in love with glory can achieve it if he relies on intelligence to outdo the wealthy and the fortunate, though the latter two characters tend to enjoy fame despite their rapacious behaviour.

Philodoxeos is not, then, a perfect copy of an antique comedy, despite the fact that its first version was so Roman in character that it passed for an ancient play by 'Lepidus'. There are other 'medieval' elements, such as the anachronisms noted by Cesarini Martinelli.[24] Also indicative of its non-classical nature is the fact that Alberti does not divide his comedy into five acts, no doubt because the manuscripts of Plautus and Terence he read had no act-divisions, only scene divisions. However, it is divided into twenty scenes, and that number actually corresponds to the average number of scenes in Terence's comedies. The most significant divergence of all, though, is the fact that it is written in Latin prose, since most humanists failed to understand the metre of Roman comedy until the end of the fifteenth century, and thought they were written in prose.[25] In these respects this early work by Alberti was very much of its transitional time.

What is more remarkable is that in his rewriting of his first play, Alberti shows certain stylistic nuances that indicate an impressive ability to distinguish the typical traits of Plautus and his language from those of Terence: one constant in his revision of the first redaction of *Philodoxeos* was an excision of Plautine elements which are often replaced by Terentian features. An obvious Plautine element was obscenity. In Scene 11, for instance, Philodoxius's evil rival Fortunius is fantasizing about what he would do if he were able to be with Doxia, and in the first version he declares: 'I will feel her, embrace her, cover her completely with love-bites, lick her all over';[26] unsurprisingly, in the more Terentian second redaction the final phrase 'lick her all over' [omnem ligurriam totam] is omitted. Cesarini Martinelli and others have noted several examples of such eliminations of Plautine vulgarity, and most recently Carmen Codoñer has studied this aspect thoroughly.[27] She concludes that, overall, the cuts in the first half of the play (especially of obscenities) and the additions in the second half transform the comedy from a Plautine farce to something more like a comedy by Terence: indeed the plot is very similar to that of the *Adelphoe* where one respectable and one wicked brother pursue two girls, one respectable, the other debauched.

The counterpart to the cutting of obscene remarks is the insertion of moralizing *sententiae*, and this too adds to the Terentian feel of the second redaction of the play. A good instance of the addition of just such a maxim is in the very first scene where in the second redaction Alberti makes the protagonist's servant Phroneus add a wry conclusion about a lover's torments (the added passages are in italics):

But, by heavens, what sort of a monster is this, *when a man can be really an enemy to himself, just because he loves somebody else. In fact, the torments a lover inflicts on himself are undoubtedly greater than those that come from his enemies! A lover's mind is never free of sadness, cares and worries.*[28]

There is a very similar *sententia* in the *Eunuchus* when again the servant to the protagonist says of his master in love: 'Good gods, what kind of a disease is this, that a man can be so changed by love that you don't recognize him as the same person!'[29] A similar addition can be found towards the end of the play. In another speech added to the second redaction, Tychia expatiates on the virtues of being lenient: 'How pleasing in all walks of life is leniency to those that you live with, and how useful to those who know how to exploit that very virtue! The strict man is hated both by those who know him and those who don't, whereas there is nobody who doesn't love a lenient, indulgent man. Now people can learn this very thing from my own case'.[30] These words also rework a famous Terence passage, this time from the end of the *Adelphoe*: 'By this very experience I have found that there is nothing better for a man than leniency and clemency. Anyone can realize that this is true from the case of me and my brother. [...] they all love him, and shun me'.[31]

However, Alberti's Terentian imitation extends beyond the level of content to embrace matters of dramatic technique and language. One of the most striking changes in technique in a rewritten passage is the one in Scene 12 where Mnimia is telling Philodoxeos and Phroneus about the abduction of his beloved Doxia by his rival Fortunius, also known as Thrasis. In the first redaction she does so in a monologue using a sequence of verbs interrupted by suspension dots:

> MNIMIA. Along came Fortunius ... he wanted ... he broke in ... he entered ... she didn't want to ... he carried out the act ... he went off.[32]

But when he rewrites this scene in the definitive version, Alberti has Philodoxeos and Phroneus interrupt Mnimia alternately in order to render the scene more lively and dramatic (again the added words are in italics):

> MNI. Along came *Thrasis...* PHIL. *I'm afraid.* MNI... he broke in... PHRON. *Oh !* MNI... he entered... PHRON. *This is terrible.* MNI... *he abducted her...* PHIL. *Oh, I am the unhappiest man alive!*[33]

Some critics have worked out a 'liveliness factor' for plays by dividing the number of scenes by the number of characters in a play. Thus according to Stoppelli, Machiavelli's *Mandragola* has a liveliness factor of 4.6 (37 scenes divided by 8 characters), which is similar to that of Bibbiena's 1513 comedy, *Calandra*, at 4.8, but these figures are far above the average in Terence's comedies which lies somewhere between 1.8 and 2.[34] If we adopt the same method for the *Philodoxeos*, we get a figure of around 1.8 (20 scenes divided by 11 characters), so very much in line with Terentian levels of 'liveliness'.

It is worth also examining Alberti's use of comic lexis in the two versions of his comedy. There is regular use of archaic forms of Latin, though many of these, but not all of them, are eliminated when Alberti writes the second redaction of the play: for instance, the nineteen occurrences of the archaic form 'bone' as an adverb (instead of 'bene') are all eliminated in the second redaction, and the five uses of 'vortere' (instead of 'vertere') are also systematically replaced. Nevertheless some archaic forms do survive into the later redaction: three instances of 'lubet' (for 'libet') remain from the five in the earlier redaction, there are still seven examples of the form 'peximum' (for 'pessimum'), and so on. So Alberti wanted his comedy to have an archaic flavour, but not so excessively archaic as in the first version. Consistent with this tendency is the fact that in rewriting Alberti excises other, more extreme archaisms. In one instance he cuts an allusion to a classical intertext, as in the following speech by Chronos: 'Forte credideris, quia *gravascellus* sim depontave, minime quod valeam cursu' [Perhaps you might have thought that because I am a bit overweight or with one foot in the grave, I am unable to run] (*Philodoxeos*, pp. 208, 210). In the second redaction this becomes: 'Forte hoc tibi persuades, quod me admodum gravem *et morosum ac, veluti aiunt*, depontam conspicias, ideo me cursu minime valere' [Perhaps you thought that because I am overweight *and morose and, as they say*, with one foot in the grave, I am unable to run] (*Philodoxeos*, p. 209). The unusual diminutive adjective, 'gravascellus', is found only in one line of Plautus ('sed quis haec est muliercula et ille gravastellus qui venit?', *Epidica*, 620), but clearly Alberti felt that this diminutive form was too archaic and rare, so he replaces it with two classical adjectives: 'gravem et morosum', and he also softens the impact of that other rare adjective 'deponta' (literally 'fit for throwing off the bridge') by adding 'veluti aiunt', to show he is quoting an ancient source (the late grammarian Festus).[35] Here he was clearly excising Plautine lexis in his desire to make the second redaction of the comedy more Terentian.

In other descriptions he has specific passages from Terence in mind: when Phroneus is telling Philodoxeos about the wealthy man Ditonus, he describes him in the first version as '*niger, subflavus* barba et capillo multo, magno indutus pellicio, *claudus et quasi cecus*' [dark-skinned, with a slightly blonde beard and lots of hair, he wears a huge fur cloak, he limps and is almost blind] (*Philodoxeos*, p. 152). In the second redaction this is modified to become '*fuscus*, barba et capillo *prolixus*, *claudicans, cesius* [dark-skinned, with lots of hair and a beard, he limps and has blue-grey eyes] (*Philodoxeos*, p. 153). Clearly the later details in this alliterative list derive from two alliterative descriptions in Terence: '*capillus* passus, *prolixus*, circum caput | reiectus negligenter' [she had masses of hair, spread out, tossed artlessly behind her] (*Heautontimoroumenos*, 290), and 'magnus rubicundus crispus crassus *caesius* | cadaverosa facie' [he is tall, ruddy, with curly hair, blue-grey eyes and a cadaverous face] (*Hecyra*, 439–41). There are several significant alterations here: the shift from the more predictable 'niger' to the less usual 'fuscus';[36] the deletion of a compound adjective ('subflavus'), despite it being part of a description of Augustus in Suetonius ('capillum subflavum', *Divus Augustus*, 79), and its replacement by an adjective ('prolixus') that instead recalls a description in Terence: the change of 'capillo multo' into 'capillo prolixus' clearly echoes more closely Terence's 'capillus passus, prolixus' [lots of hair, spread out] (*Heautontimoroumenos*, 290); also here we find a reduction of the size of the list by the cancellation of one element, probably for its unclassical noun ('magno indutus pellicio') [clothed in a huge fur cloak]; lastly in this description Alberti changes 'quasi cecus' to 'cesius' because the latter, rather rare adjective is also found in two famous descriptions in Terence: 'magnus rubicundus crispus crassus caesius | cadaverosa facie' [he is tall, ruddy, with curly

THE RECOVERY OF TERENCE IN RENAISSANCE ITALY   123

hair, blue-grey eyes and a cadaverous face] (*Hecyra*, 439–41), and 'rufamne illam virginem, | caesiam, sparso ore, adunco naso?' [that red-head girl, with blue-green eyes, freckles on her face and a pointed nose] (*Heautontimoroumenos*, 1061–62). In fact a whole chapter of Aulus Gellius (*Noctes Atticae*, 2.26), another favourite text of Alberti, considers the range of colours implied by these four Latin adjectives 'fuscus', 'flavus', 'rufus' and 'caesius', and so Gellius as well as Terence lie behind his rewriting of this description.[37]

Finally, Alberti shows off his perception of two fundamental stylistic features that were characteristic of ancient Roman comedy: the use of lists and of alliteration. There are lists in most scenes. In the first scene we have: 'video namque ut perdite amet, ut timeat, ut expectet [...] animum et trudat et scindat et agitet' [for I see how desperately he is in love, how he's afraid and anxious [...] so that his mind is in turmoil, agitated, torn in two] (*Philodoxeos*, p. 153), which seems modelled on Terentian passages such as 'profundat, perdat, pereat' [he will fritter away, waste and ruin himself] (*Adelphoe*, 134); from the middle of the play a line like: 'O populares, opem, opem afferte, accurrite, succurrite!' [Please, people, help, bring help, come quickly, come and help!] (*Philodoxeos*, p. 157) seems to imitate a similar plea again from the *Adelphoe*: 'Obsecro, populares, ferte misero atque innocenti auxilium: | subuenite inopi' [I beg you, people, help me in my wretchedness and innocence: come to the aid of someone who is defenceless] (*Adelphoe*, 155–56); and 'Narravi parentes, mores, virtutes, probitatem ceteraque tua, ut potui, omnia' [I spoke of your parents, your character, virtues, upright way of life, and everything else about you as best I could] (*Philodoxeos*, p. 169) seems to echo another famous list from Terence: 'parentis, patriam incolumem, amicos, genus, cognatos, ditias' [his parents, safe fatherland, friends, family, relations, wealth] (*Heautontimoroumenos*, 194).

As for alliteration, again there are plenty of instances from the beginning to the end of the comedy: 'nostrum fabricatorem fraudium conveniam Phroneum' (*Philodoxeos*, p. 185); 'aut tum ero preses popine, aut in hirneis imperabo' (*Philodoxeos*, p. 201); 'parem ut parturiat penam' (*Philodoxeos*, p. 203); 'fateor esse officium femine' (*Philodoxeos*, p. 207); 'Et quam es non similis solito, quam denique difformis!' (207); 'Sed senem convenio, *posthac ex tempore consilium capiam*' (*Philodoxeos*, p. 215). This last example was added in the second redaction and may derive from this specific alliterative passage in Terence: 'necessest, Clitipho, consilia consequi consimilia' (*Heautontimoroumenos*, 209), but there are many others in the ancient author.[38]

Overall, what is remarkable about the language of the comedy is the young Alberti's ability to reproduce even in his early first version, written at the age of twenty, a play that has so many classical elements, as well as those archaic forms of Latin typical of Plautus and Terence: his claim in the *Commentarium*, that the first version was in the comic style and had an archaic flavour ('et comicum dicendi genus et priscum quippiam redolebat', *Philodoxeos*, p. 147) is certainly justified. In fact even in the second version, as we have seen, the humanist retains several archaisms and rare words, which he often draws from the ancient lexicographers to enrich his Latin and give it a more archaic flavour.[39]

Alberti's first work, the *Philodoxeos Fabula*, is then a work of its time, typical of early Quattrocento humanism in its general imitative techniques, and also in its

124   MARTIN McLAUGHLIN

few residual medieval trappings. It is part of the humanistic revival of comedy that had begun with Pier Paolo Vergerio's *Paulus* (*c.* 1390) and Bruni's *Poliscena* (1408) and was gathering pace particularly in the 1420s, with Sicco Polenton's *Catinia* (1419), Antonio Barzizza's *Cauteriaria* (1420/25), and Pier Candido Decembrio's lost *Aphrodisia* (1420).[40] The comedy is indebted most of all to Terence, who had remained a canonical author throughout the Middle Ages. At the same time it is a remarkable work for the author's precocious assimilation of the themes, stock characters, stage devices and language of Latin comedy, especially in its precise echoing of Terentian lexis and style, and rich intertextual allusions. As Anthony Grafton noted, 'Alberti picked his Latin words and phrases with a watchmaker's delicate precision from a wide range of sources'.[41] This is certainly in evidence in Alberti's first literary work. The *Philodoxeos* was thus the closest imitation of a classical Roman comedy to have been written by that time, and — as is often the case with Alberti's works — it was a precocious precursor of a later literary trend, the Italian Renaissance revival of comedy in the following century.

Machiavelli: From the *Andria* to the *Mandragola*

When we turn to Machiavelli nearly 100 years later, many things have changed in the world of Italian humanism. The first printed editions of Plautus and Terence appeared from the 1470s onwards, the first performances of classical plays also took place in those decades, and study of Donatus's commentary, which was first printed around the text in a Venice 1476 edition, equipped scholars with the notions of unity of time and place as well as the idea that the play should be divided into five acts.[42] Machiavelli is famous for his political treatises and his study of ancient history, but he was also fascinated by Latin comedy. Around 1500, in a manuscript now in the Vatican (MS, Rossiano 884), he transcribed not only the whole of Lucretius's epic poem, *De rerum natura*, but also one of Terence's plays, the *Eunuchus*.[43] He also translated Terence's *Andria* into the Tuscan vernacular, in a first redaction that has traditionally been dated to 1517/18, and a second redaction around 1520. However, Stoppelli has recently argued for an earlier dating of the first version since the quality of its prose is so poor that it is difficult to conceive of it having been written by someone who had already composed the sophisticated prose of the *Prince* and the *Discorsi*.[44] In addition, Machiavelli was clearly aware of the early Ariosto comedies (*Cassaria, Suppositi*, 1508–09) as well as Bibbiena's *Calandra* (1513), so it is unlikely that he would merely translate rather than compose a comedy at this stage. And one further clue in favour of Stoppelli's dating is the famous reply by Davus to his master's questions: 'Davos sum, non Oedipus' [I am Davus, not Oedipus] (*Andria*, 194), for which Machiavelli offers two translations in the first redaction: 'Io son Davo, non propheta, vel non el frate' [I am Davus, not a prophet, *or* not the friar].[45] The friar in question is of course Savonarola, who had been burnt at the stake in 1498, so this allusion would make much more sense at the end of the fifteenth century, not two decades later. This first redaction also would fit in with his early transcription of the *Eunuch*, while his more polished version was almost certainly revised around the time he composed his own comedy, *La mandragola*, 1518–19.[46] Thus in the two decades from 1500 to 1520 Machiavelli moves from

THE RECOVERY OF TERENCE IN RENAISSANCE ITALY   125

the transcription of Terence to translation and finally to his own creation of a vernacular comedy in the Terentian vein.

In this second half of the chapter I examine Machiavelli's growing familiarity with the Roman playwright in more detail and how it developed and influenced his own comic creativity. Let us start by comparing his two translations of the *Andria*. One of the first features that strike the reader of the two versions is their brevity compared to the Latin original: Machiavelli regularly omits the many uses of the adjective 'miser/misera/miserum' in the play. To gives just two examples: the line 'ut me a Glycerio [miserum] abstrahat' [to tear me away from Glycerium and make me miserable] (*Andria*, 243) becomes in translation simply 'per svegliermi da Glicerio' [to tear me away from Glycerium]; 'egon propter me illam decipi [miseram] sinam?' [Shall I allow her to be deceived and made miserable on my account?] (*Andria*, 271) becomes simply 'Sopporterò io che la sia ingannata per mio conto?' [Shall I allow her to be deceived on my account?]; and so on.[47]

Another obvious characteristic of the translation is its increasing clarity, with Machiavelli's versions often being more explicit than the original. However, although one might think this clarity characteristic of the author of the *Prince*, in fact it has been shown by Edoardo Fumagalli that a number of his translation solutions are so dependent on a late Quattrocento commentary on Terence that this must have been what helped him reach some of these solutions.[48] Guido Juvenalis (Guy Jouanneaux) wrote a Latin commentary to Terence that was first published in a 1492 edition of the comedies, printed in Venice, but was reprinted several times, including in the 1515 Venice edition by Lazaro de' Soardi, which was probably the one used by Machiavelli. Amongst Fumagalli's examples proving this were the following: when Terence writes 'nodum in scirpo quaeris' [You're splitting hairs, literally 'you're looking for a knot in a bulrush'] (*Andria*, 941), Machiavelli translates this as 'Tu cerchi cinque piè al montone' [You're looking for a ram with five feet], a striking metaphor from the rural world which he must have derived from the explanation in Guido's commentary, which in turn comes from a French saying of the time: 'idest, tu quaeris in vervece quinque pedes'; similarly when Terence talks of 'vulgus servorum' [the common crowd of slaves] (*Andria*, 584), Machiavelli translates '*la maggior parte* de' servi' [the majority of slaves], relying again on Guido's commentary: 'idest *maior pars*'; or when early in the play Simo says 'haud muto factum' [I do not change this fact] (*Andria*, 40) Machiavelli's explanatory translation 'Io *non mi pento* di quello che io ho fatto' [I do not regret what I have done] is clearer and more satisfactory, but it is obvious that this too derives from Guido's commentary on this line: 'idest, *non me poenitet* id fecisse'.

In addition to Iuvenalis's commentary, the edition used by Machiavelli must have also contained Donatus's commentary, as Richardson showed, since the translation adopts some of Donatus's misunderstandings: thus the phrase 'nam quod tu speres propulsabo facile' [What you hope for I will reject utterly] (*Andria* 390) is first translated as 'Et io quel che tu speri facilmente confuterò' [What you hope for I will reject utterly], but the second redaction alters 'speri' [you hope for] to 'temi' [you fear] because at this point Donatus says that some critics take 'speres' to mean 'timeas' ('sunt qui "speres" pro "timeas" habent'); similarly at *Andria* 869, Donatus misunderstands the text, saying that the word 'pietatem' stands ironically for

126   MARTIN McLAUGHLIN

'impietatem', and Machiavelli duly translates this word as 'crudeltà', changed in the
second redaction to 'ribalderia', but both words are the opposite of 'pietatem'.[49]

Nevertheless, there is another constant in the translations which is entirely due to
Machiavelli, not to any commentary, and that is what we might call 'expressivity'.
Thus the phrase 'crucior miser' [I am wretched and tormented] (*Andria*, 851) is
rendered with a vivid image by our author: 'Io sono in su la fune' [I'm on the
rope]; and on another occasion the line 'adducti qui illam hinc civem dicant:
viceris' [if you bring witnesses who say she is a citizen, you'll have won] (*Andria*,
890) is translated with a pun: 'E, chi dice ch'ella è cittadina ateniese, abbi nome
Vinciguerra' [and whoever says she is an Athenian citizen should be called Victor!].
On occasions this liveliness of translation is toned down in Machiavelli's revised
translation: thus the question 'quid hic volt?' [What does this man want?] (*Andria*,
184) is initially translated as 'Che vuole questo cazo?' [What does this prick want?],
but in the revised translation he changes this to 'Che vuole questo zugo?' [What
does this idiot want?]; similarly the exclamation 'Perii! Metuo ut substet hospes'
[I'm done for! I'm afraid that this foreigner won't stand this] (*Andria*, 914) is initially
rendered with the vulgar 'Ehimé! Io ho paura che questo forestiero non si cachi
sotto [Damn, I'm afraid this foreigner will shit himself] before being changed in
the revised version to 'Ehimé! ho paura che questo forestiero non si pisci sotto'
[Damn, I'm afraid this foreigner will piss himself]. The very fact that he modified
these expressions in his revised translation shows that Machiavelli was aware of their
strong, expressive dimension.

Another feature of the *Andria* translation(s) is what can be called cultural transfer,
where the translator has to alter original expressions with allusions to classical
culture. We saw above that in Davus's proverbial reply Machiavelli altered the
Oedipus allusion to that of a 'prophet' (though in the end he rejected the topical
allusion to Savonarola). Similarly, in the very next line, when Simo says 'nempe
ergo aperte vis quae restant hodie me loqui?' [So you want me today to say openly
what remains to be said] (*Andria*, 195), the adverb 'aperte' [openly] is translated as 'in
big letters' (literally using apothecary's letters)': 'Quelle cose adunque che mi restano
a dirti, tu vuoi che io te le dica a lettere di speziali?' References to specifically
Roman culture and religion are also altered: thus when Davus says 'Interea introire
neminem | video, exire neminem, matronam nullam in aedibus' [I saw nobody go
into or leave the house, nor did I see any Roman matron indoors] (*Andria* 363–64),
the translator omits the second half of the sentence with the allusion to the figure of
the matron: 'Io mi fermai quivi e non vidi mai entrare né uscire persona.' Similarly
Davos's instruction to Mysis: 'ex ara hinc sume verbenas tibi | atque <ea>s substerne'
[take some foliage from the street altar and place it under the baby] (*Andria*, 726–27)
is translated but without the allusion to the altar, which was a typical feature of the
Roman stage: 'Raccogli paglie e vinciglie della via, e mettigliene sotto' [Gather up
straw and rushes from the street, and put some under the baby].

Lastly, in terms of style, it is clear that Machiavelli too, like Alberti a century
earlier, noted those two key stylistic features, Terence's fondness for alliteration and
lists. Thus in this sentence which has alliteration of the letter *v* in the first half and
the letter *m* in the second — 'verum illud verbumst, volgo quod dici solet, | omnis
sibi malle melius esse quam alteri' [That saying is true, the one that is on everyone's

THE RECOVERY OF TERENCE IN RENAISSANCE ITALY   127

lips, that everybody wishes better things for themselves than for others] (*Andria*, 426–27) — Machiavelli manages to reproduce alliteration at least in the first half: 'Vero è quel proverbio che dice che ognuno vuole meglio a sé che ad altri.' Similarly when Charinus says that everyone rejoices in the evils that befall others and takes advantage of the misfortunes of others in order to gain their own advantage — 'ut malis gaudeant atque ex incommodis | alterius sua ut comparent commoda' (627–28) — the translation also manages to reproduces the triple alliteration in the original: 'che si rallegri del male d'altri e degli incommodi d'altri cerchi i commodi suoi.' There is even an instance where we can see Machiavelli deliberately changing his first version in order to achieve an alliterative effect that is not in the original: near the beginning of the play Simo says that news of his story drove Chremes to come spontaneously to him ('hac fama impulsus Chremes | ultro ad me venit', *Andria*, 99–100), and at this point in his original version Machiavelli translates 'impulsus' [driven] with 'mosso' [moved] ('Cremete, mosso da questa buona fama, venne spontaneamente a trovarmi') but then in the second redaction he changes 'mosso' to 'spinto' [pushed] in order to use a livelier verb and one that makes an alliteration with 'spontaneamente': 'Cremete, spinto da questa buona fama, venne spontaneamente a trovarmi.'

As for lists, there are plenty of examples in the *Andria* and their effect did not go unnoticed by the translator. Near the start of the play Pamphilus itemizes the things that are tearing him apart: 'amor, misericordia huius, nuptiarum sollicitatio, | tum patris pudor' [love [for Glycerium], pity for her, worrying about the wedding, but also my reverence for my father] (*Andria*, 261–62), and Machiavelli too reproduces a list without conjunctions: 'l'amore, la misericordia, il pensare a queste nozze, la reverenza di mio padre'. Without citing all the other lists in the play, it is worth noting that at times Machiavelli even introduces a tighter list than was in the original: at one point Crito reassures Pamphilus that he will help him for a number of reasons, either for Pamphilus's own sake, or because it is the truth, or because it is what he wants for Glycerium herself ('Mitte orare. una harum quaevis causa me ut faciam monet, | vel tu vel quod verumst vel quod ipsi cupio Glycerio', *Andria*, 904–05). This final half sentence, a list linked by 'vel' three times, becomes even more concise in translation, with only one conjunction, and chimes with the brevity for which Machiavelli was famous in his other works as well: 'tu, il vero e il bene che voglio a Glicerio'. We shall see that this asyndetic cadence beginning with 'tu' will have a distinct echo in a famous line at the climax of the *Mandragola*, and it is to that play that we now turn.

The traditional dating of *La mandragola* is to the period 1518–19. Certainly the first mentions of it date from 1519–20, but recently Stoppelli has argued that Machiavelli may well have begun the comedy shortly after completing the *Prince*, around 1514, especially as it seems to contain a number of allusions to other comedies performed around 1513, particularly Bibbiena's *Calandra*, as well as having echoes of letters from Francesco Vettori to Machiavelli from 1514.[50] That would still be compatible with the author putting the finishing touches to *La mandragola* around 1518–19, at a time when he was also returning to the second redaction of his translation of the *Andria*.

La mandragola, for all its breathtaking modernity, is deeply indebted to Terence in many areas, from the contents of the prologue, to stock characters and characters'

128   MARTIN MCLAUGHLIN

names, to precise verbal echoes. Although he did not translate the prologue to the *Andria*, Machiavelli does write a prologue for his two comedies, *La mandragola* and *Clizia* (1525), the first one in verse, as in Terence's prologues, and he clearly understands its traditional ingredients. Just as each of Terence's prologues mentions the title of the comedy to be performed, so does Machiavelli in his first play: 'La favola Mandragola si chiama' (Stoppelli, p. 174), echoing closely the opening line of Terence's comedy about a mother-in-law: 'Hecyra est huic nomen fabulae' (*Hecyra*, 1); similarly the last line of the prologue — 'Né per ora aspettate altro argumento' [Do not expect any other explanation of the plot] (p. 176) — clearly echoes a line from the close of the *Adelphoe* prologue: 'dehinc ne exspectetis argumentum fabulae' (*Adelphoe*, 22). In between the beginning and end of the prologue, another characteristic element was to mention the various stock characters who will appear in the following play: Alberti had imitated this feature, as we saw, and Machiavelli does likewise though his characters are a mixture of classical stereotypes (a desperate lover, a parasite) between which he also inserts two contemporary figures (a stupid lawyer, a corrupt friar): 'Uno amante meschino, | un dottor poco astuto, | un frate mal vissuto, | un parassito di malizia il cucco, | fien questo giorno el vostro badalucco' [A desperate lover, a slow-witted lawyer, a corrupt friar, a parasite who is the personification of evil, will form your enjoyment today] (p. 174). So at the very outset of his masterpiece, a classic locus for intertextual allusions, Machiavelli's signals his homage to Terence, and even the names of two of the characters explicitly indicate his debt to the ancient author, since the servant Siro shares his name with the slaves in *Heautontimoroumenos* and *Adelphoe*, while Lucrezia's mother Sostrata has the same names as the mother figure in three Terence plays: *Heautontimoroumenos*, *Hecyra* and *Adelphoe*.

The imitation of the *Andria* is densest in the opening scenes, but there are many other phrases in the *Mandragola* that echo this and other Terence plays, as well as (to a lesser extent) passages from Plautus. Stoppelli has usefully listed most of these, but it is worth just dwelling on the opening scene to see how close this imitation is.[51] In the *Andria*, Simo's opening words to his servant — 'Sosia, | ades dum: paucis te volo' [Sosia, stay here, I want a few words with you] (*Andria*, 28–29) — and his praise of Sosia's faithfulness and taciturnity ('fide et taciturnitate', *Andria*, 34) are reproduced almost verbatim in Callimaco's opening words to his servant Siro: 'Siro, non ti partire. Io ti voglio un poco [...] Se io non ti ho detto infino a qui quello che io ti dirò ora, non è stato per non mi fidare di te' [Siro, stay here, I want a brief word with you [...] If I have not mentioned to you before what I am going to tell you now, this is not because I do not trust you] (Stoppelli, pp. 177–78). The same happens with the list of Callimaco's pleasurable and business activities when young:

> Avendo compartito el tempo parte alli studi, parte a' piaceri e parte alle faccende, ed in modo mi travagliavo in ciascuna di queste cose, che l'una non mi impediva la via dell'altra. E per questo, come tu sai, vivevo quietissimamente, giovando a ciascuno, ed ingegnandomi di non offendere persona: talché mi pareva essere grato a' borghesi, a' gentiluomini, al forestiero, al terrazzano, al povero e al ricco. (Stoppelli, pp. 179–80)

> [CA. I divided my time between study, pleasure and business, and worked at each of these things in such a way that one did not get in the way of the other.

THE RECOVERY OF TERENCE IN RENAISSANCE ITALY 129

And that was why, as you know, I lived in total tranquillity, helping everyone, and trying not to offend anyone, so much so that I think I was liked by the middle classes, aristocrats, foreigners and locals, rich and poor.]

This is clearly an imitation of the list of pursuits in which Pamphilus engaged, as recounted in the *Andria* by his father Simo:

SI. quod plerique omnes faciunt adulescentuli, | ut animum ad aliquod studium adiungant, aut equos | alere aut canes ad venandum aut ad philosophos [...] sic vita erat: facile omnis perferre ac pati; | cum quibus erat quomque una is sese dedere, | <eo>rum obsequi studiis, adversus nemini, | numquam praeponens se illis; ita ut facillume | sine invidia laudem invenias et amicos pares. (*Andria*, 55–57, 62–66)

[SI. He acted as all young men do, turning to some pursuit such as breeding horses or hounds for hunting, or studying philosophy [...] This was how he lived: tolerating everyone with equanimity, he devoted himself to whoever he was with, he followed their enthusiasms, made no enemies, never put himself above anyone else, so much so that if you behaved likewise, you would find praise without envy and peers who were your friends.]

Despite Machiavelli's stronger sociological stress on the class of people that liked Callimaco, an emphasis typical of the author of the *Prince* and the *Discorsi*, we can see that in these opening exchanges, the Renaissance author is following very closely in the ancient writer's footsteps.

The echoes of Terence continue throughout the comedy, and have been studied by scholars, but more attention has been paid to matters of content than to questions of style, and I want to end by examining Machiavelli's expertise in deploying those two characteristic stylistic features of ancient comedy, also identified by Alberti, alliteration and lists. In *La mandragola* too the author takes care to craft alliterative passages, particularly to emphasize key phrases such as proverbs or metaphors. Thus at the start of Act III, Sostrata in her soliloquy quotes the saying that it is the duty of a prudent man when faced with evil options to choose the one that is least worst: 'Io ho sempre mai sentito dire ch'egli è ufficio di uom prudente pigliare de' cattivi partiti el migliore' (p. 205); with even more insistent alliteration Fra Timoteo in his monologue in Act IV, Scene 6, also cites a proverb, the one that says that bad company leads men to the gallows: 'E' dicono el vero quelli che dicono che le cattive compagnie conducono li uomini alle forche' (p. 232); and at the start of Act IV, Callimaco in despair compares himself to a ship caught between two opposing winds, and is more afraid the nearer it is to the harbour: 'Io sono una nave vessata da dua diversi venti, che tanto più teme, quanto ella è più presso al porto' (p. 221). Here the Petrarchan image of the storm-tossed ship is heightened by the alliteration of v and p.

As for lists, Machiavelli had been fond of the effect of blunt, asyndetic lists with few or no conjunctions, in his political works, but this characteristic feature of his style was derived from or reinforced by this feature in Terence's works, as we saw in the *Andria* translation. Thus when Callimaco asks how Fra Timoteo and Lucrezia's mother can be corrupted (Act II.6), Ligurio replies with this list beginning with 'tu': 'Tu, io, e' danari, la cattiva natura loro' [You, me, money, their corrupt natures] (p. 202). As we saw above, Machiavelli had already translated two similar lists from the *Andria* (261–62; 904–05), and there is one final, even more pertinent example, when Pamphilus recalls the dying Chrysis's words when she entrusted Pamphilus to Glycerium as her husband, friend, protector and father ('te isti virum do, amicum tutorem patrem, *Andria* 295), a totally asyndetic phrase translated by Machiavelli as 'io ti do a costei marito, amico, tutore, padre' without any conjunctions. This last list in particular resurfaces at the climax of the *Mandragola* (v.4) when Lucrezia's words to Callimaco are reported by the latter as:

> CA. Poi che l'astuzia tua, la sciocchezza del mio marito, la semplicità di mia madre e la tristizia del mio confessoro mi hanno condutto a fare quello che mai per me medesima arei fatto, io voglio giudicare ch'e' venga da una celeste disposizione che abbi voluto cosí [...]. Però io ti prendo per signore, patrone, guida: tu mio padre, tu mio defensore e tu voglio che sia ogni mio bene. (p. 244)

> [CA. Since your ingenuity, my husband's stupidity, my mother's naivety and my confessor's perversity have led me to do what I would never have done on my own, I want to believe that this has been willed by divine disposition that has determined things this way. [...] Therefore I take you as my lord, defender, guide: you are my father, my defender and I want you to be the source of all my happiness.]

It is clear, I hope, from the foregoing analysis, that Terence was not just a general point of reference for these two revivers of comedy in the Italian Renaissance, but also the source of precise lexical and stylistic echoes. Alberti rewrites his first work largely in a Terentian key, and often at the expense of more Plautine farcical and lexical elements. As for Machiavelli, one might not have thought the author of the *Prince* would have had much time for the orthodox, domestic morality of Terence's plays, but not only did he transcribe and translate two of the Latin author's comedies, but his own masterpiece, *La mandragola*, takes its first steps guided very much by Terence's hand, and even some of the most 'Machiavellian' maxims in the play have their origin in or are trenchant reversals of the Latin originals. In the 100 or so years that separate the *Philodoxeos* from *La mandragola*, many things changed in the Italian humanist understanding of Latin comedy. Alberti wrote his comedy in Latin, the prestige language in Quattrocento Italy, but Machiavelli writes his comedy in the vernacular, as the new language comes to the fore at the start of the new century. Machiavelli is still reliant on commentators to understand Terence's plays, but it is also from these commentators, especially Donatus, that he learns about some things unknown to Alberti: the need to structure all comedies not just in scenes but in five acts, and the need for dramatic unities, especially the unity of time. Both the number of acts and the unity of time are explicitly and comically underlined in Fra Timoteo's final monologue (Act IV, Scene 10). Here he emphasizes that during the night the unity of time will not be broken since none of the main characters will sleep and to this metatheatrical allusion to classical conventions he adds a sexual aside to the audience that has no equivalent in Latin comedy:

> TI. Io dirò l'uffizio, Ligurio e Siro ceneranno, che non hanno mangiato oggi. El dottore andrà di camera in sala perché la cucina vadia netta. Callimaco e Madonna Lucrezia non dormiranno: perché io so, se io fussi lui e se voi fussi lei, che non dormiremo. (p. 237)

> [TI. I will say my office; Ligurio and Siro will be dining, for they have had

THE RECOVERY OF TERENCE IN RENAISSANCE ITALY 131

no food today; Dr Nicia will go from the bedroom to the main quarters, for
the kitchen has to be tidied; Callimaco and Lucrezia certainly will not sleep,
because I know that if I were Callimaco and you were her, we certainly would
not sleep.]

Alberti and Machiavelli exploit not just Terence's content, his comic scenes
and dramatic techniques but also his language and style, his emphatic lists and
alliterations. As in the best Renaissance drama, we clearly see behind the new
characters created for the stage in the *Philodoxeos* and especially *La mandragola*, the
stock stereotypes of Terence's plays. But each writer transforms the Terentian raw
materials into something of their own: Alberti uses many aspects of the ancient
model to produce an allegorical comedy that revolves around his pessimistic
obsessions with virtue pitted against power, wealth and chance; Machiavelli also
extracts his own favourite themes from the classical original (including of course
virtue and fortune), but he blends this with a striking modernity of character and
message, contemporary allusions to the wars of Italy, and a sense of the comic and
the secular that is very different from Alberti, and which contributes indispensable
elements to the rebirth of comedy in the Renaissance.

Two Scenes from the End of Machiavelli, *La mandragola* (1518)

These two scenes are the pre-penultimate and final scene of Machiavelli's comedy.
In the first scene the young lover Callimaco tells his helper Ligurio, the parasite,
about his night of love spent with the virtuous Lucrezia, wife of the old lawyer
Messer Nicia. In Lucrezia's declaration of love to Callimaco we see Machiavelli
twice use a verbal list, one of the rhetorical devices that were typical of Roman
comedies, Terence's in particular ('l'astuzia tua, la sciocchezza del mio marito, la
semplicità di mia madre e la tristizia del mio confessoro [...] io ti prendo per signore,
patrone, guida: tu mio padre, tu mio defensore [...]'), but in Terence these lists were
usually of someone's positive qualities. What is striking about this and the final
scene is the way Machiavelli has taken the stock characters and literary devices of
ancient comedy and placed them in a modern and shockingly immoral context.
Whereas ancient comedies normally ended with the young lover marrying the
girl he is in love with, *La mandragola* concludes not with a marriage but with the
beginning of an adulterous affair which is sanctioned by the Church in the person
of the fraudulent friar Timoteo. The characters' names also emphasize this sense
of reversal in a final scene which is spiced with the kind of double entendres that
would not have been found in Terence: Lucrezia's reaction to what is in effect a rape
orchestrated by her family and the Church is the opposite of the virtuous suicide
committed by her famous Roman namesake in Livy's account (*Ab urbe condita*, 1.
57–59). The duped old man Nicia is anything but the 'victor' that his Greek name
suggests, and of course the corrupt Fra Timoteo (whose name means 'honouring
God') behaves throughout the play, and especially in this final scene, as though his
only thoughts are about money. Machiavelli seems to be saying here, just as he does
in his political treatises, 'welcome to the modern world'!

132   Martin McLaughlin

Machiavelli, *La mandragola*, Act v, Scene 4

CALLIMACO, LIGURIO

CALLIMACO. Come io ti ho detto, Ligurio mio, io stetti di mala voglia infino alle nove
ore; e, benché io avessi gran piacere, e' non mi parve buono. Ma, poi che io me le fu'
dato a conoscere e ch'io l'ebbi dato ad intendere l'amore che io le portavo, e quanto
facilmente per la semplicità del marito noi potavàmo vivere felici sanza infamia
alcuna, promettendole che, qualunque volta Dio facessi altro di lui, di prenderla per
donna; ed avendo ella, oltre alle vere ragioni, gustato che differenza è dalla ghiacitura
mia a quella di Nicia e da e baci d'uno amante giovane a quelli d'uno marito vecchio,
doppo qualche sospiro disse: 'Poiché l'astuzia tua, la sciocchezza del mio marito, la
semplicità di mia madre e la tristizia del mio confessoro mi hanno condutto a fare
quello che mai per me medesima arei fatto, io voglio giudicare ch'e' venga da una
celeste disposizione che abbi voluto così, e non sono sufficiente a recusare quello che
'l Cielo vuole che io accetti. Però, io ti prendo per signore, patrone, guida: tu mio
padre, tu mio defensore, e tu voglio che sia ogni mio bene; e quel che 'l mio marito
ha voluto per una sera, voglio ch'egli abbia sempre. Fara'ti adunque suo compare, e
verrai questa mattina a la chiesa; e di quivi ne verrai a desinare con esso noi; e l'andare
e lo stare starà a te, e poterèno ad ogni ora e senza sospetto convenire insieme.' Io
fui, udendo queste parole, per morirmi per la dolcezza. Non potetti rispondere a la
minima parte di quello che io arei desiderato. Tanto che io mi truovo el più felice e
contento uomo che fussi mai nel mondo; e, se questa felicità non mi mancassi o per
morte o per tempo, io sarei più beato ch'e beati, più santo ch'e santi.
LIGURIO. Io ho gran piacere d'ogni tuo bene, ed ètti intervenuto quello che io ti dissi
appunto. Ma che facciamo noi ora?
CALLIMACO. Andiàno verso la chiesa, perché io le promissi d'essere là, dove la verrà lei,
la madre ed il dottore.
LIGURIO. Io sento toccare l'uscio suo: le sono esse, che escono fuora, ed hanno el dottore
drieto.
CALLIMACO. Avviànci in chiesa, e là aspettereno.
    [...]

Machiavelli, *La mandragola*, Act v, Scene 6

TIMOTEO, NICIA, LUCREZIA, CALLIMACO, LIGURIO, SOSTRATA

TIMOTEO. Io vengo fuora, perché Callimaco e Ligurio m'hanno detto che el dottore e le
donne vengono alla chiesa. Eccole.
NICIA. *Bona dies*, padre!
TIMOTEO. Voi sete le ben venute, e buon pro vi faccia, madonna, che Dio vi dia a fare un
bel figliuolo maschio!
LUCREZIA. Dio el voglia!
TIMOTEO. E' lo vorrà in ogni modo.
NICIA. Veggh'io in chiesa Ligurio e maestro Callimaco?
TIMOTEO. Messer sì.
NICIA. Accennateli.
TIMOTEO. Venite!
CALLIMACO. Dio vi salvi!
NICIA. Maestro, toccate la mano qui alla donna mia.
CALLIMACO. Volentieri.
NICIA. Lucrezia, costui è quello che sarà cagione che noi aremo uno bastone che sostenga
la nostra vecchiezza.

The Recovery of Terence in Renaissance Italy

Machiavelli, *La mandragola*, Act v, Scene 4

CALLIMACO, LIGURIO

CALLIMACO. My dear Ligurio, as I told you, I was uncomfortable being there up till about the ninth hour [2 am], and although I enjoyed great pleasure, it did not seem right. But then Lucrezia got to know me thoroughly and I made her realize how much I loved her, and how easily, given the naivety of her husband, we could live in happiness without any risk of scandal, promising her that I would marry her should God dispose otherwise of him; and apart from all these reasons, after she tasted the difference between what it was like being in bed with me and what it was like with Nicia, as well as the difference between a young lover's kisses and those of an old man, she sighed a little and said: 'Since your ingenuity, my husband's stupidity, my mother's naivety and my confessor's perversity have led me to do what I would never have done on my own, I want to believe that a divine disposition has determined things this way, and I am not strong enough to reject what heaven wants me to accept. So I take you as my lord, defender, guide: you are my father, my defender and I want you to be the source of all my happiness. And what my husband wanted to happen for one night I want for ever. So you must become the child's godfather, and you will come to the church this morning; and after that you must come and eat with us; and you can come and go into our house at your will; and you and I can be together at any time, without arousing suspicion.' On hearing these words, I was really on the point of dying for pleasure. I couldn't speak a tenth of what I would have liked to say. So now I feel I am the happiest and most contented man on earth; and if this happiness is not cut short by death or time, I would be more blest than the blessed, more ecstatic than the saints.

LIGURIO. I am very happy for all your blessings, and what has happened to you is precisely what I predicted.

CALLIMACO. Let us head towards the church, because I promised Lucrezia I'd be there: she herself, her mother and husband will be going.

LIGURIO. I hear sounds at her door. There are the two women coming out with Dr Nicia behind them.

CALLIMACO. Let's head off to the church and wait for them there.

    [...]

Machiavelli, *La mandragola*, Act v, Scene 6

TIMOTEO, NICIA, LUCREZIA, CALLIMACO, LIGURIO, SOSTRATA

TIMOTEO. I have come out here because Callimaco and Ligurio told me that the lawyer and the two women are coming to the church. Here they are.

NICIA. Bona dies, Father!

TIMOTEO. You are all welcome, and my lady, may this all turn out well and may God give you a fine baby boy!

LUCREZIA. May God will it!

TIMOTEO. He will want it to happen certainly.

NICIA. Is that Ligurio and Dr Callimaco that I see in the church?

TIMOTEO. You do, sir, yes.

NICIA. Go and tell them.

TIMOTEO. Come!

CALLIMACO. God save you all!

NICIA. Dr Callimaco, give your hand to my wife here.

CALLIMACO. Gladly.

NICIA. Lucrezia, this is the man who will provide a good stiff rod to support our old age.

LUCREZIA. Io l'ho molto caro, e vuolsi che sia nostro compare.

NICIA. Or benedetta sia tu! E voglio che lui e Ligurio venghino stamani a desinare con esso noi.

LUCREZIA. In ogni modo.

NICIA. E vo' dar loro la chiave della camera terrena d'in su la loggia, perché possino tornarsi quivi a loro comodità, che non hanno donne in casa, e stanno come bestie.

CALLIMACO. Io l'accetto, per usarla quando mi accaggia.

TIMOTEO. Io ho avere e danari per la limosina?

NICIA. Ben sapete come, domine, oggi vi si manderanno.

LIGURIO. Di Siro non è uomo che si ricordi?

NICIA. Chiegga, ciò che io ho è suo. Tu, Lucrezia, quanti grossi hai a dare al frate, perentrare in santo?

LUCREZIA. Dategliene dieci.

NICIA. Affogaggine!

TIMOTEO. E voi, madonna Sostrata, avete, secondo che mi pare, messo un tallo in sul vecchio.

SOSTRATA. Chi non sarebbe allegra?

TIMOTEO. Andianne tutti in chiesa, e quivi direno l'orazione ordinaria; dipoi, doppo l'uficio, ne andrete a desinare a vostra posta. Voi, aspettatori, non aspettate che noi usciàno più fuora: l'uficio è lungo, io mi rimarrò in chiesa, e loro, per l'uscio del fianco, se n'andranno a casa. Valète!

Bibliography

ALBERTI, LEON BATTISTA, *Philodoxeos fabula*, ed. by Lucia Cesarini Martinelli, *Rinascimento*, 17 (1977), 111–234

ANDREWS, RICHARD, *Scripts and Scenarios: The Performance of Comedy in Renaissance Italy* (Cambridge: Cambridge University Press, 1993)

ARBIZZONI, GUIDO, 'Il teatro in età umanistica', in *Storia di Ferrara*, vol. VII: *Il Rinascimento: la letteratura*, ed. by Walter Moretti (Ferrara: Librit, 1987), pp. 266–95

BARTON, ANNE, *The Names of Comedy* (Oxford: Clarendon Press, 1990)

CASELLA, ANGELA 'Presentazione', in *Tutte le opere di Ludovico Ariosto*, ed. by Cesare Segre, vol. IV: *Commedie*, ed. by Angela Casella, Gabriella Ronchi, Elena Varasi (Milan: Mondadori, 1974)

CODOÑER, CARMEN, 'La doble versión del *Philodoxeos* albertiano', in *Leon Battista Alberti umanista e scrittore. Filologia, esegesi, tradizione. Atti dei Convegni internazionali del Comitato Nazionale VI centenario della nascita di Leon Battista Alberti (Arezzo, 24–25–26 giugno 2004)*, ed. by Roberto Cardini, Mariangela Regoliosi, 2 vols (Florence: Polistampa, 2008), I, 191–219

DECEMBRIO, ANGELO, *Politiæ literariæ Angeli Decembrii mediolanensis oratoris clarissimi ad summum pontificem Pium II libri septem [...]* (Augsburg: H. Steynerus, 1540)

FAVARETTO, MATTEO, 'Un anonimo volgarizzamento rinascimentale del II e IV atto dell'*Andria* di Terenzio', *Filologia italiana*, 7 (2010), 81–105

FUBINI, RICCARDO, and ANNA MENCI GALLORINI, 'L'autobiografia di Leon Battista Alberti. Studio e edizione', *Rinascimento*, 12 (1972), 21–78

FUMAGALLI, EDOARDO, 'Machiavelli traduttore di Terenzio', *Interpres*, 16 (1997), 204–39

——'Machiavelli e l'esegesi terenziana', in *Il teatro di Machiavelli*, ed. by Gennaro Barbarisi and Anna Maria Cabrini (Milan: Cisalpino, 2005), pp. 125–46

GRAFTON, ANTHONY, 'Leon Battista Alberti: The Writer as Reader', in his *Commerce with the Classics: Ancient Books and Renaissance Readers* (Ann Arbor: University of Michigan Press, 1997), pp. 53–92

LUCREZIA. He has been very good to me, and we should make him the godfather.

NICIA. God bless you. Lucrezia! And I want him and Ligurio to come and eat with us today in our house.

LUCREZIA. Certainly.

NICIA. And I want to give them the key to the ground-floor bedroom, which looks onto the loggia, so that they can come back here whenever they need to, for they have no women in their own house and live like animals.

CALLIMACO. I accept this kind offer, so I can use the room whenever the need arises.

TIMOTEO. And am I to have anything for my charitable work?

NICIA. You know well, domine, that the money will be given to you today.

LIGURIO. Has nobody remembered about Siro?

NICIA. Let him ask what he wants: what I have is his. You, Lucrezia, how much money have you got to give the friar so you can be blessed?

LUCREZIA. Give him ten grossi.

NICIA. Heaven help me!

TIMOTEO. So, madam Sostrata, you have managed to graft a new shoot onto the old trunk, as far as I can see.

SOSTRATA. What woman would not be happy at this?

TIMOTEO. Let us all go into the church, and we will say the ordinary prayers; then after I say the office, you will all go home to dine at your house. [To the audience] And you spectators, do not wait for us to come back out: the office is long, I will stay in the church while they go back home by the side door. Farewell!

Humanist Comedies, ed. by Gary R. Grund (Cambridge, MA: Harvard University Press, 2005)

HERRICK, MARVIN T., *Italian Comedy of the Renaissance* (Urbana: University of Illinois Press, 1966)

MACHIAVELLI, NICCOLÒ, *Teatro: Andria, Mandragola, Clizia*, ed. by Guido Davico Bonino (Turin: Einaudi, 2001 [1979])

MARASCHIO, NICOLETTA, 'Aspetti del bilinguismo albertiano nel *De pictura*', *Rinascimento*, 12 (1972), 183–228

MARTELLI, MARIO, 'La versione machiavelliana dell'*Andria*', *Rinascimento*, 8 (1968), 203–74

MASTROROSA, IDA, 'La tradizione memorialistico-antiquaria romana in Leon Battista Alberti: Valerio Massimo e Gellio', in *Leon Battista Alberti e la tradizione: Per lo «smontaggio» dei mosaici albertiani. Atti del Convegno internazionale del Comitato Nazionale VI centenario della nascita di Leon Battista Alberti (Arezzo, 23–24–25 settembre 2004)*, ed. by Roberto Cardini, Mariangela Regoliosi (Florence: Polistampa, 2007), pp. 383–414

McLAUGHLIN, MARTIN, 'Alberti's *Canis*: Structure and Sources in the Portrait of the Artist as a Renaissance Dog', *Albertiana*, 14 (2011), 55–83

—— 'From Lepidus to Leon Battista Alberti: Naming, Renaming and Anonymizing the Self in Quattrocento Italy', *Romance Studies*, 31.3–4 (November 2013), 152–66

PANDOLFI, CLAUDIA, 'Il *Commentarium* e la dedica della *Philodoxeos fabula*. Osservazioni sui paratesti', in *Leon Battista Alberti. Actes du Congrès International 'Gli Este e l'Alberti: Tempo e misura'* (Ferrara, 29. XI. — 3. XII. 2004), ed. by Francesco Furlan & Gianni Venturi, 2 vols, special issue of *Schifanoia*, 30–31 (Pisa-Rome: Serra, 2010), I, 99–117

PERRY, JON, 'A Fifteenth-Century Dialogue on Literary Taste: Angelo Decembrio's Account of Playwright Ugolino Pisani at the Court of Leonello d'Este', *Renaissance Quarterly*, 39 (1986), 613–43

PIERI, MARZIA, *La nascita del teatro moderno in Italia tra XV e XVI secolo* (Turin: Bollati Boringhieri, 1989)

POLIZIANO, ANGELO, *La commedia antica e l'Andria di Terenzio. Appunti inediti*, ed. by Rosetta Lattanzi Roselli (Florence: Sansoni, 1973)

136   Martin McLaughlin

Reynolds, Leighton D. (ed.), *Texts and Transmission: A Survey of the Latin Classics* (Oxford: Clarendon Press, 1986)

—— 'Donatus', in Reynolds 1986, pp. 153–56

—— 'Plautus' in Reynolds 1986, pp. 302–07

—— 'Terence', in Reynolds 1986, pp. 412–20

Ribuoli, Riccardo, *La collazione polizianea del codice bembino di Terenzio. Con le postille inedite del Poliziano e note su Pietro Bembo* (Rome: Edizioni di Storia e Letteratura, 1981)

Richardson, Brian, 'Evoluzione stilistica e fortuna della traduzione machiavelliana dell'*Andria*', *Lettere italiane*, 25 (1973), 319–38

Stäuble, Antonio, *La commedia umanistica del Quattrocento* (Florence: Istituto Palazzo Strozzi, 1968)

Stoppelli, Pasquale, *La mandragola: storia e filologia. Con l'edizione critica del testo secondo il Laurenziano Redi 129* (Rome: Bulzoni, 2005),

Terentius in sua metra restitutus, ed. by Benedictus Philologus (Florence: Giunta, 1505)

Villa, Claudia, *La 'Lectura Terentii'*, vol. i: *Da Ildemaro a Francesco Petrarca* (Padua: Antenore, 1984)

Notes to Chapter 6

I am very grateful to Dr Giuseppe Pezzini for his expert advice on ancient comedy in general, and on Terence's comedies in particular.

1. For instance, Marvin T. Herrick, *Italian Comedy of the Renaissance* (Urbana: University of Illinois Press, 1966); Marzia Pieri, *La nascita del teatro moderno in Italia tra XV e XVI secolo* (Turin: Bollati Boringhieri, 1989); Richard Andrews, *Scripts and Scenarios: The Performance of Comedy in Renaissance Italy* (Cambridge: Cambridge University Press, 1993), esp. pp. 24–56.

2. For the textual transmission of Terence in the Middle Ages and Renaissance, see Claudia Villa, *La 'Lectura Terentii'*, vol. i: *Da Ildemaro a Francesco Petrarca* (Padua: Antenore, 1984); Leighton D. Reynolds, 'Terence', in his *Texts and Transmission: A Survey of the Latin Classics* (Oxford: Clarendon Press, 1986), pp. 412–20.

3. On Plautus, see Reynolds, *Texts and Transmission*, pp. 302–07; on Donatus, ibid., pp. 153–56.

4. Reynolds, *Texts and Transmission*, p. 419; Guido Davico Bonino, 'Introduzione', in Niccolò Machiavelli, *Teatro: Andria, Mandragola, Clizia*, ed. by Guido Davico Bonino (Turin: Einaudi, 2001 [1979]), pp. viii–ix. Poliziano's course on the *Andria* can be found in Angelo Poliziano, *La commedia antica e l'Andria di Terenzio. Appunti inediti*, ed. by Rosetta Lattanzi Roselli (Florence: Sansoni, 1973). Poliziano also knew the importance of the Codex Bembinus of Terence: see Riccardo Ribuoli, *La collazione polizianea del codice bembino di Terenzio. Con le postille inedite del Poliziano e note su Pietro Bembo* (Rome: Edizioni di Storia e Letteratura, 1981).

5. See Matteo Favaretto, 'Un anonimo volgarizzamento rinascimentale del II e IV atto dell'*Andria* di Terenzio', *Filologia italiana*, 7 (2010), 81–105 (p. 82, n. 2).

6. For the precise dating of Ariosto's comedies, see Angela Casella, 'Presentazione', in *Tutte le opere di Ludovico Ariosto*, ed. by Cesare Segre, vol. IV: *Commedie*, ed. by Angela Casella, Gabriella Ronchi, Elena Varasi (Milan: Mondadori, 1974), pp. ix–xlix. On humanist (mis)understanding of the metre of Latin comedy, see *Humanist Comedies*, ed. by Gary R. Grund (Cambridge, MA: Harvard University Press, 2005), p. x, and Reynolds, 'Terence', in his *Texts and Transmission*, pp. 417–18: once Poliziano had read the Bembinus manuscript of Terence, in 1491, he was able to see that the plays were written in verse: 'Erat enim liber in versus digestus' (Ribuoli, *La collazione polizianea del codice bembino di Terenzio*, p. 64). This interest in metre soon led to a first printed attempt to present the comedies in verse, in Benedictus Philologus's edition of *Terentius in sua metra restitutus* (Florence: Giunta, 1505).

7. 'In ea quidem aegritudine suos perpessus est affines non pios neque humanos. Idcirco consolandi gratia, intermissis iurium studiis, inter curandum et convalescendum scripsit *Philodoxeos* fabulam, annos natus non plus viginti' [And it was during that illness that he discovered that his relations showed him neither sympathy nor humanity. As a result, in order to console himself,

THE RECOVERY OF TERENCE IN RENAISSANCE ITALY   137

he interrupted his law studies, and in the process of looking after himself and returning to full health, he wrote the comedy *Philodoxeos*, when he was not more than twenty years old]. See Riccardo Fubini, Anna Menci Gallorini, 'L'autobiografia di Leon Battista Alberti. Studio e edizione', *Rinascimento*, 12 (1972), 21–78 (p. 69).

8. 'Denique annos decem [comedia] vagata est': for the text of both redactions see 'Leon Battista Alberti, *Philodoxeos fabula*, edizione critica a cura di Lucia Cesarini Martinelli', *Rinascimento*, 17 (1977), 111–234 (p. 147). Future references to the two redactions will be from this edition and will be given in the text of this chapter, using the abbreviation '*Philodoxeos*' followed by the page number. As for the obscene elements, the editor of the *Philodoxeos* rightly doubts that these were added by others since that would have given rise to an intermediate redaction of which there is no trace in the manuscripts. In fact there are some scurrilous passages in Alberti's first version which he took care to eliminate in the second: see *Philodoxeos*, p. 112, n. 1 for a list. The second redaction of the *Philodoxeos* with a facing page English translation (not always accurate) can be found in *Humanist Comedies*, ed. by Grund, pp. 70–169.

9. On the significance of Alberti's pseudonym, see Martin McLaughlin, 'From Lepidus to Leon Battista Alberti: Naming, Renaming and Anonymizing the Self in Quattrocento Italy', *Romance Studies*, 31.3–4 (November, 2013), 152–66.

10. Terence features prominently in the discussions between Leonello, Guarino and other humanists, in Chapters 3, 17, 21–22 and 58 of Angelo Decembrio's famous Latin dialogue which offers a portrait of Leonello's Court in the mid-1430s: *Politiæ literariæ Angeli Decembrii mediolanensis oratoris clarissimi ad summum pontificem Pium II libri septem [...]* (Augsburg: H. Steynerus, MDXXXX). On Leonello's and his Court's enthusiasm for Latin comedies, see Guido Arbizzoni, 'Il teatro in età umanistica', in *Storia di Ferrara*, vol. VII: *Il Rinascimento: la letteratura*, ed. by Walter Moretti (Ferrara: Librit, 1987), pp. 266–95 (270); and Jon Perry, 'A Fifteenth-Century Dialogue on Literary Taste: Angelo Decembrio's Account of Playwright Ugolino Pisani at the Court of Leonello d'Este', *Renaissance Quarterly*, 39 (1986), 613–43.

11. For the paratexts that accompanied Terence's comedies in the middle ages and up to the Quattrocento, see Villa, 'La *Vita Terentii* di Francesco Petrarca', in '*La "Lectura Terentii"*', pp. 191–216. Perhaps the fact that Terence too was driven by envy to defend himself in his prologues was another reason why Alberti identified with the Roman comedian: Petrarch's *Life of Terence* states that it was his rivals' envy of him that drove the ancient author to write prologues ('quibus [prologis] scribendis emulorum invidia causam dedit', cited by Villa, p. 205).

12. 'Hercle, et bellula est: insunt qui ament, qui decipiant, qui construant festos. Certiores vos reddo: hec est fabula, Philodoxios dicitur fabula' (*Philodoxeos*, First Prologue, p. 149).

13. Cf. *Eunuchus*, Prologue, 35–41: 'currentem servom [...], | bonas matronas [...], meretrices malas, | parasitum edacem, gloriosum militem, | puerum supponi, falli per servom senem, | amare odisse suspicari' [slaves running about, good women, wicked prostitutes, a greedy parasite, a boastful soldier, changelings, an old man being tricked by his servant, love affairs, hatred, suspicion]; and *Heautontimoroumenos*, Prologue, 37–39: 'servo' currens, iratus senex, | edax parasitu', sycophanta autem inpudens, | avaru' leno' [a slave running about, an angry old man, a greedy parasite, a cheeky sycophant, a miserly pimp].

14. At the end of *Adelphoe*, the son who has witnessed his authoritarian father become more relaxed about his son's marriage calls him 'very charming' (*lepidissume*) and the father then replies 'Great, now they say I'm charming [*lepidus*] [...] I have become charming [*lepidus*] and have become popular' ('Euge, iam lepidus vocor [...] ego lepidus ineo gratiam', *Adelphoe*, 911–14). In fact, the *Adelphoe* is of all Terence's comedies the one that has most influence on the *Philodoxeos*.

15. *Philodoxeos*, p. 144. See also Claudia Pandolfi, 'Il *Commentarium* e la dedica della *Philodoxeos fabula*. Osservazioni sui paratesti', *Leon Battista Alberti. Actes du Congrès International 'Gli Este e l'Alberti: Tempo e misura'* (Ferrara, 29 Nov–3 Dec 2004), ed. by Francesco Furlan & Gianni Venturi, 2 vols, special issue of *Schifanoia*, 30–31 (Pisa and Rome: Serra, 2010), I, 99–117.

16. All in all, Terence uses the verb 'occipere' once in *Hecyra* and in *Phormio*, twice in the *Andria* and *Heautontimoroumenos*, four times in *Adelphoe*, and five times in *Eunuchus*, including one instance in the prologue — 'magistratus quom ibi adesset occeptast agi' (line 22).

17. 'Phimiamque ... vitiat' (p. 150) in the first redaction becomes 'Phimiam rapit' (p. 151) in the second, and 'ut sedatis omnibus hanc compressam hic teneat' (p. 150), is replaced by 'ex quo

138   MARTIN McLAUGHLIN

hic raptam tenuit' (p. 151). The verb 'vitiare' appears already in the summary of the *Eunuchus* ('introiit, vitiat virginem', *Eunuchus*, 10), as well as on four other occasions in the play (654, 704, 857–58, 953); it is also used twice in the Summary of *Adelphoe* (lines 8, 13), and twice more in the play itself (466–67, 686); and 'comprimere' is used three times in the *Hecyra* (572, 828, 832); and once each in *Phormio* (1017–18) and *Adelphoe* (474–75).

18. See McLaughlin, 'From Lepidus to Leon Battista Alberti', pp. 156–58.

19. See above, n. 10.

20. Notably Vergerio's *Paulus* (c. 1390) and Polenton's *Catinia* (1419) had plots based on *novelle*: see Antonio Stäuble, *La commedia umanistica del Quattrocento* (Florence: Istituto Palazzo Strozzi, 1968), pp. 10, 19, 26. See also Alberti, *Philodoxeos fabula*, p. 113; *Humanist Comedies*, pp. viii–ix.

21. *Philodoxeos*, p. 113, n. 3.

22. In *De amicitia* Cicero had pointed out that it would have been sufficient for Gnatho to say to Thraso that Thais was very grateful, not hugely so: ' "Magnas vero agere gratias Thais mihi?" Satis erat respondere: "magnas"; "ingentes" inquit' (*De amicitia*, 98). In Scene 4 when Philodoxus thanks Phroneus profusely — 'Tibi etiam ingentes gratias — et utinam condignas exoptatasque! — pro tuo hoc tanto facinore referam' [I will bear you huge gratitude — and I hope it will be appropriate gratitude and something you wished for — for this wonderful deed of yours] (pp. 166–67) — the wording clearly shows that it derives from the Terence and Cicero passages (and in any case Cicero's treatise on friendship was one of Alberti's favourite texts). The protagonist seems initially to be guilty of flattery in thanking Phroneus using the exaggerated adjective 'ingentes' but the addition of 'condignas exoptatasque' shows that he wants to avoid such a charge, and has Cicero's (and possibly Dante's) condemnation of flattery in mind.

23. For such 'Cratylic' names, see Anne Barton, *The Names of Comedy* (Oxford: Clarendon Press, 1990), p. 45.

24. *Philodoxeos*, p. 115, n. 1.

25. See above, note 6.

26. 'Tractabo, amplectar, morsibus cunctam insignibo, omnem ligurriam totam' (*Philodoxeos*, p. 192).

27. Carmen Codoñer, 'La doble versión del *Philodoxeos* albertiano', in *Leon Battista Alberti umanista e scrittore. Filologia, esegesi, tradizione. Atti dei Convegni internazionali del Comitato Nazionale VI centenario della nascita di Leon Battista Alberti (Arezzo, 24–25–26 giugno 2004)*, ed. by Roberto Cardini, Mariangela Regoliosi, 2 vols (Florence: Polistampa, 2007), I, 191–219.

28. 'Sed, proh deum, quid hoc monstri est, *hominem, quod alium amet, sibi ipsi admodum esse inimicum? Ne vero maiora procul dubio tormenta sunt que amans ipse sibi afferat, quam que ab inimicis deveniant! Amantis animus nunquam tristi est cura et sollicitudine vacuus est*' (*Philodoxeos*, p. 153).

29. 'di boni, quid hoc morbist? adeon homines inmutarier | ex amore ut non cognoscas eundem esse!' (*Eunuchus*, 225–26).

30. '*Quam est in omni vita facilitas imprimis et grata is, cum quibus vivas, et utilis his, qui isthac eadem virtute sciant uti! Difficilem omnes et noti et ignoti odere, facilem atque indulgentem nemo non diligit. Id quidem ipsum modo perdisci licet ex me*' (*Philodoxeos*, p. 213).

31. 're eapse repperi | facilitate nihil esse homini melius neque clementia. | id esse uerum ex me atque ex fratre quoiuis facilest noscere. | [...] illum amant, me fugitant' (*Adelphoe*, 860–72).

32. 'Venit Fortunius... voluit... rupit... introivit... noluit... fecit... abiit' (*Philodoxeos*, p. 196).

33. MNI. Venit *Thrasis*... PHIL. *Metuo*. MNI.... rupit... PHRON. *Hem*. MNI... introivit... PHRON. *Malum*. MNI.... rapuit... PHIL. O me infelicissimum! (2nd version, *Philodoxeos*, pp. 197–99).

34. Pasquale Stoppelli, *La mandragola: storia e filologia. Con l'edizione critica del testo secondo il Laurenziano Redi 129* (Rome: Bulzoni, 2005), p. 55.

35. For the phrase 'ut aiunt' and its equivalents signalling the quotation from a classical source, see Martin McLaughlin, 'Alberti's *Canis*: Structure and Sources in the Portrait of the Artist as a Renaissance Dog', *Albertiana*, 14 (2011), 55–83 (pp. 71–72).

36. Similarly in his description of Apelles' painting of *Calumny* in *De pictura* (3. 53) Alberti opts for the less usual 'pulla veste' where Guarino had used the more common 'obscura veste': see Nicoletta Maraschio, 'Aspetti del bilinguismo albertiano nel *De pictura*', *Rinascimento*, 12 (1972), 183–228 (p. 216, n. 2; p. 217).

37. For Alberti's reading of Aulus Gellius, see Ida Mastrorosa, 'La tradizione memorialistico-

antiquaria romana in Leon Battista Alberti: Valerio Massimo e Gellio', in *Leon Battista Alberti e la tradizione: Per lo «smontaggio» dei mosaici albertiani. Atti del Convegno internazionale del Comitato Nazionale VI centenario della nascita di Leon Battista Alberti (Arezzo, 23–24–25 settembre 2004)*, ed. by Roberto Cardini, Mariangela Regoliosi (Florence: Polistampa, 2007), pp. 383–414.

38. For instance: 'quo pacto porro possim | potiri, consilium volo capere una tecum' (*Eunuchus*, 613–14); 'hic est vietus, vetus, veternosus senex' (*Eunuchus*, 688); 'profundat, perdat, pereat' (*Adelphoe*, 134), and so on.

39. Cesarini Martinelli (*Philodoxeos*, p. 232) gives a list of such words: some of these, such as 'heritudo' (p. 162), 'flagrio' (p. 194) and so on, are omitted or modified, but many others are retained: 'bellitudo' (pp. 192–93), 'consuetio' (pp. 182–83), 'deponta' (208–09), and in one case Alberti actually eliminates the classical form ('famulus', p. 154) for an archaic one ('famel', p. 155).

40. Stäuble, *La commedia umanistica del Quattrocento*, pp. 10–25.

41. Anthony Grafton, 'Leon Battista Alberti: The Writer as Reader', in his *Commerce with the Classics: Ancient Books and Renaissance Readers* (Ann Arbor: University of Michigan Press, 1997), pp. 53–92 (p. 58).

42. Reynolds, *Texts and Transmission*, p. 155.

43. See Davico Bonino, 'Introduzione', pp. v–vi.

44. Stoppelli, 'La datazione dell'*Andria*', in *La mandragola: storia e filologia*, pp. 25–41. He also argues for a later dating of the second redaction, perhaps as late as 1525–27.

45. References to Machiavelli's translations in what follows will be from Machiavelli, *Teatro: Andria, Mandragola, Clizia*, ed. by Davico Bonino, cit., pp. 9–61, except for any references to the first redaction which can be found in the textual apparatus in Mario Martelli, 'La versione machiavelliana dell'*Andria*', *Rinascimento*, 8 (1968), 203–74.

46. Martelli, 'La versione machiavelliana dell'*Andria*', cit.

47. Other examples of the omission of the adjective are at *Andria*, 351, 616 etc.

48. Edoardo Fumagalli, 'Machiavelli traduttore di Terenzio', *Interpres*, 16 (1997), 204–39, and 'Machiavelli e l'esegesi terenziana', in *Il teatro di Machiavelli*, ed. by Gennaro Barbarisi and Anna Maria Cabrini (Milan: Cisalpino, 2005), pp. 125–46; see also Brian Richardson, 'Evoluzione stilistica e fortuna della traduzione machiavelliana dell'*Andria*', *Lettere italiane*, 25 (1973), 319–38.

49. Richardson, 'Evoluzione stilistica e fortuna', pp. 320–21.

50. Stoppelli, 'La composizione del testo', in *La mandragola: storia e filologia*, pp. 69–89.

51. Stoppelli, *La mandragola: storia e filologia*, pp. 52–55, n. 27.

CHAPTER 7

❖

Palimpsestuous Phaedra:
William Gager's Additions to Seneca's
Tragedy for his 1592 Production at
Christ Church, Oxford

Elizabeth Sandis

Merton College, Oxford

In 1592, an impressive theatrical display akin to a drama festival was produced at Christ Church, Oxford.[1] The three plays performed were composed by the same author, the jurist William Gager (1555–1622), and staged on consecutive nights: *Ulysses Redux* (6 February); *Rivales* (7 February); *Panniculus Hippolyto Senecae Tragoediae Assutus* (8 February). In contrast to Gager's previous productions, the arrangement of such entertainments had not been occasioned by the visit of any dignitary and there had been no instructions issued from Court, as there would be the following September for Queen Elizabeth's visit. There was, however, rising tension within the University over the practice of staging plays in colleges, with opinion on both sides becoming increasingly outspoken. The season of plays at Christ Church seems to have been motivated by a desire to promote academic drama and lead by active example,[2] placing Gager in the firing line for criticism by objectors such as the theologian John Rainolds.[3] This is an important context for interpreting the plays, though too often scholarly engagement with the Gagerian corpus has failed to move beyond the Rainolds controversy, resulting in a tradition of regular but superficial references to the plays. Thus Gager's work has become familiar as evidence for the historical context, but the plays themselves deserve closer attention.

This is most notably the case with Gager's *Panniculus Hippolyto Senecae Tragoediae Assutus* [Little Patch Sewn on to Seneca's *Hippolytus*], where the entrance of Momus at the end of the epilogue is regularly cited, but references to the play very rarely move beyond a reiteration of Rainolds's suspicions that in the figure of Gager's Momus he was personally depicted.[4] In focusing on the finale to the *Panniculus* we forget the main rationale behind the composition of the play, which offers a display of creativity in tension with self-conscious appropriation of Senecan rhetorical techniques. As the title suggests, Gager's technique in the *Panniculus*

142   ELIZABETH SANDIS

is to offer his audience both the Senecan play they knew so well ('Quem Seneca vestrum lateat?' [For which of you does not know Seneca?], line 30, Prologue to *Pann.*) and a variety of scenes of his own invention.[5] In layering the canonical work with fresh innovations, Gager makes conspicuous advertisement of his engagement with the Senecan tradition, positioning himself as a direct follower of Seneca's rhetorical methods. When we examine his new scenes in detail and investigate their impact upon the rest of the play, we discover that, far from offering the audience a wholesome, moralizing narrative, as Gager was tempted into arguing in reactionary defensiveness to Rainolds's criticism, his interventions in Seneca's *Phaedra* actually serve to problematize the play's moral structure.[6] To take an example, we may observe how he approaches the treatment of the figure of Phaedra. His very conscious handling of Phaedra as a *literary* persona prioritizes word-craft and inter-textual conversations over moral messages, with an emphasis on rhetoric that illuminates the larger story of Senecan imitation operating within the *Panniculus*. Through an examination of Phaedra's characterization we can see how Gager implements Seneca's rhetorical methods by inventing self-referential, set-piece speeches, sewn on as new layers on top of the character's existing literary heritage. Phaedra thus speaks not with the voice of a single character but that of a literary palimpsest.

One of the key elements of Seneca's portrayal of Phaedra, to which we see Gager providing a creative response, is her intriguingly disjointed sense of identity, which frees her to pick up and drop new guises at will. As has often been noted, Phaedra is apt to rewrite her own character as suits the moment, employing something akin to shape-shifting tactics in her efforts to win Hippolytus, most famously at *Ph.* 609–11: 'Matris superbum est nomen et nimium potens: | nostros humilius nomen affectus decet; | me uel sororem, Hippolyte, uel famulam uoca' ['Mother' is overly grand, too powerful a title, | my feelings call for a humbler name: | call me 'sister', Hippolytus, or call me 'servant'].

In searching for the name to fit the role she *wants* to play, Phaedra does away with any genuine sense of propriety, hoping that the right rhetoric can be used to override the inconvenience of being Hippolytus' stepmother. As Braden puts it, in Phaedra's hands, '[s]ocial bonds are, at best, ploys to be cynically manipulated'.[7] At *Ph.* 620–23, she invites Hippolytus to enter into role-play with her, offering him the position of powerful king and commanding him to rule ('rege'), whilst she will take the role of suppliant and slave under his protecting embrace ('sinu receptam supplicem ac seruam tege'). Experimenting with various permutations of the character 'Phaedra', she tries to solicit Hippolytus' attention adopting one label after another: 'miserere uiduae' [pity the widow] (*Ph.* 623), 'miserere amantis' [pity the lover] (*Ph.* 671). Yielding to the effects of her passion, *furor*, Phaedra has allowed the framework of social structure to dissolve, and substituted a fantasy world of her own making, where identities can be re-worked and re-fashioned through word play.

Ultimately, however, Phaedra's struggle to reinvent herself is futile; she cannot speak her way out of her fate, nor can she dodge the literary tradition and mythological cycle to which she belongs. Seneca has her reflect on this fact self-consciously, flinching at the pattern which she sees emerging. She sees herself

PALIMPSESTUOUS PHAEDRA   143

imprisoned in a cycle of inherited sin: first her mother Pasiphae, 'fatale miserae matris agnosco malum' [I recognize poor mother's fateful sin] (*Ph.* 113), and then her sister Ariadne, 'nulla Minois leui | defuncta amore est, iungitur semper nefas' [No daughter of Minos has made it through a love affair unscathed; it is always a route to infamy] (*Ph.* 127–28). There is a comical edge to Phaedra's doom-laden commentary here, as if the character is addressing the audience, well aware of the mythological cycle involving the House of Minos, King of Crete, and its various treatments in drama and poetry.[8] The Nurse's reaction to the tradition contributes to the same effect: 'natura totiens legibus cedet suis, | quotiens amabit Cressa?' [must nature always abandon her laws, every time a Cretan woman loves?] (*Ph.* 176–77). When it comes to Cretans, it seems, we have all heard the stories, we know to expect the worst, and this is as true of Seneca in the first century as it is for Gager and his audience in the sixteenth. Making a joke of the tradition, Gager remarks in the prologue which he adds to Seneca's play: 'Tellure dira, tale quae genuit nefas, | Quod tam remota est, gratulor nostrae Insulae' [thank goodness our own island [of Britain] lies as far away as it does from the dreadful land [of Crete] which spawned such sin!] (*Pann.* 13). As theatregoers we inhabit the world of the characters for a limited period, but we are fortunate enough to leave when we want to; Phaedra carries her burden wherever she goes, tied to her Cretan heritage and the serial misdemeanours of her notorious family.

Gager savours and extends this vision of a Phaedra gripped by the forces of tradition, combining two ideas inherited from Seneca's method: the author displaying wit in controlling a character who claims to be able to reinvent herself, and the presentation of new material set in a self-conscious relationship with earlier works on the same subject. For example, Gager adds a new sequence of scenes following the first act of Seneca's play, where Hippolytus enters to give a joyful soliloquy on the virtues of hunting,[9] and is interrupted by two encounters which both mar his peace of mind and prefigure the fatal encounter with Phaedra. His first confrontation is with Pandarus, a mysterious figure who meets Hippolytus in the woods and hands the young man a letter without introducing himself. Much emphasis is put upon the fact that the letter purports to be anonymous, but naturally we know very well who has written it, and Gager seems to enjoy having engineered another scenario in which Phaedra can try to talk her way out of her own identity. The letter reads as follows (*Pann.* 200–07):

> *Charissimo suo Hippolyto S.*
>
> Hippolyto mittit pectus suffixa salutem,
>   Mittere si forsan, qua caret ipsa, potest.
> Ne quaeras quae sim, pudet ah pudet addere nomen,
>   Tractari sine quo iam mea causa potest.
> Nolim ante esse tibi (quid enim me nosse iuvabit?)
>   Cognita, quam voti spes mihi parva foret.
> Perlegis? An feritas prohibet tua? Perlege, quaeso,
>   Non haec hostili est littera scripta manu.

[*Greetings to her own dearest Hippolytus*

Transfixed through the heart, she sends good health to Hippolytus, if indeed she can send that which she lacks herself. Do not ask who I am; it is shameful, ah!, it is shameful to add my name, and now I can plead my case without it. I should not wish to be known to you (for how will it help to know me?) until I have some small hope of my desire. Are you reading this to the end? Or does your brutishness prevent you? Read it through, I beg; this letter is not written by an enemy hand.]

The speaker is immediately identifiable, and not simply because of the plot line we are anticipating. The voice that rings out in those familiar, plaintive tones is that of Ovid's Phaedra from the *Heroides*, whose style our sixteenth-century author has carefully imitated. The famous opening lines of Ovid's poem run as follows: '*Quam nisi tu dederis, caritura est ipsa, salutem | mittit Amazonio Cressa puella viro*' [With wishes for the welfare which she herself, unless you give it her, will ever lack, the Cretan maid greets the hero whose mother was an Amazon] (*Heroides* IV.1–2).[10] Conspicuous similarities in phrasing place both Phaedras in parallel, but just as noticeable is that which is *not* said: Gager's Phaedra removes the reference to her Cretan heritage from Ovid's text, effectively editing herself out of this tradition, so that she can cut the ties to her shameful identity. This is in striking contrast to Ovid's brazen heroine, who reflects very openly on her family history and race in her letter to Hippolytus, offering up the details of the past as an explanation for her current behaviour.[11] In the *Panniculus*, Gager follows Seneca in playing the game of silence: Phaedra's plea to remain nameless ('*Ne quaeras quae sim, pudet ah pudet addere nomen*' [Do not ask who I am, it is shameful, ah it is shameful, to give my name], *Pann.* 202), is a pointedly hopeless gesture, celebrating the fact that her name does not *need* to be spoken because Gager has successfully imitated the sound of the past and brought Phaedra alive.

In giving his work the title *Panniculus Hippolyto Senecae Tragoediae Assutus* [Little Patch Sewn on to Seneca's *Hippolytus*], Gager signals that Seneca's composition lies at the heart of his own, and, since Seneca's verses greatly outnumber his own, it is an underestimation to say that Seneca's play is the main model. However, as we have seen, Gager makes a point of showing that it is not his only model and he demonstrates Seneca's own debt to Ovid as an important part of Phaedra's literary history.[12] Looking further back in time, beyond Seneca, to some of their mutual sources, Gager also engages with Euripides' version of the play, evoking Phaedra's use of the letter device to speak to Theseus from beyond the grave. Finding the tablet upon her body, Theseus is presented with Phaedra's version of events, written in her own words, including the false story of Hippolytus' rape, fabricated to cover the shame of having tried to seduce him and the anger of having been rejected by him. Euripides' choice of language to describe the letter, seen 'suspended from her hand' ('ἐκ φίλης χερὸς | ἠρτημένη', *Hippolytus* 856–57) emphasizes Phaedra as the author trying to script her own tale, shaping and controlling events right up until the last moment when her hand falls limp in death.[13] It is interesting that Seneca does away with the intermediary of the written object in his version of the play, giving Phaedra the opportunity to tell her duplicitous tale to Theseus in person, and yet the result does not diminish Seneca's debt to Euripides as an important model. As Segal notes, 'Seneca's *Phaedra* is at nearly every point conscious of its literary ancestry and therefore of its literariness. The ghost of Euripides haunts every line.'[14] Yet there are many differences between the Greek play and its Roman offspring. Writing in the sixteenth century, Gager makes his own creative contribution to the tradition, where the insertion of new elements such as the letter scene into Seneca's play does not produce a seamless homage to one main model, but a composite of multiple Phaedras viewed as intertextual layers.[15]

This palimpsestuous technique is, of course, reflected in the metaphor of Gager's title, which expresses the act of tacking new scenes on without editing or removing content from Seneca's play, so that the additions are layered, rather than blended, and can potentially be cut away, leaving the original intact. Gager's method of publication reinforces this idea; instead of publishing the full sequence of scenes as they would have been performed on the night, he selects only the material which he had penned and divides it between two separate volumes. His prologue and three epilogues are published soon after performance in 1592, appended to the text of another of Gager's plays, *Ulysses Redux*,[16] which was performed on the same occasion, whilst the main scenes of his invention form the appendix to his *Meleager*,[17] published the following year.

When we observe Gager's and Seneca's scenes side by side, we can see how the rationale behind the detached structure of the *Panniculus* draws its inspiration from Seneca's own method of composition. Focusing upon the rhetorical potential of each single speech (rather than its contribution to plot momentum), Seneca moves us through a series of virtuoso displays, each one operating as a self-contained moment as well as part of a greater whole. One of the most striking examples is the melodramatic monologue he creates for Phaedra at *Ph*. 387–403. Here we linger on a moment of pure indulgence while the Queen declaims upon the subject of her fantasy, and threatens to remove all her royal finery, assume the appearance of a huntress maiden and, in this new guise, head into the woods: 'talis in siluas ferar' [thus will I go into the woods] (*Ph*. 403). The act of throwing off her robes and jewels and letting her hair run free is a symbolic rejection of her identity as the wife of King Theseus, father of Hippolytus, and the superficial glitter of the courtly life. However, Phaedra performs the process of undressing as a rhetorical act, self-consciously describing the removal of each layer of artifice covering her body. Thus she betrays through her use of sensuous language that the impulse to change the way she looks is more about a seduction of Hippolytus (keen advocate of the simple life) than genuine interest in purity of living.[18] Parading her colours like a peacock, she offers a luxurious display of her silk robes daubed with purple and gold ('purpura atque auro inlitas'), enriching her description with details of the ingredients used to make them: the scarlet of Tyrian dye and silken threads gathered from the branches of trees by faraway peoples. Her earrings, likewise, are made not simply of pearl, but 'niueus lapis | [...] Indici donum maris' [snow-white stone, | [...] the gift of the Indian sea]. She cannot resist adding a touch of fragrance, 'odore crinis [...] Assyrio uacet' [my hair is to be free of Assyrian perfume], inviting the listener *not* to notice her perfumed hair.

146   ELIZABETH SANDIS

When it comes to choosing a new costume to replace her former finery, it is thoughts of a hairstyle which preoccupy Phaedra. Dreaming of the freedom to run and let her hair down, 'sic temere iactae colla perfundant comae | umerosque summos' [My hair is to be tossed like this any which way, spread over my neck and the tops of my shoulders] (*Ph.* 394–95), she takes a lesson from the nymphs of the *Metamorphoses*, masters in the art of the dishevelled look (cf. *Metamorphoses* I.497, where Apollo is attracted to Daphne by her natural-flowing hair: 'spectat inornatos collo pendere capillos' [he sees her hair draped loose over her neck]). Qualifying this description further, she lingers on the image of the flowing hair, declaring 'cursibus motae citis | ventos sequantur' [stirred by my flight, let it stream on the winds] (*Ph.* 395–96). Our mind may still be on the figure of Daphne escaping Apollo's advances, but with this additional phrase a new model enters the picture, the very opposite of an Artemisian nymph: 'venatrix, dederatque comam diffundere ventis' [like a huntress, she had loosened her hair to let it stream in the winds] (*Aeneid* I.319). This is the goddess Venus, who adopts the disguise of a virgin huntress, just for fun. Phaedra's emulation of her, whether subconsciously or deliberately, seems justly apt, and adds another inter-textual layer to Seneca's portrayal of Phaedra. In such a boldly rhetorical speech, the stylistic models adopted by the character Phaedra for her own self-representation are seen to form a neat parallel with Seneca's *imitatio* of his literary predecessors.

The rhetorical mode is Phaedra's *modus vivendi*; she savours the verbal enactment of a physical action she is powerless to achieve. The freedom she craves and momentarily seems to enjoy as she luxuriates in the language of letting her hair down is a short-lived and artificial joy; Hippolytus' sylvan world remains out of reach and can only be experienced by Phaedra through carefully crafted literary conceits. However, we are caught up in the moment with her and enjoy the fantasy while she delivers this speech. It is pieces such as these which make up the patchwork of scenes in Seneca's play, where the author allows the power of rhetoric to dominate the narrative structure, slowing the pace, and marginalizing concerns of plot.[19]

The more elaborate the disguise which Phaedra creates, the less we believe in it. Seneca's handling of rhetoric easily punctures the indulgent fantasy with ironic touches which remind us of the writer who is really in control. Phaedra ends her dramatic speech by imagining herself bravely entering battle, dressed like an Amazonian warrior carrying her crescent shield, a defiant image one might think, but, unfortunately for Phaedra, one which evokes the very person she is most anxious to avoid any association with, the Amazon queen Antiope, Hippolytus' mother. (We may remember Ovid's Phaedra addressing Hippolytus as the 'Amazonio [...] viro' in *Heroides* IV.) She simultaneously fears and fantasizes about her role as *noverca*, stepmother to Hippolytus acting *in loco parentis*.[20] The taint of an incestuous desire is part and parcel of the tradition of unnatural love in her family, as she expressed in her first speech of the play (*Ph.* 127–28), and we can feel the sense of an inevitable slide towards her destined role. She will take her place amongst the bevy of 'saeuas | [...] nouercas' [cruel stepmothers] (*Ph.* 356–57), as Seneca terms them in his first choral ode.[21]

Some of the most memorable moments of Seneca's *Phaedra*, and of Gager's *Panniculus* following in its footsteps, result from the self-conscious presentation of the author, who draws on the audience's knowledge of the fate of the characters to lace their words with dramatic irony. For example, Seneca invites us to share a joke at Hippolytus' expense when the young man laments the loss of a Golden Age and concludes his rant against the evils of the world with the comment: 'taceo nouercas' [I say nothing of stepmothers] (*Ph.* 558). This remark is perfectly timed to maximize our enjoyment of dramatic tension and Seneca's ironic treatment of the *noverca* theme: Hippolytus is, at this moment, gloriously ignorant of his own stepmother's intentions, just when Phaedra is preparing to manufacture the rhetorical snares with which to proposition him. This will very shortly culminate in the famous speech in which she will attempt to circumvent the inconvenience of her role as *noverca* by asking her stepson not to call her 'mother' (see above on *Ph.* 609ff.). Gager responds to this with particular wit at *Pann.* 157–64, having Pandarus describe at length the signs of Phaedra's love and admiration for him, only for Hippolytus to praise Phaedra's parenting skills with genuine enthusiasm. The stepson concludes with the hilariously inappropriate, though completely innocent, decision to reward Phaedra for such devotion by upgrading her status from stepmother *to mother*: 'Nec enim novercae, sed dehinc matris locum | Supplebit.' [She will fulfil the role not of stepmother indeed, but, henceforth, of mother] (*Pann.* 161–62).

Once Pandarus has fulfilled his task of handing over the letter, Hippolytus is left alone again, furiously brooding on the impertinence of the anonymous woman's addresses. Since he has not identified her, he has no one person to focus his outrage upon, but instead denounces all women with an intensity of bitterness both extravagant and breathtaking. Gager clearly did not want to miss an opportunity to compose another set-piece speech, and the resulting soliloquy (*Pann.* 216–52) combines two particular literary models, Euripides' *Hippolytus* and Baptista Mantuanus' *De natura mulierum* (*Eclogue* IV),[22] in addition to Seneca. The figure of Umber in Mantuan *Eclogue* IV delivers a lengthy diatribe against women (lines 110–241) which is as fearsome as it is famous; together with his other eclogues it quickly found favour with schoolmasters across Europe as an instructive *exemplum* of style and diction and continued to be used as a textbook in the English grammar schools right into the seventeenth century. Mantuan includes a direct reference to Phaedra as one of Umber's 'exempla', though it is fleeting and fairly commonplace. What is important, however, is the list-structure which Gager borrows for Hippolytus' torrent of accusations, and also the final flourish, a self-conscious literary conceit which transforms Mantuan's rather basic *sententia* 'The poem's not long; the folly of women *is*' into the following vivid, meta-poetic quadruplet (*Pann.* 248–51):

> Non tota tellus charta si, et caelum forent,
> Et omnis atramentum aqua, et fluvio, et mari,
> Lignum omne calami, quisque scribendi artifex,
> Nequitia vel sic faeminea queat exprimi.

[If all the earth and all the sky were paper, and all the water in both river and sea were ink, and if every piece of wood were a pen, and every person skilled in writing, the wickedness of woman could not even thus be expressed.[23]]

Phaedra, though Hippolytus does not know it, is the one who stands in the dock accused of the 'nequitia [...] faeminea', on behalf of womankind.[24] The Mantuan model enables the portrayal of Phaedra as a generic type, (man)handled by the conventions of the literary topos which Mantuan had brought to the mainstream.

Gager's use of meta-poetic figures in the quadruplet above is an interesting example of the kind of sophistic embellishment taught in the grammar schools and prescribed by popular manuals such as Vida's *De Arte Poetica* (1527).[25] Vida refers to figures of speech as *indicia*, or *colores*, recommending the employment of such ornaments for achieving poetic elegance in one's manner of speaking. Here Gager uses the imagery of the writer's craftsmanship, 'scribendi artifex' [master of the art of writing] (250), to remind us of the literary forces which shape and mould the character of Phaedra. As Segal puts it in relation to Seneca, '[t]he power and suggestiveness of his characterization work in large part through the *figurative language* into which he recasts the mythical and literary material of his predecessors.'[26] Gager reformulates his material with a subtlety of variation that harks back to his grammar-school training: Mantuan's 'insidiatur' (*Ecl.* IV.197) becomes 'mulierum insidiis' (*Pann.* 237), 'si retia cervi | [...] si damma canem' (*Ecl.* IV.193–94) becomes 'si retia ferae, si canem cervus' (*Pann.* 239),[27] whilst the serpents of Medusa, 'columbros' (*Ecl.* IV.201) lose their mythological mask to become 'in messe serpens, anguis in gremio latet' (a twist on the now proverbial 'snake in the grass' of Virgil's third *Eclogue*, line 93). Gager's adaptation of Euripides *Hippolytus* 618–24 sees the transfer of Hippolytus' utopia from the pagan temples of the Olympians (where men might go to buy offspring with gifts of bronze, iron, or gold) to Nature's garden, where he suggests woman banished as the procreative vessel in favour of the asexual reproduction of trees: 'Natura, quin nos arborum potius modo | Tellure nasci sponte voluisti editos' [Nature, why did you not rather wish us to be born from the earth, after the manner of trees?[28]] (*Pann.* 224–25). Like the Ovidian letter introduced in the previous scene, Hippolytus' soliloquy (*Pann.* 216–52) is a self-contained piece, recognizable as imitation of but also independent from its models, loosely tethered to Seneca's play so that it contributes a small piece to a larger patchwork. Gager's set-piece of invective looks ahead to the Senecan Hippolytus' parting shot at the end of his Golden Age speech (*Ph.* 483ff.), in which he points the finger at women as the chief source of evils, 'dux malorum femina' (*Pann.* 559), and makes that wonderfully pertinent remark, 'taceo novercas' [I say nothing of stepmothers], *Ph.* 558.

Gager structures Hippolytus' encounter with Pandarus and his outraged reaction as the first of two episodes prefiguring his confrontation with Phaedra. The second of these, following on directly from Hippolytus' diatribe against women, introduces the figure of Nais, whose name reflects her symbolic value as the archetypal nymph. Nais offers the audience an image of the persona which Phaedra most wishes to emulate, the pure huntress maiden living a simple life in the woods (matching Hippolytus' own eutopia), and her drive toward imitation is given a neat meta-poetic treatment by Gager. Nais's solicitation of Hippolytus comes just before Phaedra's famous undressing scene (*Ph.* 387–403, discussed above), strengthening the comparison via juxtaposition. In setting Hippolytus in dialogue with Nais, Gager has arranged a dramatic preview of how a scene between Phaedra, dressed as huntress maiden, and her youthful prey would play out.

This serves to intensify the tragic irony in the next scene, when we witness Seneca's Phaedra gesticulating with animated delight at the fantasy of her new costume. The momentary escape from herself is, as we have seen, a fleeting pleasure, a rhetorical conceit. When Seneca's Phaedra faces Hippolytus in person, the futility of her self-deception is given a deeper tragic poignancy, since she cannot regain her purity by merely donning new clothes: 'respersa nulla labe et intacta, innocens | tibi mutor uni' [Stained by no dishonour, untouched, innocent, I am changed for you alone[29]] (*Ph.* 668–69). Even Nais, generic representative of the *virgo intacta*, and certainly portrayed as 'innocens' by Gager,[30] cannot penetrate Hippolytus' emotional armour and is rebuffed with such vehemence that she brings down curses upon him in a dramatic prefiguring of his death. Nais can be viewed as Phaedra's avenger,[31] or indeed the other way around, as Nais suggests with a meta-theatrical flourish at *Pann.* 361: 'vindex repulsae turpis existat brevi' [May an avenger of this shameful repulse appear in a short while].

Through his introduction of Nais, Gager offers us a view of innocent love crushed by Hippolytus' brutality (what Phaedra calls Hippolytus' *feritas*, *Pann.* 206), providing a pristine foil to the perversions of Phaedra's passion. In Gager's own words, Nais demonstrates 'the affection of honest, lawfull, vertuous, marriage-meaninge love; for no other did she profer' (*Letter to Rainolds*, f. 56).[32] The rhetorical violence of Hippolytus' rejection of Nais offers an important prelude to his rejection of Phaedra, accompanied by physical violence at *Ph.* 706–08, as he grabs her hair (in ironic mutation of her fantasy) and threatens her with his sword. Does Hippolytus' misogynistic rant and his treatment of Nais promote an underlying current of sympathy for Phaedra, her avenger? It certainly complicates our view of Phaedra and adds fresh layers to what is already a complex palimpsest rather than a one-dimensional character.[33] Gager seems to have an appreciation of the moral ambiguities of Seneca's play and in adding material to the Roman tragedy he does not use it as an opportunity to engineer a specific, didactic trajectory for his sixteenth-century audience.

By contrast, Alexander Nowell attempted to do just that, in his production of Seneca's *Hippolytus* at Westminster School in the 1540s, whilst he was headmaster there.[34] The prologue which Neville composed for the occasion has been preserved in a manuscript notebook of his, Bodleian MS. Brasenose Coll. 31 (fol. 27^r–28^v),[35] and this production is, in fact, the first recorded performance of a classical tragedy in England. Smith summarizes Nowell's prologue as an 'attempt to bend ethical complexities into straight moral lines' and to style Phaedra as playing solely one role, that of the wicked temptress.[36] Elizabethan writers frequently diverted Seneca's moral outlook towards a Christian hermeneutic, and contemporary interest in translating Seneca's tragedies produced a significant group of examples which Thomas Newton gathered together in a collected volume of translations, entitled *Seneca his Tenne Tragedies* (1581).[37] This includes, for instance, Alexander Neville's translation of Seneca's *Oedipus*, first published in 1563 while Neville was an undergraduate at Cambridge, and later revised for Newton's 1581 publication.[38] In considering the approach taken by Gager in his 1592 adaptation of the *Phaedra*, this corpus of translations from Seneca is doubtless an important backdrop, but I would argue that his adaptation in Latin, written as a stage entertainment before being published, cannot be put squarely in the same box without further consideration. This is the fate of Gager's *Meleager* in Norland's recent analysis, where little evidence is offered to justify the sweeping statement that Gager's portrayal of fortune in the *Meleager* shows him '[f]ollowing the precedent of Senecan translators whose collected edition published in 1581 frequently added a Christian dimension to his tragedies'.[39] The work of Nowell and Neville is not strictly contemporary with Gager's *Panniculus* of 1592, nor is that of Studley, whose translation of Seneca's *Phaedra* likewise appeared in Newton's *Tenne Tragedies* (1581) but had already been published during the mid-1560s.[40] McCabe concludes of Studley's version that it is 'very much a misogynistic play', with Hippolytus' character eulogized as the supreme model of chastity and a defence of patriarchy so starkly delineated that it 'dwarfs the female figures to the level of crouching demons.'[41] The *Panniculus*, by contrast, presents characters fashioned more as rhetorical models than moral ones.

Whatever moralizing Gager may offer in his much-quoted letter to Rainolds, it should be remembered that he is looking back upon the production six months down the line with the need to defend it. It is easy for us to forget that any retrospective justification which Gager gives is in direct response to Rainolds's criticism, and that his initial intention in staging the plays had more than a moral focus. As McCabe puts it, 'Gager was forced to defend himself on moral grounds although his real sympathies were aesthetic since the portrayal of sin makes for good drama.'[42] Good drama, for Gager, however, was strictly that of the amateur kind, staged at the two universities and the Inns of Court, and not the output of any commercial theatre companies. He drew a distinction that ran deeper than issues of contrasting content in academic and commercial plays, deeming the style of delivery just as important in differentiating the two forms: 'we differ from them alltogether in the manner bothe of setting owte Playes, and of actinge them. Thay did it with excessyve charge; we thriftely, warely, and allmost beggerly; [...] we may seeme, compared with them, eyther for skill, or diligence, rather *recitare*, which you doe not dislike, than *agere*.' (*Letter to Dr. John Rainolds*, fol. 47, my emphasis). Here he is reacting defensively against Rainolds's diatribe, attempting to draw a distinction between *recitatio* and *declamatio* as practised in university drama and *actio* as practised by the professional players, whilst undercutting the point about rhetorical mode of delivery with an air of mock modesty regarding the talents of his student cast. His jovial prologue to the *Panniculus* repeats the point when he makes the traditional plea for audience attention, 'Attentionem quaeso praestetis Gregi' [Pay attention, I beg, to our troop], familiar from many a Roman comedy,[43] but adds the following flourish of his own: 'Saltem theatro quanta vulgari datur' [at least as much [attention] as is given in the popular theatre]. His jesting comparison between the academic stage at Oxford University and 'theatro vulgari', professional theatre performed in the vernacular, pokes fun at the idea of the two stages in competition with one other, in the process reinforcing the idea that they are two very distinct phenomena.[44]

At the same time, however, in the very first scene of the *Panniculus* he introduces opportunities for the kind of stage effects associated with the popular theatre, clearly intended to contribute to the audience's enjoyment of the play rather than their moral enrichment. He first brings the winged figure of Cupid on stage, followed by the vengeance-bringing fury Megaera, both figures drawn up from the ghostly caverns of the underworld. Brooke describes the underlying contradiction in Gager's work thus: 'On the one hand, he never gave up the opinion, often repeated in later years, that drama in English was unworthy of scholars and gentlemen. [...] And yet he could not write a Latin play without admitting into its emotion and structure traces at least of the larger freedom of the vulgar stage.'[45] His decision to introduce the visual spectacle of the fury and, through her, another strand of revenge motivation, panders to contemporary taste for ghost scenes and the personified figures of revenge or *furor* (cf. Thomas Kyd's *The Spanish Tragedy, or Hieronimo is Mad Again* in the late 1580s, Shakespeare's *Titus Andronicus* in the early 1590s, and *Macbeth* a few years later). This adds another layer of complexity to our analysis of Phaedra as we delve further into Gager's aims as a dramatist and consider the various forces shaping his choices. The distribution of guilt or *culpa* amongst the characters for the tragic events of the play is certainly affected by the introduction of the Cupid-Megaera scene as the new opening to the play, but, as I will show, Gager turns our attentions towards the literary, as opposed to moral, implications of this new strand of causation.

In introducing divine machinery to kick-start the tragic plot, Gager adds to the tangle of causal streams already at work in Seneca's play, including, as discussed above, meta-poetic references to the inevitable pull of the mythological cycle determining the characters' fate. When forced to defend herself in the wake of Hippolytus' fury, Seneca's Phaedra claims an inability to escape the family curse: 'Et ipsa nostrae fata cognosco domus' [I recognize that fate of my house] (*Ph.* 698), adding 'fugienda petimus; sed mei non sum potens' [We hunt for what we ought to run away from; but I am powerless over myself] (*Ph.* 699). With the intervention of the fury Megaera in Gager's version, we now witness the staged instigation of *furor*, which formally undermines Phaedra's control over her own actions, before we see Phaedra herself. This may remind us of the opening to Euripides' *Hippolytus*, where the intervention of Aphrodite provides a divine strand of causation in addition to the narrative of characters committing their own crimes. The passion is portrayed as taking hold of Phaedra with alarming speed: 'flagrabit', says the fury, 'et iam flagrat' [She will be inflamed, and already she is inflamed] (*Pann.* 50). Once Megaera has decided to exert her power over the narrative, it is immediately felt. Revenge is already in motion, and before she has even appeared on stage, Phaedra has a claim to the status of passive victim.

Literary precedents for such an opening, signalled by verbal patterning, reinforce the sense of unavoidable fate or destiny. When Megaera asks the rhetorical question 'cur tam diu scelere haec vacat | domus nefando?' [why has this house gone so long without abominable crime?] (Pann. 47–48), she is not only stating her intent to reintroduce the troubles but identifying the whole family, 'domus', as her target, contextualizing the tragic chain of events in the play as part of the perpetual cycle of evil for the House of Theseus. That this is a *literary* cycle as well as a mythological one is strengthened by Megaera's use of formulaic terminology, linking the *Panniculus* to its predecessors verbally as well as thematically. Gager's own play,

152   ELIZABETH SANDIS

the *Meleager*, opens with the figure of Megaera emerging from the underworld to unleash revenge upon the House of Oeneus, father of Meleager: 'cur adhuc tanto vacat | Althaea scelere? quam diu est domus innocens?' [Why is Althaea still free of crime? How long is this house to remain blameless?] (Mel. 100–01). This, in turn, is a reworking of two passages in Seneca's *Thyestes*, 'dextra cur patrui uacat? | nondum Thyestes liberos deflet suos?' [Why does the hand of the uncle lie empty? Does Thyestes not yet weep for his own children?] (*Thy.* 57–58), spoken by the (unnamed, generic) fury inciting the ghost of Tantalus, and 'tam diu cur innocens | seruatur Atreus?' [Why has Atreus remained innocent so long?] (Thy. 280–81), spoken by Atreus himself (whose self-conscious characterization shares ground with Seneca's and Gager's portrayals of Phaedra). These linguistic parallels between *Meleager, Panniculus,* and their mutual source in Seneca's *Thyestes*, reinforce our sense of the framework which enmeshes Phaedra and the predetermined, typecast role she must play as a member of both the House of Minos and the House of Theseus. Through his introduction of Megaera the fury, Gager's over-determination of the action complicates questions of guilt and responsibility, but at the same time opens up attractive *poetic* possibilities, allowing threads of characterization and plot to be absorbed from a variety of sources, including other plays of his own making.

Gager has Hippolytus add yet another dimension with his engendered view of causation, 'Totam mariti mulier evertit domum' [A woman overturns her husband's whole house] (*Pann.* 245), where 'domum' is used by the character as a commonplace for the household or home but is also understood by the audience to mean the written cycle of tragedy in which generations of characters participate. Gager's Hippolytus provides a dissenting voice to match that of Seneca's Nurse,[46] when he rejects the view that the evils of the past should be allowed to contaminate the present: 'Absiste, quaeso, vulnus antiquum domus | Refricare nostrae' [Cease, I entreat, to scratch open that ancient wound of our house[47]] (*Pann.* 129–30). We may admire Hippolytus' sense of defiance here, but later we will encounter him in Seneca's portion of the play asking why he has not yet been punished by Jupiter's thunderbolt with the words 'cur dextra, diuum rector atque hominum, uacat | tua [...]?' [Why, ruler of gods and men, does your hand lie empty?] (*Ph.* 680–81). His heavily ironic use of this familiar formula signals the literary framework in which the characters operate and emphasizes the powerlessness of both Hippolytus and Phaedra to deviate from tradition.

Seneca's emphasis upon Theseus' share of culpability for the events of the play has often been remarked upon,[48] and as Armstrong points out, 'it is in Ovid and Seneca that the motif of Theseus' infidelity towards Phaedra [...] is most fully exploited.'[49] Therefore, whilst the injection of divine machinery into the *Panniculus* may draw Gager's Phaedra closer to her Euripidean counterpart, Megaera's emphasis upon Theseus' violence in the underworld and his neglect of his own household sharply contrasts with Euripides' Theseus, the uxorious figure who is only absent because he is visiting an oracle, and puts *Panniculus* in closer alignment with its Ovidian and Senecan models. Megaera draws our attention to Theseus' absence from home with the sarcastic rhetorical question: 'nil habet, quod agat domi?' [Does he have nothing to do at home?] (*Pann.* 46), followed by the sinister 'Habebit' [He will have]. Gager

PALIMPSESTUOUS PHAEDRA   153

also inserts the figure of Pandarus as Phaedra's advocate; Pandarus rails against the wrongs done to Phaedra and her kindred by Theseus, looking ahead to the Queen's own accusations that in pursuing his adventures in the underworld her husband is shirking his duty at home: 'profugus en coniunx abest' [See, my husband is playing truant and runaway[50]] (*Ph.* 91).

Neglect and infidelity may provide mitigating circumstances for Phaedra, but it is the violence of Theseus' impulses which Megaera wants revenge for. Whilst Cupid tuts at the chaos Theseus has provoked in the underworld ('Tumultuatum est', a phrase which resounds with contemptuous alliteration), Megaera condemns Theseus' attempted violation of 'thalamos Ditis, et Proserpinae' [the bedchamber of Dis and Proserpina] (*Pann.* 44) and is aghast that this crime might go unavenged (note the anaphoric repetition of 'impune' in three consecutive lines, *Pann.* 44). Megaera's expression of anger prefigures the Senecan Phaedra's complaints that her husband is committing 'stupra et illicitos toros' [the outrage of adulterous liaisons] in Acheron (*Ph.* 97). Megaera's use of 'Violet' (*Pann.* 45) supports Phaedra's branding of Theseus as the rapist snatcher of Proserpina, 'raptorem' (*Ph.* 627), making Phaedra's discontented and troubled mind seem less monstrous and more human. We may contrast the lack of humanity in Studley's depiction of Phaedra, which removes this causal link between Theseus' treatment of Phaedra and Phaedra's actions, preventing the audience from feeling any empathy with her plight. In Gager's version, a variety of voices are heard and the distribution of *culpa* becomes more complicated and uncertain. As McCabe puts it, his insertion of the Megaera motivation 'distorts the emphasis of the Senecan drama'.[51] In addition, Gager's introduction of the sweet figure of Nais into the frame, sent packing by the vehement Hippolytus, tugs at our sympathies for anyone unfortunate enough to fall in love with this young man, and he words Nais's reactionary curse upon Hippolytus in such a way as to suggest that Phaedra will come to act as poor Nais's avenger, 'vindex' (*Pann.* 361).

The appearance of Cupid alongside Megaera is perhaps one of the most damaging of Gager's additions for anyone trying to argue for a strait-laced moral trajectory to his *Panniculus.* Drawing upon and mocking literary (especially elegiac) conventions for portraying the god of love, the sixteenth-century playwright deliberately cultivates comic effects which poke fun at our attempts to come to moral judgements in the story of Phaedra and Hippolytus. In an ironical rejection of his role in the several episodes of Ovid's *Metamorphoses*, Cupid protests at Megaera's plans, since being implicated in an incestuous love would spoil his reputation ('nomen', *Pann.* 55). He huffily predicts that everyone will blame him for what happens ('Nam quis per orbem ... | non mihi culpam imputet?' [For who in the world would not assign the blame to me?], *Pann.* 56–57), offers Phaedra the choice of any other man except Hippolytus, and lectures her about propriety in love: 'amandus, Phaedra, privignus tibi est, | Sed ut novercae' [You should love your stepson, Phaedra, but *as a stepmother*] (*Pann.* 63–64). That Gager's mind is on his display of inter-textual wit is demonstrated by his decision to set a conspicuous fragment of Ovid's *Metamorphoses* into Cupid's speech here, remoulding 'ex omnibus unum | elige, Myrrha, virum: dum ne sit in omnibus unus' [O Myrrha, choose one man out of all of them, so long as from amongst them all it is *not this one*], (*Met.* X.317–18) into 'O Phaedra, amicum delige unum ex omnibus, | Dum non sit unus omnium.' [O Phaedra, choose one special friend from amongst them all, so long as it is *not this one* out of them all] (*Pann.* 60–61). Through this inter-textual link Gager adds a further subtext to his portrayal of Phaedra by engineering a parallel with Myrrha as the incestuous lover of her father Cinyras, a warning to Phaedra against her own inappropriate desires. There is not a little irony in Gager's substitution of 'amicum' for 'virum' here, which gives Cupid's speech an added coyness. The cheeky love god may be self-righteous in claiming, for once, to be trying to prevent a disastrous love affair, but his rejection of a role so familiar from the *Metamorphoses* comes just at the moment he is heard quoting from this text. Once again Gager has demonstrated the comic potential of having his characters attempt and fail to escape the pull of literary tradition, muddying the moral waters by focusing on meta-poetic elements to their portrayal.

Gager's additions of Megaera and Cupid inject greater poignancy, but also comic force, into Phaedra's set piece speech articulating the emotions which have overtaken her (*Ph.* 177–94). The fact that, in Gager's version, we have already seen these feelings embodied as personifications walking about the stage ironizes the Queen's use of the term *furor* to identify her emotion and her recognition of the intervention of some unnamed but awesome winged deity: 'uicit ac regnat furor, | potensque tota mente dominatur deus. | hic uolucer omni pollet in terra impotens' [Fury has conquered and is in command, and a mighty god controls my whole mind. This winged god prevails, out of control, in every land] (*Ph.* 184–86).

Gager's physicalization of Cupid on stage in his opening scene also adds an ironic flourish to the following speech, put in the mouth of the Nurse at *Ph.* 195–217, in which she remonstrates with Phaedra that the god of Love is simply made up ('finxit [...] | [...] finxit [...]'). His use of literary conceits further lowers the tone when he constructs a face-off between the two anthropomorphized depictions of passion, Love and Revenge. The physical attributes of these deities are continually evoked in order to play upon the conventions of love elegy ('Abesse telis crimen hoc longe meis' [this misdeed has nothing at all to do with my darts], says Cupid at *Pann.* 59) and Gager pitches Megaera's torches against those of Cupid in a farcical competition which drives Cupid off stage even after he has just stubbornly declared his intention to stay ('stabo, et arcebo nefas' [I will stand fast, and I will ward off this evil[52]], *Pann.* 53). This makes rather a mockery of Seneca's first choral ode, a hymn to the universal and destructive power of Love.

Thus, in his *Panniculus Hippolyto Senecae Tragoediae Assutus* [Little Patch Sewn on to Seneca's *Hippolytus*], Gager offers his sixteenth-century audience an intriguing literary puzzle built from a variety of models and traditions. Through examining the impact which Gager's additions have on the characterization of Phaedra we gain important insights into Elizabethan views of Seneca *tragicus* as the central rhetorical model, and the use to which Seneca's writing was put by university dramatists aiming to please audiences and prove their own academic credentials. Building upon Seneca's own method, Gager construes Phaedra as a literary palimpsest, overlaying her portrayal with new layers of composition which bring self-conscious intertextualities to the surface. Gager's additions to Seneca's *Phaedra* problematize the moral structure of the play in the interests of meta-literary conversations which take place between his own plays, the Senecan corpus, and the canonical texts which feed the work of both playwrights. The result is a witty and inventive example of Senecan adaptation which allows Gager's additions to stand out from the Roman poet's original scenes, winning both dramatists their own applause.

Bibliography

Manuscripts

Corpus Christi College, Oxford, MS. 352 (Gager, *Letter to Dr. John Rainolds*)
Bodleian, Brasenose MS. Coll. 31 (Nowell's prologue to Seneca's *Hippolytus*)

References

ARMSTRONG, REBECCA, *Cretan Women: Pasiphae, Ariadne, and Phaedra in Latin Poetry* (Oxford: Oxford University Press, 2006)

BALDWIN, THOMAS, *William Shakespere's small Latine & lesse Greeke*, 2 vols (Urbana: University of Illinois, 1944)

BARRETT, WILLIAM S., ed., *Hippolytos* (Oxford: Clarendon Press, 1964)

BINNS, JAMES, ed., 'William Gager's Additions to Seneca's *Hippolytus*', *Studies in the Renaissance*, 17 (1970), 153–91

—— *William Gager, Meleager, Ulysses Redux, Panniculus Hippolyto Senecae Tragoediae Assutus*, First series, vol. 2 of *Renaissance Latin Drama in England* (New York: Hildesheim, 1982)

BOAS, FREDERICK, *University Drama in the Tudor Age* (Oxford: Clarendon Press, 1914)

BOYLE, ANTHONY JAMES, 'In Nature's Bonds: A Study of Seneca's *Phaedra*', *Aufstieg und Niedergang der römischen Welt*, II.32.2 (1985), 1284–1347

—— *Tragic Seneca: An Essay in the Theatrical Tradition* (London: Routledge, 1997)

BRADEN, GORDON, *Renaissance Tragedy and the Senecan Tradition: Anger's Privilege* (London and New Haven, CT: Yale University Press, 1985)

BROOKE, CHARLES FREDERICK TUCKER, 'The Life and Times of William Gager (1555–1622)', *Proceedings of the American Philosophical Society*, 95 (1951), 401–31

DAVIS, PETER, '*Vindicat omnes natura sibi*: A Reading of Seneca's *Phaedr*', in *Seneca Tragicus: Ramus Essays on Senecan Drama*, ed. by Anthony James Boyle (Victoria, Australia: Aureal Publications, 1983), pp. 114–27

FITCH, JOHN, ed., *Seneca. Volume VIII Tragedies I: Hercules, Trojan Women, Phoenician Women, Medea, Phaedra* (Cambridge, MA, and London: Harvard University Press, 2002)

FREEMAN, ARTHUR, ed., *Th'overthrow of stage-playes, by the way of controversie betwixt d. Gager and d. Rainoldes* (New York: Garland, 1974)

HARRISON, GEORGE, ed., *Seneca in Performance* (London: George Duckworth, 2000)

HUNTER, G. K., 'Seneca and the Elizabethans: A Case Study in Influence', *Shakespeare Survey*, vol. 20 (Cambridge: Cambridge University Press, 1967), pp. 17–26

MCCABE, RICHARD, *Incest, Drama and Nature's Law, 1550–1700* (Cambridge: Cambridge University Press, 1993)

MIOLA, ROBERT, *Shakespeare and Classical Tragedy: The Influence of Seneca* (Oxford: Oxford University Press, 1992)

MUELLER, MELISSA, 'Phaedra's Defixio: Scripting Sophrosune in Euripides' Hippolytus', *Classical Antiquity*, 30 (2011), 148–77

NEWTON, THOMAS, ed., *Seneca: His tenne tragedies | translated into English; edited by Thomas Newton, anno 1581; with an introduction by T. S. Eliot* (London: Constable, 1927)

NORLAND, HOWARD, *Neoclassical Tragedy in Elizabethan England* (Newark: University of Delaware Press, 2009)

156   ELIZABETH SANDIS

PEARSON, ALFRED CHILTON, ed., *The fragments of Sophocles | edited, with additional notes from the papers of Sir R. C. Jebb and Dr W. G. Headlam* (Cambridge: Cambridge University Press, 1917)

PIEPHO, LEE, ed., *Adulescentia: The Eclogues of Mantuan* (New York: Garland, 1989)

SEGAL, CHARLES, *Language and Desire in Seneca's Phaedra* (Princeton, NJ: Princeton University Press, 1986)

SHENK, LINDA, 'Gown before Crown: Scholarly Abjection and Academic Entertainment under Queen Elizabeth I', in, *Early Modern Academic Drama*, ed. by Jonathan Walker and Paul D. Streufert (Aldershot: Ashgate, 2008), pp. 19–44

SHOWERMAN, GRANT, ED. and TRANS., *Heroides and Amores* (Cambridge, MA: Harvard University Press, 1958)

SPEARING, EVELYN M., *The Elizabethan Translations of Seneca's Tragedies* (Cambridge: Heffer, 1912)

SMITH, BRUCE, *Ancient Scripts & Modern Experience on the English Stage, 1500–1700* (Princeton, NJ: Princeton University Press, 1988)

SUTTON, DANA, ed., *William Gager: The Complete Works*, 4 vols (New York: Garland, 1994)

TARRANT, RICHARD J., ed., *P. Ovidi Nasonis Metamorphoses* (Oxford: Clarendon Press, 2004)

WATSON, PATRICIA A., *Ancient Stepmothers: Myth, Misogyny and Reality* (*Mnemosyne Supplement*, 143) (Leiden: E. J. Brill, 1995)

WINSTON, JESSICA, 'Seneca in Early Elizabethan England', in *Renaissance Quarterly*, 59 (2006), 29–58

YOUNG, KARL, 'William Gager's Defence of the Academic Stage', *Transactions of the Wisconsin Academy of Sciences, Arts, and Letters*, 18 (1916), 593–638

ZWIERLEIN, OTTO, ed., *L. Annaei Senecae tragoediae* (Oxford: Clarendon Press, 1986)

Notes to Chapter 7

1. See Chapter 12 for further discussion of English university drama (eds).
2. As argued by Charles Frederick Tucker Brooke, 'The Life and Times of William Gager (1555–1622)', *Proceedings of the American Philosophical Society*, 95 (1951), 401–31 (p. 420).
3. A fellow of The Queen's College, Oxford, and shortly to become President of Corpus Christi, John Rainolds vociferously attacked Gager for his productions in a series of letters — see *Th'overthrow of stage-playes, by the way of controversie betwixt d. Gager and d. Rainoldes*, ed. by Arthur Freeman (New York: Garland, 1974). Gager, followed by Gentili, made an attempt to counteract — see Karl Young, 'William Gager's Defence of the Academic Stage', *Transactions of the Wisconsin Academy of Sciences, Arts, and Letters*, 18 (1916), 593–638.
4. A trend unhappily continued by Howard Norland, *Neoclassical Tragedy in Elizabethan England* (Newark: University of Delaware Press, 2009), who, in his recent study of Gager's works, otherwise offers useful inroads into discussion of the Gagerian corpus. His references to the *Panniculus*, however, are restricted to the Rainolds connection (p. 41 and p. 192), Momus' mention of another of Gager's plays, *Ulysses Redux* (p. 184), the date of the performance of *Panniculus* at Christ Church (p. 47), and the passing comment that, for his production of Seneca's tragedy, 'Gager added 339 lines extending Hippolytus's role and emphasizing his chastity' (p. 180). In the absence of in-depth studies devoted to the *Panniculus*, the paratexts to the two editions of the play, by James Binns, 'William Gager's Additions to Seneca's *Hippolytus*', *Studies in the Renaissance*, 17 (1970), 153–91 (153–63 and 184–91), and by Dana Sutton in *William Gager: The Complete Works* (New York: Garland, 1994), remain the fullest treatments to date, together with Frederick Boas, *University Drama in the Tudor Age* (Oxford: Clarendon Press, 1914), pp. 197–201 and 233–40.
5. These new scenes are inserted as openings to the first and second acts, leaving the rest of Seneca's play to run its course. All translations are my own unless otherwise indicated.
6. We should not read too much into Gager's use of *Hippolytus* as the title of Seneca's play (in place of the now more widely used *Phaedra*), since the 'A' MSS (one of two manuscript branches,

PALIMPSESTUOUS PHAEDRA 157

A and E) transmit the play with *Hippolytus* as the title. It does not appear to reflect a judgement on Gager's part as to the importance of Phaedra as a protagonist. Following modern practice, I refer to Seneca's play as the *Phaedra* (abbreviated to *Ph.* hereafter), taking all quotations from the OCT edition by Otto Zwierlein (1986). All references to Gager's additional scenes (labelled with the abbreviation *Pann.* for *Panniculus*) are taken from Binns's 'William Gager's Additions to Seneca's *Hippolytus*'; however, I follow the line numbers assigned by Sutton in preference to Binns's division by act and scene.

7. Gordon Braden, *Renaissance Tragedy and the Senecan Tradition: Anger's Privilege* (London and New Haven, CT: Yale University Press, 1985), p. 35.

8. For an analysis of the treatment of the Cretan mythological in poetry, see Rebecca Armstrong, *Cretan Women: Pasiphae, Ariadne, and Phaedra in Latin Poetry* (Oxford: Oxford University Press, 2006).

9. This is Gager's contribution to an important topos in Seneca's play. Peter Davis, '*Vindicat omnes natura sibi*: A Reading of Seneca's *Phaedra*', in *Seneca Tragicus: Ramus Essays on Senecan Drama*, ed. by Anthony James Boyle (Victoria, Australia: Aureal Publications, 1983), pp. 114–27 and others have demonstrated that Seneca's use of the hunting motif offers further scope for role-play, giving eloquent expression to the constantly shifting dynamics of power between Phaedra and Hippolytus, as they move back and forth between the positions of hunter and hunted. Gager's addition of Hippolytus' hymn to hunting develops the ironic contrast between the young man's illusion of control and his impending victimhood.

10. This English rendering is taken from Grant Showerman's edition of Ovid's *Heroides*.

11. See *Heroides* IV.53–62.

12. As Robert Miola, *Shakespeare and Classical Tragedy: The Influence of Seneca* (Oxford: Oxford University Press, 1992), p. 4 points out, Ovid is 'erroneously considered at times a distinct alternative to Seneca. As sources in the Renaissance, Ovid and Seneca run routes parallel, identical, contiguous, and intersecting.' We may also note Gager's extensive engagement with Ovidian material in his play *Meleager*, often misrepresented as a 'Senecan play'.

13. See Melissa Mueller, 'Phaedra's *Defixio*: Scripting *Sophrosune* in Euripides' *Hippolytus*', *Classical Antiquity*, 30 (2011), 148–77 (pp. 164–65) for a summary of critical analysis exploring the visual dimension to Phaedra's entanglement with her own words.

14. Charles Segal, *Language and Desire in Seneca's Phaedra* (Princeton, NJ: Princeton University Press, 1986), p. 202. Not only Euripides of course, but a wide variety of other influences, including Ovid (as above). See also *The fragments of Sophocles | edited, with additional notes from the papers of Sir R. C. Jebb and Dr W. G. Headlam*, ed. by Alfred Chilton Pearson (Cambridge: Cambridge University Press, 1917), *passim*, and William Spencer Barret's critical edition of the *Hippolytos* (Oxford: Clarendon Press, 1964), *passim*, on Sophocles' *Phaedra*, now in fragmentary form.

15. Gager's insertion of the letter into the play interposes a passage of elegiac couplets which breaks with the metric sequence. This focuses our attention on the presence of Ovid's *Heroides*, conspicuous as one of the traditions underpinning Gager's portrayal of Phaedra. However, it also strengthens our impression of the independence of Gager's additions from the rest of Seneca's play.

16. *Ulysses Redux* (1592), F2^v–F6^v.

17. *Meleager* (1593), E8^r–F5^v.

18. Phaedra's fantasy demonstrates the disparity between her own ideas of virtue and Hippolytus'; her desire for the life of the huntress is, as Armstrong, *Cretan Women*, p. 99 puts it, 'a distorted reflection' of Hippolytus' devotion to Artemis. See note 9 above on Seneca's interest in the topos of hunting.

19. Here we intersect with the debate over the performability and performance history of Seneca *tragicus*, issues which have long dominated scholarship on his works. The debate has yet to be decisively settled, as shown by *Seneca in Performance*, ed. by George Harrison (London: George Duckworth, 2000), a collection of essays offering contrasting views. Gager's adaptation of Seneca's *Phaedra*, which illustrates a conspicuous desire to promote Senecan rhetoric at the expense of other concerns, reflects the Elizabethan aesthetic interest in *recitatio* and the practical emphasis which was placed upon oratorical skills as training for public service. (Cf. Gager's own oration, *Eloquentiae Encomium* (1585), delivered while Rhetor of Christ Church, in which he combines the Horatian partnership of *utile* and *dulce* (*Ars Poetica*, 343) with an exhortation to return to ancient *exempla* to improve one's eloquence). An appreciation of Seneca's plays as

158   ELIZABETH SANDIS

recitationes does not, however, prevent Gager from actively cultivating opportunities for visual effects on stage (see below). The Elizabethan reception of Seneca may provide illuminating *comparanda* for modern debates over the original performance context for Seneca' plays, though this topic lies beyond the scope of the present study.

20. Ovid's Phaedra makes an interesting comparison here, since she does not perceive the role of *noverca* as an obstacle. Far from it, she even suggests that it is to the lovers' advantage, for anyone who sees them embracing will offer praise for a stepmother and stepson clearly getting on so well. (See *Heroides* IV. 129–46, especially line 140).

21. The survey of the *noverca* figure presented in Patricia Watson, *Ancient Stepmothers: Myth, Misogyny and Reality* (*Mnemosyne Supplement*, 143) (Leiden: E. J. Brill, 1995) establishes the full extent to which this proverbial menace makes her mark on Greek and Roman literature and mythology, and notes that, in the *Phaedra*, 'Seneca avails himself of the opportunity offered by his theme to exploit conventional ideas about wicked stepmothers' (p. 111).

22. In his turn, Mantuan may have drawn upon Juvenal, *Satire VI* as a model.

23. I adopt Binns' translation here.

24. A range of evidence exists in relation to Gager's personal views on women, marriage, and celibacy, but, as Sutton, *William Gager: The Complete Works*, vol. I, pp. xvii–xix points out, this evidence is not only inconclusive but can be used to overturn the assumptions which have been made in the past. Gager's personal view of Phaedra as a moral *exemplum* lies outside the parameters of this article, but it is interesting to note that in his prologue to the *Panniculus* he makes a point of trying to limit the potential for misinterpretation by stating that the play does not intend to criticize *all* women, 'impudicas, non bonas' (22). Tongue-in-cheek though the prologue is, it includes the statement that Hippolytus is to take the blame, 'culpam' (23) and he 'will pay to womankind the penalty he deserves.' (27).

25. Much could be said about the education which Gager received at Westminster (and subsequently as a Queen's Scholar at Christ Church) in relation to his composition methods in the *Panniculus*. Regrettably, this lies outside the scope of the present study, except to say that, as a rule, the schoolboy experience of Seneca was as a series of fragments isolated from their dramatic context, rhetorical treasures culled from the text and printed in *florilegia* to be copied out into students' commonplace books under *loci communes* (thematic headings). Gager's prioritization of Senecan rhetoric and literary conceits reflects contemporary pedagogical culture and panders to the audience tastes and expectations influenced by that culture.

26. Segal, *Language and Desire*, p. 15, my emphasis.

27. Much of Hippolytus' imagery in Gager's speech draws on the natural world, as it does elsewhere in both Gager and Seneca. Note particularly the recurrent emphasis on traps and snares, portraying man as the prey of woman the hunter. See note 9 above on the significance of the hunting topos in Seneca's play as a whole.

28. Binns's translation.

29. Translation by John Fitch, ed., *Tragedies* (Cambridge, MA, and London: Harvard University Press, 2002).

30. See Sutton, *William Gager: The Complete Works*, vol. III, p. 237, who points out that, in his use of Ovid *Metamorphoses* IV.320–28 as the model for Nais's first speech (*Pann.* 253ff.), Gager deliberately removes the compromising line in which Salmacis says that she is willing to accept 'furtiva voluptas' [stolen joy], if Hermaphroditus already has a betrothed: '[T]he fact that Gager offers no equivalent for 327 in this passage demonstrates his intent of representing the Naiad as a genuinely chaste and wholesome creature.' Binns, 'Additions to Seneca's *Hippolytus*' concurs, referring to Nais's proposition of 'a legitimate love' (p. 160).

31. As an avenger, Nais appropriates the language of Ariadne and Dido in her repudiation of Hippolytus' ancestry and her curse upon him: 'Nec tibi, superbe, mater Antiope fuit. | Sed hirta duro Caucasi tigris iugo;' [Arrogant man, your mother was not Antiope, but some shaggy tigress on a hard ridge of the Caucasus] (*Pann.* 345–46). In reworking Catullus LXIV.155 and Virgil *Aeneid* IV.365–67, Gager, through the association of Nais and Phaedra together wreaking vengeance upon Hippolytus, adds to the palimpsest of Phaedra's *persona*. The Catullan link here has interesting resonances for Phaedra's fantasy at *Ph.* 661–66, where she imagines her sister Ariadne falling for the son Hippolytus in place of the father Theseus.

32. Corpus Christi College, Oxford, MS. 352, fol. 56.
33. 'Nais's love seems, in fact, so ingenuous that Gager manages to confuse the moral issue rather than clarify it', says Bruce Smith, *Ancient Scripts & Modern Experience on the English Stage, 1500–1700* (Princeton, NJ: Princeton University Press, 1988), p. 214.
34. The date of the performance was 'probably for the Christmas of 1546' according to Thomas Baldwin, *William Shakespere's small Latine & lesse Greeke*, 2 vols (Urbana: University of Illinois, 1944), vol. I, p. 177. Gager would later attend Westminster as a pupil.
35. This record is, in fact, a rough draft of the prologue scribbled hastily into his notebook (in which he kept various accounts and lists of books), with several corrections and insertions made, one of which spills over onto the previous page, where he had drafted his prologue to Terence's *Adelphi* (26ᵛ).
36. Smith, *Ancient Scripts*, p. 235. See ibid. pp. 199–202 for a full discussion of the biblical parallel which Nowell offers in his prologue (the wife of Potiphar's attempt to seduce Joseph, 'the Christian Hippolytus'). As Smith points out, Nowell's interpretation requires some 'selective hearing of Seneca's lines' in an attempt to force the *Hippolytus* into the generic mould of a medieval morality play.
37. On the Elizabethan interest in translating Seneca's tragedies, see Evelyn M. Spearing, *The Elizabethan Translations of Seneca's Tragedies* (Cambridge: Heffer, 1912) and G. K. Hunter, 'Seneca and the Elizabethans: A Case Study in Influence', *Shakespeare Survey*, vol. 20 (Cambridge: Cambridge University Press, 1967), pp. 17–26.
38. See Eliot's introduction to Newton's edition (London: Constable, 1927), p. xlv.
39. Norland, *Neoclassical Tragedy*, p. 165.
40. Eliot suggests a date of 1567 (London: Constable, 1927), p. xlv.
41. Richard McCabe, *Incest, Drama and Nature's Law, 1550–1700* (Cambridge: Cambridge University Press, 1993), p. 112.
42. McCabe, *Incest, Drama and Nature's Law*, p. 115.
43. For example, Plautus' *Casina* (21–22) and Terence's *Eunuchus* (44).
44. The need to differentiate had become increasingly important by this time, as demonstrated by Linda Shenk, 'Gown before Crown: Scholarly Abjection and Academic Entertainment under Queen Elizabeth I', in *Early Modern Academic Drama*, ed. by Jonathan Walker and Paul D. Streufert (Aldershot: Ashgate, 2008), pp. 19–44.
45. Brooke, 'The Life and Times of William Gager', p. 405.
46. See above on *Ph.* 176–77, 'must nature always abandon her laws, when a Cretan woman loves?', and also her sarcastic tone at *Ph.* 174, 'cur monstra cessant? aula cur fratris uacat?' [Why have the monsters ceased? Why is your brother's hall empty?], since tradition expects that there should always be a Minotaur in the labyrinth, ready for Theseus' arrival and the re-enactment of the rest of the cyclical narrative.
47. I follow Binns's translation here.
48. See, for example, Boas, *University Drama*, who concludes that Gager's adaptation 'made the awful catastrophe that overwhelms the house of Theseus the direct result of his impious attempt upon the bride of the ruler of the shades' (p. 199).
49. Armstrong, *Cretan Women*, p. 279.
50. Translation by Fitch.
51. McCabe, *Incest, Drama and Nature's Law*, p. 113.
52. Binns's translation.

CHAPTER 8

The Power of Transformation in Guillén de Castro's *El caballero bobo* (1595–1605) and *La fuerza de la costumbre* (1610–15): Translation and Performance

Kathleen Jeffs

Gonzaga University, WA

'*La fuerza de la costumbre*, de don Guillén de Castro, por la bizarría del verso y por la invención merece el inmortal laurel, así como *La dama duende* de Calderón'

BALTASAR GRACIÁN, *Arte de ingenio*, Madrid, 1642[1]

In the final decades of the sixteenth century, the Valencian playwright Guillén de Castro (1569–1631) was writing innovative and challenging dramas and comedies that drew from the dramatic tradition that preceded him, and which anticipated the popular *comedia nueva*.[2] Castro, the star of the active playwriting scene in Valencia until he moved to Madrid at age fifty, is best known for his two-part *Las mocedades del Cid*, upon which Corneille based his renowned *Le Cid*. Three of Castro's plays were directly inspired by Cervantes.[3] Yet his lasting legacy is an engagement with the art form of the three-act Spanish play that provides a bridge between sixteenth- and seventeenth-century works for the theatre, treading a line between violence and love, between death and life, between ruin and *honor*. In this chapter, which is based on my experience of translating these plays for the stage, I will argue that his early play, *El caballero bobo*, sheds light on the developing mind of Castro, illuminating his more mature work, *La fuerza de la costumbre*.

The main challenge to a contemporary theatre company approaching Guillén de Castro's *La fuerza de la costumbre* in production is the ending. How should the actors playing the long-lost brother and sister portray a simplistic gender transformation that seems to undermine the work the playwright has done in showing the complexities of that aspect of the human experience? The play is ostensibly about gender, but I will argue that the siblings undergo a transformation that goes deeper than sexuality, and touches on the very formation of identity. But we must look at the issue of gender in the ending first, as it is foremost. *La fuerza de la costumbre* is difficult because of the transformation, at the eleventh hour, of the Amazon

162   KATHLEEN JEFFS

warrior, the girl Hipólita. At the conclusion of the play, in a way which defies verisimilitude, she becomes a shrinking violet, weak and prone to fainting.[4] She has a sexual encounter with the man who has won her admiration, and the experience teaches her 'what it means to be a woman'. The monologue she delivers, recounting the 'miraculous' event, is as follows:

CASTRO, *La fuerza de la costumbre*[5]

Allí, madre, allí atrevidos,
que todo amante lo es,
sacamos las dos espadas...
Yo una punta le tiré,
desvióla, retiróse;
tiréle segunda vez;
hizo ganancia en mi espada;
metió el brazo y no excusé
el quedar dél abrazada
y el abrazarme con él.
Forcejamos un gran rato,
cada uno por vencer;
más es jabón en la yerba
el rocío... Resbalé
y dando traspiés, caí
de mi enemigo a los pies.
Y aun esto no fuera nada,
pero después de caer,
hizo, ¡ay, madre!, cierta cosa,
que nunca la imaginé.
Revolvióme toda el alma
y mudóme todo el ser,
diciendo: 'Para que vea,
pues es mujer, que lo es.'
Creí con tal desengaño
que lo soy, y ya no sé
sino llorar tiernamente
su ausencia, y quiérole bien;
y en efecto, madre mía,
desde entonces soy mujer. (73–74)

JEFFS, trans., *The Force of Habit*[6]

There, mother, there, daringly,
for every lover is daring,
both of us drew our swords...
I thrusted, he parried and drew back;
I thrusted a second time;
he overpowered my sword;
he took hold of my arm
and I could not resist his grasp
and found myself locked in his embrace.
We wrestled for a long time,
but the dew on the grass was slippery as
soap...
I slipped and stumbled, I fell,
at the feet of my enemy.
And as if this were not enough,
after I fell, he did, O mother, such a thing,
that I never could have imagined.
My soul turned,
my being changed,
saying, 'Now you see
what it means to be a woman,
for that is what you are.'
I see so clearly now, I believe that I am.
Now I love him when I am with him,
and weep tenderly when I am not.
Mother, since that moment, I am a woman.

How should the actress portray this moment? Her *aria* in this particularly earnest key seems disingenuous after three acts of delightfully ironic comic twists and turns exposing the constructed games of gender (the arts of shoes and swords have to be learned, after all, and Castro hilariously exposes the lessons learned in both areas of study). However, help may be at hand if we view this speech alongside Castro's sixteenth-century play, *El caballero bobo*, and gain a deeper understanding of Castro's nascent thinking on the transformative power of love.

Let us begin with a comparison of the brother–sister sibling pairs in both plays, to gain context and a sense of the personalities at play. In *La fuerza*, we have the cross-dressed siblings Hipólita and Félix, who have each been raised by one parent in a particularly challenging situation: Hipólita grew up fighting the war in Flanders with her father, who was a soldier, and Félix stayed at home with his terrified mother, who kept him in the long robes of early childhood, and who did not let him out into the street lest he be injured in some duel or scrap. Their love interests are another brother–sister pair, Luis and Leonor, whose parents are not on the scene. Luis is a typical *galán* with a well-developed sense of honour and the gift of eloquence when falling in love. He woos Hipólita by luring her into a private spot for a 'duel', appealing to her desire to fight, and overpowers her in an altercation that leads to her seduction described above.[7] His sister, Leonor, is a pretty *dama* with a lovely singing voice and a manipulative nature. She, unlike her brother who loves Hipólita for her strength and personal qualities, demands that her love-interest change completely before she will accept him. She demeans Félix until he wins her favour by committing an act of violence against his rival, Otavio, for her love.

Turning to *El caballero bobo*, it is unlikely that readers will be familiar with the plot, so I will paraphrase it here. The King of Hungary has one son, Lotario, and one daughter, Aurora. Like Segismundo in *La vida es sueño*, Aurora has been locked up her entire life due to a prophecy given at her birth.[8] Her brother is violent and libidinous (as his name implies), and he decides near the start of the play to kill Aurora to rid his family of the threat of her discovery and their associated ruin if anyone were to see her face before her wedding day. Due to Aurora's cunning plan for the cousins to swap places, he is unsuccessful. The King's brother, the Duke, has a son and daughter as well: Anteo and Estrella. Anteo, like Semiramis from *La hija del aire*, lives as a savage and eschews marriage. His sister, Estrella, is sweet at the beginning of the play, but she later reveals herself to be clever and ambitious, traits that grow stronger as she glimpses the possibility of a marriage that would lead to her ascent to the throne as Queen.

Toward our purpose of shedding light on *La fuerza de la costumbre*, it is helpful to draw some very rough parallels between the four siblings in each play. Crudely, our hero Luis aligns with Anteo, in his admiration of strong women and his acceptance of a female partner who displays typically masculine qualities. Luis's sister Leonor aligns with Estrella, in that both of them display typically feminine qualities (Estrella is girlish at the start of *El caballero bobo*), and they both admire masculinity in their potential partners. Félix, the feminized young man raised by his mother to sew and fear thunder, aligns interestingly with Lotario, though this comparison is less obvious because, certainly at the beginning of both plays, the characters could not appear more different from one another. Comparing Félix and Lotario is fruitful if we look at their motivations for committing the violence that they perpetrate: Lotario will kill his sister because she has betrayed him by loving the man who tried to kill him, so he attempts to kill for genuine revenge and out of personal anger and retribution. Félix, on the other hand, will kill Otavio because he has to; he is not motivated by anger, but is following the instructions of his lady-love and the mandate of his bloodthirsty father. Félix knows that his personal safety is at risk if he does not defeat Otavio, because his father will kill him or at least disown him, and, if unsuccessful, he will not be able to marry, and he would thus have no place in society. So, Lotario lashes out for reasons of revenge and self-preservation of a very direct kind, while Félix attacks out of fear that he will be killed or rejected in fundamental and dangerous ways. Both Félix and Lotario fight for their own protection, though their methods and demeanours may be very different on the surface.

Comparing some of the siblings' exchanges will illuminate the depth of characterization in both plays. Félix's initial words to Leonor, are, at first glance, similar to the courtly, stock-phrased love that Lotario professes for Estrella:

CASTRO, *La fuerza de la costumbre*	JEFFS, trans., *The Force of Habit*
FÉLIX: No se ha visto en el oriente con más hermosura el sol. LEONOR: Poco resplandor le debes, pues está puesto en tus brazos. FÉLIX: Y en mi [sic] ojos amanece. (49) [...] LEONOR: (*Ap.*) Mucho me mira don Félix. FÉLIX: Esto sin duda es amor, pues me regala y me ofende. (50)	FÉLIX: The sun in the east has never appeared with more beauty. LEONOR: It radiates upon you, for it is placed in your arms. FÉLIX: And its dawn is in my eyes. [...] LEONOR: (*Aside.*) Don Félix is staring at me. FÉLIX: (*Aside.*) This no doubt is love, for it rules and compels me.
CASTRO, *El caballero bobo*	JEFFS, trans., *The Foolish Gentleman*
LOTARIO: Mas ¡ay Dios; qué bellos ojos! ¡Ay, qué divina hermosura! ¡Qué luz hermosa y serena! ¡Qué centro de la memoria! ¡Qué pena que ofrece gloria! ¡Qué gloria que ofrece pena! ¿Qué extraña mudanza has hecho en mi alma y mi sentido? Sin duda el daño temido de tu cara está en mi pecho. (54)	LOTARIO: But, oh God, what lovely eyes! Oh, what divine beauty! Such beautiful and serene light! How it burns straight into my mind! What pain offers such glory? What glory offers such pain? What strange change have you made in my soul and in my senses? No doubt the wound we feared your face would strike is gaping in my heart.

This is meant to be 'love at first sight' in both cases. Félix is surprised by his feelings, since he has apparently never before seen a woman to whom he was attracted. She thinks and speaks highly of herself, continuing his metaphor by comparing herself to the sun. Lotario, though he thinks he has uncovered the face of his sister, and thus believes his attraction to be incestuous, is so carried away by her beauty that he fears the curse against her may be coming true right within his heart. He, like Félix, uses the language of light and the sun, of eyes that shine with a light that burns the soul.

Hipólita and Luis, for their part, enjoy a similar moment of mutual admiration tinged with a sense of personal defeat, in their case in the midst of a duel:

The Power of Transformation in Guillén de Castro 165

CASTRO, *La fuerza de la costumbre*

LUIS:
Tente, señora, por Dios,
no me mates, rendiréme;
que aunque con la espada tiras,
pero con los ojos hieres,
con mucha ventaja riñes.
HIPÓLITA:
Con lo bien que te defiendes,
sin ofender, has mostrado
que eras animoso y fuerte,
y por eso no he querido
ni matarte ni ofenderme.
LUIS:
Ya me ha muerto tu hermosura
pero ha sido dulcemente. (49)

JEFFS, trans., *The Force of Habit*

LUIS:
Wait, my lady, by God,
do not kill me, I will surrender;
for although you fight with the sword,
you wound with the eyes,
which have defeated me.
HIPÓLITA:
You defended yourself with skill,
showing me your spirit and strength,
and so I have decided to let you live.
LUIS:
Your beauty has killed me
but it has been a sweet death.

There is a nice symmetry between Luis's captivation by Hipólita and the ending, in which the tables are turned. Here Hipólita does not yet know Luis's identity, but she recognizes the codes and behaviour of her own class of fighter. Castro's penchant for introducing lovers in high-stakes situations is reflected in the dangerous straits in which Anteo and Aurora first meet, which also entail a case of mistaken identity:

CASTRO, *El caballero bobo*

AURORA:
¿Quién ha sido
tan loco y tan atrevido
que osó descubrir mi cara?
[...]
ANTEO:
Alumbrado de sus ojos
descubre más su hermosura.
Si cuando estaban cerrados,
daban cuidados tan ciertos,
agora que están abiertos,
¿cuáles serán los cuidados? (56–57)

JEFFS, trans., *The Foolish Gentleman*

AURORA:
Who has been
so mad and so bold
that he dared to uncover my face?
[...]
ANTEO:
Illuminated by her eyes
her beauty shines all the brighter.
If, when they were closed,
they struck me with such passion,
now that they are open,
what passions will they now inspire?

The seeds of transformation are sown in these first moments when the lovers' eyes lock, and each one seems to either hint at or explicitly state the personal danger they feel as a result of being struck. Now that we have a sense of the first step of each pair of lovers' journey toward marriage, I will break the couples down into units in order to more closely examine the parallels and lessons that can be taken from *El caballero bobo* when interpreting *La fuerza de la costumbre*. If both plays begin with conventional love-language about the power of love generated through sight and the eyes, their journeys become increasingly unconventional as the stakes of love and loss grow higher and more dangerous.

Two Men Who Admire a *mujer varonil*

Let us continue our exploration of the transformative power of love, and its eventual consequences, by looking at how these seeds of love begin to germinate in the hearts of the young lovers. Beginning with Anteo and Luis, these two heroes enjoy a similar moment when their lady-loves declare themselves ready to fight on the side of their man. Aurora boldly declares herself a General, and Anteo's response is to say that he did not know what a woman was until he saw her strength and capabilities in that moment. As this is the theatre, and not a novel, he must physically enact his inner state, and his response is to bend down to kiss her feet, indicating the traditional shift in balance of power of the courtly lover abasing himself to his lady (see *El perro del hortelano* [The Dog in the Manger]) and he says:

CASTRO, *El caballero bobo*

ANTEO:
Y será cierto el vencer
con tan fuerte General.
AURORA:
Para mostrar mi caudal
he dejado el ser mujer.
Las lágrimas y el dolor
por la braveza he trocado,
que yo quiero esposo honrado,
y tú lo has de ser, señor.
Y así es bien, con sangre mía,
comprar tu honor y mi gusto.
ANTEO:
Y que yo te adore es justo,
loco y muerto de alegría.
Y aun no será por ser tanta
bastante indicio la muerte:
mujer bella, mujer fuerte,
mujer linda, mujer santa.
[...]
Y si un tiempo aborrecía
hasta el nombre de mujer,
sin duda debió de ser
porque no las conocía.
Sumo bien, suma belleza,
por mi gusto e interese,
deja que los pies te bese;
pondré en ellos la cabeza. (82)

JEFFS, trans., *The Foolish Gentleman*

ANTEO:
Victory will be certain
with so strong a General.
AURORA:
In order to show my mettle
I have ceased to be a woman.
I have exchanged tears and
wringing hands for ferocity;
for I want an honourable husband,
and that must be you, Sir.
And so, is right that
I should purchase your honour
and my pleasure with my own blood.
ANTEO:
And for me to adore you it is right
that I am insane and half-dead with joy;
even death is not a sufficient sign
of how much I love you,
but no, it's for you,
my beautiful, strong,
lovely, and holy woman.
[...]
And if at one time I myself
abhorred even the name of 'woman',
undoubtedly that had to be
because I did not truly know them.
The height of all good and beauty,
for my pleasure and in my interest
leave your feet here so I can kiss them,
I will put my head at their level.

The power balance shift is courtly, but we get the sense that it is not pure formality. His words and actions express a human connection as well as depict the typical image of a knight on bended knee. He is a willing student in the lessons of love, and has the capacity to be astonished by his lady's bravery and to re-define his understanding of womanhood. It is noteworthy that Castro's character is open and able to make this change in his understanding of something so culturally 'fixed' as the nature of a woman.

Anteo's disbelief at the happy chance of finding such a strong woman is echoed by Luis when he first discovers Hipólita and tells his friends, 'quiero mujer para mía | que nunca lo supo ser' (52) (to highlight this discovery I translated this line for performance as: 'I want her for my wife; I never thought there could be someone like her'). As the plot develops, the lovers find themselves in a literal battle as Hipólita believes herself wronged, and fights him to reclaim her reputation. In their witty exchange as they go off to fight, Luis displays his passion for the militant Hipólita:

CASTRO, *La fuerza de la costumbre*	JEFFS, trans., *The Force of Habit*
LUIS: Pues tras de aquella alameda te espero.	LUIS: I will wait for you behind that poplar grove.
HIPÓLITA: Mueve los pies, y allí que tengo has de ver de mujer no más del nombre.	HIPÓLITA: Move your feet, and there you will see that only in name am I a woman.
LUIS: Y allí verás que soy hombre para más de una mujer. Has de probar, vive Dios, de mis fuerzas los extremos.	LUIS: And there you will see that I am man enough for one who is more than a woman. You will see, by God, the extent of my strength.
HIPÓLITA: Camina, que allí veremos cuál se rinde de los dos.	HIPÓLITA: Walk, for there we will see which of us is the stronger.
LUIS: [*Ap.*] Y allí, fortuna, ha de ser logrado mi buen deseo.	LUIS: [*Aside.*] And there, fortune, I will achieve what I desire.
HIPÓLITA: [*Ap.*] El me engaña, ya lo veo, pero no lo quiero ver. (71)	HIPÓLITA: [*Aside.*] He is deceiving me, I see that, but I do not want to see it.

In both plays, the men are forced, by both habit and love, to re-examine their definition of a woman and the effect the person they love can have on their own understanding. Luis is focused on the goal of realizing his passion in this moment, but he knows that the way to this particular woman's heart is through her sword, and he is willing to adapt his wooing strategy to suit her tastes.

'Man up or go home': Estrella and Leonor

Looking at Estrella and Leonor there are comparisons that can be made throughout the plays, because neither one is a simple love-interest character fulfilling the role of *segunda dama*. Castro's understanding of relationships is as complex with these secondary characters as it is with his protagonists. In *El caballero bobo*, Estrella is perhaps not as clever as her more prominent cousin Aurora, but she is in love, and that lends her cunning. The key difference between Castro's early lady, Estrella, and the more complex character of Leonor in *La fuerza de la costumbre*, is the manipulative tactics of Leonor which do not serve to build up and reify her lover, but instead wear him down and destroy his morale until he is forced to do her will, as she leaves him no option. Let us look first at Leonor's tactics, which are pure bullying:

CASTRO, *La fuerza de la costumbre*	JEFFS, trans., *The Force of Habit*
LEONOR:	LEONOR:
Ya os aborrezco, y no en vano	I detest your cowardice.
por vileza semejante,	If you had defended my glove,
y advertid que fuera llano,	perhaps you could have deserved my hand.
si defendierais el guante,	But despite receiving my favour,
quizá el merecer la mano.	you chose to act in your own silly way.
Con todo, favorecido	If you were to appear
habéis de ir a vuestro modo,	how you look in my eyes,
que es falta el no haber tenido	you would wear these feathers!
plumas para ser del todo	*She drops some feathers from her headpiece.*
lo que veo que habéis sido.	You could put these pretty plumes on,
Dale una pluma que se quita del tocado.	and you'd look just like the chicken you are.
Estas os podéis poner,	
aunque, a ser yo más curiosa,	
para vos habían de ser	
de otra ave menos hermosa,	
pero mejor de comer. (61)	

Though difficult to translate, her intention is clearly to emasculate Félix. In performance, this scene conveys its meaning through the visual composition of the actors, because Leonor is up on her balcony and Félix makes easy prey down below. Leonor in this scene is not pretty, but pretty horrible.

Estrella in *El caballero bobo*, on the other hand, does everything humanly possible to follow and help her husband. When the family fighting sparks off and she must choose a side, she instantly turns against her cousin and friend Aurora, saying to Lotario,

CASTRO, *El caballero bobo*	JEFFS, trans., *The Foolish Gentleman*
ESTRELLA:	ESTRELLA:
Y haz que tu gusto permita	You can do what you like;
porque el Rey y señor mío	the King my lord sees how
vea cómo ofrece brío	Love lends us courage
el amor, y no le quita,	and does not take our strength from us.
que salga contigo yo,	I go out with you,
porque se venga a entender	so that it may be seen and understood
que agravios de una mujer	that the offences of one woman
otra mujer los vengó:	can be avenged by another;
que para que no te afrente	so that you are not offended
salir con empresa tal,	by such an enterprise,
yo saldré por General	I will go out as the General
de tu campo y de tu gente.	of your side and of your people.
Gobernaréla, y de hecho	I will govern them and
el orgullo pienso dar. (82)	I will take pride in my leadership.

THE POWER OF TRANSFORMATION IN GUILLÉN DE CASTRO   169

It is Estrella who 'mans up' in this case. Though her actions are extreme and perhaps intended to be comic (aligning herself implicitly as the teleological Marian figure redeeming the sins of Eve?), Estrella is serious, and pulls her weight in the conflict. Her additional motivations begin to become clear in the latter half of the second act, as she desires the throne: 'Dichosa Reina he de ser' ['I'll be Queen, and blessed']. As her star and fortune rises, she begs fortune not to continue its typically cyclical behaviour, 'Fortuna no me levantes | para dejarme caer' [Fortune, do not raise me up | only to see me fall] (*El caballero bobo* 71).

In contrast, Leonor fights dirty, indirectly, and spurs her lover on not with offers of military assistance or leadership, but by shaming him into action, churlishly throwing feathers at him, and calling him a chicken. Leonor's diatribe follows the exit of Hipólita, whose method of direct action aligns her with the ladies' leadership strategy shown in *El caballero bobo* (Hipólita takes the responsibility upon herself and heads out to fight on Félix's behalf, perhaps seen in her precursor 'Generals' Estrella and Aurora). In sharp relief, Castro shows another side to women's weaponry in the character of Leonor, who has no weapons except her words (and feathers). However, Leonor's weapons are arguably more dangerous, because they inspire in Félix not necessarily bravery, but the knowledge that he has no choice now but to attack. This is a winning dramaturgical strategy, because it drives the action of the play to its inexorable climax.

Lotario and Félix as Defenders of Themselves

Rather than save the marriages for the end of the play in what will become traditional Lopean fashion, Castro matches up the couples in the middle of *El caballero bobo*. Lotario and his beloved Estrella are married in the midst of the action, but there is still plenty of meat left on the play before its conclusion. The war between the English and the Hungarians, which has been brewing ever since Anteo killed the English Ambassador's son Henrico (thinking it was Lotario), is now in full force, and the King is mustering forces to take them on and protect his territory. He interrupts Lotario and Estrella's honeymoon in order to rally him to war, cajoling him:

CASTRO, *El caballero bobo*

REY:
El pecho gallardo y fiero
cubre de aceradas piezas,
si, enseñado a estas ternezas,
puede sufrirte el acero.
Al campo sal, y defiende
tu gusto, vida y honor;
deja el amor, que el amor,
si te regala, te ofende:
que un hombre no ha de querer
de suerte a la mujer bella,
que el recelo de perdella
cobarde le pueda hacer.
Ea, hijo.

JEFFS, trans., *The Foolish Gentleman*

KING:
The brave heart and sharpest steel sword
must now replace the tenderness of home,
if you can remember how to handle steel,
after becoming used to a softer touch.
Go out to the field,
and defend your pleasure, life and honour;
leave off love,
for love in your heart now will
only serve to weaken you:
a man must not come to
love a beautiful woman in such a way
that the fear of losing her
can turn him into a coward.
So, my son ...

LOTARIO:
Padre, baste;
que tan sobrado anduviste,
que en lo que aquí me dijiste
es cierto que me afrentaste.
Yo saldré donde esas gentes
puedan probar mi rigor
¿quién hace sino el amor
a los cobardes valientes?
Al amor la culpa has dado
que mil palmas me asigura;
¿quién ha visto, por ventura,
un cobarde enamorado? (81)

LOTARIO:
Father, enough;
one word from you would be enough,
of course I will go.
I will go where those people
can test my strength;
who but Love can turn
cowards to valiant men?
You have blamed love
but a thousand of love's gifts assure me;
who has seen, peradventure,
a coward in love?

The King's understanding of the power of love is that it can transform a man for the worse. He cajoles his son, warning him that love might turn him into a coward if he becomes accustomed to the comforts of home and the softness of domestic happiness. Lotario's self-protective strategy is to turn that logic on its head and say that the reverse is true: love imbues the lover with a renewed strength, because he will do anything to protect and defend his beloved. In *La fuerza*, the patriarch's position is to rally his son's bravery in order to harden him and train him in the ways of masculinity, and he is much more insulting as he berates his son. If the King's words are an attempt to encourage his son to take action by appealing to his sense of masculinity in the face of threat, Pedro's intent is similar, but he uses a variety of cajoling speeches in various attempts to reach this goal. In one scene, Pedro tries a tactic that is distinct from his usual threats and name-calling, and brings not only his future son-in-law, Luis, but also a trusted advisor, a Captain from Pedro's fighting days in Flanders, to give Félix some military advice. During that scene, he encourages Félix to focus his mind and ignore all distractions:

CASTRO, *La fuerza de la costumbre*

JEFFS, trans., *The Force of Habit*

PEDRO:
Tú, solamente guiado
de tu honor, piensa, atrevido,
sólo en que te han ofendido,
si quieres quedar vengado,
pues si das en discurrir,
en temeroso has de dar,
y nunca acierta a matar
quien teme que ha de morir. (63)

PEDRO:
Guided by your honour and your daring,
you must think only on your enemy
if you want to achieve vengeance.
Because if you admit distractions,
you will find yourself giving way to fear,
and the man who is afraid to die
will never be able to kill.

Rather than fix his mind on his lady or his love, Pedro says that action can only be taken if one concentrates on the enemy, on defeating the opponent in front of him. Thinking of his love may cause him to fear his own death, which has a tinge of the King's argument above about the power of love to weaken a man in the face of danger. The fruit of comparing the patriarchs' logic in the two plays is even more helpful when we consider Pedro's representative, the Tutor, in the first act of *La fuerza de la costumbre*, when he tells Pedro that Félix's unmanly nature is the result of mollycoddling by his mother, Costanza:

THE POWER OF TRANSFORMATION IN GUILLÉN DE CASTRO

CASTRO, *La fuerza de la costumbre*

AYO:
En su niñez dió señales
de naturaleza altiva,
de caballeroso brío,
que causara honrada envidia;
pero su amorosa madre,
femenilmente encogida,
previniendo los peligros
y temiendo las desdichas,
con diligencias piadosas,
prudencia mal entendida,
sus acciones reformaba
y su natural vencía.
Cuando a varoniles cosas
inclinarse pretendía,
divertíale con otras,
de afeminadas, indignas;
[...]
Siempre a su cuello colgado,
entre alcorzadas caricias
con regalos lo enviciaba,
con temores le ofendía. (44)

JEFFS, trans., *The Force of Habit*

TUTOR:
In his childhood he showed signs
of gentlemanly spirit.
But his loving mother
clothed him inappropriately,
thinking that would keep him safe.
Her actions overcame his nature.
When he tried to incline himself
to manly occupations,
she distracted him with
feminine things, unworthy of him.
His mother always hung her arms
around his neck with sweet caresses,
spoiling him with gifts,
and instilling girlish fears.

The Tutor leaves no doubt about who should bear the blame for Félix's condition as an *hombre femenil*; not himself as the boy's teacher, and not even the boy — rather, the blame is levelled clearly at Costanza, where it rests in Pedro's estimation for the remainder of the play, and presumably their lives. Thinking back to the King's words in *El caballero bobo*, we can see that the threats that comforts of home (personified by wives and mothers) may have a weakening effect is something that preys on the minds of men in both plays. The actions of the younger generation in Luis, Anteo and Lotario are all the more interesting given this deep-seated suspicion of the damaging effects of a woman's love in both plays.

Predictably, Félix does not immediately prove himself a man in quite the way his father had hoped. Disappointed, Pedro's admonishments are harsh and forbidding. Félix's response is to desire to please his father, so he summons his anger and hurt and transforms it into violent energy. Félix, no longer a mouse, is now transformed into a lion:

CASTRO, *La fuerza de la costumbre*

PEDRO:
Pues, ¡vive Dios!, hijo indigno
deste nombre que te doy,
que has de cortalle la mano
con que el guante te quitó,
o has de dejar en las mías
pedazos del corazón.

JEFFS, trans., *The Force of Habit*

PEDRO:
By God, you are unworthy
to be called my son,
for you must cut the hand
that took the glove from you,
or you will cut my heart in pieces.

FÉLIX:
Padre, no me afrentes más,
porque ya de suerte estoy,
que habré de empezar en ti
a cobrar nueva opinión.
Ya el agravio recebido,
esta invidia, este dolor
de tantas afrentas juntas
me ha convertido en león;
[...]
Seré otro Martín Peláez,
que cobarde se corrió
de que le quitó el escaño
el famoso Campeador,
y fué un asombro después.
Por el divino Hacedor,
que he de ser rigor del cielo,
y en su esfera a todo el sol
pondré nubes coloradas
siendo de sangre el vapor:
mil víboras me han picado,
todo de veneno soy. (62)

FÉLIX:
Father, do not insult me further,
because now my fortune is such
that I am going to inspire in you
a better opinion of me.
The grievance I have suffered,
the envy, the pain
of so many offences together
have changed me into a lion.
[...]
I will be another Martin Peláez,
the coward who ran from battle
until he was unseated by
the famous Champion, El Cid,
and he was a terror after that.
By the divine maker,
I must be Heaven's scourge,
and from the sky up to the sun
I will colour the clouds
and vapour with his blood;
a thousand vipers have bitten me,
and I am all poison.

By this point in the play the audience is supposed to see evidence that Félix is making the transformation from a weak, girlish boy into a warrior ready for battle, but the reasons for it, which are clear in this speech, are not those his father intended. While his *padre* hoped that he would reach down into his own noble blood and find fencing ability located in his very marrow, instead it is the 'grievance I have suffered, the envy, the pain of so many offences together' that transforms him. He has learned the history lessons and lore, including the myths of the minor characters inspired (and shamed) by El Cid into bravery, and he uses examples to prove he has been listening. Arguably it is not love at all that turns Félix into a man; it is rage at the bullying and mistreatment of him by his father and by Leonor. If we compare the subject of the sentence in which he says that it is *agravio* that has turned him into a lion, it is very different from how Castro understood love's power to make us brave in *El caballero bobo*, when Lotario argued that love would guide his powerful hands due to the desire to protect and defend his beloved lady. Yet it is not romantic love for Leonor that spurs Félix on to commit acts of 'bravery' (violence); it is pain.

So, once Félix has made this transformation and is ready to carry out his bloody deed, he must come up with a plan to do it. The enactment of this plan ensures the preservation of his *honor*. To shed light on his methodology, it is helpful to look at his analogue in a particularly dastardly moment in *El caballero bobo*. Lotario's decision to kill his sister by strangulation rather than to spill their family's precious noble blood is an absurdly comic move made according to the twisted logic of honour. Even he prepares to kill her, clever Aurora desperately searches for a way to stay his hand, and she appeals to their family bloodline:

THE POWER OF TRANSFORMATION IN GUILLÉN DE CASTRO

CASTRO, *El caballero bobo*

AURORA:
¡Ay, hermano! Y ¿qué dirán
de que tu sangre vertiste?
¿Merece la tierra fría
llevar entre sus arenas
una sangre de mis venas
que es tan tuya como mía?
¿No es hidalga? ¿No es leal?
Mi razón ha de obligarte.
LOTARIO:
De otra suerte he de matarte;
espera, no dices mal.
Tu sangre no verteré
porque es mía, y por hacello
echaréte un lazo al cuello
y con él te mataré
para que el mundo no diga
que la vierto.
Desátase una atapierna
y échale un lazo al cuello. (84)

JEFFS, trans., *The Foolish Gentleman*

AURORA:
Oh, my brother! What will they say
if you spilled your own blood?
Does our blood deserve to be spilled
out here among the rocks,
to rest in the cold, hard ground?
Is it not noble? Is it not loyal?
My reasons must oblige you.
LOTARIO:
Wait, you are right;
I must kill you in another way.
I will not spill your blood,
because you are right, it is mine,
but I will put a cord around your neck
and kill you that way instead.
That way no one can say
I shed our blood.
He takes off his sock-garter
and makes a noose around her neck.

Aurora, ever the clever one, finds a method of deterring her brother from his murderous intent, even if only to stall him for a moment. Lotario finds a way to get what he wants and protect his own reputation. Castro uses these twists again with his later anti-hero, Félix, as he also operates within the codes of honour using questionable means. The advice that the Captain (Félix's father's trusted friend from the fighting in Flanders) offers him gives Félix a way to ensure he is successful, though perhaps not through conventional ways: 'Con tal disimulacion [*sic*], | en hallando a tu enemigo, | le saca al campo contigo, | que no impidan tu intención, | y en el lugar apartado, | donde ninguno lo impida, | quítale el guante o la vida' [Contrive a reason to draw your enemy | to a secret place where no one may intrude, | and there you must take from him | the glove or his life] (65). The Captain, who echoes Pedro's advice to focus on his enemy, also encourages the young man to make sure no one is around to see whether his reputation was reclaimed honourably, or not.

This advice plays out like a script for performance. Félix implements the plan to the letter: once he has his rival Otavio out in the field and is ready to fight, he changes the location so that no one might bear witness to the fray:

CASTRO, *La fuerza de la costumbre*

OTAVIO:
¿Agrádate este lugar?
FÉLIX:
Más escondido le quiero.
OTAVIO:
Por algún despeñadero
a un valle puedes bajar;
que hasta el abismo mayor
te seguiré, que deseo
verte solo.

JEFFS, trans., *The Force of Habit*

OTAVIO:
Does this location suit you?
FÉLIX:
I'd prefer one that is more secluded.
OTAVIO:
I hope you find a cliff
over a deep valley to fall from;
for I'd follow you to the deepest realm of hell;
I only want to see you alone.

174   KATHLEEN JEFFS

FÉLIX:
Yo lo creo
de tu nobleza y valor.
Detrás de aquellas paredes
iremos.
OTAVIO:
Iré tras ti;
ve, que aunque me toca a mí
señalar puesto, bien puedes...
FÉLIX:
Que lo estimo te prometo,
que es mucho para estimar;
pero si busco lugar
tan escondido y secreto,
es porque gente no acuda,
y porque no tenga al vella
una espada tan doncella
vergüenza de estar desnuda. (72)

FÉLIX:
I have full faith in your nobility and
valour.
We're just going behind those walls.
OTAVIO:
I'll follow after you;
for although custom dictates
that I would choose the spot, you can...
FÉLIX:
I promise you that I trust you,
and it is a great leap to do so;
I seek a hidden, secret place
so that people do not burst in on us,
and so that I will not have to show
my maidenly sword to anyone else,
she is ashamed to be seen naked.

Like Lotario, Félix finds a method of eliminating his victim that suits his purpose but requires him to think in alternative ways. Rather than using the normal duelling-ground for his fight with Otavio, Félix lures him to another place where, honourably or by whatever means available in order to be successful, he can defeat him. There is a hint of foul play in the Captain's monologue where he recounts the events (he alone watched the duel from a place of safety, and then tells the tale in lofty *octavas* for the entire family later):

CASTRO, *La fuerza de la costumbre*

JEFFS, trans., *The Force of Habit*

CAPTAIN:
Otavio se afirmó gallardamente:
pero asióle la espada, y se le arroja
don Félix tan furioso y tan valiente,
que por un hombro desvió la hoja,
y con la guarnición nariz y frente
le hizo pedazos, y su sangre roja,
cuando sobre la yerba dió de espaldas,
en rubís convirtió las esmeraldas.
Perdió sombrero y guante, y aturdido,
perdiendo espada y todo, al cielo invoca,
repitiendo: 'No mates a un rendido',
con voz turbada en la sangrienta boca. (75)

CAPTAIN:
Otavio held himself gracefully,
but Félix grabbed his sword, and
with a flourish he cut his nose and forehead
into pieces, and his red blood,
jewelled the emerald grasses with rubies.
Otavio, without his hat, the glove,
                            or his sword,
was stunned, and he invoked heaven,
repeating, 'Do not kill one who surrenders',
with a broken voice in his bloody mouth.

The colourful language of the red blood staining the emerald grasses adds a touch of decorative lyricism, and almost a grace, to the description of the sensitive Félix's moment of victory. If the violent climax in *La fuerza de la costumbre* ends with Félix humiliating and wounding his enemy, and all for the sake of reclaiming his honour, it has a revelatory parallel in the end of *El caballero bobo*, though with a very different scenario. As the climactic final scene begins, the two brothers are punishing their wayward sisters for their *liviana* behaviour, most of which consisted of declaring themselves Generals and committing acts of 'bravery' (violence), but for the wrong side. Each brother has hold of his sister and is about to kill her: Lotario is strangling

The Power of Transformation in Guillén de Castro 175

Aurora with his sock-garter while Anteo is dangling poor Estrella off a cliff. The husbands both notice that the other man has his beloved wife in his clutches, and each one pleads for mercy:

CASTRO, *El caballero bobo*

ANTEO:
Deja tú la que es mi Aurora
y es mi señora, y mi cielo.
LOTARIO:
Esta mataré, y a darte
el castigo subiré.
ANTEO:
Tente.
LOTARIO:
Tente.
ANTEO:
Espera.
LOTARIO:
Espera,
no arrojes el cielo al suelo.
ANTEO:
No subas el suelo al cielo
tan sin tiempo.
LOTARIO:
Muera.
ANTEO:
Muera.
Para que se haga pedazos
los brazos abrir podré.
LOTARIO:
Y yo el lazo apretaré
en abriendo tú los brazos.
ANTEO:
¿Qué haré ahora?
LOTARIO:
¿Qué he de hacer?
ANTEO:
¿Estoy loco?
LOTARIO:
Loco estoy.
ESTRELLA:
Mira que tu esposa soy.
AURORA:
Mira que yo lo he de ser.
Ablanda el pecho insensible. (84–85)

JEFFS, trans., *The Foolish Gentleman*

ANTEO:
You must leave her, my Aurora,
my dawn and my lady.
LOTARIO:
I must kill this one,
and afterwards I will come down and
punish you.
ANTEO:
Stop.
LOTARIO:
Stop.
ANTEO:
Wait.
LOTARIO:
Wait,
do not be so quick
to cast the heavens down to earth.
ANTEO:
Do not raise her up
to Heaven so soon.
LOTARIO:
Die.
ANTEO:
Die,
I will open my arms,
cast you down,
you will break to pieces.
LOTARIO:
And I will tighten the noose
when you open your arms.
ANTEO:
What will I do now?
LOTARIO:
What can I do?
ANTEO:
Am I insane?
LOTARIO:
I must be insane.
ESTRELLA:
Look at me, I am your wife.
AURORA:
I am to be yours.
Soften your unfeeling heart.

If the production achieves this moment of tension, and the audience is not laughing at this extreme scenario, they should be on the edge of their seats. Though there

176   KATHLEEN JEFFS

should be a sense of real danger here, these are comedies; Félix does not kill Otavio, and Lotario does not kill Aurora. In *El caballero bobo*, the violence is stopped in a climactic, taut moment when the brother–sister pairs are at the height of murderous desperation, and the patriarchs appear to stay the violence, each man begging for the life of his beloved daughter:

CASTRO, *El caballero bobo*

Sale el DUQUE *arriba y el* REY *abajo y detienen a cada uno.*
DUQUE:
¡Hijo!
REY:
¡Hijo!
DUQUE:
Tente.
REY:
Tente.
De tus rigores me espanto.
LOTARIO:
Suelta, señor.
REY:
No podré.
ANTEO:
Arrojaréla.
DUQUE:
¡Ay de mí!;
advierte que el ser le di.
REY:
Advierte que la engendré.
DUQUE:
A mí me quitas la vida.
REY:
¿No es la tuya la de Estrella?
LOTARIO:
Habré de caer tras ella
pues la tengo al alma asida.
REY:
Quita el rigor, pierde el brío,
ponme ese lazo o cordel
ahogarásme con él,
que, al fin, ese cuello es mío.
DUQUE:
Cuando mi hijo no fueras
a mis canas respetaras.
REY:
Si mis lágrimas miraras
lo que te suplico hicieras.
ANTEO:
No soy yo tan inhumano.
LOTARIO:
Ni yo tan mal hijo he sido.
Suéltanlas, y sale el CONDE *y* CLAUDIA. (85)

JEFFS, trans., *The Foolish Gentleman*

Enter the DUKE *above, and the* KING *below, and they each detain one of the younger men.*
DUKE:
Son!
KING:
Son!
DUKE:
Stop!
KING:
Stop!
Your ferocity frightens me.
LOTARIO:
Let go, my lord.
KING:
I will not.
ANTEO:
I'll throw her off.
DUKE:
Can't you spare a man his daughter?
KING:
Can't you see she's my child?
DUKE:
If you kill her, you kill me.
KING:
Is your life not shared by Estrella?
LOTARIO:
I will have to share the fall with her
as I share my soul with her.
KING:
Stay your anger, temper your pride,
put this noose around my neck
and choke me, for, in truth,
that neck belongs to me.
DUKE:
If you will not respect me as a father
at least show respect for me as an old man.
KING:
If you can see my tears,
you will do what I beg of you.
ANTEO:
I am not so inhuman.
LOTARIO:
Nor am I such a disobedient son.
They let the women go. Enter the COUNT
and CLAUDIA [*and the scene continues...*]

The pain that a parent feels when his or her child is in danger is unbearable. Reading these two plays together illuminates small moments in *La fuerza de la costumbre* that might otherwise go unnoticed: mental torment is experienced by both Costanza and Pedro as they anxiously await the return of Félix during his fight with Otavio:

CASTRO, *La fuerza de la costumbre*	JEFFS, trans., *The Force of Habit*
COSTANZA:	COSTANZA:
¡Qué desdicha tan cruel!	What cruel misfortune!
Todos saben de mi hijo,	Everyone knows what's happened to my son,
y yo sola no lo sé. (73)	and I alone have no news of him.
[...]	[...]
PEDRO:	PEDRO:
Soy padre, en fin, y apriétame el cuidado;	I am a father, and concern
pero estoy previniendo la venganza,	for my son grips my heart.
si me matan mi hijo. ¡Ay, hijo amado! (74)	But I must prepare myself
	to take revenge immediately
	if he is killed. Oh, beloved son!

Pedro's outcry reminds us of King David lamenting the death of his beloved, but deeply flawed son, Amón, in Tirso's *La venganza de Tamar*. The pull of paternal love is strong, and the fathers in these plays seem bound by a force of this 'natural' impulse however much they may disapprove of their sons' actions. And the feeling, despite the fathers' irascible behaviour, is mutual. Ultimately, Anteo and Lotario relent out of love and respect for their fathers, not for love of their wives or mercy for their sisters. It is the protection of the patriarchs from the broken heart of losing a daughter that finally moves the sons to mercy. Is the play thus a showcase of the transformative power of romantic love, or the irresistible power of a parent's love for a child? In the final moments of crisis for Anteo, Lotario, and Félix, they do not pull back from killing their rival because of the power of love for a woman, but out of a sense of duty. Félix relents and does not kill Otavio, but is satisfied with disarming and wounding him, because of his adherence to a code of honour in which he is unable to kill a man who has surrendered, and he wishes more than anything to please his father, which means adhering to his clear instructions to follow that code. Anteo and Lotario, blind with rage, do not ultimately murder their sisters, but they stay their hands out of love and respect for their fathers (Anteo is not so 'inhuman' as to deprive a father of his child, but until he sees it this way he is ready to murder his own flesh and blood).

Seen in this light, Félix relents because he needs his father to see that the transformation he so fervently desired is complete. Félix has learned the codes required of him and appealed to the noble blood that Pedro always knew would speak to him when he needed it to guide his noble hand. Félix as a 'lion' is not an unthinking animal, but a rational man. But it is not at all convincing as an act of love for Leonor, and there is a whiff of this absence when he presents himself to her as a worthy husband, offering up Otavio's sword and saying, 'Recíbele de mi mano, | si tus desdenes lo sufren' [Receive it from my hand, | if your disdain will suffer it] (75). He has won her, but he has done it by numbers, and lost touch with the person he has been his whole life, as part of the process. Worse still for him, his relationship with his beloved mother will never be the same as his fears from the beginning come painfully true: 'La pérdida será mucha | si a mi madre he de dejar' [It will be even worse for me | if I have to leave my mother] (43).

Aurora and Hipólita: The Transformative Power of Actual Loss

For the two women in the position of *primera dama*, Aurora and Hipólita, the loss they experience in the plays is material, not just internal, and the consequences of it are profound and transformative. As we did when comparing Félix with Lotario, let us look at the motives for the transformation of Hipólita and Aurora for clues that will shed light on them both.

Aurora is willing to use and manipulate people (like her cousin Estrella) as pawns for self-protection. When she declares herself the General of Anteo's and the Duke's forces, uniting with the English against her own father and her own country, she betrays her father the King, her brother Lotario, her cousin Estrella, and her fellow citizens of Hungary all with one move. She is motivated by love of Anteo, and the cost of her love is her family and homeland. It is also accomplished without lamentation or much acknowledgement that this sacrifice has taken place; it is presented as a 'given' that she would give up everything for the man she loves.

Hipólita's loss is different. From the beginning she is warlike, and reminiscent of Anteo in her misogyny and how she explicitly says 'woman; I despise that name' (El nombre me ha reportado, | afrentoso para mí (48)). She transforms, for love, into the thing she abhors: she becomes, literally, a weak and feeble woman. If we find a past analogue in Aurora for the more complex Hipólita, it is fruitful here to compare their words directly:

CASTRO, *El caballero bobo*	JEFFS, trans., *The Foolish Gentleman*
AURORA: Para mostrar mi caudal he dejado el ser mujer. Las lágrimas y el dolor por la braveza he trocado (82)	AURORA: In order to show my mettle I have ceased to be a woman. I have exchanged tears and wringing hands for ferocity;

Aurora's moment recalls Shakespeare's Lady Macbeth as she implores Heaven to 'unsex me here' and rid her of the feminine part of her nature in order to commit acts of bloody violence. The reverse happens to Hipólita when an act of sexual violence is perpetrated upon her:

CASTRO, *La fuerza de la costumbre*	JEFFS, trans., *The Force of Habit*
HIPÓLITA: Ya olvido, como mujer, el ser valiente en la guerra desde que la paz probé. Ya me espanta un arcabuz, y para mí no ha de haber tratar en cosas de acero, si no es que opilada esté; ya me duele, si me pica la punta de un alfiler, y si hay sangre, será cierto el desmayarme después. (73)	IPÓLITA: I now forget, as a woman, how to be brave in war since I have tasted peace. Now I shall be frightened of a harquebus, and I will not touch anything made of steel, if it is not a needle; I'll cry out with pain if I prick my finger, and if there is a drop of blood, it is certain that I will faint immediately.

Aurora has exchanged her femininity for masculinity, while Hipólita exchanges her strength for weakness. Looking at the two plays together illuminates them both, because it shows us a glimpse of Castro's understanding of how, in his character Otavio's words, 'Fuertemente es poderosa, más que papas, más que reyes; | divinas y humanas leyes | puede hacer' [[t]hese customs are strong and powerful, | they command us more than popes, more than kings; they make divine and human laws] (51). If love is the root of the transformation which takes place in both siblings in *La fuerza de la costumbre*, and causes them to dig deep and make fundamental identity changes, it is more powerful even than habit, which commands us more than popes, more than kings. Rooted in *El caballero bobo*, the protagonists' changes in *La fuerza de la costumbre* show the characters' capacity to harness the transformative power of love and lend us the strength we do not know we possess; even, in Hipólita's case, the strength to submit to a code and custom of identity she finds repugnant.

It is not *costumbre* but the indomitable, hard, unfeeling, crushing rock of love that transforms and partially destroys Hipólita, even as it delivers her the highest prize: reciprocated true love. As the marriages are agreed, Hipólita's last verb is fascinatingly in the past tense, and it speaks for itself:

CASTRO, *La fuerza de la costumbre*	JEFFS, trans., *The Force of Habit*
FÉLIX:	FÉLIX:
¡Dicha grande!	Such blessings!
LUIS:	LUIS:
¡Grande gloria!	Great glory!
LEONOR:	LEONOR:
Yo la tengo.	I have it.
HIPÓLITA:	HIPÓLITA:
Yo la tuve. (76)	I had it.

The two heroines experience the power of love through loss. Aurora, motivated by love for Anteo, loses 'all' in turning against her family and homeland. Hipólita, motivated by love, changes and then loses 'all' ('y como mudara el valor | mudara el género y todo' [And I, who must change, | change my valour... gender... everything] (46)). That is a compelling way to understand Hipólita's eleventh-hour transformation; it did not happen all at once after all, but between 1595 and 1615 as Castro grew in his understanding of the high price of love, and the extent of personal loss we are willing to endure.

Conclusion

On the face of it, *El caballero bobo* and *La fuerza de la costumbre* are very different plays. One is an early work, penned toward the end of the turbulent sixteenth century, which displays its values of bravery, loyalty, and is infused with a late medieval hangover of astrology and the threat of ancient enemies. The play uses biblical themes such as salvation and redemption and incestuous love (the theme of Amón's love for his sister Tamar will be dramatized by Tirso and Calderón, and receives a double airing here with both Lotario and Anteo each believing they have fallen in love with his own sister, and proceeding with plans to marry her anyway).

The figure of Anteo, our *caballero salvaje*, is a type well known to readers of the Spanish sentimental and chivalric novel. Yet *El caballero bobo* is more than a sum of its parts; when the Duke declares at the end that a truce will be declared so that the fighting will stop for one month, we have no reason to believe that anything will change after the end of that brief happiness. As the lovers declare 'Sumo bien' and 'inmensa gloria' as they do at the end of many *comedias* that end happily, everyone is smiling through gritted teeth because they know the old enmities will spring up immediately after that one month. The new brothers experience fraternal love (Lotario gains Anteo: 'yo ganaré un hermano' [I will gain a brother]), but are not likely to forget that one attempted to kill the other. As the English Ambassador leaves at the very end to inform his king of the truce, he mutters under his breath: 'rabiando voy de pesar' [Regret and rage weigh upon me].

The end of *El caballero bobo*, with its ostensible happiness, makes a productive analogue to the end of *La fuerza de la costumbre*. From the beginning, the Moncada family is in an unheard-of situation, part of the *ingenio* of the work, as the cross-dressed siblings attempt to realize their potential and find their place in a society that fundamentally rejects them at every turn. Their alliances are ultimately as tentative and fragile as the family 'unity' at the end of *El caballero bobo*, a 'happy-ending' moment in which Estrella's feet are barely back on the ground and Aurora is rubbing her throat after being nearly strangled by her brother. In choosing to stage these plays now, we must consider the extent of the transformation that we may realistically believe to have occurred by the end: we know that bitterness and the isolating pain of constant bullying has transformed Félix into an honour-bound rule-minder, and he performs the acts required of him with no enjoyment, including the moment when he is forced to propose to a woman who has done nothing but torment him. Her first words to Félix are about what she sees in Félix's eyes: herself. Tellingly, there is one song in the play, sung by Leonor, and its subject is her 'ojos negros, ojos tristes', her sad, black eyes, full of tears, longing for something she does not find (56). Félix experiences the literal fear of groping around in the dark like a blind man, armed only with a heavy sword he does not know how to use ('Como ciego o como loco, | tropiezo con las esquinas, | no acostumbrados mis ojos | a ver entre las tinieblas' [Like a blind man or a madman | I trip at every corner. | My eyes are not accustomed | to this half-light of dusk] (57)). His father put him in this situation to test him, and although his actions are designed to build up Félix's bravery, they only serve to harden the boy into a dangerous, bitter, calculating lion. His sister Hipólita, transformed into a meek mouse, gains a husband who really loves her, but whose love robs her of the qualities that attracted him to her in the first place. Seen in the context of the international war brewing behind the final moments of *El caballero bobo*, Castro's understanding of the power of transformation in these plays is shown to be fascinatingly partial. *Plus ça change, plus c'est la même chose.*

Bibliography

ANONYMOUS, *Hic mulier: Or, the Man-Woman and Haec-vir: Or, the Womanish-Man*. Facsimile editions of originals printed in London for J. Trundle in 1620 (Exeter: The Rota at the University of Exeter, 1973)

BARNES, RUTH, and JOANNE B. EICHER, *Dress and Gender: Making and Meaning* (New York and Oxford: Berg, 1992)

BEREK, PETER, 'Cross-Dressing, Gender, and Absolutism in the Beaumont and Fletcher', *Studies in English Literature, 1500–1900, Tudor and Stuart Drama*, 44 (2004), 359–77

BOND, R. WARWICK, 'On Six Plays in Beaumont and Fletcher, 1679', *The Review of English Studies*, 11.43 (1935), 257–75

BOYLE, CATHERINE, and DAVID JOHNSTON with JANET MORRIS, eds, *The Spanish Golden Age in English: Perspectives on Performance* (London: Oberon, 2007)

BRADBURY, GAIL, 'Irregular Sexuality in the Spanish *Comedia*', *Modern Language Review*, 76 (1981), 566–80

BRUERTON, COURTNEY, 'The Chronology of the *Comedias* of Guillén de Castro', *Hispanic Review*, 12 (1944), 89–151

BUTLER, JUDITH, *Bodies that Matter: On the Discursive Limits of 'Sex'* (New York: Routledge, 1993)

—— *Gender Trouble: Feminism and the Subversion of Identity* (New York: Routledge, 1990)

CANAVAGGIO, JEAN, 'Los disfrazados de mujer en la Comedia', in *La mujer en el teatro y la novela del siglo XVII: Actas del Segundo Coloquio del Grupo de Estudios sobre Teatro Español* (Toulouse: France-Ibérie Recherche, 1979), pp. 135–45

CASA, FRANK P., 'Affirmation and Retraction in Golden Age Drama', *Neophilologus*, 61(1977), 551–64

CASTRO, GUILLÉN DE, *El caballero bobo*, in *Obras de Guillén de Castro y Bellvís*, ed. by Eduardo Juliá Martínez, vol. 1 (Madrid: Real Academia Española, Imprenta de la Revista de Archivos, Bibliotecas y Museos, 1925), pp. 47–86

—— *La fuerza de la costumbre*, in *Obras de Guillén de Castro y Bellvís*, ed. by Eduardo Juliá Martínez, vol. 3 (Madrid: Real Academia Española, Imprenta de la Revista de Archivos, Bibliotecas y Museos, 1925–27), pp. 39–76

CLARK, SANDRA, ' "Hic Mulier", "Haec Vir", and the Controversy over Masculine Women', *Studies in Philology*, 82.2 (1985), 157–83

—— *The Plays of Beaumont and Fletcher: Sexual Themes and Dramatic Representation* (New York and London: Harvester Wheatsheaf, 1994)

CONNOR (Swietlicki), Catherine, 'Marriage and Subversion in Comedia Endings: Problems in Art and Society', in *Gender, Identity, and Representation in Spain's Golden Age*, ed. by Anita K. Stoll and Dawn L. Smith (Cranbury, NJ: Associated University Press, 2000), pp. 23–46

COTARELO Y MORI, EMILIO, *Bibliografía de las controversias sobre la licitud del teatro en España* (Madrid: Revista de Archivos, Bibliotecas y Museos, 1904)

DONNELL, SIDNEY, *Feminizing the Enemy: Imperial Spain, Transvestite Drama, and the Crisis of Masculinity* (Cranbury, NJ: Associated University Press, 2003)

DUNCAN, ANNE, 'It Takes a Woman to Play a Real Man: Clara as Hero(ine) of Beaumont and Fletcher's *Love's Cure*', *English Literary Renaissance*, 30.3 (2000), 396–407

EICHER, JOANNE B., and MARY ELLEN ROACH-HIGGINS, 'Definition and Classification of Dress: Implications for Analysis of Gender Roles', in *Dress and Gender: Making and Meaning* (New York and Oxford: Berg, 1992), pp. 8–28

FISCHER, SUSAN, *Reading Performance: Spanish Golden Age Theatre and Shakespeare on the Modern Stage* (Woodbridge: Tamesis, 2009)

182   KATHLEEN JEFFS

FRIEDMAN, EDWARD H., 'Sign Language: The Semiotics of Love in Lope's *El perro del hortelano*', *Hispanic Review*, 68 (2000), 1–20

GARCÍA LORENZO, LUCIANO, *El teatro de Guillén de Castro* (Barcelona: Planeta, 1976)

LOFTIS, JOHN, *Renaissance Drama in England and Spain: Topical Allusion and History Plays* (Princeton, NJ: Princeton University Press, 1987), pp. 252–56

MCKENDRICK, MELVEENA, *Woman and Society in the Spanish Drama of the Golden Age* (London: Cambridge University Press, 1974), pp. 98–102

—— *Theatre in Spain 1490–1700* (Cambridge: Cambridge University Press, 1989), pp. 127–29

—— *Identities in Crisis: Essays on Honour, Gender and Women in the 'Comedia'* (Kassel: Reichenberger, 2002)

MORENO, CHARO, '"Qué haré entre tantas confusiones?" Sobre los padres dubitativos en el teatro de Guillén de Castro', *Criticon*, 87–89 (2003), 507–17

PAUN DE GARCÍA, SUSAN, and DONALD LARSON, eds., *The 'Comedia' in English: Translation and Performance* (London: Tamesis, 2008)

RIVERS, ELIAS L.,'Indecencias de una monjita mejicana', in *Homenaje a William L. Fichter: estudios sobre el teatro antiguo hispánico y otros ensayos*, ed. by A. David Kossoff and José Amor y Vázquez (Madrid: Castalia, 1971), pp. 633–37

RUBIERO, JAVIER, 'Encuentros de galán y dama en el espacio de la casa', *Insula: Revista de Letras y Ciencias Humanas*, 714 (2006), 17–21

SHAKESPEARE, WILLIAM, *The Taming of the Shrew* (videorecording), dir. by Franco Zeffirelli (London: Cinema Club, 1997) [film made in 1967]

—— *The Taming of the Shrew*, dir. by Jonathan Miller (British Broadcasting Corporation in association with Time-Life Television, broadcast on 23 October 1980)

—— *Shakespeare Re-Told: The Taming of the Shrew*, written by Sally Wainwright, dir. by David Richards (British Broadcasting Corporation, broadcast on 21 November 2005)

SIMERKA, BARBARA,'The "Efemination" of Flor: Satire and Sexuality in Ruiz de Alarcón's *Ganar amigos*', *Romance Languages Annual*, 4 (1993), 580–83

STOLL, ANITA K., and DAWN L. SMITH, eds., *Gender, Identity, and Representation in Spain's Golden Age* (Cranbury, NJ: Associated University Press, 2000)

STROUD, MATTHEW D., 'Performativity and Sexual Identity in Calderón's *Las manos blancas no ofenden* (White Hands Don't Offend)', in *Gender, Identity, and Representation in Spain's Golden Age*, ed. by Anita K. Stoll and Dawn L. Smith (Cranbury, NJ: Associated University Press, 2000), pp. 109–23

—— *Plot Twists and Critical Turns: Queer Approaches to Early Modern Spanish Theater* (Cranbury, NJ: Associated University Press, 2007)

TADDEO, SARA,'"Ahógame este vestido": La amazona y la mujer-paje en *La fuerza de la costumbre* y *Love's Cure*', in *Vidas paralelas: el teatro español y el teatro isabelino, 1580–1680*, ed. by Anita K. Stoll (London and Madrid: Tamesis, 1993), pp. 63–75

THACKER, JONATHAN, 'Yearning to Play the Part: Social Role-Play in Guillén de Castro's *La fuerza de la costumbre*', in *A Society on Stage: Essays on Spanish Golden Age Drama*, ed. by H. J. Manzari and Donald D. Miller (New Orleans: University Press of the South, 1998), pp. 223–37

—— *Role-Play and the World as Stage in the 'comedia'* (Liverpool: Liverpool University Press, 2002)

—— *A Companion to Golden Age Theatre* (Woodbridge: Tamesis, 2007)

WEIGER, JOHN G, 'Another Look at the Biography of Guillén de Castro', *Bulletin of the Comediantes*, 10.1 (1958), 3–5

—— 'Forced Marriage in Castro's Theatre', *Bulletin of the Comediantes*, 15.1 (1963), 1–4

WEIMER, CHRISTOPHER B., 'Going to Extremes: Barthes, Lacan, and Cervantes' *La gran sultana*', in *Gender, Identity, and Representation in Spain's Golden Age*, ed. by Anita K. Stoll and Dawn L. Smith (Cranbury, NJ: Associated University Press, 2000), 47–60

WILSON, WILLIAM E., *Guillén de Castro* (New York: Twayne, 1973)

THE POWER OF TRANSFORMATION IN GUILLÉN DE CASTRO   183

Notes to Chapter 8

1. Quoted by García Lorenzo, *El teatro de Guillén de Castro* (Barcelona: Planeta, 1976), p. 25.
2. In the early years of the seventeenth century, Castro was directly influenced by his friend Lope de Vega, who admired him so much that he dedicated his play *Las almenas de Toro* to the Valencian (Thacker, *A Companion to Golden Age Theatre* (Woodbridge: Tamesis, 2007), p. 72).
3. Castro's plays *El curioso impertinente*, *Don Quijote de la Mancha*, and *La fuerza de la sangre* are all drawn from Cervantes.
4. See Thacker, 'Yearning to Play the Part: Social Role-Play in Guillén de Castro's *La fuerza de la costumbre*', in *A Society on Stage: Essays on Spanish Golden Age Drama*, ed. by H. J. Manzari and Donald D. Miller (New Orleans: University Press of the South, 1998), pp. 223–37, and his *Role-Play and the World as Stage in the* comedia (Liverpool: Liverpool University Press, 2002).
5. Citations from Guillén de Castro's plays *La fuerza de la costumbre* and *El caballero bobo* are taken from the editions by Eduardo Juliá Martínez. As the lines are not numbered, I give the page numbers. All translations into English are my own.
6. Citations from *The Force of Habit* are from my production text, which was performed at the Magnuson Theatre, Gonzaga University, 22, 23, and 28 February and 1, 2 and 3 March 2012. It is therefore not a 'literal' translation, but a script for performance.
7. A theatre company staging this play must decide if Hipólita is complicit in what happens to her out in the field with Luis. Thacker has used the word 'rape', and though the play is not explicit on this point, after working with the translation and directing the play in production, I would agree with that interpretation. See Thacker, 'Yearning to Play the Part', p. 235.
8. Wilson compares the two plays: '*The Foolish Young Gentleman* [...] has so many points in common with Calderón's *Life is a Dream*, that it is probable that Calderón did borrow several details from it when he composed his masterpiece' (*Guillén de Castro* (New York: Twayne, 1973), p. 131).

PART II

Theatre and Performance

CHAPTER 9

❖

Amateurs Meet Professionals: Theatrical Activities in Late Sixteenth-Century Italian Academies

Lisa Sampson

University of Reading

Lo studio è necessario per saper, occorrendo, trattare di tutte le materie non solo in comedia, ma nelle Academie: poiché pure vi sono Academie illustrissime che, per testimonio che i comedianti che fan[n]o l'arte loro come si conviene non sono indegni d'essere ammessi nelle loro adunanze, hanno accresciuto il numero de gli academici accettando e uomini e donne che ordinariamente comparivano in iscena, come avenne in Pavia alla signora Isabella Andreini, ed in Firenze a suo figlio, che l'una negl'Intenti e l'altro ne' Spensierati, furono accolti [...].[1]

[Study is required to be able to discuss, if necessary, not only all subjects in comic theatre but also in Academies: for there are even some most illustrious Academies which have increased their membership by accepting men and women who have regularly appeared on stage, as is evident from the fact that those actors who practise their art as they should are considered worthy of being admitted to their gatherings. This happened in Pavia to Madame Isabella Andreini, and in Florence to her son [Giovan Battista], she being admitted to 'The Academy of the Intent' [Intenti] and he to 'The Academy of the Carefree' [Spensierati].]

In 1623, the working actor Domenico Bruni presented membership of a literary academy as a clear sign of the great recognition awarded to some of the leading actors of his age, and mentions as examples the legendary actress and writer Isabella Andreini (in 1601) and her actor-dramatist son, Giovan Battista (in 1604). Bruni even cites such membership alongside the imperial honours awarded to another prominent actor, Pietro Maria Cecchini. Five years later, yet another learned actor, Nicolò Barbieri, would similarly consider academic affiliation as the acme of an actor's career.[2] For Bruni, such an honour clearly illustrated the dignity that he was claiming for his profession (or *arte*), which he argued was based not only on *art*, that is, study and learning, but also natural talent which could not necessarily be learned even by intellectuals. To put this view into perspective, only a few decades earlier it would have been unimaginable for most learned academies, institutions founded

188 Lisa Sampson

by intellectuals especially from the 1540s for virtuous education and learned recreation, to have admitted what were typically considered 'unlettered', itinerant
and immoral, mercenary actors (*zanni*) into their hallowed throng. As Richard
Andrews observes, despite some aspects of mutual influence, the mid-century in
Italy witnessed an increasing separation 'in which the professional performers of
farce and the gentlemanly composers of literary comedy went their separate ways'.[3]
However, with the more or less coetaneous appearance of formally constituted
companies of actors, first documented in Padua in 1545 in the case of the 'fraternal
compagnia' of Ser Maphio detto Zanini, this split seems to have intensified while
becoming more problematic to sustain.[4]

Something of the sense of intellectual opposition towards — and fascination
for — such professional groups is captured in the satirical verse of the unorthodox
Florentine poet and dramatist, Anton Francesco Grazzini (1504–1584), himself
a member of the Accademia degli Umidi, the more unruly predecessor of the
Medici-sponsored Accademia Fiorentina:

> Hanno i poeti questa volta dato
> del cul, come si dice, in sul pietrone,
> poi che il nuovo salone sverginato
> stato è da Zanni per lor guiderdone,
> onde delle commedie hanno acquistato
> la Gloria tutta e la riputazione:
> così da i Zanni vinti e superati
> possono ire a impiccarsi i letterati.
> > (*Le rime burlesche*, c. 1552)[5]

> [This time the poets have fallen
> on their backsides on the floor, one might say,
> as the new hall has been sullied
> by *zanni* [comic actors] for their profit;
> their comedies have gained them
> all the glory and reputation:
> now the literati, beaten and outdone by the *zanni*,
> can go hang themselves.]

While it is unclear to which performance or hall Grazzini (known as 'Il Lasca') is
referring here, there is no mistaking the disruptive effect of the performances of
these troupes which had rapidly became popular in northern and central Italy. As this
academician facetiously suggests, such companies presented a competitive challenge
to the groups of serious 'poets' or literati which also began to be formally constituted
around the same time, and who likewise pursued public acclaim and glory, among
other things in the field of theatre. Grazzini's lively and contradictory account of
arte performances in his various festive poems suggest that these presented a popular
alternative to the scripted humanist plays written and staged by academies, which
were typically characterized by long set-piece descriptions and careful attention to
the classical ideals of verisimilitude and decorum. Whether performed by dignified
professionals or street players, 'the new theatre provides a richer signifying system,
complementing voice with actions, manners, and gestures'.[6]

So does the fact that the Andreini, mother and son, were members of an academy by the early 1600s indicate altered and improved relations between these two kinds of 'institutions' as far as theatrical production was concerned? Or at least an opening of *some* academies towards some select *comici* in the later sixteenth century? If so, what kind of social and cultural forces can explain this? And what pressures did the opening of membership in the case of the Intenti or Spensierati academies, respectively of Pavia and Florence, bring to bear on the institutions themselves and their theatrical production?

This chapter can only begin to touch upon the broader questions surrounding the still obscure and complex relationship between the new professional theatrical companies and the Italian literary academies. This is due in part to the difficulty in providing an overview of 'academic theatre' in the period, given the great diversity of academies in their typology and activities across the peninsula. There is a shortage of systematic, in-depth analysis of this phenomenon, especially compared to the comprehensive scholarly documentation of the comparatively sparse surviving evidence for *arte* practices in the early decades of its existence. Nonetheless, scholarship has begun to touch upon specific relations between actors and academies.[7] Research on late sixteenth-century Italian academy theatre, moreover, is often coloured by a prevailing negative view which holds that dramatic practices were informed by pettifogging literary debate and archaizing tastes. Academies should, however, properly be regarded as forming a third, somewhat hybrid and culturally vibrant sphere for the production of theatre in the late sixteenth- and early seventeenth-century Italy, alongside the traditional sphere of the princely courts, and the newly emerging professional marketplace. This would explain why *comici* were aware of the need to engage with these flourishing and predominantly secular institutions, especially in the transition period between *c.*1585, when court-sponsored theatre became less frequent, and 1637 when the foundation of professional opera theatres in Venice began to provide a more steady income stream for actors.

Academies vs *comici dell'arte*: Antagonism or Overlap?

During this time, academies could offer economic or practical benefits as well as the social validation that many learned actors like Bruni sought. Less clear, though, is why an academy would admit a professional actor to their sodality. As Grazzini's verse suggests, academies and their members typically liked to present themselves in their theatrical practices as distinctly superior, and even antagonistic, to professional troupes — now known by the eighteenth-century term of *commedia dell'arte*.[8] *Arte* actors in the sixteenth century were often disparagingly termed by literati as *comici della gazzetta* ('tuppenny actors', referring to a Venetian low value coin). Battista Guarini, the author of the *Pastor fido* (first printed 1589), famously described them as 'sordid and mercenary people', who have profaned comedy.[9] Like his colleague, Angelo Ingegneri, in his treatise on theatre (*Della poesia rappresentativa*, 1598), Guarini does however distinguish between corrupting practitioners of this potentially noble art, and virtuous thespians — a distinction that actors themselves would soon apply. The 'othering' of professional *comici* was of course sanctioned by religious discourse

190   LISA SAMPSON

and political legislation. It must also reflect a sense of competition on the part of aristocratic intellectuals and, as Roberto Tessari suggests, represent a defensive response on their part to what they perceived to be a contaminating act of theft perpetrated against them by the 'ignoble plebeians'.[10]

Such distinctions between traditions have traditionally been perpetuated in criticism. As mentioned, academies are often viewed as favouring humanist-inspired, literary, and antiquarian forms of theatre (as epitomized by the first academy theatre in Vicenza, the Teatro Olimpico), typically influenced by critical (mostly Aristotelian) theoretical considerations, and cultivated predominantly by amateurs. Professional companies, on the other hand, are considered to be based broadly on popular, oral culture, using freer 'modern', improvised forms, as well as fixed characters or 'masks' and dialect. However, recent scholarship has shown that such ideas require careful nuancing. Studies of *commedia dell'arte* have demonstrated extensively that there was much productive cross-fertilization between this artform and learned culture both in terms of performance practices, content, and rhetorical style. From the 1570s, numerous leading *arte* practitioners began to imitate, adapt and challenge more official 'literary' forms and ideas through their dramatic, literary and theoretical writings. On the other hand, the academies could be laboratories for changing conceptions of dramatic genre and theatre design: the Olimpici Academy of Vicenza developed new technical devices for lighting, while the Alterati Academy and the Camerata de' Bardi of Florence were instrumental in pioneering the explicitly modern dramatic genre of *melodramma* (opera). The Intronati Academy of Siena has been studied especially for its performances of trend-setting, collectively written plays.[11]

These two kinds of 'microsocieties', each relatively closed and self-regulated in their distinct ways — and for different reasons — may then have sought ostensibly to promote different kinds of theatrical experience, but they also increasingly came into contact (at least in the case of the leading companies) within the context of Court theatre during the later sixteenth century.[12] Aristocratic patrons made use of both academies and professional troupes to deliver the most spectacular and innovative theatrical events possible for important political occasions, doubtless engendering both rivalry and emulation among the different kinds of theatre producers as they converged. Notably, at the much lauded 1589 Medici wedding celebrations in Florence, an academic comedy (*La Pellegrina* [The Lady Pilgrim]) by Girolamo Bargagli, a member of the Intronati who had died in 1586, was staged by young amateurs from the same academy. The lavish and innovative *intermedi* which were interspersed between the acts of the play, probably against the wishes of the academicians, were designed by the leading Florentine nobleman and academician Count Giovanni de' Bardi as well as others, but executed by a variety of leading professionals in different fields. These mythological interludes were repeated several times during the festivities and probably accompanied the virtuoso performances of first Vittoria Piissimi with the Gelosi troupe in *La Cingana* [The Gypsy] (perhaps based on a comedy by Gigio Giancarli) and then, a few days later, of her rival leading lady, Isabella Andreini, in *La Pazzia d'Isabella* [The Madness of Isabella]. For practical reasons, all these performances were held in the same recently remodelled Medici Theatre in the Uffizi.[13]

While such aspects of convergence and rivalry especially in courtly contexts have received great attention from historians of theatre and especially of *commedia dell'arte*, research into specific cases of professional actors approaching or belonging to formal 'literary' academies before and around 1600 has been more limited. Why and how were they accepted? And what form did their association take? Mostly, scholars are content simply to repeat uncritically the assertion that actors (especially Isabella Andreini) *were* admitted in this period.[14] Studies documenting links between (and even borrowings from) actors and celebrated playwrights of the time, like Battista Guarini and Gabriello Chiabrera, who belonged to numerous academies as well as informal aristocratic circles, provide a context for this kind of investigation. So too does the evidence of professional artists and musicians joining literary circles and more experimental academies, especially in Rome, Florence, Siena, and Milan from around 1600.[15] Nonetheless, unlike their fellow *virtuosi* musicians and even artists, actors in this period — and indeed for long after — presented a more oblique relationship with the liberal arts generally cultivated in academies (notably with rhetoric through the arts of memory, oratory, and invention), and faced particular prejudice because of their unconventional and apparently immoral, even irreligious, lifestyle.

This chapter aims to add some further evidence for interactions between early professional actors and academies, which will help to nuance Bruni's assertion quoted above. It will also question why, and which, academies accepted actors as members. First, the academic context will be introduced, then there will be a brief examination of some specific cases of interactions between the actors Adriano Valerini and Isabella Andreini with academies in Northern Italy around the end of the sixteenth century. Closing observations on Giovan Battista Andreini will signal further developments in the next century.

Theatrical Practices in Sixteenth-century Italian Academies

From the mid-sixteenth century secular theatre was one of the specific activities most cultivated by academies, which were commonly at this time interdisciplinary in character, though marked by a strong penchant for ritual and spectacle. Indeed, theatrical activities formed the major concern of two of the earliest academies formed, the above mentioned Intronati of Siena (1525) and the somewhat anomalous Congrega dei Rozzi (1531), as well as of others such as the Olimpici of Vicenza (1555) and the Innominati of Parma (1574). These institutions to different extents led the way in innovating dramaturgical and technical practices, in addition to theatre-building during the later sixteenth century. Such high profile examples were merely the tip of the iceberg: Amedeo Quondam's important survey essay on Italian academies calculates that 4.2% of the 2,000 or so academies listed in Michele Maylender's encyclopedia (itself a somewhat problematic source) had a special interest in theatre in the sixteenth century. This interest remained at about the same level in the seventeenth century (4.3%), rising to 6.6% in the eighteenth century.[16] In some centres this specialization was more marked. In Florence from the sixteenth to the eighteenth centuries it has been calculated that about 42% (45 of 106 documented academies) cultivated theatre in a sustained fashion, though a large proportion of these fall in the later part of the period surveyed.[17]

192   LISA SAMPSON

Such cultivation of theatre was in some cases a hangover from earlier more socially mixed groups, including 'bourgeois' confraternities, and festive societies like the Compagnia della Cazzuola of Florence, which included the freelance actor Domenico Barlacchia.[18] For more exclusive academies, there must have been some continuity with the earlier sixteenth-century practices of festive companies of young patrician elites like the Venetian *compagnie della calza* [companies of the hose], upon whose constitutions the notarized contract of the first professional group was based.[19] These *compagnie* were active until 1565, first performing and then patronizing comedies. This explains why public, dramatic spectacles were usually staged by academies for occasional or festive events (*feste*) before distinguished invited audiences and, importantly, why they were not commercially motivated.[20]

In hosting or staging public performances academies typically sought to exploit the power of spectacle to gain prestige and honour for their institution, reflected glory for their members and city, as well as potentially to attract political patronage and public recognition. For this reason, if the occasion demanded it, they would recruit high-profile professional musicians, artists and scenographers, following the practice of courtly sponsors. The dramatic texts selected for performances could be by academy members or outsiders, though in either case they were subjected to close collective scrutiny usually by censors (*censori*), who were specially appointed. (One wonders whether improvised comedies with *arte* style 'masks', widely documented from the 1620s, were practised much in Italian academy contexts before 1600, as they had been for the famous 1568 performance at the Munich Court in Bavaria.[21]) As at the 1589 *La Pellegrina* performance in Florence, however, the *actors* were normally amateurs and male in the sixteenth century, following earlier and continuing courtly practices.[22] Nonetheless, as we shall see, there is some rare evidence of women on stage in plays put on by academies in the late sixteenth-century academy.

By this time, however, the distinction between amateur and professional was complicated by the presence of a few highly specialized, semi-professional actors. In northern Italy they were associated particularly with Ferrara, rather than Florence and Mantua, the more remunerative centres for *arte* performances. As Alessandro Marcigliano has documented, actors of this kind like Giovan Battista Verato were highly valued for their practical skills within courtly and academic spheres, and carefully presented as virtuoso *amateurs*.[23] The specialized team of amateur actors led by the literato and actor-dramatist 'Ruzante' (Angelo Beolco, d. 1542), a protégé of the patrician Alvise Cornaro in Padua who at one time worked with Ariosto, also provides a transitional model for the evolution between amateur and professional theatrical groups.[24]

The performance in 1585 of Orsatto Giustinian's translation of Sophocles's *Oedipus Rex* to inaugurate the magnificent theatre of the Accademia Olimpica of Vicenza provides a well-documented example of both traditional and innovative aspects of academic theatre. Innovations abounded in the theatre itself, designed by Andrea Palladio with additions by Vincenzo Scamozzi, in the lighting technologies by Antonio Pasi, the music by the organist of St Mark's Venice, Andrea Gabrieli, and the splendid costumes probably designed by the artist-member Giambattista

Maganza. By contrast, the director, the Venetian literato Angelo Ingegneri, was a highly skilled amateur, as were (it appears) the actors taking the speaking roles, thus allowing the academy to circumvent Venetian theatre legislation which pertained to professionals.[25] The eight speaking parts were played by dramatists and writers as well as (initially) university professors from the Veneto area. There was also a chorus of fifteen, and nearly one hundred other non-speaking parts on stage, including, unusually, young women and children ('putti'). Surviving eye-witness accounts report favourably on the staging aspects. However, of the actors, Giacomo Dolfin singled out for praise only the experienced semi-professional, Giovan Battista Verato, who played Tiresias, the priest of Apollo, and, unusually for a public academy performance, his daughter, who played Jocasta. Both had been brought to Vicenza by their sponsor, Battista Guarini. Dolfin praises the girl's control of voice and gesture, but especially her extremely moving performance in the recognition scene. However, Antonio Riccoboni in his more critical account found it to be lacking 'affetto' or emotional power; and criticized the inappropriate casting of this 'giovinetta, assai bella putta' [very pretty young girl] as Oedipus's older consort (and mother).[26] Others commended the off-stage singing and playing by two sisters, Elisabetta and Lucia Pellizzari, who served the academy as salaried musicians (1582–87), though not in the capacity of full members.[27] Two further very young girls appeared in the *esodo* (as Antigone and Ismene).

This performance thus provides unusually early evidence of women performing on stage for an official, public academy event, at a time of significant restrictions on theatre in the Veneto, even for noble academies. A continuum may in this respect be seen with the Olimpici's private musical performances, for example by the professional Maddalena Casulana in 1583 and perhaps by the noblewoman poet Maddalena Campiglia. Such entertainment undoubtedly reflects contemporary courtly practices, especially in Ferrara with the celebrated *musica secreta* performed in private first by skilled amateurs and then by professionals. It also looks forward to a greater inclusion in academies, from the turn of the seventeenth century, of virtuoso female poet-musician-performers, sometimes as full members, despite the usual formal constitution of academies as male-only preserves. Virginia Cox has gathered significant new evidence in this respect. An important example is the exceptional intellectual and poet Margherita Sarocchi's active participation in academy debates and literary activities in Rome; first with the Umoristi, founded for a performance in 1600, then as a founder of its offshoot, the Ordinati Academy (1608).[28] Similar involvement may perhaps be hypothesized for the noble Sienese musician-poet Ippolita Benigni Manfredi, who became a member of the Affidati of Pavia, the Insensati of Perugia, and perhaps the Informi of Ravenna (by 1609) — as well as for the actress Isabella Andreini.

The question of female performance within academies — of music, poetry and drama — still requires further examination, but could present an important motive for contacts between the worlds of the academies and *commedia dell'arte*. As is well known, *commedia dell'arte* practices changed significantly with the appearance of actresses (documented in Italy from 1564) who, together with a number of learned actors, could in the mask of the *innamorata* play more socially elevated roles and engage with 'serious' and moral genres, while often performing as singers. This created a more hybrid form of theatre, mixing higher with the traditional lower registers.[29] At around the same time some actors and their companies began to gain wider recognition in Italian princely courts and the royal Court of France. From the 1570s a few actors also began to venture into print to seek commercial success, fame and honour ('symbolic capital') for themselves, and increasingly sought to defend and commemorate their profession.[30] In this way, higher-level, educated actors began to encroach on the theatrical preserve of *letterati* and academies, competing for the same patronage and print markets. This tendency towards upward social mobility and transcendence of the material aspects of the art must also explain the fantastic names and emblems that some of the most distinguished *commedia dell'arte* companies took on, which are evocative of academies, starting with 'I Gelosi' [The Jealous], who adopted the emblem of the Janus face.[31] For this reason, it is sometimes difficult to distinguish between these groups where the only surviving documentation relates to theatrical performances.

Despite the efforts by academies with theatrical interests to distinguish themselves in name and style from professional companies, there was still some blurring of the boundaries. Naturally, if academies themselves took on the production of drama, they were obliged to adopt a corporate approach and could over time assume specialized 'roles' as in professional troupes. The Intronati Academy of Siena also appear to have composed their plays collaboratively under a collective name in the mid-sixteenth century, and in ways suggesting the modular approach of the *commedia dell'arte*.[32] Furthermore, as we have seen, various skilled amateur directors and actors like their professional counterparts were peripatetic, including Battista Guarini, Angelo Ingegneri, and Luigi Groto, who operated across courtly and academic venues in northern Italy (like their courtly predecessors) and worked closely with their preferred musicians, engineers and architects — as well as actors.[33] Such collaboration by academies and their members with professionals of this kind could stimulate innovations especially in scenography and theatre design, which allowed them (as in the case of the Olimpici of Vicenza) to compete with princely patrons, and distinguished their productions from the public ones of itinerant *comici*. However, an academician's openness to effective stage practices and appeal to modern sensibilities could, if extended to *dramaturgy*, result in outcomes that to other academic critics smacked pejoratively of *arte* practices. Notably, the Paduan university professor Giason Denores publicly argued in 1586, and again in 1590, that Guarini's tragicomedy *Pastor fido* not only lacked the novelty the dramatist claimed for his work but, worse still, it imitated *arte* productions. The vehemence with which in 1593 the dramatist (presumably) — under the academic pseudonym 'L'Attizzato Ferrarese' — denies any such hybrid and low-brow precedent in his erudite play, and defends the nobility of the actor Verato (who supposedly penned the first defence of the play in 1588), testifies to the contested nature of amateur 'academic' status in this case.[34]

Given the blurring between 'academy' and 'professional' theatrical practices and dramaturgy, it is striking how little concrete evidence there is of actual contacts between these *milieux* up to at least 1600, when the Roman Umoristi academy was founded and began to open up to singers, semi-professional actors, and women.[35] If one sets aside the unusual example of the Intronati of Siena, which more than others straddles the divide between amateur and professional, it would seem that by 1604 the only securely documented instance of a professional actor becoming a full member of a literary academy is Isabella Andreini. This actress joined the Intenti academy of Pavia in 1601, with the nickname 'L'Accesa' [The Enflamed], as attested by the local contemporary historian and poet laureate, Antonio Maria Spelta. After Andreini's death, the editors of her literary works and pastoral play (*Mirtilla*) also emblazoned her academic identity on printed editions. Notably, a cluster of compositions by the Intenti are placed prominently and highlighted typographically in the second part of the 1605 edition of Isabella Andreini's *Rime*.[36]

The evidence for her son Giovan Battista's membership of the still little known Accademia degli Spensierati of Florence (documented in print publications from 1600), stated as fact by Domenico Bruni and others, is a little less conclusive. Giovan Battista, a Florentine citizen despite his itinerant existence, and educated at Bologna university, clearly demonstrates his connections with this academy in his early print publications. As Fabrizio Fiaschini has detailed, four printed works (dated between 1604 and 1606), including his tragedy *Florinda* (1606), refer to the academy and its members in their dedicatory letters, through internal references, the inclusion of verse by members, and other circumstantial links.[37] Importantly, a portrait engraving preceding the text of *Florinda* pictures the actor wearing a medal with a symbol that evokes the emblem of the academy, which was possibly given to him in recognition of his services or merit. However, the medal does not fully reproduce the academy emblem (there is no motto for example). In addition, unlike in the case of other dramatist members of this academy (including Vincenzo Panciatichi, Francesco Vinta and Giovanni Soranza), there is no mention of Andreini's academic nickname in the linked publications. After 1606, Andreini's publications no longer mention this association, though the academy was still publishing theatrical and other literary works after this time. This may reflect the actor's physical distance from the academy and a consequent break in connections, perhaps prompted by the academy itself. Though, as has been suggested, it may also indicate Andreini's sense that he no longer needed academic validation of his success.[38]

Earlier on, the supposed association between the Veronese actor, Bernardino Lombardi, and the Rinnovati academy of Ferrara, on the basis of a play published in 1579 under an academic pseudonym, is now thought to originate from the actor's own attempt at plagiarism.[39] Yet there is some evidence of connections from the 1560s between *arte* actors and academies that specialized in the visual arts, because of their mutual interest in hybrid and even anti-literary cultural forms, in impersonation, and in the expression of the 'affects'. As Elena Tamburini has shown, Simone Panzanini of Bologna, famous for taking the Bergamasque porter role in the Gelosi company, among others from the group, had connections with the more socially and culturally heterogeneous and marginal Accademia della Val di Blenio (near Milan). This Academy was founded in 1560 and presided over for many years by the painter and theorist Giovanni Paolo Lomazzo.[40] By 1585, Isabella Andreini also became close to some leading members of this and other more

196   LISA SAMPSON

'serious' Milanese academies, including the important cultural operator and poet Gherardo Borgogni, a member of the Inquieti academy of Milan and the Intenti of nearby Pavia.

However, printed works by actors often exude a sense of separateness from more official academic circles. Like many novice writers, some explicitly express fear of hostile criticism from academicians versed in the art of poetics rather than performance. In the manner of Grazzini, various cultured professional actor-writers also exploited the opposition in polemic and parodic vein. For example, the popular collection of facetious letters by Cesare Rao (*L'argute e facete lettere*, first printed in Brescia, 1562) presents much academic satire, through pillorying pedants, mocking academic-style *conclusioni* and orations, and even a paradoxical address from the 'Academy of the Zanni' to the 'Academy of the Ignorant' (Accademici Ignoranti).[41] Rao is addressed in these both as the 'presidente' and 'Lo Svegliato' [The Awakened] of the Academia Peregrina, which coupled with a mention of Anton Francesco Doni in the address just mentioned, apparently suggests his connection to the fictitious academy invented by this *poligrafo*. These letters in fact uniquely turn out to plagiarize Doni's — an act that Rao would not, Giorgio Masi argues, have dared to contemplate for any other academy.[42] A contemporary Sicilian *comico* Vincenzo Belando ('il Cataldo'), author of *Lettere facete e ghiribizzose* (Paris, 1588) similarly signs himself in one as 'el Dottor incognito Accademic Balord' [The Unknown Doctor, the Idiot Academician].[43] As late as 1655, Bartolomeo Bocchino or Zan Muzzina's works are accompanied by sonnets by such unlikely *comici* academicians as Zan Gurgola, Academico Frullato [The Whirled Up Academician] and Zan Scaramuzza, Academico Sdruciolato [The Slipped Over Academician].[44]

It seems then that more elite and formal academies tried to maintain an outward segregation of their theatrical practices from those of the professional *comici* in this formative period before the opening of Venetian opera theatres in 1637. They did this through controlling access to membership and their performance spaces, and by differentiating performance practices and actors involved. How far then did these theatrical economies — professional vs 'serious' literary academies — actually converge and cohabit in the period before the 1620s–30s when, as we shall see, the crossover between *arte* and amateur theatrical styles became more widely consolidated? To answer this, let us now turn to two cases around the end of the sixteenth century where actors were involved with literary academies.

Adriano Valerini and the Accademia Filarmonica of Verona

My earliest example is of the celebrated actor, Adriano Valerini (*c.* 1546–*c.* 1592), a *comico* famed for his role as lover (*innamorato*) in the Gelosi company, who made various approaches to the local Accademia de' Filarmonici [Philharmonic Academy] of Verona in the 1580s. Founded in 1543, this academy was known especially for its exceptional musical activities, but it also staged scripted comedies and pastoral plays from 1549 — including notably, an early production of Tasso's *Aminta* (1581). Valerini's print publications show from the start how he cultivated academies favourable to theatre to elevate his social status by association, and presumably to gain patronage. His first and best known work, probably the first of any *arte* actor in print, was compiled to celebrate his beloved colleague in the Gelosi, Vincenza Armani, on her untimely death in 1569, a publication which would spawn a fertile tradition of literary compilations for female actors and singers. Valerini's oration alludes to the praise of the Intronati Academy of Siena — in which there flourished 'the cult of the stage' — for Armani's eloquence in improvised performance, which exceeded that of the most expert authors 'in carefully contemplated writing'.[45] This is the only direct reference to a cultural authority in the work, and is confirmed in the closing collection of verse by two sonnets by the Intronati (or by a key member, Scipione Bargagli, as Laura Riccò suggests).[46] Additionally, there is verse here by the Accademia degli Ortolani, by Leone de' Sommi the Jewish semi-professional dramatist for the Invaghiti academy of Mantua (but identified only as L.S.H.), and by the Filarmonici Academy member Francesco Mondella, who would later author a Senecan tragedy (*Irifile*, 1582) in the manner of Valerini's *Afrodite* (1578).

In 1583, when the actor was domiciled in Verona with his family, Valerini is recorded as having sent to the Filarmonici a possibly autograph manuscript copy (now lost) of Count Federico Asinari's still unprinted tragedy *Tancredi*, with a dedication.[47] The summary of the manuscript *atti* of the academy notes that it was judged according to the usual procedures for works submitted to them by a committee of three members. No subsequent verdict or recognition is recorded, which is intriguing particularly since the play would later be pirated by a fellow actor, Bernardino Lombardi, and printed under the false name of Torquato Tasso as *La Gismonda, tragedia* (Paris, 1587). The correct attribution was exposed in the 1588 edition by Gherardo Borghini, who was close to Isabella Andreini.[48] It is possible then that Valerini was hoping to gain credit with the Filarmonici by supplying a rare manuscript copy of a text then circulating among actors, perhaps because he was aware of their interest in theatre.

Three years later, Valerini tried a different approach. His lengthy prose encomium of his native city, *Le bellezze di Verona* (Verona, 1586), contains a section explicitly praising the celebrated local academy.[49] It is very likely, as Gian Paolo Marchi has suggested, that the actor hoped thereby to curry favour with the local cultural, civic and religious authorities, so as to receive a permanent licence to perform in the city. Certainly, like his other eight existing printed works, the *Bellezze* shows off his humanist erudition and his close contacts with important intellectual and aristocratic circles in the city — but, significantly, it makes no mention of his status as an actor. Valerini seems intent on positioning himself as a literato, already with privileged access to cultural networks, in his bid for more public recognition from the most famous lay cultural institution of the city.[50] Nonetheless, it is perhaps no coincidence that this encomium appeared shortly after the inaugural performance of the Olympic Theatre in nearby Vicenza, at a time when we know that the Filarmonici were themselves engaged in semi-private theatrical performances, including the staging twice of Antonio Ongaro's pastoral play *Alceo*.[51]

Despite these approaches to the Accademia Filarmonica there is no indication of any *official* acknowledgement of Valerini on their part. This could of course simply be down to the patchy state of the archival documentation for these years. It seems

198   LISA SAMPSON

unlikely that this was solely because of the actor's modest family background, since he had a humanist training and highly placed connections. Although the academy was increasingly becoming populated by noblemen, it still admitted professional members who were of lower social extraction, including the high-profile painters, Domenico Brusasorci and later his son Felice (who appear to have been involved with the academy theatricals), as well as musicians of great renown — though these did not always have full membership status.[52] It seems probable, therefore, that the academy ignored Valerini because of his status as an *arte* actor, perhaps exacerbated by his association with Armani and other actresses. They doubtless wished to avoid any potential run-ins over the issue of theatre with the civic and religious authorities of Verona — both of which were strongly opposed to secular dramatic performances. Notably, in 1591 the authorities even turned down a request by the Duke of Mantua to allow his troupe (headed by Valerini) to perform there.[53] Even so, there must have been a strong and continued local interest in *comici* in this period, given the unprecedented success with Veronese presses of the pastoral play *Mirtilla* (published in Verona in 1588, in two editions, and again in 1599) by the actress Isabella Andreini.[54]

Archival evidence about the Filarmonici provides a somewhat different picture. There are suggestions that they cultivated amateur theatre in a private, even secretive manner; and some prominent members also had connections — probably in less official contexts — with professional *comici*, including Valerini. Some new evidence of this is suggested by a manuscript verse anthology in the State Archive of Verona, which has hitherto been examined only in relation to music.[55] The volume posthumously commemorates Alberto Lavezzola, an honoured 'padre' (protector) of the academy, who was clearly interested in theatre. This manuscript contains sonnets by and for Valerini among verse by Lavezzola himself and various *letterati*, including several Filarmonici members and other Veneto dramatists. One presumably posthumous sonnet appears to commemorate Valerini's tragedy, *Afrodite* (Verona, 1578):

> *Per Adriano Valerini, al suo tempo comico famoso*
>
>   Come possa un meschin ne i lacci involto
> Chieder mercè da duo benigni lumi
> Come il foco eshalar, che lo consume
> Far men grave il dolor nel petto accolto
>   Come di donna far cader dal volto
> Di freddo cor, di perfidi costumi
> Per la pietà duo lagrimosi fiumi,
> Valerin mostri in stil purgato, e colto.
>   Per dar conforto a l'amorosa piaga
> E quetar nostre passioni acerbe
> Huopo non è di Circe, o di arte maga
>   Or, che poi senza incanti, o succhi di herbe
> D'alma sdegnosa, e d'ogni stratio vaga
> Le voglie humiliar crude, e superbe.

[For Adriano Valerini, in his day a famous actor

How a poor wretch caught in love's snares
can beg for mercy from a pair of kind eyes;
how releasing the fire that consumes him
can lessen the heavy grief in his heart;
    how he can make the eyes of a cold-hearted,
treacherous-natured lady start to flow
with twin rivers of tears out of pity:
let Valerini show all this in his pure and learned style.
    But to comfort my wounds of love
and to calm my bitter passions
there is no call for Circe or magic arts,
    now that without enchantments or herbal draughts,
you can humiliate the cruel and bold will
of a disdainful and blood-thirsty soul.]

This poem clearly celebrates Valerini's rather gruesome tragedy for its learned style ('stil purgato, e colto', l. 8) as well as for its masterly control of the affects, aspects that suggest a learned appreciation probably in circles that overlapped with the Filarmonici. The *rime* involving Valerini and other theatrical figures in the manuscript are, however, not found in the printed volume put together for Lavezzola posthumously by Francesco Mondella (*Rime del S. Alberto Lavezzola*, Verona, 1583).

Valerini also seems to have had contacts with another 'protector' of the academy, Count Mario Bevilacqua, who headed a famous private musical and cultural gathering (*ridotto*) in his Verona palace. Kathryn Bosi has indicated that this aristocrat knew and supported various actors and dramatists in Verona (and Vicenza), including Isabella Andreini and Valerini, from the late 1580s. There seems to be some reference to this relationship in the considerably annotated copy of Valerini's verse collection, *Rime diverse* (1577), dedicated to Bevilacqua, which is held in the Accademia Filarmonica library.[56] The undated comments, to my knowledge not previously examined, would in another context merit further discussion, especially for their sometimes negative judgements on style. A later manuscript inventory (1628) shows that two further editions of Valerini's works (now lost) — but not his tragedy — were held in the academy. Whatever dealings Valerini had with the Filarmonici, therefore, seem to have been at a purely private and not an officially recognized level. Finally, it seems that Valerini gave up on this avenue for patronage in the face of the Filarmonici's lack of interest, and decided to dedicate his last work to the Olympic Academy of Vicenza.[57]

Isabella Andreini's Academic Networks

The Filarmonici appear to have officially maintained this blind spot for more 'public' and controversial forms of theatre also later on. Curiously, when Battista Guarini was accepted as an 'absent' member in 1601, the academy minutes note his 'dottiss[im]e prose, et le leggiadrissime rime' [most learned prose and delightful verse], but do not even mention his dramatic masterpiece, *Il Pastor fido*, which had by then attracted much debate in other academies in the Veneto region.[58]

So it is perhaps not surprising that when in the following year (June 1602) the famous actress, Isabella Andreini, sent the Filarmonici an encomiastic sonnet, the academicians agreed to honour her with a reply, but avoided a corporate response, which some feared the actress would print. Instead, an individual member was asked to respond, and five other members voluntarily did likewise.[59]

Importantly, though, the Filarmonici could not ignore this *grande dame* of the stage (now aged forty) as they had done Valerini. In contrast to her fellow Gelosi member, Isabella's reputation was founded not only on virtuosity and learning, but also on personal virtue — bolstered by her patronage by Cardinal Cinthio Aldobrandini, as well as important friends in exclusive cultural circles including that of Cardinal Federico Borromeo in Milan and the Accademia degli Inquieti in the same city. Importantly, she was an academic *equal*, as in 1601 she had been made a member of the distinguished Accademia degli Intenti of Pavia. Her membership of the academy was preceded by many years of literary and social connections with academy members and local elites, such as Gherardo Borgogni, and was reinforced by publications and regular performances in the nearby capital Milan from the 1570s.[60] Her invitation to join the Intenti was probably precipitated more specifically by the recent publication of her very first organic volume of *Rime* printed under her own name, dedicated to Aldobrandini in Milan (1601). This successfully advertised her highly placed contacts and her innovative poetic skills, both of which she would have known were of interest to the Intenti. In addition, she may have been extended membership in recognition of her 'diplomatic' role in performing with her troupe in Pavia in March 1601, at the time of a political conclave involving the papal legate Cardinal Pietro Aldobrandini, the Duke of Savoy and the governor of Milan, Conte de Fuentes.[61]

When Isabella joined the Intenti (founded in 1593 by two members of the Barnabite order), the Academy included numerous prominent ecclesiastics (such as Cardinals Cinthio Aldobrandini and Federico Borromeo) as well as several secular princes. In addition, there were political authorities and other civic officials, university professors and intellectuals from across the arts and sciences. The institution had a strong interest in politics and poetry, as well as music; but it seems unclear whether they were engaged in *theatrical* activities too.[62] Andreini and her company were certainly performing in Pavia by 12 March 1601 and were working in Milan the following summer. She had become a member of the Pavia academy by 14 November, where she apparently stayed at least until 24 December. In the following year Andreini returned to Milan in April, and she was in Pavia again in December, when Spelta was completing the *Aggionta* to his *Historia*, a work which shows his strong interest in political and carnival spectacle. He records her 'exquisite eloquence' in Pavia in the winter of 1601, and her performance of a pastoral play which inspired him to write verse and an encomium for her, perhaps as a collegial gesture.[63] So *if* Andreini actually attended academic gatherings during her stays in the city, and performed or improvised verse or dramatic works there, or contributed to debates and lectures, one wonders *how* she did this, unless chaperoned, without contravening decorum, as the sole representative of her sex in the academy. This was of course a problem for the exceptional few female academicians generally.

However, as mentioned, there were precedents of actresses/singers in the Olimpici of Vicenza, and of singers like Vittoria Archilei performing for private male gatherings involving clergymen. Isabella Andreini is also said (perhaps not reliably) to have improvised poetry in the domestic 'academy' of Cardinal Aldobrandini in Rome.[64] On an official level, the admission of Andreini as an iconic *virtuosa* performer and poet would undoubtedly have been calculated to raise the profile of the Intenti to rival their sister-academy, the Affidati, which included two other female poets or singers.[65] This pattern of academic rivalry with female figure-heads has been identified by Virginia Cox also in other academies, and compares interestingly with *commedia dell'arte* groups — often known by their leading actress.

For Andreini herself, this membership of a literary academy apparently brought her the award of a doctoral degree ('laurea dottorale') and further opportunities for patronage as well as for display of her erudition and poetic expertise.[66] Notably, her verse is featured straight after the dedicatory letter to Antonio Maria Spelta's *La curiosa e dilettevole aggionta*, 1602. This also describes the actress's aggregation to the academy and presents a glowing tribute to her as well as showcasing four more of her poems, all of which were included in the second edition of her *Rime* (Milan, 1605, Part 2). This posthumous volume, which, Chiara Cedrati argues, Isabella Andreini had probably in large part organized herself for a re-edition in 1602, highlights the actress's membership of the Intenti Academy both visually and poetically, by including in Part 2 various new poetic exchanges with this academy and its members, as well as with the Filarmonici of Verona and the Olimpici of Vicenza.[67] This seems to prove the point made by Bruni and Barbieri that academic membership added dignity to actors and their profession. Yet, curiously, in Part 3 Andreini's earlier play, *Mirtilla*, though presented again as a composition of a 'Comica Gelosa e Accademica Intenta', is addressed to and invokes a specifically female rather than an academic (male) audience.[68] Like Valerini, Andreini's academic identity seems therefore to be deliberately and predominantly connected with her status as a *poet* rather than as a dramatist or *arte* performer.

Giovan Battista Andreini, *comico-accademico*

The two facets seem to have been combined in the case of her son, Giovan Battista Andreini, a distinguished *comico* and *letterato* who was associated with the Accademia degli Spensierati of Florence from 1604. This private academy functioned relatively independently from the circuits of grand-ducal power, and was connected to broader literary, religious and political circles across northern Italy in which Isabella operated. As Fabrizio Fiaschini has analysed in detail, the publications of the academy members reflect a growing openness to experiments with mixed genres and the contamination of verse, musical and theatrical forms, as practised also in other contemporary, private Florentine academies.[69] Importantly, Andreini's wife, the great actress and singer Virginia Ramponi, known by the stage name 'Florinda', seems to have been a stimulus in this respect. Circumstantial evidence suggests that she may have made her debut in the title role of her husband's tragedy *Florinda*, performed in some way (but not fully staged) for the Spensierati in 1604, or have been involved in other performances. However, there is no direct confirmation of this in the sole surviving printed edition of *Florinda* from 1606 (the 1604 edition was apparently destroyed by the author because Acts IV and V were poorly printed).[70] Nonetheless, this lavish edition, which features an engraving of the author and another depicting the stage setting (entitled 'La scena si finge nelle Foreste di Scozzia', fol. 12/B2^v), is introduced by a small collection of verse, 'Sonetti D'Alcuni Illustriss. Signori Accademici Spensierati, Et altri dotti Scrittori, in lode dell'Opera, e dell'Autore', of which the first two of the seven authors are prominently identified as Spensierati members. Furthermore, the first of Virginia Ramponi Andreini's two sonnets included here is composed for the Spensierati Academy 'in ringratiamento d'alcune Rime sopra di lei da gli stessi composte' [to thank them for some verse which members composed about her]. Emily Wilbourne has argued that the actress is referring here to a small printed collection of verse by five Spensierati from 1604, which were composed alongside ones for *Florinda*, of which others were perhaps lost with the earlier destroyed edition. This tragedy and Andreini's other three printed works connected with the academy mark a crucial first stage of his strategy for self-affirmation and to ennoble his profession.[71] In turn, it has been argued by Wilbourne that the academicians were influenced in their compositions by Virginia Andreini's performance.

From the early decades of the seventeenth century some *comici* were becoming more accepted and their performance styles were even imitated in polite, literary society, reflecting a growing interest in novel, hybrid dramatic forms mixing styles and genres, following a trend for which Guarini was an important pioneer. Numerous 'academies' of a more open and less formal type, devoted to theatrical activities, began to be formed especially in Florence and Rome (until 1627) involving skilled amateur actor–dramatists like Giovanni Briccio, who wrote and performed plays based on or incorporating the improvised dialect comedy of professionals (*commedia ridicolosa*).[72] In Naples, Don Pedro Fernandez de Castro, viceroy between 1610 and 1616, also founded an 'academy' of noble amateur actors at Court. The Immobili [The Immobile Academy] of Florence, headed by Jacopo Cicognini, were heavily involved in improvised performances and even began to run a private theatre with Medici support from *c.* 1650.[73] As Nicolò Barbieri observed in his famous defence of the arte (*La supplica*, 1634): 'I comici mercenari sovente recitano le stesse [commedie] delle accademie e perciò sono onorati' [professional actors often perform the same [comedies] as academies and for this reason they are honoured]. At the same time, it seems, the professional actor Pier Maria Cecchini planned to set up an 'accademietta' in Rome in which amateurs could be trained privately.[74] Nonetheless, the rapport between amateurs and professionals was destined to remain problematic and the two groups followed broadly separate pathways throughout the seventeenth century.[75]

Characteristically, Giovan Battista Andreini made theatrical capital of this blurred and changing relationship between specialized *arte* practitioners and their amateur counterparts in one of his most self-consciously meta–theatrical comedies, *Le due commedie in commedia* [Two Comedies in One] (1623). The title refers to two 'improvised comedies' (with *arte* characters) that are staged in a private courtyard for the same Venetian audience, first by a group of 'accademici' and then by a professional company. This sets up an implicitly competitive structure of the kind beloved in *commedia dell'arte* performances. Inevitably, the usual distinctions are made between the groups: i.e. the *comici* are *itinerant* and *paid*, but, predictably, they are also more inventive and skilled than the *accademici*. As usual, there is also much ambiguity: Lelio (the *nome d'arte* of Andreini himself) directs and acts with both groups as well as writing sketches, while we learn that the leader of the *comici* (Fabio) is in fact an educated nobleman who has often performed in academies.[76] Two things are striking about this comedy, I would suggest, in the light of our discussion. Firstly, the term 'accademici' is understood very loosely and informally here, compared to such institutions as the Filarmonici and Intenti at least: this is simply a group of pseudo-courtly amateur performers, friends and servants of a wealthy patron, who meet at his house to perform plays for which they are trained. Secondly, the female performers play a key role in the group's overall success. The 'accademici' perform with the patron's daughter, Lidia, a talented amateur, while the all-male group of *comici* are allotted the patron's skilled musician-actress, Florinda (*nome d'arte* of Virginia Ramponi), whose particularly moving qualities in the final act bring about the full moral and Christian potential of theatre which Andreini promoted.

Andreini's dramaturgy in the early seventeenth century marks a decisive step forward on the part of this actor-literato in re-evaluating the status and function of professional drama, and bridging the 'academic'/'professional' divide. The comedy highlights the increasingly unstable notion of 'academy' over the period, and suggests the critical role of female performers in breaking down divisions between the theatrical practices of 'literary' academies and *comici dell'arte* — as seen in the cases of Isabella Andreini and Virginia Ramponi — and in encouraging the development of new genres and styles of performance. This the Intronati had already foreshadowed with their strong interest in female characters and, more covertly, in female performers like Vincenza Armani. But as Valerini's rapport with the Filarmonici shows, the task of historically reconstructing such relations seems to be obscured by the mythomania of actors and by self-censorship on an official level by academies, as well as, until recently, by a tendency for disciplinary separatism in modern theatre scholarship. So, to give a provisional answer to my initial question about how far *accademici* and *comici* interacted in this period, one might conclude that they did at first occasionally, though rarely openly or corporately. Increasingly, though, the increased blurring between the practices of these groups suggests that the rhetoric of mutual antagonism coexisted with unacknowledged coalescence.

204   LISA SAMPSON

Appendix

Extracts from Giovan Battista Andreini,
Le due comedie in comedia. Suggetto stravagantissimo
(Venice: Gherardo e Giuseppe Imberti, 1623)

1. Act II, Scene 3

Lelio, the servant of Rovenio a nobleman living in Venice, has been asked to stage at short notice a comedy to delight the latter's beloved (Solinga) and various invited locals. In this scene the group of nine male academicians (*accademici*) have appeared, whom Lelio has already begun to rehearse and train in improvisation ('parlar all'improviso') together with Rovenio's daughter, Lidia. They will perform a comedy that they have started rehearsing, involving *commedia dell'arte* masks and entitled *Commedia d'incerto fine* [Comedy with an Unknown Ending].

ROVENIO, ZELANDRO, ARMINIA, FILINO, GILENIO, TRIBINO, ALFESIMORO, RICCIARDO, RUBENIO, TERBUONO, LUCRANO, [LELIO]

ROVENIO	O signori Accademici, o figliuoli miei amati, quant'obligo a tutti voi tengo! Ma vedete, alla libera, perché sapete ch'io non son corteggiano. Madonna Arminia, Lelio.
ARMINIA	Son qui, signor, per ricever i suoi carissimi comandamenti.
ROVENIO	Zelandro.
ZELANDRO	Rovenio mio, che volete? Mi pare la vostra casa un museo di virtù.
ROVENIO	Tale esser doveva per ricever voi, ch'avete del Giove. Messer Filino, la vostra parte?
FILINO	Eccola in scritto nel foglio, ma stampata poi nella mente.
ZELANDRO	E voi Gilenio, voi Tibrino, voi Alfesimoro, voi Ricciardo, Rubenio, Terbuono, Lucrano, come vanno le cose?
FILINO	Benissimo, signor, ed ecco come ogni Accademico ha la sua parte in mano e tra sé la va ruminando.
ZELANDRO	A farsi onore, vedete, perché avete Rovenio e che oltre il lodarvi v'ama di cuore. La signora Lidia, figlia del mio caro amico, pur sa benissimo la sua parte, e così ben discorre che sembra comica avvezzata a far pompa di sé ne' maggiori teatri, non solo sparsi per la città, eretti fra le Accademie, ma innalzati da' più famosi principi e più felici regi.
CALANDRA	Son qui, son qui anch'io, fratelli, con la mia parte in mano.
ROVENIO	Olà, oh ecco il resto del carlino! Zelandro, s'apparecchia, or ora, che appunto abbiam desinato, un bellissimo trattenimento.

Appendix

Extracts from Giovan Battista Andreini,
Two Comedies in One (1623)
(translated by Lisa Sampson)

1. Act II, Scene 3

ROVENIO, ZELANDRO, ARMINIA, FILINO, GILENIO, TRIBINO, ALFESIMORO, RICCIARDO, RUBENIO, TERBUONO, LUCRANO, [LELIO]

ROVENIO   O noble and dear Academicians of mine, I'm much obliged to you all! Although of course I'm under no obligation myself, because, as you know, I am no courtier. Madonna Arminia, Lelio!

ARMINIA   Here I am, my Lord, eagerly awaiting your every command.

ROVENIO   Zelandro.

ZELANDRO   My dear Rovenio, what do you want? Your house is like a museum of virtues.

ROVENIO   Just as it should be to receive you, who resemble Jove himself. Master Filino, where is your part?

FILINO   Here it is, written down on this sheet, but also imprinted on my mind.

ZELANDRO   And you Gilenio, you Tibrino, you Alfesimoro, you Ricciardo, and Rubenio, Terbuono, Lucrano, how are things coming along?

FILINO   Very well, my lord, look how all the Academicians are holding their script and thinking it over.

ZELANDRO   So as to gain honour, you see, for you have Rovenio's support; indeed, he praises you and also loves you dearly. Lady Lidia, my dear friend's daughter, knows her part perfectly too and speaks so well that she seems like a professional actress who is accustomed to displaying her virtues in the greatest theatres — not only those in this city, or in Academies but also those of princes of great repute and the highest royalty.

CALANDRA   [*Arriving*] I'm here now, I'm here too, brothers, and I have my script.

ROVENIO   Oh look who's here to complete the cast! Zelandro, as soon as we have dined, we can look forward to a treat of a performance.

206   LISA SAMPSON

2. Act IV, Scene 2

After their performance, two of the *accademici*, Calandro and Filino encounter a troupe of professional *comici*. Led by the Roman nobleman Fabio, these actors have recently arrived in Venice looking for honour and employment from among the many interested patricians. The scene exposes the pompous and naïve amateur courtier-actors (*accademici*) to the ridicule of the sophisticated, self-reliant *comici*, and parodies some of the markers of academy status.

CALANDRA Vi so dir, Filino, ch'avete filato fil sottile mentre ch'eravate in teatro; con quella parte di Narciso vi farete un grand'Accademico comico.

FILINO E voi, Calandra, qual passero solitario, qual caponero, qual rusignolo nella dolcezza della favella vi pareggiò mai? Ma chi son costoro con tant'oro in dosso, con tante piume in capo? Sono tutti signori? E dove sono i servi? [...]

FABIO Costoro fanno un gran rimirare, lasciate fare a me. Galantuomini, siete voi stampatori?

CALANDRA Messer, signorsì, perché? Volete far istampar alcun bando?

FABIO Non bando, ma bandiere.

CALANDRA Che siete alfieri?

FABIO Alfieri di virtù che in candida bandiera, entrovi affisse note vere, facciamo al comparir di quelle radunar per piazza e per cantoni genti diverse, intente al mirarne ed ammirarne.

CALANDRA Fratello io non l'intendo. [...]

FABIO Oh povera gente, s'andarebbe dietro un pezzo se con una dolcezza d'un mendicato ambiguo volessi attorniarvi. Il candido stendardo, entrovi affisse note nere, sono que' cartelli di commedie che si veggono per le città, i quali, mentre son letti e per piazza e per cantoni, riducono alle stanze gran numero di popolo. Siamo alfieri di virtù, poiché al vagar di queste insigne per la città invitiamo gente molta a vederne. Ministriamo morti, maneggiamo teste, poiché le tragedie così fatte cose ricercano: siamo comici alfine.

FILINO Comici?

CALANDRA O signori comici, che siate benedetti sopra i legni, parlo sui vostri teatri: e noi siamo Accademici.

ORAZIO Accademici?

FILINO Accademicissimi, poiché noi duo siamo i più virtuosi e graziosi.

CALANDRA Anzi, che or ora abbiamo fatta una commedia intitolata *Commedia d'incerto fine*, e siamo stati tanto eccellenti ed Accademici senza pari, che una nemicizia di vent'anni abbiamo convertita in pace e parentela; e la nostra Accademia s'addimanda l'*Incerta Speranza*, per le incertezze che'l nostro capo sperando disperava; ma pure alfine sortì l'effetto conforme alle cose sperate.

FILINO Signori comici, se conoscerete la vostra fortuna, noi altri signori Accademici vi favoriremo, e vi faremo guadagnar ben bene; ma se non siete virtuosi, non ci venite a recitar davanti, perché noi altri signori Accademici non vogliam cose se non degne d'Accademia o d'Accademici accademicissimi.

FABIO Sono Accademico anch'io, e mi domando l'Afflitto.

CALANDRA Ed io il Morto di fame.

FILINO Ed io di sete; e la mia impresa è 'l fiasco vuoto col motto: 'Mi muoio di sete, aspettate, aspettate'. Oh di casa! Oh di casa! Signor Rovenio, signor Zelandro, fuori! Fuori Accademici, comici, sine numero! [*Bussano*]

[Italian text cited from Siro Ferrone, ed., *Commedie dell'Arte* (Milan: Mursia, 1985), vol. 2, pp. 41–42, 66–68.]

2. Act IV, Scene 2

CALANDRA I can tell you, Filino, you wove a subtle tale while you were in the theatre; you will become a great actor-academician playing the part of Narciso.

FILINO As for you, Calandra, what lonely sparrow, tit, or nightingale could ever compare in sweetness to your voice? But who are those men over there all dripping with gold and with those great plumes in their hats? Can they all be masters? Where are their servants? [...]

FABIO Those men over there are observing us closely. Let me deal with them. Gentlemen, are you printers?

CALANDRA Yes, my Lord, why do you ask? Do you want to have a notice printed?

FABIO Not a notice, but a banner.

CALANDRA Are you standard-bearers?

FABIO We are standard-bearers of virtue. On seeing our white banner with true signs, all kinds of people gather in the piazzas and on street corners, eager to see and admire us.

CALANDRA My friend, I don't understand. [...]

FABIO Ah you poor people, we wouldn't get very far if I kept on confounding you with a sweet and deliberate pun. The white standard with black signs refers to the notices of comedies that you see displayed around the cities. When these are read in the piazzas and on street corners they draw large crowds to the halls. We call ourselves standard-bearers of virtue as we invite many people to come to see us by taking these banners around the city. We administer deaths and handle decapitated heads, which are needed for tragedies. We are, you see, a troupe of actors.

FILINO Actors?

CALANDRA O gentle Actors, blessed be you on stage — I mean in your theatres. We are Academicians.

ORAZIO Academicians?

FILINO Most academic academicians, and we two are the most virtuoso and gracious.

CALANDRA In fact, we've just performed a comedy entitled *Comedy with an unknown ending* and we were so skilled — better than all other Academicians — that we converted a twenty-year enmity into peace and a family bond. Our Academy is called the 'Uncertain Hope' because of the uncertainty with which our leader despaired in hope; but in the end what he hoped for came to pass.

FILINO Actors, sirs, if you recognize your good fortune, we Academicians will look kindly on you, and have you earn substantially. But if you are not *virtuosi* don't come before us to perform, because we Academicians want only what is worthy of an Academy and of the most Academic Academicians.

FABIO I'm also an Academician and my nickname is 'The Afflicted'.

CALANDRA And I'm the 'The Starving Hungry'.

FILINO And I'm 'The Parched with Thirst': and my emblem is an empty flask with the motto 'I die of thirst, wait, wait'. Hey, you inside, open up! Open up! Signor Rovenio, Signor Zelandro, come out! Come out all of you Academicians, there's a whole group of actors here! [*They knock*]

208   LISA SAMPSON

Bibliography

Archival sources

Archivio di Stato, Verona
    Fondo Dionisio-Piomarta, ms 634, *Summario degli atti dell'Accademia Filarmonica*
    Fondo Dionisio-Piomarta, ms 637, *Rime* dedicated to Alberto Lavezzola
Archivio dell'Accademia Filarmonica, Verona
    Atti dell'Accademia Filarmonica, b. 41

Printed works

ALBONICO, SIMONE, ed., '*Sul Tesin piantāro laureti': poesia e vita letteraria nella Lombardia spagnola (1535–1706)* (Pavia: Cardano, 2002)

ALONGE, ROBERTO, and GUIDO DAVICO BONINO, eds, *Storia del teatro moderno e contemporaneo* (Turin: Einaudi, 2000)

ANDREINI, ISABELLA, *Rime* (Milan: Appresso Girolamo Bordone, & Pietromartire Locarni, 1605)

—— *La Mirtilla. Fauola pastorale ... Di nuouo dall'istessa riueduta, et in molti luoghi abbellita* (Verona: per Francesco dalle Donne, & Scipione Vargnano suo genero, 1599)

—— *Mirtilla* (Verona: Girolamo Discepolo, 1588; Sebastiano dalle Donne and Camillo Franceschini, 1588)

ANDREWS, RICHARD, *Scripts and Scenarios: The Performance of Comedy in Renaissance Italy* (Cambridge: Cambridge University Press, 1993)

ARCAINI, ROBERTA GIOVANNA, 'I comici dell'arte a Milano: accoglienza, sospetti, riconoscimenti', in *La scena della Gloria: drammaturgia e spettacolo a Milano in età spagnola*, ed. by A. Cascetta and R. Carpani (Milan: Vita e pensiero, 1995), pp. 268–76

BARBIERI, NICOLÒ, *Discorso famigliare ...* (Venice, 1628), in *La commedia dell'arte*, Pandolfi, III, 369–98

BOSI, KATHRYN, 'Accolades for an Actress: On Some Literary and Musical Tributes for Isabella Andreini', *Recercare*, 15 (2003), 73–117

BOUTIER, JEAN, and MARIA PIA PAOLI, 'Letterati cittadini e principi filosofi: i milieux intellettuali fiorentini tra cinque e settecento', in *Naples, Rome, Florence: une histoire comparée des milieux intellectuels italiens* (XVIIe–XVIIIe siècles), ed. by Jean Boutier, Brigitte Marin and Antonella Romano (Rome: École Française de Rome, 2005), pp. 331–403

BRUNI, DOMENICO, *Fatiche comiche di Domenico Bruni detto Fulvio, Comico di Madama Serenissima Principessa di Piemonte* (Paris, 1623), in Marotti and Romei, *La commedia dell'arte e la società barocca*, II, 347–48

CALENDOLI, GIOVANNI, 'Le Compagnie della Calza, Ruzante e la compagnia Padovana del 1545', in *Il convegno internazionale di studi sul Ruzante*, ed. by Giovanni Calendoli and Giuseppe Vellucci (Venice: Corbo e Fiore, 1989), pp. 325–31

CAMPIGLIA, MADDALENA, *Flori: A Pastoral Play* [1588], ed. by Virginia Cox and Lisa Sampson, trans. by Virginia Cox (Chicago, IL: Chicago University Press, 2004)

CEDRATI, CHIARA, 'Isabella Andreini: la vicenda editoriale delle "Rime"', *ACME — Annali della Facoltà di Lettere e Filosofia dell'Università degli Studi di Milano*, 60.2 (May–August 2007), 115–42 <http://www.ledonline.it/acme/allegati/Acme-07-II-05-Cedrati.pdf>

COCCO, ESTER, 'Una compagnia comica nella prima metà del secolo XVI', *Giornale storico della letteratura italiana*, 65 (1915), 50–70

COMI, SIRO, *Ricerche storiche sull'accademia degli Affidati e su altri analoghi stabilimenti in Pavia* (Pavia: Comino, 1792)

COX, VIRGINIA, *The Prodigious Muse: Women's Writing in Counter-Reformation Italy* (Baltimore, MD: Johns Hopkins University Press, 2011)

—— *Women's Writing in Italy, 1400–1650* (Baltimore, MD: Johns Hopkins University Press, 2008)

CRIMI, GIUSEPPE, 'Appunti per il testo e il commento delle Lettere di Cesare Rao', in *Dissonanze concordi: temi, questioni e personaggi intorno ad Anton Francesco Doni*, ed. Giovanna Rizzarelli (Bologna: Il Mulino, 2013), pp. 353-74

DELLA VALLE, CAMILLO, *Fillide, egloga pastorale* (Ferrara: Vittorio Baldini, 1584)

—— [attrib.] *La Fillide, fauola pastorale, dell'Acceso Academico Rinouato* (Ferrara: Vittorio Baldini, 1579)

DI PASQUALE, MARCO, 'Intorno al patronato della musica della Accademia Filarmonica di Verona nel Cinquecento: riflessioni e congetture', *Recercare*, 23.1–2 (2011), 35–63

FENLON, IAIN, *Music and Patronage in Sixteenth-Century Mantua*, 2 vols (Cambridge: Cambridge University Press, 1980)

FERRONE, SIRO, 'La Commedia dell'Arte senza commedia', *Biblioteca teatrale*, 3 (2011), 163–74

—— *Attori mercanti corsari: la Commedia dell'Arte in Europa tra Cinque e Seicento* (Turin: Einaudi, 1993)

—— ed., *Comici dell'Arte: corrispondenze*, 2 vols (Florence: Le Lettere, 1993)

—— ed., *Commedie dell'Arte*, 2 vols (Milan: Mursia, 1985)

FIASCHINI, FABRIZIO, *L'Incessabil agitazione': Giovan Battista Andreini tra professione teatrale, cultura letteraria e religione* (Pisa: Giardini, 2007)

FUMAROLI, MARC, 'Academia, Arcadia, Parnassus: trois lieux allégoriques de l'éloge du loisir lettré', in *Italian Academies of the Sixteenth Century*, ed. by D. S. Chambers and F. Quiviger (London: Warburg Institute, 1995), pp. 15–35

GALLO, ALBERTO, *La prima rappresentazione al Teatro Olimpico, con i progetti e le relazioni dei contemporanei*, preface by Lionello Puppi (Milan: Il Polifilo, 1973)

GUARINI, G. B., *Compendio della poesia tragicomica tratto dai duo Verati* [1602], in *Il Pastor fido e Compendio della Poesia Tragicomica*, ed. by Gioachino Brognoligo (Bari: Laterza, 1914), pp. 219–88

—— *Delle Opere del Cavalier Battista Guarini*, 4 vols (Verona: Tumermani, 1737–38)

HENKE, ROBERT, *Performance and Literature in the Commedia dell'Arte* (Cambridge: Cambridge University Press, 2002)

INGEGNERI, ANGELO, *Della poesia rappresentativa e del modo di rappresentare le favole sceniche* [1598], ed. by Maria Luisa Doglio (Modena: Panini, 1989)

JOHNSON, EUGENE J., 'The Short, Lascivious Lives of Two Venetian Theaters, 1580–85', *Renaissance Quarterly*, 55.3 (2002), 936–68

MACNEIL, ANNE, *Music and Women of the 'Commedia dell'Arte' in the Late Sixteenth Century* (Oxford: Oxford University Press, 2003)

MAINO, MARZIA, 'Dispositivi illuminotecnici e spettacolo a Vicenza: L'Accademia Olimpica, l'inaugurazione del Teatro e gli influssi sul contesto spettacolare' (unpublished PhD dissertation, Padua University, 2009)

MAMONE, SARA, *Dèi, Semidei, Uomini: lo spettacolo a Firenze tra neoplatonismo e realtà borghese (XV–XVII secolo)* (Rome: Bulzoni, 2003)

MARCHI, G. P., 'L'esperienza teatrale di Adriano Valerini', in *La commedia dell'arte tra Cinque e Seicento in Francia e in Europa. Atti del Convegno Internazionale di Studio, Verona-Vicenza, 19–21 Oct. 1995*, ed. by Elio Mosele (Fasano: Schena, 1997), pp. 173–80

MARCIGLIANO, ALESSANDRO, 'Giovan Battista Verato: un attore nella Ferrara del Cinquecento', in *Scenery, Set and Staging in the Italian Renaissance: Studies in the Practice of Theatre*, ed. by Christopher Cairns (Lewiston, NY: Edwin Mellen, 1996)

MARITI, LUCIANO, *Commedia ridicolosa: comici di professione, dilettanti, editoria teatrale nel Seicento, storia e testi* (Rome: Bulzoni, 1979)

MAROTTI, FERRUCCIO, and GIOVANNA ROMEI, *La commedia dell'arte e la società barocca. 2. La professione del teatro* (Rome: Bulzoni, 1991)

Masi, Giorgio, 'Coreografie doniane: L'Accademia Pellegrina', in *Cinquecento capriccioso e irregolare: eresie letterarie nell'Italia del classicismo*, ed. by Paolo Procaccioli and Angelo Romano (Rome: Vecchiarelli, 1999), pp. 45–85

Materassi, Marco, *Il Primo Lauro. Madrigali in onore di Laura Peperara. Ms 220 dell'Accademia Filarmonica di Verona [1580]* (Treviso: Diastema Fiori Musicali, 1999) <http://web.tiscali.it/ensemble900/Diastema/Libri/Schede/Materassi.pdf>

Maylender, Michele, *Storie delle Accademie d'Italia*, 5 vols (Bologna: Cappelli, 1926–30)

Mazzoni, Stefano, 'Lo spettacolo delle accademie', in Alonge and Davico Bonino, eds, *Storia del teatro moderno e contemporaneo*, pp. 869–903.

——*L'Olimpico di Vicenza: un teatro e la sua 'perpetua memoria'* (Florence: Le Lettere, 1998)

——'Genealogia e vicende della famiglia Andreini', in *Origini della Commedia Improvvisa o dell'Arte*, ed. by M. Chiabò and F. Doglio (Rome: Torre d'Orfeo, 1996), pp. 107–61

Megale, Teresa 'Lombardi, Bernardino', *DBI* 65 (2005), <http://www.treccani.it/enciclopedia/bernardino-lombardi_(Dizionario-Biografico)/>

Palisca, Claude V., 'The Alterati of Florence, Pioneers in the Theory of Dramatic Music', in *New Looks at Italian Opera: Essays in Honor of Donald J. Grout*, ed. with intro. by William W. Austin (Ithaca, NY: Cornell University Press, 1968), pp. 9–38

——'The First Performance of *Euridice*', in *Queens College Department of Music: Twenty-fifth Anniversary Festschrift*, ed. by Albert Mell (New York: Queens College Press, 1964), pp. 1–23

Pandolfi, Vito, ed., *La commedia dell'arte: storia e testi*, 6 vols (Florence: Sansoni, 1957–1961)

Pieri, Marzia, '"Il Pastor fido" e i comici dell'arte', *Biblioteca teatrale*, 17 (1990), 1–15

Pignatti, Franco, 'Grazzini, Antonfrancesco (detto il Lasca)', *Dizionario Biografico degli Italiani*, 59 (2002); online at <http://www.treccani.it/enciclopedia/antonfrancesco-grazzini_%28Dizionario-Biografico%29/>

Pirrotta, Nino, and Elena Povoledo, *Music and Theatre from Poliziano to Monteverdi*, trans. by Karen Eales (Cambridge: Cambridge University Press, 1982)

Povoledo, Elena, 'Una rappresentazione accademica a Venezia nel 1634', in *Studi sul teatro Veneto fra rinascimento ed età barocca*, ed. by Maria Teresa Muraro (Florence: Olschki, 1971), pp. 119–69

Quondam, Amedeo, 'L'Accademia', in *Letteratura italiana*, I, *Il letterato e le istituzioni* (Turin: Einaudi, 1982), pp. 823–98

Rao, Cesare, *L'Argute et facete lettere [...] nelle quali si contengono molti leggiadri Motti, & solazzevoli Discorsi* (Vicenza: Appresso Perin Libraro, & Giorgio Greco compagni, 1585)

Regali, Maria Cristina, 'Le ricerche storiche sull'Accademia degli Affidati di Siro Comi: edizione delle postille dell'autore' (Como: Litografia New Press, 1999)

Riccò, Laura, *La 'miniera' accademica: pedagogia, editoria, palcoscenico nella Siena del Cinquecento* (Rome: Bulzoni, 2002)

Rigoli, Paolo, 'L'architettura effimera: feste, teatri, apparati decorative', in *L'architettura a Verona nell'età della Serenissima (sec. XV–sec. XVIII)*, ed. by Pierpaolo Brugnoli and Arturo Sandrini, 2 vols (Verona: Banca popolare di Verona, 1988), I, 1–86, 391–414

Sampson, Lisa, *Pastoral Drama in Early Modern Italy: The Making of a New Genre* (Oxford: Legenda, 2006)

Saslow, James M., *The Medici Wedding of 1589: Florentine Festival as Theatrum Mundi* (New Haven, CT: Yale University Press, 1996)

Seragnoli, Daniele, *Il teatro a Siena nel Cinquecento: 'progetto' e 'modello' drammaturgico nell'Accademia degli intronati* (Roma: Bulzoni, 1980)

Spelta, Antonio Maria, *Historia ... De' fatti notabili occorsi nell'universo, & in particolare del Regno de' Gothi, de' Longobardi, de i Duchi di Milano, [...] Con una nuova aggiunta* (Pavia: Pietro Bartoli, 1602)

Tamburini, Elena, '"Comedia dell'arte": An Enquiry and Some Incursions into the

Meaning of This Term', trans. by Mark Weir, *Acting Archives Essays*, 15 (April 2012), 1–35 [from ' "Commedia dell'arte": immagini e percorsi intorno a un'ipotesi', *Drammaturgia*, 5 July 2010, <www.drammaturgia.it>)

——'Comici, cantanti e letterati nell'Accademia Romana degli Umoristi', *Studi Secenteschi*, 50 (2009), 89–112

——'I comici Gelosi e l'Accademia della Val di Blenio', *Teatro e storia*, 3 (2011), 175–96

TAVIANI, FERDINANDO, ' "Bella d'Asia": Torquato Tasso, gli attori e l'immortalità', *Paragone letteratura*, 35 (1984), 3–76

TESSARI, ROBERTO, 'Il mercato delle Maschere', in ALONGE AND DAVICO BONINO, eds, *Storia del teatro moderno e contemporaneo*, pp. 119–91

——*La Commedia dell'arte nel Seicento: 'industria' e 'arte giocosa' della civiltà barocca* (Florence: Olschki, 1969)

TURRINI, G., *L'Accademia Filarmonica di Verona dalla fondazione (Maggio 1543) al 1600 e il suo patrimonio musicale antico* (Verona: Tipografica Veronese, 1941)

VALERINI, ADRIANO, *Le bellezze di Verona* [1586], ed. by G. P. Marchi (Verona: Stamperia Valdonega, 1974)

——*Rime diverse et origine della famiglia della famiglia Bevilacqua* (Verona: per Sebastiano dalle Donne e fratelli, [1577])

——*Oratione ... In morte della Divina Signora Vincenza Armani, Comica Eccellentissima. Et alcune rime dell'Istesso e d'altri Auttori, in lode della medesima. Con alquante leggiadre e belle Compositioni di detta Signora Vincenza* (Verona: Per Bastian dalle Donne, & Giovanni Fratelli, n.d. [1570?])

VAZZOLER, FRANCO, 'Chiabrera fra dilettanti e professionisti dello spettacolo', in *La scelta della misura. Gabriello Chiabrera: l'altro fuoco del barocco italiano*, ed. by Fulvio Bianchi and Paolo Russo (Genoa: Costa & Nolan, 1993), pp. 429–66

WILBOURNE, EMILY, 'La Florinda: The Performance of Virginia Ramponi Andreini' (unpublished PhD dissertation, New York University, 2009)

——' "Isabella ringiovinita": Virginia Ramponi Andreini before Arianna', *Recercare*, 19.1–2 (2007), 54–67

ZANRÉ, DOMENICO, *Cultural Non-conformity in Early Modern Florence* (Aldershot: Ashgate, 2004)

ZAPPERI, ADA, 'Barlachia (Barlacchia, Barlacchi), Domenico', *DBI*, 6 (1964)

Web-based resources:

British Library Database of Italian Academies (1525–1700): <http://www.bl.uk/catalogues/ItalianAcademies/>

Dizionario Biografico degli Italiani: <http://www.treccani.it/biografie/>

COX, VIRGINIA, 'Members, Muses, Mascots: Women and Italian Academies', conference paper delivered at 'The Italian Academies, 1525–1700: The First Intellectual Networks of Early Modern Europe', 17 September 2012, British Library, London. Available as a podcast on: <http://backdoorbroadcasting.net/2012/09/virginia-cox-members-muses-mascots-women-and-italian-academies/>

SAMPSON, LISA, ' "Gir' in porto a le degn'opre Intenta": Isabella Andreini and the Intenti Academy of Pavia' [2014], podcast on <http://www.casaitaliananyu.org/content/isabella-andreini-and-intenti-academy-pavia-2014>

212   LISA SAMPSON

Notes to Chapter 9

This research has been supported by the Arts and Humanities Research Council UK as part of the *Italian Academies, 1525–1700* project [ref. AH/H023631/1], and by a Gladys Krieble Delmas Foundation grant. I am grateful for the comments of Jane Everson and the editors in preparing the essay.

1. Domenico Bruni, *Fatiche comiche di Domenico Bruni detto Fulvio, Comico di Madama Serenissima Principessa di Piemonte* (Paris, 1623), in Ferruccio Marotti and Giovanna Romei, *La commedia dell'arte e la società barocca. 2. La professione del teatro* (Rome: Bulzoni, 1991; repr. 1994), pp. 347–48. This quotation appears in 'Prologo da ragazzo' [Prologue played by a boy], which Bruni claims he was instructed to recite as a boy by Francesco Andreini, husband of Isabella and father of Giovan Battista. All translations are mine, except where indicated.

2. 'molti comici per mezzo dell'Arte loro si sono resi capaci di molti honori havuti da Imperatori, da Regi, da Principi, e da Illustrissime Academie' [several actors have through the development of their Art gained many honours from emperors, kings, princes and most illustrious academies] (Nicolò Barbieri, *Discorso famigliare...* (Venice, 1628), in *La commedia dell'arte: storia e testi*, ed. by Vito Pandolfi, 6 vols (Florence: Sansoni, 1957–1961), III, 369–98). However, like Bruni, Barbieri only provides specific details for academy membership for Isabella and Giovan Battista Andreini.

3. Richard Andrews, *Scripts and Scenarios: The Performance of Comedy in Renaissance Italy* (Cambridge: Cambridge University Press, 1993), p. 168.

4. For notarized contracts and other documents regarding this group of eight, mostly artisanal, actors, see Ester Cocco, 'Una compagnia comica nella prima metà del secolo XVI', *Giornale storico della letteratura italiana*, 65 (1915), 55–70; Robert Henke, *Performance and Literature in the Commedia dell'Arte* (Cambridge: Cambridge University Press, 2002), pp. 69–74.

5. Roberto Tessari, 'Il mercato delle Maschere', in *Storia del teatro moderno e contemporaneo*, ed. by Roberto Alonge and Guido Davico Bonino (Turin: Einaudi, 2000), pp. 119–91 (citation p. 119). On Grazzini, the author of eight surviving prose comedies, see also Franco Pignatti, 'Grazzini, Antonfrancesco (detto il Lasca)', *Dizionario Biografico degli Italiani*, 59 (2003); online at <http://www.treccani.it/enciclopedia/antonfrancesco-grazzini_%28Dizionario-Biografico%29/> [accessed 9 September 2013]. On his much studied problematic relations with the Accademia Fiorentina and involvement in alternative cultural spaces, see for example Domenico Zanré, *Cultural Non-Conformity in Early-Modern Florence* (Aldershot: Ashgate, 2004), pp. 59–85, 144–45.

6. Henke, *Performance and Literature*, p. 78; see also pp. 74–79.

7. For an essential overview, but less focused on the actor, see Stefano Mazzoni, 'Lo spettacolo delle accademie', in *Storia del teatro moderno e contemporaneo*, ed. by Roberto Alonge and Guido Davico Bonino (Turin: Einaudi, 2000), pp. 869–903. On academy theatre in the Veneto see Elena Povoledo, 'Una rappresentazione accademica a Venezia nel 1634', in *Studi sul teatro Veneto fra rinascimento ed età barocca*, ed. by Maria Teresa Muraro (Florence: Olschki, 1971), pp. 119–69. See also the studies by Tamburini, Mazzoni, Mamone and Fiaschini cited below, and for Adriano Valerini and Isabella Andreini consult the bibliography.

8. For relations between English actors and the *commedia*, see Chapter 10, section 3.

9. G. B. Guarini *Compendio della poesia tragicomica tratto dai duo Verati* [1602], in *Il Pastor fido e Compendio della Poesia Tragicomica*, ed. by Gioachino Brognoligo (Bari: Laterza, 1914), pp. 219–88 (p. 245). The two earlier treatises on which the *Compendio* draws (*Verato*, 1588; *Verato secondo*, 1593) are named after the distinguished (semi-professional) actor Giovan Battista Verato, who is also defended in the second treatise. For academic hostility to mercenary actors, see Tessari, 'Il mercato delle maschere', pp. 122–23. Compare Angelo Ingegneri, *Della poesia rappresentativa e del modo di rappresentare le favole sceniche* [1598], ed. by Maria Luisa Doglio (Modena: Panini, 1989), p. 6.

10. Tessari, 'Il mercato delle maschere', p. 123; and his 'Comici e letterati', in *La Commedia dell'arte nel Seicento: 'industria' e 'arte giocosa' della civiltà barocca* (Florence: Olschki, 1969), pp. 56–68.

11. On the Olimpici, see Marzia Maino, 'Dispositivi illuminotecnici e spettacolo a Vicenza: l'Accademia Olimpica, l'inaugurazione del Teatro e gli influssi sul contesto spettacolare'

(unpublished PhD dissertation, Padua University, 2009); Stefano Mazzoni, *L'Olimpico di Vicenza: un teatro e la sua 'perpetua memoria'* (Florence: Le Lettere, 1998). On the Alterati, see Claude V. Palisca, 'The Alterati of Florence, Pioneers in the Theory of Dramatic Music', in *New Looks at Italian Opera: Essays in Honor of Donald J. Grout*, ed. with intro. by William W. Austin (Ithaca, NY: Cornell University Press, 1968), pp. 9–38; and his 'The First Performance of *Euridice*', in *Queens College Department of Music: Twenty-fifth Anniversary Festschrift*, ed. by Albert Mell (New York: Queens College Press, 1964), pp. 1–23. For the much studied Intronati, see for example Daniele Seragnoli, *Il teatro a Siena nel Cinquecento: 'progetto' e 'modello' drammaturgico nell'Accademia degli intronati* (Roma: Bulzoni, 1980); and Laura Riccò, *La 'miniera' accademica: pedagogia, editoria, palcoscenico nella Siena del Cinquecento* (Rome: Bulzoni, 2002).

12. On *comici dell'arte* as a 'microsocietà', see Tessari, 'Il mercato delle maschere', p. 132; for an interesting exploration of the symbolic and ritual separation inherent in the idea of the academy, see Marc Fumaroli, 'Academia, Arcadia, Parnassus: trois lieux allégoriques de l'éloge du loisir lettré', in *Italian Academies of the Sixteenth Century*, ed. by D. S. Chambers and F. Quiviger (London: Warburg Institute, 1995), pp. 15–35.

13. James M. Saslow, *The Medici wedding of 1589: Florentine Festival as Theatrum Mundi* (New Haven, CT: Yale University Press, 1996), esp. pp. 150–62, 169–70; Andrews, *Scripts and Scenarios*, pp. 227–37.

14. For important exceptions, see Fabrizio Fiaschini, *L''Incessabil agitazione": Giovan Battista Andreini tra professione teatrale, cultura letteraria e religione* (Pisa: Giardini, 2007), and the studies of Elena Tamburini.

15. For Guarini, see Marzia Pieri, '"Il Pastor fido" e i comici dell'arte', *Biblioteca teatrale*, 17 (1990), 1–15; see also Franco Vazzoler, 'Chiabrera fra dilettanti e professionisti dello spettacolo', in *La scelta della misura. Gabriello Chiabrera: l'altro fuoco del barocco italiano*, ed. by Fulvio Bianchi and Paolo Russo (Genoa: Costa & Nolan, 1993), pp. 429–66; Elena Tamburini, '"Comedia dell'arte": An Enquiry and Some Incursions into the Meaning of this Term', trans. by Mark Weir, *Acting Archives Essays*, 15 (April 2012), 1–35 (from '"Commedia dell'arte": immagini e percorsi intorno a un'ipotesi', *Drammaturgia*, 5 July 2010, <www.drammaturgia.it>); and Sara Mamone, *Dèi, Semidei, Uomini: lo spettacolo a Firenze tra neoplatonismo e realtà Borghese (XV–XVII secolo)* (Rome: Bulzoni, 2003).

16. Amedeo Quondam, 'L'Accademia', in *Letteratura italiana*, I, *Il letterato e le istituzioni* (Turin: Einaudi, 1982), pp. 823–98 (pp. 870–71). These statistics are acknowledged to be hard to quantify precisely. However, Quondam's analysis is based on the 2,050 institutions that he classifies as academies from the over 2,270 listed in Michele Maylender, *Storie delle Accademie d'Italia*, 5 vols (Bologna: Cappelli, 1926–30). Maylender's encyclopedia still remains a valuable guide, but recent scholarship has highlighted some inconsistencies, errors and limitations. For ongoing research by the AHRC funded Italian Academies project, see the publicly accessible British Library Database of Italian Academies (1525–1700): <http://www.bl.uk/catalogues/ItalianAcademies/>.

17. Jean Boutier and Maria Pia Paoli, 'Letterati cittadini e principi filosofi: i milieux intellettuali fiorentini tra cinque e settecento', in *Naples, Rome, Florence: une histoire comparée des milieux intellectuels italiens (XVIIe–XVIIIe siècles)*, ed. by Jean Boutier, Brigitte Marin and Antonella Romano (Rome: École Française de Rome, 2005), pp. 331–403 (pp. 371–73); and for an updated alphabetical index of Florentine academies, pp. 684–88.

18. See Mamone, *Dèi, Semidei, Uomini*, pp. 13–25. On Barlacchia, whose name (meaning 'stupid') recalls facetious academic nicknames, see Ada Zapperi, 'Barlachia (Barlacchia, Barlacchi), Domenico', *DBI*, 6 (1964), on <http://www.treccani.it/enciclopedia/domenico-barlachia_%28Dizionario-Biografico%29/> [accessed 20 August 2013]. See also Alison Brown, 'Defining the place of academies in Florentine culture and politics', forthcoming in *The Italian Academies 1525–1700: Networks of Culture, Innovation and Dissent*, ed. by Jane E. Everson, Denis V. Reidy and Lisa Sampson (Oxford: Legenda).

19. Giovanni Calendoli, 'Le Compagnie della Calza, Ruzante e la compagnia Padovana del 1545', in *Il convegno internazionale di studi sul Ruzante*, ed. by Giovanni Calendoli and Giuseppe Vellucci (Venice: Corbo e Fiore, 1989), pp. 325–31 (pp. 326–29).

20. On the seasonal and repetitive nature of *arte* performances, see Anne MacNeil, *Music and Women*

214   LISA SAMPSON

of the 'Commedia dell'Arte' in the Late Sixteenth Century (Oxford: Oxford University Press, 2003), p. 5 n. 10, p. 8 n. 13.

21. On the Bavaria performance, see Nino Pirrotta and Elena Povoledo, *Music and Theatre from Poliziano to Monteverdi*, trans. by Karen Eales (Cambridge: Cambridge University Press, 1982), pp. 108–11. For seventeenth-century amateur improvised comedy, see Luciano Mariti, *Commedia ridicolosa: comici di professione, dilettanti, editoria teatrale nel Seicento, storia e testi* (Rome: Bulzoni, 1979); and Elena Tamburini, 'Comici, cantanti e letterati nell'Accademia Romana degli Umoristi', *Studi Secenteschi*, 50 (2009), 89–112. For the Intronati's imitation of comic masks in their games (*veglie*) as opposed to their dramaturgical techniques, see Riccò, *La 'miniera' accademica*, pp. 130–39.

22. The same is true of plays performed by the Accademia Fiorentina (Zanré, *Cultural Non-Conformity*, p. 150), and for court performances of Guarini's *Pastor fido* in the 1580s–90s, see Lisa Sampson, *Pastoral Drama in Early Modern Italy: The Making of a New Genre* (Oxford: Legenda, 2006), pp. 179–81.

23. Alessandro Marcigliano, 'Giovan Battista Verato: un attore nella Ferrara del Cinquecento', in *Scenery, Set and Staging in the Italian Renaissance: Studies in the Practice of Theatre*, ed. by Christopher Cairns (Lewiston, NY: Edwin Mellen, 1996), pp. 81–99. See above, n. 9.

24. Calendoli, 'Le Compagnie della Calza', pp. 328–30.

25. On Venetian theatre legislation, see Eugene J. Johnson, 'The Short, Lascivious Lives of Two Venetian Theaters, 1580–85', *Renaissance Quarterly*, 55.3 (2002), 936–68 (pp. 939–44, 946–57). For the actors of the Vicenza performance, see Mazzoni, *L'Olimpico*, pp. 141–48. The Olimpici in 1605 may even have dropped a planned performance of Guarini's *Idropica* with a professional company (the Gelosi?) because of the scandal it would cause, ibid., pp. 64–69.

26. Alberto Gallo, *La prima rappresentazione al Teatro Olimpico, con i progetti e le relazioni dei contemporanei,* preface by Lionello Puppi (Milan: Il Polifilo, 1973), pp. 33–37 (Letter by Giacomo Dolfin to Battista Guarini, Venice, 9 March 1585); pp. 39–51 (Letter from Antonio Riccoboni to Benedetto Zorzi, Podestà of Vicenza, Padua, post 3 March 1585) (pp. 35, 49, 50). See also Mazzoni, *L'Olimpico*, pp. 87–207.

27. Dolfin, in Gallo, ibid., p. 35. On the Pellizzari sisters (and for Maddalena Casulana below), see Iain Fenlon, *Music and Patronage in Sixteenth-Century Mantua*, 2 vols (Cambridge: Cambridge University Press, 1980), I, 127–28; also the praise by Maddalena Campiglia, *Flori: A Pastoral Play* [1588], ed. by Virginia Cox and Lisa Sampson, trans. by Virginia Cox (Chicago, IL: Chicago University Press, 2004), III.6, p. 183, p. 320 n. 74.

28. See Virginia Cox, 'Members, Muses, Mascots: Women and Italian Academies', forthcoming in Everson et al. (eds), *The Italian Academies 1525–1700*; for the podcast of the paper delivered at the conference on 'The Italian Academies, 1525–1700: The First Intellectual Networks of Early Modern Europe', 17 September 2012, British Library, London, see <http://backdoorbroadcasting.net/2012/09/virginia-cox-members-muses-mascots-women-and-italian-academies/>. Cox explores fourteen cases of academy membership for women between 1543 and 1650, and other kinds of association by women with academies 'beyond membership'. See also her *The Prodigious Muse: Women's Writing in Counter-Reformation Italy* (Baltimore, MD: Johns Hopkins University Press, 2011), esp. pp. 13, 15–19, 95–96, 233–34. For Sarocchi, see also Tamburini, 'Comici, cantanti e letterati', pp. 96, 105.

29. Henke, *Performance and Literature*, pp. 85–105; Siro Ferrone, 'La Commedia dell'Arte senza commedia', *Biblioteca teatrale*, 3 (2011), 163–74.

30. Siro Ferrone, 'Introduzione' to *Commedie dell'Arte*, 2 vols (Milan: Mursia, 1985), I, 5–69; and *Attori mercanti corsari: la Commedia dell'Arte in Europa tra Cinque e Seicento* (Turin: Einaudi, 1993), pp. 203–24.

31. Tessari, *La Commedia dell'artecento*, p. 57; MacNeil, *Music and Women*, p. 1.

32. Andrews, *Scripts*, pp. 91–92, 100–07.

33. Mazzoni, *L'Olimpico*, pp. 145–47.

34. *Il Verato Secondo ovvero Replica dell'Attizzato Accademico Ferrarese in difesa del Pastor fido... [1593]*, in *Delle Opere del Cavalier Battista Guarini*, 4 vols (Verona: Tumermani, 1738), III, 1–384 (pp. 29–31, 44–47). On this episode, see Pieri, ' "Il Pastor fido" ', pp. 4–9.

35. Tamburini, 'Comici, cantanti'.

36. Antonio Maria Spelta, *Historia ... De' fatti notabili occorsi nell'universo, & in particolare del Regno de' Gothi, de' Longobardi, de i Duchi di Milano, [...] Con una nuova aggiunta* (Pavia: Pietro Bartoli, 1602), 'Aggiunta', p. 170. On Andreini's academic name and emblem, see Ferdinando Taviani, '"Bella d'Asia": Torquato Tasso, gli attori e l'immortalità', *Paragone letteratura*, 35 (1984), 3–76 (p. 5). For a reference to the actress's association with another Pavia academy, the Affidati, but without further supporting documentation, see, ed., *'Sul Tesin piantàro laureti': poesia e vita letteraria nella Lombardia spagnola (1535–1706)*, Simone Albonico (Pavia: Cardano, 2002), pp. 22, 188. On Isabella Andreini's two volumes of *Rime*, see ibid., pp. 312–18, and esp. Chiara Cedrati, 'Isabella Andreini: La vicenda editoriale delle "Rime"', *ACME — Annali della Facoltà di Lettere e Filosofia dell'Università degli Studi di Milano*, 60.2 (May–August 2007), 115–42 <http://www.ledonline.it/acme/allegati/Acme-07-II-05-Cedrati.pdf> [accessed 19 March 2013]; and Anne MacNeil, 'Introduction' to *Selected Poems of Isabella Andreini*, ed. by Anne MacNeil, trans. by James Wyatt Cook (Lanham, MD: Scarecrow Press, 2005), pp. 1–28. See also Lisa Sampson, '"Gir' in porto a le degn'opre Intenta": Isabella Andreini and the Intenti Academy of Pavia' (2014), podcast on <http://www.casaitaliananyu.org/content/isabella-andreini-and-intenti-academy-pavia-2014>.

37. Fiaschini, *L''Incessabil agitazione'*, pp. 15–16, 21–49.

38. Stefano Mazzoni, 'Genealogia e vicende della famiglia Andreini', in *Origini della Commedia Improvvisa o dell'Arte*, ed. by M. Chiabò and F. Doglio (Rome: Torre d'Orfeo, 1996), pp. 107–61 (p. 130). For Giovan Battista's *La venetiana* (two editions 1619), published with the pseudo-academic name Sier Cocalin dei Cocalini da Torzelo Academico Vizilante ditto el Dornioto, see Ferrone, *Attori mercanti corsari*, pp. 205, 211–12. For the Venetian Accademia dei Vigilanti (recorded from 1602), see Maylender, v, 459–62.

39. *La Fillide, fauola pastorale, dell'Acceso Academico Rinouato* (Ferrara: Vittorio Baldini, 1579). See the caustic comment by the printer of a later edition on the importance of establishing legitimate authorship, in Camillo Della Valle, *Fillide, egloga pastorale* (Ferrara: Vittorio Baldini, 1584), Dedicatory letter, fols A2^v–A3^r. On Bernardino Lombardi (of the Confidenti or Uniti troupe), author of a comedy *L'Alchemista* (Ferrara, 1583) and a known plagiarist, see *Commedie dell'Arte*, ed. by Siro Ferrone, 2 vols (Milan: Mursia, 1985), i, 15, 16, 18, 73–74; and Teresa Megale 'Lombardi, Bernardino', *DBI*, 65 (2005), <http://www.treccani.it/enciclopedia/bernardino-lombardi_(Dizionario-Biografico)/> [accessed 2 April 2013].

40. Tamburini, 'Commedia dell'Arte', pp. 26–29; and her 'I comici Gelosi e l'Accademia della Val di Blenio', *Teatro e storia*, 3 (2011), 175–96. On Borgogni, his multiple academy membership and his close involvement with Andreini, see Kathryn Bosi, 'Accolades for an Actress: On Some Literary and Musical Tributes for Isabella Andreini', *Recercare*, 15 (2003), 73–117; and Taviani, '"Bella d'Asia"', passim; also *Sul Tesin*, ed. by Albonico, pp. 20, 21, 110–11.

41. Cesare Rao, 'L'Accademia de' Zanni a voi Accademici gnoranti desidera salute, e perpetua felicità', in *L'Argute et facete lettere [...] nelle quali si contengono molti leggiadri Motti, & solazzevoli Discorsi* (Vicenza: Appresso Perin Libraro, & Giorgio Greco compagni, 1585), fols 59^v–61^v, see also fols 33^r–45^r. On Rao's performance-oriented letters on the model of Andrea Calmo (reprinted at least fifteen times by 1622), and those of other professional *comici* like Vincenzo Belando, see Ferrone, *Commedie dell'Arte*, i, 19–20; Marotti and Romei, *La commedia dell'arte*, ii, 97–104.

42. Rao, *L'Argute et facete lettere*, fols 59^v (Doni reference), 46^v–48^v, 111^r–113^r. On the evidence for the Accademia Pellegrini, which revolves solely around Doni and the printer Francesco Marcolini, see Giorgio Masi, 'Coreografie doniane: L'Accademia Pellegrina', in *Cinquecento capriccioso e irregolare: eresie letterarie nell'Italia del classicismo*, ed. by Paolo Procaccioli and Angelo Romano (Rome: Vecchiarelli, 1999), pp. 45–85 (p. 70). Giuseppe Crimi, 'Appunti per il testo e il commento delle *Lettere* di Cesare Rao', in *Dissonanze concordi: temi, questioni e personaggi intorno ad Anton Francesco Doni*, ed. Giovanna Rizzarelli (Bologna: Il Mulino, 2013), pp. 353–74.

43. Cited in Pandolfi, *La commedia dell'arte*, ii, 20–22; for Belando's fears of linguistic criticism of his comedy (*Gli amorosi inganni*, 1609) by 'colonies of academicians', like that of the Crusca for Tasso's epic, see pp. 162–63.

44. *Il Trionfo di Scappino parte prima: di Bartolomeo Bocchini detto Zan Muzzina...* (Modena: Bartolomeo Soliani, 1655) and *Del Trionfo di Scappino e della Zagnara Di Zan Muzzina Parte seconda*, cited in Pandolfi, *La commedia dell'arte*, iv, 191–92.

216 LISA SAMPSON

45. *Oratione d'Adriano Valerini Veronese, In morte della Divina Signora Vincenza Armani, Comica Eccellentissima. Et alcune rime dell'Istesso e d'altri Auttori, in lode della medesima. Con alquante leggiadre e belle Compositioni di detta Signora Vincenza* (Verona: Per Bastian dalle Donne, & Giovanni Fratelli, n.d. [1570?]), fol. 7^v. Valerini's oration without the verse is transcribed in Marotti and Romei, eds, *La commedia dell'arte*, II, 31–41; on Valerini, see pp. 27–30.

46. Valerini, *Oratione*, fols 17^v, 20^v–21^r, 31$^{r–v}$, 35$^{r–v}$; Riccò, *La 'miniera' accademica*, pp. 131, 142–43, 147–52, 155–64; see also Tessari, *La Commedia dell'arte*, p. 56.

47. Archivio di Stato, Verona, *Summario degli atti*, Fondo Dionisio-Piomarta, ms 634 [henceforth *Summario*], 13 April 1583 c. 58 t.o (folios not numbered in sequence). For the possibility that this manuscript copy may correspond with that of Asinari's tragedy in Valerini's hand sent to the Filarmonici, as registered in the 1734 index of books of Giulio Saibante, see Adriano Valerini, *Le bellezze di Verona*, ed. by G. P. Marchi (Verona: Stamperia Valdonega, 1974), pp. xxvii–xxviii.

48. Ferrone, *Commedie dell'arte*, I, 73–76.

49. Valerini, *Le bellezze*, ed. by G. P. Marchi, pp. xxxiii, 97–98.

50. On continuing ambiguous attitudes of Italian actors engaged in literary activities towards their practical art even in the later seventeenth century, see Tessari, *La commedia dell'arte*, pp. 61–62.

51. *Summario* (for performances of *Alceo* see entry 15 May 1585). A manuscript inventory of the academy from this year also shows they had a theatrical stage set and properties, see G. Turrini, *L'Accademia Filarmonica di Verona dalla fondazione (Maggio 1543) al 1600 e il suo patrimonio musicale antico* (Verona: Tipografica Veronese, 1941), p. 186; Paolo Rigoli, 'L'architettura effimera: feste, teatri, apparati decorative', in *L'architettura a Verona nell'età della Serenissima (sec. XV–sec. XVIII)*, ed. by Pierpaolo Brugnoli and Arturo Sandrini, 2 vols (Verona: Banca popolare di Verona, 1988), I, 1–86, 391–414 (p. 55).

52. See Marco Di Pasquale, 'Intorno al patronato della musica della Accademia Filarmonica di Verona nel Cinquecento: riflessioni e congetture', *Recercare*, 23.1–2 (2011), 35–63. On the role of the Brusasorzi and more generally on theatre in Verona, see my forthcoming 'Gentlemen of Verona: Theatre in the Accademia Filarmonica, 1543–1608'.

53. Bosi, 'Accolades', pp. 87–89; G. P. Marchi, 'L'esperienza teatrale di Adriano Valerini', in *La commedia dell'arte tra Cinque e Seicento in Francia e in Europa. Atti del Convegno Internazionale di Studio, Verona-Vicenza, 19–21 Oct. 1995*, ed. by Elio Mosele (Fasano: Schena, 1997), pp. 173–80 (pp. 173–74).

54. Isabella Andreini, *Mirtilla* (Verona: Girolamo Discepolo, 1588; and Sebastiano dalle Donne and Camillo Franceschini, 1588); *La Mirtilla. Fauola pastorale ... Di nuouo dall'istessa riueduta, et in molti luoghi abbellita* (Verona: per Francesco dalle Donne, & Scipione Vargnano suo genero, 1599).

55. ASVer, Archivio Dionisi-Piomarta, ms 637 [unpaginated], *Rime* dedicated to Alberto Lavezzola [1590?]. This fair copy codex in many hands includes verse by Filarmonici academicians using their nicknames, and by (named) dramatists, who were not members: Giovanni Fratta, Luigi Groto d'Adria, Vincenzo Giusti as well as Valerini himself. On the manuscript, see Marco Materassi, *Il Primo Lauro. Madrigali in onore di Laura Peperara. Ms 220 dell'Accademia Filarmonica di Verona [1580]* (Treviso: Diastema Fiori Musicali, 1999), p. VII [available on <http://web.tiscali.it/ensemble900/Diastema/Libri/Schede/Materassi.pdf>]. Cf. the 'secret' evidence of relations between Intronati and professional practitioners in Riccò, *La 'miniera' accademica*, p. 141. My thanks to Martin McLaughlin and Nicola Gardini for their assistance in translating the sonnet for Valerini.

56. Adriano Valerini, *Rime diverse et origine della famiglia della famiglia Bevilacqua* (Verona: per Sebastiano dalle Donne e fratelli, [1577]), edition held in the Archive of the Accademia Filarmonica, Verona, Coll. 202. For a 1628 inventory of the library holdings, see Turrini, *L'Accademia Filarmonica*, p. 195. On Bevilacqua, see Bosi, 'Accolades', pp. 84–91.

57. Marchi, 'L'esperienza teatrale', p. 175.

58. Archivio dell'Accademia Filarmonica, Verona, *Atti*, b. 41, fol. 8^r.

59. On this episode, see Bosi, 'Accolades', pp. 91–95. The verse was indeed printed under the Academy's name in Isabella Andreini's *Rime* (Milan: Appresso Girolamo Bordone, & Pietromartire Locarni, 1605), Part 2, p. 28.

60. For Andreini's networks, see Bosi, 'Accolades', pp. 102–04; Fiaschini, *L'Incessabil agitazione'*, pp. 17, 55–62. For Isabella Andreini and the Gelosi's performances in Milan, see the chronology

in Macneil, *Women and Music*, pp. 187–263; Roberta Giovanna Arcaini, 'I comici dell'arte a Milano: accoglienza, sospetti, riconoscimenti', in *La scena della Gloria: drammaturgia e spettacolo a Milano in età spagnola*, ed. by A. Cascetta and R. Carpani (Milan: Vita e pensiero, 1995), pp. 268–76. For the importance of Pavia academies in poetic production, see *Sul Tesin*, ed. by Albonico, pp. 18–19, 21, 27, and the various entries on verse publications.

61. Macneil, *Music and Women*, pp. 2, 250–51, 285; on the *Rime* of 1601, see Cedrati, 'Isabella Andreini', pp. 116–28; *Sul Tesin*, ed. by Albonico, pp. 312–15.

62. On the Intenti, see Siro Comi, *Ricerche storiche sull'accademia degli Affidati e su altri analoghi stabilimenti in Pavia* (Pavia: Comino, 1792), pp. 47–58; now in a modern edition with manuscript revisions by Comi, in Maria Cristina Regali, 'Le ricerche storiche sull'Accademia degli Affidati di Siro Comi: edizione delle postille dell'autore' (Como: Litografia New Press, 1999), pp. 218–24; see also, based on Comi, Maylender's entry (III, 319–23). On membership, see Fiaschini, *L'Incessabil agitazione'*, pp. 55–62.

63. For Andreini's whereabouts, see Macneil, *Music and Women*, pp. 250–56. For Andreini's performance and verse for her, as Accademica Intenta, see Spelta, *Aggionta*, pp. 169, 172. See also the somewhat ambiguous admiration for her eloquence by the Flemish university professor and Intenti member Erycius Puteanus, in Macneil, ibid., pp. 305–23 (esp. 311).

64. Taviani, 'Bella d'Asia', pp. 25, 27–29. For Archilei, see Macneil, *Music and Women*, p. 21.

65. Isabella Cervoni (before 1599) and Ippolita Benigni (by 1609) belonged to the Affidati. In the 1550s, the poet Alda Lunato Torelli served the Affidati as a cultural muse and figurehead, see Cox, *The Prodigious Muse*, pp. 13, 15; Virginia Cox, *Women's Writing in Italy, 1400–1650* (Baltimore, MD: Johns Hopkins University Press, 2008), pp. 102–03, 306 n.106; *Sul tesin*, ed. by Albonico, pp. 148–50.

66. Comi, *Ricerche storiche*, ed. by Regali, p. 224.

67. Cedrati, 'Isabella Andreini', pp. 123, 124–25, 127–29, 136–39, 141.

68. Andreini, *Rime*, 1605, dedicatory letter by the printers to Margherita Casati, which mentions performances by Isabella for her and other Milanese ladies (fol. A2^{v}).

69. Fiaschini, *L'Incessabil agitazione'*, pp. 12–13, 15–16, 21–49. The following discussion draws on this source.

70. See Andreini, *La Saggia Egiziana: dialogo spettante alla lode dell'arte scenica* (Florence: Volcmar Timan, 1604), dedication to Don Antonio de' Medici.

71. Fiaschini, *L'Incessabil agitazione'*, p. 15. Andreini's first publications are connected in various ways with the Spensierati Academy: his dialogue on theatre, *La Saggia Egiziana*, recalls in the dedicatory letter the academy's contribution of verse to his 1604 edition of *Florinda*; his religious poem *Divina Visione in soggetto del beato Carlo Borromeo* (poemetto) (Florence: Volcmar Timan, 1604) is dedicated to the academy (23 Dec. 1604); academy members contributed to the verse added to his *Florinda, tragedia* (Milan: Bordoni, 1606), pp. 5–11 (British Library copy consulted, shelf-mark C.73.c.10); and see the 'poemetto' *Pianto d'Apollo, Rime funebri in morte d'Isabella Andrini Comica Gelosa...* (Milan: Bordoni e Locarni, 1606). For a complete list of Giovan Battista Andreini's publications, see *Comici dell'Arte: corrispondenze*, ed. by Siro Ferrone (Florence: Le Lettere, 1993), I, 71–75. No correspondence relating to this early period of Andreini's career, or his links with the Spensierati appears in this volume. On the connections between Virginia Ramponi Andreini (Florinda) and the Spensierati, including their *Rime in lode della signora Verginia Ramponi Andreini, comica Fedele, detta Florinda* (Florence: Volcmar Timan, 1604), see Emily Wilbourne, '"Isabella ringiovinita": Virginia Ramponi Andreini before Arianna', *Recercare*, 19.1–2 (2007), 54–67; and on academic verse for Virginia esp. in the Raccolta Morbio, I, Milan, Biblioteca Braidense, Milan, see Wilbourne, 'La Florinda: The Performance of Virginia Ramponi Andreini' (unpublished PhD dissertation, New York University, 2009), pp. 185–216; 221–24.

72. Tamburini, 'Comici, cantanti e letterati'. Mariti, *Commedia ridicolosa*.

73. Mazzoni, 'Lo spettacolo', pp. 888, 891; Tessari, *La commedia dell'arte*, pp. 62–63 (Barbieri citation).

74. '[Frittellino (i.e. Cecchini) vuole] inviarsi a Roma, et colà porre un accademietta in piedi e alcuna volta privata', Letter from Giovan Battista, Turin, to Duke Vincenzo Gonzaga, Mantua, 14 August 1609, in *Comici dell'Arte: corrispondenze*, I, 91.

75. Tessari, *La commedia dell'arte*, pp. 56–68.
76. Giovan Battista Andreini, *Le due commedie in commedia*, in *Commedie dell'Arte*, ed. by Siro Ferrone, II, 17–105; IV.1, p. 66; IV.2, p. 68 (Fabio's nickname). On Virginia Ramponi Andreini, see above n. 71.

CHAPTER 10

❖

Competing with Continentals:
The Case of William Kemp

Katherine Duncan-Jones

Somerville College, Oxford

i. Shakespeare's Clowns: Kemp in Context

Three exceptionally talented comic performers were well known to Shakespeare: Richard Tarlton (d. 1588), William Kemp (d. 1610?) and Robert Armin (1563–1615). Kemp will be the chief subject of this chapter, but I would like to open by situating him in the context both of Shakespeare and of the other two 'fools'. There is little doubt that Kemp and Armin were the original performers of several significant 'fool' or 'clown' roles (the terms were then interchangeable) in Shakespeare's plays. Roles of which Kemp was the earliest performer include those of Costard in *Love's Labour's Lost*, Peter in *Romeo and Juliet* and Dogberry in *Much Ado About Nothing*, while Robert Armin premiered as Touchstone in *As You Like It*, Feste in *Twelfth Night*, Clown 1 in *Hamlet* and the Fool in *King Lear*. All were evidently outstanding players, but Kemp alone was celebrated beyond England.

The oldest of the three, Richard Tarlton, died on 3 September 1588. We have no hard evidence that he and Shakespeare knew each other, but it's possible that they did. There may have been a period when Shakespeare was a member of the Queen's Men, alongside the hugely popular Tarlton. The company had been established in March 1583 under the patronage and general oversight of Sir Francis Walsingham, and incorporated talented performers from other existing companies, such as Leicester's Men. The majority of the Queen's Men's performances took place in the provinces, rather than in London or at Court.[1] Shakespeare could plausibly have been recruited to this company in the second half of 1587. Four years after the company's formation, on the evening of 13 June 1587, William Knell, a versatile leading Queen's Man, was fatally wounded in a sword fight with John Towne, a fellow actor and a company sharer. The players' scuffle took place while the company was performing at Thame, in Oxfordshire. Despite this grim misadventure the Queen's Men continued to tour and perform during the later months of 1587. But with William Knell dead, and John Towne in prison facing charges of manslaughter, they were in urgent need of two more performers.[2] The company was in the Midlands from mid-July, and reached Stratford-upon-Avon on 17 December. Either then, or a couple of years earlier, a youthful William Shakespeare could have been recruited to this company as a 'hired man' — that is a performer who was not a full 'sharer' in the company, and was therefore not mentioned in the company's records, which relate only to payments to the nine full 'sharers'. As a versatile young man, skilful both in writing plays and performing in them, he could have been extremely useful to the Queen's Men during this difficult summer. This is all entirely speculative, but there is no doubt that Shakespeare was deeply familiar with many plays in the Queen's Men's repertoire of the late 1580s. As McMillin and Maclean point out,

> The plots of no fewer than six of Shakespeare's plays are closely related to the plots of plays performed by the Queen's Men.
> It appears that Shakespeare's composition of these plays indicate[s] an unusually substantial and detailed knowledge of the Queen's Men plays.[3]

Whether or not Shakespeare was familiar with Tarlton as a colleague, there is little doubt that he witnessed some of his comical performances, and was fully aware of his unique and memorable success in entertaining audiences in public venues in London as well as in the provinces, and more privately both in great men's houses and at Court. Tarlton's attested fans range from unlearned playgoers — such as some of those described in *Tarltons Jests* — to distinguished academics, such as Gabriel Harvey. Notoriously, Tarlton was also strongly favoured by the Queen herself.

The celebrated graveyard scene in Shakespeare's *Hamlet* Act v Scene 1 seems to pay tribute to Tarlton's distinctive gifts as a Court jester. A disguised Hamlet returns from supposed exile in England to find an old grave being dug up by two men who, in all of the play's three earliest editions, are described as 'Clowns'. After a lively discussion of such diverse topics as corrupt lawyers and the mad Prince's banishment from Denmark to England, Hamlet closely interrogates Clown 1 — the insignificant Clown 2 having gone off to fetch a 'stoup of beer' — concerning the identity of the latest skull that he has unearthed: 'This same skull, sir, was, sir, Yorick's skull, the king's jester', says the Clown (*Hamlet*, v. 1. 138 — 9). Clown and Prince proceed to exchange their own vivid and personal recollections of the Court fool Yorick, 'a fellow of infinite jest', who once baptized the Clown by pouring 'a flagon of Rhenish' on his head, and frequently carried the boy prince playfully on his broad shoulders. The name 'Yorick', emphatically enunciated four times in the Q1 text of *Hamlet*, suggests 'Your Rick [Tarlton]' — a uniquely popular performer equally well loved by princes and clowns, actors and audiences. As David Wiles has remarked: 'When the grave-digging "clown" gives Hamlet the skull of the Queen's jester, the actor Armin is able to pay a vicarious tribute to his mentor Tarlton.'[4] Shakespeare seems here to have provided his first audiences with pleasing reminders of the most celebrated clown of the age, a man whose name and fame were to endure for many decades after his sudden death. The fact that this death — probably from plague — took place only three weeks after the so-called 'defeat' of the Spanish Armada, in mid-August 1588 — the most serious invasion attempt to occur in the whole of Elizabeth I's forty-five-year reign — made it especially memorable. An astonishing and apparently miraculous triumph for England and her Queen was quickly succeeded by a sad cultural loss.[5]

COMPETING WITH CONTINENTALS 221

In that celebrated graveyard scene Shakespeare was doing something else, in addition to reminding his audience about the life and death of Richard Tarlton. He is reminding them emphatically that the events they see represented on stage take place 'here in Denmark', where the Clown has been sexton 'man and boy, thirty years' (*Hamlet*, v. 1. 153–54). There are other plays in which Shakespeare frequently reminds his audience of the country in which all or most of the action takes place. *The Merchant of Venice*, for instance, includes nineteen allusions to 'Venice' and four to 'Venetian'; *Othello* has seventeen allusions to 'Venice', four to 'Venetian', and one to 'Venetians'. But *Hamlet* has the largest number of such reminders, with twenty-one allusions to 'Denmark' or 'Denmark's', six uses of the term 'Dane', five of 'Danish' and one of 'Danskers'.[6] The audience is never permitted for very long to forget this play's geographical location — a location that was probably familiar to some of the play's original performers, as well as to audience members.

As early audience members were surely aware, England is only a short distance away across the North, or 'German', Sea. There was considerable mutual understanding, commercial, cultural and diplomatic, between these two northern European Protestant countries. During the period when *Hamlet* was composed, around 1600/01, their interactions were about to be more fully realized. In the spring of 1603, as widely anticipated, Elizabeth I was peacefully succeeded by a male Scottish monarch married to a Danish royal princess, Anne 'of Denmark'. Both the Scottish King and the Danish Queen proved to be generous patrons of their respective playing companies.

Playing companies frequently travelled between England and other countries. As Jerzy Limon has shown, from the late sixteenth century onwards various principalities along the Baltic coast, and inland from it, were visited by groups of English performers — musicians, players, fools, dancers and acrobats in various combinations. Though most of these overseas tours were seasonal, carefully timed to coincide with local fairs and religious festivals, there were some English companies which even achieved resident status. These performers, whose names are by definition not very familiar to English scholars, 'found service at noblemen's, ducal, or even royal courts, where they stayed for many years, undertaking only occasional travels or none at all'.[7] However, although the Queen's Men, generally including Richard Tarlton, toured extensively within England, travelling as far West as Plymouth, and as far North as York, there is no reason to suppose that Tarlton ever set foot in continental Europe.[8] This is one of the major differences between Tarlton's career and that of the 'fool' who will be the chief focus of this chapter, William Kemp. Kemp was in every sense mobile, both at home and overseas.[9] His outstanding physical fitness and personal resourcefulness were major factors in his success. In the second and third sections of this chapter evidence will be presented that suggests that Kemp was the first English actor to achieve a genuinely international reputation.

Before turning to Kemp and 'Continentals', however, something should be said about Robert Armin, who succeeded Kemp as the leading comic performer of the Lord Chamberlain's Men, later to become an even more handsomely retained and rewarded King's Man. Armin was apparently chosen by Richard Tarlton as

222   KATHERINE DUNCAN-JONES

his professional heir, being talent-spotted when, as a boy apprenticed to a leading London goldsmith, he ran errands to one of the City taverns owned and managed by Tarlton:

> *Tarlton* keeping a Taverne in Gracious street, hee let it to another, who was indebted to *Armins* Master, a Gold smith in Lumbard street: yet he himself had a Chamber in the same house. And this *Armin* being then a wag[10] came often thither to demaund his Masters money, which hee sometimes had, and sometimes had not: in the end the man growing poore, told the boy he had no money for his Master, and he must beare with him. The mans name being *Charles*, *Armin* made this verse, writing it with chalke on a waine-scot:

> > O world how wilt thou lie, thou *Charles* the great?[11]
> > That I denie:
> > Indeed *Charles* the great before,
> > But now *Charles* the lesse, being poore.

> *Tarlton* coming into the roome reading it, and partly acquainted with the boyes humor, coming often thither for his *Masters* money, tooke a piece of chalke, & writ this rime by it.

> > A wag thou art, none can prevent thee,
> > And thy desert shall content thee:
> > Let me divine, as I am, so in time thou'lt be the same.
> > My adopted sonne therefore be,
> > To enjoy my Clownes suite after me.

> And so it fell out: the Boy reading this, so loved *Tarlton* after, that regarding him with more respect, used to [attend] his playes, and fell in a league with his humour, and private practice brought him to present playing, and at this houre performs the same, where at the Globe on the Bancke-side men may see him.

This account of an Elizabethan actor's professional apprenticeship, through close study and mimicry of an outstanding senior performer, has been surprisingly little discussed. It may well be authentic, since Armin himself was almost certainly the author of *Tarltons Jests*, along with other works that celebrate Tarlton after his death, such as *Tarltons News out of Purgatorie*. *Tarltons Jests* was originally published in 1600, though no copy of that printing survives. The closing phrase of the anecdote quoted above — 'where at the Globe on the Bancke-side men may see him' — clearly relates to the year 1600, when the Globe was a splendid newly built playhouse, and Armin a leading comic performer formally recruited to the Lord Chamberlain's Men after the departure of William Kemp. Armin may already have been an occasional performer for the company.

In contrast to Tarlton, who was strong, pugnacious and broad-shouldered, Armin was small in stature, and perhaps slightly frail in appearance. The only image we possess of him, a woodcut on the title-page of his comedy *The Two Maides of Moreclack*, shows him costumed in a long blue gown as the celebrated City simpleton 'John of the Hospital' and gazing upwards, as if he is smaller than the people around him. When Tarlton first met Armin, as a 'wag', he may have been as young as fourteen or fifteen — a plausible age for starting an apprenticeship. But even when he was older his small stature may have enabled him appear to be younger than he really was. It may have equipped him particularly well, in later years, for the role of the child-like and nameless Fool of *King Lear*, who seems frail and vulnerable, and repeatedly addresses the aged King as his 'nuncle'. Two of the English names that Armin used when clowning solo, 'Pink'[12] and 'Snuffe', suggest diminutive stature. One of *OED*'s definitions of 'pink' as a noun, sense 6, is 'A very small person or creature; a brat; an elf'; while 'snuff', in sense 1b, is used 'In comparisons [...] to describe what is faint, feeble, or on the point of extinction.' As a verb, 'to pink' could mean to blink or flicker. Rather strikingly, the two words occur in close proximity in *Pappe with an Hatchet* (1589), an anti-Marprelate satire written possibly by Thomas Nashe, possibly by John Lyly: 'A wit worn into the socket, twinkling and pinking like the snuffe of a candle.'[13] Though Armin is not known to have performed abroad, later in his career he was in the habit of giving himself Italianate nicknames such as 'Clunnico de Curtanio Snuffe' [Snuff, the Clown of The Curtain Theatre], later updated to 'Clunnico del Mondo Snuff' [Snuff, the Clown of the Globe Theatre].[14]

If Armin ever travelled beyond England — and we have no evidence that he did — it is unlikely that he got as far as Italy. Yet it's clear that he had a good working knowledge of the Italian language. During the severe plague of 1608–10, when the public theatres were closed, Armin raised some money from the stationers by re-packaging and re-framing his book *Foole upon Foole* as *A Nest of Ninnies*, and also by translating and adapting a comic poem from the Italian of Straparola, *The Italian Taylor and his Boy* (1608) — or possibly, again, re-packaging a poem he had prepared some years earlier.[15] This playful account of a boy apprentice's magical metamorphoses into different shapes, hotly pursued by his tyrannical master, also a shape-changer, may be read as an allegory of Armin's own lively and varied career as it approached its close. He seems to have retired from the stage in about 1610.

Armin probably learned Italian from some of the 'Lombard' goldsmiths denizened in London. As indicated in the anecdote from *Tarltons Jests* quoted above, his master, a leading goldsmith, had his workshop in 'Lumbard Street'. This had been designated as the goldsmiths' and silversmiths' quarter as long ago as the reign of Edward I, and most of its craftsmen came from northern Italy. As an apprentice goldsmith Armin spent long days working alongside these highly skilled Italian craftsmen, acquiring a good working knowledge of the Italian language by that means. The *novelle* of Straparola approximate to children's literature, or what we might now categorize as fairy tales, providing congenial and not very taxing material for Armin to study in the original Italian. However, unlike Kemp, Armin displays little awareness of Italian stage comedians, or of the conventions of Italian drama. Five of the six fools whose careers he chronicled in *Foole upon Foole* were native Englishmen, while one, Jemy Camber, was a Scot.

ii. Competing with Continentals: Kemp overseas

Most of the earliest allusions to William Kemp are associated with performances overseas. In May 1585 he is recorded as a member of Leicester's Men, a playing company that enjoyed the patronage of Elizabeth I's long-term favourite Robert

224   KATHERINE DUNCAN-JONES

Dudley, Earl of Leicester, who had repeatedly declared himself willing to lead a military expedition on the Queen's behalf. The longstanding friendship between Leicester and the Queen had become rather fraught since his marriage to the widowed Countess of Essex, Lettice Knollys, yet Leicester's continued association with the Queen ensured considerable status for his playing company. It was from this group that new recruits were regularly selected for the Queen's Men.

In the summer of 1585 Leicester's players were rewarded with £5, and on the same day 'William Kympe one of the pleyers' was individually rewarded with ten shillings, presumably for a freestanding comic turn such as a 'merriment' or 'jig'. £5 may have been Leicester's normal rate of payment to a company for performance of a full play, since the same sum had been paid to 'the Quenes majesties players' at Leicester House on 20 April 1585. Earlier still, according to an entry in Leicester's accounts dated 30 March 1585, a payment of 40 shillings was made to 'William foole at his goyng from Wansted to my Lord of Essex'. Given Kemp's attested role as a bearer of letters a little later, it seems probable that this entry also relates to him, connecting Kemp, not implausibly, to Leicester's stepson Robert Devereux, Second Earl of Essex.

The 1585 performances at Leicester House took place during a period of high excitement and expectation. Leicester was preparing ambitiously to lead a large expeditionary force to the Netherlands to provide English support to provinces resistant to Spanish rule, which had been left leaderless by the assassination of William of Orange in Delft on 10 July 1584. There was much delay and prevarication on the part of the Queen, who postponed assent to Leicester's appointment as General of the English troops until 23 September. Even then, she issued only a verbal request, not a written commission.[16] However, when Leicester's troops finally sailed from Harwich, reaching Flushing by noon on 10 December 1585, he led an impressively large fleet. It was composed of

> over a hundred vessels of varying sorts bearing six to seven hundred cavalry [...].The household included chaplains and physicians, a steward, four Secretaries, two engineers, pages, grooms, trumpeters [... and] there was even a troop of players to beguile the time in an alien land.[17]

Kemp figures in two main ways in surviving records of the Netherlands expedition: as a performer immediately popular with strangers; and as a letter-bearer, skilled and speedy in travel, both at home and overseas. In combination with his performative gifts, these skills were to distinguish Kemp for the remainder of his career.

The English forces were received with magnificent celebrations as they travelled Northwards, via inland waterways, to Rotterdam, Delft and The Hague. In Delft, Leicester reported that the Dutch staged 'the greatest shows that ever I saw'.[18] We should remember that Leicester himself was something of an expert on such displays, having sponsored exceptionally magnificent shows in his time, most notably at Kenilworth in July 1574. Enormous sums had been spent on banquets and allegorical pageants by the bigwigs of Delft, and even larger ones on the troops' 'solemn entry in the Hague', 'where [Leicester] determined to keep his standing court'.[19] The next staging post, with yet more civic splendour, was the University city of Leiden. Here, however, Leicester made the appalling blunder of accepting 'the rule and government general' of the United Provinces, including the title of 'Excellency', something the Queen had explicitly forbidden him to do — he was supposed always to be designated as her current deputy, not as an autonomous 'governor', and certainly not as any kind of long-term leader of what she saw as rebel provinces. In the Netherlands, too, Leicester's acceptance of the Governorship soon proved a false move, for the youthful Prince Maurice of Nassau, son of William of Orange, was rapidly emerging as both a genuinely popular leader and an energetic and effective combatant.

It took some time for news of the Queen's severe displeasure to arrive.[20] Meanwhile, Leicester's retinue's slow progress proceeded to Utrecht, where the English Garter Feast — for St George's Day, 23 April 1586 — was celebrated with yet more magnificent banqueting and pageantry, this time paid for and performed by the English. This was the first major opportunity for the English players and musicians to show off their considerable talents.

Meanwhile, the light-footed Kemp had travelled back to England, where he delivered letters, returning to the Netherlands in time to take a leading role in the English Garter Feast. On 1 January 1585/86 Leicester gave 'William Kempe the player' thirteen shillings for his contribution to what was evidently a merry New Year's day (New Style), in the course of which Leicester played many games of cards — 'doble hand Lodam'[21] — with Prince Maurice and the Earl of Essex, and lost thirty shillings. Later that same day Leicester gave 'William Kempe the player' twenty shillings 'for his charges into England'.

Kemp was entrusted with a budget of letters home from Leicester, Essex, Sidney and probably other English noblemen currently resident in the Netherlands. However, some of these were mis-delivered. We learn of this from an often-cited letter from Philip Sidney to Sir Francis Walsingham dated 24 March 1586, according to which he had sent a letter to Walsingham, his father-in-law:

> [...] by Will my lord of lester jesting plaier, enclosed in a letter to my wyfe. and I never had answer thereof, it contained something to[22] my Lord of lester. and council *that* som wai might be taken to stai my ladi there. I since dyvers tymes have writ to know whether y<ow> had received them. but yow never answered me *that* point. I since fynd *that* the knave deliverd the letters to my ladi of lester. but whether she sent them yow or no I know \not/ but earnestly desire to do.[23]

Since the letters that Sidney entrusted to 'Will' have not survived, it is hard to work out exactly what happened. Perhaps the endorsement on the outside of Sidney's letter to his wife used the formula 'To my Lady', though as the wife of a knight she was of course 'Lady Sidney'. In haste, or for some other reason, such as poor reading skills, Kemp may have construed this as a direction 'To my Lady [Leicester]'. The incident is worth recording because one of Kemp's most celebrated roles in a play by Shakespeare — as Peter, in *Romeo and* Juliet — was to be as a semi-literate letter-bearer — a mistake that plays a key role in the plot.

As well as delivering letters, Kemp's New Year trip to England probably required him to assemble additional performers, costumes and props for the forthcoming St George's Day feast in Utrecht. Kemp was almost certainly the athletic star turn of this show, which was notable enough to be chronicled by John Stow. It entailed 'dancing, vaulting, and tumbling, with the forces of Hercules, which gave great delight to the strangers, for they had not seen it before'.[24] The chosen theme was a narrative familiar to all present, whether English or Continental. It could be enacted visually, with much physical action and few words, showcasing the exceptionally fit Kemp who surely brought athleticism, broad comedy and physical inventiveness to the performance of the Seven Labours of Hercules.

There had been an earlier episode in which Kemp distinguished himself in the eyes of at least one foreign spectator. Probably many more were present. He was given the substantial reward of five shillings 'after his leaping into a ditch before your Ex[cellency] & the Prince Elector as you [i.e. Leicester] went a walking at Amersfoord'.[25] The 'Prince Elector' was the Protestant Archbishop of Cologne, who had fled to the Netherlands in 1583. When transcribing this item into his master's household accounts Leicester's secretary may have misunderstood the precise nature of Kemp's spectacular feat. I strongly suspect that it entailed leaping 'over a dyke', rather than 'into a ditch'. This seems especially plausible given Kemp's more fully documented stunt in 1599 when, reaching the end of his dancing progress from London, he leapt clean over the churchyard wall of St John's, Maddermarket, in Norwich.[26]

Kemp saw which way the wind was blowing for Leicester's extravagant mission. He abandoned the Earl's retinue soon after those notable St George's Day performances in the Netherlands. In a sequence that was to recur throughout his career, he decided to build on recent personal success by travelling and performing semi-independently, rather than as part of a regular and full-size playing company. Returning to London later in May, he soon joined the entourage of the Danish ambassador, Henrik Ramel, travelling to Denmark with five 'instrumentalists and tumblers', who performed for the Danish Court for a period of three months. What may have been Kemp's last journey abroad, in 1600–01, was also the most ambitious, and ultimately the least successful, in so far as he had many misadventures on the way home, limping back penniless after his return journey across the Alps.[27]

Early nineteenth-century Shakespeare scholars speculated that Kemp had quarrelled with fellow members of the Lord Chamberlain's Men, and that this was what led to his 'going solo' in 1599. However, there is no evidence to support this. In the very knowing Cambridge play *The Return from Parnassus* Burbage is depicted as a close friend and colleague of Kemp's,[28] but the evidence should, I think, be read to the contrary. The fact that Kemp continued as a member of the Lord Chamberlain's Men for so long a period as five or six years indicates that this company made sufficiently resourceful and congenial use of his talents for him to be content to work with them for a longer continuous period than he appears to have done with any other company. The Chamberlain's Men's plays, and especially those written by Shakespeare, incorporated excellent roles for Kemp — roles which were designed to showcase his distinctive gifts while minimizing his limitations. Some also reflect his competitive relationships with Continental performers, which I shall examine in the next section.

iii. Competing with Continentals: Kemp on the English Stage

Testimony to Kemp's reputation as a performer who could hold his own either among, or in comparison with, Continental entertainers, can be encountered both in non-dramatic texts and in plays. One of the earliest non-dramatic accounts occurs in the anti-Marprelate treatise *An Almond for a Parrat*, printed early in 1590. Its author was almost certainly Thomas Nashe, writing here under the satirical pseudonym of 'Cutbert Curry-Knave'.[29] *An Almond* is dedicated 'TO THAT MOST Comicall, and conceited Cavaleire Monsieur du Kempe' — a Frenchified form of nomenclature that is typical of Kemp's many Continental aliases. As early as November 1585 a man called Thomas Doyley, in a letter to the Earl of Leicester, alluded to him as 'Don Gulihelmo Kempino'.[30] This was presumably one of the names he assumed when performing in the Netherlands, where the Spanish title 'Don' would presumably function as mockery of the enemy.

In the epistle prefaced to *An Almond*, Cutbert/Nashe describes an encounter that he claims to have had with an Italian Harlequin in Bergamo — a city celebrated for its fools — who had apparently heard much about the Kemp's artistry:

> [...] comming from Venice the last Summer, and taking Bergamo in my waye homeward to England, it was my happe, sojourning there some foure or five dayes, to light in felowship with that famous Francatrip'[31] Harlicken, who, perceiving me to bee an English man by my habit and speech, asked me many particulars of the order and maner of our playes, which he termed by the name of representations: amongst other talke he enquired of me if I knew any such Parabolano[32] here in London as Signior Chiarlatino Kempino. Very well, (quoth I,) and have beene oft in his company.[33]

The title 'Signior Chiarlatino Kempino' identifies Kemp as an honorary member of the traditional cast of the *commedia dell'arte*. The *ciarlatino* was the mountebank, or quick-patter salesman, who was one of the *commedia*'s leading and most resourceful members.[34] Although the encounter in Bergamo is no doubt an elaborate comic fiction, it suggests that Nashe — or whoever wrote *An Almond for a Parrat* — viewed Kemp as a performer who could be fancifully imagined as having something to teach to northern Italian companies.

A more explicit and extended fictionalization both of Kemp and of his familiarity with the *commedia dell'arte* occurs much later, in a play belonging to 1607. This is *The Travels of the Three English Brothers*, a highly topical travelogue written jointly by John Day, William Rowley and George Wilkins.[35] Their triple collaboration probably reflected pressure to get the play written as quickly as possible. The much travelled soldier of fortune Sir Thomas Shirley had returned to England in the spring of 1606, after the most prolonged and unfortunate of his five voyages to what we now call the Middle East, some of which had even taken him as far as Russia.[36] In this final voyage, starting from Gibraltar, Shirley's small fleet of three ships sailed in slow stages Eastwards across the Mediterranean to the island of Kea, 'the most north-westerly of the Cyclades Islands, and Ottoman territory'.[37] Together with two other officers, Shirley was captured by the Ottomans, while the remainder of the crew escaped and almost immediately 'without their captain [...] captured a rich Venetian galleon'.[38] Meanwhile Thomas Shirley and his companions were imprisoned by the Turks first in Negroponte (Euboea), and later in Constantinople. The grim conditions of Shirley's imprisonment, chained day and night to a captured slave, were considerably improved in April 1604 when a draft of money arrived from his father and namesake. In the winter of 1605/06 Shirley was finally released, after thirty-three months of imprisonment, and made a deliberately leisurely journey back to England, accumulating topographical notes and observations. His eventual return, in December 1606, was received as a piece of sensational news, provoking great excitement and curiosity. Shirley immediately set about to compose a 'Discours of the Turkes' — savagely hostile to his captors — which also included a detailed description of his year-long return journey from Constantinople to London.[39] Shirley's reports were immediately drawn on by Anthony Nixon in his eulogistic prose account of *The Three English Brothers* (1607). This, in turn, was speedily drawn on by Day, Rowley and Wilkins for their play, both performed and printed in the summer of 1607.

That is where Kemp comes in. As Anthony Parr and H. Neville Davies have observed, *The Travels of the Three English Brothers*, inevitably episodic, given its three narrative strands, nevertheless has definite symmetry built into its design. It is constructed around a mid-point, the central episode being 'sandwiched between the Zariph scenes, which in turn are enclosed by episodes featuring Thomas Sherley's adventures and his brother Robert's attempts to ransom him'.[40] This central scene is located in Venice. It opens with the middle brother, Sir Anthony Shirley, sending and receiving letters. An unnamed gentleman arrives from England, with 'Nothing of import' to deliver. Next comes the Shylock-like Jew Zariph, who presses Sir Anthony hard for payment for a splendidly rich jewel which the latter plans to give to the 'Sophy' — that is, the Shah of Persia. Things then suddenly liven up, with news of the imminent arrival of 'an Englishman', who 'calls himself Kemp'. Immediately after the announcement comes the stage direction: 'Enter WILL KEMP and a boy.' Anthony Shirley addresses him as 'honest Will' and 'Jesting Will' — forms of address that identify him both as a welcome visitor, and as a man with whom Sir Anthony is already acquainted. This lends some support to the theory that Kemp was related to the Shirley brothers, whose mother was the well-born Anne Kempe, from Ollantighe, in Kent. But it may be simply that Sir Anthony had seen Kemp perform, and was already one of his fans.

Next, Sir Anthony Shirley inquires after the welfare of Kemp's fellow players — as ever, they are short of money — and 'any good new plays'. This discussion culminates in Kemp's account of the fraudulent play *England's Joy*. It was advertised for performance at the Swan on 6 November 1602 by one Richard Venner, who took a good deal of money in advance, and then attempted to flee when it became apparent that there was no play and no actors. It may seem odd that a well-known incident from 1602 should be retailed as amusing news in a play both composed and performed in 1607. However, the date fits very well with the period of Sir Anthony's residence in Venice, 'engaged as a spy for both the Spanish and Scots [... from] late 1601 until the end of 1604.'[41] Kemp returned from what was probably his last, as well as his most ambitious, Continental journey in September 1601. He

COMPETING WITH CONTINENTALS   229

may well have travelled from Rome to Venice earlier that year, and while in Venice could have received news-letters from his fellow actors back in England. The encounter represented in this scene is therefore plausible, and may even be based on a genuine incident.

Soon, 'a Harlequin and his wife' enter, and Shirley asks Kemp to 'play a part with them'. Tellingly, Kemp confesses that he is not very good at memorizing lines: 'I am somewhat hard of study, and like your honour; but if they will invent any extemporall merriment, I'll put out the small sack of wit I ha' left in venture with them.' A 'merriment', or 'mirth', was one of the terms used to describe the short, often partly improvised, comic entertainments also known as 'jigs'.[42] Sir Anthony reassures him, in a couplet that sums up Kemp's gifts:

> We neither look for scholarship nor art,
> But harmless mirth, for that's thy usual part.

Shirley then exits, leaving Kemp and the Harlequin to devise their joint entertainment. The latter keeps tumbling into pits dug by himself. Despite being designated as 'Harlequin', he chooses to play the role of the elderly, avaricious and jealous Pantaloon:

> *Harlequin.* Marry, sir, first we will have an old Pantaloon.
> *Kemp.* Some jealous coxcomb.
> *Harlequin.* Right, and that part I will play.
> *Kemp.* The jealous coxcomb?
> *Harlequin.* I ha'played that part ever since —
> *Kemp.* Your wife played the courtesan.
> *Harlequin.* True, and a great while afore.

The whole thrust of this proposed 'merriment', thanks to Kemp's relentless interjections, is towards the conclusive humiliation and cuckolding of the Harlequin. Kemp attempts to kiss the Harlequin's wife — and may have succeeded in doing so, depending on how the scene was performed. Digging yet another pit for himself, the Harlequin goes on to say:

> *Harlequin.* Then, sir, we must have an Amorado that must make me cornuto.
> *Kemp.* O for love sake, let me play that part.
> *Harlequin.* No, you must play my man's part, and keep my wife.
> *Kemp.* Right: and who so fit to make a man a cuckold as he that keeps his wife?

Next, the Harlequin freely confesses to being 'a true Italian', who 'can be jealous for nothing', thus setting up the stereotypical comic scenario in which a husband already subject to unreasonable jealousy is deliberately inflamed to even greater jealousy. He proposes that a Magnifico must be included 'that must take up the matter between me and my wife'. What the Harlequin presumably means to suggest is that a high-ranking Magnifico will arbitrate between the Harlequin and his (possibly adulterous) wife. However, as Parr points out, 'taking up the matter' between the Harlequin and his wife could also denote lifting up the latter's skirts — just the kind of saucy innuendo that was characteristic of English clowns.

The scene concludes with a dispute over the order in which the characters leave the stage. Despite the latter's protestations, Kemp compels the Harlequin to exit first, since 'In our country 'tis the custom of the master to go in before his wife, and the man to follow the master.' This ensures that the Harlequin leaves Kemp in triumphant possession of his (silent) 'wife'. He has efficiently despatched the Harlequin to 'Cuckolds-haven: Saint Luke be your speed'. St Luke was regarded as the patron saint of cuckolds, while 'Cuckolds Haven' was a notorious bend in the Thames three miles East of St Paul's that was marked with an upright pole adorned with horns.

What we have here is a rather brutal contest between the traditional performances of the Italian *commedia dell'arte* — whose treatment here is of course a travesty — and the freer, coarser, largely extempore performances of English fools. Though Kemp has confessed to being 'hard of study', his natural wit is supple and opportunistic. Through swift interruptions and improvisations he finally subjects the supposedly native-born Venetian performer to humiliating defeat: Kemp gains full possession of the girl. But perhaps even more importantly, he has compelled the Harlequin to leave the stage, so that Kemp and two boy performers — Kemp's boy was probably the player on tabor and pipe who was his usual accompanist — can command the full attention of the audience with their singing and dancing.

If — as I believe — Kemp was still alive and active in 1607, he may have appeared in person in *Travels*, playing the part of 'himself', as he was always apt to do.[43] The play was performed by Queen Anne's Men both at the Curtain and the Red Bull. By this date the Queen's Men had absorbed Worcester's Men, a company to which Kemp undoubtedly belonged in 1602–03.[44] The appearance of such a celebrated performer in a play of intense topical interest would be sure to have attracted large audiences, helping to account for the play's manifest popularity. I have discussed *Travels* at this point because it offers the simplest and most graphic illustration of Kemp's notorious success in 'competing with Continentals'. It may also relate to a genuine encounter between Kemp and a Harlequin in Venice in 1601.

But there is a much earlier, and surely far better, comedy in which Kemp had already been portrayed as engaging in such competition. Shakespeare's *Love's Labour's Lost* — probably first composed in 1594 — provides an exceptionally rich array of comic characters, as well as complex thematic, topical and linguistic interest, and this particular aspect has not been exhaustively discussed.

There is good reason to suppose that Kemp was the original performer of the rustic clown 'Costard'. The name associates him with a common breed of apple, as well as being a comic term for the human head. Admittedly, the case for Kemp's participation in *Love's Labour's Lost* is not quite so conclusive as it is for his appearance as 'Peter' in *Romeo and Juliet*, where a stage direction '*Enter Will Kemp*' appears as cue for one of Peter's entrances,[45] but it is strong, and essentially persuasive.[46] A broad connexion with Kemp is Costard's employment as a letter-bearer, and an incompetent one at that. This parallels both the real-life Will Kemp (see above) and Kemp's fictional role as Peter in *Romeo and Juliet*, in which he is unable to deliver Lord Capulet's party invitations because he can't decipher the list of names. In *Love's Labour's Lost*, Costard is entrusted with a love letter from Berowne to Rosaline and also one from Armado to Jaquenetta, but predictably mixes them up.

A further reason for identifying Costard as a 'Kemp' role is his style of dialogue.

COMPETING WITH CONTINENTALS   231

He has a habit of relentless interruption with a strong resemblance to the passages I have quoted from the 1607 *Travels*. This is exemplified in Costard's interruptions of the King of Navarre in the play's long opening scene. The King is reading aloud the verbose and pretentious letter written by the braggart Spaniard Don Armado:

> *King.* [...] There did I see that low-spirited swain, that base minnow of thy mirth–
> *Costard.* Me?
> *King.* That unlettered small-knowing soul —
> *Costard.* Me?
> *King.* That shallow vassal —
> *Costard.* Still me?
> *King.* Which, as I remember, hight Costard —
> *Costard.* O, me![47]

These comical interruptions are analogous to those made by 'Kemp' in the 'Harlequin' scene discussed above. They are notably monosyllabic, and would pose little challenge to a performer who was seen, as above, as being 'hard of study', that is, bad at memorizing scripted lines. Costard's role in *Love's Labour's Lost* is fairly extensive, but many of his speeches, especially in passages of dialogue, are very brief.

Costard's speech at the close of the long opening scene of *Love's Labour's Lost* may, I suggest, have originally preceded a solo routine which retained Kemp/Costard on stage for a while in sole command of the audience's attention — the position that enabled him to perform best. On the evidence of Don Armado's long letter, Costard has been found guilty of adultery with the rustic wench Jaquenetta, and is supposed to be handed over for a week's punitive detention under the keepership of Armado — who is, however, absent. The King and two of his companions evidently exit at line 290, leaving the playful Berowne to 'see him deliver'd o'er' to his keeper. Berowne's closing words to Costard convey both Berowne's impatience and Costard's reluctance: 'Sirrah, come on' (*LLL* 1. 2. 294). In early performances, Costard/Kemp may have remained on stage for a few minutes more after Berowne has left to join his fellow courtiers. Addressing Berowne directly, Costard shamelessly acknowledges his sin — or, as he quibblingly defines it, his sexual triumph:

> I suffer for the truth, sir, for true it is, I was taken with Jaquenetta,
> and Jaquenetta is a true girl. (*LLL* 1. 2. 295–96)

Here, I suspect, Berowne should exit, leaving Costard/Kemp to delight the audience with his cheerful indifference to everyone else's disapproval. Like 'Kemp' in *The Travels*, he is sexually competitive, and views seducing a country girl as a pleasing triumph. Only twelve more words are scripted for Costard, but they appear to be a cue for a song and/or some comic business:

> Affliction may one day smile again, and, till then, sit thee down, sorrow.
> (*LLL* 1.2.298–99)

'Affliction' is presumably a malapropism for 'affection', while the phrase 'sit thee down, sorrow' is a slightly adapted quotation from an elegiac poem by Nicholas Breton. The words 'Sorrow, come sit thee downe' open *An Epitaph on the death of a*

232   KATHERINE DUNCAN-JONES

noble Gentleman, a poem in poulter's measure included in Nicholas Breton's *Brittons Bowre of Delights* (1591). No musical adaptation of this appears to have survived, but it is possible that a song based on the poem once existed. The subject of Breton's elegy appears to have been a favourite courtier, mourned by the Queen herself:

> Me thinks I see a Queene come covered with a vaile,
> The Court all stricken in a dumpe, the Ladies weepe and waile.

The phrase 'sit thee down, sorrow' is echoed by Berowne at the beginning of IV. 3, yet he seems to know it only by repute. This confirms my suspicion that in I. I. Berowne should exit immediately after Costard's line 'Jaquenetta is a true girl', leaving Costard/Kemp to perform some memorably comic business, of which Berowne's comment at IV. 3 is a pleasing reminder:

> Well, set thee down, sorrow, for so they say the fool said, and so say I, and I
> the fool. (*LLL* IV. 3. 3–5)

It seems that Berowne did not hear precisely what 'the fool said', but has gathered that the fool's delivery of the phrase to the audience was extremely memorable. Further support for the notion that Berowne should exit before Costard's last script-ed line in I. I — 'Affliction [...] sorrow' — is provided by the Folio text, in which the speech is followed by the stage-direction '*Exit*', which suggests that Costard is finally alone on stage at the scene's close. In tune with his cheerful refusal to express shame, rather than pride, about his seduction of Jaquenetta, Costard/Kemp may have performed some merry capers which entailed singing, 'sitting down' in mock-sorrow, and suddenly leaping up again with joy.

Though he is supposedly the prisoner of Don Armado, assisted by Constable Dull, Costard is once again left alone on stage at the end of IV. I. This is the scene in which he gives the Princess Don Armado's letter addressed to Jaquenetta, instead of Berowne's letter addressed to Rosaline. Armado's rhetoric, by turns ridiculously inflated and tediously pedantic, provides the Princess, her ladies, and her faithful attendant Lord Boyet, with richly comic entertainment. Like most of Act IV, the scene is leisurely and playful. Gradually, however, as in Act I Scene I, all the courtiers exit, leaving Costard free once again to seize command of the theatre audience. His nine-line speech is mostly composed of lumpish rhyming couplets. Indeed, so lumpish are they that I am tempted to wonder whether they could be the composition of Will Kemp rather than of Will Shakespeare. However, their drift is clear: Costard delightedly triumphs first over the silky-smooth Boyet, the Princess's faithful attendant lord, whom he calls 'a most simple clown', and then over the swaggeringly absurd Don Adriano de Armado, whose desperate attempts at courtship and courtiership are so laughably ill-judged. Thirdly and finally, Costard ridicules Armado's diminutive boy page, Moth:

> And his page o'th'other side, that handful of wit!
> Ah, heavens, it is a most pathetical nit!

As reinforced in performance by cruel mimicry of the three characters satirized, Costard/Kemp's solo performance once again establishes him as the paramount comic performer amid an unusually large array of comic characters.

COMPETING WITH CONTINENTALS   233

It is with 'the Braggart' Armado that Costard/Kemp most blatantly and explicitly 'competes'. 'Armado', it's perhaps worth mentioning, was a common Elizabethan variant of the word for the Spanish fleet of 1588 now described as the 'Armada'. Shakespeare used the word in this form in *The Comedy of Errors* III. 2. 135, in the phrase 'whole Armadoes of carracks'. Don Adriano de Armado is both a swashbuckling Spanish nobleman and a one-man embodiment of the Spanish fleet. In setting up extreme opposition between a posturing Spaniard and a versatile rustic, whose name suggests that he is English, even though the play is notionally set in France, Shakespeare offers his most explicit depiction of 'competing with Continentals'.

He draws broadly on an earlier comedy, by Robert Wilson, *The Three Lords and Three Ladies of London* (printed 1590) — a play that modern scholars have surprisingly often conflated with Wilson's earlier play *The Three Ladies of London* (printed 1584).[48] It is surprising how little the later play has been examined either in its historical context, as a lively example of post-Armada triumphalism, or in its literary context, as a play surely influential on *Love's Labour's Lost*. Wilson himself must have been known to Kemp, for he too was among the English performers who travelled to the Netherlands in the retinue of the Earl of Leicester in 1585–86, and, like Kemp, Wilson was sometimes employed as a letter-bearer between England and the Netherlands.

Like Shakespeare in *Love's Labour's Lost*, Wilson in this City drama plays games with numbers.[49] Three 'Lords of London', each accompanied by a page, compete with three 'Lordes of Spaine', likewise accompanied by pages. The Spanish lords' transparently symbolic names are Pride, Ambition and Tiranny, while their pages' names are Shame, Treachery and Terror. Conventional and extensive comic diversion is provided by the clown 'Simplicity', probably performed by Wilson himself, who, among much else, pays rich tribute to the lately dead Richard Tarlton and displays a picture of him. In clear contrast to the Spanish lords are three 'Lordes of Lincolne', whose names, Desire, Delight and Devotion, identify them as highly desirable suitors. The play reaches a climax with the impending arrival in London of those 'proud usurping Spanish tyrants', who seek to marry the London ladies. They are received, however, not with arms or overt hostility, but with lavish shows of festive entertainment that will take the wind out of their presumptuous sails. This is commanded by Lord Pollicie:

> Lord Pompe, let nothing that's magnificall,
> Or that may tend to *London*'s gracefull state
> Be unperform'd. As showes and solemne feastes,
> Watches in armour, triumphes, Cresset-lightes,
> Bonefieres, belles and peales of ordinance.
> And *pleasure*, see that plaies be published,
> Mai-games and maskes, with mirth and minstrelsie,
> Pageants and school-feastes, beares, and puppit plaies [...]
> That *John* the Spaniard wil in rage run mad,
> To see us bend like Oakes with his vain breath[50]

Great English and Spanish pomps and pageants ensue, with massed displays of

234   KATHERINE DUNCAN-JONES

weapons, shields and banners. With symbolism that is more sexual than heraldic, the 'English Boies' — pages to the Lords of London — cause the Spanish pages to 'put downe the tops' of their lances. Predictably, the Spanish lords are finally dismissed as deceptive and malign:

> Spanish *Ambition*, Honor would be cal'd,
> And *Trecherie*, his page, term'd *Action*.
> Their *Tyranny* was cleped Government,
> *Terror*, his page, was (falsly) nam'd Regard,
> But God above had given them their reward.

In *Love's Labour's Lost*, written at least six years, and possibly more, after the so-called 'defeat' of the Spanish Armada, there is nothing so crudely jingoistic.[51] Nevertheless, it is evident from the opening scene, in which the King receives and then reads out 'A letter from the magnificent Armado' (I. I. 181), that the Spaniard is laughably over-ambitious. He appears to take himself entirely seriously, while providing everyone else with welcome opportunities for teasing and merriment. Don Adriano de Armado — even the name seems inflated to English ears — belongs broadly to the Plautine type of *miles gloriosus*, or braggart soldier. He lays claim to great expertise both in fighting and in wooing. (I. 2. 72). but he foreshadows the great Don Quixote, in so far as the object of his blind devotion is a low-born country wench. We see him, however, not in the company of Jaquenetta, but in that of his diminutive page, Moth, who runs rings round him while pretending to teach him how to win his beloved's love — most notably in III. I.

Ridiculous though he is, however, Armado is acknowledged by the King of Navarre as a genuine courtier and nobleman. It is Armado who brings news to the lower-rank characters that the King wishes to delight the Princess of France 'at her pavilion [...] with some delightful ostentation, or show, or pageant or antic, or firework' — a proposal immediately fleshed out by the Pedant Holofernes as a theatrical parade of the Nine Worthies (*LLL* v. I. 80–115). Having been physically absent in Act IV — though represented *in absentia* by a ridiculous love-letter — Armado moves into a position of considerable prominence and authority in the closing act. Costard/Kemp has already had two major opportunities to capture audience attention, one at the end of I. I, the other at the end of IV. I.

The close of a scene, or, even more so, the close of a complete play, was a traditional space into which improvised 'merriment' could be inserted. But this comedy, as its title forewarns us, ends differently. After news of the death of the King of France, the betrothals agreed by the four young couples are rendered provisional. Their unions will be completed only on condition that the young noblemen spend a full year studying and doing penance for their excessive frivolity, in breach of the solemn oath they took at the beginning of the play. As the Princess and her ladies prepare to depart, and amid a farcical showdown for possession of Jaquenetta between Armado (as Hector of Troy) and Costard (as Pompey the Great), the messenger Marcade arrives with news of the Princess's father's death.

As the Princess and her ladies prepare to depart, and an apparent closing line is spoken by Berowne — 'That's too long for a play'— a fifth nobleman, Armado, re-appears, and it is he who presides over the play's bittersweet afterpiece. The four

Navarrois noblemen — especially Berowne — are doubtful about whether they can succeed in performing the penances imposed on them, Armado, in contrast, is confidently committed to his own beloved:

> I am a votary; I have vowed to Jaquenetta to hold the plough for her for her sweet love three years.

Depending on how this speech is delivered, it can come across either as ridiculous — after all, Jaquenetta is apparently already pregnant by Costard, so Armado, when he marries her, will be a cuckold — or else as distinctly and surprisingly impressive. After all, Armado's pledge of three years' service trumps the single year's penance imposed on the King of Navarre and his companions. Here, again, we may see Don Armado as foreshadowing Don Quixote. He is a nobleman whose sense of chivalric purpose can be viewed simultaneously as heroic and absurd.

Armado next presides over the two 'sides', of 'Hiems, winter', and 'Ver, the spring', on whose behalf two songs are performed in the reverse order: spring first, then winter. In the 1598 Quarto text Armado's closing reflection both on the songs and on the play's close are printed in extra-large type:

The words of Mercury are harsh after the songs of Apollo.

In the Folio text, Armado delivers a further line, 'You that way, we this way', which perhaps distinguishes the ladies who are travelling back to France from the characters who will remain in Navarre.

Embedded within Shakespeare's complex and sophisticated comedy we can trace the outline of a 'jig' plot, in which the clown succeeds in stealing a young woman, or wife, from her possessive husband or lover. That is the scenario invoked in the Kemp/Harlequin scene in *The Travels of the Three English Brothers*. But by placing Armado, rather than Costard, centre stage at the close, Shakespeare challenges the 'jig' formula, and apparently reinforces the status of Armado. There has been keen competition between Costard and Armado both for sexual conquest and for theatrical dominance. With characteristic boldness and originality, Shakespeare implies that the winner here is the Spaniard. Kemp, it seems, was not always seen as victorious when he 'competed with Continentals'.

Bibliography

ADAMS, SIMON, ed., *Household Accounts and Disbursement Books of Robert, Earl of Leicester*, Camden Society Fifth Series, vol. VI (Cambridge: Cambridge University Press, 1995)

ANON, *The Life of Long Meg of Westminster* (London: John Beale for Robert Bird, 1635)

ANON, *Pappe with an hatchet* (London: Imprinted by Thomas Orwin, 1589)

ARMIN, ROBERT, *Foole upon Foole* (London: E. Allde for William Ferbrand, 1600)

—— *Foole upon Foole* (London: for William Ferebrand, 1605)

BUTLER, MARTIN, 'Kemp, William (*d.* in or after 1610?)', *Oxford Dictionary of National Biography*, Oxford University Press, 2004; online edn, Jan 2011 <http://www.oxforddnb.com/view/article/15334> [accessed January 2014]

Calendar of state papers, foreign series, of the reign of Elizabeth: preserved in the Public Record Office, vol. XX [September 1585–May 1586], ed. by Sophie Crawford Lomas (London: His Majesty's Stationery Office, 1921)

Camden Miscellany XVI, CS 3rd Series, 52 (1936), item 2, pp. i–ix, 1–45

CHAMBERS, EDMUND K., *The Elizabethan Stage*, 4 vols (Oxford: Oxford University Press, 1923)

DAVIES, DAVID WILLIAM, *Elizabethans Errant* (Ithaca, NY: Cornell University Press, 1967)

DUGDALE, GILBERT, *A True Discourse of the practices of Elizabeth Caldwell* (London: By James Roberts for John Busbie, 1604)

DUNCAN-JONES, KATHERINE, 'MS Rawl. Poet 185: Richard Tarlton and Edmund Spenser's "Pleasant Willy"', *The Bodleian Library Record*, 20.1–2 (2007), 76–101

—— 'The Life, Death and Afterlife of Richard Tarlton', *Review of English Studies, n.s.*, 65.286 (2013), 18–32

—— 'Retired from the scene: did William Kemp live on as "Lady Hunsdon's Man?"', *Times Literary Supplement*, 13 August 2010, pp. 13–15

FEATHER, JOHN P., 'Introduction', in *Works of Robert Armin*, vol. II [*The Italian Taylor*] (New York and London: Johnson Reprint Corporation, 1972), s.p.

FLORIO, JOHN, *Queen Anna's new world of words, or dictionarie of the Italian and English tongues* (London: Melch. Bradwood [and William Stansby], for Edw. Blount and William Barret, 1611)

KEMP, WILLIAM, *Kemps Nine Daies Wonder* (London: Printed by E. Allde for Nicholas Ling, 1600)

KUIN, ROGER, ed., *The Correspondence of Sir Philip Sidney*, 2 vols (Oxford: Oxford University Press, 2012)

LEISHMAN, JAMES B., ed., *The Three Parnassus Plays (1598–1601)* (London: Ivor Nicholson & Watson, 1949)

LIMON, JERZY, *Gentlemen of a Company: English Players in Central and Eastern Europe, 1590–1660* (Cambridge: Cambridge University Press, 1985)

MCMILLIN, SCOTT, and SALLY-BETH MACLEAN, *The Queen's Men and their Plays* (Cambridge: Cambridge University Press, 1998)

NASHE, THOMAS, *Works*, ed. by R. B. McKerrow, with corrections by F. P. Wilson, 5 vols (Basil Blackwell: Oxford, 1966)

RAISWELL, RICHARD, 'Sherley, Sir Thomas (1564–1633/4)', *Oxford Dictionary of National Biography*, Oxford University Press, 2004 <http://www.oxforddnb.com/view/article/25436> [accessed January 2014]

SHAKESPEARE, WILLIAM, *Romeo and Juliet*, ed. by Rene Weis (Bloomsbury: Arden Shakespeare, 2012)

—— *Love's Labour's Lost*, ed. by Henry R. Woudhuysen (Bloomsbury: Arden Shakespeare, 1998)

SPEVACK, MARVIN, *Complete and Systematic Concordance to the Works of Shakespeare* (Hildesheim: Georg Olms, 1968–75)

STRONG, ROY, and JAN ADRIANUS VAN DORSTEN, *Leicester's Triumph: An Account of his Progresses in the Low Countries in 1585–86* (Leiden: Leiden University Press; London: Oxford University Press, for the Sir Thomas Browne Institute, 1964)

Three Renaissance Travel Plays, ed. by Anthony Parr (Manchester: Manchester University Press; New York: St. Martin's Press, 1995)

WILES, DAVID, *Shakespeare's Clown: Actor and Text in the Elizabethan Playhouse* (Cambridge: Cambridge University Press, 1987)

WILSON, ROBERT, *The Three Ladies of London* (London: Roger Ward, 1584)

—— *The Pleasant and stately Morall, of the three Lordes and three Ladies of London* (London: R. Ihones, 1590)

—— *A right excellent and famous comedy called the three ladies of London* (London: printed by John Danter, 1592)

Notes to Chapter 10

1. Scott McMillin and Sally-Beth Maclean, *The Queen's Men and their Plays* (Cambridge: Cambridge University Press, 1998), pp. 24–31.
2. Towne received a royal pardon on 15 August 1587.This example of the Queen's support for the company under her nominal patronage has not been much discussed. Cf. Katherine Duncan-Jones, 'MS Rawl. Poet 185: Richard Tarlton and Edmund Spenser's "Pleasant Willy"', *The Bodleian Library Record*, 20.1–2 (2007), 76–101 (p. 88).
3. McMillin and Maclean, *The Queen's Men*, p. 161, p. 165.
4. David Wiles, *Shakespeare's Clown: Actor and Text in the Elizabethan Playhouse* (Cambridge: Cambridge University Press, 1987), p. 151.
5. For a more detailed discussion of Tarlton's career and reputation, see Katherine Duncan-Jones, 'The Life, Death and Afterlife of Richard Tarlton', *Review of English Studies, n.s.*, 65.286 (2013), 18–32.
6. Figures from Spevack Concordance: Marvin Spevack, *Complete and Systematic Concordance to the Works of Shakespeare* (Hildesheim: Georg Olms, 1968–75).
7. Jerzy Limon, *Gentlemen of a Company: English Players in Central and Eastern Europe, 1590–1660* (Cambridge: Cambridge University Press, 1985), p. 6 and *passim*.
8. McMillin and Maclean, *The Queen's Men*, pp. 175–78.
9. For detailed accounts of Kemp's whole career, see Wiles, *Shakespeare's Clown*, and Martin Butler, 'Kemp, William (*d*. in or after 1610?)', *Oxford Dictionary of National Biography*, Oxford University Press, 2004; online edn, Jan 2011 <http://www.oxforddnb.com/view/article/15334> [accessed January 2014].
10. Wag: cf. *OED* 'wag' *n*. 1 A mischievous boy.
11. i.e. 'do you believe yourself to be Charlemagne?'
12. See Armin's commendatory epistle to the widowed Lady Chandos appended to Gilbert Dugdale, *A True Discourse of the practices of Elizabeth Caldwell* (London: By James Roberts for John Busbie, 1604).
13. Anon, *Pappe with an hatchet* (London: Imprinted by Thomas Orwin, 1589), sig. E1ᵛ.
14. See the title pages of Robert Armin, *Foole upon Foole* (London: E. Allde for William Ferbrand, 1600) and *Foole upon Foole* (London: E. Allde for William Ferbrand, 1605).
15. See John P. Feather, 'Introduction', in *Works of Robert Armin*, vol. ii [*The Italian Taylor*] (New York and London: Johnson Reprint Corporation, 1972), s.p.
16. See 'Appendix II', in *Household Accounts and Disbursement Books of Robert, Earl of Leicester*, ed. by Simon Adams, Camden Fifth Series, vol. vi (Cambridge: Cambridge University Press, 1995), p. 388.
17. Roy Strong and Jan Adrianus van Dorsten, *Leicester's Triumph: An Account of his Progresses in the Low Countries in 1585–86* (Leiden: Leiden University Press; London: Oxford University Press, for the Sir Thomas Browne Institute, 1964), p. 32.
18. Strong, van Dorsten, *Leicester's Triumph*, p. 40.
19. Strong, van Dorsten, *Leicester's Triumph*, p. 43.
20. Strong, van Dorsten, *Leicester's Triumph*, pp. 56–63.
21. An ancestor of the card game now known as 'Hearts'; the records are in Adams, *Household Accounts*, p. 371.
22. Cf. *OED* 'to' *preposition* 22, in respect of, concerning.
23. Slightly adapted from text in *The Correspondence of Sir Philip Sidney*, ed. by Roger Kuin, 2 vols (Oxford: Oxford University Press, 2012), ii, 1214. Oddly, Kuin identifies 'Will' as the player William Johnson. Though a member of Leicester's Men, and later of the Queen's Men, William Johnson is nowhere singled out for comic gifts.
24. From John Stow, *Chronicle* 717, quoted in Edmund K. Chambers, *The Elizabethan Stage*, 4 vols (Oxford: Oxford University Press, 1923), ii, 90.
25. Adams, *Household Accounts*, p. 374. The record is of a repayment of the sum to Leicester's steward; but the leap itself had taken place during a brief visit to Amersfoort by Leicester from 18 to 20 April, which makes it clear that Kemp had returned from England in ample time for the Garter Feast.

238   KATHERINE DUNCAN-JONES

26. William Kemp, *Kemps Nine Daies Wonder* (London: Printed by E. Allde for Nicholas Ling, 1600), sig. D1^r.
27. For a fuller account, and bibliography, see Butler, 'Kemp, William'.
28. *The Three Parnassus Plays (1598–1601)*, ed. by James B. Leishman (London: Ivor Nicholson & Watson, 1949), pp. 336–43.
29. This decidedly 'English' name was derived from the probably apocryphal account of the exploits of the splendidly pugnacious virago Long Meg of Westminster. Meg assumed the name of Cutbert Curry-Knave when, disguised as a man, she entered into a violent quarrel with a constable; cf. Anon, *The Life of Long Meg of Westminster* (London: John Beale for Robert Bird, 1635), p. 16.
30. *Calendar of state papers, foreign series, of the reign of Elizabeth: preserved in the Public Record Office*, vol. xx [September 1585–May 1586], ed. by Sophie Crawford Lomas (London: His Majesty's Stationery Office, 1921), pp. 162–63.
31. Francatrippe: cf. John Florio, *Queen Anna's new world of words, or dictionarie of the Italian and English tongues* (London: Melch. Bradwood [and William Stansby], for Edw. Blount and William Barret, 1611), 'Francatrippa, *a logger-head, a greasie scullion-like foolish fellow.*'
32. Cf. Florio, *Queen Anna's World of Words*: 'Parabolano [...]. *a Mountebank, a pratler, a babler*'; also the name of a character in Pietro Aretino's *Cortigiana*.
33. Thomas Nashe, *Works*, ed. by R. B. McKerrow, with corrections by F. P. Wilson, 5 vols (Basil Blackwell: Oxford, 1966), III, 342.
34. For further information about the *commedia*, see Chapter 9 (eds).
35. For a modern edition, see *Three Renaissance Travel Plays*, ed. by Anthony Parr (Manchester: Manchester University Press; New York: St. Martin's Press, 1995). Wilkins was soon to collaborate with Shakespeare in *Pericles*, another episodic play involving exotic travel.
36. For a full biography, see Richard Raiswell, 'Sherley, Sir Thomas (1564–1633/4)', *Oxford Dictionary of National Biography*, Oxford University Press, 2004 <http://www.oxforddnb.com/view/article/25436> [accessed January 2014]. See also David William Davies, *Elizabethans Errant* (Ithaca, NY: Cornell University Press, 1967), pp. 172–80.
37. Raiswell, 'Sherley, Sir Thomas'.
38. Ibid.
39. An edition of the text is to be found in *Camden Miscellany XVI*, CS 3rd Series, 52 (1936), item 2, pp. i–ix, 1–45.
40. *Three Renaissance Travel Plays*, p. 14.
41. Raiswell, 'Sherley, Sir Thomas'.
42. Cf. *OED* 'merriment' *n.* 2a, 'a brief, comic, dramatic entertainment'.
43. For evidence that Kemp may have lived until 1610/11, see Katherine Duncan-Jones, 'Retired from the scene: did William Kemp live on as "Lady Hunsdon's Man?" ', *Times Literary Supplement*, 13 August 2010, pp. 13–15.
44. See Martin Butler, 'Kemp, William'.
45. Cf. William Shakespeare, *Romeo and Juliet*, ed. by Rene Weis (Bloomsbury: Arden Shakespeare, 2012), IV. 5. 99.
46. For a discussion of the issue, see Shakespeare's *Love's Labour's Lost*, ed. by Henry R. Woudhuysen (Bloomsbury: Arden Shakespeare, 1998), pp. 4, 61.
47. Shakespeare, *Love's Labour's Lost*, I. 1. 239–46.
48. See, for instance, *Love's Labour's Lost*, 65n.: this note rightly alludes to the second printing of *The Three Ladies of London* (London: Iohn Danter, 1592), published in 1592, but no mention is made of the later, and, surely more relevant, *Three Lords and Three Ladies*, published in 1590.
49. For a detailed discussion of number-games in *Love's Labour's Lost*, see pp. 26–31 of the edition by Woudhuysen.
50. Robert Wilson, *The Pleasant and stately Morall, of the three Lordes and three Ladies of London* (London: printed by John Danter, 1592), sig. F2^v.
51. For a discussion of the play's possible date(s), see *Love's Labour's Lost*, pp. 59–61.

CHAPTER 11

❖

Gil Vicente, a Source for a Heritage Made of Scraps

José Camões

Centro de Estudos de Teatro, Universidade de Lisboa

When dealing with the history of Portuguese theatre, researchers usually have a preference for the sixteenth century. However, a mere glance at what is being studied and published easily shows that they all have a common theme, which can be summarized as 'Gil Vicente and the rest'.

Leaving aside the question of the birth of Portuguese theatre, an issue that has occupied the minds of some scholars for the last 150 years, the fact is that Gil Vicente is the most significant personality in early sixteenth-century Iberian drama. He wrote verse plays in Portuguese and Castilian, often using both languages in the same play, and covered an enormous range of themes and forms. His work has been regarded as a forerunner of the *auto sacramental* and the *comedia*, two of the main genres of Spanish Golden Age of theatre. But his accomplishments cannot be confined to writing plays. He was essentially a man of the theatre, involved in directing, rehearsing, finding ways to interact with the structure and acoustics of the venue, exploring or devising staging patterns, finding or designing costumes and props, and selecting or composing the music.

His *autos* (i.e., plays and theatrical entertainments) were not produced for the playhouse.[1] Christmas entertainments and other plays written to celebrate events in the liturgical calendar were usually performed in chapels, churches and monasteries, while those written to honour the births of royal children, their marriages, and royal entries were presented in the palace, either indoors, in chambers and great halls, or outside, in the gardens.

Taking advantage of the venues, the characteristics of the audience and the circumstances of the occasion, Gil Vicente exploited the coincidence between the venue and the space within the play, and at the same time brought the spectators into the action. He would often revert to this 'circumstantial theatre' throughout his career. However, a closer study of his work shows a gradual deviation from this standard over time. If in the earlier plays the characters stepped into the places where the audience was accustomed to assemble, sometimes speaking directly to a few chosen spectators and involving them in the action, in later plays a new understanding of theatrical experience allowed him to move on towards modernity and the Renaissance separation of performers and audience.

240   José Camões

A noticeable testimony to this transformation is the way that the circumstance that was the motive for the play's composition fades away as the themes and structures of the piece are developed. This phenomenon is especially visible in the *autos* composed for the celebrations of royal births and of Christmas, and becomes more obvious as the reign of D. Manuel is succeeded by that of D. João III.

The author himself was conscious of the need for change in his style and for a loftier rhetoric, as he states in the Prologue of *Dom Duardos*, addressing D. João III: 'Como quiera (excelente príncipe y rey muy poderoso) que las comedias, farsas y moralidades que he compuesto en servicio de la reina vuestra tía (cuanto em caso de amores), fueron figuras baxas, en las cuales no había conveniente retórica que pudiese satisfacer al delicado spíritu de vuestra alteza, conoscí que me cumplía meter más velas a mi pobre fusta. Y así con deseo de ganar su contentamiento hallé lo que en estremo deseaba, que fue Don Duardos y Flérida, que son tan altas figuras como su historia recuenta, con tan dulce retórica y escogido estilo, como se puede alcanzar en la humana inteligencia' [Since (excellent prince and most powerful king) the comedies, farces and morality plays I wrote in service of the Queen your aunt (in the case of love) were low figures, with no proper rhetoric that might satisfy the delicate spirit of your Highness, I realized that I should give more sail to my poor pinnace. And thus, wishing to gain your contentment, I found what I most wanted, Dom Duardos and Flérida, lofty figures, as their story tells, with as much sweet rhetoric and well-chosen style as human intelligence can achieve].

The fact that the author uses the word 'rhetoric' in this short text, associating it with his work, may not be due to chance, since at the time he already held the office of Master of Rhetoric of the Performances. Later, in 1531, after a violent earthquake, it may have been in that capacity that D. João III sent him to Santarém to persuade 'with his art' the friars who were alarming the population to refrain from their intolerant impulsiveness.

The Vicente *corpus* consists of fifty plays that have survived chiefly in the *Copilaçam de Todalas Obras*, a book which he himself did not complete, published in 1562 by his son and daughter, well after his death, and organized in five books: Works of Devotion (*Visitação, Pastoril Castelhano, Reis Magos, Sebila Cassandra, Fé, Quatro Tempos, Mofina Mendes, Pastoril Português, Feira, Alma, Barca do Inferno, Barca do Purgatório, Barca da Glória, História de Deos, Ressurreição de Cristo, Cananea, São Martinho*); Comedies (*Rubena, Viúvo, Devisa de Coimbra, Floresta de Enganos*); Tragicomedies (*Dom Duardos, Amadis de Gaula, Nau d'Amores, Frágua d'Amor, Exortação da Guerra, Templo d'Apolo, Cortes de Júpiter, Serra de Estrela, Inverno e Verão, Romagem dos Agravados*); Farces (*Quem tem farelos?, Índia, Fama, Velho da Horta, Fadas, Inês Pereira, Juiz da Beira, Ciganas, Almocreves, Clérigo da Beira, Lusitânia, Físicos*); and Minor Works, a book composed of assorted poems, notably a paraphrase of *Psalm L*, and his own epitaph.

This work put him in a high position in the table of intellectual value. This is evident in the testimonies of his contemporaries which always mention his literary and theatrical qualities, even allowing him authority in the use of the language.

In 1531, as part of the festivities to celebrate the birth of Prince Manuel, there was a performance of a comedy by Gil Vicente in Brussels, *Jubiléu de Amor* [Jubilee of Love], attended by the humanist André de Resende. In his account of the revels (*Genethliacon Principis Lusitani*, Bologne, 1533) he mentions the success of the *auto*, complimenting the author whom he places alongside the great names of Antiquity, while lamenting the fact that he does not use the Latin language.[2] The text of the humanist indicates the double quality of Gil Vicente as an author and an actor.

Gillo Vincentius Poeta comicus

Cunctorum hinc acta est magno comoedia plausu,
quam Lusitana Gillo auctor et actor in aula
egerat ante, dicax atque inter vera facetus,
Gillo, iocis levibus doctus perstringere mores.
Qui si non lingua componeret omnia vulgi,
et potius Latia, non Graecia docta Menandrum
ante suum ferret, net tam Romana theatra
Plautinosve sales lepidi vel scripta Terenti
iactarent. Tanto nam Gillo praeiret utrisque
quanto illi reliquis, inter qui pulpita rore
oblita Corycio digitum meruere faventem.

[Next a comedy was performed, with loud applause all round which its author and actor, Gil Vicente, had produced before the Portuguese Court, Gil, sharp and witty with the truth, clever at criticizing foibles with light humour.

If he had not composed in the vernacular, but rather in Latin, then learned Greece would not prefer its Menander to him, nor would Roman theatre boast so highly of Plautus' wit, or of the comedies by elegant Terence. For Gil would surpass both of them by as much as they surpass the others who earned the people's applause on stages smeared with Parnassian dew.]

Unfortunately this is one of the plays that has not survived time. Although we know it was printed — it is prohibited in the *Rol dos livros defesos* [List of prohibited books], of 1551 — no copy has yet been found.

The first Portuguese grammarian, Fernão de Oliveira, in Chapter XIV of his *Gramática* [Grammar] (1536) tries to establish norms for the use of the letter H, regretting that his usage differs from that of Gil Vicente: 'Mas, entre nós, eu não vejo alguma vogal aspirada senão nestas interjeições: *uha* e *aha* e nestoutras de riso: *há-há*, *hé*, ainda que não me parece bom riso português, posto que assim o escreva Gil Vicente nos seus *Autos*' [But among us I do not see any aspirated vowel apart from these exclamations: *uha* and *aha* and these others for laughter *ha*, *ha*, *he*, even though they do not seem to me good Portuguese laughter, in spite of being written in this fashion by Gil Vicente in his plays].

Apparently written in the same year, but published twenty years later, the *Miscelânea* by Garcia de Resende includes verses (ll.1951–60) that have become the most quoted testimony about Gil Vicente's activity:

E vimos singularmente
Fazer representações
D'estilo mui eloquente
De mui novas envenções
E feitas por Gil Vicente;
Ele foi o que inventou

242   JOSÉ CAMÕES

> Isto cá e o usou
> Com mais graça e mais doutrina
> Posto que João del Encina
> O pastoril começou

[And we saw some remarkable spectacles, in an eloquent style and with new inventions, put on by Gil Vicente. It was he who invented this here and who practised it with more grace and learning, though Juan del Encina began the pastoral]

A reductive reading of these verses has upheld the tradition of attributing to Gil Vicente the introduction of theatre in Portugal. In fact, the verb 'invented' (l. 1556) should not be read exclusively with today's meaning ('to be the first to have an idea or discover a novelty') but as a hypothetical *invencionar*, to create *invenções* [to adorn with artifice or efabulation]. One should note that the praise is immediately softened by the reference to Juan del Encina.

In 1540 João de Barros, in his *Diálogo em louvor da nossa linguagem* [Dialogue in praise of our language] (fol. 55ᵛ), praises Gil Vicente's discernment and good taste which did not allow for the creation of a such a disreputable character as Centúrio in the *Celestina*, by Fernando Rojas, deemed incompatible with the Portuguese language: 'E Gil Vicente, cómico, que a mais tratou em composturas que algũa pessoa destes reinos, nunca se atreveo a introduzir um Centúrio português: porque, como o não consente a nação, assi o não sofre a linguagem' [And Gil Vicente, comedian, who composed more in this vein than any other person in this realm, did not dare to introduce a Portuguese Centúrio: because, just as the nation does not consent to it, so neither does the language allow it]. As well as being a testimony to the author's reputation, these citations prove the wide circulation of the printed and performed plays, long before they were collected in volumes by his son and daughter.

In one of his tragicomedies — *Frágua de Amor* [Forge of Love] — Vicente depicts the figure of Justice as a deformed cockeyed old woman leaning on a broken rod, who comes to the forge hoping to get a makeover. Cupid, who is in charge of it, orders the blacksmiths to gather up the scraps that will come out of her. These are, as one may easily guess, items suggesting bribery and corruption: chickens, partridges, purses filled with coins.

What I think happened to the theatrical tradition set up by Gil Vicente is somewhat similar to what happened to Justice in his tragicomedy. The scraps are not tempting objects but memories of a *modus theatralis* that were subject to minor reinvention throughout the century.

Only the playwrights who used prose, Sá de Miranda, António Ferreira and Jorge Ferreira de Vasconcelos, escaped what amounts to a Vicentine curse. Among those who used verse, only António Prestes seems to have taken a more original route. He wrote an immensely long religious allegory, the *Auto da Ave Maria* [The *Auto* of the Hail Mary], which has thirty characters and more than 2600 lines, both figures greatly surpassing those to be found in the work of the majority of his contemporaries, as well as six other plays, all of them set in Lisbon. The leading characters come from a middle class that is without economic worries, for example, people with important positions in the administration of justice and ambitious for social advancement, which is also open to their servants. For the first time such people have the leading roles on stage — uniquely in Portuguese sixteenth-century drama — though the novelty consists more in their social status than in their theatrical function, somewhat underplayed, which celebrates, at least up to a point, marriage as a family institution, with a certain predilection for the theme of conjugal love.

In fact, few scholars have studied the so-called followers of Gil Vicente, either those who came after him or those who followed his style and who are commonly known as 'the school of Gil Vicente'.

In Portugal, besides Gil Vicente's works, seventy-nine other sixteenth-century play texts are known, by a variety of writers, which, added to Gil Vicente's forty-six, amount to one hundred and twenty-five in total — in other words, not much more than one for each year of the century. Among them are prominent figures in literary history, like Sá de Miranda, António Ferreira, and Luís de Camões. It is not surprising that their dramatic works are few, for it is plausible that their writings for the stage were a digression from their poetry; Sá de Miranda wrote two comedies, António Ferreira wrote two comedies and a tragedy, and Luís de Camões three comic plays, or *autos*.

What is indeed surprising is that we find some authors — they are little more than mere names now — who are supposed to have written only one text in their whole lives, and oddly enough that single work is a play. Such is the case of Jorge Pinto (*Auto de Rodrigo e Mendo*) [Auto of Rodrigo and Mendo], Anrique Lopes (*Cena Policiana*) [Policiano's Scene], and Jerónimo Ribeiro (*Auto do Físico*) [Auto of the Physician]. Moreover, it is quite startling that only an average of four plays have survived by authors who wrote exclusively for the stage — or playwrights as we would call them today — such as Afonso Álvares, Baltesar Dias, and António Ribeiro Chiado.

A good example is given by a volume published in Lisbon in 1587, bearing the title *Primeira Parte dos Autos e Comédias Portuguesas, feitas por António Prestes e por Luís de Camões* [First part of the autos and comedies by António Prestes and by Luís de Camões].[3] The publisher included only two plays by Camões (and he probably mentioned him in the title to catch the attention of the buyers: by this time *Os Lusíadas*, first published in 1572, had gone through three editions). As the title and colophon indicate, we have reason to believe that the publisher intended to produce at least a second volume, but he never did. With the exception of the plays by Camões, all the texts in this collection had to wait until the nineteenth century for a second edition.

The tradition established by Gil Vicente produced a significant number of plays — four — that use the theatre within the theatre device (in none of the plays do we find the structure of a play within a play), and stage the staging, recreating the milieu in which they were first performed, rather than using two plots. In them is visible the familiarity that the Portuguese had with the theatre in the sixteenth century, as frequently they require a knowledge of theatrical codes. I shall comment briefly on those four plays that witness a literary fashion that, in Portugal, also owes its development to Vicente. As we shall see, the topic of the overcrowded audience will be frequent in those plays.

244   José Camões

In his *Auto da Lusitânia* [*Auto* of Lusitania], the theatre within the theatre device is taken further, and the author comments on himself in what we may call a Pirandellian mode *avant la lettre*.

The introito is a short story that tells of a happy Jewish family living in Lisbon, not at all different from any other family, even, and specially, I think, from Christian families. The father has gone out, a young child is sleeping in its crib, while the mother is taking care of the house and doing the cleaning. At the same time, the mother is trying to get the help of her daughter who is more interested in a Christian nobleman, outside in the street, who is attempting to court her. The arrival of the father completes the domestic scene. Suddenly a friend of the family arrives with the news that the King is coming to town with his new-born son who has never been to Lisbon (these are historical facts: D. João III made an entry into Lisbon with the new-born prince in July 1532, and it is likely that the city council ordered all the communities and guilds to prepare a celebration). The Jews decide that the theatre is their thing. After a brief discussion about their talent as performers, they choose to go out in search of inspiration. Fortunately Gil Vicente is presenting a new excellent play, as they explain to the audience, so they decide to watch and learn from it.

And so the *Auto* of Lusitania begins. A learned man who is in charge of the prologue has a different opinion from the Jews. He maintains that Gil Vicente is not a good author and does not have sufficient merit to '...trovar e escrever | as portuguesas façanhas' [chant and write | the feats of the Portuguese]: 'Gil Vicente o autor | me fez seu embaixador | mas eu tenho na memória | que pera tam alta história | naceu mui baixo doutor' [Gil Vicente the author | made me his ambassador | but I hold in my memory | that too low a scholar was born | for such a lofty tale] — a scholar to whose 'lowness' a genealogy is attributed: a rustic, the son of a midwife and a halberdier, and the grandson of a drummer.

This ability to merge different levels of fiction is unique in the first half of the sixteenth century in Portugal. As already noted, there are four plays that try to assemble the bits and pieces gleaned in Vicente's work: *Auto da Geração Humana* [The *Auto* of Human Generation], *Auto dos Sátiros* [The *Auto* of the Satyrs], both by anonymous author(s), *Auto da Natural Invenção* [The *Auto* of Natural Invention], by António Ribeiro Chiado, and *Auto del rei Seleuco* [The *Auto* of King Seleucus], by Luís de Camões.

I shall focus my approach on some mainly structural and formal aspects. As for the themes, they are all to be found in Vicente's works, if not exactly, at least insofar as they follow Gil Vicente's habit of digging into previous material and cultural references to seek scraps with which to begin.[4] All stage the theatre-going public and the preparations for a performance. One (*Geração Humana*) goes no further and the two planes do not intersect. *Seleuco* keeps the same distance between the two planes, but, at the end of the play, the metatheatrical opening is recalled. In the other two plays (*Sátiros* and *Natural Invenção*) the two planes touch constantly, although in entirely different ways: the former in parallel and the latter by convergence.

The *Auto da Geração Humana* is the simplest of the group. Two farmers go to a village to watch a religious play of which they have heard. They are welcomed by the actor who will go on to play an Angel. The dialogue between him and the

GIL VICENTE, A SOURCE FOR A HERITAGE MADE OF SCRAPS   245

two spectators is a kind of introduction, in which he explains to the peasants, who are very excited by the idea of watching a play, what they are about to see. This pedagogical opening has an ancestor in Vicente's *Auto da Fé* [*Auto* of the Faith]. The show then begins. It deals with the Biblical version of the creation of mankind, with Adam arguing with allegorical characters such as Justice and Reason and also with two little devils, while they wait for the Samaritan Christ who will carry Adam to an inn where he can rest. The inn that awaits him is the Church which is occupied by the four doctors of the Church. There is a very similar programme in Gil Vicente's *Auto da Alma* [*Auto* of the Soul].

A first glimpse at the text of the *Auto* of Seleucus shows us two noticeable features: it uses both prose and rhyming verse and is spoken in Portuguese and in Castilian, by the Doctor and his Boy, in the manner of Gil Vicente. Bilingualism is indeed a trait of Vicente's plays, and he used it to achieve different goals. It is possible that his first compositions used the Castilian of the writers who inspired him, like Juan del Encina. Vicente seems also to have chosen to use Castilian in his plays in order to raise them to the level of their subject matter, formed by a new rhetoric, especially in the tragicomedies *Dom Duardos* and *Amadís de Gaula* [Amadis of Gaul], as he himself explains in the prologue dedicated to D. João III in *Dom Duardos*.

But soon the use of the language begins to serve other purposes than simple imitation. Sometimes the plot requires a certain Spanish character or characters to speak in their mother tongue, thus leaving room for humour and mockery. Although a considerable number of later plays resort to this device, the truth is they do not take bilingualism further than this.

The alternation of prose and verse is not so easy to explain, although in the present case they appear to correspond to different sequences of the plays. In Vicente's *Lusitania* only the argument presented by the player 'who speaks the prologue' is in prose, the choice being justified because prose is easier to understand ('Para a obra não ir escura | direi em prosa o argumento' [I will put the summary in prose, so that the work is not obscure]).

In Camões's play the use of prose and verse is also very straightforward. The theatrical spectators speak in prose. In the play which they watch, the characters express themselves in verse, perhaps to conform to normal practice, which was to use verse in *autos*.[5] Just as in the *Auto da Geração Humana*, we see a stage performance being prepared. This time it is not in a public space but in a private house, where the householder has commissioned a performance for his friends. While we wait for the piece to begin, the master of the house discusses with his servant the logistical reasons for the delay in starting: props missing, all the places taken, and yet the servant is asked to notify some squires, the master's friends, that the performance will take place. Once they have arrived, the delay in starting leads to general conversation on trivial matters, including poetry, and this gives the opportunity for a comic number about ways of versifying. From time to time, the public is invited to sit closer together. The play begins with the traditional entry of a stage manager, who introduces, in prose, the piece which is about to be staged. The introduction is a flop, commented on humorously by the invited guests. Finally, the long-awaited play about Seleuco and Estratónica, husband and wife, begins. It is in verse, and

246   JOSÉ CAMÕES

continues to the end without interruption. Once the play is over we return to the initial setting which, it seems, will serve a space in which to serve supper to the actors.

The *Auto dos Sátiros* [*Auto* of the Satyrs] is more complex. The starting point is also a performance in a private house, belonging to a well-educated man. Part of the audience he gathers to watch the play he is offering is made up of his friends and is thus a sort of elite which will comment on the action throughout. When one guest asks who is the author of the play they are about to watch the host can easily answer: 'Mordomo: É comédia de Terêncio | cousa de muito primor' [It's a comedy by Terence, a very fine thing], knowing that his friends will know who and what he is talking about.[6] And so the play within the play starts, using both Spanish and Portuguese, as in *El-rei Seleuco*. It is not a play by Terence, though, but a simple love story concerning a Spanish Austrian Prince and a Portuguese maiden, told through a disruptive narrative structure that allows for the change between different spaces and gives room for commentaries on what the audience is watching. The play, which takes place on the outskirts of Lisbon, also evokes vaguely the world of chivalry. As with Duardos and Flérida in Gil Vicente's *Dom Duardos*, the garden is the *locus amoenus* where the love-making will take place. And if Vicente's adaptation of romances of chivalry comes to mind, so does the technique of merging the spaces of the various levels of representation.

At some point the Prince comments on the magnificence of the architecture and the beauty of the garden of the heroine Ulinea's palace, and the views from the hills, naming some of the villages that may be seen. By no coincidence, those are the very same villages the spectators comment on before the play starts, and one can also imagine that the palace and garden are the ones built by the Count of Castanheira in a village near to where the performance is taking place.[7] Vicente used this exact device more than once. For instance in the Comedy *Devisa da Cidade de Coimbra* [Arms of the City of Coimbra], of 1527, in which the mountain where the action takes place is suddenly transformed, towards the end of the play, into a domestic space when Belicastra, announcing the lineage of the Castro family, says: 'As molheres de Crasto são de pouca fala | fermosas e firmes como sabereis | pola triste morte de dona Inês | a qual de constante morreu nesta sala' [The women of the Castro family spare their words, they are beautiful and loyal, as you know from the grievous death of Dona Inês who died in this very room for being constant].

In the *Comédia do Viúvo* [The Comedy of the Widower], of 1514, a play which has some spatial affinities with *Devisa*, the interference is much more abrupt and the set changes are never announced. From a household space, the widower's house — the space within the play — the action moves on, with no continuity scheme, to a space at Court, a room in the palace — the space of the performance — where a royal personage in the audience, the (then) adolescent Prince João, will be asked to decide about the marriage of the characters in the play:

> Tirou dom Rosvel o chapeirão e ficou vestido como quem era, e firamse as moças a el rei dom João III sendo príncipe (que no serão estava) e lhe perguntaram dizendo:
> — Príncipe que Dios prospere | en grandeza principal | juzgad vos | la una Dios casar quiere | decidnos señor real | cuál de nos.
> Julgou o dito senhor que a mais velha casasse primeiro.

GIL VICENTE, A SOURCE FOR A HERITAGE MADE OF SCRAPS 247

[Dom Rosvel took off his large, rustic hat and stood in the attire which was proper to him, and the girls went to King João III, who was then a prince and sat in the audience, and asked him: 'Prince, may you prosper in royal greatness, you shall judge the matter: God has intended that she should marry one of us. Tell us, royal sir, which of us.' The aforesaid lord determined that the eldest should marry first.] (105c)

The most interesting of these plays is, without doubt, the *Auto da Natural Invenção* [The *Auto* of Natural Invention], by António Ribeiro Chiado. It is a quite unique piece of theatre, as the theatre is, after all, the main theme of the play. The title itself, or at least the one given by the chapbook that has survived to the present day — in only one copy, by the way, as so often happens — is at once very enigmatic and very accurate. What is shown is real life, or so it seems.

As in all the others, particularly *El-rei Seleuco* and *Auto dos Sátiros*, it takes place in a private house. The *dramatis personae* could be one of Vicente's: the host, or the owner of the house, a servant, a black man, two ruffians or bullies, the author or theatre company manager, a player who speaks the prologue, a young peasant coming to town, a cousin of his, a squire, an old woman — all urban types that Vicente depicted on stage. The play starts with the preparation for a performance at a wealthy man's house. He has decided to open his home to the public and put on a show. He already regrets his idea as too many people have turned up, and he fears trouble, especially because there is a delay. The players have not yet arrived and the audience is starting to show some impatience. Eventually everything and everybody is in place and the show may start. And, as it was often the case, there is a Prologue spoken by a senior player. It reads like this:

> *Representador*:
> Os antigos costumavam
> como lereis nessas rúbricas
> representar às repúbricas
> por figuras o que usavam.
> E ordenavam
> dos seis cônsules os quatro
> que houvesse aí teatro
> onde se representavam
> e nos dias feriais
> eram tal seus exercícios
> pera escusar outros vícios
> doutros vícios desiguais.
> Que cuidais
> Era esta ũa arte sobida
> discreta mas mal sentida
> de nécios irracionais
> uns lhe chamaram comédias
> outros representações
> outros arremediações
> e outros a soltas rédeas
> tinham mil openiões.
> Outros, de baixa gramática
> que vós tendes cá por cautos

248 José Camões

lhes foram pôr nome autos
outros nam senão que é prática
quem tal inventou per regra
achou por saber celeste
a altura de leste a oeste
da cousa que mais alegra.
Foi esta galantaria
perdendo de dia em dia
como mui claro se vê
a qual há mister que lhe dê
outra vez de sesmaria
sabeis a quanto mal veio
esta mui sobida graça?
Que se vende nessa praça
por quaisquer dous réis e meo
mas o bom come-o a traça.

[*The player who speaks the Prologue*: In ancient times it was the usage — as you can read yourselves in the preliminaries — to turn the customs of the times into plays, staged before the republic. And four of the six consuls ordered that there should be a theatre in which the presentation would take place.

Thus the ancients passed the time of a festive day, safe from the harm of improper vices. What do you think?

The theatre was a lofty art, high above the grasp of the mindless rabble.

Some called it by the name of comedy, some would say play, and others imitations, and some gave themselves free rein to think up countless other names. Men, who have little knowledge of Latin but are believed to be prudent, would call it Auto; others disagree, and call it Dialogue.

He who devised such a thing well, discovered, by divine inspiration, the longitude of joy.

But this gallant entertainment is waning day by day, as we can see, and it needs to be reallocated to those who will make use of it.

Do you know to what ill this lofty delight came? Because it's sold for next to nothing in the town square... and good things lie mouldering away.]

When the piece ends, the master of the house's friends agree that though it is not a masterpiece, the play they have watched has the merit of being 'natural', that is, a representation of life as it is: 'Tomada assi em geral | não é de todas o cume | todavia tem chorume | de discreta e natural' [Taken all in all, it's not the best thing ever. All the same, it has some clever and natural substance].

The *Auto da Natural Invenção* seems to me to be crucial to the understanding the aesthetic principle which underlies performance. If we confine ourselves exclusively to the theatre we find as far back as Gil Vicente the expression of a 'naturalistic' or 'realistic' theory. In the *Devisa da Cidade de Coimbra*, Vicente states:

ordena o autor de a representar
por que vejais
que cousas passaram na serra onde estais
feitas em comédia mui chã e moral
e os mesmos da história polo natural
e quanto falaram nem menos nem mais.

[The author had it performed so that you can see what happened in the mountains, where you are, turned into a very simple, moral comedy, and the characters of the story are natural and so is what they said, to which nothing has been added or taken away.]

At one point one of the members of the audience who was watching the *Auto dos Sátiros* comments: 'Mordomo: O natural é milhor | no representar das farsas' [Master: It is best to be natural when you're acting a farce].

This taste for natural imitation is also in line with what was expected of painting. Taking examples from other plays, here is a comment from the *Auto de Guiomar do Porto* [*Auto* of Guiomar from Porto]: 'Vosso rostro por igual | que parte do mal lhe tira | tirou tanto ao natural | que Apeles não fez tal' [He made a natural likeness of your face, one that not even Apelles could do, and this excuses him from some of the fault].

And here is another comment from the *Comédia Aulegrafia*, by Jorge Ferreira de Vasconcelos:

> Por esta razão, portanto, me escolheu e manda por seu autor a Comédia Aulegrafia, que pretende mostrar-vos ao olho o rascunho da vida cortesã, em que vereis ũa pintura que fala e vos fará vente e palpável a vaidade de certa relé, cuja compostura trasladada ao natural vos será representada per corrente e aprazível estilo de certos almogáveres que correm o campo fazendo ũa salsada de gente manceba.

> [For this reason, then, he chose me and sends, by the hand of its author, the *Comédia Aulegrafia*, which aims to show you a sketch of courtly life, in which you will see a speaking picture and which will make visible and palpable to you the vanity of a certain set of people, whose behaviour, copied naturally, will be represented in a fluent and agreeable style by certain Moorish ruffians who range over the country making a disarray of young people.]

It may well be this taste for the natural that allowed the popularity of the farce, to the detriment of more elevated tragedy. If we consider what was written for the stage in Portuguese in the sixteenth century, the suspicion can easily be proved. Of the 125 titles known, only two avoid 'representação polo natural': *Castro* and *Vingança de Agamemnon* [Agamemnon's Revenge].

Though there are dangers in giving documentary value to artistic texts, it is possible to find in them information about the history of the theatre in Portugal. It would be too much of a coincidence if these four examples were merely a literary convention and were not the reflection of everyday life when private houses are used as settings, for which plays were certainly commissioned. The character of the owner of the house is also referred to in Gil Vicente, *Auto da Festa*, to whom Truth addresses her speech. The equivalent is the *Mordomo* (the person who pays for the show or the festive event). He is so-called in the *Auto of the Satyrs*, and *Seleucus* gives us the answer to whatever issues of semantics the nouns might raise by making them synonymous in the initial rubric: the *Mordomo*, or master of the house.

And so, as we have seen, there is quite a variety of dramatic snippets which enable us to put together a history of theatrical practice in the sixteenth century, including elements of stagecraft. This is possible because the constituent parts of a drama are discussed by the actors, and the preliminaries also contain information about how plays functioned. We have to recognize that in Portugal there is hardly any dramatic theory in the sixteenth century (and the little material that exists has yet to be brought together), so play texts themselves become first-hand sources for the study of precepts, especially when they make explicit reference to the norms and modes of theatrical practice.[8]

The documentary character of these autos is not confined to metatheatrical detail. These texts bear witness to the establishment of a 'naturalist' taste which demands a space in the theatre, derived from the real world, for the portrayal of a reality known to the public. These spaces are organized in a linguistic geography which was familiar to Portuguese audiences of the period, including Portugal itself, Spain, Italy, etc., and even the figurative characters of allegory are everyday people.

The characters of plays continue to be the stock types of theatrical tradition: fathers, mothers, daughters, uncles, nephews, amorous squires and noblemen, youthful servants, black and white, maids, boastful Castilians, as well as wage-earners and administrators, and in addition mythological figures, both classical and Christian. However, there was room for minor and exotic innovations, like the satyrs.

What we see during the fifty years following Vicente's death is a theatre of manners, staging social concerns in ways which neatly combine entertainment and direct protest, and for a public which was accustomed to plays and which was self-consciously knowledgeable about the theatre.

Regardless of the intrinsic value, large or small, of individual plays, one can say that all of them contribute productively to a reassessment of the very few histories of drama which exist in Portugal, all of which, since the days of Teófilo Braga (writing in the nineteenth century) have been satisfied with the term 'Vicentine school'.

Bibliography

BARROS, JOÃO DE, *Gramática da Língua Portuguesa. Cartinha, Gramática, Diálogo em Louvor da nossa linguagem e Diálogo da viciosa vergonha* [Olyssipone: apud Lodouicum Rotorigiu Typographum, 1540], intro. and commentary by Maria Leonor Carvalhão Buescu (Lisbon: University of Lisbon, 1971)

OLIVEIRA, FERNÃO DE, *A gramática da linguagem portuguesa*, ed. Maria Leonor Carvalhão Buescu (Lisbon: Imprensa Nacional–Casa da Moeda, 1975)

Primeira parte dos Autos e Comédias Portuguesas, prefaced by Hernâni Cidade (Lisbon: Lysia, 1973)

RESENDE, ANDRÉ DE, *On Court Life*, ed. and trans. by John R. C. Martyn. (Bern : Peter Lang, 1990)

RESENDE, GARCIA DE, *Crónica de D. João II e Miscelânea*, ed. by Joaquim Veríssimo Serrão (Lisbon: Imprensa Nacional — Casa da Moeda, 1973)

Online Sources

Teatro de Autores Portugueses do Século XVI — Centro de Estudos de Teatro, University of Lisbon: <www.cet-e-quinhentos.com>

Notes to Chapter 11

1. No evidence has come to light of spaces constructed specifically for theatrical performance before the end of the century.
2. André de Resende, *On Court Life*, ed. and trans. by John R. C. Martyn. (Bern : Peter Lang, 1990), p. 103.
3. There is a full bibliographical account of this volume in Chapter 13 (eds).
4. This happened with Vicente, for instance in *D. Duardos* or *Amadis*, or less notably, in one of the sketches that form part of *Floresta de enganos* [Forest of Deceits], where he uses the literary material of 'Le conseiller au buletau' [The lawyer and the bolting-mill], a tale collected by Antoine de la Sale in the mid-fifteenth century in *Cent nouvelles nouvelles* (*One Hundred Merrie And Delightsome Stories*, n° 17).
5. The poet makes a more complex employment of both literary forms in *Filodemo*, a work in which, for no apparent reason, the characters randomly use prose and verse.
6. This is the only reference to the name of Terence in the Portuguese theatre of the sixteenth century, apart from those by Sá de Miranda and Jorge Ferreira de Vasconcelos, who lived, almost literally, in another world.
7. Though there is nothing in the text which allows us to date it precisely, it seems probable that it was written in the reign of D. João III, at the end of the 1530s.
8. There are examples of such an analysis in Chapter 5 (eds).

PART III

Theatre and Society

CHAPTER 12

Plautus and Terence in Tudor England

Peter Brown

Trinity College, Oxford

The comedies of Plautus and Terence occupied a central place in sixteenth-century education in England, as in continental Europe: students learnt tags from both authors, read their plays at least in extracts, and took part in performances of entire plays. It is thus not surprising that their influence can be seen in comedies written during the century, both in Latin and in English. My aim in this chapter is to give some examples to illustrate that influence. I cannot include every play that might be thought relevant, but I hope to draw attention to some of the most significant cases, in terms both of verbal echoes and of similarities in plot construction, and to show how thoroughly embedded Latin comedy was in the developing dramatic culture of the period. I do not mean to imply, of course, that such echoes and similarities are the key to all interpretations of the plays in question, but they are important ingredients in the mixture, and they are what I as a classical scholar am best qualified to discuss.

Part of the interest of this subject for a classicist is that in adapting Plautus and Terence the English writers were doing something similar to what Plautus and Terence themselves had done, since their plays were versions of Greek comedies which had been written 100 to 150 years previously. However, we do not have the Greek comedies that they were adapting, except that we have been able since 1968 to compare about 100 lines of one of Plautus's plays (*Bacchides*) with its Greek model. We can see that Plautus there preserves the basic story line and follows the same sequence of scenes but also cuts some of the material altogether and expands and rearranges what he has not cut: he is clearly writing a version of the Greek play, and his play is still set in Greece and portrays Greek society, but it is a creative adaptation, not a close translation. We believe that this was typical of the approach of both Plautus and Terence, and Terence tells us in some of his Prologues that he has combined material from more than one Greek play in composing his Latin version. In the case of sixteenth-century English writers we are in a position to make many more direct comparisons at first hand, and, as we shall see, they were generally even freer in their adaptations and combinations than the Latin authors had been.[1]

Performances of Plautus and Terence

Throughout the century comedies by Plautus and Terence were performed in Latin at various venues in England, starting with an unspecified play of Terence at King's Hall, Cambridge, in 1510/11; thirty-two further productions of plays by Plautus or Terence are known to have taken place at Cambridge colleges between 1516/17 and 1591/92.[2] The records for the Oxford colleges are sparser, but performances of Plautus and Terence are attested for 1559, 1566/67, 1567/68, 1581/82, and 1583/84.[3] Under Wolsey, there were productions for Henry VIII: an unspecified comedy of Plautus in 1519/20, Plautus's *Menaechmi* in 1527, and Terence's *Phormio* in 1528.[4] The last of these was performed by boys from St Paul's School,[5] and other school performances included 'Terentian plays' at Ipswich School in 1525,[6] and at least five productions by the boys of Westminster School.[7] There must have been many other school performances of which we have no record.

Comedies in Latin: *Hymenaeus, Pedantius, Bellum Grammaticale*

There were also newly composed Latin comedies performed at the two universities, often including idioms that derived from Plautus and Terence but not following the plots of any of their plays. Thus *Hymenaeus*, performed at St John's College, Cambridge in 1578/79 and based on a story in Boccaccio's *Decameron* (as the Prologue itself proclaims in lines 26–33), contains 'dozens of quotations both from Plautus [...] and Terence [...], never verbatim but slightly modified either by the omission of single words or by changed word order'.[8] These quotations are often put in a completely different context, and sometimes echoes of different plays are combined in one passage, showing how thoroughly the author had absorbed the comic style. When the young lover Erophilus is told by the father of the girl he loves that he is not a welcome guest in their house, he replies (I. 3. 46–49):

> Aecastor, cum uerba haec mecum considero,
> nonnullam te puto mihi facere iniuriam,
> quam, etsi ego dignus essem maxime,
> at tu minime dignus, Alphonse, qui faceres.

> [My god, when I reflect on what you say, I think you do me no small wrong. Even if it were entirely proper for me to be treated like that, even so it wasn't at all proper for you to do it, Alphonsus.]

These lines contain three borrowings from plays by Terence, the first line from *Heautontimoroumenos* 385 *et quom egomet nunc mecum in animo uitam tuam considero* [And now that I reflect on the sort of life you live] (one prostitute talking to another), the second from *Adelphoe* 148 *nonnullam in hac re nobis facit iniuriam* [does us no small wrong in this matter] (a father complaining about his son's behaviour), the third and fourth from *Eunuchus* 865–66 *nam si ego digna hac contumelia | sum maxume, at tu indignus qui faceres tamen* [If it's entirely proper for me to be insulted like that, even so it wasn't proper for you to do it] (a prostitute reproaching a boy for raping a girl in her care); in this case, Terence's contrast of *digna* [...] *maxume*

PLAUTUS AND TERENCE IN TUDOR ENGLAND   257

with *indignus* is made even more pointed by the replacement of the latter term with *minime dignus*. Overall the play, the earliest University play known to have been based on an Italian source, is rightly praised by Boas:

> The more closely *Hymenaeus* is examined, in relation to its source and to the conditions under which it was performed, the more favourable will be the view taken of its author's dramatic talent. It would be difficult to point to any comedy in the vernacular, written before 1579, which equals it in technical dexterity, economy of action and dialogue, and effective blending of humour and pathos.[9]

The Prologue boasts in lines 41–42 that *haec a Bocatij fabula longe magis est alia,* | *quam a Colace Menandri Eunuchus Terentij* [this play differs far more from Boccaccio's story than Terence's *Eunuchus* does from Menander's *Colax*]. As Moore Smith says in his note on p. 74, 'The writer of course knows nothing about the *Colax* of Menander or its relation to the *Eunuchus* beyond what Terence says in the Prologue to his play';[10] but he clearly expects his audience to know Terence's Prologue.

Another case is *Pedantius*, performed at Trinity College, Cambridge in 1580/81 and not known to derive from any particular source.[11] This shows a pedantic humanist in love with a slave girl and not only has him quoting Cicero extensively but also includes (for example) the following account of scholarly life in his mouth in Act I Scene 4 (lines 592–94 Moore Smith = 445–47 Sutton): *Nos omnia habemus, nec quicquam habemus, id est animos tranquillos, nummos nullos; nil enim est, nil deest tamen: pecuniam cum non habemus, non desideramus* [We have everything without having anything; that is to say, we have tranquil minds but no cash. There's nothing in the bank, but there's no shortage either; though we have no money, we don't feel the need of it]. This echoes the parasite Gnatho's praise of his lifestyle at Terence, *Eunuchus* 243: *omnia habeo neque quicquam habeo; nil quom est, nil defit tamen* [I have everything without having anything; although there's nothing in the bank, there's no shortage either], and similar echoes are found elsewhere in the play.

Even a self-professed 'tragicomedy' whose plot is utterly dissimilar from those of Plautus and Terence, the *Bellum Grammaticale* [*Grammatical War*] by Leonard Hutten, is full of echoes of their plays. This was performed in the presence of Queen Elizabeth at Oxford in 1592 but had been written and first performed in 1581.[12] It is 'a dramatized version of one of the most popular publications of the Renaissance period, the *Bellum Grammaticale* of the Italian humanist Andrea Guarna, originally published at Cremona in 1511', whose 'fundamental idea is to explain the irregularities of Latin grammar as the result of a civil war between the various parts of speech'.[13] The major powers in this war are the nouns and the verbs, commanded by their kings, respectively Poeta and Amo. The influence of Latin comedy is clear from the start of the play, since Hutten has attached the traditional figure of the parasite to each king, and the play opens with a lengthy monologue by Ille, the parasite of Poeta, which starts as follows:

> O populares, ecquis me uiuit hodie fortunatior? Nemo hercle quisquam, nam in me dii penario qui praesunt potestatem omnem ostendere suam, in cuius uentrem tot subito confluxerunt bellaria. Nunc est profecto cum interfici me possum perpeti, ne felicitatem adimat fames ieiunio aliquo.

258   PETER BROWN

[Citizens, is there anyone luckier than me alive today? No, not a single person. In my case the gods in charge of the larder have displayed all their power: so many puddings have suddenly been poured into my belly! Now, now is the time when I could put up with death, so that hunger couldn't remove my happiness with any fast!]

This combines in reverse order two passages from Terence's *Eunuchus*, both in the mouth of Chaerea, celebrating the fact (a) that he has succeeded in raping the girl he has fallen for, and later (b) that she has been betrothed to him. The second is at lines 1031–33:

> O populares, ecquis me hodie uiuit fortunatior?
> nemo hercle quisquam, nam in me plane di potestatem suam
> omnem ostendere, quoi tam subito tot congruerint commoda.

[Citizens, is there anyone luckier than me alive today? No, not a single person. In my case the gods have clearly displayed all their power: so many good things have suddenly come together for me!]

The first is at lines 551–52:

> Nunc est profecto interfici quom perpeti me possum,
> ne hoc gaudium contaminet uita aegritudine aliqua.

[Now, now is the time when I could put up with death, so that life couldn't spoil this joy with any sorrow!]

As can be seen, Terence's wording is followed very closely, except that details appropriate to a parasite have been added. Similarly at the beginning of the second scene a new character, the Neuter Adjective (*Adiectivum in neutro genere*), being unsteady on his feet, enters with words that reproduce almost verbatim the drunken entry of Pseudolus at Plautus, *Pseudolus* 1246–48 and immediately adds a close echo of a similar drunken entry at *Eunuchus* 729. The author displays an intimate acquaintance with the plays of Plautus and Terence and deploys his material imaginatively. By no means all the new Latin plays were comedies, but those that were display profound awareness of their ancestry.

Richard Rowland, in an interesting and informative discussion, has drawn attention to the fact that echoes of Plautus and Terence in these plays are neither explicitly acknowledged nor exact quotations,[14] but I am puzzled by his reference to 'an almost clandestine anonymity' in the way that the influence of ancient comedy made its presence felt (p. 161), and by his conclusion from this fact alone that 'Roman comedy thus appears to have occupied a precarious position within the hierarchy of classical writing' (p. 162). Rather, the position of Roman comedy in academic culture was so assured that the authors could take for granted that their audiences would see what games they were playing. There were debates in some quarters about the possible morally corrupting effects of the ancient plays (also discussed by Rowland), but those debates did not deter these authors from showing off their knowledge of the texts.

In echoing the language of Plautus and Terence without reproducing their plots, these plays continued the tradition of earlier Humanist Latin comedies such as Pier Paolo Vergerio's *Paulus* (*c.* 1390), Leon Battista Alberti's *Philodoxus* (1426),

PLAUTUS AND TERENCE IN TUDOR ENGLAND 259

Enea Silvio Piccolomini's *Chrysis* (1444), and the seven comedies of Tito Livio dei Frulovisi, written in the 1430s.[15] On the other hand, a work such as Giovanni Armonio's *Stephanium* (*c.* 1500) shows closer involvement with the plots of Plautus's *Aulularia* and (above all) Terence's *Andria*, as well as including elements derived from Plautus's *Amphitruo*, *Mercator*, and *Pseudolus*;[16] and a number of plays written in Italian also show engagement with more than turns of phrase from Plautus and Terence. For example, Niccolò Machiavelli's *Clizia* (1525) is quite freely modelled on Plautus's *Casina*, Vincenzo Gabiani's *I Gelosi* (1545) combines Terence's *Andria* with his *Eunuchus*, and Giovan Maria Cecchi's *La Moglie* (1556) combines the *Andria* with Plautus's *Menaechmi*. All these plays (whether Latin or Italian, and whether or not incorporating plot-elements from Plautus and Terence) tend to be set in the contemporary world of the author and sometimes combine classical elements with features derived from vernacular dramatic traditions; but all wear their Plautine and Terentian hearts on their sleeves, and some reproduce ancient plot structures combined in unexpected ways. Italian comedies in particular were in many cases important intermediaries between ancient and Elizabethan comedy; I cannot give a full account of their influence in this chapter, but I include two examples in the next section.[17]

Comedies in English: (i) *Calisto and Melebea*, *Supposes*, *The Buggbears*

Just as in Latin and Italian, so too in English there were plays showing the influence of Plautus and Terence in various ways. We do not always know where they were performed, but when we do the evidence points to a variety of venues: schools and universities, Inns of Court, and (by the end of the century) public playhouses. These plays do not normally advertise the fact that they have been influenced by Latin comedy, and in some cases the influence is indirect. But it sometimes reveals itself in very precise echoes, as I shall try to show in much of what follows.

I start with an example of indirect influence in one of the early scenes in the first English play to be advertised as a comedy, *Calisto and Melebea*.[18] This play, of unknown authorship, dates from the 1520s and is said on the title page to be 'A New Commodye in Englysh in Maner of an Enterlude'. Calisto is passionately in love with Melebea, and at lines 116–18 he says:

> For I fele sharp nedyls within my brest,
> Peas, warr, truth, haterad, and injury,
> Hope and suspect, and all in one chest.

Shortly afterwards, at 147–48, he says to his servant Sempronio:

> What counsell can rule hym, Sempronio,
> That kepyth in hym no order of counsell?

These passages are clearly based on Terence, *Eunuchus* 57–63, where the slave Parmeno says to his young master:

> Ere, quae res in se neque consilium neque modum
> habet ullum, eam consilio regere non potes.
> in amore haec omnia insunt uitia: iniuriae,
> suspiciones, inimicitiae, indutiae,   60

260   PETER BROWN

> bellum, pax rursum: incerta haec si tu postules
> ratione certa facere, nihilo plus agas
> quam si des operam ut cum ratione insanias.

[Sir, if a matter has no plan or control to it at all, you can't manage it according to a plan. Love contains all the following faults: wrongs, suspicions, enmities, truces, war, then peace again. These are uncertain things, and if you expected to make them certain by thinking about them you wouldn't get any further than if you worked on a method for being mad.]

Parmeno's words in lines 57–58 are closely echoed by Calisto's at lines 147–48, and the list of the characteristics of love in Calisto's mouth at 117–18 is so similar to the list in lines 59–61 of Terence's play that it strengthens the case for changing the English text in line 117 to read 'truce' rather than 'truth' (which does not really belong in this list), since the Latin in line 60 has *indutiae*. Those who remember Terence's play can derive further amusement from noticing that what was said by the slave to the lover in the Latin text is said by the lover to the slave in the English text.

However, the author of *Calisto and Melebea* was translating not directly from Terence but from Fernando de Rojas's popular Spanish novel-in-dialogue *The Tragicomedy of Calisto and Melibea*, which came to be called *Celestina* (first published in 1499 as *Comedia de Calisto y Melibea*, and in an expanded version in 1502 as *La Tragicomedia de Calisto y Melibea*). Large portions of the play, including this scene, have been translated quite closely. Here is Calisto's list of the characteristics of love in the Spanish work: 'paz: guerra: tregua: amor: enemistad: injurias, pecados: sospechas, todo a vna causa' [peace, war, truce, love, enmity, injuries, wrongs, suspicions, all caused by one thing]: here 'tregua' seems to confirm that we should read 'truce' and not 'truth' in the English text.[19] And a little later on he says: 'qual consejo puede regir lo que en si no tiene orden ni consejo?' [What planning can control something that contains no order or plan?] Surely Rojas was well aware that he was following Terence closely in this piece of dialogue; and many people in the audience of the English play no doubt smiled with satisfaction on recognizing the ultimate source of these lines. But in this case Terence came to them through an intermediary, and overall this play is very different indeed from a Roman comedy, becoming an exhortation to Christian virtue and chastity.

A similar case, though closer in spirit to Roman comedy, is George Gascoigne's *Supposes* (i.e. *Mistaken Suppositions*, as Gascoigne explains in his teasingly playful 'Prologue or Argument') of 1566, apparently the first English comedy to be written in prose.[20] This contains a number of situations that seem to derive from different Latin comedies: a master and his servant change places, each pretending to be the other, as in Plautus's *Captivi*; the master uses his disguise as a servant to get into the house of the woman he loves and sleep with her, as in Terence's *Eunuchus*; a stranger is persuaded to pretend to be the father of this young man (a motif somewhat similar to one in Plautus's *Poenulus*), which leads to scenes which have something in common with Plautus's *Amphitruo*; at the end a father discovers his long-lost son, in a scene with some echoes of a similar scene at the end of Terence's *Andria* and also (again) of *Captivi*. But Gascoigne's work is a translation of Ludovico Ariosto's

PLAUTUS AND TERENCE IN TUDOR ENGLAND   261

comedy *I Suppositi* (prose version 1509, subsequently rewritten in verse), and that is the route by which these echoes of Plautus and Terence have reached the English public.

Another work taken from an Italian comedy is the anonymous English comedy *The Buggbears* (*c.* 1564), an adaptation of Antonfrancesco Grazzini's *La Spiritata* (1561), itself based on Plautus's *Mostellaria* and *Aulularia*. However, this incorporates additions not only from the anonymous comedy *Gl'Ingannati* (*c.* 1531) but also — more interestingly for our purposes — from Terence's *Andria*.[21] From Terence's play the author takes the motifs that the young lover has made his girl friend pregnant, that he is under pressure from his father to marry a different girl altogether, and that another boy is in love with that other girl. This leads to some very close echoing of Terence's lines, particularly in Act II Scene 3 where the young lover Formosus assures Tomasine, the nurse of his beloved Rosimunda, that he will never desert Rosimunda, and in Act II Scene 5 where Formosus assures Manutius that he has no desire to marry Manutius's beloved Iphigenia. These scenes reproduce *Andria* 265–98 and 301–35 respectively, the former a scene full of passionate declarations of fidelity by Pamphilus to his beloved's maid Mysis, the latter more comic with its contrasts of the differing reactions of Pamphilus and Charinus to the notion of marrying Charinus's beloved Philumena. One example will show how closely the author follows Terence's text, *Buggbears* II. 3. 95–102:

> FORMOSUS: Doth she think me such a dastard?   95
> So unkind, so brutish, so degenerate a bastard
> From common humanity to yield to such a wrong,
> That neither her acquaintance, whom I have known so long,
> Nor her most loyal love, nor my shame, nor her courtesy,
> Nor our faiths in wedlock plight can stay me from such villainy?   100
> TOMASINE: I know she hath deserved to be remembered of you.
> FORMOSUS: Remembered? O Tomasine, Tomasine, 'tis most true.

Compare *Andria* 277–82:

> PAMPHILUS: adeon me ignauom putas,
> adeon porro ingratum aut inhumanum aut ferum,
> ut neque me consuetudo neque amor neque pudor
> commoueat neque commoneat ut seruem fidem?   280
> MYSIS: unum hoc scio, hanc meritam esse ut memor esses sui.
> PAMPHILUS: memor essem? O Mysis, Mysis...

> [PAMPHILUS: Do you think I'm so feeble, or so ungrateful or unfeeling or
>   savage, that neither our relationship nor my love and respect could move or
>   motivate me to stay true to her?
> MYSIS: All I know is that she's earned the right to be remembered by you.
> PAMPHILUS: Remembered by me? O Mysis, Mysis...]

There can be no doubt that the author had Terence's text in his mind as he composed these scenes and at a few other points as well.[22] The play ends with a song that includes the line 'We boys are glad our pain is past', suggesting that it was written for performance by schoolchildren.

262   PETER BROWN

(ii) *Jacke Jugeler* and *Roister Doister*

Echoes of Plautus and Terence are also found in works not based on Italian models,
for instance in two plays written in the middle of the century, perhaps both in
the early 1550s, and perhaps both by the same author, Nicholas Udall. These are
Jacke Jugeler and *Roister Doister*. *Jacke Jugeler* contains several passages that are closely
modelled on Plautus's *Amphitruo*.[23] Again I shall give just one example. At lines
364–67 Jacke Jugeler says:

> Now, fistes, me thinkithe yesterday seven yers past
> That four men a sleepe at my fete you cast.   365
> And this same daye you did noo manar good,
> Nor were not washed in warme blod.

Jenkin Careawaye overhears him and says:

> What whoreson is this that washith in warme blod?
> Sum divell broken loose out of hell for wood?
> Four hath he slayne, and now well I see   370
> That it must be my chaunce the fift to bee.

This is clearly modelled on *Amphitruo* 302–07:

> MERCURY: agite, pugni, iam diu est quom uentri uictum non datis:
> iam pridem uidetur factum heri quod homines quattuor
> in soporem conlocastis nudos.
> SOSIA: formido male
> ne ego hic nomen meum commutem et Quintus fiam e Sosia: 305
> quattuor uiros sopori se dedisse hic autumat;
> metuo ne numerum augeam illum.

> [MERCURY: Come on, fists: you haven't provided food for my stomach for ages.
> It seems a long time since yesterday when you stripped four men and put them
> to sleep. SOSIA: I'm dreadfully afraid that I may change my name here and turn
> from Sosia into Quintus [the Fifth]. This man says he's put four men to sleep:
> I'm afraid I may increase that number.]

We have every reason to think that the author was working directly from Plautus's
play, not least because the Prologue proclaims that the main theme of the play is
taken 'out of Plautus first commedie' (line 64): *Amphitruo* is the first in alphabetical
order of Plautus's surviving plays, and for that reason the first in manuscripts and
editions of the author. The theme which has been borrowed from Plautus is the
theme introduced in the opening scene of his play, in which the god Mercury,
disguised as the slave Sosia, bullies Sosia himself into believing that Mercury has
taken over his identity and that he himself is no longer Sosia. Plautus's scene is
unusually long, but it forms only the first quarter of the play: Mercury's theft of
Sosia's identity matches Jupiter's theft of Amphitruo's identity, and both Mercury
and Jupiter have assumed these disguises so that Jupiter can sleep with Amphitruo's
wife Alcumena. The scene with Sosia gets the play off to a very entertaining start,
and it introduces the theme of identity confusion which runs through the play, but
in the working out of the plot it is subordinated to the concerns of other characters.
Jacke Jugeler is more limited in its scope. As we have seen, the characters who

PLAUTUS AND TERENCE IN TUDOR ENGLAND   263

correspond to Mercury and Sosia are Jacke Jugeler and Jenkin Careaway, and the scene between them fills very nearly half of the play. Jacke wishes to punish Jenkin because they have fallen out for some reason, and essentially that is what the play is about: how Jacke Jugeler gets his revenge on Jenkin Careaway by stealing his identity and throwing him into confusion. Some passages in the scene between the two of them correspond very closely with passages in Plautus's play, and a later scene between Jenkin and his master Boungrace (lines 774–906) also contains some very close echoes of the equivalent scene in Plautus's play between Sosia and his master Amphitruo (551–628). But there is no one to correspond to Jupiter, Boungrace has very little in common with Amphitruo, and the setting of the play is London in the sixteenth century; the play is in no sense a slavish translation of Plautus, but the author clearly knew Plautus's play very well. The Prologue makes it clear that the play was written for schoolchildren to perform ('little boyes', line 76), and the quarto editions published in the sixteenth century proclaim it to be an 'Enterlued for children to playe'. (This may perhaps explain why the theme of adultery has been almost entirely eliminated from the play.) The editions also name Jacke Jugeler himself in the cast-list as 'The Vyce', thus advertising a continuity with the traditional mischievous character of medieval English drama even in a play which proclaims itself in the Prologue to be based on Plautus.

Roister Doister is twice as long as *Jacke Jugeler* and has a more complex plot; it has often been referred to as 'the first regular English comedy', or at least as one of the first, in the sense that it has been constructed in five acts and can be analysed in terms of *protasis*, *epitasis*, and *catastrophe* in accordance with classical theories that were well known at the time.[24] The Prologue invokes the precedent of Plautus and Terence as the acknowledged masters of Comedy, but it does not specify any particular play as the model (lines 15–21):[25]

> The wyse poets long time heretofore,
> Under merrie Comedies secretes did declare,
> Wherein was contained very vertuous lore,
> With mysteries and forewarnings very rare.
> Suche to write neither Plautus nor Terence dyd spare,
> Whiche among the learned at this day beares the bell;
> These with such other therein dyd excell.

Like *Jacke Jugeler*, the play has a contemporary English setting, and nearly all the characters have good English names such as Madge Mumblecrust and Tom Truepenny. However, it is not difficult to detect the influence of Plautus's *Miles Gloriosus* and above all of Terence's *Eunuchus*. These influences have been analysed in some detail by Gianni Guastella,[26] and I shall cite here only some of the more obvious examples.

At lines 1403–12 Roister Doister calls to his servants off-stage:

> Sirs, see that my harnesse, my tergat, and my shield,
> Be made as bright now as when I was last in fielde,
> As white as I shoulde to warre againe tomorrowe: 1405
> For sicke shall I be, but I worke some folke sorow!
> Therfore see that all shine as bright as Sainct George,
> Or as doth a key newly come from the smith's forge.

I woulde have my sworde and harnesse to shine so bright,
That I might therwith dimme mine enimies' sight;   1410
I would have it cast beames as fast, I tell you playne,
As doth the glittryng grasse after a showre of raine.

This echoes and elaborates the opening four lines of *Miles Gloriosus*:

Curate ut splendor meo sit clupeo clarior
quam solis radii esse olim quom sudumst solent,
ut, ubi usus ueniat, contra conserta manu
prasestringat oculorum aciem in acie hostibus.

[See that the shine of my shield is brighter than the sun's rays tend to be on a
clear day, so that, when the need arises, when battle is joined, it may dazzle the
field of vision of my enemies in the field.]

In general, Roister Doister clearly stands in the tradition of boastful soldiers that
goes back to Plautus's play; the tradition had developed a life of its own, as has been
shown with a wealth of detail by Daniel C. Boughner,[27] and when we come across
Falstaff at the end of the century we are not necessarily put in mind of Plautus's
play in particular. But here and elsewhere in *Roister Doister* the echo is too clear to
be missed.

Roister Doister is accompanied by Matthew Merrygreek, a character who would
be labelled a 'parasite' in Latin comedy but who can also, like Jacke Jugeler, be seen
as a descendant of the medieval Vice, since he manipulates Roister Doister and leads
him on to his own destruction far more actively than parasites in Latin comedy
tend to do. In the opening scene of *Miles Gloriosus* the soldier is accompanied by
a parasite, but it is in Terence's *Eunuchus* that we see the parasite Gnatho playing
a far larger part as he accompanies the soldier Thraso, and this play contributes
more than Plautus's play to the plot of *Roister Doister*. The following are the main
similarities.

(1) Merrygreek introduces himself and Roister Doister to the audience in a monologue at the start of the play, just as Gnatho introduces himself to the audience on
his first appearance in Terence's play, at lines 232–64, and his speech contains some
verbal echoes of Gnatho's monologue (*Roister Doister* 75–80, with *Eunuchus* 248–53):

Then must I sooth it, whatever it is:
For what he sayth or doth cannot be amisse;
Holde up his yea and nay, be his nowne white sonne,
Prayse and rouse him well, and ye have his heart wonne,
For so well liketh he his owne fonde fashions
That he taketh pride of false commendations.

est genus hominum que esse primos se omnium rerum volunt
nec sunt: hos consector; hisce ego non paro me ut rideant,
sed eis ultro adrideo et eorum ingenia admiror simul.
**quidquid dicunt laudo; id rursum si negant, laudo id quoque;
negat quis: nego; ait: aio**; postremo imperavi egomet mihi
omnia adsentari. is quaestus nunc est multo uberrimus.

[There's a class of men who want to pass as outstanding in everything, but who
aren't; they're the ones I hunt down. I don't lay myself on as entertainment

PLAUTUS AND TERENCE IN TUDOR ENGLAND   265

for *them*; *I'm* the one who laughs at *their* jokes, and I praise their wit at the same time. **Whatever they say, I express my approval; if they then say the opposite, I approve of that too! If a man says no, I say no; if he says yes, I say yes.** In short, I've given orders to myself to **agree to everything.** That's the trade with much the fattest profits nowadays!]

Once again, the translation is by no means literal, but it is clear that the Terentian passage lies behind the English one.

(2) At the end of Act IV Roister Doister and Merrygreek attack the house of Dame Custance, the widow with whom Roister Doister is in love, just as Thraso and Gnatho come to attack the house of the prostitute Thais at *Eunuchus* 771–816.

(3) At the end of both plays the parasite negotiates a deal by which the soldier will be welcomed at the table of his rival in love, even after he has been driven off quite ignominiously.

However, large parts of the play do not derive from Plautus or Terence, and the fact that the prostitute has become a widow engaged to marry another man makes quite a significant difference to the ethos of the piece. I do not entirely agree with Howard Norland's thesis that the play is Aristophanic in character,[28] but it is certainly in many respects non-Plautine and non-Terentian, although the author has clearly used Plautus and Terence both in matters of detail and in some aspects of overall structure. Guastella brings out all of these points.[29]

(iii) William Shakespeare (*The Comedy of Errors, The Taming of the Shrew*) and Ben Jonson (*The Case is Altered*)

The Comedy of Errors, dating from the early 1590s, must count as the most notable use of Plautus in the whole period.[30] The main plot-line is based on Plautus's *Menaechmi*, about two identical twin brothers who have been separated since early childhood and who get mistaken for one another, with all sorts of confusions ensuing, because no one realizes there are two of them. They find themselves quite independently in the same town, the town where one of them lives and the other has just arrived from elsewhere, and of course everyone who meets the visiting brother takes him to be the one who lives there. Shakespeare has added to this the notion that the two servants accompanying the two brothers are themselves identical twins who have been separated since early childhood: this creates a whole new dimension of additional comedy and confusion between the masters and the servants. A similar doubling of the twin motif is found in a number of Italian comedies,[31] but ultimately the notion that both masters and servants are identical can be traced back to Plautus's *Amphitruo*, which has both Jupiter and Amphitruo identical in appearance and also Mercury and Sosia — these are not twins in either case, but they do look identical. In addition, one central scene in *The Comedy of Errors* can be seen as influenced by a comparable scene in *Amphitruo*: Act III Scene 1, where, while the wife of the local brother entertains the other brother to dinner (believing him to be her husband), her true husband is locked out of her house because everyone thinks that he is already indoors; compare *Amphitruo* 1009 ff.

266   PETER BROWN

On the other hand, *The Comedy of Errors* does not follow the text of either of Plautus's plays nearly as closely as *Jacke Jugeler* does, and it has very few even of the occasional echoes that we find in *Roister Doister*; it was claimed by J. A. K. Thomson that 'while the structure of the play is Plautine, the superstructure is the work of a man who appears never to have looked at the *Latin* of Plautus at all'.[32] Thomson concluded that Shakespeare had not read Plautus's plays for himself but had come across summaries of them; it seems more likely, though, that Shakespeare had so completely absorbed Plautus's two comedies that he was able to combine and transform them into a work that is much more tightly constructed than either of them and in which the situations are worked out without detailed reference to the Latin text. Like Plautus, he sets the play in the Greek world, but he has changed the setting from Epidamnus to Ephesus, and in addition to the twin servants he has added two characters who turn out to be the parents of the twin boys, with the result that there are multiple reunions and recognitions at the end of the play. The mother is an abbess at Ephesus, a clear Christianizing detail: the play does not have a carefully preserved antique setting. The heart of the play, and much of its skeleton, unmistakeably derive from Plautus's *Menaechmi*, but the outer surface, the skin, is Shakespeare's own. It is widely believed that Shakespeare in fact had a further source, and that the two parents, together with the setting at Ephesus, derive from John Gower's *Confessio Amantis*.[33] But it is not clear that he had any of these texts open in front of him as he composed.

Shakespeare's one direct quotation from Terence in Latin comes in another of his early comedies, *The Taming of the Shrew* I. I. 161–62 (in the Arden Shakespeare edition of Brian Morris),[34] where Tranio advises his young master Lucentio 'If love have touch'd you, naught remains but so, | *Redime te captum quam queas minimo*' [Ransom yourself out of your captivity for as little as possible]. This is *Eunuchus* 74–75, not exactly in the form in which Terence wrote it (*ut te redimas captum quam queas minimo*) but as it is found in the standard grammar book of Shakespeare's day, William Lily's *A Shorte Introduction of Grammar*. However, Niall Rudd has shown that Shakespeare appears to have remembered ('however dimly') the context of the quotation in Terence's play, the very scene echoed in *Calisto and Melibea* that I discussed earlier in this chapter.[35] It may be worth adding that shortly before this, in lines 155–56, Lucentio has said 'Tranio, I burn, I pine, I perish, Tranio, | If I achieve not this young modest girl', echoing a line from later in Terence's play (*Eunuchus* 888), *emoriar si non hanc uxorem duxero* [I shall die if I don't get her as my wife].[36]

Later in the 1590s Ben Jonson wrote *The Case is Altered*, which was perhaps an attempt to be even more adventurous in his combination of Plautine plots than Shakespeare had been in *The Comedy of Errors*: Shakespeare combined two plays that had quite a lot in common; Jonson combines two that are utterly dissimilar.[37] The play is set in Milan at a time of warfare between Milan and France, but the main plot is very similar to that of Plautus's *Captivi*, with two French prisoners of war pretending to be one another, and one of them leaving Milan to negotiate an exchange of prisoners with the French that apparently concerns the one left behind but in fact concerns himself. Count Ferneze, the father of the Milanese soldier who has been captured by the French, is so angry on discovering the deception that he threatens to execute the French prisoner who has been left behind, who is in fact (though he does not realize it) a long-lost son of his own. But fortunately the other Frenchman returns just in time, bringing with him Count Ferneze's other son, the one who had been captured by the French; the true identity of the long-lost son is discovered, and all ends happily. That is essentially all taken from Plautus's *Captivi*. But *Captivi* is famous for having no love interest; it is unique in Latin comedy in this respect. Jonson follows the example of Ariosto and Gascoigne (see above on *Supposes*) in adding a love interest, partly by giving Count Ferneze two daughters, but above all by importing a character who obsessively hoards his hidden treasure and also has a daughter (or a girl everyone thinks is his daughter) who is desired by various characters in the play. This sub-plot derives from Plautus's *Aulularia*, a play that one might not expect to find combined with *Captivi*. As with *The Comedy of Errors*, the influence of Plautus shows itself more in the overall situations and themes than in verbal echoes, but I believe this is Jonson's closest engagement with Roman comedy in his plays.[38] His later plays certainly develop character types that can be traced back to Roman comedy, and occasionally even follow a sequence of lines quite closely, but the plots on the whole have rather less in common with Plautus and Terence.

Translations

To return to *The Comedy of Errors*, I think it is now generally accepted both that Shakespeare, having attended his local grammar school, was well able to read the plays of Plautus in Latin and that there is no reason to suppose he had encountered William Warner's English translation of *Menaechmi* before its publication in 1595;[39] Wolfgang Riehle tried to show that Shakespeare was indeed influenced by Warner's version, in addition to reading the plays in Latin,[40] but I cannot see that any of the examples he adduces has any probative value. However, it may be worth ending this chapter with some remarks about English translations of Plautus and Terence in the sixteenth century. The first point to make is that England was slower than some other countries to start producing translations of Latin comedy.[41] Stuart Gillespie has written that 'On a pan-European view from the beginning of printing in the mid-fifteenth century to 1600, and speaking quantitatively, classical translation moved fastest in Italy and France, with German, Spanish and English following some distance behind';[42] in the case of Plautus and Terence, England lagged behind Germany and Spain as well and produced remarkably few translations before 1600. R. R. Bolgar's charts, even if not entirely reliable, show that Italian and German versions of plays by both authors started to be published before 1500, Spanish versions of plays by Plautus from 1517, and a complete Spanish Terence in 1577. The two French versions of Terence's plays that Bolgar dates to *c.* 1466 and *c.* 1470 were in fact published in *c.* 1500, and their authorship and date of composition are not certain;[43] he also lists several French translations of individual plays of Terence from 1541 onwards, and French versions of two plays of Plautus in 1567 and 1580.[44] For Terence, Giovanni Cupaiuolo gives further details and also lists a large number of reprints of some volumes during the sixteenth century.[45] By contrast,

268   PETER BROWN

the only English translations of Terence produced during this period were two versions of the *Andria* published in the 1520s (together with the Latin text) and 1588 respectively, and a translation of all the plays published with the Latin text in 1598,[46] while the only translation of Plautus was William Warner's version of *Menaechmi*. (Since readers may well come across the claim that there was also a translation of *Amphitruo* published in the 1560s and written by Edward Courtenay, the first Duke of Devonshire,[47] it is perhaps worth pointing out that there was no such translation: the claim is based on a confusion with *Jacke Jugeler*, of which a printed copy was at one stage in the possession of a later Duke of Devonshire.[48] Also, the *Vulgaria quaedam abs Terentio in anglicam linguam traducta*, first published at Oxford in 1483 and reprinted several times in the late fifteenth and early sixteenth centuries,[49] was not a complete bilingual edition, as is sometimes claimed, but a selection of phrases from Terence's plays with their English equivalents — though that of course is a stepping-stone towards a more complete translation.)

There is clear evidence that translators of Latin texts into English expected to meet with disapproval,[50] and translators of Terence were no exception. The translation of the *Andria* from the 1520s (evidently written by more than one hand) has a Prologue and an Epilogue, explaining and justifying what the translators have done.[51] In the Prologue they say in lines 29–31 that they

> all discreet men now do beseech,
> And specially learned men, to take no disdain
> Though this be compiled in our vulgar speech.

And in the Epilogue (lines 15–21):

> And, for this thing is brought into the English tongue,
> We pray you all not to be discontent:
> For the Latin book which hath be used so long
> Was translate out of Greek: this is evident.
> And since our English tongue is now sufficient
> The matter to express, we think it best be may
> Before Englishmen in English it to play.

They say they have only treated Terence the way Terence treated his Greek source, and anyway if you are performing in England you might as well do it in English. This shows that they intended their translation to be performed, and it seems they envisage that at least some people in the audience have the learning to appreciate the play in Latin and will not altogether approve of its being put on in English. But we do not know whether it was in fact performed or in what sort of context they thought it might be.

Maurice Kyffin in 1588 similarly expects to meet with disapproval of his translation of the *Andria*, not for doing it at all but for using 'the most known, vsuall, and familiar phrases in common speech'. This is in his Preface, which is quoted entire in the brief account of Kyffin's translation by Henry Burrowes Lathrop.[52] Interestingly, Kyffin suggests that Terence was no longer much taught in English schools, saying 'And surely, great is the pity, that Terence were not more used of maisters in teaching, and made more familiar to schollers in learning, than commonly it is'.[53] Kyffin commends Terence as the best possible source 'for the

PLAUTUS AND TERENCE IN TUDOR ENGLAND   269

true knowledge and puritie of the Latin tong', but he is slightly apologetic about
the quality of the play itself and says: 'it was no part of my meaning to translate the
same, as a thing either pleasing to be played, or very delightful to bee read [...] but
especially, for that the Latin is pure & eloquent [...] & right requisite to be studied,
& understood of all such, as would attaine to the knowledge of right speaking,
and readines of wel writing, in the Latin tong.' (These claims for the excellence
of Terence's Latin were of long standing in Renaissance discussions of the author.)
Lathrop also quotes extracts from an introductory letter in which Kyffin says that
he had first translated almost the whole play into verse but then 'playnely saw, that
such manner of forced translation must needs be both harsh and vnpleasant to the
Reader, and also not halfe seemely befitting the sweete style and eloquence of the
Author'; so he has finally done it in prose.

According to Anne Henry, Kyffin's version has earned a place in the history
of printing as the first published play in English to use dashes to indicate that a
sentence is interrupted or left incomplete.[54]

Lathrop discusses Richard Bernard's 1598 translation of the whole of Terence,
which includes Kyffin's *Andria* slightly rewritten. Lathrop concludes that 'the book
as a whole in spite of its abundance of English colloquial expressions is nothing
more than a creditable school-book'.[55] In his dedicatory and introductory prefaces
Bernard commends the moral lessons to be learnt from the study of Terence
(another long-standing claim made by Terence's supporters) and also follows the
authors of the 1520s *Andria* in justifying the practice of translation into English by
pointing out that Terence himself had translated from Greek into Latin.

William Warner's translation of *Menaechmi* has a preface by the printer saying
that he has insisted on publishing it 'although I found him [the author] very loath
and unwilling to hazard this to the curious view of envious detraction (being as he
tels mee) neither so exactly written, as it may carry any name of a Translation, nor
such libertie therein used, as that he would notoriously varie from the Poets owne
order'. In other words, Warner feared that he would be criticized not for translating
at all but for falling between two stools; and it is doubtless a sign of his nervousness
that he marks with an asterisk passages where 'the Poets conceit is somewhat altred,
by occasion either of the time, the country, or the phrase'. I have counted twelve
of these asterisks, some of them at places where the Latin is in fact followed very
closely; I have also spotted at least as many further places where it would have
been appropriate to use an asterisk, particularly to indicate either expansions or
(sometimes quite considerable) abbreviations. Warner does not follow Plautus's
Latin nearly as closely as the rarity of his asterisks might lead us to believe, but I
think most readers would none the less judge that it is indeed 'so exactly written as
it may carry [the] name of a Translation'. As Gordon Braden says, 'Other changes
are not marked, and the translation would be unreliable for the schoolroom, but
it is respectful enough, and its virtues resemble those of Kyffin's *Andria*'.[56] Warner
certainly reproduces the overall structure of Plautus's play more closely than does
the anonymous translation of *Amphitruo* published as *The Birthe of Hercules* at the
start of the seventeenth century and discussed by Braden on pp. 284–85: this follows
the text closely but increases its length by nearly a third by adding a second slave

(Dromio) to complement Sosia and by making some further additions discussed by Smith.[57]

The case of Nicholas Udall provides further evidence for disapproval by learned men of the activity of translation from Latin in the sixteenth century. In 1534, well before *Jacke Jugeler* or *Roister Doister* was written, Udall applied to be awarded the status of Master of Arts at Oxford University. This was granted to him, but the Register of the University shows that at first they wanted to impose a condition, which they later withdrew. What is written in the Register is: *concessa sic quod in posterum non traducat ullos libros e Latina lingua in uernaculam nostram linguam* [granted on condition that in future he does not translate any books from Latin into our native language]; this condition has then been crossed out.[58] Shortly before this, Udall had published *Floures for Latine Spekynge: selected and gathered out of Terence, and the same translated in to Englyshe, together with the exposition and settynge forthe as well of such latyne wordes, as were thought nedefull to be annoted, as also of dyuers grammatical rules, very profitable & necessarye for the expedite knowledge of the latine tongue.*[59] This proved to be a very popular work and was reprinted several times. It is not strictly speaking a translation of Terence but rather (like the *Vulgaria* that it superseded) a selective commentary on three of his plays, going through the text in order and translating and explaining in particular the linguistic idioms which schoolchildren might at first find puzzling, with the aim of helping them to speak conversational Latin. Apparently that was what irritated someone at Oxford in 1534: we do not know of any other work of Udall's that could have provoked that reaction at that time. According to C. H. Conley the Universities were in general not in favour of translations and believed that Latin texts should be preserved for those capable of reading them in Latin; perhaps Oxford's first reaction to Udall's *Floures* was that it came dangerously close to making Terence easy to read.[60]

Robert Hornback has made what as far as I can judge is a very powerful case for regarding *Roister Doister* as subversive of Roman Catholic ritual in a number of ways.[61] Hornback further suggests that Udall also subverts the authority of Terence as the idol of the humanists, by writing in English, and sometimes even a ludicrously archaic, rustic sort of English, in a play that observes the regularities of the five-act structure with great care, and (what is more) that he was subverting the authority of Terence already in *Floures for Latine Spekynge* by selecting all the most colloquial expressions to elucidate. He suggests that Udall 'must have felt ambivalence about reverence for the Latin language and Roman dramatic form in the curriculum' (p. 39), since he was hostile to the use of Latin in the Roman Catholic Church. My own instinct about this is that translating Terence into English is rather different from translating the Bible or the Prayer Book; and in any case Hornback exaggerates the lowness of Terence's colloquial idioms. In fact it was Terence's highly original achievement to reproduce in his plays the style of cultivated conversation, the language we find in Cicero's *Letters*, and *Floures for Latine Spekynge* offers much more by way of elucidation than simply colloquial English equivalents for Terence's idioms. Udall was keen to bring Terence to life and to get students to think about how to translate him most effectively, but I do not see that as subversive of Terence's authority.

Conclusion

It will be clear from all the above that the influence of Plautus and Terence showed itself in a number of different ways in sixteenth-century drama in England, both in Latin and in English, both in close adaptations and in free combinations, sometimes explicitly acknowledged, sometimes not. *The Comedy of Errors* is a particularly striking example of a play that is both clearly based on Latin sources and very free in the way it adapts them, but others before Shakespeare had produced vigorous combinations of classical material with native elements. England was not alone in this, but it was as enterprising as any other country.

Bibliography

Andria. The first Comoedie of Terence, in English. A furtherance for the attainment vnto the right knowledge, and true proprietie, of the Latin Tong. And also a commodious meane of help, to such as haue forgotten Latin, for their speedy recouering of habilitie, to vnderstand, write, and speake the same. Carefully translated out of Latin, by Maurice Kyffin (London: T. East for T. Woodcocke, 1588)

AUSTEN, GILLIAN, *George Gascoigne*, Studies in Renaissance Literature, 24 (Cambridge: D. S. Brewer, 2008)

BALDWIN, THOMAS WHITFIELD, *William Shakspere's Small Latine and Lesse Greeke*, 2 vols (Urbana: University of Illinois Press, 1944)

—— *Shakspere's Five-Act Structure: Shakspere's Early Plays on the Background of Renaissance Theories of Five-Act Structure from 1470* (Urbana: University of Illinois Press, 1947)

BERTINI, FERRUCCIO, 'Un rifacimento del XVI secolo dell'*Amphitruo* plautino: il *Jack Juggler* di Nicholas Udall', in *Estudios sobre teatro romano: el mundo de los sentimientos y su expresión*, ed. by Rosario López Gregoris (Saragossa: Libros Pórtico, 2012), pp. 453–66

BLUME, HORST-DIETER, 'Plautus und Shakespeare', *Antike und Abendland*, 15.2 (1969), 135–58

BOAS, FREDERICK S., *University Drama in the Tudor Age* (Oxford: Clarendon Press, 1914)

BOLGAR, ROBERT RALPH, *The Classical Heritage and its Beneficiaries* (Cambridge: Cambridge University Press, 1958)

BOUGHNER, DANIEL C., *The Braggart in Renaissance Comedy* (Minneapolis: University of Minnesota Press, 1954)

BRADEN, GORDON, 'Comedy', in *The Oxford History of Literary Translation in English*, ed. by Gordon Braden, Robert Cummings and Stuart Gillespie (Oxford: Oxford University Press, 2010), vol. II: *1560–1660*, pp. 280–92

BROWN, PETER, 'Terence and Greek New Comedy', in *A Companion to Terence*, ed. by Antony Augoustakis and Ariana Traill (Malden, MA, Oxford and Chichester: Wiley-Blackwell, 2013), pp. 17–32

BULLOUGH, GEOFFREY, ed., *Narrative and Dramatic Sources of Shakespeare*, 3rd impression (London: Routledge & Kegan Paul; New York: Columbia University Press, 1964)

BURROW, COLIN, *Shakespeare and Classical Antiquity* (Oxford: Oxford University Press, 2013)

CHAMBERS, EDMUND K., *The Elizabethan Stage*, 4 vols (Oxford: Clarendon Press, 1923; repr. Oxford University Press, 2009)

CONLEY, CAREY H., *The First English Translators of the Classics* (New Haven, CT: Yale University Press, 1927)

CUPAIUOLO, GIOVANNI, *Bibliografia Terenziana (1470–1983)* (Naples: Società editrice napoletana, 1984)

DUCKWORTH, GEORGE E., *The Nature of Roman Comedy* (Princeton, NJ: Princeton University Press, 1952; repr. Bristol: Bristol Classical Press, 1994)

DUNCAN, DOUGLAS, '*Gammer Gurton's Needle* and the Concept of Humanist Parody', *Studies in English Literature, 1500–1900*, 27.2 (1987), 177–96

Early Plays from the Italian, ed. by R. Warwick Bond (Oxford: Clarendon Press, 1911)

Four Tudor Comedies, ed. by William Tydeman (London: Penguin, 1984)

FRULOVISIIS, TITUS LIVIUS DE, *Opera hactenus inedita T. Livii de Frulovisiis de Ferraria*, ed. by C. W. Previté-Orton (Cambridge: Cambridge University Press, 1932)

GARCÍA-HERNÁNDEZ, BENJAMIN, *Gemelos y sosias: la comedia de doble en Plauto, Shakespeare y Molière* (Madrid: Ediciones Clásicas, 2001)

GILLESPIE, STUART, *English Translation and Classical Reception: Towards a New Literary History* (Malden, MA, Oxford and Chichester: Wiley-Blackwell, 2011)

GUASTELLA, GIANNI, 'Pirgopolinice, Trasone, Ralph Roister Doister: evoluzioni di un paradigma classico', in *Lecturae Plautinae Sarsinates XII: Miles Gloriosus*, ed. by Renato Raffaelli and Alba Tontini (Urbino: QuattroVenti, 2009), pp. 53–109

HANDLEY, ERIC W., *Menander and Plautus: A Study in Comparison* (Inaugural Lecture, University College, London, 1968)

HARNISCHMACHER, WIBKE E., *Andrea Guarnas* Bellum Grammaticale: *Einführung, Text, Übersetzung, Kommentar*, Bochumer Altertumswissenschaftliches Colloquium, Band 94 (Trier: Wissenschaftlicher Verlag Trier, 2013)

HENRY, ANNE, '*Quid ais Omnium?* Maurice Kyffin's 1588 *Andria* and the Emergence of Suspension Marks in Printed Drama', *Renaissance Drama*, n.s., 34 (2005), 47–67

HORNBACK, ROBERT, 'A *Dirige* and Terence "in the Briers": Mock-Ritual and Mock-Classicism as Iconoclastic Translation in Udall's *Ralph Roister Doister*', *Research Opportunities in Medieval and Renaissance Drama*, 48 (2009), 22–47

—— 'Reformation Satire, Scatology, and Iconoclastic Aesthetics in *Gammer Gurton's Needle*', in *A Companion to Tudor Literature*, ed. by Kent Cartwright (Malden, MA, Oxford and Chichester: Wiley-Blackwell, 2010), pp. 309–23

HOSLEY, RICHARD, 'The Formal Influence of Plautus and Terence', in *Elizabethan Theatre*, ed. by John Russell Brown and Bernard Harris, Stratford-upon-Avon Studies, 9 (London: Edward Arnold, 1966), pp. 131–45

Humanist Comedies, ed. and trans. by Gary R. Grund, The I Tatti Renaissance Library, 19 (Cambridge, MA, and London: Harvard University Press, 2005)

HUTSON, LORNA, *The Invention of Suspicion: Law and Mimesis in Shakespeare and Renaissance Drama* (Oxford: Oxford University Press, 2007)

HUTTEN, LEONARD, *Bellum Grammaticale*, hypertext edition with English translation by Dana F. Sutton, first posted 8 October 2007 (revised version 7 January 2008) at <www. philological.bham.ac.uk/bellum/> [accessed February 2014]

Leonard Hutton (?), Bellum Grammaticale sive Nominum Verborumque Discordia Civilis (printed 1635); Thomas Snelling, Thibaldus sive Vindictae Ingenium (printed 1640), prepared with an introduction by Lothar Cerny, Renaissance Latin Drama in England — first series, vol. 12, ed. by Marvin Spevack and J. W. Binns (Hildesheim and New York: Georg Olms Verlag, 1982)

Hymenaeus, ed. by George C. Moore Smith (Cambridge: Cambridge University Press, 1908)

Hymenaeus, Victoria, and *Laelia*, ed. by Horst-Dieter Blume, Renaissance Latin Drama in England — second series, vol. 13, ed. by Marvin Spevack, J. W. Binns, and Hans-Jürgen Weckermann (Hildesheim, Zurich and New York: Georg Olms Verlag, 1991)

Ioannis Harmonii Marsi Comoedia Stephanium, ed. by Walther Ludwig (Munich: Wilhelm Fink Verlag, 1971)

LATHROP, HENRY BURROWES, *Translations from the Classics into English from Caxton to*

Chapman, 1477–1620, University of Wisconsin Studies in Language and Literature, 35 (Madison: University of Wisconsin, 1933; repr. New York: Octagon Books, 1967)

LAWTON, HAROLD WALTER, *Contribution à l'histoire de l'humanisme en France: Térence en France au XVIe siècle, éditions et traductions* (Paris: Jouve, 1926; repr. Geneva: Slatkine, 1970)

LEA, KATHLEEN MARGUERITE, *Italian Popular Comedy: A Study in the Commedia dell'Arte, 1560–1620, with Special Reference to the English Stage* (Oxford: Clarendon Press, 1934)

LEVENSON, JILL, 'Tragedy', in *The Cambridge Companion to English Renaissance Drama*, ed. by A. R. Braunmuller and Michael Hattaway, 2nd edn (Cambridge: Cambridge University Press, 2003), pp. 254–91

MAXWELL, JAMES C., '"Amphytrio" or "Jack Juggler"', letter to the *Times Literary Supplement*, 17 May, 1957

Menaecmi. A pleasant and fine Conceited Comaedie, taken out of the most excellent wittie Poet Plautus. Chosen purposely from out of the rest, as least harmefull, and yet most delightfull. Written in English, by W[illiam]. W[arner] (London: T. Creede, 1595), available in *Early English Books Online*

MIOLA, ROBERT S., *Shakespeare and Classical Comedy* (Oxford: Clarendon Press, 1994)

——'Aristophanes in England, 1500–1660', in *Ancient Comedy and Reception: Essays in Honor of Jeffrey Henderson*, ed. by S. Douglas Olson (Berlin and Boston, MA: De Gruyter, 2014), pp. 479–502

MOTTER, THOMAS HUBBARD VAIL, *The School Drama in England* (London, New York and Toronto: Longmans, Green and Co., 1929)

NØRGAARD, HOLGER, 'Translations of the Classics into English before 1600', *The Review of English Studies*, n.s., 9.34 (May 1958), 164–72

NORLAND, HOWARD B., *Drama in Early Tudor Britain, 1485–1558* (Lincoln and London: University of Nebraska Press, 1995)

Pedantius, ed. by George C. Moore Smith (= *Materialien zur Kunde des älteren Englischen Dramas* vol. 8, Louvain / Leipzig / London: A. Uystpruyst / O. Harrassowitz / David Nutt, 1905)

Pedantius, hypertext edition with English translation by Dana F. Sutton, first posted 23 January 1998, at <www.philological.bham.ac.uk/forsett/>

RADCLIFF-UMSTEAD, DOUGLAS, *The Birth of Modern Comedy in Renaissance Italy* (Chicago, IL, and London: University of Chicago Press, 1969)

Records of Early English Drama: Cambridge, ed. by Alan H. Nelson, 2 vols (Toronto, Buffalo, NY, and London: University of Toronto Press, 1989)

Records of Early English Drama: Oxford, ed. by J. R. Elliott, Jr, A. H. Nelson, A. F. Johnston, and D. Wyatt, 2 vols (London and Toronto: The British Library and University of Toronto Press, 2004)

RIEHLE, WOLFGANG, *Shakespeare, Plautus and the Humanist Tradition* (Cambridge: D. S. Brewer, 1990)

ROWLAND, RICHARD, *Thomas Heywood's Theatre, 1599–1639: Locations, Translations, and Conflict* (Farnham: Ashgate, 2010)

RUDD, NIALL, '*The Taming of the Shrew*: Some Classical Points of Reference', *Hermathena*, 129 (1980), 23–28

——*The Classical Tradition in Operation* (Toronto, Buffalo, NY, and London: University of Toronto Press, 1994)

——*The Common Spring: Essays on Latin and English Poetry* (Exeter: Bristol Phoenix Press, 2005)

SALINGAR, LEO, *Shakespeare and the Traditions of Comedy* (Cambridge: Cambridge University Press, 1974)

SEGAL, ERICH, *The Death of Comedy* (Cambridge, MA, and London: Harvard University Press, 2001)

SHAKESPEARE, WILLIAM, *The Comedy of Errors*, ed. by R. A. Foakes, The Arden Shakespeare (London: Methuen & Co. Ltd, 1962)

—— *The Taming of the Shrew*, ed. by Brian Morris, The Arden Shakespeare (London: Methuen & Co. Ltd, 1981)

SMITH, BRUCE R., *Ancient Scripts & Modern Experience on the English Stage, 1500–1700* (Princeton, NJ: Princeton University Press, 1988)

STEGGLE, MATTHEW, 'Aristophanes in Early Modern England', in *Aristophanes in Performance*, ed. by Edith Hall and Amanda Wrigley (London: Legenda, 2007), pp. 52–65

Supposes and Jocasta: two plays translated from the Italian, ed. by John W. Cunliffe (Boston, MA, and London: D. C. Heath, 1906)

TANNER, LAWRENCE E., *Westminster School*, 2nd edn (London: Country Life 1951)

Terence in English. Fabulae comici facetissimi et elegantissimi poetae Terentii omnes Anglicae factae primumque hac noua forma nunc editae (Cambridge: J. Legatt, 1598)

Terence in English, ed. by Meg Twycross, Medieval English Theatre Modern Spelling Texts, 6 (Lancaster: Lancaster University, 1987)

Terens in englysh. The translacyon out of latin into englysh of the first comedy of tyrens callyd Andria (London: J. Rastell, 1520–30)

The Bugbears; A Modernized Edition, ed. by James D. Clark (New York and London: Garland Publishing, 1979)

The Cambridge Edition of the Works of Ben Jonson, ed. by David Bevington, Martin Butler, and Ian Donaldson (Cambridge: Cambridge University Press, 2012)

Therence en francois, prose et rime, auecques le latin (Paris: A. Vérard, *c.* 1500)

THOMSON, JAMES ALEXANDER K., *Shakespeare and the Classics* (London: George Allen & Unwin, 1952; repr. 1966)

Three Rastell Plays, ed. by Richard Axton (Cambridge: D. S. Brewer; Totowa, NJ: Rowman and Littlefield, 1979)

Three Tudor Classical Interludes, ed. by Marie Axton (Cambridge: D. S. Brewer; Totowa, NJ: Rowman and Littlefield, 1982)

UDALL, NICHOLAS, *Nicholas Udall's Roister Doister*, ed. by Gustave Scheurweghs, Materialien zur Kunde des älteren Englischen Dramas, New Series, 16 (Louvain : Librairie universitaire, C. Uystpruyst, 1939)

—— *Floures for Latine Spekynge: selected and gathered out of Terence, and the same translated in to Englyshe, together with the exposition and settynge forthe as well of such latyne wordes, as were thought nedefull to be annoted, as also of dyuers grammatical rules, very profitable & necessarye for the expedite knowledge of the latine tongue* (London: T. Berthelet, 1533), available in *Early English Books Online*

VAN ELK, MARTINE, ' "Thou shalt present me as an eunuch to him": Terence in Early Modern England', in *A Companion to Terence*, ed. by Antony Augoustakis and Ariana Traill (Malden, MA, Oxford and Chichester: Wiley-Blackwell, 2013), pp. 410–28

VON REINHARDSTOETTNER, KARL, *Plautus. Spätere Bearbeitungen plautinischer Lustspiele* (Leipzig: Verlag von Wilhelm Friedrich, 1886; repr. Hildesheim and New York: Georg Olms Verlag, 1980)

Vulgaria quaedam abs Terentio in anglicam linguam traducta (Oxford: T. Rood and T. Hunt, 1483)

WALTON, J. MICHAEL, 'Business as Usual: Plautus' *Menaechmi* in English Translation', in *Ancient Comedy and Reception: Essays in Honor of Jeffrey Henderson*, ed. by S. Douglas Olson (Berlin and Boston, MA: De Gruyter, 2014), pp. 1040–61

WILSON, FRANK PIERCE, *The English Drama, 1485–1585*, ed. by George K. Hunter (Oxford: Clarendon Press, 1969)

PLAUTUS AND TERENCE IN TUDOR ENGLAND   275

Notes to Chapter 12

1. On the place of Plautus and Terence in the educational curriculum see, for example, Martine van Elk, ' "Thou shalt present me as an eunuch to him": Terence in Early Modern England', in *A Companion to Terence*, ed. by Antony Augoustakis and Ariana Traill (Malden, MA, Oxford and Chichester: Wiley-Blackwell, 2013), pp. 410–28, with references to earlier discussions. On Plautus' adaptation of Menander in his *Bacchides* see Eric W. Handley, *Menander and Plautus: A Study in Comparison* (Inaugural Lecture, University College, London, 1968). On Terence's adaptations of Greek plays see Peter Brown, 'Terence and Greek New Comedy', in *A Companion to Terence*, pp. 17–32. There is an overall survey of English Renaissance comedy and its sources by Jill Levenson in *The Cambridge Companion to English Renaissance Drama*, ed. by A. R. Braunmuller and Michael Hattaway, 2nd edn (Cambridge: Cambridge University Press, 2003), pp. 254–91. For Aristophanes, the other ancient comic playwright whose works were known at the time, see Matthew Steggle, 'Aristophanes in Early Modern England', in *Aristophanes in Performance*, ed. by Edith Hall and Amanda Wrigley (London: Legenda, 2007), pp. 52–65 and Robert S. Miola, 'Aristophanes in England, 1500–1600', in *Ancient Comedy and Reception: Essays in Honor of Jeffrey Henderson*, ed. by S. Douglas Olson (Berlin and Boston, MA: De Gruyter, 2014), pp. 479–502.

2. See the 'Chronological List of College Performances', in *Records of Early English Drama: Cambridge*, ed. by Alan H. Nelson, 2 vols (Toronto, Buffalo, NY, and London: University of Toronto Press, 1989), II, 963–76. There is a summary list of the productions of identified plays in Bruce R. Smith, *Ancient Scripts & Modern Experience on the English Stage, 1500–1700* (Princeton, NJ: Princeton University Press, 1988), p. 138; as Smith says on p. 139, 'Perhaps it is more than the chance survival of good records that marks off the 1550s and 1560s as a particularly strong period for classical comedy at Cambridge'.

3. See *Records of Early English Drama: Oxford*, ed. by J. R. Elliott, Jr, A. H. Nelson, A. F. Johnston, and D. Wyatt, 2 vols (London and Toronto: The British Library and University of Toronto Press, 2004), II, 847–49.

4. See Edmund K. Chambers, *The Elizabethan Stage*, 4 vols (Oxford: Clarendon Press, 1923; repr. Oxford University Press, 2009), III, 19–20; Smith, *Ancient Scripts*, pp. 134–38.

5. I do not know on what evidence Frank Pierce Wilson, *The English Drama 1485–1585*, ed. by G. K. Hunter (Oxford: Clarendon Press, 1969), p. 103, thought it possible that the first also was performed by them, though of course that may be true. Chambers, *The Elizabethan Stage*, II, 12, n. 1 accepts that they did not perform the second, against his own earlier view.

6. So Thomas Hubbard Vail Motter, *The School Drama in England* (London, New York and Toronto: Longmans, Green and Co., 1929), p. 237, unfortunately without citing any source.

7. The database of the *Archive of Performances of Greek and Roman Drama* at <www.apgrd.ox.ac.uk> [accessed 4 April 2013] lists two productions in 1545 as well as two in 1564 and one in each of 1566, 1567, and 1569. It is not certain that the first two took place, but the Head Master wrote drafts of prose prologues which were clearly intended to be spoken before performances: see Lawrence E. Tanner, *Westminster School*, 2nd edn (London: Country Life, 1951), p. 99; Smith, *Ancient Scripts*, pp. 141–47.

8. Horst-Dieter Blume on p. 5 of his edition of *Hymenaeus, Victoria*, and *Laelia*, vol. 13 of the Second Series of *Renaissance Latin Drama in England*, ed. by Marvin Spevack, J. W. Binns, and Hans-Jürgen Weckermann (Hildesheim, Zurich and New York: Georg Olms Verlag, 1991). Since that volume reproduces manuscripts of the plays, readers may prefer to consult the edition with notes of *Hymenaeus* by George C. Moore Smith (Cambridge: Cambridge University Press, 1908). There are summaries of the play in Frederick S. Boas, *University Drama in the Tudor Age* (Oxford: Clarendon Press, 1914), pp. 124–40 and (with more attention to the relationship with ancient comedy) in Blume, pp. 1–14. Boas in his book discusses some other Latin plays not discussed here.

9. Boas, *University Drama* p. 139.

10. *Hymenaeus*, ed. by George C. Moore Smith (Cambridge: Cambridge University Press, 1908).

11. For a summary of the play see Frederick S. Boas, *University Drama*, pp. 148–56. There is an edition

276   PETER BROWN

by George C. Moore Smith (= *Materialien zur Kunde des älteren Englischen Dramas* vol. 8, Louvain / Leipzig / London: A. Uystpruyst / O. Harrassowitz / David Nutt, 1905), and also a hypertext edition with English translation by Dana F. Sutton, first posted 23 January 1998, at <www.philological.bham.ac.uk/forsett/>. *Pedantius* is in one sense Aristophanic, in that it was evidently a sustained caricature of Gabriel Harvey, a noted figure of the contemporary academic world.

12. For an account of the Queen's visit and of the play see Boas, *University Drama*, pp. 252–67. There is a hypertext edition with English translation by Dana F. Sutton, first posted 8 October 2007 (revised version 7 January 2008) at <www.philological.bham.ac.uk/bellum/>, and a facsimile reproduction of the 1635 printing of the play in *Leonard Hutton (?), Bellum Grammaticale sive Nominum Verborumque Discordia Civilis (printed 1635); Thomas Snelling, Thibaldus sive Vindictae Ingenium (printed 1640)*, prepared with an introduction by Lothar Cerny, Renaissance Latin Drama in England — first series, 12, ed. by Marvin Spevack and J. W. Binns (Hildesheim and New York: Georg Olms Verlag, 1982). The other play performed before the Queen, William Gager's *Rivales*, has unfortunately not survived, but we do have two Prologues and an Epilogue written by Gager for this production of *Bellum Grammaticale*. The Epilogue and one of the Prologues can be found in Sutton's hypertext edition; the other Prologue is briefly summarized by Boas, *University Drama*, at the top of p. 266.

13. Boas, *University Drama*, p. 257. There is an edition of Guarna's work by Wibke E. Harnischmacher, *Andrea Guarnas Bellum Grammaticale: Einführung, Text, Übersetzung, Kommentar*, Bochumer Altertumswissenschaftliches Colloquium, Band 94 (Trier: Wissenschaftlicher Verlag Trier, 2013).

14. Richard Rowland, 'Stages of Translation in Early Modern England', in *Thomas Heywood's Theatre, 1599–1639: Locations, Translations, and Conflict* (Farnham: Ashgate, 2010), pp. 157–72 (pp. 160–62).

15. *Paulus, Philodoxus*, and *Chrysis* are included in *Humanist Comedies*, ed. and trans. by Gary R. Grund, The I Tatti Renaissance Library, 19 (Cambridge, MA, and London: Harvard University Press, 2005). The comedies of Frulovisi were edited by Charles-William Previté-Orton in *Opera hactenus inedita T. Livii de Frulovisiis de Ferraria* (Cambridge: Cambridge University Press, 1932). All these works are discussed briefly by Douglas Radcliff-Umstead, *The Birth of Modern Comedy in Renaissance Italy* (Chicago, IL, and London: University of Chicago Press, 1969), pp. 25–42, with plot summaries on pp. 245–53. For a fuller discussion of *Philodoxus* see Martin McLaughlin's chapter in this volume.

16. See *Ioannis Harmonii Marsi Comoedia Stephanium*, ed. by Walther Ludwig (Munich: Wilhelm Fink Verlag, 1971), pp. 43–71.

17. See Richard Hosley, 'The Formal Influence of Plautus and Terence', in *Elizabethan Theatre*, ed. by John Russell Brown and Bernard Harris, Stratford-upon-Avon Studies, 9 (London: Edward Arnold, 1966), pp. 131–45; Leo Salingar, *Shakespeare and the Traditions of Comedy* (Cambridge: Cambridge University Press, 1974), pp. 175–242.

18. Included in *Three Rastell Plays*, ed. by Richard Axton (Cambridge: D. S. Brewer; Totowa, NJ: Rowman and Littlefield, 1979). The play is discussed by Howard B. Norland, *Drama in Early Tudor Britain, 1485–1558* (Lincoln and London: University of Nebraska Press, 1995), pp. 244–54.

19. See *Three Rastell Plays*, p. 142.

20. Available e.g. in *Supposes and Jocasta: two plays translated from the Italian*, ed. by John W. Cunliffe (Boston, MA, and London: D. C. Heath, 1906), in *Early Plays from the Italian*, ed. by Richard Warwick Bond (Oxford: Clarendon Press, 1911), and in *Narrative and Dramatic Sources of Shakespeare*, ed. by Geoffrey Bullough, 3rd impression, vol. 1 (London: Routledge & Kegan Paul; New York: Columbia University Press, 1964), pp. 111–58. On pp. 66–68 Bullough discusses briefly the use made by Shakespeare of Gascoigne's play in *The Taming of the Shrew*, also discussed by Hosley, 'The Formal Influence of Plautus and Terence', pp. 142–45. There is a brief overview of the play in Gillian Austen, *George Gascoigne*, Studies in Renaissance Literature, 24 (Cambridge: D. S. Brewer, 2008), pp. 48–52; see also Lorna Hutson, *The Invention of Suspicion: Law and Mimesis in Shakespeare and Renaissance Drama* (Oxford: Oxford University Press, 2007), pp. 185–207.

21. See *The Bugbears; A Modernized Edition*, ed. by James D. Clark (New York and London: Garland Publishing, 1979). The play is also included in *Early Plays from the Italian*.

PLAUTUS AND TERENCE IN TUDOR ENGLAND   277

22. Clark, *The Bugbears; A Modernized Edition* has a chart summarizing the author's use of his various sources on pp. 92–93.
23. This play is included in *Three Tudor Classical Interludes*, ed. by Marie Axton (Cambridge: D. S. Brewer; Totowa, NJ: Rowman and Littlefield, 1982) and in *Four Tudor Comedies*, ed. by William Tydeman (London: Penguin, 1984). There is a survey of the play's debts to Plautus by Karl von Reinhardstoettner, *Plautus. Spätere Bearbeitungen plautinischer Lustspiele* (Leipzig: Verlag von Wilhelm Friedrich, 1886; repr. Hildesheim and New York: Georg Olms Verlag, 1980), pp. 186–90. For a more recent account of the play, including a discussion of its relationship to *Roister Doister*, see Ferruccio Bertini, 'Un rifacimento del XVI secolo dell'*Amphitruo* plautino: il *Jack Juggler* di Nicholas Udall', in *Estudios sobre teatro romano: el mundo de los sentimientos y su expresión*, ed. by Rosario López Gregoris (Saragossa: Libros Pórtico, 2012), pp. 453–66.
24. See above all Thomas Whitfield Baldwin, *Shakspere's Five-Act Structure: Shakspere's Early Plays on the Background of Renaissance Theories of Five-Act Structure from 1470* (Urbana: University of Illinois Press, 1947); Baldwin discusses the structure of *Roister Doister* on pp. 386–401, rightly stressing the play's debts to Terence. Another comedy that can be analysed in similar structural terms is *Gammer Gurton's Needle*, written for performance at Christ's College, Cambridge, probably in the early 1550s and possibly a few months before the first performance of *Roister Doister*. Douglas Duncan, '*Gammer Gurton's Needle* and the Concept of Humanist Parody', *Studies in English Literature, 1500–1900*, 27.2 (1987), 177–96 presents a strong case for seeing that play as a parody of Terence as he was interpreted in commentaries with which the student audience would have been familiar; see also Robert Hornback, 'Reformation Satire, Scatology, and Iconoclastic Aesthetics in *Gammer Gurton's Needle*', in *A Companion to Tudor Literature*, ed. by Kent Cartwright (Malden, MA, Oxford and Chichester: Wiley-Blackwell, 2010), pp. 309–23. But the play cannot be closely related to specific Plautine or Terentian prototypes.
25. This play is included in *Four Tudor Comedies*, edited by Tydeman who lists other twentieth-century editions on pp. 97–98. The circumstances of its first performance are a matter of conjecture.
26. Gianni Guastella, 'Pirgopolinice, Trasone, Ralph Roister Doister: evoluzioni di un paradigma classico', in *Lecturae Plautinae Sarsinates XII: Miles Gloriosus*, ed. by Renato Raffaelli and Alba Tontini (Urbino: QuattroVenti, 2009), pp. 53–109, citing earlier discussions. As Guastella brings out, the plot is indebted to *Eunuchus*, whereas *Miles Gloriosus* provides 'una significativa serie di motivi complementari' (p. 62).
27. Daniel C. Boughner, *The Braggart in Renaissance Comedy* (Minneapolis: University of Minnesota Press, 1954). Guastella , 'Pirgopolinice, Trasone, Ralph Roister Doister', pp. 84–85, points out a number of differences between the tradition that had developed and the portrayal of Roister Doister. Also, on pp. 71–78, he discusses the interlude *Thersytes*, perhaps also by Udall, performed probably by schoolboys or students in 1537. This was based on a brief dialogue in Latin hexameters written by the French humanist Ravisius Textor in the 1520s and showed Thersites as a vainglorious soldier who shows some trepidation even in fighting against a snail; a text is included in Marie Axton's edition of *Three Tudor Classical Interludes*.
28. See Chapter 19 of *Drama in Early Tudor Britain, 1485–1558*. My picture of Aristophanes is rather different from his, and some of the features he points to seem to me as much Plautine as Aristophanic.
29. Guastella, 'Pirgopolinice, Trasone, Ralph Roister Doister'.
30. For accounts of Shakespeare's use of Plautus in this play see (among many others) Horst-Dieter Blume, 'Plautus und Shakespeare', *Antike und Abendland*, 15.2 (1969), 135–58; Wolfgang Riehle, *Shakespeare, Plautus and the Humanist Tradition* (Cambridge: D. S. Brewer, 1990); Robert S. Miola, *Shakespeare and Classical Comedy* (Oxford: Clarendon Press, 1994), pp. 20–38; Niall Rudd, *The Classical Tradition in Operation* (Toronto, Buffalo, NY, and London: University of Toronto Press, 1994), pp. 32–60 ; Erich Segal, *The Death of Comedy* (Cambridge, MA, and London: Harvard University Press, 2001), pp. 286–304; Benjamin García-Hernández, *Gemelos y sosias: la comedia de doble en Plauto, Shakespeare y Molière* (Madrid: Ediciones Clásicas, 2001), pp. 163–202. Colin Burrow, *Shakespeare and Classical Antiquity* (Oxford: Oxford University Press, 2013), pp. 143–51 includes a discussion of this play in a chapter (pp. 133–61) showing how wide-ranging and pervasive the influence of Plautus and Terence was in Shakespeare's works.

278 PETER BROWN

31. See Kathleen Marguerite Lea, *Italian Popular Comedy: A Study in the Commedia dell'Arte, 1560–1620 with Special Reference to the English Stage*, 2 vols (Oxford: Clarendon Press, 1934), I, 173.
32. James Alexander K. Thomson, *Shakespeare and the Classics* (London: George Allen & Unwin, 1952; repr. 1966), p. 49.
33. See *The Comedy of Errors*, ed. by R. A. Foakes, The Arden Shakespeare (London: Methuen & Co. Ltd, 1962), pp. xxxi–xxxii.
34. London: Methuen & Co. Ltd, 1981.
35. Niall Rudd, *The Common Spring: Essays on Latin and English Poetry* (Exeter: Bristol Phoenix Press, 2005), pp. 118–19 [the end of the chapter '*The Taming of the Shrew*: Some Classical Points of Reference', reprinted from *Hermathena*, 129 (1980), 23–28].
36. I wonder too about IV. v. 42, 'This is a man, old, wrinkled, faded, wither'd': cf. *Eunuchus* 688, *hic est uietus uetus ueternosus senex* [This one's an old man, sunken, senile, and soporific], in each case correcting an apparent misperception. For larger-scale similarities (and significant differences) between the two plays see Miola, *Shakespeare and Classical Comedy*, pp. 70–74, in a discussion of Shakespeare's play (pp. 62–79) which also covers other classical points of comparison and contrast, particularly in Plautus' *Mostellaria* and *Captivi*.
37. This play, edited by Robert Miola, is included in volume I of *The Cambridge Edition of the Works of Ben Jonson*, ed. by David Bevington, Martin Butler and Ian Donaldson (Cambridge: Cambridge University Press, 2012).
38. Cf. Rowland, 'Stages of Translation in Early Modern England', p. 164: 'Jonson's most extensive debt to Plautus'; Rowland there mentions Charles Fitzgeoffrey's Latin epigram accusing Jonson of plagiarism in following Plautus so closely.
39. *Menaecmi. A pleasant and fine Conceited Comaedie, taken out of the most excellent wittie Poet Plautus. Chosen purposely from out of the rest, as least harmefull, and yet most delightfull. Written in English, by W[illiam]. W[arner]* (London: T. Creede, 1595), available in *Early English Books Online*.
40. Riehle, *Shakespeare, Plautus and the Humanist Tradition*, pp. 279–83.
41. Portugal was another country where there were few translations. See Chapter 5 (eds).
42. Stuart Gillespie, *English Translation and Classical Reception: Towards a New Literary History* (Malden, MA, Oxford and Chichester: Wiley-Blackwell, 2011), p. 6.
43. *Therence en francois, prose et rime, auecques le latin* (Paris: A. Vérard, *c.* 1500), containing two versions, one in prose and one in verse. For a detailed and highly critical discussion of these, see Harold Walter Lawton, *Contribution à l'histoire de l'humanisme en France: Térence en France au XVIe siècle, éditions et traductions* (Paris: Jouve, 1926; repr. Geneva: Slatkine, 1970), pp. 350–425. In the same volume Lawton discusses other French translations of Terence.
44. Robert Ralph Bolgar, *The Classical Heritage and its Beneficiaries* (Cambridge: Cambridge University Press, 1958), pp. 532–33 (for Plautus) and pp. 536–37 (for Terence).
45. Giovanni Cupaiuolo, *Bibliografia Terenziana (1470–1983)* (Naples: Società editrice napoletana, 1984), with brief summaries of the evidence on pp. 13–14 and 16–17.
46. (1) *Terens in englysh. The translacyon out of latin into englysh of the first comedy of tyrens callyd Andria* (London: J. Rastell, 1520–30). (2) *Andria. The first Comoedie of Terence, in English. A furtherance for the attainment vnto the right knowledge, and true proprietie, of the Latin Tong. And also a commodious meane of help, to such as haue forgotten Latin, for their speedy recouering of habilitie, to vnderstand, write, and speake the same. Carefully translated out of Latin, by Maurice Kyffin* (London: T. East for T. Woodcocke, 1588). (3) *Terence in English. Fabulae comici facetissimi et elegantissimi poetae Terentii omnes Anglicae factae primumque hac noua forma nunc editae* (Cambridge: J. Legatt, 1598).
47. For instance, George E. Duckworth, *The Nature of Roman Comedy* (Princeton, NJ: Princeton University Press, 1952; repr. Bristol: Bristol Classical Press, 1994), p. 413 n. 61 remarks that 'Courtney's translation of the *Amphitruo* seems to have been overlooked by many scholars'. The translation is also listed at Bolgar, *The Classical Heritage and its Beneficiaries*, p. 532.
48. See Holger Nørgaard, 'Translations of the Classics into English before 1600', *The Review of English Studies*, n.s., 9.34 (May 1958), 164–72 (p. 164), and the letter of James C. Maxwell to the *Times Literary Supplement* of 17 May 1957.
49. Cupaiuolo, *Bibliografia Terenziana (1470–1983)*, p. 269, nos 2724–32.
50. C. H. Conley, *The First English Translators of the Classics* (New Haven, CT: Yale University Press, 1927), p. 85: 'hardly any other one topic receives the amount of attention in the dedications and prefaces that the opposition to the translation of the classics does'.

51. There is an edition of this version by Meg Twycross, *Terence in English*, Medieval English Theatre Modern Spelling Texts, 6 (Lancaster: Lancaster University, 1987). The title might seem to evoke that of the French translation of all of Terence's plays cited in n. 38, but the English translation is far more accurate, and I see no sign that its authors knew the French versions.

52. Henry Burrowes Lathrop, *Translations from the Classics into English from Caxton to Chapman, 1477–1620*, University of Wisconsin Studies in Language and Literature, 35 (Madison: University of Wisconsin, 1933; repr. New York: Octagon Books, 1967), pp. 223–26.

53. T. W. Baldwin, *William Shakspere's Small Latine and Lesse Greeke*, 2 vols (Urbana: University of Illinois Press, 1944), II, 262–64 documents a slight weakening in the position of Terence in some schools at this time but does not suggest that it had gone very far and certainly not that Terence was no longer being read.

54. Anne Henry, '*Quid ais Omnium?* Maurice Kyffin's 1588 *Andria* and the Emergence of Suspension Marks in Printed Drama', *Renaissance Drama*, n.s., 34 (2005), 47–67.

55. Lathrop, *Translations from the Classics into English*, pp. 291–93

56. Gordon Braden, 'Comedy', in *The Oxford History of Literary Translation in English*, ed. by Gordon Braden, Robert Cummings and Stuart Gillespie (Oxford: Oxford University Press, 2010), vol. II: *1560–1660*, pp. 280–92, (p. 285). However, J. Michael Walton quotes several instances of lively and spirited translation in Warner's version in 'Business as Usual: Plautus' *Menaechmi* in English Translation', in *Ancient Comedy and Reception: Essays in Honor of Jeffrey Henderson*, ed. by S. Douglas Olson (Berlin and Boston, MA: De Gruyter, 2014), pp. 1040–61 (pp. 1044–47).

57. Smith, *Ancient Scripts & Modern Experience on the English Stage*, pp. 164–68.

58. See *Nicholas Udall's Roister Doister*, ed. by Gustave Scheurweghs, Materialien zur Kunde des älteren Englischen Dramas, New Series, 16 (Louvain : Librairie universitaire, C. Uystpruyst, 1939), pp. xv–xvi, xix n.4.

59. London: T. Berthelet, 1533, available in *Early English Books Online*.

60. Conley, *The First English Translators of the Classics*, pp. 89–90, p. 124.

61. Robert Hornback, 'A *Dirige* and Terence "in the Briers": Mock-Ritual and Mock-Classicism as Iconoclastic Translation in Udall's *Ralph Roister Doister*', *Research Opportunities in Medieval and Renaissance Drama*, 48 (2009), 22–47.

CHAPTER 13

❖

Diffusing Drama:
Manuscript and Print in the
Transmission of Camões's Plays

Vanda Anastácio

Universidade de Lisboa

Among the works attributed to Camões there are three plays — *Enfatriões*, *Filodemo* and *Seleuco* — probably written between 1540 and 1560. These have often been considered by the critics as 'minor' achievements, sometimes even as *oeuvres de jeunesse*, which is to say, texts which do not reflect either the maturity or the full capabilities of an author best known for the epic poem *Os Lusíadas*, and whose lyric poems have been received by posterity both as the height of poetic perfection and as a model to be followed.[1]

One possible explanation for this interpretation could be the apparent simplicity of these plays. In fact, as far as their structure is concerned, Camões's plays are very close to the *auto*, an Iberian dramatic form of late medieval origin, used in liturgical plays associated with church celebrations like Christmas or Easter. The *auto* was a relatively short text (500 to 1000 verses) intended to be performed without interruption (presenting no divisions into acts and scenes), and composed in the traditional short metres of the verse-forms known as *redondilhas* (verses of seven or five syllables and hemistichs rhyming with them, also called *quebrados*) organized into five- or ten-verse stanzas.[2] One should note, however, that not all Camões's plays have the same structure: *Enfatriões* is written entirely in verse, but *Filodemo* and *Seleuco* both combine the traditional peninsular metres and forms with prose.[3]

The subjects chosen by Camões for his plays have in common the fact that they are all of erudite or bookish origin, although they had such a large circulation at the time that they were probably also known outside learned circles. *Enfatriões* is an adaptation of Plautus's *Amphitruo*, *Seleuco* dramatizes an episode found in Plutarch, Valerius Maximus, and other Roman authors, and the intrigue of *Filodemo* was clearly inspired both by the fifteenth-century *Tragedia de Calixto y Melibea* better known as *Celestina* by Fernando de Rojas (1465–1541), and by the *Eufrosina* by the Portuguese Jorge Ferreira de Vasconcelos (1597–1632). It also makes use of a number of *topoi* taken from the sentimental and chivalresque novels then in vogue.[4]

Instead of analysing the plays, I would like to concentrate on their transmission, and try to shed some light on the way plays have circulated in Portugal from the introduction of print, until the eighteenth century.

As is often the case with early modern authors, there are no autographs of the three plays attributed to Camões. Two of them, *Enfatriões* and *Filodemo*, were printed for the first time in Lisbon, in 1587, around seven years after the death of the author, in a miscellaneous compilation of works for theatre published by Antonio Lopes and Andres Lobato. The third play, *Seleuco*, remained unknown until 1645, when it was included by the printer Paulo Craesbeeck at the end of an edition of the complete works of the poet.[5] For *Enfatriões* and *Seleuco* there is only one surviving witness before 1700. For *Filodemo* however, a second contemporary source is known: one version of this play was copied in a handwritten *Cancioneiro* by Luís Franco Corrêa who, in the first page of this compilation, explains that he started making copies in 1557 and finished in 1589, claiming to have collected only texts which were never printed before, and refers to himself as 'a companion in the state of India as well as a close friend of Luís de Camões'.

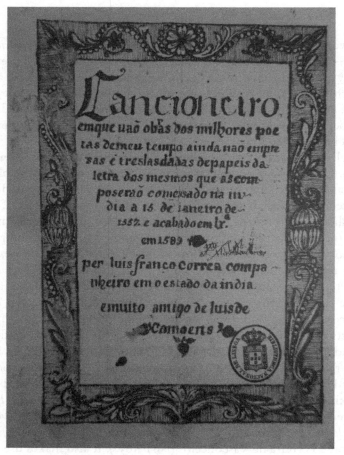

FIG. 1. Frontispiece of MS *Cancioneiro de Luis Franco Correa*

Cancioneiro | em que uão obras dos milhores poe | tas de meu tempo ainda
não empre | sas e tresladadas de papeis da | letra dos mesmos que as com |
poserão, comessado na india a 15 de janeiro de | 1557 e acabado em Lx.ª | em
1589 | per luis franco correa compa | nheiro em o estado da india | e muito
amigo de luis de | Camoens.

[Song-book with the works of the best poets of my time not yet printed and
copied from papers in the hand of those who wrote them, started in India
15th of January 1557 and finished in Lisbon in 1589 by Luís Franco Correa
companion in the state of India and a close friend of Luís de Camões.]

Although Correa's bragging about his close friendship to Camões leaves margin
for interpretation — allowing us to think, for instance, that Camões's celebrity
might have been a factor by the time he wrote the title page of his *Cancioneiro* — I
would like to take another direction and show how the fact that two sixteenth-
century versions of *Filodemo* have been preserved allows for a comparison between
the manuscript and the printed version of this play which can be extremely
revealing.[6]

The Manuscript *Cancioneiro de Luís Franco Correa*

The *Cancioneiro de Luís Franco Correa* belongs to the Portuguese National Library
in Lisbon. According to Carolina Michaelis de Vasconcelos it was acquired by
the institution in 1840.[7] This *Cancioneiro* was first described by the Viscount of
Juromenha in his monumental edition of Camões's works, of 1861,[8] and by Carolina
Michaelis de Vasconcelos, who examined it when preparing her critical edition
of Sá de Miranda, published in 1885,[9] and it has continued to be of interest to
scholars since then.[10] The MS is of 297 folios to which the title page, displaying a
pen-and-ink decoration imitating a printed book, was added later. The cordovan
leader binding dates from the seventeenth century: Roger Bismut, Eduardo Borges
Nunes and Dinah Rodrigues, who examined the manuscript personally, coincide in
stating that the three sorts of paper present in the manuscript, as well as the ink and
handwriting, date from the sixteenth century. They also point out that one of the
sorts of paper found in the document only started to be manufactured in the 1570s.[11]
Another relevant feature of this document is that it consists of twelve gatherings of
unequal size, which started to be filled independently, a process which continued
after they were bound.

Luís Franco Correa's manuscript includes around 330 texts, mostly poems in the
'new' genres in vogue in Europe in the second half of the sixteenth century: sonnets,
canzoni, eclogues, elegies, and so on. The poems are attributed to a relatively small
number of contemporary poets (twelve, to be precise: Sá de Miranda, Camões,
Hurtado de Mendoza, Dom Manuel de Portugal, Diego de Meneses, Diogo
Bernardes, Andrade Caminha, Francisco de Andrade, Prince Dom Luís, Jorge de
Montemor, Jerónimo Corte-Real, Francisco de Morais), but most of the texts (255
out of the 303) have no indication of authorship. This fact can either indicate that
Correa did not know to whom they belonged, or that the authors of the works were
so well known that he felt no need to write down their names.

284 VANDA ANASTÁCIO

One of the texts by Camões found in this *corpus* is the first *Canto* of the *Lusíadas*, near the end of the volume, in the eighth gathering. Under the last verse of this *Canto* there is the indication: 'Não continuo | porque saiu à luz' [I do not continue because it has been printed]. This can be interpreted as a confirmation of the compiler's claim that he was collecting only unpublished material. If this was the case, this note allows us to date this text approximately, since the first edition of the epic dates from 1572. Since the version of *Filodemo* is placed after the canto from *Os Lusíadas* in the volume compiled by Luís Franco Correa, one might consider the decade of 1570 as a possible date for the inclusion of the play in his collection. The possibility of dating the copy to the 1570s is especially interesting because the transcription of *Filodemo* is placed even closer to the end of the volume, occupying gatherings 11 and 12 with no allusion whatsoever to the existence of printed versions of the play.

Now, if Luís Franco collected the play during the decade of 1570, it means that he had copied it more than ten years after its first performance. In fact, the only information referring to the actual performance is a note in Correa's manuscript which states that *Filodemo* was 'feita por Luís de Camões' [made by Luís de Camões] and 'representada na India a Francisco Barreto' [performed in India for Francisco Barreto], who was Governor between 1555 and 1558. But even this information is far from being precise: did the performance take place upon the Governor's arrival? During his mandate? Or at the time of his departure?

This time span also allows us to wonder about the nature of the 'papers' mentioned by Correa as a basis for his copy: could he be sure, after ten years, that these were 'in the very hand' of their authors (in this case, of Camões)? These questions invite the hypothesis that there may have been other copies, other links in the chain of transmission between the originals or the first clean copy or copies made by the author, and Correa's version.

Let us look now into the printed version of this same text published in 1587.

The *Primeira parte dos Autos e Comédias Portuguesas*

The book in which *Filodemo* was published for the first time is a collective volume containing twelve plays, by different playwrights (António Prestes, Jerónimo Ribeiro and Anrique Lopes). These were brought together by Afonso Lopes, 'moço de Capela de sua Magestade' [Officer of His Majesty's Chapel]. The title page states that the edition was made 'à sua custa' [at his expense] with the technical support of Andres Lobato, a Spanish printer working in Portugal in a scheme we could describe as 'printing on demand' *avant la lettre*.[12] For this, Lopes enjoyed a ten-year privilege granted by the King.[13] Both the print quality and its material features, of 'extreme simplicity' as Pina Martins has remarked, indicate that it was intended for what we would call today the 'general reader':[14]

> PRIMEIRA | PARTE DOS AVTOS | E COMEDIAS PORTVGVESAS | Feitas por Antonio Prestes, & por Luís de Camões, & por | outros Autores Portugueses, cujos nomes vão nos princi | pios de suas obras. Agora novamente juntas & emen- | dadas nesta primeira impressão, por Afonso | Lopez, moço da Capella de sua | Magestade, & a sua custa. | Impressas com licença & priuilegio Real. | Por Andres Lobato Impressor de Liuros. | Anno M. D. Lxxxvij.

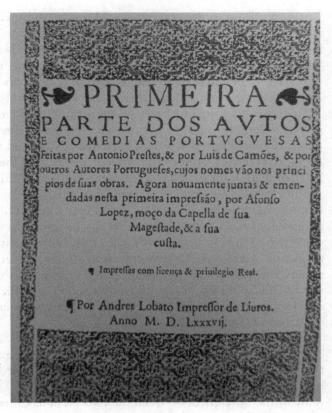

Fig. 2. Frontispiece of *Primeira Parte dos Autos e Comédias Portuguesas* (Lisbon, 1587)

[The first part of the Portuguese *autos* and comedies, written by António Prestes and Luís de Camões, and by other Portuguese authors whose names are stated at the beginning of their works. Now newly collected and emended, in this first printed edition, by Afonso Lopez, officer of His Majesty's Chapel, and at his expense. Licensed to be printed and with the royal privilege. By Andres Lobato, printer. 1587]

As a way of publicizing the work, on the title page Lopez tells his reader that the plays he publishes are *collected* and *emended* ('juntas & emendadas'). If the first statement suggests that we probably have before us an anthology of plays which had circulated previously separately in single editions, the second alerts us to the fact that the texts have been reworked, with the intention of improving them. The comparison of the published text of *Filodemo* with Franco Correa's manuscript copy provides further data allowing for a deeper understanding of Lopes's interference.

Some of the divergences between the printed text and the manuscript version compiled by Correa can be attributed to Lopes. He certainly chose the plays and it was most likely he who decided the sequence in which they should appear in the volume. One can assume that it was Lopes who corrected irregular spellings, metres and rhymes (frequent in a text meant to be recited), and suppressed or changed a few words and popular expressions in order to improve the style. Other differences, like the ones resulting from applying Spanish spelling conventions to Portuguese

286   VANDA ANASTÁCIO

words, resulting in the correction of Lusisms and spelling mistakes in the Spanish passages can be attributed to Andres Lobato (and/or to typographers working with/ for him) since he was a native speaker of Spanish. It is more difficult to decide who was responsible for the inclusion of stage directions in the printed version, since they seem to be intended to help readers and directors to imagine the performance, and could have been added either by Lopes or by Lobato.

Since the book had to have the approval of the censor in order to be printed, it is wise to look for signs of possible interference of the inquisitor 'revedor de livros' [book reviser] Frei Bartolomeu Ferreira, who signed the licence for publication.[15] As a matter of fact, most of the differences between the two versions of the play can be attributed, with a high degree of probability, to this censor's action.

This is the case with the ideological changes, made in accordance with the inquisitorial practice of the time,[16] and which consist of the suppression of elements potentially offensive to religion, to the clergy or to Christian morals (as well as explicit or implicit allusions to the body, to sexuality or to superstition — like magic or astrology). One of the longest cuts detectable when comparing the manuscript version and the printed text corresponds to the monologue of around forty verses spoken by a servant named Solina, in which she defends the idea that it is better for a woman to act according to her wishes and be happy than to observe chastity and live frustrated.[17]

Nevertheless, however clear the identification of alterations resulting from the censor's activity may be, it should not induce us to limit the relationship between the manuscript and the printed versions of *Filodemo* to the suppressions and minor linguistic or typographical interferences that have been discussed here. In fact, some of the differences between the two versions cannot be attributed either to the typographers, or to the editor, or to the censor, and they alert us to the possibility that these two texts may not be directly related, in a process of transmission where several intermediaries have left their marks.

Some of the variants which can be observed in the passages in prose, for instance, correspond to real *reconstructions* which may be the result of a process of memorization, consisting of rephrasing, summarizing or expanding stanzas and verses, while remaining faithful to the meaning. Often, the same information is formulated in slightly different ways, and details were added which seem to add little to the intrigue or to the meaning of the play.

In short, the printed version is not the equivalent of the manuscript version *without* the mistakes emended by Lopes, or *without* the elements suppressed by the inquisitorial censor. It is a *changed* version where additions have been introduced, with the intention of adding details of the dramatized intrigue or of making them more specific. Some of these elements cannot be clearly attributed to the typographers, the editor or the censor and they undoubtedly alert us to the fact that we are dealing with two witnesses not directly related to each other in the process of textual transmission. There are elements in the printed text that do not exist in the manuscript, and that *make sense*, to the point of giving credence to the hypothesis that they may have belonged to a previous version of the play, closer to the author's final version.

Let us take, for instance, the two versions of the following passage of a dialogue between Duriano and Solina:

Cancioneiro de Luís Franco Correa

DURIANO

Quão longe estará agora a senhora
Solina, de cuidar que já canso de cuidar
em como meus cuidados não cansam.
Se esta rapariga da Fortuna, minha
senhora, em pago de tantos danos,
consentisse que pudesse meu desejo
deitar ua âncora em vossa fermosura,
eu tomaria de vós vingança de fogo
e sangue.

Primeira parte dos Autos e Comédias

DURIANO

Ah, quão longe estará agora
Minha senhora Solina,
De saber qu'estou bem fora
De ter outra por senhora
Segundo Amor determina.
Porém se determinasse
Minha bem aventurança
Que de meu mal lhe pesasse
Ata que nela tomasse
Do que lhe quero vingança.

In this case, the difference between the way in which the same message is formulated seems to suggest that the manuscript preserves a prosification of the versified text found in the printed version, as if for some reason (lapse of memory, deterioration of the condition of the transcribed text, etc.) it had been changed to a *lectio facilior*. There is another revealing variant in the monologue where Venadouro explains how he got lost in the woods. The printed version includes a five-verse stanza which disappeared from the manuscript:

Cancioneiro de Luís Franco Correa

Junto desta fonte pura
Não sei quem cuido que está
Mas no coração me dá
Que aqui me guarda a Ventura
Algua Ventura má.
Oh, que fermosa serrana
À vista se me oferece!
Deosa dos montes parece,
E se é certo que é humana,
A serra mal a merece!
O monte não na merece!

Primeira parte dos Autos e Comédias

Junto desta fonte pura
Não sei quem cuido que está
Mas no coração me dá
Que aqui me guarda a Ventura
Algua Ventura má.
Ou ganhando ou bem perdido
Faça enfim o que quiser
Que eu o fim disto hei-de ver
Que já venho apercebido
A tudo quanto vier.

Oh que fermosa serrana
À vista se me oferece!
Deosa dos montes parece,
E se é certo que é humana,
O monte não na merece!

When compared to the manuscript, the five verses included in the printed version do not correspond to a real change of meaning. They just add a detail to the characterization of Venadouro, prolonging his speech and contributing, to a certain extent, to the creation an effect of suspense by announcing that something is about to happen: 'Que eu o fim disto hei-de ver | Que já venho apercebido | A tudo quanto vier' [I mean to see the end of this, because I am prepared for whatever may come]. There is no clear reason for attributing these verses to the printer, to the editor, or to the censor. These verses could simply have been omitted during the process of transmission. In this case, there must have been at least another version of the play, previous to the one transmitted by Luís Franco Correa which included these five verses absent from his manuscript. We find a similar situation in the speech addressed by the Pastor to D. Lusidardo where he explains the birth of Filodemo and Florimena:

Cancioneiro de Luís Franco Correa	*Primeira parte dos Autos e Comédias*
Fui en fin, certificado	Soy, en fin, certificado
Que la madre de los dos	Que la madre de los dos
Fue Princesa d'alto estado,	Fue Princesa d'alto estado,
Y por un caso nombrado	Y por un caso nombrado
Los truxo a la sierra Dios.	La traxo a esta tierra Dios.
Y si más quiere, señor,	*El macho como creció*
De mi arte, prestamente	*Desseoso de otro bien*
Dello le haré sabedor,	*A la corte se partio*
Mas ha de ser de tenor	*La hembra es esta por quién*
Que no lo sepa esta gente.	*Nuestro hijo se perdió*
	Y si más quiere, señor,
	De mi arte, prestamente
	Dello le haré sabedor,
	Mas ha de ser de tenor
	Que no lo sepa la gente.

These five 'supplementary' verses do not bring new elements to the progression of the action either. However, by explaining and summarizing information which was given at the beginning of the play, they recall to the listener/reader the aristocratic origins of Filodemo and Florimena, and anticipate the final unveiling of their identity. Here, also, there is no objective reason why these verses should not be attributed to the playwright: the drama does not lose much without them, but their presence *makes sense*.

Finally, I would like to comment on the largest element added in the printed version which is absent from the manuscript. It is a passage not directly connected to the evolution of the intrigue, where Vilardo (Filodemo's servant) appears with another servant named Doloroso accompanied by two musicians and suggests that they rehearse a couple of love songs to cheer up his beloved Solina, also a servant. This passage is, in fact a musical *intermezzo*, which could have been added on a specific occasion to make use of available musicians in the performance.

The introduction of a scene like this, where servants perform music, recite mock lyrical poems of their own composition, tell jokes or court each other, is a very common strategy used in popular Portuguese plays. It is well known to scholars working with eighteenth-century plays printed as chapbooks (Port.: *folhetos* or Sp.: *pliegos*) often sold on the streets by blind vendors. These plays are known as *teatro de cordel* and were designated by contemporaries as *teatro ao gosto português* which could be translated as 'suitable' or 'adapted' to the Portuguese taste. These plays consisted mostly of adaptations of previously existing plays, from classical as well as contemporary authors (the most popular being by Goldoni, Metastasio, Apostolo Zeno, Voltaire and Calderón), which were submitted to a process of manipulation along two main lines: the reinforcement of the love intrigue, achieved by the addition of one or more love stories in the plot; or the inclusion of *graciosos* (funny or clown-like characters), usually servants, whose language, gestures and performances were meant to entertain and provoke laughter.

The inclusion of this musical *intermezzo* presented and performed by *gracioso*-like characters opens the possibility that, in the case of the printed version of *Filodemo*, we may be dealing with a similar kind of interference in a pre-existing version.

The differences between the two versions of *Filodemo* can help us question the 'nature' of the written versions of plays circulating in the early modern period, as well as their relationship to the play as performed, in the sense that they may correspond to different moments of textual transmission, or to different stages/states of the text, and may even have had different functions: the written text could relate to the performance as a sort of 'script', a prompt guide or an *aide-mémoire*; but it could also have been used as way to continue, to remember, or to enable the repetition of the performance.

In the case of Camões' play *Filodemo*, these verifications allow us to hypothesize the existence of various chains of textual transmission, in manuscript and in print form, of which the versions collected by Lopes and by Correa are only two examples:

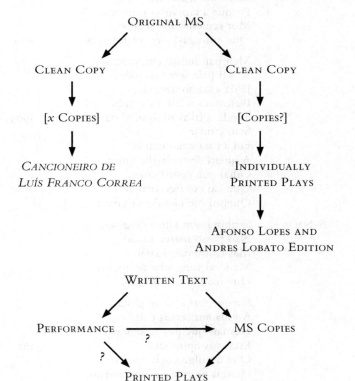

Above all, they show us very clearly that what we know of Camões' plays are texts altered by transmission, which, in some aspects, can be quite far from what their author originally wrote.

Appendix

This is the dialogue from Camões's *Auto de Filodemo* that was eliminated by the inquisitorial censor. The speakers are the heroine of the play, Dionisa, and her rebellious servant, Solina. Dionisa feels guilty about her relationship with a young man whom she believes (incorrectly, as it turns out) to be her social inferior. Solina, however, urges her mistress to take advantage of the absence of her father and her brother to meet her lover, using arguments which go against moral and social norms. The verses in italic are a quotation from a well-known popular song of the period.

DIONISA. Ó Solina, minha amiga,
Que todo este coração
Tenho posto em vossa mão!
Amor me manda que o diga,
Vergonha me diz que não.   1595

Que farei?
Como me descobrirei?
Porque a tamanho tormento
Mor remédio lhe não sei,
Que entregá-lo ao sofrimento.   1600

Meu pai, muito entristecido,
Se vai pela serra erguida,
Já da vida aborrecido,
Buscando o filho perdido,
Tendo a filha mais perdida!   1605
Sem cuidar,
Foi a casa encomendar
A quem destruir-lha quer:
Olhai que gentil saber,
Que vai comigo deixar   1610
Que[m] me não deixa viver!

SOLINA. Senhora, em tanto desgosto
Não posso meter a mão,
Mas como diz o rifão,
Mais val vergonha no rostro,   1615
Que mágoa no coração.

De que serve assim gastar
A vida em tantas paixões,
Nomais que por sostentar
Estas vãs opiniões   1620
Que o vulgo foi inventar?
Honras grandes, nome eterno,
De que servem ou que são?
Nenhũa outra cousa dão,
Que pera as almas Inferno   1625
E dores no coração.

Quem não pretende morar
Hipócrita, em ũa ermida,

DIFFUSING DRAMA   291

[DIONISA.   Oh, Solina, my friend,
           I have put all my heart
           Into your hands!
           Love commands me to say yes,
           and shame tells me to say no.

           What shall I do?
           How shall I show myself?
           For such a torment
           I can find no other remedy
           Than to abandon myself to suffering.

           My father, so sad,
           Left and went across the hills,
           Displeased with life;
           He went looking for his lost son,
       ·   While his daughter is so lost here!
           Without thinking twice
           He left his house in charge
           Of someone who wants to destroy it:
           Look at his gentle wisdom!
           He went away and left me
           With him who does not let me live!

SOLINA.   My Lady, in such a sorrow
           I can have no part,
           But I'll quote the old saying:
           It is better to have shame in your face
           Than to have sorrow in your heart.

           What good is it to waste
           Your life in so many upsets,
           If it is only to uphold
           Opinions that are so vain,
           Invented by common people?
           Great honours, eternal name,
           What use have they, what are they?
           They give you nothing but
           Hell in your soul
           And pain in your heart.

           Who doesn't try to live
           Hypocritically in a hermitage,

Quem não há-de jejuar
Deciplinar-se a chorar   1630
Pera fengir santa vida?
Porque não se logrará
Do tempo que tem nas mãos,
Ou porque sostentará
Honras falsas, nomes vãos,   1635
À custa da vida má?

Certamente que m'espanto
Desta opinião errada,
Como está tão arreigada,
Que custando a vida tanto,   1640
Enfim, em fim, não é nada!

Dela naceram as guerras,
Os danos e mortes de gente,
Por ela só se consente
Correr mares, buscar terras   1645
Pola sostentar somente.
Por esta nossa inimiga
Vereis logo o mundo vão
Ter em má openião
A molher que o amor obriga   1650
A natural afeição.

Assi que é meu parecer
Quem estas verdades mede,
Pois no mundo quer viver,
Deve certo de fazer   1655
O que lhe a vontade pede.
Se me nisto replicais
Que ofendo as leis dos Céos,
Os que as honras sostentais
Dizei-me: servis a Deos?   1660
Mas errai-lo muito mais!

Ora, senhora, este error
Consinto que seja culpa,
Nenhũa lhe podem pôr
Porque tão sobejo amor   1665
Todos os erros desculpa.
Bofé, que se tanto amasse,
E visse tempo e sazão
Sem seu pai e seu irmão,
Que a triste nuvem tirasse   1670
De cima do coração!...

DIONISA.   Ah, mana, que tenho medo
Que se eu tal consentisse,
Logo o mundo o sentisse,
Porque nunca houve segredo   1675
Que em fim não se descobrisse!

Who doesn't go there and fast
Mortifying themselves and weeping,
Just to fake a life of sainthood?
Why not make use
Of the time one has at hand,
Or why keep up
False honours, empty names
In exchange for a miserable life?

I certainly am astounded
That such a wrong opinion
Can be so deeply rooted
For although life is so precious
In the end it's only nothing!

This is where wars are born,
And the destruction and deaths of people,
Because of it, people go
Across the seas, seeking new lands
Just in order to defend it [honour].
Because of this common enemy
You see how the vain world
Has a very bad opinion
Of the women forced by love
To feel a natural affection.

Therefore it is my view
That she who measures these truths,
If she wants to live in this world
She must certainly do
Whatever she wishes.
If you answer to me about this
That I offend Heaven's laws,
Just tell me, you who defend your honours,
Do you think you are serving God?
For you fail him even more!

So, My Lady, about this mistake
Though I admit it may be guilt,
I say there is no reason to condemn it,
For such an incommensurable love
Can justify all mistakes!
By God, if I loved like this
And saw the time and the season
Without a father or brother
I would free myself from that dark cloud
Which was covering my heart!...

DIONISA.   Oh, my friend, I am so scared
That if I give my consent
All the world would hear about it,
For there was never a secret
That was not discovered sooner or later!

294 VANDA ANASTÁCIO

> SOLINA. Se eu tantas dobras tivesse
> Como quantas houve erradas
> Sem que o mundo o soubesse,
> À fé que eu enriquecesse   1680
> E fosse das mais honradas!

Bibliography

ALMEIDA, FRANCISCO VIEIRA DE, 'Le Théâtre de Camões dans l'histoire du théâtre portugais', *Bulletin d'Histoire du Théâtre Portugais*, 1.2 (1950), 250–66

ANASTÁCIO, VANDA, 'El Rei Seleuco, 1645 (reflexões sobre o *corpus* da obra de Camões)', *Península*, 2 (2005), 327–42

——'Nota Breve acerca de *El-Rei Seleuco*, *Santa Barbara Portuguese Studies*, special issue: 'Luís Vaz de Camões Revisitado', 7 (2003 [published in 2006]), 213–20

——'As duas versões de *Filodemo*', in *Teatro completo de Camões* (Porto: Caixotim, 2004), pp. 53–63

AZEVEDO FILHO, LEODEGÁRIO DE, 'Paul Teyssier e o teatro de Camões', *Revista Camoniana*, 12 (2002), 101–09

BERARDINELLI, CLEONICE, 'Cancioneiro de Luís Franco Correa', in *Estudos Camonianos* (Rio de Janeiro: Nova Fronteira, 2000), pp. 275–76

BISMUT, ROGER, *La Lyrique de Camões* (Paris: Fondation Calouste Gulbenkian, 1970)

——'Les Compositions poétiques camoniannes du *Cancioneiro Luís Franco Correa*', *Arquivos do Centro Cultural Português*, 15 (1980), 25–109

CAMÕES, LUÍS DE, *Obras de Luiz de Camões. Precedidas de um ensaio biográfico no qual se relatam alguns factos não conhecidos da sua vida*, ed. by Vicount of Juromenha, 6 vols (Lisbon: Imprensa Nacional, 1861)

CORREA, LUÍS FRANCO, *Cancioneiro de Luís Franco Correa* (facsimile: Lisbon: Comissão Executiva do IV Centenário da publicação d'Os Lusíadas, 1972)

DÍEZ BORQUE, JOSÉ MARÍA, *Los géneros dramáticos en el siglo XVI: el teatro hasta Lope de Vega)* (Madrid: Taurus Ediciones, 1987)

FRANCO CORREA, LUÍS, *Cancioneiro de Luís Franco Correa*, presented by Maria de Lurdes Belchior (Lisbon: Comissão Executiva do IV Centenário da Publicação de *Os Lusíadas*, 1972)

LE GENTIL, GEORGES, *Camões* (Lisbon: Portugália Editora, 1969)

MENEGAZ, RONALDO, 'O *auto de Filodemo*: dos romances de cavalaria à expressão maneirista', *Revista Camoniana*, 11 (2002), 69–90

MILLER, NEIL TED, 'O elemento pastoril no Auto de Filodemo de Luís de Camões', *Arquivos*, 1 (December 1972), 46–58

——'Algumas considerações sobre o auto de *Filodemo* de Camões', *Anais do I Congresso Internacional de Camonologia* (Maringá-Paraná: n.pub., 1972)

NUNES, EDUARDO BORGES, 'Algumas sugestões para exame do cancioneiro de Luís Franco Correa', in 'Apêndice I', Dinah Morais Nunes Rodrigues, 'Os cadernos de poesia de Luís Franco Correa', 2 vols (unpublished master's dissertation, Pontifical Catholic University — Rio de Janeiro, 1979)

PÉREZ PRIEGO, MIGUEL, *El teatro en el Renacimiento* (Madrid: Ediciones el Laberinto, 2004)

PICCHIO, LUCIANA STEGAGNO, *História do teatro português* (Lisbon: Portugália, 1969)

PINA MARTINS, JOSÉ V., 'Nota Bibliográfica e Crítica', in *Primeira parte dos Autos e Comédias Portuguesas*, pref. by Hernani Cidade (Lisbon: Lysia, 1973), pp. 1–13

Primeira parte dos autos e comédias portuguesas (Lisbon: Afonso Lopes, 1587; facsimile: Lisbon: Lysia, 1973)

DIFFUSING DRAMA   295

SOLINA.   If I had as many gold coins
As women who do these things
Without the world ever knowing
I swear that I would be rich
And would be covered with honours!]

SÁ DE MIRANDA, FRANCISCO, *Poesias de Sá de Miranda*, ed. by Carolina Michaelis de Vasconcelos (Halle: Max Niemeyer, 1885)

SENA, JORGE DE, 'O Cancioneiro de Luís Franco Correia', *Arquivos do Centro Cultural Português*, 13 (1978), 105–25 [reprinted in *Trinta Anos de Camões, 1948–1978: estudos camonianos e correlatos*, 2 vols (Lisbon: Edições 70, 1980), I, 135–56]

TAVARES DE PINHO, SEBASTIÃO, 'Critérios e métodos de Censura na edição dos Piscos d'*Os Lusíadas* de Camões e no poema *De Senectute* de Lopo Serrão, de 1579', in *Actas da IV Reunião de Camonistas* (Ponta Delgada: University of Azores, 1984), 459–73 [repr. in *Decalogia Camoniana* (Coimbra: Centro Interuniversitário de Estudos Camonianos, 2007), 37–51]

——'As variantes: critérios de censura', in *Lopo Serrão e o seu Poema da Velhice* (Coimbra: INIC, 1987), pp. 98–117

TEYSSIER, PAUL, 'As duas versões do *Auto de Filodemo*', *V Reunião Internacional de Camonistas*, ed. by Seabra Pereira and Manuel Ferro (São Paulo: Faculdade de Letras e Ciências Humanas, 1987), pp. 383–91

VASCONCELOS, CAROLINA MICHAELIS DE, 'Introduction', in *Poesias de Sá de Miranda* (Halle: Max Niemeyer, 1885), pp. lx–lxv

Notes to Chapter 13

1. This was, for instance, the opinion of Francisco Vieira de Almeida, who wrote, in his article 'Le Théâtre de Camões dans l'histoire du théâtre portugais', *Bulletin d'Histoire du Théâtre Portugais*, 1.2 (1950), 250–66 (p. 254): 'L'imagination de Camões, lyrique, verbale, subtile et descriptive ne s'adapte que difficilement aux besoins de la scène'. Years later Georges Le Gentil mentioned Camões's plays in his *Camões* (Lisbon: Portugália Editora, 1969), p. 195: 'They have only a secondary value, and it does not even seem that Camões set much store by them [...]. It was a line that he did not continue. He must have embarked on it just to satisfy a request of his friends or of some influential patron, unless he wanted to prove, as a kind of bet,that he was at home in all genres.' Luciana Stegagno Picchio in her *História do Teatro Português* (Lisbon: Portugália, 1969), p. 123 states: 'In the overall context of Camões's work, which include the sonorous and pompous epic, *Os Lusíadas*, as well as the more limpid beauty of the lyrics, the three *autos* which make up his work for the stage do not amount to more than a curious diversion.' All translations in the notes are by the editors.
2. For more information on the *Auto*, see José María Díez Borque, *Los géneros dramáticos en el siglo XVI: el teatro hasta Lope de Vega* (Madrid: Taurus Ediciones, 1987) and Miguel Perez Priego, *El teatro en el Renacimiento* (Madrid: Ediciones el Laberinto, 2004).
3. This can be interpreted as an interference of other dramatic models circulating at the time in the Iberian literary field, like the prose comedy derived from the medieval Neo-Latin tradition or the Italian-style humanistic comedy which had attracted authors like Sá de Miranda in the generation before Camões. One should note, however, that there is no division into acts and scenes even in the plays where prose is introduced, which indicates a fundamental difference: one could say that Camões subordinates or incorporates prose into the structural logic of the *auto*.
4. See Ronaldo Menegaz, 'O *auto de Filodemo*: dos romances de cavalaria à expressão maneirista', *Revista Camoniana*, 11 (2002), and Neil Ted Miller, 'O elemento pastoril no Auto de Filodemo de Luís de Camões', *Arquivos*, 1 (December 1972), 48–58, and *idem* 'Algumas considerações sobre o

296 Vanda Anastácio

auto de *Filodemo* de Camões', *Anais do I Congresso Internacional de Camonologia* (Maringá-Paraná: n.pub., 1972).

5. Vanda Anastácio, 'El Rei Seleuco, 1645 (reflexões sobre o *corpus* da obra de Camões)', *Península*, 2 (2005), 327–42, and *idem*, 'Nota breve acerca de *El-Rei Seleuco*', *Santa Barbara Portuguese Studies*, special issue: 'Luís Vaz de Camões Revisitado', 7 (2003 [published in 2006]), 213–20.

6. The first critic to point out the importance of the variants between the two versions of *Filodemo* was Paul Teyssier 'As duas versões do *Auto de Filodemo*', in *V Reunião Internacional de Camonistas*, ed. by Seabra Pereira and Manuel Ferro (São Paulo: Faculdade de Letras e Ciências Humanas, 1987), pp. 383–91. His views have been criticized by Leodegário de Azevedo Filho, 'Paul Teyssier e o teatro de Camões', *Revista Camoniana*, 12 (2002), 101–09, and discussed by Vanda Anastácio, 'As duas versões de *Filodemo*', in *Teatro completo de Camões* (Porto: Caixotim, 2004), pp. 53–63.

7. A facsimile edition of this *Cancioneiro* was published, in 1972, by the Comissão Executiva do IV Centenário da Publicação de *Os Lusíadas*.

8. Carolina Michaelis de Vasconcelos, 'Introduction', in *Poesias de Sá de Miranda* (Halle: Max Niemeyer, 1885), pp. lx–lxv. See also volume II of Luís de Camões, *Obras de Luiz de Camões. Precedidas de um ensaio biográfico no qual se relatam alguns factos não conhecidos da sua vida*, ed. by Vicount of Juromenha, 6 vols (Lisbon: Imprensa Nacional, 1861).

9. de Vasconcelos, 'Introduction', pp. lx–lxv.

10. See, for instance, Jorge de Sena, 'O Cancioneiro de Luís Franco Correia', *Arquivos do Centro Cultural Português*, 13 (1978), 105–25 [reprinted in *Trinta Anos de Camões, 1948–1978: estudos camonianos e correlatos*, 2 vols (Lisbon: Edições 70, 1980), I, 135–56; see also, and Cleonice Berardinelli, 'Cancioneiro de Luís Franco Correa', in *Estudos Camonianos* (Rio de Janeiro: Nova Fronteira, 2000), pp. 275–76.

11. Roger Bismut, *La Lyrique de Camões* (Paris: Fondation Calouste Gulbenkian, 1970), and *idem*, 'Les Compositions poétiques camoniannes du *Cancioneiro Luís Franco Correa*', *Arquivos do Centro Cultural Português*, 15(1980), 25–109. See also, Eduardo Borges Nunes, 'Algumas sugestões para Exame do Cancioneiro de Luís Franco Correa', in 'Apêndice I', Dinah Morais Nunes Rodrigues, 'Os cadernos de poesia de Luís Franco Correa', 2 vols (unpublished master's dissertation, Pontifical Catholic University — Rio de Janeiro, 1979).

12. On the possibility that Andres Lobato was an itinerant printer who worked on his clients' property, see Vanda Anastácio, 'Preface', in *Luís de Camões, Teatro completo*, pp. 41–53.

13. The privilege was printed immediately before the text, and dates from 21 March 1587.

14. J. V. de Pina Martins has described the work in a 'Nota Bibliográfica e Crítica', in *Primeira parte dos Autos e Comédias Portuguesas*, prefaced by Hernani Cidade (Lisbon: Lysia, 1973), pp. 1–13.

15. The inquisitor's licence is transcribed immediately after the title page and says: 'I have seen by His Highness's orders this book, *Autos & Comedias Portuguesas*, and it has nothing against faith and morals, there being no reason why it should not be printed. F. Bertolameu Ferreyra'. This is followed by the licence of the Royal Court (*Mesa do Desembargo do Paço*) which states: 'The information has been considered and the book may be printed. When it has been printed it should be returned to this Board to be compared to the original and be given a licence to circulate, in Lisbon, 2nd September 86. Iorge Serrão. Antonio de Mendoça'.

16. Sebastião Tavares de Pinho, 'Critérios e métodos de Censura na edição dos Piscos d'*Os Lusíadas* de Camões e no poema *De Senectute* de Lopo Serrão, de 1579', in *Actas da IV Reunião de Camonistas* (Ponta Delgada: University of Azores, 1984), pp. 459–73 [Reprinted in *Decalogia Camoniana* (Coimbra: Centro Interuniversitário de Estudos Camonianos, 2007), pp. 37–51.

17. This passage, with a translation, is printed as an appendix to the chapter (eds).

CHAPTER 14

❖

From the Catholic Mystery Play to Calvinist Tragedy, or the Reinvention of French Religious Drama

Michael Meere

Wesleyan University

In the sixteenth century, the rediscovery of ancient tragedy and comedy caused undoubtedly the most profound shift in French theatre. Sparked by humanist translators, teachers, and playwrights such as Lazare de Baïf, Guillaume Bochetel, George Buchanan and Marc-Antoine Muret,[1] a young generation of poets, some of whom formed what would become known as the Pléiade, began penning, in the French language, tragedies and comedies in the style of Euripides, Sophocles, Aristophanes and in particular Seneca, Plautus and Terence.[2] Etienne Jodelle, Jean Bastier de La Péruse and Robert Garnier are just three major figures of French (Catholic) literature who produced tragedies (Jodelle, La Péruse, Garnier) and comedies (Jodelle). Garnier also wrote the first (extant) French tragicomedy, *Bradamante* (1582), inspired by Ariosto's *Orlando furioso*. At the same time, Protestant humanists were also experimenting with tragedies and comedies — the circles were not necessarily mutually exclusive, either — and poets such as André Rivaudeau, Jacques Grévin and Jean and Jacques de La Taille wrote several tragedies and comedies that generally followed and promoted Horatian and at times Aristotelian precepts rather than medieval ones.[3]

Nevertheless, medieval theatrical traditions did not disappear, and French Renaissance drama was very much influenced by the earlier theatre. Théodore de Bèze, for instance, Jean Calvin's right-hand man in Geneva, composed and had performed *Abraham sacrifiant* [A Tragedie of Abrahams Sacrifice] in *c.* 1550, which arguably more resembles a medieval religious drama (with a Protestant message) than a classical tragedy, and yet he chose to label his play a 'tragédie'.[4] It would not be too bold a statement, in fact, to suggest that Bèze's immensely successful tragedy reinvented French religious drama.[5] For, while some humanists such as Jodelle (*Cléopâtre captive*, 1552) and La Péruse (*Médée*, 1556) preferred tragic subjects inspired by historical and mythological sources, and while they tended to imitate Senecan tragedy and divided their plays into five acts, Calvinist reformers of the 1550s and early 1560s were producing dramas whose subject matter came from the

298   MICHAEL MEERE

Old Testament, and they preferred to divide their plays into a various number of sections separated by pauses and musical interludes rather than by a chorus.[6]

The Protestant plays, although heavily influenced by medieval religious drama, were nonetheless moving away from this Catholic model to find a Protestant one, particularly through the choice of hero. Indeed, in his address to the reader, Bèze states that three biblical heroes illustrate God's 'plus grands merveilles, à scavoir Abraham, Moise, et David: en la vie desquels si on se miroit aujourdhuy, on se congnoistroit mieux qu'on ne faict' (p. 46) [his greatest wonders: namely Abraham, Moses, and David: in the liues of whome if men would nowe a dayes looke upon them selues, they should knowe them selues better then they do] (p. 4). For Bèze, Calvin's successor at Geneva, staging biblical plays that depicted Abraham, Moses and David would have direct and immediate urgency for the reformers. Taking his cue from Bèze's statement, Michel Jeanneret concludes that Calvinist playwrights give their plays an edifying message and are not afraid to point out their topical nature, for the project is only interesting, in their eyes, if it offers a mirror to their followers of their situation and a solution to their problems.[7] To be sure, the very first lines spoken by Bèze's Abraham relate the biblical plot to the situation of exiled and persecuted Protestant spectators and readers:

> Depuis que j'ay mon païs delaissé,
> Et de courir çà et là n'ay cessé,
> Helas mon Dieu, est il encor' un homme,
> Qui ait porté de travaux telle somme? (ll. 49–52)

> [Alas my God, and was there euer any
> That hath endured of combrances so many
> As I have done by fleeting too and fro
> Since I my natiue countrie did forgo?] (ll. 1–4)

Two of Bèze's contemporaries, the Calvinist pastors Joachim de Coignac and Louis Des Masures, would follow his suggestion and example, both in subject matter and in form, as they chose to write tragedies about the famous duel between David and Goliath. Coignac composed *La Desconfiture de Goliath* [The Defeat of Goliath] (1551),[8] while Des Masures's *David combattant* [Fighting David] appeared as part of his *Holy Tragedies* trilogy in 1563.[9] Moreover, instead of implementing a five-act structure with choruses, Coignac and Des Masures, like Bèze, divided their plays with 'pauses' and musical interludes, hymns taken from the Book of Psalms. As Corinne Meyniel has suggested, their tragedies are perfectly hybrid: they maintain a medieval structure and mode of performance but they also are quite modern. The authors' edifying goals concern the spiritual just as much as the political spheres, exhorting their brothers and sisters in faith to resist Catholic domination, not by force or intelligence that everyone can hope to have, but by exemplary faith.[10] Thus, Coignac and Des Masures evoke the Reformation and the reformers' tribulations in order to give their followers hope in the face of Roman Catholic domination.

But what is more, Coignac and Des Masures, like their playwright contemporaries such as Rivaudeau,[11] were writing and preaching during the uncertain situation of reformers in the mid-sixteenth century, just before and after the outbreak of the first official religious war in 1562.[12] Their tragedies, however, as opposed to Bèze's

FROM THE CATHOLIC MYSTERY PLAY TO CALVINIST TRAGEDY 299

Abraham or Rivaudeau's *Aman*, graphically stage the duel between David and Goliath, and the characters rejoice in the latter's death and decapitation. At the same time, unlike other humanist tragedies inspired by the cruelty of Senecan plots such as *Thyestes* or *Medea*, Coignac and Des Masures stage the bloodbath not to invoke fear or horror in the spectators, but as a celebratory victory of good (David) over evil (Goliath). In turn, this bloody spectacle, I should like to argue, which has been overwhelmingly neglected in the scholarship on these plays,[13] raises questions of the legitimacy of violence in the light of Calvinist ethics, thus highlighting the tensions between human, temporal violence, and divine, spiritual violence.

To attain a clearer understanding of the dramatic, theological and ethical implications of the physically staged violence, in this article I will first compare the Catholic *Mystére du Viel Testament* [Mystery of the Old Testament] and Coignac's and Des Masures's plays in order to show how the Calvinist plays diverge from the Catholic model, both in terms of drama and theology. From there, I will provide in-depth analyses of the Calvinist tragedies and their paratextual dedicatory letters in order to argue that Coignac's and Des Masures's plays gesture towards militant and transcendent violence, but violence that only a certain elect few have the authority to control and regulate.

David and Goliath on Stage in the Catholic Tradition

Calvinist tragedies about the Old Testament had Catholic precedents, notably the illustrious sixteenth-century *Mistére du Viel Testament*.[14] The staging of the violence of the David and Goliath story in this late-medieval mystery play and the Calvinist tragedies are very similar, as they each depict the slaying of the giant on stage. Yet there are important differences between them that indicate a transformation of the biblical story from one of individual salvation (the mystery) to one of collective jubilation and redemption (Calvinist tragedies).

The *Mystére du Vieil Testament* is the most famous and complete mystery from the sixteenth century that stages biblical stories from the Old Testament. This 49,386-line play begins with Creation and ends with the popular medieval legend of Octavian and the Sibyl. In the Rothschild edition of the play, the David and Goliath story occupies a mere 346 lines (ll. 29,750–30,096).[15] The brief episode between David and Goliath exemplifies the practice of retelling the biblical story in its simplest form in order to fulfil its primary civic and religious function: to instruct the usually illiterate lay audience without glosses or commentaries on the events. The mystery thus follows the Vulgate nearly verbatim, with neither polemical overtones nor references to the spectators' contemporary situations. Unlike other episodes in the *Mistére du Viel Testament* and in other medieval mysteries, the author of the David and Goliath episode does not add comical aspects, save perhaps for David's awkwardness in Saul's armour (ll. 29,988–96).[16] There is also an absence of supernatural characters, such as God, Satan, angels or demons. However, like the Bible's version of the story, the drama abruptly shifts from the Philistine camp to the Hebrews, Isai's home and David's fields, hence adhering to the medieval aesthetic and practice of multiple decors.

300   MICHAEL MEERE

In the mystery and in the Vulgate, David insists that the battle between the Hebrews and the Philistines is God's battle, and that God will defeat the monstrous giant. When David refuses to wear Saul's armour, David reassures the king, saying 'Et aussi les gens font les armes, | Mais Dieu seul la victoire donne' [And also men make weapons, but only God gives victory] (ll. 29,995–96). Then, while David and Goliath banter back and forth before fighting, David shouts 'Nostre Seigneur, le Dieu des ostz | D'Israel, te delivrera | Entre mes mains' [Our Lord, the God of the inhabitants of Israel, will deliver you unto my hands] (ll. 30,035–37). Finally, about to fight Goliath, David proclaims 'Que Dieu ne sauve, en substance, | Nul par espée ne par lance, | Car, ainsi qu'il nous apparest, | Toute la bataille luy est' [That God does not save, in substance, neither by sword nor by lance, for, as he appears to us, all the battle is his] (ll. 30,044–47). The Vulgate reads in a similar fashion: David yells out to Goliath 'This day, and the Lord will deliver thee into my hand [...] And *all this assembly* shall know that the lord saveth not with sword and spear: for it is his battle, and he will deliver you into *our* hands' (I Samuel 17. 46–47, emphasis added). Both the mystery and the Catholic Vulgate depict God as giving David the power and courage to defeat Goliath and the Philistines, yet a subtle difference in possessive pronouns is to be noted. The mystery play has David say 'mes mains' ('my hands'), while the Vulgate states 'our hands'. In the play, David faces the forces of evil alone, while the rest of the Hebrews and the Philistines watch passively and silently. They are virtually absent from the action occurring on stage, and David makes no reference to 'nous' ('we', 'us') or, as we see in the Vulgate, to 'all this assembly'. Unlike the Vulgate, and as we will remark in the Calvinist tragedies, David's defeat of Goliath in the mystery does not recount a story of collective victory and redemption, but rather one of David's singular history, for the mystery play underscores David's individual freedom in the face of evil. It may be God's battle, yet it is David who is in control of his stones and who decides himself to decapitate the giant: God 'te delivrera | Entre *mes* mains, *puis* on verra | Que c'est que de toy *je feray*: | Au jour d'uy, le chef te *osteray*' [will deliver you into *my* hands, *then* we will see what it is that *I will do* with you: Today, *I will take off* your head] (ll. 30,036–39, emphasis added). The adverb 'puis' ('then') dislocates God's providence and David's free will: it is David who chooses what to do with Goliath once God has delivered the enemy into his hands.

The medieval mystery shows the duel between David and Goliath in its entirety, from the slinging of the stones to Goliath's beheading (ll. 30,049–64). In the Vulgate, David silently cuts off Goliath's head (I Samuel 17. 51), yet in the mystery, David speaks these words just before committing the act: 'Je fais veu a Dieu et prometz | Que maintenant de ton espée | Tu auras la gorge coupée, | Pour te monstrer que tu as tort (*Il luy coupe la teste*)' [I make a vow to God and promise that now with your sword you will have your throat slit, to show you that you are wrong (*He cuts off his head*)] (ll. 30,061–64). This speech has a very practical purpose, for it underscores the special effect that is about to occur, for a fake body was likely substituted for the actor playing Goliath during the unravelling of the action.[17] On a more serious note, David's words get the audience's attention for the big moment that is coming and it explains the message that Goliath is wrong to have blasphemed God and

FROM THE CATHOLIC MYSTERY PLAY TO CALVINIST TRAGEDY 301

that God is almighty and just.[18] Finally, this short exclamation also justifies David's violent act, a justification that does not exist in the Vulgate.

In the mystery play, David does not say another word after beheading Goliath, and there is no jubilation or exasperation on the part of the internal spectators. In fact, as mentioned above, the Hebrew and Philistine troops are mute characters during the battle between David and Goliath. Instead, the Hebrew troops reap the benefits of David's victory and chase after the Philistines who have taken flight. The silent internal spectators exit the stage, while David remains on stage and walks calmly towards Saul and Jonatas, 'la teste portant de Goullias' [carrying Goliath's head]. David humbly presents 'Le chef de Goullias' [Goliath's head] that he 'en ceste heure presente, | Par le voulloir de Dieu desconfit' [in this present hour, by the will of God, slaughtered] (ll. 30,082–84). Saul's acceptance of David into his household ends the David and Goliath episode in the *Mistére*.[19] Again, then, the mystery play concentrates on David and seems to neglect the collective aspect of David's victory. His defeat of Goliath is an individual act that establishes David as God's elected one *after* the fact. As we will see, the Calvinist tragedies, on the other hand, present David as God's elected one *before* the duel actually begins, and they depict the battle between Good and Evil, Life and Death, David and Goliath, in terms of a collective victory for the entire community. The Hebrew and Philistine troops take on a discursive role in the tragedies, commenting on the events that unfold before them. Moreover, after the slaying of Goliath, Coignac's and Des Masures's tragedies integrate choral songs celebrating David and their liberation from evil, which implicates the onlookers in the staged violence and reinforces the ethical messages of resistance and transcendence.

Militant and Transcendent Violence

The famous biblical story of Goliath's defeat became a commonplace in the reformers' collective consciousness as a reflection of their own struggle.[20] The simple shepherd defeats the proud and blasphemous giant, which in turn saves the chosen people of Israel from the Philistines. In this schema, David represents the reformers, and Goliath symbolizes the Roman Catholic Church, whose leader (*chef* or head) is the Pope. Theological, symbolic, metaphorical, and polemical interpretations of the David and Goliath story are at work in Coignac's and Des Masures's tragedies. They could very well have given a messenger a detailed monologue to relate the violence, a dramaturgical technique practised by other playwrights such as Buchanan or the anonymous Philone in *Josias*, yet they chose to stage the duel. In fact, Des Masures's prologue announces the violence and the reasons he has chosen to stage it, insisting on the visual aspect of the battle scene and God's responsibility: 'Combattre le [David] *verrez*, non d'un vouloir soudain [...] Ains celui de son Dieu, *auteur de l'entreprise*' [You *will see* David fight, not with a sudden fancy [...] But that of God, *the author of the undertaking*] (l. 29; l. 32, emphasis added). God has prepared this duel in advance: it has not happened by chance, nor is it David's decision to defeat Goliath. Moreover, the spectators will *see* the action with their own eyes. As I will argue, this dramaturgical decision has implications for the ethics of resistance and rebellion.

The battle and ultimate slaying of Goliath are the main subjects of the tragedies, as their titles indicate. Des Masures chooses the present participle 'combattant' to describe David, which places the emphasis on the duel, while Coignac titles his tragedy *La Desconfiture de Goliath*. In the sixteenth century, the term 'desconfiture' meant 'défaite' [defeat] or 'victoire sur' [victory over], but could also signify 'massacre, tuerie' [massacre, slaughter] and 'amas de cadavres après une bataille' [pile of cadavers after a battle].[21] Hence, Coignac underscores the violent and bloody aspect of his tragedy; as we will see, he ends his tragedy not only with the bloody death of Goliath, but also with that of the Philistine soldiers. In this sense, too, then, we can understand what Des Masures and Coignac had in mind when labelling their plays 'tragedies', since theoreticians such as Peletier du Mans believed that in tragedy 'la fin est tousjours luctueuse e lamantable, ou horrible a voir' [the end is always sad and lamentable, or horrible to see].[22] In other words, tragedies often end in blood and death that the spectators *see* with their own eyes.

This type of ending is precisely the kind Coignac and Des Masures chose to incorporate into their tragedies. But, beyond what we have noticed thus far, they differ from the Catholic mysteries in even more important ways. First, Coignac and Des Masures draw out the battle scene and give David and Goliath many more lines than we find in the late medieval play, which allows them not only to make references to the Bible but also to reinforce the reformers' current situation in the face of the papal threat.

Second, before the battle begins, Coignac has David explain why he has come to fight Goliath and why the latter will fall:

> Du SEIGNEUR est ceste bataille,
> Au SEIGNEUR mesme tu te prens:
> Pour-tant DIEU puissance nous baille
> Contre ce que tu entreprens.
> Tu fais au SEIGNEUR DIEU la guerre,
> Car c'est luy qui est nostre chef:
> Pour ce tu tomberas par terre,
> En vengence de ce meschef. (p. 63)

[This is the LORD's battle; you are fighting the LORD himself. However, GOD gives us power against that which you are undertaking. You are making war with the LORD, for he is our leader. For this you will fall to the ground, as revenge for this attack.]

David will defeat Goliath only if God wants him to do so. David thus acts as a vessel for God to overcome evil, to carry out divine justice and revenge. Coignac employs (easy yet effective) wordplay: as God is the leader ('chef') of the Israelites, David will cut off the head ('chef') of the enemy of God. In Des Masures's tragedy, David's response to Goliath echoes that of Coignac's hero:

> Je viens *au nom de Dieu*, du Dieu des exercites,
> Du grand Dieu d'Israël contre qui trop petites
> Sont les forces de toi. *Par lui* comme une bête
> Tu viendras en mes mains et t'ôterai la tête.
> *Par lui* ferai les corps des Philistins méchants
> Paître aux oiseaux du ciel et aux bêtes des champs

FROM THE CATHOLIC MYSTERY PLAY TO CALVINIST TRAGEDY 303

> Afin que près et loin sache la terre toute
> Qu'Israël a un Dieu et qu'ici nul ne doute
> Que notre Dieu puissant, non par glaive ni lance
> Donne victoire aux siens, mais par autre vaillance
> Dont tes gens aujourd'hui en ruine cherront,
> Mais premier dessous moi tomber *ils te verront*
> Et le *verra* ensemble Israël à ses *yeux*.
> (ll. 1593–1605, emphasis added)

[I come *in the name of God*, of the God of armies, of the great God of Israel against whom your forces are too small. *In his name* like a beast you will come into my hands and I will take off your head. *In his name* I will make the evil Philistine bodies food for the birds of the sky and for the beasts of the fields so that near and far the whole world may know that Israel has a God and that no one here will doubt that our powerful God, by neither sword nor lance gives victory to his own, but by another kind of valiance which your people, today destroyed, will cherish. But first beneath me *they will see* you fall and all of Israel *will see* it with their own *eyes*.]

By the repetition of 'Par lui' [In his name], David emphasizes that supernatural forces control the imminent duel, and that, because Goliath has sinned against the chosen people of Israel, God will punish him. Des Masures, like Coignac, underscores the visibility of the duel ('Ils te verront', 'le verra', 'ses yeux') in order that Goliath may serve as an example of God's victory and divine justice to both the internal (Philistines and Israelites) and external (Francophone) spectators.

Next, after Goliath insults and mocks David, Coignac includes internal stage directions for the fight scene, which David narrates, placing emphasis on the visibility of the scene: 'J'espere que de ceste pierre, | Je te renverseray par terre [...] *La voilà* par terre, la beste. Il me luy faut coupper la teste, [...] Maintenant de ta propre espée, Te sera la teste couppée. *Comme ceste rapiere tranche!* [...] *Le voyla* donques deffailly, | *Et voicy* la grand'teste fole, Qui avoit espoir en l'idole [...] Et si avoit fait entreprise, | De ruïner la vraye Eglise' [I hope that with this stone, I will throw you to the ground [...] *There he is* on the ground, the beast. I must cut off his head, [...] Now with your own sword, your head will be cut off. *How this blade slices!* [...] *There he is* now dead, and *here is* his great foolish head, who had hope in a false god [...] And so he had tried to destroy the true Church] (pp. 64–65, emphasis added). The repetition of the defective verbs 'voilà' [there] and 'voici' [here] as well as the adverb 'maintenant' [now] underscore the visibility of the staged violence and act as internal yet explicit stage directions. David thus gives the spectators a running narrative as the violent events unfold before them, from the start of the duel ('J'espere que de ceste pierre'), to the slicing off of Goliath's head with his own sword ('Comme ceste rapiere tranche!'), to the end ('Et voicy la gran' teste fole'). The combination of narration and action engages the spectators more effectively than the action alone, for hearing and seeing merge together and to form a deeper impression on them. Holding up the head for the audience to see, moreover, reinforces the violent yet liberating act, for foolish Goliath attempted to destroy the true (i.e., reformed) Church.

Des Masures's version includes external stage directions as to how the duel should

304   MICHAEL MEERE

take place (the external stage directions are italicized in parentheses):

GOLIATH   Que maudit à jamais sois-tu de tous nos dieux.
             Or' va sous les Enfers.
             (Il le pense frapper de sa hache et faut d'atteinte.)
DAVID   Il a failli son coup.
GOLIATH   Me feras-tu tourner et retourner beaucoup?
             Si t'aurai-je!
DAVID   Il s'oublie, il est tout aveuglé
             De fureur, il se perd, son pas est déréglé.
             Seigneur, dresse ma main!
             (David tire son coup. Goliath tombe avec la pierre au front.
             David court et se met sur lui.)
TROUPE D'ISRAEL   Victoire en Dieu!
DEMI-TROUPE D'ISRAEL   Victoire!
TROUPE DES PHILISTINS   Tout est perdu.
ECUYER   Fuyons!
DEMI-TROUPE DES PHILISTINS Fuyons ce territoire!
GOLIATH*(par terre)*   Je dépite le Ciel. Je dépite et déteste
             En mourant, s'il est rien de déité céleste.
             Le père soit maudit, maudite soit la mère
             Dont je fus onques né pour souffrir mort amère!
             Maudit soit Israël! Maudite soit ma race
             Quand il faut qu'en ce point un berger me terrasse!
             (Cependant David lui tire son épée et lui en coupe la tête.)
                                              (ll. 1606–18)

[GOLIATH   Be forever cursed by all our gods. Now go to Hell.
             (He tries to strike David with his axe but misses.)
DAVID   He failed his blow.
GOLIATH   Are you going to make me turn around again and again?
             So I've got you!
DAVID   He is forgetting himself. He is completely blind.
             Out of fury, he is losing himself, his step is unbridled.
             Lord, guide my hand!
             (David shoots. Goliath falls with the stone in his brow. David runs
             and stands on top of him.)
TROOP OF ISRAEL   Victory in God!
HALF-TROOP OF ISRAEL   Victory!
TROOP OF PHILISTINES   All is lost.
HORSEMAN   Let us flee!
HALF-TROOP OF PHILISTINES Let us flee this land!
GOLIATH *(on the ground)*   I spite the heavens. Dying, I spite and hate, if
             any celestial deity exists. Cursed be my father, cursed be my
             mother of whom I was born to suffer such a bitter death!
             Cursed be Israel! Cursed be my race since a shepherd has cast
             me down!
             (Meanwhile David takes out his sword and cuts off his head.)]

Two violent passions, fury and rage, blind Goliath and cause his inability to strike
David. In turn, David calls God to draw his sling ('dresse ma main'), and it is God
who is responsible for David's aim and guides the stone to strike Goliath between

FROM THE CATHOLIC MYSTERY PLAY TO CALVINIST TRAGEDY 305

the eyes, hence creating more wordplay: Goliath is blinded by passion, and thereafter blinded by the stone, while the audience watches the duel with their own eyes. We also notice once again the visibility of the event, for the Hebrew troops/choruses witness and rejoice in God's victory, while the Philistine troops flee out of fear.

Des Masures and Coignac add yet another new element to the David and Goliath story, for, whereas the mystery, the Vulgate, and the Geneva Bible depict David decapitating Goliath and then discreetly returning to Saul's tent, the two playwrights reinforce the collective, celebratory aspect of the duel. David, after using Goliath's sword to dismember Goliath on stage, takes the giant's head in his hands and lifts it up for all to see. In Coignac's and Des Masures's versions, David, 'tenant la tête coupée' [holding the decapitated head], utters very similar sentiments:

> Mais DIEU qui n'a peur de surprise,
> Par une merveilleuse atteinte,
> A renversé son entreprise.
> Celuy qui faisoit tant du brave,
> N'a plus ne vie ne vertu:
> Avec son orgueilleuse bave,
> *Le voilà mort et abbatu.*
> Ainsi sera tousjours battu,
> Qui à DIEU voudra contredire.
> Ames ne valent un festu,
> Pour luy resister en son ire.
> Ainsi les obstinez mechans,
> Qui n'ont point DIEU en leur pensée,
> S'en iront à-bas tresbuschans.
> (Coignac, 65–66, emphasis added)[23]

> A toi, Seigneur, qui ton peuple visites
> Soit, à toi seul, ô Dieu des exercites,
> A toi qui es mon glaive et mon écu,
> A toi qui as le Philistin vaincu,
> A toi qui mets les ennemis en route,
> Honneur sans fin, gloire et puissance toute!
> Qui le petit et humble oublié n'as
> Qui du plus grand as rué bas,
> Qui les hauteurs et puissances humaines
> En un instant à rien réduis et mènes,
> C'est à toi seul non à moi qui rien suis,
> Toi en qui tout et sans qui rien ne puis,
> C'est à toi seul, ma force, à toi,
> C'est toi à qui la victoire je dois!
> (Des Masures, ll. 1609–21)

[But GOD who fears not surprise, by a marvellous blow, reversed his undertaking. He who thought to be so brave, no longer has life nor strength. With his proud drivel, there he is dead and cast down. Thus will forever more be defeated he who wants to go against GOD. Souls are not worth a chip, to endeavour against him in his ire. Hence the evil, stubborn ones who have not got GOD in their thoughts, will go down stumbling.]

306   MICHAEL MEERE

[To you, Lord, whom your people visit utter, to you alone, o God of armies, to you who are my sword and my shield, to you who have defeated the Philistine, to you who send enemies away, endless honour, glory and all power! Who has not forgotten the small and humble one, who has struck down the largest one, who reduce and lead in an instant human heights and powers, it is yours alone and not mine, I who am nothing, you in whom all and without whom nothing is possible. It is yours alone, my force, yours, it is you to whom I owe the victory!]

In both versions, David attributes his victory to God alone, and the young shepherd reinforces his own humility and human limitations in God's grand scheme. It is God who has punished Goliath's pride and arrogance through David. The gesture of lifting up the lifeless head and preaching to the internal audience of Israelites as well as the external Francophone audience underscores the liberating and just action that has just occurred. In turn, David gives hope to the internal and external audience members to have unconditional faith in divine power and justice, and the internal onlookers manifest their joy in collective song. At the same time, the shepherd preaches that anyone who attempts to revolt against God will be unable to resist His anger. In this way, David has thus liberated the Hebrew soldiers in another way, for they no longer are inhibited to fight against the Philistines.

Thou Shalt (Not) Kill?

With all of this blood and violence on stage, one must ask what kinds of ethical messages these playwrights are endorsing. Perhaps we can begin finding the answer by turning to Jean Calvin for, as Calvinist pastors, Coignac and Des Masures were presumably respected men in their religious communities who closely adhered to the their founder's teachings. As we will see, the tragedies provide moral instruction to the audience and aim to give hope and courage to the oppressed spectators, but they also raise essential questions: what role does the representation of violence play in Calvinist ethics? and under what circumstances is killing allowed?

The essence of Calvin's *oeuvre*, according to Lucien Febvre, was not so much to 'composer des livres, de prononcer des sermons, de formuler et de défendre des dogmes', but to 'dresser les hommes'.[24] Calvin's historical importance and influence lies in the ways in which he shaped 'le type humain du Calviniste'.[25] If this is true, we can presume that the Calvinist pastors who wrote these tragedies intended to transmit Calvinist ideas and ethics. However, because of the limited space of this article, I will only briefly look at Calvin's writings in order to focus on the plays in question, to discern a certain number of principles in his ethics and theology regarding the functions of physical violence, and how his followers were to interpret certain events with which they were faced.

In Book 2 of the *Institution de la religion chrétienne*, Calvin explains the sixth commandment, 'Tu n'occiras point' (Thou Shalt Not Kill), in some detail,[26] yet it is not until the fourth and most pragmatic book that Calvin makes the distinction between who has the right to inflict violence and who must remain obedient. Calvin underscores that the *peuple* must always respect the Laws, as well as their authorities. If the magistrates (e.g., kings, princes, judges) abuse their power, the

FROM THE CATHOLIC MYSTERY PLAY TO CALVINIST TRAGEDY   307

people must consider it as divine punishment, and they must not rise up against them but must obey the evil leaders. Even so, the people may resist them in their hearts and pray for their salvation and redemption.[27]

In the case of Des Masures, he dedicated his play to a fellow pastor, Le Brun, and the two men were members not of the magistrates or the ruling classes, but of the *peuple*. In turn, David's literal slaying of Goliath takes place in the Old Testament, before Christ's own suffering for the salvation of God's chosen people. Jesus's symbolic victory over his enemies represents the spiritual manifestation of David's literal victory over the evil Philistine soldiers.[28] Thus, in Book 2 of the *Institution*, Calvin distinguishes between the literal, mortal and temporal law of the Old Testament, and the spiritual, vivifying and eternal Scriptures.[29] For the Calvinists, then, who live in this world according to the Word of the Scriptures and spiritual salvation, David's defeat of Goliath can be read on a figurative level insomuch as it announces the redemption, salvation of humankind thanks to Jesus's defeat of sin and damnation. Calvinist followers may understand the story of David in Goliath through the lens of the (peaceful) life and teachings of Jesus Christ.

Still, in the last lines of Des Masures's *épître* to Philippe Le Brun, the playwright promotes an ambiguously militant message regarding the imitation of David as an exemplar for the reformers of the Church:

> Or toi, mon Brun, mon frère, et moi, si en nous vit
> La vraie et ferme foi qui anima David,
> A l'exemple de lui marchons de bon courage
> Tout à travers du monde, encontre tout orage,
> *Nous assurant en Dieu dont la main nous a mis*
> *Au combat pour défaire enfin nos ennemis.*
> Et jà de sa faveur la vraie expérience
> Nous montre *la victoire en notre patience.*
> [...]
> Combattons en David, tirant son coup de fonde,
> Mais combattons en Christ qui a vaincu la monde!
>   (ll. 223–34, emphasis added)

[Now you, my Brun, my brother, and me, if in us lives the true and firm faith that emboldened David, following his example let us walk forward with courage throughout the world, against all odds, *assuring ourselves that God whose hand has put us in battle to undo finally our enemies.* And already from his favour the true experience shows us that *victory lies in our patience.* [...] Let us fight as David did, shooting his slingshot, but let us fight as Christ who overcame the world!]

Des Masures's message is ambiguous, for on the one hand he seems to advise the persecuted reformers to take up arms against their enemies as David did against the Philistines, yet on the other his verses gear the spectator towards a peaceful, spiritual victory, following the example of Jesus Christ.

Coignac's message is much less ambiguous. He dedicated his play to the young Edward VI of England, who was only nine years old when proclaimed king in 1547. Coignac compares the English king, now roughly eighteen years old, to David in their struggle against comparable giant enemies:

308 MICHAEL MEERE

> Combien qu'il [David] fust encores jeune enfant,
> Si fit-il là un acte triomphant,
> Bien digne d'estre en celebre memoire.
> Ainsi de vous n'est pas moindre la gloire,
> Roy fleurissant, excellant et tresdigne [...] (p. 3)

[How he [David] was still a young child, thus he did a triomphant act, worthy to be celebrated in memory. Your glory, blossoming, excellent and very worthy king is no less great [...]]

At the end of the dedicatory preface Coignac evokes divine election and providence, underscoring the belief that God has elected Edward VI, who is just a child, to stand up to the giant Catholic Church, and to save the followers of the true Religion from the proud and bloody oppressor:

> Le toutpuissant, le Createur du monde,
> Qui conduisoit de son David la fonde,
> Et qui tousjours puis apres se servit
> Du jeune Roy et Prophete David:
> Vueille de vous tant se servir (ô Sire)
> Que de son FILS le royaume et l'empire
> Soit fleurissant, en grand' perfection,
> En vostre regne et domination:
> Et tant en vous, avec voz ans accroisse
> Ses riches dons, que par tout on cognoisse
> En nostre temps, que de l'Eglise sienne
> Il a le soing: comme de l'ancienne
> Il se monstra excellent defenseur,
> Contre le fier et sanglant oppresseur. (p. 12)

[The omnipotent, the Creator of the world, who guided David's sling, and who afterward always took benefit from the young King and Prophet David, may he also take benefit from you [Sire] so that from his SON the kingdom and empire may be blooming and in great perfection, in your reign and domination. And so much in you, that with your years may his rich gifts grow, that everywhere we may know in our time that he has taken care of his Church, as of his ancient Church he showed himself to be an excellent defender against the proud and bloody oppressor.]

Coignac thus refers directly to the papacy and the tyranny of the Roman Catholic Church, comparing Catholicism to the sacrilegious Goliath, and instils a glimmer of hope that God will soon give Edward and his allies the strength, courage and grace to conquer evil and defeat the domination of the Pope. Because Calvinist doctrine dictates that only princes and magistrates have the power to inflict violence through the power of divine election, Coignac seems to be making a plea to Edward VI, elected by God to be King of England, to rise up against the tyrannous papacy and save the Reformed peoples from oppression. The spectators would watch this spectacle with the hope that a courageous, divinely elected ruler might be able to overthrow the papacy.

Both Coignac and Des Masures thus evoke allusions to the Catholic Church that would have been obvious to a contemporaneous spectator by means of the *figura* and, by extension, the *tableau spirituel*, techniques that allow the poet and pastor Coignac, a self-proclaimed elected individual, to make the link between divine Word and the Book of the world.[30] In this respect, David defeats the giant who has faith in idols and who attempted to destroy the 'vraye Eglise', or the Reformed Church. By cutting off Goliath's/the Papacy's/the Antichrist's head, David dislocates the leader ('chef') from its body. Goliath's head represents the Pope, while his body symbolizes the papacy; the rest of the Philistines represent the Pope's soldiers, the leaders and members and components of the Catholic Church.

While there is a shift from the physical to the allegorical, this shift does not displace or reduce the power of the literal interpretation of the violence on stage. Rather, the physical violence between David and Goliath has a powerful and immediate effect upon the internal and external audience members, and by watching and experiencing the staged violence they transform the physicality of the spectacle into spiritual terms. Moreover, the allegorical shift gives this violence its full ethical and ideological dimensions. God's justice transcends the sword and spear, yet in order for this transcendence to occur, we are obliged to pass through the physicality of violence. It is the poet's responsibility to depict and decipher physical, terrestrial signs in order to show the rest of the people the presence of eternal life on earth.[31] In order to do so, the playwrights stage violence so that the audience may see for themselves that sin and evil pervade their daily existences, and it is through expunging these evil forces, represented by Goliath and the Philistines, that they can ultimately attain freedom and salvation.

La Desconfiture de Goliath and *David combattant* underscore the idea that God has chosen them and their addressees to defeat their enemies, and to imitate David and Christ in their battle against evil and oppressors. They transmit these messages similarly in three ways, as we have seen. First, they draw out the battle scene and give David and Goliath many more lines than we find in the medieval versions of the story or even in the Geneva Bible. In doing so, Coignac and Des Masures slightly distort the Bible in order to reinforce the reformers' current situation in the face of the papacy and threats of religious persecution. Second, they reinforce the celebratory aspect of David's (and God's) victory. For, whereas the medieval mystery, the Vulgate, and the Geneva Bible depict David decapitating Goliath and then discreetly returning to Saul's tent, the two Calvinist playwrights have David pick up Goliath's lifeless head, show it to the spectators, and preach to them. This gesture represents the liberating and just action that has occurred before them, and encourages the audience members to have unconditional faith in God's divine power. Third, both playwrights insist upon the duel's visibility, in order that the internal and external spectators may *see* with their own eyes Goliath's death and mutilation. His demise hence serves as an example of God's divine justice, justice which ultimately transcends the sword and the spear.

However, the playwrights' ultimate aims and effects on the addressee and the spectators are quite different. Des Masures calls for patience and courage during their suffering, which will allow the reformers to attain eternal salvation. While the kings, princes, and leaders have the moral obligation to wage war when necessary, only an elect few have the right to carry out God's divine justice in the Calvinist system in which the three uses of the law must be obeyed in order to maintain civil and political order.[32] Coignac, however, promotes a very militant and proactive message by addressing his tragedy to Edward VI of England. Coignac seems to urge the audience to wait patiently for the 'chosen one' to overtake the Catholic Church. His representation of the victory of David over Goliath as an unleashing of the collective inhibitions of the Hebrew soldiers to attack and annihilate the Philistines translates into a fully polemical text, which, on the one hand inspires hope and courage in the readers in order to resist their enemies, and, on the other entices them to take up arms and *physically* kill the Pope and Catholics. Coignac's tragedy seems to suggest that the *peuple* shall not kill — unless, of course, they are told to do so.

Bibliography

BEAM, SARA, *Laughing Matters: Farce and the Making of Absolutism in France* (Ithaca, NY: Cornell University Press, 2007)

BÈZE, THÉODORE DE, *Abraham sacrifiant* [Geneva, 1551], ed. by Keith Cameron, Kathleen M. Hall and Francis Higman (Geneva: Droz, 1967)

——*A Tragedie of Abrahams sacrifice* [London, 1577], trans. by Arthur Golding [1575], ed. by Malcolm W. Wallace (Toronto: University of Toronto Library, 1906)

BIET, CHRISTIAN, et al., eds., *Théâtre de la cruauté et récits sanglants en France (XVIe–XVIIe siècle)* (Paris: Robert Laffont, 2006)

BIET, CHRISTIAN, MARIE-MADELEINE FRAGONARD et al., *Tragédies et récits de martyres en France (fin XVIe–début XVIIe siècle)* (Paris: Classiques Garnier, 2009)

BLUM, CLAUDE, *La Représentation de la mort dans la littérature française de la Renaissance*, 2 vols (Paris: Champion, 1989)

BORDIER, JEAN-PIERRE, *Le Jeu de la passion: le message chrétien et le théâtre français, XIIIe–XVIe siècle* (Paris: Champion, 1998)

BUCHANAN, GEORGE, *Baptistes* (London, 1578)

——*Jephthes* (Paris, 1557)

CALVIN, JEAN, *Institution de la religion chrétienne*, 4 vols (Geneva: Labor es Fides, 1957)

——*The Institutes of the Christian Religion*, trans. by Henry Beveridge (Grand Rapids, MI: Christian Classics Ethereal Library, n.d.)

CHARPENTIER, FRANÇOISE, 'Naissance de la tragédie poétique en France: Jodelle, la Péruse', in *Par Ta colère nous sommes consumes: Jean de La Taille auteur tragique*, ed. by Marie-Madeleine Fragonard (Orléans: Paradigme, 1998), pp. 73–86

——*Pour une lecture de la tragédie humaniste: Jodelle, Garnier, Montchrestien* (Saint-Etienne: Publications de l'Université Saint-Etienne, 1979)

COIGNAC, JOACHIM DE, *La Desconfiture de Goliath* (n.p., n.d. [1551?])

DES MASURES, LOUIS, *David combattant* [1563], ed. by Michel Dassonville, in *La Tragédie à l'époque d'Henri II et de Charles IX*, series 1, vol. 2 (Florence: Olschki; Paris: Presses Universitaires de France, 1989), pp. 215–441

DOMINGUEZ, VÉRONIQUE, *La Scène et la Croix: le jeu de l'acteur dans les Passions dramatiques françaises (XIVe–XVIe siècles)* (Turnhout: Brepols, 2007)

ENDERS, JODY, *Medieval Theater of Cruelty: Rhetoric, Memory, Violence* (Ithaca, NY: Cornell University Press, 2002)

FEBVRE, LUCIEN, *Au cœur religieux du XVIe siècle*, 2nd edn (Paris: S.E.V.P.E.N, 1968)

FORSYTH, ELLIOT, *Tragédie française de Jodelle à Corneille: le thème de la vengeance (1533–1640)* (Paris: Champion, 1994)

FRAGONARD, MARIE-MADELEINE, ed., *Par Ta colère nous sommes consumes: Jean de La Taille auteur tragique* (Orléans: Paradigme, 1998)

FRONTAIN, RAYMOND-JEAN, ed., *The David Myth in Western Literature* (West Lafayette, IN: Purdue University Press, 1980)

FUCHS, ERIC, *La Morale selon Calvin* (Paris: Cerf, 1986)

GATTON, JOHN SPALDING, '"There must be blood": Mutilation and Martyrdom on the Medieval Stage', in *Violence in Drama*, ed. by James Redmond (Cambridge: Cambridge University Press, 1991), pp. 79–91

GOSSELIN, EDWARD A., *The King's Progress to Jerusalem: Some Interpretations of David during the Reformation Period and their Patristic and Medieval Background* (Malibu: Undena Publications, 1976)

GREVIN, JACQUES, *Le Théâtre de Jacques Grévin* (Paris: Vincent Sertenas, 1561)

GRIFFITHS, RICHARD, *The Dramatic Technique of Montchrestien: Rhetoric and Style in French Renaissance Tragedy* (Oxford: Oxford University Press, 1970)

HUGUET, EDMOND, ed., *Dictionnaire de la langue française du seizième siècle*, 7 vols (Paris: Librairie Ancienne Édouard Champion, 1925)

JEANNERET, MICHEL, *Poésie et tradition biblique au XVIe siècle: recherches stylistiques sur les paraphrases des 'Psaumes', de Marot à Malherbe* (Paris: J. Corti, 1969)

JODELLE, ETIENNE, *Cléopâtre captive*, ed. by Françoise Charpentier, Jean-Dominique Beaudin and José Sanchez (Mugron: J. Feijóo, 1990)

JONDORF, GILLIAN, *French Renaissance Tragedy: The Dramatic Word* (Cambridge: Cambridge University Press, 1990)

LA PÉRUSE, JEAN BASTIER DE, *Médée* [1566], ed. by James A. Coleman (Exeter: University of Exeter Press, 1985)

LATAILLE, JEAN, 'De l'art de la tragédie', in *Saul le Furieux, Tragedie prise de la Bible, Faicte selon l'art et à la mode des vieux Autheurs Tragiques* (Paris: Frederic Morel, 1572)

THE LATIN VULGATE BIBLE, <http://vulgate.org/> [accessed 31 July 2013]

LAUDUN D'AIGALIERS, PIERRE DE, *Art poétique français*, ed. by Jean-Charles Monferran et al. (Paris: Société des Textes Français Modernes, 2000)

LAZARD, MADELEINE, *Le Théâtre en France au XVIe siècle* (Paris: Presses Universitaires de France, 1980)

LEBÈGUE, RAYMOND, *La Tragédie religieuse en France: les débuts (1514–1573)* (Paris: Champion, 1929)

——*Etudes sur le théâtre français*, 2 vols (Paris: Nizet, 1977)

LEBLANC, PAULETTE, *Les Écrits théoriques et critiques français des années 1540–1561 sur la tragédie* (Paris: Nizet, 1972)

LIGNIM, H. LAMBRON DE, 'Recherches sur l'origine du théâtre en Touraine', *Mémoire lu dans la Séance générale du Congrès scientifique de France, le 6 septembre 1847* (Tours: Imprimerie Lecense et Alf. Laurent, 1848)

LOUVAT, BÉNÉDICTE, 'Le Théâtre protestant et la musique (1550–1586),' in *Par la vue et par l'ouïe: littérature du Moyen Age et de la Renaissance*, ed. by Michèle Gally and Michel Jourde (Fontenay Saint Cloud: ENS Editions, 1999), pp. 135–58

LOUVAT-MOLOZAY, BÉNÉDICTE, *Théâtre et musique: dramaturgie de l'insertion musicale dans le théâtre français (1550–1680)* (Paris: Honoré Champion, 2002)

MAZOUER, CHARLES, *Le Théâtre français de la Renaissance* (Paris: Champion, 2002)

MEYNIEL, CORINNE, 'De la Cène à la scène: la tragédie biblique en France pendant les guerres de religions (1550–1625)' (unpublished doctoral thesis, Université Paris X–Nanterre, 2010)

Mistère du Viel Testament, ed. by James de Rothschild, 6 vols (Paris: Firmin Didot et cie, 1878–91)

Le Mystère de Judith et Holofernés: une édition critique de l'une des parties du 'Mistere du Viel Testament', ed. by Graham A. Runnells (Geneva: Droz, 1995)

312   MICHAEL MEERE

PELETIER DU MANS, JACQUES, *Art poëtique* (Lyon: J. de Tournes, 1555)
PETIT DE JULLEVILLE, LOUIS, *Histoire du théâtre en France. Les Mystères* (Paris: Hachette, 1880)
RIVAUDEAU, ANDRÉ DE, *Aman, de la perfidie* (Poitiers: N. Logeroys, 1566)
STAWARZ-LUGINBÜHL, RUTH, *Un théâtre de l'épreuve: tragédies huguenotes en marge des guerres de religion en France, 1550–1573* (Geneva: Droz, 2012)
STONE, DONALD, *French Humanist Tragedy: A Reassessment* (Manchester: Manchester University Press, 1974)
STREET, JOHN SPENCER, *French Sacred Drama from Bèze to Corneille: Dramatic Forms and their Purposes in the Early Modern Theatre* (London, New York and Melbourne: Cambridge University Press, 1983)
TERNAUX, JEAN-CLAUDE, ed., *Le Théâtre du XVIe siècle et ses modèles* (Paris: Société française d'étude du XVIe siècle, 2010)
VAILLANCOURT, PIERRE-LOUIS, 'Théologie du sacrifice dans la tragédie renaissante', in *Les Arts du spectacles au théâtre (1500–1700)*, ed. by Marie-France Wagner and Claire Le Brun-Gouanvic (Paris: Champion, 2001), pp. 15–33
WEINBERG, BERNARD, ed., *Critical Prefaces of the French Renaissance* (Evanston, IL: Northwestern University Press, 1950)
ZEPPE DE NOLVA, CLAUDIO, 'Tragédie italienne et française au XVIe siècle', in *Par Ta colère nous sommes consumes: Jean de La Taille auteur tragique*, ed. by Marie-Madeleine Fragonard (Orléans: Paradigme, 1998), pp. 59–71

Notes to Chapter 14

1. Lazare de Baïf translated Sophocles's *Electre* in 1537, Guillaume Bochetel and Baïf both translated Euripides's *Hecuba* into French in 1544 and 1550, respectively, while George Buchanan and Marc-Antoine Muret translated and penned tragedies in Latin for pupils at various *collèges*, including the Collège de Guyenne and the Collège de Boncourt.

2. For a concise synthesis of dramaturgical poetics and practices in the early 1550s in France, see Françoise Charpentier, 'Naissance de la tragédie poétique en France: Jodelle, la Péruse', in *Par Ta colère nous sommes consumes: Jean de La Taille auteur tragique*, ed. by Marie-Madeleine Fragonard (Orléans: Paradigme, 1998), pp. 73–86.

3. See Rivaudeau's 'Avant-Parler' which precedes his tragedy *Aman* (*Œuvres* (Poitiers: Nicolas Logeroys, 1566)); La Taille, 'De l'art de la tragédie', in *Saul le Furieux, Tragedie prise de la Bible, Faicte selon l'art et à la mode des vieux Autheurs Tragiques* (Paris: Frederic Morel, 1572); Grévin, 'Brief discours pour l'intelligence de ce Theatre', in *Le Théâtre de Jacques Grévin* (Paris: Vincent Sertenas, 1561). All three authors evoke Aristotle's *Poetics*, but they are arguably more influenced by Horace and Italian commentators of Aristotle than by the *Poetics*. See, for example, Claudio Neppo de Nolva, 'Tragédie italienne et française au XVIe siècle', in *Par Ta colère nous sommes consumes: Jean de La Taille auteur tragique*, ed. by Marie-Madeleine Fragonard (Orléans: Paradigme, 1998), pp. 59–71.

4. Théodore de Bèze, *Abraham sacrifiant* [Geneva, 1551], ed. by Keith Cameron, Kathleen M. Hall and Francis Higman (Geneva: Droz, 1967). The play was translated in 1575 by Arthur Golding, *A Tragedie of Abrahams sacrifice* [London, 1577], ed. by Malcolm W. Wallace (Toronto: University of Toronto Library, 1906). The English quotations of Bèze's play will come from this edition.

5. Madeleine Lazard, *Le Théâtre en France au XVIe siècle* (Paris: Presses Universitaires de France, 1980), pp. 97–98 succinctly sums up Bèze's tragedy: '[sa tragédie] ouvrait la voie à une tragédie moderne, engagé, celle des protestants. Bon helléniste, Bèze a tiré de la Bible le sujet de la pièce, le sacrifice d'Isaac par Abraham, dont la structure s'inspire de la tragédie grecque, d'*Iphigénie à Aulis* notamment, tout en conservant certains procédés des mystères: apparition de l'Ange et de Satan, simplicité du style [...], absence de division en actes. Des cantiques chantés par les bergers tiennent lieu de chœurs. L'intervention divine permet un dénouement heureux. Si l'œuvre de Bèze, humaniste et ami de Ronsard passé au protestantisme militant, ne manque pas de mérite littéraire, elle propose avant tout un enseignement religieux qui s'adresse à un large public, non

From the Catholic Mystery Play to Calvinist Tragedy 313

aux seuls lettrés.' It should be noted that George Buchanan's *Jephthes* (perf. *c.* 1545, printed in 1554) is also modelled after Euripides's *Iphiginea at Aulis* and that the subject of sacrifice and divine oaths were an important topic of discussion and debate during the Reformation. On oaths, see Raymond Lebègue, *La Tragédie religieuse en France: les débuts (1514–1573)* (Paris: Champion, 1929), pp. 229–31; on sacrifice, see Pierre-Louis Vaillancourt, 'Théologie du sacrifice dans la tragédie renaissante', in *Les Arts du spectacles au théâtre (1500–1700)*, ed. by Marie-France Wagner and Claire Le Brun-Gouanvic (Paris: Champion, 2001), pp. 15–33. All translations are mine unless otherwise noted.

6. Indeed, as Donald Stone has asserted, French humanist tragedy 'followed two rather distinct forms. One, used by Théodore de Bèze in *Abraham sacrifiant*, did not employ the term act, saw no need to divide its plot into five episodes, had choruses that spoke and sang, but did not serve to separate the main blocks of the action' (*French Humanist Tragedy: A Reassessment* (Manchester: Manchester University Press, 1974), p. 131).

7. 'confient à leurs pièces un message édifiant et ne craignent pas d'en préciser l'actualité, car l'entreprise n'a d'intérêt, à leurs yeux, que si elle propose aux fidèles un miroir de leur situation et une solution à leurs problèmes', *Poésie et tradition biblique au XVIᵉ siècle: recherches stylistiques sur les paraphrases des 'Psaumes', de Marot à Malherbe* (Paris: J. Corti, 1969), pp. 124–25.

8. No modern edition of Coignac's tragedy exists. I have consulted and will cite from the microfilmed copy at the Bibliothèque Nationale de France, reference RES-YF-4349. There is no place of publication, and the date 1551 is written in by hand. Another edition exists at the British Library with a title page, reference C.65.c.11.

9. Des Masures's *David combattant* comprises the first tragedy in his David trilogy, the other plays bearing the titles *David triomphant* and *David fugitif*. The Bibliothèque Nationale de France (Arsenal) contains the 1566 edition printed by François Perrin at Geneva (reference 8-BL-13906 [1]) and the Richelieu and Arsenal sites have the 1582 edition printed by N. Sollmans at Anvers (Richelieu: 8-RF-1209; Arsenal: GD-1644). I have consulted all of the editions; however, I will cite from the critical edition by Michel Dassonville in *La Tragédie à l'époque d'Henri II et de Charles IX*, series 1, vol. 2 (Florence: Olschki; Paris: Presses Universitaires de France, 1989), pp. 215–441.

10. Corinne Meyniel, 'De la Cène à la scène: la tragédie biblique en France pendant les guerres de religions (1550–1625)' (unpublished doctoral thesis, Université Paris X–Nanterre, 2010), p. 93.

11. His biblical tragedy *Aman, de la perfidie [Aman, of Perfidy]* was performed in 1561 and printed in Poitiers in 1566.

12. We do not know much about Coignac, besides that he preached in Thonon and Grenoble before taking refuge in Switzerland, and that he also printed a polemical comedy, titled *Deux satires, l'une du pape, l'autre de la papauté* [Two Satires, One of the Pope, the Other of the Papacy] (Lausanne: Jean Rivery, 1551). The date of publication of *La Desconfiture de Goliath* is uncertain, although critics have deduced that it was printed in the same year (Lebègue, *Tragédie religieuse*, p. 319). We know more about Des Masures's life and publications: he converted to Calvinism during Francis I's reign, frequented humanist circles and made a name for himself as a translator of Virgil's *Aeneid* (first four books printed in Lyons in 1552). Hence, Des Masures's 'objection to the embellishment of the neo-classical style, its flights of rhetoric which he approximates to lying, and mythological allusions which could lead to obscurity' was not insignificant (John Spencer Street, *French Sacred Drama from Bèze to Corneille: Dramatic Forms and their Purposes in the Early Modern Theatre* (London, New York and Melbourne: Cambridge University Press, 1983), p. 47). Although there are no known traces of performance of Coignac's tragedy, it is highly likely that it was put on stage, and it is clear that Coignac and Des Masures intended that they be performed in front of an audience. There is one document (13 February 1627) that relates a performance of Des Masures's *David combattant* by students at the duke's castle in the Protestant city of Montbéliard (Lebègue, *Tragédie religieuse*, p. 368). Nonetheless, it is equally probable that Des Masures's tragedy was performed during the sixteenth century.

13. The most recent, thorough work on these plays is Ruth Stawarz-Luginbühl's *Un théâtre de l'épreuve: tragédies huguenotes en marge des guerres de religion en France, 1550–1573* (Geneva: Droz, 2012), pp. 397–441 for Coignac and pp. 493–589 for Des Masures. However, Stawarz-Luginbühl entirely ignores the staged violence in these plays as she is more interested in how they support

314   MICHAEL MEERE

her thesis that the plays stage '*le passage — effectif ou manqué — du désespoir à la confiance*, cette crise, de nature intellectuelle, existentielle et spirituelle, qui place le protagoniste et la communauté à laquelle il appartient [...] face à la rupture apparente du contrat initial [...] qui les sépare d'une hypothétique délivrance' (p. 17). She does, nonetheless, offer insightful analyses on tragedy as the chosen form of these Calvinist playwrights (pp. 399–407; 507–23).

14. In the sixteenth century, the *Mistére du Viel Testament* was printed three times: *c.* 1500, 1520 and 1542, following the performance of the *Mistére* in Paris by the Confrérie de la Passion in the same year (1542). Other parts of the *Mistére* were performed later in the century throughout France, such as *Judith et Holofernés* in Puy en Velay in 1585 (Graham A. Runnalls, Introduction, *Le Mystère de Judith et Holofernés: une édition critique de l'une des parties du 'Mistere du Viel Testament'* (Geneva: Droz, 1995), p. 44). For detailed and erudite studies on the medieval *mystère*, Louis Petit de Julleville's *Histoire du théâtre en France. Les Mystères* (Paris: Hachette, 1880) and Raymond Lebègue's *La Tragédie religieuse en France* remain extremely useful and informative. Other leading authorities on the mystery and medieval religious drama are Maurice Accarie, *Le Théâtre sacré de la fin du Moyen Âge: étude sur le sens moral de la 'Passion de Jean Michel'* (Lille: Atelier national de reproduction des thèses, 1983), Jean-Pierre Bordier, *Le Jeu de la passion: le message chrétien et le théâtre français (XIIIe–XVIe siècle)* (Paris: Champion, 1998), Graham A. Runnalls, *Etudes sur les mystères* (Paris: Champion, 1998), and Véronique Dominguez's *La Scène et la Croix: le jeu de l'acteur dans les Passions dramatiques françaises* (Turnhout: Brepols, 2007). John Spalding Gatton's article '"There must be blood": Mutilation and Martyrdom on the Medieval Stage', is also useful in regard to the staging of medieval theatre but it does not propose any arguments regarding the theological aspects of this drama (in *Violence in Drama*, ed. by James Redmond (Cambridge: Cambridge University Press, 1991), pp. 79–91). Finally, Jody Enders's *Medieval Theater of Cruelty* remains a leading theoretical work on the staging of violent medieval theatre and its relationship with rhetoric and memory (Ithaca, NY: Cornell University Press, 2002).

15. The story of David and Goliath is the eleventh episode in the thirty-third mystery in the Rothschild edition of the Mistére du Viel Testament. Mystery XXXIII runs to a total of 1536 lines (ll. 28,802–30,358). Rothschild divides the mystery into thirteen separate episodes, including: 'De Isay, pére de David, et comme ledit David estoit pasteur; Comme Saül fut fait roy; du Règne de Saül et de Samuel; des Batailles de Saül contre Amalech; de la Mutacion du Régne de Saül; comme David, par le commendement de Dieu, fut oinct; comme David tue ung ours; comme David combat ung lyon; comme David sonne de la harpe devant Saül; de Goullias; comme David tue Goullias; de l'Alliance de David et de Jonathan, filz de Saül; comme Saül voulut tuer David; du Mariage de David et de Michol' (xvj).

16. This aspect of the story exists in the Vulgate (I Samuel 17. 39).

17. In sixteenth-century Tours, in preparations for a performance of this mystery, for example, a local painter Henri Matthieu, who was often hired for making props, made 'le moule de Golyas et moule et estouffé dessus ledit moulle de painture ainsi quil appartient et fait les cheveux et le chappeau tous pains et fait dedans la teste de Golyas une faincte qui rendoit le sang' in H. Lambron de Lignim, 'Recherches sur l'origine du théâtre en Touraine', *Mémoire lu dans la Séance générale du Congrès scientifique de France, le 6 septembre 1847* (Tours: Imprimerie Lecense et Alf. Laurent, 1848), p. 26. These special effects were undoubtedly recycled for the performances of tragedies.

18. Enders would argue that the violence in this play, as a pedagogical device, serves to remind the audience of what they see (p. 100).

19. The main prize for defeating Goliath was marrying Saul's daughter (l. 29,910; Vulgate, I Samuel 17. 25).

20. Charles Mazouer, *Le Théâtre français de la Renaissance* (Paris: Champion, 2002), p. 215. For a general panorama of the story of David in literature, see *The David Myth in Western Literature*, ed. by Raymond-Jean Frontain and Jan Wojcik (West Lafayette, IN: Purdue University Press, 1980). On the interpretations of David in the Reformation, see notably Edward A. Gosselin, *The King's Progress to Jerusalem: Some Interpretations of David during the Reformation Period and their Patristic and Medieval Background* (Malibu: Undena Publications, 1976).

21. *Dictionnaire de la langue française du seizième siècle*, ed. by Edmond Huguet, 7 vols (Paris: Librairie Ancienne Édouard Champion, 1925), III, 51.

From the Catholic Mystery Play to Calvinist Tragedy 315

22. Jacques Peletier du Mans, *Art poëtique* (Lyon: J. de Tournes, 1555), p. 72.
23. Just after his tirade, David orders the Hebrews to chase after the Philistines, which empties the stage in order to allow the 'filles d'Israël' [daughters of Israel] to sing their hymn which ends the tragedy (pp. 67–69). On the use and importance of songs in Calvinist theatre, which reinforces the communal and spiritual aspects of these plays, see Bénédicte Louvat, 'Le Théâtre protestant et la musique (1550–1586),' in *Par la vue et par l'ouïe: littérature du Moyen Age et de la Renaissance*, ed. by Michèle Gally and Michel Jourde (Fontenay Saint Cloud: ENS Editions, 1999), pp. 135–58, as well as her *Théâtre et musique: dramaturgie de l'insertion musicale dans le théâtre français (1550–1680)* (Paris: Honoré Champion, 2002), pp. 219–55.
24. Lucien Febvre, *Au cœur religieux du XVIe siècle*, 2nd edn (Paris: S.E.V.P.E.N, 1968), p. 263.
25. Ibid., p. 263.
26. Calvin first published the Latin version of the *Institution* in 1536. The French version appeared in 1541. A revised and augmented Latin version appeared in 1559, while its translation into French hit the presses in 1560. I am citing the 1560 edition, 4 vols (Geneva: Labor es Fides, 1957), II, VIII, 39, pp. 161–62. For the English translation, I cite John Calvin, *The Institutes of the Christian Religion*, trans. by Henry Beveridge (Grand Rapids, MI: Christian Classics Ethereal Library, n.d.), 2.8.39, pp. 329–30.
27. *Institution*, IV, XX, 22–29, pp. 471–78; *Institutes*, 4.20.22–29, pp. 1184–90.
28. The most common literal and metaphorical relationship between David and Jesus is the fact that David was a shepherd of actual sheep, whereas Jesus was a shepherd of humans' souls.
29. *Institution*, II, xi, 7–9, pp. 215–16; *Institutes*, 2.11.7–9, pp. 371–72.
30. Blum: 'Au sens stricte, on a *figura* lorsqu'une série d'événements (dans l'*Ancien Testament*) annonce une deuxième série d'événements (dans le *Nouveau Testament*) qui accomplit la première.' *La Représentation de la mort dans la littérature française de la Renaissance*, 2 vols (Paris: Champion, 1989), II, 579, n. 27.
31. Blum, II, 575–76.
32. See Eric Fuchs, *La Morale selon Calvin* (Paris: Cerf, 1986), pp. 49–56.

CHAPTER 15

❖

The Renaissance Meets the Reformation: The Dramatist Thomas Naogeorg (1508–1563)

Helen Watanabe-O'Kelly

Exeter College, Oxford

During the century before the outbreak of the Reformation, German Humanists were steadily disseminating Latin drama north of the Alps. German scholars such as Enea Silvio Piccolomini (later Pope Pius II, 1405–1464) and Rudolf Agricola (1444–1485) who visited Italy played an important part in this.[1] Once the German invention of printing had taken root in Italy, Latin texts printed in Rome and Venice could reach the Empire by a variety of routes, where they could in turn be copied and distributed by the rapidly multiplying number of German printers.[2] Some of these print shops, such as those of Amerbach and Froben in Basel, acted as veritable clearing houses for classical texts and Humanist ideas, but Basel was only one important centre. Terence's plays were printed by Johann Mentelin in Strasburg in 1470, Plautus's works were printed there 1508,[3] Terence's were printed again in Wittenberg in 1514,[4] and editions of these two dramatists continued to appear in the Empire during the sixteenth century.[5]

Not all of the newly discovered texts came from Italy, however. Giovanni Aurispa (1376–1459) had found Donatus's commentary on Terence in Mainz in 1433, for instance, while Nikolaus von Kues (Nicolaus Cusanus, 1401–1464) discovered twelve comedies by Plautus, probably in Fulda, in the middle of the fifteenth century. German Humanists began themselves to edit Latin plays. Conrad Celtis (1459–1508), the great Nuremberg Humanist, edited two of Seneca's tragedies, *Hercules furens* and *Cena Thyestis*, in 1487 and went on to publish Terence's comedies with the commentaries of Aelius Donatus in 1499,[6] while Jacob Locher (1471–1528) edited and published three Senecan tragedies in 1520.[7] German Humanists also began to translate Latin dramas into German. Albrecht von Eyb (1420–1475) translated Plautus's *Menaechmi* and *Bacchides* around 1474 (as well as Ugolino Pisani's *Philogenia*)[8] and Hans Neidhart (*c.* 1430–after 1502) translated Terence's *Eunuch* in 1486.[9] In his inaugural lecture in 1492 as professor at the University of Ingolstadt, Conrad Celtis presented drama as being central to Roman political and civic life, saying that it should be adopted for similar reasons in the German-speaking world.

318   HELEN WATANABE-O'KELLY

All these factors led, towards the end of the fifteenth century, to the development of original drama in Latin in the Empire on the Roman model.[10] *Stylpho* by Jacob Wimpfeling (1450–1528), first performed in 1480, is usually claimed as the first such play, though Dietl points out that it began life as a dialogue and was only turned into a play by a student of Wimpfeling's when it was published in 1494.[11] *Stylpho* praises the new learning, as do *Codrus* (1485) by Johannes Kerckmeister (*c.*1450–*c.*1500), *Comoedia de optimo studio iuvenum* [A play about the best kind of study for young men] (1501) by Heinrich Bebel (*c.* 1472–1518) and *Virtus et Fallacicaptrix* [Virtue and Madam Pleasure] (1497) by Joseph Grünpeck (1473–1540). *Scenica Progymnasmata* [Rhetorical Exercises in Dramatic Form] (first performed in 1497 and printed in 1498), better known as *Henno*, by Johannes Reuchlin (1455–1522), is a so-called *ludus anilis* or unrefined comedy. It is the first play to be divided into acts and scenes with a chorus at the end of each act. It stages the conflicts between good and bad students and academics and was so popular that it was reprinted thirty-one times up to 1531.

Latin plays were often written about contemporary political events, for tragedy, as the Humanists saw it, should by definition concern itself with public affairs, while comedy rather had to do with private ones. Two plays by Jacob Locher exemplify the role of the dramatist as commentator on the important events of the day. Locher's *Historia de rege Frantie I* [The History of the King of France] (1495) takes as its subject the invasion of Italy by Charles VIII of France (1470–1498) which took place in the year the play was written. Locher had been in Italy at the time of the invasion and he structures the action so as to present the rise and fall of Charles and his defeat by the Emperor Maximilian I (1459–1519) at the end of the play — even though this had not yet happened in real life! Locher's next play was *Tragedia de Turcis et Suldano* [A Tragedy about the Turks and the Sultan] (1497), which again portrays Maximilian in a heroic light as the victor over the Turks. Conrad Celtis was another Humanist who put his pen at the service of Maximilian. He composed what are usually called festival plays, that is, panegyric entertainments to be performed at Court. One of these is *Ludis Diana* [The Play of Diana] (1501), in which divine figures such as Diana, Bacchus and Mars/Silenus praise the Emperor. Another is *Rhapsodia, laudes et victoria de Boemannis* [Rhapsody, Praise and Victory over the Bohemians] (1504) which lauds Maximilian's defeat of the Bohemians at the Battle of Wenzenberg in September of that year.

It was said in the first decades of the sixteenth century, and has been said many times since, that the Humanists in the Empire paved the way for the Reformation. Chief among them was Desiderius Erasmus (*c.* 1466–1536), who, though born in Rotterdam, was always regarded in his own time as a German. Erasmus never went over to the Reformers — indeed, he objected to the identification of Humanism with Protestantism — but it was claimed in his own day that he 'laid the egg that Luther hatched'. It was he who discovered and published Lorenzo Valla's collation of Gospel manuscripts: *In Latinam Novi Testamenti Interpretationem ex Collatione Graecorum Exemplarium Adnotationes* [Notes on the Latin Translation of the New Testament, Based on a Collation of Greek Manuscripts, 1505]. Likewise, it was he who first published a Greek New Testament with a revised version of the Vulgate

THE RENAISSANCE MEETS THE REFORMATION   319

in 1516 (the *Novum Instrumentum* or New Instrument).[12] His satirical pen excoriated abuses in the Church and his support for the writings of the ancients contributed to the questioning of old certainties. Many other Humanists also applied their expertise in textual scholarship and their questioning of orthodoxy to matters of religion and Church organization in their own day.

What has this got to do with drama and its reinvention in the sixteenth century? Quite simply, Luther saw the theatre as a vital tool to convert people to the new doctrine, to educate them in its central tenets, to teach them about the Bible, and to inculcate in them certain social teachings. That Luther's right-hand man, Melanchthon, was of the same mind is made clear in the latter's *Epistola de legendis Tragoediis et Comoediis* (1545).[13] Reformers, therefore, quickly followed Luther's call to write dramas which would present the new beliefs. Gulielmus Gnapheus (Willem van de Voldersgraft, 1492–1568) was a headmaster in Elbing and Königsberg and initiated the flood of Reformation plays on the theme of the Prodigal Son with his *Acolastus sive de filio prodigo* [Acolastus or the Prodigal Son] (1529). The topic was so popular because it illustrated the central Lutheran doctrine of justification by faith, not works. *Acolastus* was first published in Antwerp in 1529 and was constantly reprinted, translated and performed throughout the sixteenth century. Even when an author did not himself go over to Luther, like Georg Macropedius (Joris van Lanckvelt, 1487–1558) who remained a Catholic, his Everyman play about faith and repentance, *Hecastus* (first performed in Utrecht in 1538 and published in 1539), was nonetheless thought to be so close to central Protestant notions about salvation that Macropedius was heavily criticized by his own Church.

Luther exhorted his followers to dramatize Bible stories in order to promulgate his ideas about social behaviour, in particular about marriage and the family. In his Preface to the Book of Tobias in the 1544 edition of his translation of the Bible Luther writes:

> VND Gott gebe | das die Griechen jre weise | Comedien vnd Tragedien zu spielen | von den Jüden genomen haben | Wie auch viel ander Weisheit vnd Gottesdienst etc. Denn Judith gibt eine gute | ernste | dapffere Tragedien | So gibt Tobias eine feine liebliche | gottselige Comedien. Denn gleich wie das Buch Judith anzeigt | wie es Land vnd Leuten offt elendiglich gehet | vnd wie die Tyrannen erstlich hoffertiglich toben | vnd zu letzt schendlich zu boden gehen. Also zeigt das Buch Tobias an | wie es einem fromen Bawr oder Bürger auch vbel gehet | und viel leidens im Ehestand sey | Aber Gott jmer gnediglich helffe | vnd zu letzt das ende mit freuden beschliesse. Auff das die Eheleute sollen lernen gedult haben | vnd allerley leiden | auff künfftig hoffnung gerne tragen | in rechter furcht Gottes vnd festem glauben.[14]

> [And God ordained that the Greeks took their way of acting comedies and tragedies from the Jews, like much other wisdom and divine service, etc. For [the Book of] Judith is material for a good, serious, brave tragedy and in the same way [the Book of] Tobias is a fine, pleasant and godly comedy. For just as the Book of Judith shows how a country and a people often suffer and how tyrants first of all rage vaingloriously and in the end are ignominiously defeated, so the Book of Tobias shows how things go badly too for a decent peasant or townsman and how much he suffers in his marriage. But God always helps graciously and finally brings about a joyous ending, so that the married

> couple may learn patience and how to put up with all suffering gladly for the
> sake of future hope and with a firm and god-fearing faith.]

This gave rise to large number of dramas, not just on the subject of the Prodigal Son, but also about Susanna, Esther, Judith and the marriage feast at Cana. That these plays could be in Latin as well as in German, depending on the context in which they were to be performed, is illustrated by the work of Sixt Birck (1501–1554). He taught first at a grammar school in Basel from 1534 and then went to Augsburg in 1536 to be the headmaster of the Latin school there. He wrote a series of biblical plays in German verse for his Basel pupils (among them *Zorobabel*, *Ezechias, Joseph, Susanna,* and *Judith*) and then translated some of them into Latin for performance by his Augsburg pupils.[15] *Susanna* and *Judith* were reprinted again and again throughout the sixteenth century.

At around the time that Birck was active, there came onto the scene a powerful dramatist and polemicist in the Protestant cause, all of whose plays are in Latin. This is Thomas Naogeorg (whose real name was Kirchmair, *c.* 1508–1563). Born in Straubing in Bavaria he entered the Dominican order, only to leave it in 1526, convinced by Luther's teachings. He then became a Lutheran clergyman but his teachings on such subjects as the Eucharist led him into conflict with Lutheran orthodoxy throughout his life and towards the end of his life he was accused of Calvinist leanings. Hans-Gert Roloff, the editor and scholar best acquainted with Naogeorg's work, makes a convincing case for Naogeorg as both a Reformer and a thorough-going and highly competent Humanist.[16] Naogeorg wrote all his works, not just his plays, in Latin and did not consider the vernacular to be its equal. He was also expert in Greek and in the period between 1552 and 1558 translated a substantial body of Greek texts into Latin. Apart from patristic literature, such as the speeches of Chrysostomos, he translated seven works by Plutarch — he was the first to translate Plutarch into Latin — works by Isocrates, and, most important of all, the whole of Sophocles.[17] He wrote also wrote satires and a series of educational works on both sacred and secular subjects between 1538 and 1552.[18]

The first of his six plays was published in Wittenberg, the very centre of the Lutheran Reformation, by Hans Lufft, who four years before had published the first full edition of Luther's translation of the Bible. It is the powerful and hard-hitting *Tragoedia nova Pammachius* [The Warmonger] (1538). It is dedicated to Thomas Cranmer, Archbishop of Canterbury (1489–1556), in the same year in which a delegation from the German Lutherans led by Friedrich Myconius (1490–1546) came to England to bring about a rapprochement between the English and German Reformers. Cranmer was known in Germany, for he had served as English ambassador to Charles V in 1532, had met Andreas Osiander (1498–1552), the leader of the Reformation in Nuremberg, and had even, in contravention of his vow of celibacy, married Osiander's wife's niece Margarete. Cranmer's German sympathies were, therefore, well known to the German Lutherans. In the dedication to Cranmer, Naogeorg says that he has written the play to convey a picture of papal tyranny to young people and that he is dedicating it to Cranmer to show him how much Cranmer's efforts to reform the Church and remove abuses are admired abroad.

THE RENAISSANCE MEETS THE REFORMATION   321

Naogeorg follows this with a verse epistle to Luther himself, in which he justifies dealing with contemporary events in the play (unlike the ancients) even though he knows it will attract opprobrium:

> qui praesentes audeam
> Et serias res et plenas periculo
> Infido plerumque theatro committere.
> Sanè veteres, qui scripserunt Tragoedias
> Praeterita tum tractarunt argumenta, nec
> Res praesentes quisquam ausus est proponere. (Roloff 1, 18)

> [I dare to commit often to the theatre present situations both serious and full of danger. Certainly the ancients, who wrote tragedies, dealt with arguments well over long before their time, and none of them dared to put on present events.] [19]

The ancients lived in safety because of this policy, he says, whereas he knows that putting contemporary events onto the stage will make him hated. Naogeorg calls this play and all his other plays a tragedy, which in the Humanist conception of the genre meant that the subject matter would be political, illustrating the fall of a contemporary tyrant.[20]

Like all of Naogeorg's plays, *Pammachius* is about the struggle between good and evil. Pure good is represented by Christ and his disciples Peter and Paul and by Truth with her chatty maid Parrhesia [Free Speech].[21] Pure evil is represented by Satan and his four attendant devils and his amoral and comic servant Dromo. Between these two forces stand the human characters. On the side of evil are Pammachius, the Bishop of Rome, with his wily henchman Porphyrius the sophist. They have no scruples about becoming accomplices of Satan in order to achieve their own ends, which are wealth and world domination. To achieve this they have to overcome the emperor Julianus, who is well-meaning but weak, and his wise but powerless chancellor Nestor. The play takes us from early Christian Rome to sixteenth-century Germany.

Act 1 begins with Christ telling a horrified Peter and Paul that the Church is in a lamentable state and that the man who should be protecting it, Pammachius, the Bishop of Rome, once a virtuous follower of the lord, has become puffed up with vanity and power and has gone over to Satan. Instead of intervening to prevent Pammachius's further rise to power, Christ decides to release Satan from his thousand-year captivity to roam unchecked in the world, as this is the only way to purify humankind. He orders Truth to leave, lest she be defiled and insulted. The scene shifts to a meeting between the emperor Julian and his chancellor Nestor, who are rejoicing at their recent conversion to Christianity. Then we meet Pammachius, who tells Porphyrius, his two-faced adviser, that he finds Christian precepts such as loving your enemy, turning the other cheek and giving your goods away to the poor ridiculous and contrary to common sense. He wants to become an adherent of Satan who will give him wealth and an elevated worldly position but he wishes to attain it under the cloak of faithfulness to Christ and realizes that he will have to push Julian aside in order to get his way. In the next scene Pammachius and Porphyrius instruct Julian to cede unlimited power to them and give them and all churchmen as much wealth as they desire. Julian refuses to comply, saying that this is contrary to Christian doctrine. Porphyrius tells Pammachius that he knows how to ensure that Julian will ultimately do their bidding and that they will be able to convince the faithful that all their wicked actions are carried out in the service of God.

Act II begins with the arrival of Satan and the departure of Truth and Free Speech. Dromo, Satan's servant, tells him that, because of his long absence, things are not completely under his sway anymore. Satan's four devil henchmen appear and tell him that they have done their best to corrupt mankind during Satan's imprisonment. Porphyrius and Pammachius appear and beg to serve Satan. Why should I accept you? says Satan. Are you not my enemies? The eloquent Porphyrius explains to Satan that this churchman Pammachius is so outstandingly impious that he will make an excellent disciple and tool of the devil and describes him like this:

> Hic est vir ille, qui regno dudum abstulit
> Opinam predam, nempe Caesarem, potens
> In Scripturis, nugis multo potentior,
> Avaricia tumens morbo tibi placito, et
> Superbia dederit secundas nemini,
> Impietate egregius. Audet resistere
> Vel ipsi Christo, vel quidquid potentiae
> Adversatur tibi tuisque commodis.
> Hic vel totam fidem novit subvertere.
> His mutuis valet odiis connectere
> Quidquid in orbe est regum, ducum, atque Principum.
>
> (Roloff 1, 182–83)

[He is the man who for a long time has taken greater booty even than Caesar the emperor from your kingdom: he is powerful in his writings, much more powerful in idle speeches, swollen with avarice, a disease pleasing to you, and in pride he takes second place to no one; he is outstanding in his impiety. He dares to resist even Christ himself or any power that opposes you and your advantages. He knows how to undermine even complete trust; he is strong enough to join by mutual hatreds all the kings, leaders and princes in the world.]

When we remember that the figure of Pammachius represents the Pope, we realize how hard-hitting Naogeorg's polemic is.

Satan gives Pammachius a crown of darkness and blindness and agrees that he may work for his cause, though under the cloak of opposition to the devil. Act III shows us how weak Julian's opposition is. As soon as he realizes that Pammachius has simply deposed him and that all his subjects have defected, he decides that he has only two alternatives — either go to war or placate Pammachius. If he does not do the latter, someone else will come along and do it in his stead, so against Nestor's advice he decides to subordinate himself to Pammachius. Pammachius is now drunk on magnificence and power, a true tyrant. Comic relief is provided by Free Speech, who is allowed into the Papal Court as an observer, provided she keeps silent, but who constantly interrupts with critical comments. Julian agrees to subordinate himself completely to Pammachius in order to retain his imperial crown. He prostrates himself before him and even swears that the Pope is above

THE RENAISSANCE MEETS THE REFORMATION   323

the emperor, that he holds sway over him in all things and that the emperor has no power to do anything whatsoever without the Pope's agreement. Pammachius agrees that he have the title of emperor under these conditions and packs him off scornfully.

Pammachius needs servants, however, so he decides to create cardinals and Porphyrius is made the first of them, saying:

> Placet pater venatio.
> Ferae pingues solent esse in Germania,
> Illic primo tendam casses. (Roloff 1, 352)

[Hunting pleases me, Father. There are usually fat wild creatures in Germany. There I will first of all set snares for them.]

Pammachius boasts to Satan of how he has not just created cardinals but monks, relics, temples, statues, monasteries. Satan explains that he has also done something very clever in order to destroy Christianity: he has raised up a prophet called Mahomet. Act IV begins with Free Speech reporting to Truth what is happening on earth, how she has been insulted and how no one is interested in Truth any longer. Then, in a highly effective scene, Satan celebrates his success with a depraved banquet in hell at which Pammachius, his cardinals and all his monks and priests are guests of honour. Satan asks Dromo to bring a whore for each of them and then dishes out the food, whereupon we realize that what they are feasting on is the corpses of the sinful faithful — a prince, a rich man and a widow, for instance. Satan does his best to make them all drunk and then brings on a bag of money to see them fight over it. The scene shifts to heaven and to Christ, Peter, Paul and Truth. Christ shows himself fully cognizant of the appalling depravity that now prevails on earth. Truth mourns her exile from the world and asks for a place where she can find a home:

CHRISTUS.	Vides Germaniam?
VERITAS.	Video.
CHRISTUS.	Ad boream vide.
VERITAS.	Heu, num me etiam vis macerare frigore?
CHRISTUS.	Confide, calesces plus satis. Albis ubi fluit?
VERITAS.	Video Illic ex Bohemia magno alveo
	Per Mysiae campos et per fortes Saxones,
	In Oceanum devolvitur Germanicum..
CHRISTUS.	Rectè. Hinc eunti trans Albim est sita civitas
	Bis longitudine vincens latitudinem.
	Arx est in parte quae occidentem respicit,
	Quam Saxonum Dux condidit, qui primus est
	Conversus ad fidem.
VERITAS.	Quid postea? In angulum
	Illum me divertere iubes?
CHRISTUS.	Scilicet. Abi.
VERITAS.	Ad quem?
CHRISTUS.	Ad Theophilum. (Roloff, 1, 416–18)

[CHRIST.   Do you see Germany?

TRUTH.	I do.
CHRIST.	Look towards the north.
TRUTH.	Alas, surely you don't also wish to torture me with cold?
CHRIST.	Trust me. You'll be more than warm enough. See where the Elbe flows?
TRUTH.	I do. There from Bohemia by a wide channel through the plains of Mysia and through the doughty Saxons it rolls along into the German Ocean.
CHRIST.	Right. As you go from here across the Elbe there lies a state twice as long as it is wide. In part it is a fortress, which looks back to the west; it was established by the Saxon leader who was first converted to the faith.
TRUTH.	What after that? You bid me to trek to that corner?
CHRIST.	Certainly. Off you go.
TRUTH.	To whom?
CHRIST.	To Theophilus.]

Saxony, the territory to which Truth is sent, is of course the cradle of the Reformation and Wittenberg is a Saxon town. The audience will instantly realize too that Theophilus is Luther the Saxon. Truth asks to have Paul as her companion, which again the audience will understand: it was by lecturing on Paul's Letter to the Romans that Luther arrived at his central doctrine of justification by faith and Paul is the authority whom he quotes most often.

The next scene takes us back to the banqueting hall in Satan's palace and the place is awash with vomit and littered with the bodies of diners, sleeping off their excesses of the night before. Dromo rushes in to waken them and alert them to the danger of the uprising among the Germans led by Luther. They are casting off Pammachius's yoke, are preaching justification by faith, are disputing the authority of the Pope and saying that the Mass and the sacraments are not necessary for salvation. The act ends with a meeting between Satan, his devils, Pammachius and Porphyrius to find a solution to this threat. The devils will corrupt the universities, sow dissension among the reformers, get the common people to rise up in the name of reform, thus discrediting it, bring in the Turks and buy support from others.

We then expect the denouement to be staged in a fifth act, but there is no fifth act. Instead an epilogue tells us that we must now go out into the real world to see how the action continues. This is where the stratagems announced by the devils in the fourth act are being acted out and, though we can be confident that Christ will one day bring about a solution, this has not yet come to pass, so what we shall see wars and disasters. The verve and conviction of this play are compelling, lightened here and there by an admixture of comedy in the figures of Parrhesia, who cannot keep her mouth shut no matter the danger, and Dromo, Satan's servant, who like all Plautine servants is never cowed by his master. The Machiavellian Porphyrius, the initially well-meaning but ultimately venal emperor Julian, and the sinister Pammachius and evil Satan are all nicely differentiated from one another.

Naogeorg's third play *Incendia seu Pyrgopolinices* [The Conflagration or the Fireraiser] (1541) is a kind of sequel to *Pammachius* which refers directly to contemporary events in the Empire, the fireraiser of the title being Duke Heinrich the Younger of Braunschweig-Wolfenbüttel (1489–1568), a leading light of the Catholic

THE RENAISSANCE MEETS THE REFORMATION 325

League.[22] Again the forces of good and evil are ranged against each other in the struggle to reform the Church. As before, Satan is in league with Pammachius the Pope and his righthand man is again Porphirius [sic], who was created a cardinal at the end of the earlier play. The play is divided into five acts with a chorus at the end of each act. The entire first act shows us Satan, Pammachius and Porphirius engaged in dastardly machinations to achieve world domination. Act II shows them drawing an archbishop called Oncogenes and a hypocritical bishop called Disidemonades into their conspiracy. Pyrgopolinices, an aggressive warrior duke, then appears to offer himself as the scourge of the heretic and as a loyal supporter of the Pope. The third act sees Pyrgopolinices in discussion with three knights who, like him, are fireraisers, prepared to bring destruction to the world in order to rid it of anyone who is disloyal to the Pope. After all these scenes peopled by characters of unremitting evil, it is a relief when the fourth act brings on the Elector Philalethes [Lover of Truth], and his companion Probus, the virtuous chancellor (who resembles Nestor, the emperor's chancellor in *Pammachius*). Philalethes calls Pyrgopolinices to a council in an attempt to stop the burning and destruction of the countryside. Far from being repentant, Pyrgopolinices laments the fact that he has not managed to burn more German towns to the ground, for it is right to burn heretics and he is doing so on the authority of the Pope in Rome. Pyrgopolinices says the fate of the ordinary people is of no interest to him — he wishes to protect the 'old faith'. This gives Philalethes the opportunity to expound the reformed faith and its tenets at some length. Pyrgopolinices cannot be punished on earth, as he does not accept the jurisdiction of either the courts or the emperor; his fate will have to be determined by the judgement of Christ. Duke Heinrich the Younger in fact outlived Naogeorg by five years and died in 1568, a Catholic hardliner to the last.

Each of Naogeorg's other four plays dramatizes the struggle between good and evil and all of them but one bring Satan onto the stage. His second play *Mercator seu judicium* [The Merchant or the Judgement], written in 1540, is a comedy with a serious message.[23] It illustrates the central Lutheran doctrine that only faith can save a soul and that works and the sacrament of confession are useless. The central figure is a dishonest merchant, a kind of Everyman, to whom Lyocares, the messenger of the dead, appears, to tell him of his imminent demise. Conscience tries to get him to repent, while Satan informs him that he is lost and bound for Hell. A priest comes to hear the merchant's confession but he is constantly interrupted by the devil's farting, so that he cannot be given absolution, no matter how much money he gives the Church. Christ intervenes to send St Paul and Cosmas down to earth to assist Conscience. Comas gives the merchant a purgative so that he vomits up all his popish practices such as pilgrimages and fasting. He is now able to repudiate works and express his faith, so he sets off on his last journey with Lyochares. On the way they encounter a bishop, a prince and a Franciscan monk who refuse to depart from their Catholic beliefs and so are claimed by the devil. The play ends with an anti-papal chorus of five stanzas of which each of the first four begins: 'Papatus pereat' ([let the papist perish], while the fifth states firmly: 'Papatus cecidit' [the papist has fallen] (Roloff II, 508–10).

As is clear from the titles of Naogeorg's last three plays — *Hamanus* (1543),

Hieremias (1551) and *Iudas Iscariotes* (1552) — each of them presents a bible story. They do so, however, in Naogeorg's typical fashion. *Hamanus* is a dramatization of the Esther story, which was extremely popular with German Reformation playwrights because it presented a model for the good Lutheran wife.[24] Naogeorg, however, does not focus on the virtuous Esther but on Haman, the villain of the piece, who is out to ruin the Jewish people. He is the very type of the evil counsellor at Court, ambitious, venal, two-faced. Naogeorg's other two biblical plays might almost be called devil plays, because they present so vividly the influence on earth of Satan and his minions. In *Ieremias* the prophet Jeremiah is pitted against Satan and his henchman Raschates, who open the play and appear frequently throughout its course.[25] As in the Pammachius plays, the wily Satan is pulling the strings and Jeremias as the representative of godliness has his work cut out to counter his influence. Naogeorg depicts at length the depravity of humankind in order to illustrate the enormity of Jeremiah's task in calling it to repentance. Again in *Iudas Iscariotes*, which deals with Judas's betrayal of Christ, Satan is a central figure. He and his henchman Sargannus tussle with Conscientia for Judas's soul but he cannot believe in divine forgiveness and, driven by his conscience, kills himself. Judas is to be understood not just as the betrayer of Christ, but also as representing those who, in Naogeorg's eyes, are traitors to the Lutheran cause. The prime examples are Melanchthon and Johannes Agricola, both of whom played a part in 1548 in those attempts at compromise between the two confessional camps known as the Augsburg Interim and the Leipzig Interim. The third arch-traitor was Moritz, Elector of Saxony, who played the Protestants and the Emperor off against each other for his own ends. In many ways, Naogeorg is a true disciple of Luther, for all his quarrels with him. Like his teacher, Naogeorg is certain of his own point of view and intolerant of those who think differently. His writing is eloquent and lively and seeks, like Luther's, to overwhelm his audience with his rhetoric rather than subtly to convince them.

Naogeorg was an influential playwright, as the many reprintings and translations of his work attest. *Pammachius* was reprinted in 1539 and 1540. It was translated into German three times in 1539, namely, by Justus Menius, by Thomas Kirchbaur, and again anonymously. It was translated again in 1540 by Johann Tyrolf, a version authorized by Naogeorg himself, and in 1565 by Georg Bömich. His other plays have a similar history. *Mercator* was reprinted in 1560 and 1590 and translated into German by Thomas Neubaur in 1541, by Jacob Rulich in 1595 and again anonymously in the sixteenth century. *Incendia* was printed twice in 1541, translated into German in the same year and reprinted in 1617, the centenary of the Reformation. *Hamanus* was reprinted in 1547 and translated into German in 1546 and 1607, while a third, undated, translation also appeared in the late sixteenth century. *Ieremias* was reprinted in 1603 and again in 1620 and a German translation was published in 1603. *Iudas* was printed twice in 1552 and translated into German in 1556. What is striking about these dates is that they show that, apart from *Iudas*, Naogeorg's reception extends well into the seventeenth century.

Naogeorg's influence also reached beyond the German-speaking world. Roloff points out (I. 588) that copies of his plays can be found in all the major European

THE RENAISSANCE MEETS THE REFORMATION   327

libraries with a provenance going back to their original date of publication. Some of his plays were also translated into languages other than German. *Pammachius* was translated into Czech in 1546. *Mercator* appeared in a French translation in 1558, reprinted in 1561, in a Low German translation in 1593, and in a Dutch one in 1613. Roloff has found a record of a lost translation into English of *Pammachius* by John Bale from 1538–39.[26] Whether this ever existed or not, John Bale does refer to the play in his *The image of both Churches after the most wonderfull and heauenly Reuelation of sainct Iohn the Euangelist* (1570).[27] In the same year, 1570, Barnaby Googe translated Naogeorg's treatise *Regnum papisticum* (Basel, 1553) into English under the title 'The Popish Kingdom',[28] dedicating it to Elizabeth I of England and to Philip, Landgrave of Hesse (1504–1567), one of Luther's earliest and strongest supporters among the German princes.

We might claim that the most important German-speaking dramatist writing in Latin in the second half of the sixteenth century, Nicodemus Frischlin (1547–1590), follows in some ways in Naogeorg's footsteps. He, like Naogeorg, strongly espoused the Protestant cause. Like Naogeorg, he too wrote biblical plays, such as *Rebecca* (1576) and *Susanna* (1578), and his last play, *Plasma*, takes the same vigorous line on the controversies of the Reformation as do *Pammachius* and *Pyrgopolinices*. *Plasma* was first performed in 1580 on the fiftieth anniversary of the Augsburg Confession, but could not be published until 1592 because Frischlin's opponents saw Calvinist tendencies in it. *Plasma* brings a heroic Luther onto the stage to refute the arguments of Zwingli, the papal legate Tommaso Campeggio, the Wittenberg iconoclast Andreas Karlstadt and the crypto-Anabaptist Kaspar von Schwenkfeld. It introduces the devil as the power behind the Council of Trent and shows the impact of Reformation conflict on ordinary people. Some of Frischlin's works have no precedent in Naogeorg's, however, such as his *Hildegardis magna* (1578), about Charlemagne's wife. His *Priscianus vapulans* [The Beaten Priscian], published posthumously in 1592, but first performed for the centenary of the founding of the University of Tübingen, is a comic staging of the difficulties of a Humanist battling ignoramuses in the University (Erasmus and Melanchthon have to come on to support the harassed Priscian). And his *Julius Redivivus* [Julius Caesar Reborn] (1585) brings the German hero Arminius back from the dead, together with Caesar and Cicero, so that he can show them such splendid new German inventions as gunpowder, the cannon and the printing press, while the German Humanist Eobanus Hessus (1488–1540) demonstrates to Cicero the eminence of German classical learning.

If we look at the bulk of drama in the century after the Reformation, however, we have to acknowledge that, while it certainly took on a vibrant new life, it did so above all in the service of confessional dissension.[29] This meant that it was more and more frequently written in two different languages for two different confessional camps. The two dramatists just discussed were not the only supporters of the Reformation to write in Latin — we saw how Sixt Birck wrote in Latin for use in his school and he was not alone in this. Protestant dramatists were more likely than Catholic ones to write in the vernacular, however, not only to reach ordinary people but also to distinguish themselves from their religious opponents. Luther

328   HELEN WATANABE-O'KELLY

had, after all, nailed his colours to the mast from the beginning by writing in the vernacular in order to reach the uneducated, by translating the Bible into German, and by explaining his linguistic policy so firmly in the treatise which justifies his translation practice, the *Sendbrief vom Dolmetschen* [An Open Letter on Translation] (1530). The language of his Bible translation, he says, in a famous phrase, is that of: 'die mutter im hause | die kinder auff der gassen | der gemeine mann auff dem marckt' [the mother in the home, the children on the street, the common man in the marketplace].[30] This gave a strong impetus to Lutheran dramatists to write in German and a large number of them did so, among them Joachim Greff (1510–1552), Johannes Chryseus (fl.1540s), Hans Sachs (1494–1576), Paul Rebhun (1500–1546), Jörg Wickram (*c.* 1500/05–1560/02), Andreas Pfeilschmidt (*c.* 1555), Thomas Brunner (*c.* 1535–1571), and Georg Rollenhagen (1542–1609).[31] For a shoemaker such as Hans Sachs, it was clear that the language of his dramas had to be German. Those dramatists with a Humanist education, though, and especially those who were schoolmasters, were torn between their allegiance to Latin as the language of education and German as the language of the Reformation.

At the same time, drama in Latin was espoused by the new Jesuit colleges.[32] The Society of Jesus first established itself in the Empire in Cologne in 1544, then in Munich in 1549. It was formally invited by Ferdinand I (1503–1564), the future Holy Roman Emperor, while he was ruler of the Austrian lands, to found a college in Vienna, in 1551. From very early on, Latin theatre was a central element in the Jesuits' educational programme, so, as they expanded and set up new Colleges throughout the German-speaking lands, they equipped them with theatres. *Euripus* by Livinus Brecht, which had been written in the Netherlands in 1548, was the first Jesuit play performed in the Empire, at Vienna in 1555.

The conclusion that can be drawn from all this is that, while the coming together of Humanism and the Reformation could give rise to a dramatist with the verve of a Naogeorg, all kinds of drama in the Empire were centrally, if not quite exclusively, concerned with questions of theology and religious practice. The advent of the Reformation and the subsequent Counter-Reformation ensured that the available dramatic talent did not evolve as secular drama but wrote in support of its respective confessional allegiance. This also meant that different types of drama became associated with different regions. Those territories such as Bavaria and Austria that remained Catholic put on drama in Latin; those such as Saxony that were strongly Lutheran or others such as Brandenburg that became Calvinist put on drama in German. It was not until the great Silesian dramatists of the seventeenth century, Andreas Gryphius (1616–1664) and Daniel Caspar von Lohenstein (1635–1683), that Senecan tragedies on subjects taken from Roman or contemporary history were written in German.

Bibliography

ALEXANDER, JOHN, 'Early Modern German Drama', in *Early Modern German Literature, 1350–1700*, ed. by Max Reinhart, The Camden House History of German Literature, vol. IV (Rochester, NY: Camden House, 2007), pp. 357–94

BALE, JOHN, *The image of both Churches after the most wonderfull and heauenly Reuelation of sainct*

Iohn the Euangelist, contayning a very fruitfull exposition or paraphrase vpon the same. Wherin it is conferred vvith the other scriptures, and most auctorised histories. Compyled by Iohn Bale an exyle also in thys lyfe, for the faithfull testimony of Iesu. (London: Thomas East, [*c.* 1570])

BIRCK, SIXT [Xystus Betuleius], *Svsanna comoedia tragica* (Augsburg: n.pub., 1537)

—— *Ivdith Drama comicotragicvm. Exemplum Reipublice rectè institutae. Vnde discitur, quomodo arma contra Turcam sint capienda* (Augsburg: Rudolf Gwalther, 1539)

—— *Svsanna comoedia tragica* (Augsburg: n.pub., 1541)

DIETL, CORA, *Die Dramen Johann Lochers und die frühe Humanistenbühne im süddeutschen Raum* (Berlin: de Gruyter, 2005)

—— 'Neo-Latin Humanist and Protestant Drama in Germany', in *Neo-Latin Drama in Early Modern Europe*, ed. by Jan Bloemendal and Howard B. Norland (Amsterdam: Brill, 2013), pp. 103–84

ERASMUS, DESIDERIUS, *Novum Instrumentum omne, diligenter ab Erasmo Rot. Recognitum et Emendatum, non solum ad Graecam veritatem verum etiam ad multorum utiusq; linguae codicum eorumq; veterum simul et emendatorum fidem, postremo ad probatissimorum autorum citationem, emendationem et interpretationem, praecipue, Origenis, Chrysostomi, Cyrilli, Vulgarij, Hieronymi, Cypriani, Ambrosij, Hilaryj, Augustini, una cum annotationes, quae lectorem doceant, quid qua ratione mutatum sit* (Basel: Froben, 1516)

FÜSSEL, STEPHEN, *Gutenberg and the Impact of Printing* (Aldershot: Ashgate, 2005)

KÜHLMANN, WILHELM, VOLKER HARTMANN and SUSANN EL KHOLI, eds., *Die deutschen Humanisten: Dokumente zur Überlieferung der antiken und mittelalterlichen Literatur in der frühen Neuzeit*, 4 vols (Turnhout: Brepols, 2005)

LUTHER, MARTIN, *Die gantze Heilige Schrifft Deudsch* [Wittenberg, 1545], ed. by Hans Volz, assisted by Heinz Blanke, 2 vols (Darmstadt: Wissenschaftliche Buchgesellschaft, 1972)

MELANCHTHON, PHILLIP, *Melanchthons Werke in Auswahl*, ed. by Robert Stupperich, vol. III, *Humanistische Schriften*, ed. by Richard Nürnberger (Gütersloh: Verlagshaus Mohn, 1961)

NAOGEORG, THOMAS, *Tragoediae septem, latino carmine redditae, et annotationibus illustratae; Coll. sunt etiam gnōmai, dictaque proverbialia ex hisce tragoediis, per eundem, adque finem operis adiectae graecè et latinè / Sophocles* (Basel: Oporinus, 1558)

—— *The popish kingdome, or reigne of Antichrist, written in Latine verse by Thomas Naogeorgus, and englyshed by Barnabe Googe. Regnum papisticum. Popish kingdome, or Reigne of Antichrist. Spirituall husbandry. Reigne of Antichrist* (London: Henrie Denham, Richarde Vvatkins, 1570)

—— *Sämtliche Werke*, ed. by Hans-Gert Roloff, vols I–IV (Berlin: De Gruyter, 1975–87)

PLAUTUS, TITUS MACCIUS, *Plautus Poeta Comicus* (Strasburg: Grüninger, 1508)

—— *Maccii Plauti comoediae sex: a mendis purgatae, ac numeris suis ... restitutae* (Magdeburg: Lotter, 1536)

RÄDLE, FIDEL, 'Jesuit Theatre in Germany, Austria and Switzerland', in *Neo-Latin Drama in Early Modern Europe*, ed. by Jan Bloemendal and Howard B. Norland (Amsterdam: Brill, 2013), pp. 185–292

ROLOFF, HANS-GERT, 'Thomas Naogeorg und das Problem von Humanismus und Reformation', in *L'Humanisme allemand (1480–1540)*, ed. by Joel Lefebvre and Jean-Claude Margolin (Paris: Vrin, 1979), pp. 455–75

—— 'Naogeorg, Thomas', in *Neue Deutsche Biographie*, 18 (1997), S. 729 f. <http://www.deutsche-biographie.de/pnd118785656.html> [accessed 23 January 2014]

RUMMEL, ERIKA, '*Ad fontes*: German Humanists as Editors and Translators', in *Early Modern German Literature, 1350–1700*, ed. by Max Reinhart, The Camden House History of German Literature, vol. IV (Rochester, NY: Camden House, 2007), pp. 331–53

SENECA, LUCIUS ANNAEUS, *Hercules furens: tragoedia prima, Conrado Celtis editore* (Leipzig: Martin Landsberg, 1487)

330   HELEN WATANABE-O'KELLY

——*Lutij Annei Senece Cordubensis tres selectiores Tragoediae in hoc volumine continentur. Hercules Fvrens, Thyestes Mycenevs, Octavia Romana*, ed. by Jacob Locher (Nuremberg: Friedrich Peypus, 1520)

TERENTIUS AFER, PUBLIUS, *Comoediae Sex* (Wittenberg: Lotter, 1514)

——, AELIUS DONATUS, *Comoediae* (Basel: n.pub., 1538)

——, AELIUS DONATUS, GIOVANNI CALFURNIO, *Comoediae* (Strasburg: Johann Grüninger, 1499)

——*Eunuchus* / Deutsch von Hans Neithart; gedruckt 1486 zu Ulm durch Conrad Dinckmut. Reprint edn by Peter Amelung (Dietikon-Zürich: Verlag Bibliophile Drucke, 1970)

VON EYB, ALBRECHT, *Spiegel der sitten. im latein genañt Speculum morũ: Von gũten vnd boesen sitten. Von sünden vnd tugenden dargegen. Von staenden vnd aemptern mancherlay personen. Dabey auch ... Comedien Plauti in Menechino [sic] et Bachide vnd Philegenia Vgolini. ... Die gũten zũ begreiffen vnd die boesen zũ vermeiden* (Augspurg: Rynmann, 1511)

WASHOF, WOLFRAM, *Die Bibel auf der Bühne: Exempelfiguren und protestantische Theologie im lateinischen und deutschen Bibeldrama der Reformationszeit* (Münster: Rhema, 2007)

Notes to Chapter 15

1. See Erika Rummel, '*Ad fontes:* German Humanists as Editors and Translators', in *Early Modern German Literature, 1350–1700*, ed. by Max Reinhart, The Camden House History of German Literature, vol. IV (Rochester, NY: Camden House, 2007), pp. 331–53; and *Die deutschen Humanisten: Dokumente zur Überlieferung der antiken und mittelalterlichen Literatur in der frühen Neuzeit*, ed. by Wilhelm Kühlmann, Volker Hartmann and Susann El Kholi, Heidelberger Akademie der Wissenschaften, 4 vols (Turnhout: Brepols, 2005–).

2. See Stephen Füssel, *Gutenberg and the Impact of Printing* (Aldershot: Ashgate, 2005).

3. Titus Maccius Plautus, *Plautus Poeta Comicus* (Strasburg: Grüninger, 1508).

4. Publius Terentius Afer, *Comoediae Sex* (Wittenberg: Lotter, 1514).

5. For instance: *Maccii Plauti comoediae sex: a mendis purgatae, ac numeris suis ... restitutae* (Magdeburg: Lotter, 1536); Publius Terentius Afer, Aelius Donatus, *Comoediae* (Basel: n.pub., 1538).

6. Lucius Annaeus Seneca, *Hercules furens: tragoedia prima*, Conrado Celtis editore (Leipzig: Martin Landsberg, 1487). Publius Terentius Afer, Aelius Donatus, Giovanni Calfurnio, *Comoediae* (Strasburg: Johann Grüninger, 1499).

7. Jacob Locher, *Lutij Annei Senece Cordubensis tres selectiores Tragoediae in hoc volumine continentur. Hercules Fvrens, Thyestes Mycenevs, Octavia Romana* (Nuremberg: Friedrich Peypus, 1520). See Cora Dietl, *Die Dramen Johann Lochers und die frühe Humanistenbühne im süddeutschen Raum* (Berlin: de Gruyter, 2005).

8. This first appeared in print as: Albrecht von Eyb, *Spiegel der sitten. im latein genañt Speculum morũ : Von gũten vnd boesen sitten. Von sünden vnd tugenden dargegen. Von staenden vnd aemptern mancherlay personen. Dabey auch ... Comedien Plauti in Menechino [sic] et Bachide vnd Philegenia Vgolini. ... Die gũten zũ begreiffen vnd die boesen zũ vermeiden* (Augspurg: Rynmann, 1511).

9. Publius Terentius Afer, Eunuchus / Deutsch von Hans Neithart; gedruckt 1486 zu Ulm durch Conrad Dinckmut. Reprint ed. by Peter Amelung (Dietikon-Zürich: Verlag Bibliophile Drucke, 1970).

10. See the comprehensive account by Cora Dietl, 'Neo-Latin Humanist and Protestant Drama in Germany', in *Neo-Latin Drama in Early Modern Europe*, ed. by Jan Bloemendal and Howard B. Norland (Amsterdam: Brill, 2013), pp. 103–84.

11. Dietl, 'Neo-Latin and Protestant Drama', p. 107.

12. Desiderius Erasmus, *Novum Instrumentum omne, diligenter ab Erasmo Rot. Recognitum et Emendatum, non solum ad Graecam veritatem verum etiam ad multorum utiusq; linguae codicum eorumq; veterum simul et emendatorum fidem, postremo ad probatissimorum autorum citationem, emendationem et interpretationem, praecipue, Origenis, Chrysostomi, Cyrilli, Vulgarij, Hieronymi, Cypriani, Ambrosij, Hilaryj, Augustini, una cum annotationes, quae lectorem doceant, quid qua ratione mutatum sit*, (Basel: Froben,1516)

The Renaissance Meets the Reformation 331

13. See *Melanchthons Werke in Auswahl*, ed. by Robert Stupperich, vol. III, *Humanistische Schriften*, ed. by Richard Nürnberger (Gütersloh: Verlagshaus Mohn, 1961).

14. D. Martin Luther, *Die gantze Heilige Schrifft Deudsch* [Wittenberg, 1545], ed. by Hans Volz, assisted by Heinz Blanke, 2 vols (Darmstadt: Wissenschaftliche Buchgesellschaft, 1972), II, 1731.

15. Sixt Birck (Xystus Betuleius), *Svsanna comoedia tragica* (Augsburg: n.pub., 1537); *Ivdith Drama comicotragicvm. Exemplum Reipublice rectè institutae. Vnde discitur, quomodo arma contra Turcam sint capienda* (Augsburg: Rudolf Gwalther, 1539); *Svsanna comoedia tragica* (Augsburg: n.pub., 1541).

16. Hans-Gert Roloff, 'Thomas Naogeorg und das Problem von Humanismus und Reformation', in *L'Humanisme allemand (1480–1540)*, ed. by Joel Lefebvre and Jean-Claude Margolin (Paris: Vrin, 1979), pp. 455–75; by the same author: 'Naogeorg, Thomas', in *Neue Deutsche Biographie* 18 (1997), p. 729 f. <http://www.deutsche-biographie.de/pnd118785656.html> [accessed 23 January 2014].

17. Thomas Naogeorg, *Tragoediae septem, latino carmine redditae, et annotationibus illustratae; Coll. sunt etiam gnōmai, dictaque proverbialia ex hisce tragoediis, per eundem, adque finem operis adiectae graecè et latinè / Sophocles* (Basel: Oporinus, 1558).

18. The modern historical-critical edition of Naogeorg's plays is: Thomas Naogeorg, *Sämtliche Werke*, ed. by Hans-Gert Roloff, vols I–IV (Berlin: De Gruyter, 1975–87). All the plays except *Ieremias* and *Iudas* (volume IV 1 and 2) are printed with a contemporary German translation *en face*. In the case of these two plays, the Latin is in volume IV 1 and the German in IV 2. This edition will be quoted hereafter as Roloff followed by the volume and page number.

19. English versions of the quotations are taken from the translation of *Pammachius* by C. C. Love at <http://projects.chass.utoronto.ca/rnlp/pammach3.html> [accessed 20 January 2014].

20. Dietl (2013), 150.

21. For the allegorical figure of Truth in a Catholic play, see Chapter 2 (eds).

22. Roloff, III, 1.

23. Roloff, volume II. The full title is: *Tragoedia alia nova Mercator seu Judicium, in qua in conspectum ponuntur apostolica et papistica doctrina, quantum utraque in conscientiae certamine valeat et efficiat, et qui utriusque sit exitus*.

24. Roloff, volume III 2.

25. Roloff, volume IV 1 (Latin) and volume IV 2 (German).

26. Roloff I, 619.

27. John Bale, *The image of both Churches after the most wonderfull and heauenly Reuelation of sainct Iohn the Euangelist, contayning a very fruitfull exposition or paraphrase vpon the same. Wherin it is conferred vvith the other scriptures, and most auctorised histories. Compyled by Iohn Bale an exyle also in thys lyfe, for the faithfull testimony of Iesu*. (Printed at London: By Thomas East, [c. 1570]).

28. Thomas Naogeorg, *The popish kingdome, or reigne of Antichrist, written in Latine verse by Thomas Naogeorgus, and englyshed by Barnabe Googe. Regnum papisticum. Popish kingdome, or Reigne of Antichrist. Spirituall husbandry. Reigne of Antichrist* (Imprinted at London: By Henrie Denham, for Richarde Vvatkins. Anno 1570).

29. See John Alexander, 'Early Modern German Drama', in *Early Modern German Literature, 1350–1700*, ed. by Max Reinhart, The Camden House History of German Literature, vol. IV (Rochester, NY: Camden House, 2007), pp. 357–94.

30. The German is quoted from the Weimar edition of the original text, which, together with a good English translation, can be accessed, at: <http://www.bible-researcher.com/luther01.html> [accessed 23 January 2014].

31. See Wolfram Washof, *Die Bibel auf der Bühne: Exempelfiguren und protestantische Theologie im lateinischen und deutschen Bibeldrama der Reformationszeit* (Münster: Rhema, 2007).

32. See Fidel Rädle, 'Jesuit Theatre in Germany, Austria and Switzerland', in Jan Bloemendal and Howard B. Norland (eds), *Neo-Latin Drama*, pp. 185–292.

INDEX

Accademia 187–217
   see Accademia della Val di Blenio, Accademia Fiorentina, Affidati, Alterati, Camerata de' Bardi, Compagnia della Cazzuola, Compagnie della calza, Filarmonici, Congrega dei Rozzi, Gelosi, Immobili, Informi, Innominati, Inquieti, Insensati, Intenti, Intronati, Invaghiti, Olimpici, Ordinati, Ortolani, Rinnovati, Spensierati, Umidi, Umoristi
Accademia della Val di Blenio (Milan) 195
Accademia Fiorentina (Florence) 188
accademici 187–217
act:
  one-act play, see auto
  division of plays in acts 2, 103, 120, 124, 130, 263, 270, 297, 298, 325
actio 150
Aelred of Rievaulx 44, 46, 51, 65
Affidati (Pavia) 193, 201
Agricola, Rudolf 317, 326
Alberti, Leon Battista 115–24, 129
  Philodoxeos fabula 4, 115, 116–24, 258, 276
  Commentarium to second edition of Philodoxeos fabula 116–18
  dedicatory epistle to Leonello d'Este 116, 118
  Prologus 116, 118
  Fabule Argumentum 116, 118
Aldobrandini, Cardinal Cinthio 200
Aldobrandini, Cardinal Pietro 200–01
Alighieri, Dante, Inferno 119
allegory and allegorical characters 14, 33–34, 38, 117, 223–24, 233–34, 309, 320
  Ambition 233
  Chance 120
  Church 245
  Conscience 325–26
  Delight 233
  Desire 233
  Devotion 233
  Evil 321, 322
  Fame 120
  Free Speech 321–23
  Glory 119
  Good 321–23
  Inopia 119
  Intelligence 119
  Justice 242, 245
  Luck 119
  Luxuria 119
  Memory 120
  Power 120
  Pride 233
  Providence 33
  Reason 245
  Satan 299; see also Devil
  Shame 233
  Simplicity 233
  Terror 233
  Time 120
  Treachery 233
  Truth 4, 29–30, 32–34, 38, 120, 321–23
  Tyranny 233
  Wealth 119
Alterati (Florence) 190
Álvares, Afonso 38, 243
Álvares, João 37
Amerbach, Johann 317
An Almond for a Parrat 227; see also Nashe, Thomas
Andrade, Francisco de 283
Andreini, Giovan Battista 187–88, 191
  Florinda 195, 201–02
  Le due commedie in commedia 202
Andreini, Isabella 187–88, 190–91, 193, 197, 199–201, 203
  Mirtilla 195, 198, 201
  Rime 195, 200, 201
Andreini, Virginia Ramponi 201–03
angels 299
Anne of Denmark 221, 230
Arabic Gospel of the Infancy 43–44
Archilei, Vittoria 201
Ariosto, Ludovico 115, 124, 192, 267
  I suppositi 115, 124, 260–61
  La cassaria 95–96, 115, 124
  Orlando Furioso 297
Aristophanes 275, 297
Aristotle 89, 197
  Poetics 3, 89
Armani, Vincenza 197, 198, 203
Armin, Robert 5, 219, 220, 221–23
  Foole upon Foole 223
  The Italian Taylor and his Boy 223
  A Nest of Ninnies 223
  The Two Maides of Moreclack 222
  see also Tarltons Jests, Tarltons News out of Purgatorie
Armonio, Giovanni, Stephanium 259
Asensio, Eugenio 22, 26
Asinari, Federico, Tancredi 197

334 INDEX

Augsburg Confession 327
Augsburg Interim 326
Aulus Gellius, *Noctes Atticae* 123
Aurispa, Giovanni 317
auto 91, (defined) 281
Auto da Geração Humana 38, 244–45
Auto de Deus Padre 38
Auto de Guiomar do Porto 249
Auto de la huida a Egipto 4, 41–60, 63–71
Auto de los Reyes Magos 41, 64, 70
Auto dos Sátiros 244, 246–47, 249
Aveiro, Duke of 74
Azevedo, Pedro Enriquez, Conde de Fuentes 200

Bade, Josse 93
    Praenotamenta ascensiana (1511) 93, 100–01
Bale, John, *The image of both Churches after the most
    wonderfull and heauenly Reuelation of sainct Iohn the
    Euangelist* 327
Barbieri, Nicolò 187, 202
    La supplica 202
Bargagli, Girolamo 190
    La Pellegrina 190, 192
Bargagli, Scipione 197
Barlacchia, Domenico 192
Barreto, Francisco (Governor of India) 284
Barreto, Mascarenhas 38
Barros, Gama 38
Barros, João de, *Diálogo em louvor da nossa linguagem*
    242
Barzizza, Antonio, *Cauteriaria* 124
Beauvais, Vincent de 46
Bebel, Heinrich, *Comoedia de optimo studio iuvenum* 318
Belando, Vincenzo 196
    Lettere facete e ghiribizzose 196
Belcari, Feo 50, 64, 67, 70
Bembo, Pietro 95
Benci, Tommaso 50, 67, 70
Beolco, Angelo 192
Bernardes, Diogo 283
Bevilacqua, Mario 199
Bèze, Théodore de 297–99
    Abraham sacrifiant 297–99
Bibbiena, Bernardo Dovizi da, *Calandra* 121, 124, 127
Bible 43, 319, 328
    Book of Tobias 319
    New Testament 319
    Old Testament 298–99, 307
    Psalms 298
    Geneva Bible 305, 309
    see Vulgate
    Biblical narratives:
        Amam 299
        betrayal of Judas Iscariot 325–26
        Creation 299
        David and Goliath 6, 90, 298–310
        Esther 319, 325–26

Ezekiah 320
Flight into Egypt 43–46, 54–55, 65, 69
Good Thief at Crucifixion 44–45, 65, 67, 69
Jeremiah 325
Joseph 320
Journey to Emmaus 53–55, 68
Judith 90, 319
marriage feast at Cana 319
Prodigal Son 319
Rebecca 327
the sacrifice of Abraham 297
Slaughter of the Innocents 55, 69
Susanna 319, 327
bilingualism 113, 245
Birck, Sixt:
    Zorobabel 320
    Ezechias 320
    Joseph 320
    Susanna 320
    Judith 320
The Birthe of Hercules 269–70
Bloom, Harold 11, 25
Bocage, Manuel Barbosa du 37
Boccaccio, Giovanni 256–57
    De Claris Mulieribus 99
Bocchino, Bartolomeo 196
Bochetel, Guillaume 297
Bömich, Georg 326
Borghini, Gherardo
    La Gismonda 197
Borgogni, Gherardo 200
Borromeo, Cardinal Federico 200
Braga, Teophilo 38, 250
Brecht, Livinus 328
    Euripus 328
Breton, Nicholas 231
    An Epitaph on the death of a noble Gentleman 231–32
Brittons Bowre of Delights 232
Briccio, Giovanni 202
Bruni, Domenico 187, 195
Bruni, Leonardo 118
    Poliscena 118, 124
Brusasorci, Domenico 198
Brusasorci, Felice 198
Buchanan, George 73, 90, 102, 105, 297, 301
    Baptistes 99–100
    Jephthes 102
The Buggbears 261
Buoninsegna, Duccio di 54
Burbage, Richard 226

Calderón de la Barca, Pedro 288
    La hija del aire 163
    La vida es sueño 163
Calisto and Melebea 259–60, 266; *see also* Rojas,
    Fernando de

INDEX 335

Calvin, Jean 297–98, 306–07, 327
   Institution de la religion chrétienne 306–07
Calvinism 299, 309
Calvinist tragedy 297–310
Câmara, Luís Gonçalves da 75
Cambridge 256, 275
   King's Hall 256
   St John's College 256
   Trinity College 257
Camerata de' Bardi (Florence) 190
Caminha, Pero de Andrade 283
Camões, José 30, 38
Camões, Luís de 36, 243, 281–96
   El-rei Seleuco 244–47, 249, 281–82, 295
   Enfatriões 281–82
   Filodemo 6, 77, 88, 251, 281–84, 286, 288–96
   Os Lusíadas 284
Campeggio, Tommaso 327
Campiglia, Maddalena 193
Campo, Alonso de, *Auto de la Pasión* 41
cancioneiro 27–28, 38, 282–83
caricature 27
Castanheira, Count of 246
Castiglione, Baldassare, *Il libro del Cortegiano* 90
Castro, Guillén de chapter 8; 5, 161–86
   El caballero bobo 5, 161–86
   La fuerza de la costumbre 5, 161–86
   Las mocedades del Cid 161
Castro y Andrade, Don Pedro Fernández de 202
Casulana, Maddalena 193
Cavalca, Fra Dominico 48, 52, 67
Cecchi, Giovan Maria, *La Moglie* 259
Cecchini, Pietro Maria 187, 202
Celtis, Conrad 317, 318
   Ludis Diana 318
   Rhapsodia, laudes et victoria de Boemannis 318
censorship 6, 29, 74, 77, 92, 97, 100, 105–06, 192, 241, 286–87, 290
   self-censorship 97, 100, 203
Cervantes, Miguel de 161
chapbooks 247, 288
Charlemagne 327
Charles V 326
Charles VIII of France 318
Characters in drama *see* allegory and allegorical characters; clown; *comedia nueva*; Comedy; *commedia dell'arte*; devil; fool
Chiabrera, Gabriello 191
Chiado, António Ribeiro 38, 243
   Auto da Natural Invenção 244, 247–48
chorus 2, 73, 74, 95–96, 102–04, 106, 107, 119, 146, 154, 193, 298, 301, 305, 313, 318, 325
Chryseus, Johannes 328
Chrysostomos 320
Cicero 118, 257, 327
   De amicitia 119
   De fato 117

Cicognini, Jacopo 202
La Cingana 190
Cirne, João 93
   Tragedia de los amores de Eneas y de la Reyna Dido 92
clown 5, 219, 220, 223, 227
   see also fool, Robert Armin, Richard Tarlton, William Kemp
Coignac, Joachim de 6, 299, 301, 306
   La Desconfiture de Goliath 298, 302–03, 305–09
   preface to Edward VI of England 307–08
Coimbra University 73, 75, 90
Colégio das Artes (Coimbra) 90, 92
Collège de Guyenne (Bordeaux) 101, 312
comedia nueva 161, 180, 239
   characters:
      galán 163
      hombre femenil 171
      mujer varonil 166
Comédias famosas portuguesas 74
comedy:
   definition of 95–96, 97
   Roman chapters 4, 6, 12; 76–77, 84, 93, 96, 115, 117, 118, 120, 123–24, 150, 257–58, 260, 267
   Humanist chapters 4, 5, 6, 12
   characters 117, 118, 119, 124, 128, 131
      deceiver, 117
      friend, 188
      lover, 117, 118, 128
      miles gloriosus 75, 78, 119, 234, 264, 276
      mother 118
      parasite 117, 118, 128
      rival 118
      senex 77, 118
      servus callidus 78, 118
      servus edax 78
comici dell'arte 189, 194, 196, 198, 202, 203, 206
comici della gazzetta 189
commedia dell'arte 3, 5, 189, 190, 191, 193, 194, 201, 203, 227, 228–30
   characters:
      ciarlatino 227
      cornuto 229
      francatrippa 227
      harlequin 227, 229–30, 235
      innamorato/a 193, 196, 229
      magnifico 229
      pantaloon 229
Commedia erudita see Comedy, Humanist
commedia ridicolosa 202
Compagnia della Cazzuola (Florence) 192
Compagnie della calza (Venice) 192
Congrega dei Rozzi (Siena) 191
Conde de Fuentes, *see* Azevedo, Pedro Enríquez de
contaminatio 99, 201
Cornaro, Alvise 192
Corneille, Pierre, *Le Cid* 161
Correa, Luís Franco 282–85, 287–88, 296

336 INDEX

Corte-Real, Jerónimo 283
Courtenay, Edward, first Duke of Devonshire 268
Council of Trent 327
Counter-Reformation chapters 14, 15
Craesbeeck, Pedro 282
Craig, Hugh 18, 26
Cranmer, Thomas 320
cross-dressing 5, 77, 162, 180
Crystal, David 18, 26

d'Este, Leonello, Marquis of Ferrara 116, 118
Day, John 227, 228
    The Travels of the Three English Brothers 227–28
de Baïf, Lazare 297
de' Bardi, Giovanni 190
de La Péruse, Jean Bastier 297
    Médée 297
de La Taille, Jacques 297
de La Taille, Jean 297
de' Soardi, Lazaro 125
de' Sommi, Leone 197
Decembrio, Pier Candido, *Aphrodisia* 124
decorum 97, 188, 200
declamatio 97, 150
Denores, Giason 194
Des Masures, Louis 298–99, 306–07
    David combattant 298, 301–04, 306–07, 309
    epistle to Philippe Le Brun 307
Devereux, Robert 224, 225
Devil (as play character) 33–34, 245, 299, 321–27
Dias, Baltasar 38, 243
Diomedes, *Ars Grammatica* III 93
dispositio 97
Dolfin, Giacomo 193
Don Quixote 235
Donatus, Aelius:
    commentary on Terence 93, 115, 124, 125, 129,
        317
    De Comoedia et Tragoedia 93
    'Euanthi de fabula' 99
    Vita Terenti 93
Doni, Anton Francesco 196
Doyley, Thomas 227
dramatic unity:
    of time 124, 130
    of space 124, 130
du Mans, Peletier 302
Dudley, Robert 223–25, 227
Duke of Savoy 200

Edward I 223
Edward VI 307–08, 310
Eiximenis, Francesc 55, 64, 69
El Cid 172
Elizabeth I 141 220, 223, 224, 225, 257, 276, 317
Ellrodt, Robert 12, 25
elocutio 97

Encina, Juan del 41, 64, 68–69, 242, 245
    Representación de la santíssima Resurrección de Cristo 54
England's Joy 228
Erasmus, Desiderius 88, 93, 107, 318, 327
    Novum Instrumentum 319
Euripides 2, 73, 297
    Hippolytus 147, 148, 149, 151
    Phaedra 144–45

fabella 98
fabula 98, 99, 103, 117, 128, 257
farce 2, 13–14, 27, 30, 31, 91, 120, 130, 154, 188, 234,
    240, 249
Ferdinand I 328
Fernández, Lucas 41
Ferreira, António 73, 75, 90, 97, 242–43
    Bristo/Fanchono 73, 75–79, 88, 90, 95–96, 97
    Castro 3, 73–74, 78, 80, 82–83, 88, 90, 98, 100,
        249
    Cioso 4, 73–74, 76–83, 90
    Poemas Lusitanos 73–75, 88
Ferreira, Frei Bartolomeu 286, 296
festival plays 5, 141, 318
figura 308
Filarmonici (Verona) 196, 197, 198, 199, 200, 201, 203
Fineman, Joel 14, 25–26
fool 32, 34–35
    see also clown
Francisco de Portugal, 1st count of Vimioso 30
free will 300
Frischlin, Nicodemus 327
    Hildegardis magna 327
    Julius Redivivus 327
    Plasma 327
    Priscianus vapulans 327
    Rebecca 327
    Susanna 327
Froben, Johann 317
Frulovisi, Tito Livio 259, 276

Gabiani, Vincenzo, *I Gelosi* 259
Gabrieli, Andrea 192
Gager, Wiliam 5, 141–55
    Letter to Rainolds 149, 150
    Meleager 145, 150, 151
    Panniculus Hippolyto Senecae Tragoediae Assutus 5, 141–55
    Rivales 141, 276
    Vlysses Redux 141, 145
Gammer Gurton's Needle 277
Garnier, Robert, *Bradamante* 297
Garrett, João Baptista de Almeida 37
Gascoigne, George, *Supposes* 260, 267
Gelosi 190, 195, 196, 197, 200
Giancarli, Gigio, *La Cingana* 190
La Gismonda, tragedia 197
Giustinian, Orsatto, translation of *Oedipus Rex* 192–93
Gnapheus, Gulielmus *see* van de Voldersgraft, Willem

INDEX 337

Goldoni, Carlo 288
Googe, Barnaby 327
   The Popish Kingdom 327
Gospel of Pseudo-Matthew 43, 64
Gospel of Thomas 70
Gouveia, André de 90
Gower, John, *Confessio Amantis* 266
grauitas 97
Grazzini, Anton Francesco 188, 196, 261
   La Spiritata 261
Greff, Joachim 328
Grévin, Jacques 297
Groto, Luigi 194
Grünpeck, Joseph 318
   Virtus et Fallacicaptrix 318
Gryphius, Andreas 328
Guarini, Battista 193, 199, 202
   Pastor fido 189, 194, 199
Guarna, Andrea, *Bellum Grammaticale* 257, 276

Harvey, Gabriel 220
Heinrich the Younger of Braunschweig-Wolfenbüttel
   324–25
Henno see Reuchlin, Johannes
Henry, Cardinal-Prince (of Portugal) 74, 90, 92
Herculano, Alexandre 38
Hercules 226
Herod 42
Hessus, Eobanus 327
Hildegard of the Vinzgau 327
honor 161, 172
Horace 2, 74, 95, 100, 104, 297
   Ars Poetica 93, 101–02, 103
   Epistles II 2 75
Horatianism 97
Hornback, Robert 270
Hutten, Leonard, *Bellum Grammaticale* 257, 276
hybridism 3, 189–90, 194, 195, 201–02, 298
Hymanaeus 256–57, 275–76

Immobili (Florence) 202
incest 146, 153–54, 164, 179
Informi (Ravenna) 193
Gl'Ingannati 261
Ingegneri, Angelo 189, 193, 194
   Della poesia rappresentativa 189
Innominati (Parma) 191
Inquieti (Milan) 196, 200
Insensati (Peruggia) 193
Intenti (Pavia) 187, 189, 195, 196, 200, 201, 203
Intronati (Siena) 190, 191, 194, 195, 197, 203
Invaghiti (Mantua) 197
inuentio 36, 97, 191
Isocrates 320

James I 221
jester *see* fool, clown

Jesuits 75, 92, 97
   Jesuit drama 4, 73, 97, 98, 328
   Jesuit college in Coimbra 92, 98
   Jesuit college in Évora 73
João III, King of Portugal 29, 31, 37, 240, 244
Jodelle, Etienne 297
   Cléopâtre captive 297
   Moses 298
Johannes de Caulibus of San Gimignano 46, 56 *see*
   Meditationes vitae Christi
Johnson, Samuel 24, 26
Jonson, Ben:
   The Case is Altered 266–67
   Volpone 4
Jouanneaux, Guy, commentary to Terence 125
Julius Caesar 327
Juromenha, Viscount of 283

Karlstadt, Andreas 327
Kemp, William 5, 219–38
Kempe, Anne 228
Kerckmeister, Johannes 318
   Codrus 318
King's Men 221
Kirchbaur, Thomas 326
Kirchmair, Thomas *see* Naogeorg, Thomas
Knell, William 219
Knollys, Lettice 224
Kyd, Thomas, *The Spanish Tragedy, or Hieronimo is Mad*
   Again 151
Kyffin, Maurice 268–69

La Bretonera convent 41, 52
language:
   Latin and the vernacular 94–96, 327–28
   see bilingualism
Lavezzola, Alberto 198–99
Lazarillo de Tormes 22
Le Brun, Philippe 307
Leicester's Men 219, 223
Leipzig Interim 326
Lencastre, Dom João de 74–75
Lily, William, *A Shorte Introduction of Grammar* 266
Lobato, Andres 281, 284, 286, 288–89, 296
Locher, Jacob 317
   Historia de rege Frantie I 318
   Tragedia de Turcis et Suldano 318
Lomazzo, Giovanni Paolo 195
Lombardi, Bernardino 195, 197
Lope de Vega, Félix, *El perro del hortelano* 166
Lopes, Afonso 284–86, 288–89
Lopes, Anrique 284
   Cena Policiana 243
Lopes, António 281
Lord Chamberlain's Men 221, 226
Lucretius 124
   De rerum natura 124

338 INDEX

Ludolph of Saxony 45–46, 54, 59, 64–65
ludus anilis (form of unrefined comedy) 318
Lufft, Hans 320
Luís, Prince of Portugal 283
Luther, Martin 319, 321, 324, 325, 326, 327, 328
   Sendbrief vom Dolmetschen 328
Lyly, John 223

Macropedius, Georg *see* Joris van Lanckvelt
Machiavelli, Nicolò 115, 121, 124–31, 324
   translations of *Andria* 115, 124–31
   Clizia 128, 259
   Discorsi 124, 129
   transcription of *Eunuchus* 124
   La mandragola 5, 115, 121, 124, 127–31
   Il Principe 124, 127, 129
Maganza, Giambattista 192–93
Manfredi, Ippolita Benigni 193
Manrique, Gómez:
   Lamentaciones fechas para Semana Santa 41
   Representación del Nacimiento de Nuestro Señor 41, 56,
     64, 70
Manrique, Jorge 38
Mantuanus, Baptista, Eclogue IV, *De natura mulierum*
   147–48
Manuel, King of Portugal 240
Manuel, Prince of Portugal 240
Masures, Louis de 6
Maurice of Nassau 225
Maximilian I 318
Medieval drama 2, 4, 5, 13–14, 27–28, 30, 32–34,
   41–43, 47–48, 52, 54, 90, 99, 119–20, 124, 263–64,
   281, 295 n. 3, 297–300, 302, 309, 314 n. 14
Meditationes vitae Christi 44, 46–48, 54, 56, 59, 64, 66, 69
Melanchthon, Philipp 319, 326
   Epistola de legendis Tragoediis et Comoediis 319
melodramma 190
Menander 241, 275
   Colax 257
Mendes, Fernando 38
Mendoza, Hurtado de 283
Meneses, Diego de 283
Menius, Justus 326
Mentelin, Johann 317
Metastasio, Pietro Antonio Domenico Trapassi 288
metre 34, 43, 94, 96, 100, 103–05, 115, 120, 281
Miranda, Francisco de Sá de 4, 73–74, 242–43, 251,
   283, 295–96
   Os Vilhalpandos 77
misogyny 149, 150, 178
Molière, *L'Avare* 4
Molina, Tirso de, *La venganza de Tamar* 177
Mondella, Francesco, *Irifile* 197
monologue 4, 13, 15, 16–18, 20, 21, 48, 76, 82, 84, 97,
   107, 119, 121, 129, 130, 143, 145, 147, 148, 162,
   174, 257, 264, 286, 287, 301
Montaigne, Michel de 12–13, 18

Monteiro, Gomes 38
Montemor/Montemayor, Jorge de 283
Montesino, Fray Ambrosio 45–46
Morais, Francisco de 283
morality play 27, 33, 119, 159, 240
Moritz of Saxony 326
Mouzinho, Vasco 13, 18
Muret, Marc-Antoine 297
musica secreta 193
Muzzina, Zan 196
Mystery Play 27, 39, 297–301, 305, 309, 314
Mystére du Viel Testament 299–301
Myconius, Friedrich 320

Naharro, Torres, *Propalladia* 92
Naogeorg, Thomas 2, 317, 320–27, 328
   Hamanus 325, 326
   Hieremias 326
   Incendia seu Pyrgopolinices 324–25, 326, 327
   Iudas Iscariotes 326
   Mercator seu judicium 325, 326, 327
   Pammachius 6, 320–24, 326, 327
   Regnum papisticum 327
Nashe, Thomas 223
   An Almond for a Parrat 227
   Pappe with an Hatchet 223
Neidhart, Hans 317
Neubaur, Thomas 326
Neville, Alexander 149, 150
   translation of Seneca's *Oedipus* 149
Newton, Thomas, translations of Seneca, *Tenne*
   Tragedies 150
Nixon, Anthony 228
   The Three English Brothers 228
nome d'arte 203
novella 118
Nowell, Alexander 149, 150

Officium Peregrini see *Peregrinus*
Olimpici (Vicenza) 190, 191, 194, 199, 201
Oliveira, Fernão de, *Gramática* 241
Ongaro, Antonio, *Alceo* 197
Ordinati 193
Ordo Rachelis 55–56, 69
Ortolani 197
Osiander, Andreas 320
Ovid:
   Heroides 144, 146, 148
   Metamorphoses 146, 152, 153–54
Oxford 256–57, 268, 270, 275
   Christ Church 141
   Corpus Christi College 156
   Queen's College 156
Palladio, Andrea 192
Panciatichi, Vincenzo 195
Panzanini, Simone 195
Pappe with an Hatchet 223

INDEX 339

see also Thomas Nashe, John Lyly
Pasi, Antonio 192
Patronage 74, 90, 91, 92, 116, 118, 190, 192, 194, 197, 199, 200, 201, 203, 219, 221, 223, 237, 295
Pazzia d'Isabella 190
Pedantius 257, 276
Pellizzari, Elisabetta 193
Pellizzari, Lucia 193
Peregrinus 53–54
Pérez de Oliva, Fernán, *Agaménon vengado* 92
Performance chapters 8, 9, 10, 11; 115, 124
    Children 57, 193, 256, 261, 263, 270
    hired man 220
    itinerant companies/actors 188, 194, 203, 221
    see *accademia*; sharer; theatre companies; women performers; *zanni*
Pfeilschmidt, Andreas 328
Philip I, Landgrave of Hesse 327
Philone (anon.), *Josias* 301
Piccolomini, Enea Silvio 317
    Chrysis 259, 276
Piissimi, Vittoria 190
Pinto, Jorge, *Auto de Rodrigo e Mendo* 243
Pisani, Ugolino 317
    Philogenia 317
Plautus 4, 6, 73–74, 78, 115, 117, 120, 121, 128, 241, 255–71, 275–79, 297, 317, 324
    Amphitryo 82, 259–60, 262–63, 265, 268, 281
    Aulularia 79, 92, 259, 261, 267
    Bacchides 255, 275, 317
    Captivi 92, 260, 266–67
    Casina 259
    Epidica 121
    Menaechmi 256, 259, 265–66, 268, 317
    Mercator 259
    Miles Gloriosus 263–64
    Mostellaria 77, 261
    Poenulus 260
    Pseudolus 258–59
    Stichus 92
    Trinummus 92
Pléiade 297
Plutarch 281, 320
Polenton, Sicco
    Catinia 124
Poliziano, Angelo 115
Poor Clares 41, 46, 52, 68–69
Portugal, Manuel de 283
Pratt, Óscar de 38–39
Prestes, António 4, 11, 18–24, 242–43, 284
    Ave Maria 20, 242
    Dois Irmãos 19
    Mouro Encantado 21–22
    Procurador 19–20, 23–24
prose drama 2, 26, 73–74, 92–96, 115, 120, 212 n. 5, 228, 242, 245, 251 n. 5, 260–61, 269, 275 n. 7, 278 n. 43, 281, 295

puritas 97

Queen Anne's Men 230
Queen's Men 219, 220, 221, 224
Quintilian, *Institutio Oratoria* 105

Rainolds, John 141, 142 , 149, 150
Ramel, Henrik 226
Ramponi Andreini, Virginia 201–03
Rao, Cesare, *L'argute e facete lettere* 196
La rappresentazione di San Giovanni nel deserto 50–53, 56, 59, 67–68
Rebhun, Paul 328
Recitatio 150, 157–58
redondilha (lyric metre) 281
Reformation chapters 14, 15; 90, 297–98, 301, 302, 303, 307–09
Resende, André de 251
    Genethliacon Principis Lusitani 241
Resende, Garcia de, *Miscelânea* 241
The Return from Parnassus 226
Reuchlin, Johannes 318
    Scenica Progymnasmata also known as *Henno* 318
Rhetoric 13, 24, 36, 37, 74, 91, 97, 98, 102, 105–06, 131, 141–42, 145, 146–47, 150–51, 154, 190–91, 240, 245, 313, 314, 318
Ribeiro, Jerónimo, 284
    Auto do Físico 243
Riccoboni, Antonio 193
Rinnovati (Ferrara) 195
Rivaudeau, André 297, 298
    Aman 299
Rojas, Fernando de, *Celestina/ Tragicomedia de Calixto y Melibea* 3, 242, 260, 281; *see also* Calisto and Melibea
Rol dos livros defesos 241
Rollenhagen, Georg 328
Rowland, Richard 258, 276
Rowley, William 227, 228
    The Travels of the Three English Brothers 227, 228
Rucellai, Giovanni di Bernardo 95
Rulich, Jacob 326
Ruzante, *see* Angelo Beolco

Sá de Miranda, Francisco 90, 93–95, 97
    Cleopatra 98
    Os Estrangeiros 90–91, 93, 95–97, 102
    Os Vilhalpandos 77, 90
Sabugosa, Count of 29–30, 36, 38
Sachs, Hans 328
St Anselm 45, 65
St Bonaventure 46
    see also *Meditationes vitae Christi*
St George's Day Feast 225, 226 see also English Garter Feast
St John the Baptist 42–43, 46–53, 56–58, 60, 64, 67
St Joseph 42, 55–56, 69–70

340   INDEX

St Paul's School 256
Sampaio, Manuel de 75
Santo Domingo de Silos monastery 54
Sarocchi, Margherita 193
Savonarola, Girolamo 124
Scamozzi, Vincenzo 192
scenes, division of plays into (vs. acts) 120, 298, 313
Sebastião, King of Portugal 75
Seneca 2, 5, 73–74, 327
    Hercules furens 92, 317
    Medea 92, 299
    Phaedra 141–55
    Octauia 102
    Oedipus 149
    Thyestes 92, 113, 152, 299, 317
    Troades 92, 113
sententiae 120
Ser Maphio detto Zanini 188
Serrão, Lopo, 296
Shakespeare, William 4, 11–18, 23–25, 178, 219, 220
    As You Like It 219
    The Comedy of Errors 233, 265–67, 271
    Hamlet 12–16, 18, 21, 23, 219, 220–21
    King Lear 219, 222
    Love's Labour's Lost 1, 3, 5–6, 219, 230–35
    Macbeth 151, 178
    The Merchant of Venice 221
    Much Ado About Nothing 219
    Othello 4, 221
    Richard III 11–12, 25
    Romeo and Juliet 1, 219, 225, 230
    Sonnets 12
    The Taming of the Shrew 266
    Titus Andronicus 151
    Twelfth Night 219
sharer, in theatrical company 220
Shirley, Anthony 228–29
Shirley, Thomas 227–28
    Discours of the Turkes 228
Sidney, Philip 225
Silva, Bishop Miguel da 90
Soliloquy *see* Monologue
song-book see *cancioneiro*
Sophocles 6, 92, 98, 297, 312, 320
    Electra 92
    Oedipus Rex 192
Soranza, Giovanni 195
sottie 27, 32, see also fool
Spelta, Antonio Maria 195, 200, 201
    La curiosa e dilettevole aggionta … all' Historia 200, 201
Spensierati (Florence) 187, 195, 201, 202
Stichomythia 64, 74, 103, 104, 105
Stoicism 74, 82, 104, 107
Stow, John 226
Straparola, Giovanni Francesco 223
Studley, John 150, 153
    translation of *Phaedra* 150

Suetonius, *Divus Augustus* 121

tableau spirituel 308
Tarlton, Richard 5, 219–22
Tarltons Jests 220, 222, 223
Tarltons News out of Purgatorie 222
Tasso, Torquato 13, 18, 196
    Aminta 196
Teive, Diogo de 89, 90, 97–107
    Institutio Sebastiani Primi 107
    Ioannes Princeps 4, 90, 97–107
    Iudith 90
    Opuscula Aliquot, 100–02
    Oratio funebris 98, 104–06
    Saul 90
Terence chapters 6, 12; 2, 4, 6, 73–74, 78, 151, 241,
        246, 255–71, 275–79, 297, 317
    Adelphoe 118, 119, 120, 121, 123, 128
    Andria 75, 78, 113, 115, 124–31, 256, 259–61, 268–69
    Eunuchus 76, 113, 117, 118, 119, 121, 124, 256–60,
        263–66, 317
    Heautontimoroumenos 113, 117, 119, 122, 123, 128, 256
    Hecyra 117, 122, 123, 128
    Phormio 76, 119, 256
theatre companies
    see Leicester's Men, Queen's Men, Queen Anne's
        Men, Worcester's Men
Thomson, J. A. K. 266
Towne, John 219
Tragedia de los amores de Eneas y de la Reyna Dido 92
    see Cirne, João
tragedy:
    (defined) 96, 97, 98–101, 102, 312 n. 4, 318
    See chorus; stichomythia
tragicomedy 91, 92, 194, 240, 242, 245, 257, 260, 297
The Travels of the Three English Brothers 227–30, 231,
        235
    see also Day, John; Rowley, William; Wilkins, George
Truth (allegorical figure in plays) 4, 29–30, 32–34, 38,
        120, 321–23
Tyrolf, Johann 326

Udall, Nicholas 270
    Flours for Latine Spekynge 270
    Jacke Jugeler 262–63, 266, 268
    Roister Doister 262–66
Umidi 188
Umoristi (Rome) 193, 194

Valerini, Adriano 191, 196–99, 201, 203
    Afrodite 197, 198–99
    Le bellezze di Verona 197
    Rime diverse 199
Valerius Maximus 281
Valla, Lorenzo 318
    *In Latinam Novi Testamenti Interpretationem ex Colla-
        tione Graecorum Exemplarium Adnotationes* 318

INDEX 341

van de Voldersgraft, Willem, *Acolastus sive de filio prodigo* 319

van Lanckvelt, Joris 319
  Hecastus 319

Vasconcelos, Carolina Micaelis de 38, 283

Vasconcelos, Jorge Ferreira de 26, 112 n. 10, 113 n. 24, 242, 251
  Comédia Aulegrafia 112 n. 10, 249
  Comédia Eufrosina 112 n. 10, 113 n. 24, 281
  Comédia Ulysippo 112 n. 10

Venner, Richard 228

Verato, Giovan Battista 192, 193, 194

Vergerio, Pier Paolo, *Paulus* 124, 258, 276

verisimilitude 162, 188

Vettori, Francesco 127

Vicente, Gil 1–2, 4–5, 11, 13–18, 27–37, 73, 91, 239–40
  Compilaçam de todalas obras/Livro das Obras 28, 31, 33, 35–36, 38–39, 91
  Individual Plays (*the index contains only the short titles of the plays; for the full titles of the plays, see the text*):
    Agravados 34
    Alma 34, 245
    Amadis de Gaula 245, 251
    Barca plays 34, 39
    Barca do Inferno 28, 32, 38–39
    Barca da Glória 34–35
    Breve Sumário 38–39
    Cananeia 38–39
    Ciganas 31, 33, 39
    Cortes de Júpiter 34
    Devisa de Coimbra 13, 16–17, 246, 248–49
    Dom Duardos 240, 245–46, 251
    Fé 38, 245
    Feira 33, 245
    Festa 4, 27–37, 39
    Floresta de Enganos 32, 35, 251
    Frágua de Amor 242
    Índia 13–15, 26
    Inês Pereira 28, 39
    Jubiléu de Amores 240
    Juiz da Beira 32, 38–39
    Lusitânia 243–45
    Maria Parda 39
    Monólogo do Vaqueiro 28
    Ressurreição 39
    Romagem dos Agravados 22
    Templo de Apolo 32–34, 39
    Triunfo do Inverno 33
    Viúvo 246–47

Vicente, Luís 28

Vicentine school 91

Vida, Girolamo, *De Arte Poetica* 148

villancico 42, 59

Vingança de Agamemnon see Aires de Vitória

Vinta, Francesco 195

Virgil 115
  Eclogae III 148
  Aeneid 146

Virgin Mary 33–34, 42, 46–47, 58, 65–66, 166

Visitatio sepulchri 54

Vita di Sangiovambatista 48–50, 52–53, 56, 59, 67, 70

Vitória, Aires de, *Vingança de Agamemnon* 92, 249

Voltaire (François-Marie Arouet) 288

von Eyb, Albrecht 317

von Kues, Nikolaus 317

von Lohenstein, Daniel Caspar 328

von Schwenkfeld, Kaspar 327

Voragine, Jacobus de, *Golden Legend* 43

Vulgaria quaedam abs Terentio in anglicam linguam traducta 268, 270

vulgarity 32, 116, 118, 120, 137

Vulgate 299, 300, 305, 309, 318
  I Samuel 17. 46–47 300
  I Samuel 17. 51 300

Walsingham, Francis 219, 225

Warner, William, translation of Plautus' *Menaechmi* 267–69

Westminster School 256, 275

Wickram, Jörg 328

Wilkins, George 227, 228
  The Travels of the Three English Brothers 227, 228

William of Orange 224

Wilson, Robert 233
  The Three Ladies of London 233
  The Three Lords and Three Ladies of London 233

Wimpfeling, Jacob 318
  Stylpho 318

Wittenberg 317, 320

Wolsey, Cardinal Thomas 256

Women performers 3, 187, 192–94, 195, 198, 200–03, 205

Women writers 52, 53, 60, 68, 193–95, 197, 200–01

Worcester's Men 230

zanni (itinerant actors) 188

Zeno, Apostolo 288

Zwingli, Huldrych 327